The Landscape of Truth
An Orthodox Understanding of the Biblical Testaments for the True Worshippers

by Derick Mckinnely Fuller

Published by the True Worshipper Ecclesiastical Association, Inc.

The Landscape of Truth: An Orthodox Understanding of the Biblical Testaments for the True Worshippers
Copyright © 2014 by Derick Mckinnely Fuller

Request for information should be addressed to:

True Worshipper Ecclesiastical Association (TWEA)
Germantown, Maryland 20874
http://twea.org/

ISBN: 978-0-9773714-2-6

Library of Congress Control Number: 2014938656

Unless otherwise adapted by contemporary English usage, all Scripture quotations are taken from the Authorized King James Version of the *Holy Bible*, under United States Public Domain.

All rights reserved. No part of this publication may be reproduced, stored in a retrieval system, or transmitted in any form or by any means (that is, electronic, mechanical, photocopy, recording, or any other medium) except for brief quotations in printed reviews, without the prior permission of the author.

Printed in United States of America

Contents

The Landscape of Truth...i
Contents iii
Acknowledgements xi
Introduction.. xiii
Chapter 1 1
Invocation 1
   Revelation of the Truth 1
   The Human Frailty..3
   Accepting the Reality of God...6
   The Mediator 8
   Message of Truth..10
   Values First 12
   The Holy Bible 13
   The Author's Viewpoint 15
Chapter 2..19
Y'haweh: the Totality of Truth 19
   The Pearl of Great Price...19
   The Biblical Description of *God* 22
   Identifying Biblical Harmony 26
   Truth Found in God's Love..27
   Y'haweh 31
Chapter 3..37
Immanuel's Law..37
   The Creeds of the Church 37
   Faith 41
   "The Seven Spirits of God"..43

The First Revelation of Y'haweh: *He is the Creator* 45
The Questions of Metaphysics and the Mind-Matter Explanatory Gap 47
The Ontological Commitment that Transcends Logic and Mathematics 60
Empirical Observation 69
Observing the Emerging World 70
Epiphenomenalism 74
Behaviorism 75
Cognitive Neuroscience 76
The Epistemological Question 82
The Rift between Science and Philosophy 84
Phenomenal Experience 89
The Crucial Cognitive Reality that Phenomenology Identifies . 93
The Scientific Method 98
The Rise of Newtonian Mechanics 101
How Newtonian Mechanics Failed to Describe the Immaterial Forces 104
How Natural Philosophers Employed the Scientific Method to Describe the Immaterial Forces 106
Thermodynamics 107
The Laws of Thermodynamics 108
Electrodynamics 109
Electricity's Effect upon Western Culture 112
The Consolidation of Classical Physics 113
The Deficiency of Classical Physics 114
The Enduring Contributions of Classical Physics 117
The Rational Strength of Contemporary Science 119
The Rise of Modern Physics 120
Planck's Dilemma 121

Einstein's Search for "the Old One"	123
Quantum Mechanics	125
The Standard Model	127
How the Big Bang Theory Fails to Establish a Self-sufficient Universe	132
The Question of Freewill	137
The Church's Tumultuous Quest for Orthodoxy	143
Divine Fiat	146
The Lord's Prayer	149
The Introduction and Purpose of Immanuel's Law	153
The "*A priori* Synthetic" Basis of Immanuel's Law	156
Immanuel's Law – Orthodox Judgment	161
Immanuel's Law - Theological Statements	163
Immanuel's Law - Empirical Statements	165
Immanuel's Law - Derivative Statements Introduction	178
Immanuel's Law - Derivative Statements Illustration	182
Immanuel's Law – the Critical Context of the Logos' Truth Functional Form	196
Immanuel's Law – Normalizing a World of Tropes	200
Immanuel's Law – First Derivative Statement	205
Immanuel's Law – Second Derivative Statement	219
Immanuel's Law – Third Derivative Statement	243
"In the Beginning"	250
The Choir of Angels	252
Chapter 4	257
Son of the Morning	257
Eden	257
Increasing Value by Increasing the Sense of Beauty	260
Redemption	263

Growing in Grace 266
The Golden Cities of the "Bright One" 267
Evil 273
The Veil of Sin 276
Patience—the Endowment of the Soul 280
Shadow of the Good 281
The Faithful Body—the Temple of Y'haweh 284
Marriage in the Holy City of the Kingdom of Heaven 287
Wellspring of Everlasting Life 288

Chapter 5 291
Adam 291
Scriptural Misconceptions 291
Adam's Lost Dominion 296
Creating the Knowledge of Good and Evil 299
Praying for the Kingdom 303
The Power of Prayer 305
The Two Adams 305

Chapter 6 309
The Golden Cities of the Prodigious 309
A Glimpse behind the Veil 309
The Thorns of Conscience 311
The Heart of Government 312
The Strife between Kayin and Hevel 315
The Rights of the Mighty 318
The Fraternal Orders 320
The Three Natural Forms of Human Government 322
The Prodigious 328
The Patriarch 329
Shadows of the Holy Marriage 331

- The Hallmarks of Liberty 333
- The Burden of the Patriarchs 337
- Social Disorder and Unrest 340
- Higher-level Civilizations 342
- The Gold of the Priestly King's City 345
- The Shipmaster's Law in Action 348
- "The Death of Kings" 350
- The Codified Penal Law of the Aristocrats 353
- The Covetous Oligarchs Who Initiate the Rise of Secularism . 356
- The Loss of the True Friendship 360
- The Quarrel between Secularists and the People of Faith that Necessitates the Common Wealth of Democracy 364
- The Treasures of Increasing Social Consciousness 367
- The Terrors of Anarchy 370
- The Indifferent Spirit of the Anti-Savior and His Hybrid Governmental Beast 374
- Vindication of the Faithful unto the Glory of Y'haweh 381

Chapter 7 385
The Kingdom of Heaven 385
- Optimism 385
- The Tree of Life 387
- Predestination 389
- The Second Revelation of Y'haweh: He is the Supplier of Truth and Justice 390
- The New Adam 392
- Seeking Righteousness 393
- The Course of the Gentile Nations 395
- The Third Revelation of Y'haweh: He is a Friend to His Faithful Elect 399

The Seed of Avraham That Y'haweh Plants in an Unassuming Promised Land 401

Ya`akov's Apology 407

The Power of the Holy Spirit Establishing our Personhood within the Elect Community 411

The Burden of the Children of Yisra'el 413

The Fourth Revelation of Y'haweh: He is the Governor of His Obedient and Repentant Assembly 416

Hallowed Ground 418

The Salvation Knowledge of Lord Yehoshua the Mashiach ... 420

The Law of Moshe: the Testator's Sanctification of the Church through the Commandment 424

Our Obedience Seeking the Riches of the Holy Marriage 433

The Four Phases of Y'haweh's Interim Government 440

The Interim Tabernacle of Testimony and Reconciliation 445

Righteous Judgment 455

The Fifth Revelation of Y'haweh: *He is the King of Righteousness* 458

The Sixth Revelation of Y'haweh: He is the Priest who gives the Holy Spirit of Truth 463

The Purge of the Tabernacle 464

The Diaspora, Hellenism, and Anti-Semitism 472

The Advents of Lord Yehoshua 483

The Redemption of Both Jew and Gentile 486

The Seventh Revelation of Y'haweh: He is the Husband of the Redeemed Assembly 492

The Power of Lord Yehoshua's Baptism 494

Depictions of Heaven 501

Agnus Dei, Lamb of God 505

The First Fruits of the Temple 508

The Apostle Sha'ul's Ministry of Reconciliation 519
The Death of Sha'ul 530
The Christian and Secular Successors of Rome 541
Modernity: "the Fullness of the Gentiles" 549
The Christians Who United the States of America 553
The Legal Fiction of Socialism 556
The Dominance of Protestant Germanic Kindred Groups 558
The Anti-*Christ* 560
The Totality of Y'haweh 563

Acknowledgements

Non nobis, non nobis, Domine, sed nomini tuo da gloriam.

Introduction

Liberty! Liberty is what this doctrinal treatise pursues for the true worshipper of God in Lord Jesus the savior. Only the true worshipper recognizes that liberty is a divine gift that humankind cannot fully attain—either through religious works, socio-political philosophies, scientific investigation, or domestic and civil strife—since the greatest threat to one's liberty is often one's self.

That liberty is a divine gift is the thesis of the biblical Testaments: the Testaments demonstrate that the gift of liberty is the gift of the Testator for the elect true worshippers who through faith seek the redemption of the Testator's undefiled conscience as well as God's reconciling and communal Holy Spirit. The Testaments describe how the Testator and the Holy Spirit enable the true worshippers to conduct their lives in recognition of the liberation of their reconciled consciences in brotherly love.

For the true worshipper, therefore, the biblical Testaments systematically pronounce God's gift of the Testator's liberty. First, the Old Testament and its Law demonstrate the need for God's gift of liberty. The Old Testament details God's witness to all of humankind's inequitable relationships that compromise conscience. For this reason, the Old Testament details the example that God sets forth by his creating of the people Israel, whom God issues governing covenants and laws to. As the Old Testament details the Israelites' successes and failures, the Old Testament treats the whole panoply of human relationships: using the Israelites, the Old and New Testaments treat Mesopotamian hunter-gatherer kindred groups; Mesopotamian patriarchic societies; the greater middle-east's early class-based, monarchic and aristocratic civilizations; and the disenfranchised peoples of the Greco-Roman democracies, federal republics, and Imperial Rome's multi-faceted tyrannical system.

In succession, the New Testament details how the Testator, Lord Jesus, appears at the height of human civilization to bestow the liberty of his pure conscience. In this manner, the New Testament details how the Lord's unblemished conscience fulfills the Old Testament's covenants and Law. In detail, the New Testament describes how the resurrected Lord, as the Testator of an eternal righteous Kingdom, bestows God's Holy Spirit by electing his true worshippers with the gift of faith: an election by faith that the Lord spreads abroad in every nation, despite one's male or female sex; race; kindred group; religious works; or social status.

The primary goal of this doctrinal treatise is to establish the true worshippers with an orthodox understanding, concerning how truth constitutes God's expression of the world, in a manner that pronounces God's glory and holiness, which translate as the prevailing of God's right judgment: a prevailing righteousness that becomes liberty for the true worshippers and condemnation upon humanity's shortsighted judgments. To realize the work's primary goal, the treatise's supporting objective is to establish the true worshippers with an orthodox understanding, concerning how the biblical Testaments indict the world's unjust governments, which fail to secure liberty. Thus, the doctrinal treatise concurring aim is to establish the elect true worshippers with the orthodox understanding, regarding how to overcome the world's injustices and freely conduct their lives in response to the liberty that the Testator imparts.

Requisite to the doctrinal treatise's primary goal is the treatise's championing of the understanding that God wills for Church jurisprudence to be accountable to the orthodox understanding of lay true worshippers: the treatise upholds the example set forth by Lord Jesus who entrusted the Church into the hands of uneducated fishermen. Though this work does not seek to describe how Churches are to execute and finance Church jurisprudence, the treatise champions the principle that the scholarship of Church leaders must stand upon the leaders' merit before the congregation, rather than the leaders' financial capacity to pay for their scholarship; therefore, the work holds that the Church's instruction of its leadership must stand upon the congregations' tithes and offerings, rather than tuition fees that some economically disadvantage saints cannot pay. Furthermore, in the effort to empower the laity, the treatise champions an international understanding that the laity must be free to conduct their private lives in accordance with the biblical Testaments, as understood by traditional Christian orthodoxy.

Even as we perceive the justice of our pursuit of laypeople empowerment, we initially recognize that two significant challenges encumber the Church—the Ecclesia, the Assembly of elect true worshippers—from confirming the liberty of individual true worshippers: we recognize that the first challenge is for the Church to establish its orthodoxy—its right belief—by demonstrating that God is real and that the biblical Testaments are the sole authority of God's expression of truth and salvation for humankind. Next, we recognize that the second challenge is for the Church to prevent unscrupulous ministers and congregants from exploiting true worshippers and the Church's public influence for unjust purposes.

As for the Church's addressing the first challenge of demonstrating that God is real and that the biblical Testaments are the sole repository for God's expressed truth, we partially understand the criticisms of secular historians: the secular historians, who deny the Testaments' divine authorship, justly point out that the Testaments' creation accounts in no way agree with secular scientists' understanding of the universe and its emergence. Also, the secular critics justly point out that the creation accounts mirror more ancient Mesopotamian narratives like the Mesopotamian epic of Gilgamesh. To make matters worse, we recognize that the secular critics have objective reasons for scoffing at the Church's assertion that God marshaled the writing of the Testaments: the critics observe how the biblical texts reflect a host of scribal impositions, modifications, and errors such as the case in which one author, Moses, records his own death.

Though we recognize that secular historians raise just criticisms, we also recognize that the historians do not relinquish their post nineteenth century prejudices as they critique the scriptures: instead of the critics' pursuing, first, the biblical authors' sincerity; the critics first imagine that the biblical authors have diabolically envisioned ways to deceive the readers whom the authors imagined would arise for untold millennia. For instance, contemporary critics overlook the fact that professional scribes existed long before the earliest composition of the scriptures.

Both the Old and New Testaments record instances in which the prophets and Apostles used scribes and learned men to author their epistles; therefore, it stands to reason that a biblical author such as Moses would have given the messages that he had copied from God unto the scribes to codify for posterity. Certainly, we should not expect that Moses and other prophets could have produced perfect accounts of God's impressions, after they had faced the awe and dread of God.

The most skilled and devout biblical scholars cannot satisfy all critics' concerns and so prove the biblical Testaments' validity. Notwithstanding, our doctrinal treatise—the Landscape of Truth—recognizes the following: because the Apostle Paul states that God inspired all scriptures; one cannot establish the integrity of the scriptural canon by scrutinizing the scriptural account of any one covenant that God made with an Israelite patriarch, king, or prophet. A systematic understanding of the scriptures recognizes that the covenants, which God initiated to govern the elect nation Israel, subsume under the full exposition of the biblical Testaments, which realize their inspired expression upon the advent of Rome—the height of human government: a time in which Lord Jesus the Christ appeared to bestow his liberty upon the elect true worshippers, amongst the Israelites and all nations.

Thus, holding a systematic understanding of God's full expression upon the advent of Lord Jesus, our doctrinal treatise immediately recognizes the subsequent historical means to affirm the apostolic authorship of the New Testament: because the Israelite Temple symbolizes Israel's adherence to the governing authority of the Old Testament, the Roman destruction of the Temple, in 70 AD, marks the most tumultuous period in Jewish history. We know that since the Apostles themselves were Israelites, observing the Temple's rites, the Temple's destruction would have affected them to the end that the Apostles would have addressed the Temple's destruction in their writings; especially since the Apostles had recorded Lord Jesus' foreseeing the Temple's destruction. With these considerations, we recognize that the New Testament scriptures, excepting the Apostle

John's writings, terminated when the Romans killed the Apostles prior to the Roman destruction of the Temple.

Furthermore, despite its scribal errors, our affirming the integrity of the Old Testament stands upon our affirming the apostolic authorship of the New Testament scriptures; since the New Testament records Lord Jesus' affirmation that God enjoined the Old Testament covenants with the Israelite patriarchs, kings, and prophets. Also, because the apostolic authorship of the New Testament affirms the Old Testament's divine inspiration, we refer to the testimonies of the Apostles as we ponder the Old Testament's historical record. For example, instead of imagining that the creation account derives from lyrical relics like the epic of Gilgamesh, we consider the Apostle Paul's statement in which Paul describes how the nations fell from the knowledge of God and cultivated pantheism and idol worship. And so, we are not surprised that the Old Testament's creation account recaptures the creation story by emphasizing the pursuit of an orthodoxy of belief, rather than a pursuit of an orthodoxy of pagan rites and ritual.

Likewise, we recognize that the creation accounts bear a simple narrative style that ancient illiterate societies used to retain a historical record: compositional writing styles, which make provisions for analysis, did not arise, in any significant way, until the flowering of Greek civilization. To establish the biblical Testaments' record that God created the worlds and humankind, our doctrinal treatise will secure a critical and objective proof for God's creative work. The treatise will not merely rely upon the liturgical and etymological understandings of the Church; the treatise will also present substantive and so derivative proofs that further our understanding of the creation and our relation to it. Where historical philosophers and contemporary creationists have failed to prove God's existence, our doctrinal treatise will pursue a profound course that contemporary scientists and Christian theologians have not entirely anticipated. Demonstrably, for the true worshippers, we shall deliver a concrete understanding of the way God created the world and our souls.

To be sure, a vast majority of our doctrinal treatise will address the Church's first challenge of demonstrating how God physically creates the worlds and the human soul. In so doing, the treatise will vindicate the biblical Testaments: the treatise will capture how the worlds and our human experience adhere to God's truthful expression of humanity's liberty. In this vein, the treatise will detail how our personal liberty within a just community stands upon God's expressing the worlds under God's expressed persons, Lord Jesus and the Holy Spirit. Like this, our doctrinal treatise will establish the orthodoxy of the biblical Testaments: the treatise will prove that human liberty is a divine gift to God's elect true worshippers—a gift that human civilization cannot grasp.

Not until the very end of our doctrinal treatise will we address the Church's second challenge: a challenge that arises because of the Church's ongoing struggle to affirm the divine gift of liberty that the biblical Testaments effect. To frame the second challenge, we make the subsequent observation: because the orthodoxy of the biblical Testaments stands upon liberty's being a divine gift, the Testaments by definition are not only indictments upon the world's unjust governments, but also indictments upon the efficacy of all world religions. The Testaments in their very essence indict the world religions as being actual contributors to the world's unjust civilizations.

For instance, the world religions profess that their prescribed deeds, rites, and rituals bear some efficacy in securing social justice; however, the religious practices unjustly disenfranchise people in various ways. First of all, the religions encourage senses of self-righteousness that cause a religious practitioner to ignore his or her shortcomings as he or she denounces the shortcomings of others. Along these lines, most religious practices inadvertently foster racism or classism. Case in point, many religions encourage the performance of rites and rituals such as a pilgrimage to a holy place—a rite that esteems the pilgrims and natives of the holy place over other peoples who are either not natives of the holy land or participants in the pilgrimage. Other religious practices disenfranchise segments of the population by esteeming the descendants and relatives of a holy man or prophet as being more virtuous than other unrelated or foreign peoples. Also, religious practices that encourage meditation or self-neglect inadvertently contribute to injustice as the practitioners either consider the uninitiated blameworthy for their unenlightened states, or encourage a stoicism that never liberates a person's free expression, as the person endures the abuses of the uninitiated.

Essentially, we observe that the practices and beliefs of the world's religions disenfranchise even the religions' adherents. One may readily witness that cultures, outside of orthodox Protestant Christendom, systemically tolerate high concentrations of disenfranchised peoples, due to the religions' deeming of certain peoples as less virtuous.

The biblical Testaments' unique claim upon truth and justice is this: the Testaments observe that righteousness is not a mortal person's private possession that the person may grasp through the performance of a rite or ritual. Rather, the Testaments observe that righteousness is a thing divine as exemplified by the Christ's pure conscience and as measured by the Holy Spirit's gift of faith to the elect for the purpose of overthrowing humankind's unjust social strata. We observe the efficacy of the biblical Testaments as follows: we witness the Testator's imparting measures of faith unto the elect throughout all kindred relations and societal strata to the effect that when true worshippers recognize orthodoxy and know that their righteousness is not the result of their own deeds; the true worshippers do not countenance self-righteousness by looking down upon their unbelieving peers. Likewise, the true worshippers understand that their pilgrimage is not of the rites and rituals unto a discriminatory place on the earth: the true worshippers understand that their pilgrimage is of the eye of faith unto the city of peace where their reconciled consciences abide in the Christ.

We observe the most liberal effect of the biblical Testaments when we observe the unprecedented levels of upward social mobility that nations enjoy, when the nations' social strata highly consists of true worshippers who recognize that their liberty is a divine gift, regardless of social status or religious deeds. By keeping the profound effect of the biblical Testaments in mind, we spy the second challenge that the Church faces as she seeks to affirm the true worshippers' liberty. In other words, we witness the second challenge arise as the cultural success of the Church attracts people who do not recognize that their liberty depends upon their accepting the Testator's redeeming of their faith with his pure conscience, as well as the Testator's bequeathing of God's reconciling Holy Spirit. Hence, we know that the challenge is to prevent the Church's social power from being exploited by the unfaithful who recognize the Church's immediate cultural advantages, even as they disregard the divine expression from which the Church's principles derive.

We discern three types of people who exploit the Church's prosperity. Furthermore, we recognize that the human centered efforts of all three types cloak the liberty that the Testaments express. The first group of exploiters derive from believers, themselves: what distinguishes this group of exploiters is the notion that their personal merits work in tandem with God's grace to secure justice. Charismatic types of individuals emerge from this first group to exploit worshippers and incite profound social havoc; moreover, this first group disenfranchises people by reducing the Testaments' expressed truths to the religious rites that the exploiters perform.

We define the second group of Church exploiters as those people who merely identify with and utilize the emergent Christian culture's traditional values: we define the second group as cultural Christians. The cultural Christians undermine the liberty that the Testaments effect as they consider the Lord to be a mere prophet. They also consider the scriptures to be good principles that are not binding. Instead of considering Heaven as the bounty that the Testator's good conscience imparts to reconcile the elect from the unjust nations; the cultural Christians simply consider Heaven as a place for all good people, whose personal merits earn them salvation. Too, we see that as the cultural Christians consider their observance of Church principles to be a mere cultural phenomenon, they disenfranchise other peoples who have not experienced the societal maturity that the elect true worshippers bring about.

We consider the third group of Church exploiters to be those who pose the greatest threat to the true worshippers' free expression of the liberty that the biblical Testaments effect. We define the third group as secular humanists who rightfully denounce Church corruption but wrongfully take sole credit for the societal synthesis and upward mobility that the true worshippers' Christian culture brings about. We witness the profound threat that the secular humanists pose as they equate the Church with the world religions. As we witness how the conflicting belief systems fail to achieve a just cultural synthesis, we observe the manner in which the secular humanists champion a stoic adherence to multiculturalism, to the end that the secular humanists reduce the human experience, itself, to be of no scientific worth. Unfortunately, we do not see the secular-humanists championing the liberty of an individual soul. Rather, we observe that the secular humanists rationalize individual aspirations under socialist models that impersonal and centralized bureaucracies haphazardly govern.

At the end of our doctrinal treatise, we will loosely detail the emergence of Church corruption and the emergence of today's burgeoning secular culture, which threatens the true worshippers' ability to live their lives in accordance to their faith. Our doctrinal treatise will detail the manner in which the Church and those who exploit her have respectively brought about Western civilization's profound successes and failures. First, the treatise will detail how the early Church initially consisted of elect members, while the Church endured persecution under Rome. Afterward, the treatise will show how Church corruption arose immediately after Rome ceased the persecution. At that point, the work will mention how faithless Church congregants, who bore the inclination to seek self-righteousness and personal esteem, immediately sought to deemphasize the divinity of Lord Jesus. Instead, as they sought their own aspirations, the unfaithful emphasized the Lord's humanity like their own. We shall see that the faithless congregants soon advocated the belief that one's religious works help to secure his or her salvation. Similar to an observation that the ancient Church historian Eusebius made; we here note how the pursuit of self-righteousness led unfaithful leaders and congregants to novel and heretical understandings.

Furthermore, we shall see that the only safeguards against the myriad of unorthodox doctrines that the Church exploiters spawn are the Christian creeds that articulate the orthodox understanding that the Apostles conveyed: namely, that God exists in three persons, united in one essence; that Lord Jesus is at once God and man; that salvation is by grace alone; and that the scriptures alone express the truth of God. The Creeds of Christendom—that is, the Apostles Creed, the Nicene Creeds, the Chalcedonian Creed, the Athanasian Creed, and even the underlining principles of the Westminster Confession of Faith—this work will uphold.

As an example of the profound successes that the true worshippers of the Church brought to Western civilization, the doctrinal treatise, at its end, will detail how the Church united the barbarous Germanic tribes under a single cultural identity: a feat that Roman civilization could not accomplish, due chiefly to the fact that Rome entailed a disenfranchising class structure, centered upon a ruling patrician class. The treatise will roughly detail how the Church reconciled the conflicting German kindred groups; established cultural norms across the European continent; and so enabled a cultural standardization upon which science and invention proliferated. The treatise will thereby demonstrate that the scriptural principle of the liberty of all under God eventually inspired the upward mobility of the underclass, as well as inspired universal conceptions of human rights.

Then as an example of the profound failures that the Church exploiters brought to Western civilization, the treatise will detail the ways in which the exploiters ignored the orthodox understanding that liberty is a divine gift that transcends nationality, male-female sex, and societal status. First, we will acknowledge how the bishops of Rome usurped Church authority by claiming that their authority stood upon their being inheritors of the Church that the Apostle Peter founded at Rome. In so doing, we shall see how the Roman bishops politicized the Church by discriminating against the powers of other bishops and congregants throughout the world. Second, we shall roughly detail how cultural Christians throughout the Germanic tribes began to consider Christian prosperity as a

European phenomenon, to the extent that Europeans began to see other non-European races as inferior. Lastly, we shall detail how secular powers arose to consolidate the world regions that Europeans had conquered under the auspices of the Europeans' spread of the Christian gospel. Finally, to describe the paramount threat to elect true worshippers, our doctrinal treatise will ultimately describe how the established Christian creeds' inability to predict ongoing innovations in government, science, and technology has presented secular-humanists with the opportunity to usurp the Church's power over the Western world.

At the conclusion of our treatise, we shall detail how secular-humanists have claimed authority by pointing out the Church's corruption and inability to arrest scientific knowledge. At the same time, the treatise will detail how secular-humanists' socialist programs fail to achieve the same cultural synthesis and societal enfranchisement that the elect true worshippers have inspired in European civilization. The treatise will discuss how the secular-humanists' matter-of-fact reliance upon natural laws denies the relevance of personhood, to the end that the secularists cannot grasp a universal ideal that secures universal justice, despite kindred group or societal status. As an outcome, the treatise will briefly discuss how the liberalization of markets reduces whole nations-states and individuals to commodities, leaving the disenfranchised masses imperil to the impasse between the authority of the state versus the authority of capitalist individuals. Thus, finally painting the resulting consequence and threat to the true worshippers, the doctrinal treatise will show how the secular-humanists' socialist agenda grows increasingly autocratic and centralized, as a response to the agenda's failure.

Upon its description of the threat that the autocratic secularist agenda poses to the Church, the worth of our doctrinal treatise will come into full blossom. To confound the secular-humanists' supposition that the world and humankind exist without meaning, our doctrinal treatise will decisively describe how God created the worlds and the human soul, and the treatise will describe how God completes our personhood and community in his expressed persons.

Also, to undermine the exploitive leaders and cultural Christians that weaken the Church's power and the true worshippers' freedom in the West; our doctrinal treatise will obtain a systematic theology that enables the elect to grasp an understanding of their physical and social environments as they quest for God's gift of liberty, which the Testaments effect. Decisively, the treatise will demonstrate that the liberties that Western civilization enjoys are only as strong as the true worshippers' capacity to pursue freely the redemption of the Testator's undefiled conscience, as well as God's reconciling and communal Holy Spirit. What is more, the treatise will demonstrate that the championing of liberty throughout the world is only as strong as the true worshippers' capacity to cultivate Christian societal maturity, in respect of the universality of the Testator's gift of liberty, despite male-female sex, societal status, or race.

Throughout the Landscape of Truth, we will use the Hebrew names of the Lord, the Apostles, and the Prophets wherever prudently possible. Our use of Hebrew names is not only an attempt to de-anglicize the biblical Testaments, but also an attempt to undermine historical prejudices that cloak God's truthful expression that the Testaments impart.

For the reader, we proceed to summarize how the doctrinal treatise realizes its primary goals: we recall that our first goal is to establish an orthodox understanding, concerning how God expresses his truth in such a way that the appearing worlds and human relationships pronounce God's prevailing right judgment—that is, God's imparting the liberty of the Christ's unblemished conscience upon the elect and condemnation upon human governments' compromise of conscience. Furthermore, we recall that our second goal is to establish an orthodox understanding of the biblical Testaments, in regards to how the biblical Testaments indict humanity's unjust civilizations. To realize its goals, the treatise's several chapters systematically unfold God's expressed truth as follows:

Chapter 1—Invocation

> The first chapter introduces the ways in which humanity witnesses reflections of universal truth and the ways in which humanity's shortsighted self-interests confound truth. The chapter introduces a general understanding of the ongoing social upheaval that civilization faces as it encounters innovation. Then showing a contrast between civilization's pursuit of secular self-sufficiency and Israel's perennial dependency upon Israel's God given oracles, the chapter introduces the way Israel's religious practices reflect God's influence, because the practices defeat Israel's human propensities. Following, the chapter introduces Lord Jesus as the mediator between Israel and God: the chapter briefly details how Lord Jesus demonstrates that all levels of civilization require reconciliation with God. At its close, the chapter introduces the basic conventions of the canon of Old and New Testament scriptures. Also, the chapter closes with a description of the mainstream approaches to the Holy Bible as well as the author's traditional approach.

Chapter 2—Y'haweh: the Totality of Truth

> The second chapter highlights the necessity of acquiring a systematic approach to the biblical Testaments, in order to grasp the truth that God expresses in them. The chapter begins with Lord Yehoshua's parable that draws a contrast between our temporal aspirations and Heaven's eternal truth. Thereupon, the second chapter coins the thesis of the doctrinal treatise, which is to grasp a systematic understanding that unfolds creation and the human experience into a landscape that captures God's expressed truth. Next, the second chapter briefly demonstrates that only a systematic understanding reconciles the scriptures' most profound descriptions of God's nature. For this purpose, the chapter preliminarily establishes a definition of God's expressed truth that the remainder of the work will secure an objective proof for. At its end, the second chapter introduces

how the Israelites define God's being, without confounding his eternal nature with a temporal name.

Chapter 3—Immanuel's Law

The third chapter is by far the most challenging: the chapter begins by introducing the most challenging questions that assail Church doctrine. The work introduces how it will address the tough questions as the treatise unfolds God's covenants and revelations throughout the work. Beginning with God's revelation that he is the creator, the chapter introduces the metaphysical question, concerning how theologians, philosophers, and scientists fail to resolve the mind-matter question. The chapter then surveys how empirical scientists fail to resolve the mind-matter question with logic, mathematics, empiricism, behaviorism, and cognitive neuroscience. The chapter demonstrates how the discipline of phenomenology demonstrates how empirical scientists fall short of understanding the mind-matter question. Next, the chapter details classical and contemporary physics, as well as scientists' failed attempt to encompass the advent of creation with the Big Bang theory. Then after the chapter discusses how theologians fail to describe how God expresses the creation, the chapter introduces an orthodox judgment that explains the following: why the Big Bang theory is impossible; how God extends the creation; how God creates animal and human consciousness; and how the forgoing descriptions objectively establish the orthodoxy of the biblical Testaments. Like so, the chapter defines the physicality of the human spirit and soul: the chapter strikes the balance between the liberty of personhood and personhood's identity-dependence upon ever-changing environments.

Chapter 4—Son of the Morning

The reader will not entirely grasp the significance of the fourth, fifth, and sixth chapters, until the reader assesses the chapters from the standpoint of the section entitled "the Hallmarks of Liberty," which the reader will find in chapter six. The section contrasts the nations' brief grasp of liberty with Heaven's enduring salvation.

In reference to Immanuel's Law's demonstration of how God enables human consciousness to transcend the physical world that its identity depends upon, the fourth chapter describes how the spiritual natures of evil and sin play a critical role in God's cultivating and fulfilling humanity's knowledge structure. The chapter demonstrates how the human mind cannot attain fulfillment simply by residing in a perfect physical environment. The chapter then defines evil and sin in respect to the social detriments that humanity faces upon the compromise of conscience. In this manner, the chapter defines how God cultivates his worshippers' understanding of his prevalent right judgment in the unblemished conscience of the Christ.

Chapter 5—Adam

Continuing the discussion, concerning how God cultivates his worshippers' understanding of his prevailing right judgment in the purity of the Christ, the fifth chapter surveys the story of Adam. The chapter initially addresses theologians' questions, concerning Adam's moral aptitude before Adam's fall. Then chapter details how Adam could not appreciate his being enfranchised in the Garden of Eden. The chapter then details how God cultivated Adam's understanding of the new Adam who translates Eden into the justice of Heaven.

Chapter 6—The Golden Cities of the Prodigious

The sixth chapter describes how marriage is the foundational relationship of civilization. The chapter describes how all kindred relationships arise upon the marriage unit to form communal societies where most of the population enjoys enfranchisement. The chapter then describes how higher-level-civilizations arise to govern specialized economies and how the higher-level-civilizations fail to enfranchise the entirety of the population to the extent that various degrees of liberty and oppression result. Like so, the chapter sets up the succeeding chapter seven, which demonstrates how the biblical Testaments enfranchise the elect from all nations, under eternal peace.

Chapter 7 — The Kingdom of Heaven

The seventh chapter begins with God's suzerain covenants, which fulfill the biblical Testaments by describing how God bequeaths liberty to humankind by grants that indict insufficient religious works; even as God secures the orthodoxy of belief over the orthodoxy of religious rite and ritual. The seventh chapter then proceeds to demonstrate how the biblical Testaments capture how God's unblemished lamb redeems a kindred group, that is, Israel and the adopted Church, and how God secures the elect kindred group in the higher-level-civilizations with his lamb who appears to all classes in the international civilization of Rome. The chapter afterward describes how the Church enabled the union and dominance of the Germanic kindred groups of Europe and how the excesses of European ascendency now enable a global culture to suppress the Church. Following, the chapter briefly prescribes the defensive measures that the Church must take in the securing of orthodoxy from the kindred group perspective of the elect of Israel, whom Christ shall return to redeem. Finally, chapter seven closes the Landscape of Truth with a description of God's Holy Marriage and Glory in the Kingdom of Heaven.

Chapter 1

Invocation

"Bow down your ear, O Lord, hear me.... My prayer is unto thee, O Lord... O God, in the multitude of your mercy hear me, in the truth of your salvation."
—Psalms 69:13 and 86:1

Revelation of the Truth

Surrender patiently your attention all you heavenly hosts! Lend generously your attentive ear all you God fearing people, and hear my desperate pleas for your prayers and support to help me ponder a wondrous dilemma: God continually reveals his truth unto humanity, but the human affairs unfortunately cloak truth's usefulness. It is a pitiful predicament indeed, for what greater fortune can humankind possess than the truth of God?

Surely, the attainment of God's truth would be an unparalleled accomplishment for civilization—an accomplishment that would even conclude human history. Nevertheless, this accomplishment for humanity proves to be unattainable because their worldly cares frustrate truth's aspiration.

Just imagine! If humankind possessed truth, social divisions would not exist. Medical cures and technological advancements would proliferate because the knowledge of the workings of creation would display before humanity the possibilities and boundaries of human invention. What is more, if humankind possessed truth, apprehension, animosity, and the other unsociable human emotions would cease.

Hitherto, most of humanity's contemporary thinkers deem the idea of attaining truth as fanciful or utopian because only glints of truth flicker through the cloudy midst of the cares of life in the human mind. Personal conscience (which social civility refines) and an awareness of nature's physical constants prove to be the only standards for truth that humanity accepts. Even though the hunger for truth is so inherent to human nature, truth's existence to the human mind proves to be a thing sublime. In the end, humanity considers the definitive identity of truth to be an unknown that exists with what are to them the greatest of unknowns, and that is the purposes and nature of God. To be sure, humanity rightly considers the definitive habitation of truth to be held invariably in the mind of God alone; therefore, to apprehend truth, the human mind knows that it must persistently look beyond itself to apprehend him.

In this work, however, we will conclude that a human being cannot possibly apprehend the nature of God unless God graciously reveals his nature to the human being. This fact we will establish throughout the volume of this work. Yet, for now let us say that because of its immensity, a person can only understand the nature of God, if the person receives God's miraculous revelations of himself as seen through the eye of unrelenting and selfless faith, which is a persistent look past human comprehension and ingenuity by believing on the necessity of metaphysical things that we cannot readily perceive or understand.

In fact, God miraculously revealed his nature to the people Yisra'el, and he initiated a covenant relationship with them that necessitated their observance of certain rituals and their adherence to certain cultural tenets that tentatively reflect his revealed nature. Also, though human frailty had eventually obscured God's revealed nature and had even caused Yisra'el to lack the faith and good conscience to uphold the covenant relationship, God graciously overcame human frailty by miraculously manifesting himself in the pure conscience of Lord Yehoshua[1] to finalize the revelations of himself that he had first revealed to the Yisra'elites.

In this work, therefore, we will establish the fact that Lord Yehoshua is the savior of the people who have faith in the nature of God as portrayed to the Yisra'elites, since Lord Yehoshua only

---

[1] *Adonai Yehoshua* translates from Hebrew into English as *Lord Jesus*.

retains the nature of God and fulfills God's expression of truth. In his ministry to the Yisra'elites, Lord Yehoshua disseminates God's Holy Spirit, who dispenses salvation knowledge of the Lord's unblemished conscience, unto which truth culminates in the reconciliation and liberty for all God's faithful. Thereupon, Lord Yehoshua establishes the glory of God when the Holy Spirit disseminates salvation knowledge, because they who relate to God and obtain the riches of truth (which the Holy Spirit's salvation knowledge reveals) give everlasting praise to God who creates truth.

A key goal of this work, therefore, is to apprehend liberty from God's expressed truth by encompassing the ministry of Lord Yehoshua, in whom God manifests the truth. Our goal is to come to a full understanding of how true worshippers are to relate to God through Lord Ychoshua. In this way, we will truly worship God, to overcome the natural hazards of the human condition.

The Human Frailty

Initially, we must understand the reality that when God does not gift a person with the understanding of how to relate to him in true worship, the person cannot understand the meaning and purpose of God's creation, because he or she, as a human being, has a subjective nature that his or her individual needs and concurring intellectual capacities invariably create; therefore, the person's subjective nature defies truth's manifest liberty for all, since a person's needs determines the usefulness of any experience. What is more, the person subjectively assesses his or her needs by weighing what he or she considers to be positive and negative experiences. Habitually, need conceives personal and social values; therefore, a host of misguided value systems cripple humanity because everyone's needs are different.

The differing needs of people betimes result in an individual's gross esteem of himself or herself, which is self-aggrandizement: the human frailty that is the cancer of every social relationship. Because of this frailty, strife endlessly persists within human relations, since self-aggrandizement ultimately causes everyone to seek his or her own advantage without regard for another's. Decisively, then the cloak of necessity hides from human comprehension God's purposes and truth, in which he holds the liberty for all whom he has empowered to seek his peace.

We may briefly assess the frailty of the human condition in the subsequent way: we have only to note that being without God's truth, human civilization embarks upon a never-ending quest for an equitable peace, despite the absence of truth; therefore, humanity's futile quest propels them into a never-ending tumultuous cycle of social change. And, as social conventions change, humanity's understandings and perspectives of the world around them continually change, and challenging questions then arise to plague civilization. Accepted truths (to some) become relative, and an overall meaning for creation seems inapprehensible or even inexistent. Concurrently, God's truth and purposes becomes unknowable, and his very existence then comes into question. At such a time, people make prominent in their culture any advancement in the scientific and political arts because these advancements meet the immediate needs of the people. Eventually, any quest for universal understanding becomes secondary to the people's immediate goals, because any acceptance of the existence of a universal understanding automatically implies a divine order, which (again) seems unknowable. As a consequence, humanity's conception of truth becomes subject to a status quo that corresponds with the needs of civilization.

Nonetheless, accepted conventions may suffice for day-to-day living; however, the blight of ignorance remains to haunt human civilization's stability at its very core, relentlessly. While every age brings forth new understandings of the environment, humanity seeks only an immediate advantage of the new understandings: they seek only that which facilitates any new social innovation that will create better living standards, often only for the privileged few. Social-political orders haplessly adapt to these constantly reoccurring innovations inequitably, thus causing any adaptation to occur under the duress of social turmoil. Unfortunately, the bane of newfound knowledge is prejudice and intolerance, because the new understandings usurp the societal staples of cultural tradition and ideological dogma. Thus, the ongoing process of encountering the unknown creates for civilization a never-ending cycle of political and social bewilderment. With any political settlement, one may find great skepticism among the political constituents, their thinking that there is always a more equitable way.

In summary, humankind continues to take an unfortunate approach to understanding the world around them: they constantly gather new data haphazardly, only to hope later that they might find a compatible philosophical niche to advance an understanding of the data. In their haphazard effort, humankind blindly hopes to grasp an understanding of reality.

We find many worthy illustrations of humanity's philosophical detachment with scientific progress: we have only to observe humanity's reactions to the scientific advancements made by government-sponsored programs. At the end of the twentieth century, April 24th 1990, an American space agency—the National Aeronautics and Space Administration (NASA)—launched the world's first general-purpose orbiting observatory named the Hubble Space Telescope (HST). Searching the galaxies with above ten times the visual capacity of ground based observatory telescopes, HST heralded observations in visible, infrared, and ultraviolet light. As a result, HST introduced to astronomers the ability to observe, vividly, stellar wonders never before seen, such as the colliding of spiral galaxies and the first planet directly imaged outside our solar system. What is more, due to the amazing images produced by HST, scientists increased the estimate of observable galaxies from 80 billion to 125 billion. Thus, programs like HST display to the human race a mysterious and foreboding universe of great immensity and marvel. While the size and wonder of the universe ever increase in human eyes, its mysteries for humanity increase as well.

Progressively, humanity views the earth as insignificant and lowly, its being marginalized in a girth of endless streams of galaxies. As most contemporary thinkers lower the esteem of the earth within the universe, they lower the esteem of human consciousness. When observers consider the immensity of the universe, it is not too uncommon for them to be carried away by thoughts of the sublime. Some of the Apollo astronauts, in the 1970's, were reported to have had spiritual experiences, while they were away from the earth. As often happens when studying the galaxies, they perceived an intelligence, or even a determined consciousness, pronounced in the stars. Their spiritual reaction upon encountering the great unknown is not unusual because it is a human inclination to invoke a principle greater than oneself when facing the ever-produced insecurities of ignorance. As a consequence, more common is the search for extraterrestrial intelligence, in hopes to find some distant civilization that has dealt with human civilization's problems. Desperately, people look unto the stars to find the answers to humanity's social ills.

In summary, what can be said about human nature is that the human being is the only creature on earth that does not complement its environment. Nature usually teams with itself; however, human nature does not complement any environment. The element of their conformity to the world is clearly missing: no ideology or governing system suffices to feel the intellectual void of the human soul. Of such is humanity's plight without perfect knowledge of God and his truth.

Accepting the Reality of God[1]

Yet, let us not, in despair, needlessly fall into the chasm of hopelessness without giving the sincerest effort to cross over to the other side where there are certain answers. We do not have to repeat the error of the generations. Let us not accept understandings of the universe that humanity sees through the eye of ever-changing social convenience. Rather, let us come to terms with human insecurity by

---

[1] The preliminary argument, which we present here, necessarily assumes the form of an *argumentum ad ignorantiam* (that is, an argument from ignorance), because when one initially attempts to discern the nature of God, one can only began by discovering the intellectual conventions that delineate the contrast between omniscience and finite understanding. The reader should consider the argument, as a preliminary premise. The burden of proof is incumbent upon the succeeding chapters.

looking beyond the human faculties and accepting that there is an unknown variable missing in the human equation. Let us not allow the ideological views of certain secular scientists to persuade us into believing that we must accept truth as merely the product of a status quo that society sets before itself. As well, we must not allow ourselves to fall prey to intellectual paralyses by our pondering over indefinite accumulations of scientific data. Instead, we must be true to science by identifying and dissecting a greater purpose and design. Let us accept the understanding that the missing element in humanity is purposeful because what is missing obviously figures into an overall design for the human soul.

This work of course recognizes that the biblical Testaments indict the world religions that believe that their human centered rites and rituals can secure truth's liberty. Even so, this work observes that the justification for faith in a creator—a faith that inspires the world religions to believe in the efficacy in their rites and rituals—is clearly evident, despite religions' incongruity with the accepted practices of science. Belief (or rather faith) initiates both religious and scientific inquiries into the unknown. For that reason, the faith that inspires religious pursuits finds justification together with science because of the following: while history proves that the self-determining inner constitution of human beings is incomplete (as witnessed by humanity's incompatibility with their environment), both religion and science seek to reconcile humanity with their surroundings. Essentially, the tenet of any religion is the performance of certain rites and rituals to relate to some foreign benefactor in hopes to fill a void in human consciousness. The significance of the actual rites in the face of truth is immaterial: that religion seeks a communion with an unknown is the significance, because religion is humanity's mature attitude toward its own vulnerabilities. Although the natural sciences cannot approach unto any religious system (for these systems accept the unknown, while science pursues definitive outcomes) religion and science pursue the same end: intellectual fulfillment for the soul. It is obvious, therefore, that one should not look with disdain upon religious people because their hope to grasp a greater power is a fundamental instinct of human nature. Religion is but a belief system that science does not restrain. Howbeit, although people may accept the unknown in their religious convictions, orthodox understanding and science should at some point establish that which our faith pursues, if we are to encompass truth. In a word, our faith equips us to accept the unknown, while our science pursues an end.

Having faith, therefore, we should begin any inquiry by uncompromisingly accepting that God exists, even in concert with the subsequent saying of the Apostle Sha'ul[1] who said, "He that comes to God must believe that he is, and that he is a rewarder of them that diligently seek him."[2]

To be sure, like the Apostle, we must take comfort that our general understanding of a divinely created world is sound. With this mind, we have only to pursue continuity in our approach to understanding our universe instead of trifling over degrees, because one can only understand the utility of a member when one configures the member into an overall body. Thus, we should consider any newfound data as added brilliance to the omniscient nature of God: let us rest assured that we can only grow in our appreciation of the creation's profundity.

Like so, let us progress by dismissing the word *universe* (meaning one and unto itself), and let us in our pursuit replace the word with *creation*, while we search for the creator and his cause. Finally, let us encourage ourselves with the understanding that God's place of existence can be no other place than where the definitive answers to all our questions and concerns are: let us reassure ourselves that truth, perfection, and the purpose for all things are God's habitations.

The Mediator

Still, while we comfort ourselves by accepting God's existence, we must confront the well-known fact that there have been multiplicities of belief systems that have pursued an understanding of the nature of God, in his relation to humankind. As history witnesses, most

---

[1] The Apostle Paul
[2] Hebrews 11:6

have fallen under the reproach of social progress. As stated above, we fail in obtaining a perfect understanding of the Creator because we are mentally incapable of encompassing his immensity within our intellectual state of progression. Basically, our needs and attitudes of him change as we grow. His omnipresence is uniform and unchanging, while we are confined by finite spurts of increasing knowledge: the two states of being are incompatible.

We, however, must not despair in our hope of gaining a true relationship with him because, as we have said, he has revealed his purposes. We can only proceed by knowing that a relationship with God must stand upon a sustained inquiry of trust. We initiate that trust by assuring ourselves that he is existent. As stated above, our very being bears witness to his existence by means of what is missing in our nature: even as the astronauts observed, the intelligence of creation also testifies to his existence; moreover, our lack of felicity witnesses our broken bond with him.

How then do we relate to God? While surveying human history's belief systems, we must ask ourselves has any belief system sufficed to fill our intellectual void definitively? In other words, which belief system precisely defines the nature of the invisible God?

The faith of the Yisra'elites deserves our undivided attention because theirs is the only religion that has built in mechanisms that defeat the natural human aspiration of merely reaching political stability. The Yisra'elites are truly the only people in human history who have strangled their human propensities in a belief system that is impossible to uphold. Their rites, rituals, and moral tenets portray the revealed nature of God; however, even they misunderstand their oracles because one can only appreciate the truths that they hold if one appreciates the truths within the greater scope of time. Testifying of Yisra'el's partial understanding, Yisra'el's main law giver Moshe said, "The secret things belong unto the Lord our God: but those things which are revealed belong unto us and to our children forever, that we may do all the words of this law."[1]

---

[1] Deuteronomy 29:29

The Yisra'elites' paradoxical faith evidences the intellectual divide between our Creator and us. Albeit, because the misfortunes of human nature have afflicted the Yisra'elite faith, many continue to overlook its validity, despite its large contribution to Western culture.

The very doctrines of their religious law foretell a day when there will be reconciliation between the unknown Creator and humanity. The faith of the Yisra'elites points to a mediator who stands between humanity and God, who himself is the person of God as apprehensible by humanity. In fact, the complexities of the Yisra'elites' religious Law point to the simple expression of God in a great Prophet: an eternal King, who is the missing and indelible variable in the human equation, because he eternally preserves the purity of the human soul, which matures unto him through faith and then directly relates to God.

The biblical Testaments call the Yisra'elites' mediator God's *Mashiach*[1] (Messiah), a word that means the *anointed*, that is, God's chosen. As we have noted, Lord Yehoshua, whose Hebrew name means *savior*, fulfills the Yisra'elites' prophetic scriptures in word and miraculous deed. Lord Yehoshua, therefore, is he who God chose to bring salvation to humanity by bringing them into direct fellowship with God.

Message of Truth

Using the meek nature of Lord Yehoshua, God delivered a message of truth by telling all people to turn away from malicious self-aggrandizement by humbling themselves, like Lord Yehoshua, to accept the knowledge of God in concert with others. God delivered his message to first century Yisra'elite Judea — to his people who had backslid in faith.

To the Yisra'elites, Lord Yehoshua was a man of humility because he was not socially industrious, conventionally educated, or socially classed from a distinguished family; moreover, the misguided value

---

[1] In Greek, the translation of the Hebrew word *Mashiach* is *Christos*. The English translate *Christos* as *Christ*.

systems of many of the ruling Yisra'elite priesthood led the priests to expect that the foretold Mashiach would be of great renown (as seen in human eyes). Lord Yehoshua, they did not accept as their people's savior; however, many of the common people did, because of his compelling public ministry—a ministry involving the illumination of poignant doctrinal truths and the performing of notable miracles. So distorted were the values of the priests that they viewed the works of Lord Yehoshua as unlawful. To them, Lord Yehoshua seemingly compromised Yisra'el's God given laws at every turn.

In one such event, Lord Yehoshua purposely visited an outcast woman among an outcast people called the Samaritans. At noon, even in the heat of the day, waited Lord Yehoshua for this particular Samaritan woman. She was a casualty of moral culture's conflict with human vice: she, leaving scruples and good conscience, gave herself over to promiscuity. She had married multiple times and had many lovers: from these she secured her personal welfare. An adherence to religious principles did not suffice to supply her immediate needs, although she had some knowledge and respect for the faith. So, it is ironic, indeed, that Lord Yehoshua purposed in his mind to meet this woman: so many of the religious faithful sought him, but he made a personal visit to an immoral woman who sought him not.

She, even having the Samaritans shun her, necessarily drew her water in the heat of the day and not at dawn along with her neighbors. Arriving at the well, she, immediately seeing Lord Yehoshua, instinctively avoided him (his being a Jew, a Yisra'elite).

Lord Yehoshua asked her to draw water for him, and she being stunned at his speaking to her replied, "How is it that you, being a Jew, asks a drink from me, a Samaritan woman?"

Lord Yehoshua replied, "If you knew the gift of God, and who it is who says to you, 'Give Me a drink,' you would have asked him, and he would have given you living water . . . Whoever drinks of this water will thirsts again, but whoever drinks of the water that I shall give him will never thirst. But the water that I shall give him will become in him a fountain of water springing up into everlasting life."

After asking him for the water he spoke of, she perceived that he was a prophet because he had demonstrated to her his knowledge of her checkered past; thereafter, she asked him of the correct place to worship, saying, "Sir, I perceive that you are a prophet. Our fathers worshiped on this mountain, and you Jews say that in Yerushalayim is the place where one ought to worship?"

Lord Yehoshua replied saying, "Woman, believe me, the hour is coming when you will neither on this mountain, nor in Yerushalayim, worship the Father . . . But the hour is coming, and now is, when the true worshippers will worship the Father in spirit and truth; for the Father is seeking such to worship him. God is Spirit, and those who worship him must worship in spirit and truth."

She replied saying, "I know that Mashiach is coming . . . When he comes, he will tell us all things."

Lord Yehoshua replied saying, "I who speak to you am he."

Values First

The Samaritan woman's encounter with Lord Yehoshua was a life changing experience. She (being irreligious and immoral) was humbled by the fact that the savior had actually talked to her and had shared a profound truth: God desires fellowship with those whom he empowers to look beyond their physical situation, cultural or social background, and personal aspiration by becoming one with God in the Body of Lord Yehoshua to worship God in truth. God showed his profound love and grace to the Samaritan woman when he sought her even though she did not seek him.

It is important to note that Lord Yehoshua could have shared such a truth with someone of ostensibly higher social worth. Lord Yehoshua purposely by-passed those who are seemingly more worthy of his company: the sick, the poor, the religious faithful, and the afflicted did Lord Yehoshua by-pass to meet this woman, to demonstrate the full riches of God's grace. The Lord ministered to a Samaritan woman whose profession of prostitution had undermined the foundation of the agricultural societies that relied upon legitimate children to inherit family property and social standing. By seeking the Samaritan woman, Lord Yehoshua picked the basest level of civilization's social ills: he chose a person who chooses self-gratification not only over any faith bearing religious conviction, but also over one's self-respect before his or her neighbors, as well. By ministering to the immoral woman from Samaria, Lord Yehoshua communicated that all corrupt levels of civilization are unworthy of fellowship with God: neither the oppressive and inequitable political regimes, such as the Roman Empire; or the self-serving religious societies, such as the Yisra'elite priesthood; even unto those peoples who compromise cultural moralities for self-gratification, such as the Samaritan woman, are worthy of fellowship with God. By ministering to the Samaritan woman, Lord Yehoshua affirmed the fact that any fellowship with God is solely a condition of God's grace.

In summary, God's message sent through Lord Yehoshua is the following: to have fellowship with God by worshipping him in truth, God must instill such faith that enables the person to transcend his or her physical circumstance and conform to a correct value system that holds the knowledge of God's truth (as seen through the eye of selfless faith in the nature of God as revealed unto Yisra'el and portrayed in Lord Yehoshua) above all else.

It is true, humanity's misplaced values cloak the glory of God. Thus, when those misplaced values conform to the truth that Lord Yehoshua holds, true worshippers behold God's glory.

The Holy Bible

The Samaritan woman's praise of Lord Yehoshua's ability to liberate a person's soul in a moment sings in concert with a host of others' praise. His promises to his disciples were for them guaranties. Lord Yehoshua spoke of a future existence of peace and liberty under God, calling such a place "the Kingdom of Heaven," whose composition is of "peace and righteousness," he said.

Succinctly, Lord Yehoshua answered the unutterable questions of life with an uncompromising sureness: he left his audience fulfilled and convicted, their souls left feeling complete and whole. He enlightened the bleak shadows of their ignorance with a profound new hope of an existence with meaning and purpose, where everyone achieved fulfillment without detriment to one's fellow. Lord Yehoshua's comforting words of wisdom and understanding dropped upon his anxious hearers like a morning dew revival on a parched land of skepticism and gloom.

Lord Yehoshua's disciples multiplied followers of the Lord across the globe, leaving an indelible mark on history itself. These followers formed the institution that is the foundation of Western civilization: Western civilization calls this institution the *Church*—the Ecclesia, an assemblage of the called out ones, belonging to the Lord.

The purpose of the Church is to maintenance the attributes of Lord Yehoshua's heavenly Kingdom here on earth. Its leaders preach the teachings of the Mashiach: the loving of God and neighbor, the turning away from worldly vice, the giving to the poor, and all such worldly duties befitting of a general equity among the Church goers—all such things pursuing the glory of God, whom we may see in Lord Yehoshua, humanity's salvation: of such things, they teach. The Church ministers to the world until the day in which Lord Yehoshua's Kingdom of true worshippers comes into being.

The cornerstone of the Church, therefore, is Lord Yehoshua. To this end, the Church's foundation stands upon the Old Testament canon of Jewish scriptures, which the Church couples with the New Testament writings of Lord Yehoshua's Apostles. The Church has gathered the corpus of these writings into 66 books, which prophets and Apostles wrote over a period of 1400 years. Today the world recognizes these books as the Holy Bible: a book that describes the workings of God in his relation to humanity. Buried within the annals of this great volume (the Holy Bible) is God's expressed truth that Lord Yehoshua spoke of. Within this book is the key to the health and happiness of humanity: a correct value system, which relates to God and responds to his truth.

Historically, the interpretation of the biblical Testaments has been the subject of great strife and conflict because of the political contention between the Church and the secular institutions of Western culture. Thus, the public holds the actual text of the Holy Bible under great scrutiny because of its social and political ramifications.

Generally speaking, there are three major schools of thought for biblical interpretation that have existed throughout Church history.

The three major schools are Orthodoxy, Rationalism, and Neo-orthodoxy: the first school of thought, which we identify as Orthodoxy, understands the Holy Bible to be the sole source of truth. The Orthodox assert that God used human authors with their individual personalities to compose an autographed message to humanity from God: this viewpoint predominated the greater part of two millennia. The second school of thought, which we identify as religious Rationalism, maintains that men of great talent and genius authored the biblical Testaments: the Rationalists deny that there has been any divine influence over the compositions of the Testaments. Lastly, the third school of thought, which we identify as Neo-orthodoxy, holds that the Holy Bible is only the inspired revelation of God; therefore, they believe that the Holy Bible is subject to human error. For this reason, the Neo-orthodox believe that people should only use the Holy Bible as a tool to glean whatever principles that facilitate social civility.

The Author's Viewpoint

The author of this doctrinal treatise holds that "all scripture is given by inspiration of God, and is profitable for doctrine, for reproof, for correction, for instruction in righteousness."[1] The author, therefore, considers the greater part of the Bible to be a copy of inspired messages from God that his chosen followers recorded and faithful scribes then chronicled and edited, their works being governed by divine providence to preserve the revelation of God's truth. Concurrently, the author holds that the poetry and historical accounts of the chosen followers comprise the remainder of the Bible.

Because God inspired the scriptures to reveal ultimately a truth, concerning his expressed liberty, which he unfolds throughout time, gaining an understanding of the exact meaning of particular scriptures by using rational systems of interpretation, alone, is impossible, even when one seemingly ascertains the biblical author's original intent. The biblical authors, individually, may not have been

---

[1] 2 Timothy 3:16

entirely privy to the purposes of the dispensed message, which subsumes under the expressed truth that unites all scriptures.

When we accept that God has inspired the scriptures to cultivate his worshippers, we must accept that his inspiration transcends the writing styles, grammatical usages, and cultural backgrounds of the authors, in order to communicate directly to the sensibilities of his worshippers' souls—that is, their faith, fidelity, and integrity. Indeed, only the dispensations of God's grace unto individual worshippers afford them the ability to ascertain the truth that places all scriptures into their correct context, even as the scripture declares, "this commandment that I am commanding you today is not hidden from you, neither is it far off . . . But the word is very near unto you, in your mouth, and in your heart, that you may do it."[1]

Rational approaches unto the scriptures are, therefore, without merit, when the intuitive incite of God's Holy Spirit is absent from the seeker of biblical understanding. For this cause, the Apostle Sha'ul warned, in an epistle, against the oppositions of those who only seek knowledge through vein rational approaches, despite faith.[2]

Unfortunately, modern Church institutions evaluate the status of a Church leader by the leader's ability to comprehend and apply secular interpretational conventions; whereas Church institutions should qualify a Church leader by the leader's ability to convey the underlying truth of God, in such a way that the congregation as a whole may instinctively verify biblical truth corporately, in accordance with the common inspiration of God. Rightly noting the inability to convey in writing or speech the inspiration of God, Church institutions do try to gain an understanding of the scriptures by applying the discipline of hermeneutics[3]: the study of theories and methods of interpreting any text. In this manner, Church institutions form a variety of general theories or principles as they engage the

---

[1] Deuteronomy 30:11-14
[2] 1 Timothy 6:20
[3] The word *hermeneutics* is a derivation of the Greek word *hermeneutikos*, which means *interpretation*. The Greek word derives from the name of the pagan Greek god Hermes, who is a messenger for the pagan Greek gods.

biblical canon. Following, Church institutions treat direct explanations for individual biblical passages by putting forth exegeses[1]: practical interpretations of individual text, which involves etymology, limits of passages, grammatical analysis, writing style, and historical-cultural investigation.

Notwithstanding, because Church theologies or principles do not effectively communicate God's prevailing truth to the sensibilities of all congregants, the Church's increasingly rational and inductive approach to the scriptures manifestly alienate Church leaders from a majority of the congregants, who find esoteric Church doctrines inaccessible, especially for those who are economically or physically disadvantaged. For this cause, Church corruption persists, especially as Church leaders become exploitive and the other above listed human frailties further undermine the truth of God.

This work, therefore, seeks to qualify an appropriate understanding of the entire biblical cannon by appealing to the eternal sensibilities that all congregants share, according to the dispensations of the grace of God. Once more, because God has given scripture for our personal edification, it is the author's conviction that God intends for all laypeople to understand the whole truth that the Holy Bible retains. Following Lord Yehoshua's example of directly presenting his truth to all, including working class fishermen, this work seeks to make accessible the full truth of God for laypeople, despite their lack of knowledge, in regards to Church history and the voluminous, contemporary Church doctrines that haphazardly attempt to chronicle the quintessential aspiration of God. As inferred above in the introduction, this work seeks to procure a systematic understanding of the Old and New Testaments of the Holy Bible that reconciles all the principle points of the scripture with the historical and contemporary modes of civic, social, and private life.

Although the work does not chronologically treat the entire scriptural account, the work systematically treats the governing themes of the Holy Bible, in order to demonstrate how the scriptures retain definitive truth. Our single purpose is to apprehend a

---

[1] The word *exegeses* is a plural form of the word *exegesis*.

definitive understanding of how we (whom a progressive life-experience of human frailty bind) may worship an eternal God in truth, by reconciling ourselves with God through the eternal mediator and Testator, Lord Yehoshua the Mashiach.

Chapter 2

Y'haweh: the Totality of Truth

"Show me thy ways, O Lord; teach me thy paths. Lead me in thy truth, and teach me: for you are the God of my salvation; on thee do I wait all the day."
—Psalm 25:4-5

The Pearl of Great Price

When we seek to worship God in truth eternally, we invariably seek to abide in Heaven: Heaven is the name that the biblical Testaments give to the place where God and the totality of his truth stand. The exact nature of Heaven continues to be a great mystery. Humanity's shortsighted, temporal pursuits continue to confuse Heaven's eternal meaning. The only thing certain about Heaven is that it is a place where truth bears its totality, under which all commune with God and each other in complete harmony. Undoubtedly, Heaven is a place of peace where fear and dread are absent, and surely it is a place that is so beneficial to the human soul that necessity, desire, and volition fail to add to its distinction.

We find clues that reveal Heaven's nature in certain stories told by Lord Yehoshua the Mashiach. He told one short story to describe the nature of Heaven by describing the nature of those who will gain entrance into Heaven. Lord Yehoshua told the story by saying, "The Kingdom of Heaven is like unto a merchant man, seeking goodly pearls: who, when he had found one pearl of great price, went and sold all that he had, and bought it."[1]

A correct interpretation of Lord Yehoshua's story is as follows: the merchant man in the story represents those peoples who seek

---
[1] Matthew 13:45-46

happiness by acquiring the temporal riches of this world through whatever unjust means necessary; while the merchant man's finding of the pearl of great price represents those peoples who, through faith, see the eternal riches of God in the world to come. These peoples of faith, seeing the true riches, cast away what they formerly valued in this temporal world, with all its misdeeds, and take upon themselves the duties that give them access to the true, eternal value of God in the Kingdom of Heaven.

Wisdom celebrates one who recognizes that all merchant men would cast away their worldly goods if they had the pearl of Heaven's truth, since all people would cast away their temporal vanity if they were certain of the manifold riches of truth in Heaven's eternal Kingdom. Naturally, anyone would love to possess truth and dwell within the heavens.

How involved it would be to look past our temporal perspectives; look upon truth; and forecast the nature of the Kingdom of Heaven, because truth is all encompassing. Looking upon truth would be like looking into the pearl of great price's semitransparent cascades of varying patterns, which all array themselves wonderfully and all instantly terminate at the uniform periphery of the pearl's sublime orb. Indeed, to look into truth's orb is not only to see the terminating points of the arrays as answers, finality, and conclusion; but also to see the beginning points of the arrays as causality, meaning, and purpose. Within the cascading prolific patterns of the orb, we see not only such things as the dimensions for spacetime, but also such things as the dimensions for the human emotions, like hope and despair. In the orb, we find the reason why the fundamental particle transcends time. As well, we find the origin and boundary of love.

It seems impossible for us to unfold the complex sphere of truth into a simple landscape, in order to quantify and survey its cascading patterns. If we could unfold truth's orb, we would inherently apprehend a simple understanding of the true nature of God, even though his nature seems impossible for us to comprehend. Yet, if we begin to qualify truth by what value truth is to us, we may well begin to unlock its secrets and gain an understanding of God's nature by understanding what identity of truth derives from him. Of course, ascribing a value to truth may seem daunting: what temporal monetary system can qualify its value, or what perishable possession can equal its benefits?

Still, if we measure truth by the value of its outcome—its liberating of the soul from life's drudgeries—we will find our currency. We can, therefore, affix no other value to truth's liberty than the single designation for truth as the only doorway for salvation; therefore, "the only doorway for salvation" is the composition of truth's priceless pearl, and Lord Yehoshua's Kingdom of Heaven is where salvation rests.

Unquestionably, we seek salvation when we seek truth; therefore, an understanding of salvation is the qualifying mark of an understanding of truth, because to obtain truth is to obtain freedom from the bane of ignorance. Likewise, the freedom that is liberty is salvation. Accordingly, an understanding of salvation is a qualifying mark of an understanding of the nature of God because, as we have said, truth stands with God only; therefore, salvation is a quality of God, as well. For this cause, the biblical authors used the term salvation throughout the scriptures as a key attribute that we need to appreciate the being of God. The scriptures describe God as being "clothed with salvation,"[1] and they also proclaim, "Salvation belongs to *YHWH*"[2]; moreover, the scriptures conclude by saying, "Salvation to our God which sits upon the throne."[3]

Finally, as this work seeks to detail, the scriptures invite all to know "the word of truth—the gospel [that is, the good news] of your salvation."[4]

Having an understanding and a possession of salvation is, therefore, a necessity for our having a true worshipping relationship with God. To claim salvation and truly worship God, we must distinguish his eternal nature from our temporal understandings and

---

[1] 2 Chronicles 6:41
[2] Psalm 33:8
[3] Revelations 7:10
[4] Ephesians 1:13

self-centered pursuits. In so doing, we will begin to grasps truth's totality as we look beyond our temporality.

Having our eternal salvation in mind, let us briefly grapple with the scriptures that reveal God's nature and truth. Howbeit, let us remember that we only advance by keeping in mind one thing: our work must eventually use substantive means to prove an orthodox understanding of how the scriptures record the creation's subsuming under the totality of God's truthful expression of our liberty in Lord Yehoshua.

We recognize that the biblical Testaments contain many complex understandings that some people further confuse to advance unscrupulous agendas. In our introduction, we noted how the early Church produced creeds to establish biblical orthodoxy and combat the heretics who seek to exploit and manipulate Church doctrines. Mindful of potential heresies, we appreciate that our work must secure an objective proof that transcends human prejudice and self-interests.

Later, after we systematically prove an orthodox understanding of the biblical Testaments, we will be able to exalt the valleys of ignorance with heightened comprehension. We will be able to diminish every sublime mountain of mystery with profound awareness. We will be able to make the crooked places of deception straight, as we unfold truth's orb into a landscape. At that point, we will "stand still and see the salvation of *YHWH*."[1]

The Biblical Description of *God*

For now, we proceed to underscore the need for an objective proof for biblical orthodoxy. We proceed by briefly making a systematic assessment of the complexities of the biblical Testaments' most profound doctrines, concerning God's nature.

Scattered through the Holy Bible is an extraordinary portrayal of the true nature of God in all its enormity. One cannot easily understand God's nature in its entirety, as the Holy Bible portrays, because the biblical authors composed the scriptures over the course

---

[1] Exodus 14:13

of above 1400 years, with each scripture primarily meeting the immediate needs of the author or culture at hand. Whatever divine quality sufficed to meet these needs and concluded each scriptural composition. For this cause, God's nature as revealed in the scriptures is hard to quantify in a single word or maxim. Even though we do find the biblical understanding that God's existence constitutes all things, we also find the understanding that there is but one way to identify God's person as salvation.

Though we will not prove our orthodox understanding until later, let us venture forth and begin to unfold truth's sphere (for the purpose of beginning our understanding of God's nature and salvation for us). As we recognize that God inspired the scriptures to express an eternal truth, we expect that only a systematic understanding secures orthodoxy. Taken as a whole, we may say that the subsequent systematic statement tentatively agrees with the biblical Testaments' description of God: God is a self-existent Spirit whose expressed persons comprise the totality of existence; whose every action defines love; whose will defines truth; and whose essence is the only good to all who truly worship him.

We glean the validity of the above systematic statement from a variety of scriptures, which one may find in the Holy Bible's New Testament. In summary, the New Testament describes God as a Spirit who shows his purposes and goodwill to humanity by extending himself as Lord Yehoshua the Mashiach, who delivers salvation. Lord Yehoshua, the scriptures proclaim, is God's ultimate expression to the human race. A brief survey of a few scriptures that describe God's nature, in agreement with our above systematic statement, is the following:

We start with a quotation from a letter that Sha'ul[1] the Apostle and the herald of the Christian age wrote. Sha'ul, in a letter that he sent to the new Christians in the ancient city of Colossae, wrote of the totality of God's expression in the Mashiach. In his writing, Sha'ul alluded to the fact that God had construed all things in creation

---

[1] Paul

around Lord Yehoshua. Sha'ul concluded that only Lord Yehoshua truly reflects God's nature and existence. Sha'ul wrote as follows:

> Yehoshua is the image of the invisible God, the firstborn over all creation. For by him all things were created that are in heaven and that are on earth, visible and invisible, whether thrones or dominions or principalities or powers. All things were created through him and for him. And he is before all things, and in him all things consist.[1]

Conclusively, in the above scripture, Sha'ul alludes to the fact that God expresses every aspect of creation to complete God's ultimate expression in the person of Lord Yehoshua. In this manner, God enables humanity to identify their salvation in God's good, which God expresses in this temporal world as the prevailing of his right judgment, which we see in the unblemished conscience of the Mashiach. Thus, when we consider this scripture in the context of Lord Yehoshua's life, we understand that God construed all things to underscore his definitive expression of himself to humanity through the unblemished life, death, and resurrection of Lord Yehoshua. As we shall see, God in this manner proclaims his love, comprises the dimensions for truth, and reflects the good of his person by expressing all things through Lord Yehoshua, who is the truth of God in human form.

Next, when we consider the fact that God expresses his glory through Lord Yehoshua, we especially learn that Lord Yehoshua expresses the quality of God that is most precious to us: he expresses God's love. We find God's love, being expressed through the person of Lord Yehoshua, recorded in such New Testament books like the Gospel of Yochanan[2] the Apostle. In Yochanan's Gospel, we find the most poignant scripture that testifies of God's profound love for humankind, which the life, death, and resurrection of Lord Yehoshua express. This scripture records God's sacrifice of Lord Yehoshua, God's only begotten son, for the sake of humanity; and the scripture is as follows:

---

[1] Colossians 1:13-17
[2] John

> For God so loved the world, that he gave his only begotten son, that whosoever believes in him should not perish, but have everlasting life.[1]

Yochanan's scripture, *John 3:16*, is the Holy Bible's definitive proclamation that God's salvation is an expression of his love, which the sacrifice of his son Lord Yehoshua witnesses. *John 3:16* also alludes to the fact that God glorifies himself before his true worshippers whom he empowers to receive his love as follows: God's Holy Spirit reconciles their impure consciences by redeeming their faith in the pure conscience of Lord Yehoshua, through whom they gain an everlasting life.

Equally important, we find in Yochanan's writings the understanding that Lord Yehoshua's sacrifice fulfills God's truth. For instance, Lord Yehoshua himself proclaims, "I am the way, the truth, and the life: no man comes unto the Father, but by me."[2]

Lord Yehoshua's profound truth also foreshadows God's good. We see in one scripture that Lord Yehoshua, himself, testified that God alone is good: the scripture records Lord Yehoshua rebuking a man who had addressed him as being good: Lord Yehoshua scolding the man said, "Why do you call me good? No one is good except one, God!"[3]

In effect, by simply saying that God alone is good, the Lord affirmed that God would array truth (and, therefore, his savior personage—the Mashiach) around himself. Furthermore, in another scripture, we find God himself testifying of his good to Moshe, when Moshe asked to see his glory by saying, "Please show me your glory!"

God replied to Moshe saying, "I will make all of my goodness pass before you, and I will proclaim the name of *YHWH* before you."[4]

---

[1] John 3:16
[2] John 14:6
[3] Mathew 19:17
[4] Exodus 33:18-19

And so, by saying to Moshe, "I will make all my goodness to pass before you, and I will proclaim [my name]," God signified that truth and all creation affirms the good of his first person perspective being, YHWH.

In conclusion, the affirming of God's good is the sole purpose for all creation. Our above statement systematically delineates the process through which God affirms his good. Essentially, God creates all things to express his love to us through Lord Yehoshua. Thereby he affirms his truth. Following, his truth points us to his good in the fulfillment of truth's landscape.

The Apostle Sha'ul sums up truth's totality in another letter that he wrote to the believers in the Greek City of Corinth. We see in Sha'ul's letter a glimpse of truth's landscape. Sha'ul writes that through his provision for salvation—his expression of himself in the person of Lord Yehoshua—God brings all things under his subjection that he (God) may affirm his absolute, which is his only good. The signifying quote from the letter is as follows:

> Now when all things are made subject to him, then the son himself will also be subject to him who put all things under him, that God may be all in all.[1]

The overall implication that we have from the above scripture is that God subjugated all things through his loving expression of himself as the only salvation for humanity in the person of Lord Yehoshua. This salvation affirms God's fullness, and our acquirement of God's salvation through Lord Yehoshua is the confirmation of truth and, thereby, the confirmation of all things unto God's good, which (again) is God's glory over all.

Identifying Biblical Harmony

When we juxtaposition the above scriptures next to one another and accept them at face value, the scriptures are easy to understand; however, when we analytically interpret the above scriptures apart

---
[1] 1 Corinthians 15:28

from one another and attempt to follow them through to their logical conclusions, they are at best enigmatic to some (even not understood by the learned) and at worst valueless to others (even not seen as having any validity in the eyes of secular thinkers). Although, we may glean many poignant truths and understandings from the Holy Bible, the primary truth that the Bible defines, as a whole, is unclear. Often the scriptures, themselves, invite more questions.

Most believers usually accept the above scriptures at face value, their rightly accepting that Lord Yehoshua is our only true access to God. Yet, if we qualify more lucidly the mainstream message from such scriptures, by holding our salvation in mind, we will access a more perfect understanding of not only the entirety of the scriptures, themselves; but also the nature of God, his purposes for humanity, and thereby his purpose for creation. Surely, it would be no overstatement to say that gaining this more excellent understanding would unfold truth and shed light on the answers to our social problems. In summary, what we need to qualify from such scriptures is a preliminary definition of Lord Yehoshua's truth. Later, we will secure a systematic and objective understanding of the manner in which God expresses the creation and the human experience under truth's functional form.

Truth Found in God's Love

After we have considered the above scriptures to determine an initial definition for truth, the following actuality presents itself: God affirms himself as the only good by showing his love through the sacrifice of his son Yehoshua. Thus, when we consider such, we can without hesitation say that God created all things to reflect his eternal fulfillment: a fulfillment that we progressively appreciate as God expresses his love and procures our esteem of his salvation. We will clearly see by and by that the death of Lord Yehoshua on the cross serves God's purposes. Conclusively, the underlying message from the above scriptures is that God self-determines the fulfillment of his love in us: unquestionably, the reciprocity of his love is what he purposes.

At this juncture it seems appropriate for us to put forth a definition describing the fundamental nature of love as seen in the action of God. Afterward, we will be able to apprehend our preliminary definition for truth, which we shall later prove.

The definition of love is as follows: love is a personal desire for a state of completeness that one acquires by his or her relation to the attributes of another person or thing. Thus, the person's love requires a sense of reciprocity from his or her object of love. To this end, love's fulfillment culminates in an acquired harmony between a person and another person or thing; and love's harmony is at its zenith when the wishes of a person agree with the grants of God. Categorically, therefore, love is ultimately the desire for the good, which is salvation to the true worshipper (even an enduring state of felicity) and which is to God his fullness (even *Rest* for his soul, in glory over all).

We may begin to understand how God's love precedes his truth if we consider the fact that the nature of God's love directly initiates the nature of law. For instance, the medium of law directly correlates God's sought out loving relation between himself and humankind, because the fundamental definition of law is the following: law is a sustained relation between distinct physical things and a covenant relation between two or more parties who agree upon certain principles that govern their harmonious relationship. Accumulatively, all the laws (or relations) of nature serve God's ultimate objective of sustaining a covenant relationship with his elect worshippers.

In God, love is complete and whole unto itself because he designed creation to complement himself to affirm his good. He, therefore, expectantly waits to receive the benefit of his love at a time that he predestined, as signified by the scriptures: "We love him because he first loved us."[1]

From the human perspective, God's loving endurance of the wrongs committed against him demonstrates that God's "love suffers

---

[1] 1 John 4:19

long and is kind."¹ It is important to understand, however, that God's love is the only love that can be both self-serving and beneficial to all who reciprocate his love. He determines his love to be self-serving because he is absolute: there can only be one good that a person can eternally experience as salvation when he or she reciprocates his love. Furthermore, there can only be one truth, which truth God's loving gift of salvation qualifies to uphold his ultimate good. Accordingly, the scriptures report that "there is . . . one hope . . . one Lord, one faith, one baptism [unto salvation], [and] one God and Father of all, who is above all and through all, and in you all."²

Furthermore, the Old Testament scriptures describe God's self-serving love as jealous by saying, "For I *YHWH* thy God am a jealous God."³

As well, the scriptures go on to say, "You shall worship no other god, for *YHWH*, whose name is Jealous, is a jealous God."⁴

Apart from God, a person can never truly experience the riches of love. Even if a person's love is self-serving and at the same time beneficial to others, the person's desires cannot truly find eternal fulfillment if he or she seeks to love something apart from God. Human frailty only allows people to experience sensorial gratification, which is temporary, worldly pleasure. Even, the author of the New Testament book of Jude despairingly writes of those whose love stands upon sensorial gratification, while he admonishes the faithful to seek only the true eternal love. The author poignantly writes, "These are sensual persons, who cause divisions, not having the Spirit . . . but you beloved . . . keep yourselves in the love of God."⁵

We can only find the definition of truth, therefore, in God's love: we can only find the truth in God's design to reflect his eternal completeness as he cultivates a relationship with his worshippers; because after he will have fulfilled this relationship, he will have

---

[1] 1 Corinthians 13:4
[2] Ephesians 4:4-6
[3] Exodus 20:5
[4] Exodus 34:14
[5] Jude 1:21

consummated Heaven's Kingdom. By keeping the affirmation of God's love in mind, we may qualify a general definition of truth as follows:

We equate the word *truth* with the will[1] of the self-existent Spirit (God), whose will extends God's eternal goodness and holiness as the prevailing of right judgment, which we see in the pure conscience of Lord Yehoshua. We experience truth as God's Holy Spirit condemns humanity's compromise of conscience and redeems our faith in the Lord's unblemished conscience, to the end that we receive the liberty of the Lord's righteousness, as we forsake our shortsighted pursuits. Thus, to fulfill truth, the Holy Spirit esteems the eternal good of God, which Lord Yehoshua's pure conscience reflects, as the only source of felicity (or rather the only source of salvation) for the souls whom God created: this esteem affirms God's good, which is his fulfillment that our love celebrates. Summarily, truth reflects salvation because it proves to be a medium between the human faculty of faith and God's beneficence. Truth then is the Holy Spirit's mediation between human wishes that agree with God's grants; therefore, to the true worshippers, truth is an enduring sense of fulfillment that the worshippers experience corporately as well as individually, around a single good unto God; moreover, in the eyes of God, truth culminates in the ultimate reality: the outcome of God's self-determining the totality of God's being and our complementing being within God.

More explicitly, the satisfaction of God, which he affirms in us, affirms the prevailing of his right judgment over our compromised judgments. He, being omnipotent, therefore, construed all things in existence to affirm his satisfaction in the Mashiach. In effect, all things (whether physical, emotional, thought, or action) have there being in magnifying God through Lord Yehoshua: the souls who

---

[1] The 19th Century philosopher, Arthur Schopenhauer, was the first notable thinker to surmise that the physical universe is merely a representation of an universal will, which individuals diversify and so perceive distinct objective experiences within spacetime; however, because Schopenhauer did not consider the universal will to be that of a divine creator, he conceived reality as being without purpose and chaotic. Thus, Schopenhauer perceived the human condition as harsh and meaningless, its being the product of a will-to-live that confounds universal understanding.

purposely reciprocate his love define him as their benefactor, while the souls who do not reciprocate his love define him as their judge. Every aspect of the human experience has its being in defining him, from the things that cause our most dire social ills to the things that forward the cause of our peace, as noted in one scripture: "If I ascend up into heaven, thou art there: if I make my bed in hell, behold, thou art there."[1]

It is evident that the first action of any human endeavor should be to ascertain what action best accommodates the convention that God created for our felicity. In other words, one may justly ask what action must we pursue that has its derivation in paying due homage to his love. In short, we should endeavor to claim our salvation, which we may find in his truth and realize in his love, because with this claim, we will accomplish a true relationship with God. To this end, we must encompass the unfolding will of God that occurs throughout time and culminates in his good, which we can secure from Lord Yehoshua's ministry of bringing salvation unto us.

Our acceptance of the teachings of God in the person of Lord Yehoshua is the ultimate benefit to our souls, despite whatever contentions we may endure from those who do not accept his covenants and whom God condemns. By relating to God through Lord Yehoshua, we both reciprocate the true love of God and realize our soul's completeness. Without a doubt, by reciprocating the love of him who stands clothed with salvation, we both fulfill his good and, thereby, our own good.

Y'haweh (YHWH)

It is striking that we find brilliance in the profundity of simplicity: we find the truth of all creation in God's expressing his love to humanity. We in few words dutifully declare the following: to express his love, God created all things, from the fabric of existence that creates the joy of the angels, to the state of freedom from want that creates the joy of humankind.

---

[1]Psalm 139:8

Even though the brilliance of truth is hard to quantify because the complexities of existence hide truth's simplicity, we can handedly assimilate the complexities into our understanding by proving our definition of God's truth. Indeed, we can unfurl the pearl of truth until we inherently see the uniformity of truth's landscape, even the glory God.

For the purpose of enhancing our relationship with God through Lord Yehoshua, let us proceed to encompass God's revealed truth and gain a better understanding of his nature and salvation for us. Let us begin with the understanding that all things originate from God's self-existent, spiritual nature. In truth, the word *god*, itself, is an incorrect nomination to use when describing the immensity of God's self-existent nature. For example, the word *god*, as used in the Holy Bible, is a translation of the Hebrew word *elohim*[1]. This word *elohim* is the plural form of the Hebrew word *eloi*, which means *strong one*. Accordingly, the word *god* denotes something that is supernatural and stronger than we are. For this cause, we need a more descriptive word to advance our understanding of God's self-existent, spiritual nature.

The self-existent Spirit, himself, revealed this need to Moshe a Yisra'elite Egyptian Prince around the year 1446 BC. The Spirit used a miraculous burning bush upon the mountains of Sinai to speak to Moshe, telling him that the self-existent Spirit would deliver his people from those who had enslaved them.

Moshe, who was apprehensive about relaying the Spirit's message to his people, anxiously asked for the name of him who spoke to him by saying, "When I come to the children of Yisra'el and say to them, 'The God of your fathers has sent me to you,' and they say to me, 'What is his name?' What shall I say to them?"

The Spirit answered him by saying, "I AM THAT I AM . . . this is my name forever, and this is my memorial unto all generations."[2]

Thus, *I am* are the words that Moshe brought to his people, the children of Yisra'el, to serve as a name for the God of their ancestors.

---

[1] The plural usage of the Hebrew word *eloi*, we will address at the end of chapter three.
[2] Exodus 3:13-15

Moshe and his people would eventually accept the understanding that using the words *I am* to serve as a name for their creator is a necessary rule to follow when trying to understand the self-existent Spirit. Howbeit, in truth, one may readily observe that *I am* is really not a name; it is a statement that describes an action or a state of being. By using such a statement, the Spirit communicated to Moshe that a single name cannot identify the Spirit because any single name defines and limits the thing that the name seeks to identify; moreover, names classify things apart from other things. For this cause, he who spoke to Moshe did not allow Moshe to identify him as any one thing. More importantly, he taught Moshe to know him as the composition of all things in creation. When the voice identified himself as *I am*, he identified himself as being self–existent and uncaused: one who is not subject to anything but who secures his own affirmation, definition, and purpose, by establishing truth as we have defined above. Conclusively, the statement *I am*, therefore, accurately describes the true identity of the Creator as without origin, the initiator, and the author of all things: a self-existent spirit.

In an effort to identify with the self-existent Spirit without utilizing a single name, the Hebrew speaking Yisra'elites used a Tetragrammaton—a phrase consisting of four consonants—to replace the statement *I am*. The tense of the clause *I am* is first person singular, and the Hebrew translation of the clause is *ehyeh*; however, to comprise the Tetragrammaton, the Yisra'elites translated the clause into a third person singular form to produce the statement *He Who Is*. Also, the Hebrew consonants that comprise the Tetragrammaton are *yhwh*, and the most probable pronunciation of the Tetragrammaton is *Y'haweh*[1] (Yuh-ah-wey).

In addition, the Tetragrammaton *YHWH* begins with a special indeterminate masculine pronoun that one only uses for its

---

[1] Latin scribes erroneously combined the Hebrew consonants found in the Tetragrammaton *YHWH* with the vowels found in the Hebrew name for lord *Adonai* to render the pronunciation *Y a H oe W a H*; thus, this pronunciation begets the following English derivation of the Tetragrammaton: *Yehovah* or *Jehovah*. Therefore, *Jehovah*, the erroneous pronunciation for *YHWH*, has become the English word for *Y'haweh*.

antecedent, the self-existent Spirit; therefore, if one replaces the pronoun with the words *the lord*, one renders the clause as *The Lord Who Is*. The first consonant in the clause, which one pronounces as *Yuh*, comprises the pronoun mentioned above.

In addition, the Yisra'elites used the above pronoun as a contracted form of *Y'haweh*; moreover, the Yisra'elites compounded the word *Y'haweh* with a variety of Hebrew proper nouns and phrases such as the following: *Y'haweh Yireh*, the Lord will provide; *Y'haweh Sabbaoth*, the Lord of hosts; *Y'haweh Raah*, the Lord is my shepherd; *Y'haweh Tsidkenu*, the Lord our righteousness; *Y'haweh Nakeh*, the Lord who smites; *Y'haweh Shammah*, the Lord who is present; and *HalleluYah*, praise the Lord who is.

Of most import, the Hebrew term for salvation contains the contracted form of *Y'haweh*; therefore, the Hebrew term for salvation ultimately describes Y'haweh's savior personage. In this way, the name *Yehoshua* (Jesus), which means *the Lord who is is salvation*, succinctly serves as the definitive identity for Y'haweh, which we relate to.

In brief, the Tetragrammaton YHWH does not give the self-existent Spirit a single identity; the clause only states his being. When we couple the clause with other words, the clause states the self-existent Spirit's various manifestations of himself.

In a word, we can only say that Y'haweh is much more than a god. He is far more than something that is supernatural, which merely initiates all things only to let them follow an indeterminate course outside of his will. Y'haweh is the Father and creator of all things, who stands outside the fabric of time itself (his being the beginning and the end). Y'haweh even forms the bounds of conception because his being establishes the perceptions of the souls whom he created. Y'haweh comprises all existence within his expression of himself: some receive his expression unto his edification, and others do not receive his expression unto the vindication of his judgments.

The paradigm of time exists within humanity's increasing knowledge of him, and time's completion will occur when a perfect knowledge of Y'haweh exists in the souls of humankind, even a perfect knowledge that gives humankind fulfillment in Heaven's Kingdom. At such a time, there will be a blending of human adulation with Y'haweh's exultation: a perfect liberty that will occur when Y'haweh "[highly exalts his son by giving] him a name which is above every other name,"[1] even the name salvation.

---

[1] Philippians 2:9

Chapter 3

Immanuel's Law

"The heavens declare the glory of God, and the expanse shows his handiwork. Day unto day pours forth speech, and night unto night reveals knowledge. There is no speech or language; their voice is not heard. Their measuring line has gone out through all the earth, and their words to the end of the world."

—Psalm 19:1-4

The Creeds of the Church

When we accept our definition of truth, we accept a controversial understanding that raises profound questions that the Church has struggled to reconcile for nigh two millennia. Our definition compels us to accept the understanding that Y'haweh's good and our frail existence are complementary. Our definition suggests that our succinct comprehension of Y'haweh's good as our salvation, in the Mashiach, affirms the truth of Y'haweh, while his procurement of our intelligence (by creating creation's perceptual confinements) establishes our self-awareness, through which we seek the sustenance, meaning, and purpose that find their haunt in his good.

Like many Christian theological understandings, our definition of truth essentially suggests that our reliance upon the good of Y'haweh resolves that his good pronounces our deprivations[1], which result in part from our intellectual inability to perceive his good

---

[1] The third Chapter of the Apostle Sha'ul's letter to the Romans establishes the contrast between Y'haweh's perfect state of being and our imperfect state. From the themes of Sha'ul's letter, we must stress that our imperfections do not make Y'haweh perfect; instead, our imperfections exhibit our empirical growth unto our eternal appreciation of Y'haweh's perfection, as we will detail below and in Chapter four of this work.

within creation. Our definition thus infers that Y'haweh's truth necessitates a benevolent form on him; for which cause, Y'haweh reveals himself throughout time as salvation, while our appreciation greets his benevolent form after we exhaust our own efforts in which we seek to relieve ourselves from the intellectual and environmental deprivations that his truth necessitates on us. Our definition then infers that our ignorance cloaks the glory of Y'haweh, which creation expresses, until he graciously reveals his glory as our salvation.

The most pressing questions that continue to challenge the Church and the same questions that our definition of truth raises are the following: how can Y'haweh be good and create an imperfect world that entails so much despair? And if Y'haweh can only create a world filled with despair, how can he be all powerful? For instance, why does he only save some and not others? And if he is all knowing and foresaw the need for the Mashiach, the Christ, why did he create an imperfect man, an Adam, to begin with?

The Churches that uphold the orthodox doctrines of Christianity usually answer these questions as follows: to distinguish Y'haweh's good, some may refer to the third chapter of the Apostle Sha'ul's epistle to the Romans. In the epistle, the Apostle establishes the contrast between Y'haweh's perfect state and our imperfect state, inferring that our imperfections do not make Y'haweh more perfect. Along with this understanding, we might tentatively add that our imperfections exhibit our empirical growth unto our appreciation of Y'haweh's perfection.

As for the questions concerning Y'haweh's allowance of despair and human imperfection, Christian theologians traditionally assert that Y'haweh at first created a perfect world; however, the theologians point out that Y'haweh also created free will, which entails a choice to seek out his good or suffer from the disparity of making selfish choices. Besides, the theologians point out that Y'haweh retains the sovereign power to uphold just punishment upon some, even as he retains the sovereign grace to show mercy upon others, even as the scripture says, "[I] will be gracious to whom

I will be gracious to, and will show mercy on whom I will show mercy."[1]

Too, we might underscore the fact that Y'haweh conceives the characteristics that humanity perceive to be good and evil differently, because he can only be subject to whatever constitutes a perception of the good: evil has no dominion over him because he is sovereign over all things. Truly, therefore, he cannot suffer from any misguided judgment that another makes, and he cannot suffer from any physical deprivation: he can only be subject to praise and adoration. Basically, we might consider that such is the foundation of his predisposed benevolence: Y'haweh forecasts good works upon some, while he does not prevent others from experiencing the natural hazards that human frailty exasperates. In this way, his omniscience determines the good works of some to be foreknown by him as well as the evil works of others. In fact, Y'haweh himself declares his omniscience, as recorded in the subsequent scripture:

> I am Y'haweh, and there is none else; I am God, and there is none like me; declaring the end from the beginning, and from ancient times the things that are not yet done, saying, "My counsel shall stand, and I will do all my pleasure..."[2]

While these debates persist and generate above two thousand Christian denominations that all have different approaches to these challenging questions, the cornerstones that unite the denominations are the Christian creeds. The creeds define the divinity of Y'haweh and the equal divinities of his two expressed persons who govern creation and the human epic, even as Y'haweh and his two expressed persons remain one in essence.

The principle creeds are the fourth Century AD Apostle's Creed and the Nicene Creeds; and the fifth Century AD Chalcedonian Creed and the Athanasian Creed; moreover, in the Athanasian Creed, we see the key doctrinal settlements that mark the agreed upon interpretation of the way the biblical Testaments define

---

[1] Exodus 33:19
[2] Isaiah 46:9-10

Y'haweh's nature. The key doctrinal points of the Athanasian Creed are the following:

> [We] worship one God in Trinity, and Trinity in Unity; neither confounding the Persons; nor dividing the Essence; for there is one Person of the Father; another of the Son; and another of the Holy Ghost. But the Godhead of the Father, of the Son, and of the Holy Ghost, is all one; the Glory equal, the Majesty coeternal. Such as the Father is; such is the Son; and such is the Holy Ghost. The Father uncreated; the Son uncreated; and the Holy Ghost uncreated. The Father unlimited; the Son unlimited; and the Holy Ghost unlimited. The Father eternal; the Son eternal; and the Holy Ghost eternal. And yet they are not three eternals; but one eternal. As also there are not three uncreated; nor three infinities, but one uncreated; and one infinite. So likewise the Father is Almighty; the Son Almighty; and the Holy Ghost Almighty. And yet they are not three Almighties; but one Almighty. So the Father is God; the Son is God; and the Holy Ghost is God. And yet they are not three Gods; but one God . . . [1]

The Church's use of the term "trinity"—that is, three hypostases in one ontological essence—reflects the truth that the expressed person of the Mashiach and the expressed person of the Holy Spirit are like Y'haweh, in regards to being uncaused, distinct, and eternal. Notwithstanding, the word Trinity is an incorrect and non-biblical term to use because its connotation does not grasp the epistemological structure (that is, the syntactical knowledge-structure) of Y'haweh's expressed Word through which the expressed person of the Son and the expressed person of the Holy Spirit subsists within any-possible temporal world, to reconcile the impoverished world unto Y'haweh's totality. In other words, Y'haweh's three expressed persons assume an hierarchy that one cannot equate: the self-existent Spirit Y'haweh is alone sovereign; whereas his expressed truth, which Lord Yehoshua personifies, and Y'haweh's expressed good, which the Holy Spirit communally relates, are extensively eternal, being without beginning or end,

---

[1] English translation, from The Creeds of Christendom, by Phillip Schaff, New York: Harper, 1877.

serving a qualified syntactical function. Thus, while we agree with the term "trinity" in principle, because we lack a more suitable term, we will at times employ the designation "Y'haweh's Totality" to describe the fullness of Y'haweh that his three expressed persons constitute.

Even so, to resolve the challenging questions that inhibit the Church's ability to prove and establish the orthodoxy—the right belief—of the biblical Testaments, we must pursue a critical understanding of our definition of truth by grasping the epistemological structure of Y'haweh's expressed persons. In other words, we must pursue an orthodox judgment that ascertains the higher knowledge structure of Y'haweh's expressed Word, and thereby we will understand the manner in which Y'haweh's expression fashions the physical world and the finite-knowledge-structures of our souls. Only then, will we grasp an understanding of Y'haweh's three expressed persons and the manner in which he empowers his elect to relate to him in true worship.

Faith

For now, we agree with our initial understanding of truth: we appreciate that Y'haweh's love cultivates our understanding as he cultivates our appreciation. Thus, our appreciation exists after we endure certain deprivation, our being temporarily ignorant of his good. At present, Y'haweh's glory sustains creation, as witnessed by the souls of the angels, while his eminence grows within our increasing knowledge of his *Word*, which is his expression of himself through his creating of the world before the intellectually deprived souls of humanity.

Fulfilling his truth, Y'haweh diminishes the mystery of his existence upon every revelation of himself throughout human history. In fact, his revelations discover his unknowns by stimulating humanity's innate mental ability to look beyond their senses with *faith*, which is a persistent look past social conventions by believing on the necessity and validity of things that are unseen and inapprehensible to the human senses.

When we acknowledge our intellectually frail disposition, we must conclude that it is impossible to relate to Y'haweh without faith. With this understanding in mind, the Apostle Sha'ul wrote of the necessity to have faith when relating to Y'haweh by saying, "Without faith it is impossible to please God."[1]

As well, Sha'ul wrote saying, "Faith is the substance of things hoped for, the evidence of things not seen."[2]

Our faculty of faith, therefore, is our innate awareness of the intellectual missing link between the mortal and the divine, and this innate awareness manifests itself into tangible relationships with Y'haweh, through our having faith only in his revelatory nature. So by our having faith in Y'haweh's revelations, we find that his obscure nature becomes less mysterious as his person becomes known to us, even in accordance with another of Sha'ul's scriptures that says, "For the invisible things of him from the creation of the world are clearly seen, being understood by the things that are made."[3]

Consider the case of the people of faith whom the Holy Bible chronicles. They trusted that the source of their health and eternal happiness is beyond all worldly powers. In faith, they chose the greater unseen good over any present tangible comforts. Basically, they had faith in a benevolent *God* who would ultimately reveal his good will to them through the loving nature of Lord Yehoshua, who justifies their faith, to convey Y'haweh's love.

Along these lines, we have said that Y'haweh further establishes his grace through the gift of faith that he gives to his worshippers, in order for them to believe in his revelations, which confirm that his person is their only salvation. Essentially, he couples his Word (the syntactical uniformity of creation) with his miraculous revelations (which are profound disturbances in the natural order during poignant historical moments) to speak of his rest, which social strife cloaks. He, therefore, pronounces his good in our discomforts, and he contrasts his fullness with our incompleteness. For example, we see

---

[1] Hebrews 11:6
[2] Hebrews 11:1-2
[3] Romans 1:20

that he once revealed to Sha'ul the Apostle the relationship between his largesse and the impoverished human soul by saying, "My grace is sufficient for thee: for my strength is made perfect in weakness."[1]

By knowing our place in Y'haweh's truth, we foresee our good end. We know that when we, Y'haweh's worshippers, receive the good of his Holy Spirit after enduring Y'haweh's mystery, we render to Y'haweh the appreciation that begets his eminence in our eyes. Truly, after we endure his mystery, we see that "all things work together for [the] good to them that [reciprocate the] love [of] God, to them that are called [by faith in his revelations that are] according to his purpose."[2] Then when we thus affirm Y'haweh's love, Y'haweh will express his fullness, in the glory of a new creation, and such will be time's end.

"The Seven Spirits of God"

At present, we have the understanding that Y'haweh's self-existent nature remains the same, while our understanding of Y'haweh's totality continues to evolve throughout human history. From the Holy Bible, therefore, we must quantify the most profound revelations of Y'haweh that the biblical covenants reflect and that are vital to our growing understanding of his salvation for us in Lord Yehoshua. Let us rest assured that by quantifying his revelations, we will understand his three distinct natures that fulfill truth's landscape. Thereby, we will come to a perfect understanding of him and our place of felicity.

To begin, let us understand that throughout the revelations of his truth, Y'haweh in various expressions of his will utilizes the number seven to symbolize completeness. For instance, we find the following understanding in Moshe's creation account: even though Y'haweh created all things in six days, he emphasizes the significance of the seventh day because on that day he validated the creation as good: his expression of himself within creation had been completed and his soul was then set at rest.

---

[1] 2 Corinthians 12:9
[2] Romans 8:28

While we keep the seventh day of Y'haweh's rest in mind, let us note how Y'haweh commemorated his rest by using the number seven to convey to Yochanan the Apostle how Lord Yehoshua would fulfill Y'haweh's eternal rest. Although Yochanan records in his book entitled *Revelations* a variety of symbols that Y'haweh used to reveal his truth, we find that Y'haweh conveyed most of the symbols in increments of seven. For example, Yochanan wrote the following:

> And out of the throne proceeded lightning and thundering and voices: and there were seven lamps of fire before the throne, which are the seven Spirits of God.[1]

We cannot fail, therefore, by using the symbolic number of completeness to quantify the most important revelations of Y'haweh that humanity relates to. Let us first recall from above that Y'haweh's love seeks his fulfillment by defining truth as a medium between our wishes and his grants. While considering this fact, it should be evident to us that Y'haweh's revelations of himself speak to our innermost insecurities.

If we only identify whatever missing intellectual attributes that would bring to bear our perennial wellbeing, we may well quantify Y'haweh's succinct revelations of himself to us. Considering such, we may proceed to quantify Y'haweh's several revelations of himself that are necessary for our wellbeing as follows:

First, we must consider that Y'haweh is our creator and with him is our fulfillment, that is, the meaning and purpose for our existence. Second, when never ending social turmoil afflicts us, we must rest assured that by his grace he will ultimately provide truth, justice, and judgment upon the earth. Third, we must look past social conventions with faith by trusting in his revealed nature, and we must see his continuity and fidelity within creation. Hence, we must respond to his grace by valuing the eternal things that are of him over the chaotic and ephemeral things that are of us: indeed, our response must be with rejoicing, knowing that he has predestined us

---

[1] Revelations 4:5

to become the inheritors of his grace and mercy. Fourth, we must revere his ordinance, which manifests his person and creates the laws that govern our equitable relationship with him and our fellows. Fifth, we must rest assured that one day he will reign over us eternally, ensuring peace and righteousness. Sixth, we must trust that he empathizes with our frailties and that he has overcome them by suffering the same hazards only to prevail over them with his strength. And lastly, seventh, we must trust that his love is our fulfillment, his being the supplier of all our needs.

Altogether, these several understandings define our place of felicity in the esteem of Y'haweh. Having these thoughts in mind, we will qualify several major revelatory covenants of Y'haweh as follow: 1 *he is the creator and with him is the fulfillment—the meaning and purpose for our lives*; 2 *he is the supplier of truth, judgment, and justice*; 3 *he is the eternal friend of the faithful elect*; 4 *he is the governor of us elect who are obedient to his laws, which esteem him in the midst of the elect assembly*; 5 *he is the King of righteousness*; 6 *he is the giver of the Holy Spirit of Truth, because he writes his laws upon our hearts*; lastly and above all, 7 *he is the husband of the faithful bride—the redeemed assembly*.

The First Revelation of Y'haweh: *He is the Creator*

When we take into consideration the fact that Y'haweh's Word extends all things to express the good of Y'haweh's soul, the necessity of Y'haweh's first miraculous revelation of Y'haweh's being *the Creator* becomes obvious. As we shall see, the existence of creation, itself, is inexplicable without a self-existent creator. So surely Y'haweh's simple revelation of himself as the Creator is the greatest significance; therefore, with this initial understanding of Y'haweh, we proceed.

First, let us consider the fact that to acknowledge Y'haweh as the Creator is to acknowledge his self-existence. Truly, we cannot begin any inquiry into his nature without first looking past social conventions with faith by believing that he is real: "For he who comes to God must believe that he is, and that he is a rewarder of those who diligently seek him."[1]

Subsequently, when we acknowledge Y'haweh as our creator, we acknowledge the fact that with him is the meaning of life; however, when we are without certain knowledge of him, we are uncertain of life's meaning. Afterward, we become existentially bound to a life of no reason or significance. We even become disposed to assume that survival, itself, is our life's purpose. Nevertheless, we the faithful should not despair, because Y'haweh's gracious revelations to us liberates those "who through fear of death were all their lifetime subject to bondage."[2]

Invariably, the bondage that holds people captive is the fear of dying. The following question that an ancient playwright poses, in his most famous soliloquy, resounds in the souls of all who have no faith:

> To be, or not to be, — that is the question . . .
> But that the dread of something after death, —
> The undiscovered country, from whose bourn
> No traveler returns, — puzzles the will,
> And makes us rather bear those ills we have,
> Than fly to others that we know not of?[3]

We may state in few words that the slings and arrows of life bind people who have no faith in Y'haweh's provision for our eternal salvation.

To be sure, unfortunate is the following reality: again, the only truth that many accept is that which human ingenuity arrests from their highly secularized social and physical sciences. Despite the sense of complacency that the secular institutions afford humanity, human civilization cannot sustain true peace because they lack an eternal knowledge of a good that sustains peace. The unfaithful of humanity naively comfort themselves with the knowledge that they

---

[1] Hebrews 11:6
[2] Hebrews 2:15
[3] The English playwright William Shakespeare's *Hamlet*, Act III, Scene I.

incrementally gain from their scientific observations; however, a complete understanding still eludes them. Their secularized scientific practices cannot apprehend the general purpose for existence: their science merely observes existence. In point of fact, scientists have even identified the most fundamental properties of all physical bodies by classifying them with discrete quantities of energy that they define as *quanta*. Nevertheless, humanity has no knowledge of how or why these properties came into being, because they have not perceived from the elements a functional expression of a divine purpose: they have not discerned a divine intention that they can corroborate intuitively or rationally with their senses. To humanity, existence (a coming into being from non-being) is the most baffling paradox of all, when they do not accept the reality of a creator.

The Questions of Metaphysics[1] and the Mind-Matter Explanatory Gap

To reconcile the paradox of our existence, theology and philosophy seek to facilitate the core goal of the human soul, and that goal is to know how to achieve the liberty of personal meaning and communal fulfillment, eternally. To realize this goal for society, as a whole; theologians, philosophers, and scientists, alike, seek to possess 'scientia': a systemized knowledge that objectively seeks to reconcile our cognitive experiences within a physical creation.

Christian theologians seek to reconcile all scientific discoveries with such biblical revelations that proclaim Y'haweh's metaphysical reality, while secular scientists seek material explanations that they can test and verify. The biblical approach seems trivial and exploitive to the secular scientists, because the Church's theological proclamations fail to make verifiable predictions. As a consequence, the scientists seek to liberate humankind from the Church's metaphysical speculations and oppressive religious dogma.

---

[1] An ancient editor of Aristotle's theological works first coined the term *meta ta physika* (Gk) —"after the *physika*"—when he categorized Aristotle's *First Philosophy of Theology*, as a discipline that perspective students should study after they study Aristotle's other works that addressed physical (or natural) sciences.

To counter people's reliance upon unsubstantiated Church doctrines, scientists strive to accommodate personal meaning, by discovering natural laws that explain both creation's workings and our existence. These natural explanations, scientists seek to base contemporary society's judgment upon; therefore, in public circles, scientists seek to replace religious explanations with methodological understandings that predict material behavior.

Despite the secular scientists' liberal quest, a thoughtful mind may easily discover the following oversight that the scientists suffer as they apply their naturalist approach: because the Church and philosophical disciplines have not ascertained a metaphysical proof that scientifically predicts all social, political, and phenomenal behavior; scientists irresponsibly forgo any consideration of the metaphysical origin of the natural-force-laws, themselves. They ignore the theologians' *a priori* supposition that the laws are the ultimate expression of divine intelligence.

The following rationale is an example of what compels Christian theologians and some philosophers to reason that the natural laws have a divine origin: even as the basis of our intelligence is the manner in which we involuntarily ascribe our perspective values upon all we perceive, any acceptance of natural laws is an acceptance that purposeful and determinant values transcend and sustain the physical creation that we observe. Decidedly, any recognition of a natural-force-law recognizes that we can rationally apprehend the perspective values that the identity of an object and its qualifying properties adhere to. What is more, because any given value cannot exist without an intelligent point of reference, any assessment of natural laws is functionally indeterminate, unless one conceives a perspective value that establishes the law.

For example, we shall see that scientists inescapably employ perspective values when they explain their theories. They routinely employ perspective value determinations like their considering some physical states as collapsed as opposed to fixed; evolved as opposed to adaptable; and random as opposed to contingent.

Even the ensuing anthropocentric—human centered—argument underscores the critical error of the scientists' naturalist approach: as the secular scientists hold that a material and brilliantly structured universe exists, despite divine or human intelligence, they rob the brilliant universe's structure of intelligence's point of reference. They rob creation of intelligence's contingency, quantifications, and abstractions; moreover, they rob creation of intelligence's recognition of sequence, succession, and other such qualifications that intelligence's self-aware point of reference establishes. Essentially, when secular scientists envision a structured world without intelligence, they confusingly envision knowledge without the definitive standing and targeted scope of the sentience—the self-awareness—of life.

The scientists' atheistic position basically leads to utter confusion, with no hope of satisfying any quantifiable definitions for scientific pursuits. We might add that even some scientists' agnostic perspectives, which do not avow nor disavow Y'haweh's reality, are intolerable, because agnosticism never accepts definitive truth. To sustain our social aims, agnostic scientists merely accept the utility of framing scientific theories as though divine intension exists. Though these approaches seem attractive to the liberal mind, the agnostic approaches actually leave the public without any true social mandates to advance society.

The true worth of the contemporary practices of science is that the scientific method disciplines its practitioners to overcome personal or political prejudices when they make judgments. In response to this practical benefit, we must critically establish our biblical definition of truth, in such a way that we apprehend a non-trivial treatment of Y'haweh's metaphysical nature. Instead of irrationally questioning Y'haweh's being, we must apprehend an orthodox judgment that assesses how we relate to Y'haweh in a manner that predicts and explains our interactions with his creation. Essentially, we must derive the following from the biblical Testaments' description of Y'haweh's metaphysical being: we must capture scientia by ascertaining how the intentional expanse of Y'haweh's expressed Word proceeds from Y'haweh and creates our life-experiences. To realize this end, we must ascertain how Y'haweh manifests our being in the material world through physical means.

Likewise, we must ascertain how our intentional minds relate to the world and operate upon the world to derive conclusions in a justifiable manner.

To begin, we must further underscore how the theological and scientific understandings of creation radically differ. The conflicting understandings center upon the following three undiscovered ways that the mind's qualia—even the qualitative, intentional, and sensational experiences that hallmark consciousness—relate to the material world:

First, thinkers ponder over the manner in which the qualitative mind ascends from the brain's neuronal, chemical, and other cellular processes that comprise the human brain's cortexes and extant nervous and hormonal systems. Second, thinkers ponder over the manner in which the qualitative mind remains free but contingent to the subatomic, electromagnetic, and aggregate gravitational fields of our material world. And, third, thinkers muse over the manner in which the qualitative mind intentionally assimilates, redirects, and reinterprets the external world with a universal sense of purposefulness that transcends material experience. Essentially, theologians, philosophers, and scientists continuously fail to discover the manner in which the qualitative mind ascends from matter, remains free but contingent to matter, and intentionally assimilates matter.

The qualitative senses of the human mind are of consequence because the human mind's abstractions of the world are greater than the animals' instinctive senses, which only grasp immediate environments, aesthetically. Because the human mind's qualitative sense intentionally assimilates material experiences, as representations of universal purposes, theologians assert that only a divine creator's metaphysical purposes determine our qualitative senses as being more substantial than the material world, which the creator conceived to procure our experience. In contrast, scientists hold that the mind's qualitative experience is either a fiction or a chance outcome of natural processes; therefore, scientists hold our qualitative experience as inconsequential. Many scientists even consider all qualified senses as solely the product of such anatomical processes like the hormonal systems that chemically produce moods.

The age-old metaphysical question, therefore, does not only concern the relationship between the mind and matter, but also concern the validity of our qualitative senses: indeed, the unanswered question holds in doubt the validity of our quality of life, individual freedom, and personal fulfillment; all of which serve as the bases of the human soul. As an outcome, theologians seek to establish the validity of the soul over the elements that Y'haweh conceived to create the soul; while scientists only regard the utility of our unitary thoughts when the thoughts recognize the natural-force-laws that all material experience subsume under. The validity of Judeo-Christian virtues stands upon the answer to this metaphysical problem. Presently, however, no one ascertains the structure or manner in which the qualified mind alights upon the brain's structure. This unanswered question leaves the mind residing aloft, as a ghostly synthesis of spirit hovering over the brain. Philosophers, in fact, call this unbridgeable divide *the mind-matter explanatory gap*.

Neither the theologians nor the scientists can validate their respective stances because they have not answered the mind-matter question. The mind-matter question now remains the central question that occupies the disciplines of logic, mathematics, philosophy, cosmology, physics, and theology. In brief parts of this chapter, we shall observe derivations of this question in the historical strife between rationalist philosophers and empiricist philosophers; moreover, in the latter chapters of this work, we shall see this question arise in the political conflicts between personal freedom and state sovereignty. Also, we shall discover how the answer to this question reconciles the theological argument over religious works verses Y'haweh's necessary grace. Finally, we shall see that the answer to this question resides in undiscovered manner in which Y'haweh extends himself to us, as a reflection of his own fulfillment. The answer essentially brings Heaven down to earth, as the answer captures our metaphorical pearl of truth.

In point of fact, the theologians cannot truly pronounce their knowledge of the divine mind beyond unsubstantiated revelatory claims, if they do not define how Y'haweh conceives the material world that gives rise to our intentional minds; nor can the theologians validate the mind's qualitative experiences without establishing the way divine purposes extend to us. Likewise, scientists cannot solely appeal to natural processes as an explanation for the brilliantly structured creation, if scientists do not ascertain how, why, or whether macroscopic and microscopic material systems hold nature's necessary constants and contingent functions without the mind's qualitative sense of the universal.

Although the mind-matter question remains unanswered, the theologians uphold their dogma, unapologetically. While Christian theologians have not established orthodoxy (that is, the right-belief, concerning how Y'haweh's judgment manifests the world and humanity unto the liberty of all in the Mashiach and the Holy Spirit), the theologians dogmatically maintain the following: the theologians assert that no part or degree of creation stands independent from Y'haweh's mind. This the theologians maintain, even as scientists find no otherworldly opposition to their scientific study of a "universe" that "independently" engages our minds.

Thus, scientists staunchly oppose Christian dogma. They view the theologians' metaphysical speculations as superstitious. Nearly all scientists disdain metaphysics as impossible: deriding metaphysical conjectures, scientists rather accept humanity's inability to apprehend an intelligent unified truth for the material creation. Scientists, therefore, aim to cut off 'religious superstition,' by regarding humanity's intelligent self-awareness as a fortuitous outcome of natural processes that operate, despite divine intelligence.

Our proposed orthodox judgment can only respond to the theological and scientific disagreement by establishing a critical understanding of Y'haweh's expressed truth, in a way that assimilates scientific understanding by closing the mind-matter explanatory gap. Of course, our judgment must contrast contemporary scientists' naturalist stance, which again holds that the human sense of self evolved from naturally occurring processes, without divine command. Likewise, our judgment must counter the scientists' assertion that we can possess a working knowledge of the material creation without appealing to divinity.

To counter the scientists, we must determine how Y'haweh enables our minds to transcend and correspond with the material world. Only with such a determination, can we establish a true metaphysical judgment. Without a doubt, this substantive proof will allow us to excel and assimilate scientific explanations, as we define how Y'haweh is the necessary cause and totality of creation's physical and material processes. Besides, with a demonstrable metaphysical judgment, we will describe how the very identity and corresponding essence of all things derive from an omniscient power who transcends our experience.

For us, metaphysics is the promise of a pre-material and even pre-physical synthesis between the divine mind and substance. Obviously, many thinkers, from ages old, have failed to apprehend this understanding. All have only proclaimed metaphysical realities without a determination that defines how Y'haweh physically engages our world. Besides the most favored argument that declares that an ultimate and necessary cause precedes all things; classical philosophers and Christian theologians have put forth anthropocentric—human centered—arguments: they hold that because the creation adheres to perspective values that ultimately make our perceptive experiences possible, a creator necessarily made the creation for us to perceive. Following, they seek a proof for their arguments by underscoring the impossible odds that creation spontaneously arrived to its current complex state. Using these arguments, Christian theologians hold that creation's complexity infers an intelligent designer.

Scientists then easily dismiss such anthropocentric arguments. They demonstrate how the arguments are nothing more than tautological—persistently assertive—proclamations that do not predict any outcome other than restating the proclamations.

Although traditional anthropocentric arguments are enticing, we true worshippers must look past the mere notion that necessary physical conventions prove the existence of the Creator's metaphysical reality. Instead, we must seek to prove Y'haweh's metaphysical reality by demonstrating how the expressed creation manifests the structure of knowledge, itself. To realize this end, our orthodox judgment must consist of a proof that demonstrably closes the explanatory gap between mind and matter. Thereby, our judgment will reconcile all appropriate philosophical and scientific disciplines, in a manner that derives unpredictable outcomes.

Thus, before we can prove our orthodox judgment by answering how the mind and matter unite, we must streamline previous philosophical and scientific understandings to qualify and answer this great metaphysical question. Our answer must readily appear intuitive and exemplary to all, upon analysis.

At present, let us introduce an example of the metaphysical convention through which Y'haweh orders our mind-substance coupling. Later, as we actually define the mind-matter coupling, we will put forth a definitive judgment that substantively apprehends the orthodox understanding that theologians and philosophers fail to apprehend and scientists continue to deny. For the moment, therefore, let us tentatively describe the subsequent convention: let us explain the manner in which the metaphysical essence—even the intrinsic intelligence that stands prior to our physical experience (that is, *a priori*[1])—manifests the natural-force-laws that integrally govern the material things that we perceive during and post experience (that is, *a posteriori*).

Let us begin by stating that the functional essence of any physical phenomenon is metaphysical—that is, the phenomenon's essence precedes and transcends its physical manifestation, *a priori*—because of the following: during our experience of any physical phenomenon, the phenomenon's identity depends upon its functional relationship to its attributes, as we perceive the whole physical phenomenon emerging within spacetime. Because physical relationships are ever changing within spacetime, their specific identities change; therefore, a physical phenomenon's essence concerns the manner in which Y'haweh dynamically expresses the natural-force-laws that enable the phenomenon and its attributes to relate and maintain an

---

[1] *A priori* synthetic judgments do no merely reproduce subjects, but add to them.

ontological continuity of identity that we then perceive within spacetime. Hence, the functional essence concerns an intelligible relationship between the physical phenomenon and its attributes, regardless of the specific identity of the phenomenon or its attributes. As a consequence, the essence of a physical phenomenon is the dynamic manner in which Y'haweh expresses the phenomenon to structure our knowledge as ascending beyond, while being contingent to the identity dependent, physical phenomena.

To speak particularly, we may conclude that Y'haweh expresses the functional essence of all things to establish our perspective points of reference, because our perceptions never apprehend specific physical phenomenon, as though they were idolatrously things-in-themselves. Rather, our perceptions always apprehend the perspective relationships between a perceived physical phenomenon, its attributes, and its relationship with a variety of other past, present, and future physical relations within spacetime.

A physical phenomenon's essence then is *a priori*: the essence precedes and transcends experience. Plus, a physical phenomenon's ontology—the phenomenon's operational being and identity during experience but under a metaphysical whole—is a posteriori: that is to say, post or throughout experience. What is more, because the *a priori* essence of all physical phenomena is to facilitate the genesis of knowledge, the *a posteriori* ontology of physical phenomena entails the simple expression of information. And, this informative character of a physical phenomenon's ontology concerns the manner in which the phenomenon's essence stands independent from but enables the contingent ascriptions of our minds. For instance, because the elements statistically vary within an identifiable range and thereby achieve the same aggregate macroscopic body, the relationship between a macroscopic body and its constituents is a contingent event that a natural-force-law's essence allows intelligence to identify.

At times, true ontological being seems relative to our subjective viewpoints. Yet, while the essential relationships of fundamental elements invariantly emerge unto unique macroscopic states, solely to enable our ascending thoughts; only a metaphysical power that transcends our experience holds the unified identity that informs us of the essence of all things. When we do not recognize this metaphysical reality, our understanding becomes degenerate. Our minds' intentional senses, in this way, fail to qualify meaning beyond our material experiences.

Our brief example of the metaphysical convention through which Y'haweh orders our finite-knowledge-structure may seem daunting; however, what is important for us to realize is the fact that the metaphysical essence is substantial rather than the derived material manifestations. Y'haweh's unchanging metaphysical being, which the Word's essential truth-functional order adheres to, is actuality: its being the telos and genesis of all existence.

Above all, the promise of a metaphysical reality is the promise of a universal truth that withstands the false notions of a chaotic world that exists independently for and of itself. The appeal to a divinely conferred essence is the appeal to the purposes of a creator who assimilates all experience with meaningful identities that ultimately embody our intentional sense of self. Metaphysical 'being as such that does not change' is not only an appeal to the divine, but also an appeal to the possibility of our knowledge's ascension unto meaningful truth.

From antiquity, classical philosophers pondered over metaphysical questions concerning a divine universal cause for all things. The classical philosophers, such as Aristotle, knew to look beyond the scientific study of things that are subject to change. Instead, the ancient philosophers sought for the unchanging, immutable, and metaphysical substance that transcends all phenomenal categorizations.

To achieve their ends, the ancients made a most important observation: they discerned the complementing structure that material phenomena and our mental processes purportedly share. The ancients held that all the ontological categories of understanding—such as quantity, quality, relation, and modality—underline the subject-predicate propositional form of our thoughts. And so, they concluded that the categories of understanding ascend from a non-contradictory and unified substance, which in turn proceeds from a divine consciousness. By holding this perspective, they believed that metaphysical knowledge is possible.

As they observed the metaphysical connection between mind and substance, classical philosophers portrayed the subsequent relationship: first, the classical philosophers described the metaphysical substance as either the essence of all things; the universal of all things; the genus of all things; or the subject of all things. In fact, Aristotle claimed that "a [metaphysical] substratum is that of which everything else is based, while it is itself not based of anything else."[1]

Second, the classical philosophers extended 'mind' beyond substance[2] by theorizing that a creator's mind is the first cause: the ancient philosophers held that the Creator's mind holds a universal telos-cause as the sum purpose of all things. Then under this universal cause, the philosophers envisioned subordinate causes: they listed a formal cause that describes the sum of what properties represent; a dynamic cause that describes the effectual forces of change; and a material cause that describes the actual phenomena.

Furthermore, as they upheld the principle of a first-cause creator (whose primary being is 'thinking mind'), the classical philosophers envisioned metaphysical causality, as entailing the preexisting form that all post-existing phenomena fall under. They described this causal process as the potentiality (dynamis) of phenomena falling under the preexisting actuality (energeia) of predetermined forms.

Our brief reflection upon the ancients' philosophy compels us to recognize that the ancients' metaphysical speculations are brilliant; however, because the ancients did not fully discover how the qualitative mind ascends from matter, remains contingent to matter, and intentionally assimilates matter; we advance by first noting why the ancients' understandings fell before the scientific method that scientists employ today.

---

[1] Aristotle's Metaphysics, Book VII.
[2] The term 'substance' derives from the Latin term *substantia*, which means "that which stands under."

Classical philosophers, who had held the notion that absolute space and time support their belief in an absolute metaphysical cause, fell into disarray as scientists proved that spacetime is not absolute. Too, contemporary philosophers now perceive the serious limitations of the subject-predicate scheme that the ancient philosophers employed. Revolutionary discoveries—such as genetic predispositions; short-term, long-term memory; the endocrine-exocrine hormonal systems; and the brain's limbic system—have so picked apart the ancients' ideological beliefs, to the extent that their conceptions of the mind amount to mental phantoms. As we shall see, the theories of relativity and quantum physics overturned the civil authority of not only classical philosophy, but also Judeo-Christian theology. Many contemporary philosophers now assert that metaphysical unity is merely a psychological fiction that comforts us in the face of a vast and mysterious universe.

As we described above, agnostic and atheistic scientists presently hold what thinkers term as a nominalist (or naturalist) approach to the world. We have indicated that scientists chiefly maintain their disregard for a pre-existing metaphysical essence because theological dogma does not derivatively explain how Y'haweh's metaphysical essence translates into the necessary constants and contingent functions of natural-force-laws. To draw attention to theology's shortcomings, scientists highlight how theological dogma does not explain how and why the finite, contingent, and particular things of experience, consolidated from the infinite possibilities of the divine's metaphysical unity. They ask why some things assume the mode of necessity, while other things assume the mode of potentiality. As well, they note that the theologians have not described how the necessary, non-physical, preexisting, infinite-potential, and unchanging reality physically works upon the finite world of contingent and identity-dependent material things. In the same manner, they note that theologians have failed to discover how our immaterial, contingent, and manifold thoughts command the specific, material actions of our bodies. Since theologians fail to address the scientists' questions, scientists simply accept the existence of natural-force-laws as simply a matter of fact.

We would be remiss if we did not address the theologians' failure to answer the scientists' legitimate questions. As we seek to realize our goal of establishing orthodoxy, our orthodox judgment must close the mind-matter explanatory gap; moreover, our orthodox judgment must demonstrate how our finite-knowledge-structure derives from Y'haweh's expressed truth (in such a way that we derivatively anticipate and assimilate ongoing experience beyond what we readily perceive). We must specifically describe how an infinite Y'haweh and his distinct persons create and complete our physical and social experiences of the temporal world.

In order to achieve our aims, we must dutifully use an ample portion this chapter to survey how philosophers and scientists attempt to use naturalist approaches to answer the great mind-matter question. We must ascertain the shortcomings of their resulting scientific method, which entails logical postulations, mathematical descriptions, empirical observations, and methodological analysis. We must understand how secular scientists try to ascertain a naturalist understanding of all things under the contemporary discipline that they identify as "physics": a term that derives from the Greek word "physika," meaning "nature."

We must demonstrate the shortfall of the leading philosophical and scientific approaches, which merely seek to analyze natural processes only to upkeep what atheists deem as our self-important belief in the necessity of humanity's continuance. In response to their irreverence for the human experience, we must discover why philosophers and scientists fail to ascertain the fact that the qualitative mind is a necessary aspect of creation. Only then can we reasonably submit our orthodox judgment that secures a critical understanding of truth that fully validates our qualitative experience under Y'haweh's good. After achieving such, we will finally establish a biblical orthodoxy that verifies the three persons of Y'haweh (beyond the true-beliefs of devout Christian hearts).

The Ontological Commitment that Transcends Logic and Mathematics

As we have seen, historical philosophers and scientists began their attempt to naturalize our understandings of creation when they merely accepted the preexistent nature of the natural-force-laws that govern our interaction with the material world. In this manner, they accepted the fact that distinct things relate through forces; however, they did not pursue an explanation for the actual cause or essential purpose for the natural laws that govern the forces. Dismissing the necessity of a divine metaphysical reality, the philosophers only sought to validate their belief that closed material systems emerge under natural-force-laws and then fortuitously produce our cognitive experience.

Notwithstanding, all astute philosophers necessarily accept the fact that the natural laws' metaphysical structure stands prior to the adaptive and progressive relationships between creation's material systems and our increasing awareness of them. As a consequence, philosophers necessarily accept the asymmetric way in which the laws govern the creation. What follows is that our identifying the ensuing actuality is the key to our assessing the scientists' misconceptions of the natural-force-laws: what we may describe as explanatory asymmetries define the relationships between all material phenomena and their constituent properties. In other words, physical substances and their properties do not reciprocally or equally explain one another, because metaphysically ascribed functions define unique material substances as being greater than the sum of their elemental properties.

Until we present our more critical orthodox judgment, we here note a trivial example that observes how the natural-force-laws' functional relationships render the following distinct identities between elemental properties and their macroscopic physical systems: let us note the fact that electrons have distinct identities other than the identities of atoms; however, electrons are obviously indispensable components of atoms. Likewise, atoms have distinct identities other than the identities of compounds and molecules; yet, atoms are indispensable components of all compounds and molecules. Further still, we note that the carbohydrate, protein, lipid, and other molecules that comprise our bodies' organic systems have distinct identities other than the identities of our bodies. Even so, we know that our very lives depend upon the particular functioning of these organic structures. Lastly, we observe that our nervous system has a distinct identity and functionality other than the identity of our mind's qualitative senses. Nonetheless, our brains necessarily instigate and encode our spiritual experience, as we shall discover later below.

We may formally articulate the metaphysical basis of these explanatory asymmetries as follows: while some constituent properties may stand alone, despite the constitution of their macroscopic body, only a metaphysically consigned force-law sets the functional criterion that determines how the macroscopic body assimilates the constituent properties' independent identities into its greater macroscopic whole.[1] As a result of this metaphysical consignment, a macroscopic substance cannot depend upon anything but its functional relation to its constituent properties. Thus, the constituent properties of the substance cannot be identical with the whole macroscopic substance: the properties can only exemplify universal qualities that distinguish their functional relationship with the specific macroscopic body that contains them. For example, one cannot distinguish a self-sufficient material phenomenon unto itself, because the material phenomenon cannot be an extension of itself, without integral proper parts (that is, the constituent properties) to explain itself.[2] Despite any intrinsic identities, the properties can only exhibit the existential identity that its functional relationship with the macroscopic substance incurs. Plus, the properties cannot be ever changing events that alter the identity of the macroscopic substance. Instead, the identity dependent relationship between constituent properties and their macroscopic substance is a contingent event that

---

[1] For example, 'x' can be equivalent to having the function that entails 'y' as its property, i.e., f of y; however, 'y' does not have the property of entailing 'x.'
[2] an *a priori* synthetic judgment

an asymmetric, metaphysical function assigns. As a final outcome, the essence of all properties is that they are only explanatory metaphysical ascriptions, like algorithmic sequences.

To be sure, thinkers achieve a chief benefit when they observe the natural-force-laws' metaphysical structure: they recognize the fact that the laws' ascriptions of functional relationships between distinct things make the same distinct things increasingly intelligible. First, the law's metaphysical priority compels us to look past the identities of macroscopic substances and their properties. Afterward, the law's priority directs our ascending understanding upon the causative nature of the law's function. As an outcome, the law's priority enables us to look past both substance and property unto the universal principles that the substance's properties exemplify. For instance, as we acknowledge that a substance's properties exemplify an infinite number of possible configurations within creation, we inherently cultivate analogies that misrepresent what immediately appears to us. Then, through these means, we cultivate abstract representations of the greater metaphysical whole, despite what we immediately observe.

In few words, we may conclude that without our acknowledging the metaphysical priority of the natural laws' asymmetric structure, our increasing knowledge of both mind and substance is impossible. Also, unless we acknowledge the asymmetric priority of transcending purposes, we cannot indulge the abstract inquiries of our perception.

Ironically, as philosophers and scientists seek natural explanations for the qualitative mind and the world, they unknowingly compromise two of their scientific method's key tools that the scientists utilize to make sense of the world: they undermine logic[1]—the formulated study of grammatically imparted inferences, and they undermine mathematics—the representational use of formulas to extend phenomena analytically. The scientists overlook

---

[1] The word *logic* derives from the Greek word *logos*, which means word, reasoning, or concept. Logicians practice the discipline of logic by discerning axioms and rational conditions that demonstrate valid deductions.

the fact that these two crucial tools actually stand upon what thinkers describe as our 'ontological commitment' to ascertain purposeful causes beyond the material occurrences that we perceive, ad infinitum.

In few words, we may say that both rational philosophers and empirical scientists deny the need to ascertain the divine origin of the natural-force-laws' metaphysical priority and asymmetric structure; therefore, both philosophers and scientists fail to establish their respective philosophical and scientific understandings: rational philosophers fail to apply our instinctive, rational thought processes to understand the world; and empirical scientists fail to define our thought processes and the world, by their employing empirical observations alone. The resulting strife between rationalists and empiricists, in this way, shaped the progression of Western thought.

At this juncture, let us quickly survey how that from ancient times unto the present, philosophers and scientists have transitioned from stressing rationalists' treatments of logic and mathematics unto stressing today's empiricists' treatment of the same: in the earliest philosophical societies, rational schools of thought prevailed. Of course, ancient rationalist philosophers did not know the elemental structure of matter, and they did not know the anatomical structure of the brain and the greater nervous system; however, they temporarily advanced understanding by recognizing the priority and existence of the natural laws.

The ancient philosophers' naturalist approach initially allowed the philosophers to regard both physical substances and the mind as independent and self-sufficient unto themselves. And so, with the belief in a self-sufficient and orderly relationship between mind and matter, early rationalist philosophers initially thought that they could bridge the mind-matter explanatory gap, by employing formalized logic and mathematics. Again, the striking manner in which material phenomena relate to their properties, like the immediate subjects of our thoughts relate to our predicated conceptions, compelled the early philosophers' commitment to matching observable material properties with the mind's logical and other mathematical formulations.

For instance, at the dawn of Western philosophy, the rationalist philosopher Plato championed the position that the mind has an intrinsic rational structure: he supposed that the mind's mental representations were reflections of ethereal metaphysical forms. The ancients, like Plato, initially applied logic to formalize the process through which the subjective mind ascribes descriptive predicates to the material objects that their seemingly self-sufficient minds are conscious of. In this manner, the ancients initially held that the conscious, self-sufficient mind superimposes its mental predicates upon the material world.

Much later, philosophers began to take steps towards objective perspectives of the world: they began to look past the subjective limitations of our human intuitions. The philosophers advanced the discipline of logic by applying mathematics to calculate a hypothetical object's predicated aspects that the subjective mind is not readily aware of. To accomplish this, philosophers mathematically extended formulaic grammar to observe valid inferences and logical consequences, despite personal experiences. For example, Aristotle, Plato's intellectual successor, initially championed Plato's view that the mind has intrinsic structure; however, Aristotle soon stepped away from Plato's belief that we observe a world that asymmetrically reflects a greater perfect order. Instead, Aristotle only studied the correspondence between the mind's subject-predicate relationship and substance's object-property relationship. In this manner, Aristotle stepped toward an objective, self-sufficient world that natural laws uphold. Furthermore, 17th and 18th Century Cartesian philosophers followed in Aristotle's intellectual foot-steps: they held that a self-sufficient mind corresponds with self-sufficient substances, upon which the conscious mind only adds predicated values to.

Finally, almost marrying rationalist and empiricist approaches, Immanuel Kant, an early 19th Century philosopher, asserted that our intrinsic logical capacity rests upon an apperception of space and time, which perception assimilates all material experience unto the fundamental categories of our judgment. To this end, Kant made a crucial observation that philosophers term an *a priori* synthetic judgment: he observed how we have the intuitive ability to make mathematical assessments prior to experience.

Despite its visionary scope, Kant's work (as we shall later describe) stands upon a major contradiction: Kant recognized our need to perceive the world as deriving from a divine metaphysical cause; however, Kant denied the possibility of our objectively establishing a metaphysical truth. Many influential public circles eventually accepted his conclusion that we are incapable of establishing divine or metaphysical truth. The impasse that Immanuel Kant inaugurated continues to our present day.

Soon after Kant, philosophers began to question, further, the likelihood that the brain intrinsically possesses a qualitative sense, which a divine power instilled. Too, because they did not fully understand the brain's cognitive structure, more recent naturalist philosophers began to think that the stratified order of creation solely impresses the grammatical order of our thoughts upon us. As a result, logicians applied logic to the mathematical properties of language, despite personalized inferences, altogether.

In short, we may note that despite the "intrinsically structured mind" stance that historic, rationalist philosophers like Plato upheld; later 19th and 20th Century logicians (such as Gottlob Frege, James Moore, and Bertrand Russell), held the "world's impressing structure upon the mind" position. Also, Frege, Moore, and Russell refused to uphold the earlier beliefs that objects are constituents and wholes that one's mind can intuitively comprehend. Instead, they asserted that our minds solely result from sense-impressions that logicians can analyze mathematically: they in fact believed that they could reduce the mind's "language of thought" to mathematical relations.

To their great misfortune, however, all empirical philosophers, like Frege, Moore, and Russell, could not establish the truth of their work by only using mathematics. A mathematical philosopher, Kurt Gödel (circa. 1930), proved that mathematics, itself, requires metaphysical substantiation. As we shall shortly describe, Gödel proved the fact that mathematical systems cannot prove their own validity by using their own axioms.[1]

For this cause, skeptical, existentialist philosophers arose, such as Martin Heidegger, who dismissed the subject-predicate question altogether. Heidegger submitted the idea that we impartially fall into an ordered reality of metaphysical being, which even 'god' himself must conform to. Heidegger asserted that we accordingly conform to this unified world, which we then socially adapt for ourselves.

As one would expect, however, Heidegger's sublime ideas also suffered the pitiful circumstance of being improvable. In fact, even Heidegger himself abandoned his own work after he realized that his work could not secure scientific predictions: his work could not prove or disprove anything, by using the obscure notion that we fall into a non-divine metaphysical reality of being.

Having briefly surveyed the conflicting viewpoints of rationalists and empiricists thinkers, let us not despair. Since we recognize the divine origin of the natural-force-laws' metaphysical priority and asymmetric structure, we may ascertain how both the intrinsic and existential views of logic are necessary to understand how Y'haweh expresses the world to establish our finite-knowledge-structure. First, our pending orthodox judgment can incorporate the rationalist logicians' view by describing how our material brains encode an intrinsic cognitive capacity: what remains for our orthodox judgment to discover is the manner in which our qualitative minds physically ascend to reinterpret the categorical impressions that the world makes upon us. At the same time, our pending orthodox judgment can recognize the empiricist logicians' use of logical forms: holding the propriety of the logical forms in mind, our judgment can substantively detail the systematic structuring of our subconscious thoughts that our intentional experience retrieve.

---

[1] Kurt Gödel (circa. 1930) demonstrated that all first order logical systems cannot mathematically establish their completeness by using the axioms within the systems; therefore, he ultimately concluded that the highest order logical systems are incapable of proving their own validity by using mathematics. As an outcome, Gödel demonstrated that any theory that mathematics describes is incomplete, its being unable to prove itself.

We may encompass both rationalists and empiricists' perspectives because both views entail what philosophers call an 'ought' expectancy of an order that transcends what one physically observes. As evidenced by our involuntary capacity to abstract and misrepresent what we immediately perceive, our minds seek such metaphysical meaning that precedes and assigns an intrinsic purposefulness or an existential cause for all things within our perception. Inherently, we engage all objects as ordered representations of what the objects ought to be, despite how the objects immediately appear. This 'ought' expectancy then inspires us to rationalize our thoughts into the logical forms that the historical and contemporary logicians have, respectively, identified.

The summery understanding of logic that we may secure from both the rationalists' intrinsic approach and the empiricists' existential approach is the following: logic is the conviction that an individual can existentially expound upon his or her intrinsic senses of the world by articulating inferences in an analytical form that independently derives conclusions that are not readily apparent; therefore, the whole of logic's ontological commitment for deeper and structured understanding is to ascertain whatever unified principles that material properties exemplify, beyond what our senses behold. Because the natural laws are explanatorily asymmetric, however, one cannot entirely use the mathematical elements of logic to ascertain, intrinsically, the unity that the qualitative mind perennially seeks. In a word, we can only use logic to order our thoughts, without apprehending the explicit meanings of our thoughts; therefore, we cannot use logic and mathematics, alone, to bridge the mind-matter explanatory gap.

Let us briefly relate the following explanation as an example: generally, science's contemporary logicians begin to employ logical propositions by using symbols as fixed representational meanings of the propositions' inferences. Then logicians find that propositions' inferences have truthful validity when verifiable conclusions proceed from inferential premises. In fact, logicians term this realization the logical consequence of the well-reasoned syntactical rules of grammar; moreover, these rules govern the propositions' semantic meanings.

Though logicians realize that logical consequences result from valid reasoning, they find that the intrinsic nature of the observed material phenomena remains unknown, as logic's existential forms fail to substantiate our mind's qualitative senses. We may conclude, therefore, that logical consequences only entice logicians, scientists, and other philosophers with the sense that an ongoing mathematical analysis of their judgments will justify their beliefs as true.

In fact, some scientists and contemporary philosophers actually realize that they can only utilize mathematics to ensure the integrity of mathematical formulas, even as the mathematical models fail to apprehend the deeper ontological being of physical events. What prevents other scientists from realizing mathematics' limitation is the fact that logicians can use mathematics to represent the true or false values of any inference, though mathematics cannot explicitly quantify the mind's unified, qualitative sense. The logicians can represent any inference because mathematical concepts theoretically stand upon the infinite set extension of whole and natural numbers.

Our infinite capacity to issue mathematical values seems promising. Nevertheless, the infinite capacity strangely demarcates the limited applicability of mathematics: a limitation that significantly impedes our scientific understandings of the world.

Ironically, mathematics' limitation results from the following fact: mathematics entails an infinite set of numbers, while the asymmetric nature of creation consigns natural forces to work upon discrete— even finite—material quantities, which operate in manners that exemplify but not equate the identity of the natural forces. As a result, our infinite mathematical capacity to misrepresent the extension of finite, material phenomena often yields logically consistent mathematical models that later prove to be contradictions of the world that we actually observe.

For example, if we conclude that a universe encompasses the set of all sets, our conclusion would prove to be a contradiction; because the universe set would illogically include a self-induced power set that transcends and inaugurates the universal set.

Problems like these often present sensible philosophers with questions, concerning the nature of the mathematical models: the philosophers realize that mathematical models cannot be an infinite number of entities-in-themselves. Some even wonder whether the mathematics question is an aspect of the mind-matter question. For this reason, sensible philosophers realize that our mathematical limitations are significant.

A few scientists attempt to solve the mathematical question by theorizing the existence of an infinite number of universes. Even so, these supposed universes must relate in such finite manners that allow the scientists to verify their existence. To accomplish this verification, scientists would necessarily use the infinite set extension of numbers that transcends the finite relationships between the supposed universes. So even if they accept the existence of an infinite number of universes, they still have no physical means to transcend mathematical systems to verify the truth of the systems.

Irrefutable is the fact that because the creation is asymmetric, one cannot mathematically analyze particular inferences to comprehend the whole world: one cannot scrutinize the syntactic elements of well-formed propositions to ascertain the causal meaning that appearing phenomena subsume under. For sure, one cannot use logic to analyze the metaphysical source of meaning, even though our minds are dynamic reflections of meaning. In the end, philosophers and scientists must concede that because mathematics cannot transcend its extended sets to substantiate itself, one cannot use mathematics to analyze or justify our beliefs. As a consequence, the ultimate judgments of philosophers and scientists, which solely rely upon mathematics to determine the mind's ascendant, contingent, and intentional relation to creation, stand in question.

Empirical Observation

As empirical scientists realized that formal logic and mathematical applications can neither ascertain the mind's qualitative senses, nor predict every aspect of the asymmetric creation, they did not give up their naturalist approach. In fact, when they realized that the rationalists' approach to logic and mathematics cannot explain how the qualitative mind ascends from, remains contingent to, and intentionally works upon the material creation; the scientists did not retreat to metaphysical assumptions or religious dogma. They still endeavored to find natural causes for our qualitative life-experience.

To corroborate any logical hypotheses or mathematical applications, scientists continue to stress empirical observations, as a central feature of their scientific method. Through empirical means, they seek to facilitate our ontological commitment to discover the expanse of knowledge: that is, how our minds work upon the world and how we may derive conclusions in a predictive and representational manner that justifies the conclusions.

Notwithstanding, because scientists hold that all things derive from physical causes and not a singular metaphysical cause, they diminish the qualitative mind as being a secondary product of the material world; whereas the rationalists had held the mind to be independent and self-sufficient. And so, as scientists try to discover the nature of the material world and the objective way to relate to it, scientists confound the subjective first-person perspective that perceives the quality of life.

We cannot conclusively discover the inadequacy of the secularists' application of the scientific method, unless we fully grasp how secular scientists wrongfully describe our qualitative minds as being the result of emergent material processes. Soon after, we will identify the unresolved questions, which the scientific method and the Standard Model fail to address. We, in fact, will recognize how the unresolved questions require a metaphysical understanding that extends our knowledge-structure unto a unified meaning that resides beyond the material world. At the last, this metaphysical understanding shall be the content of our orthodox judgment.

Observing the Emerging World

Above all, scientists generally explain how our mental attributes and the material world came into being, by using the concept of emergence; which is a cosmological theory that seeks to express all things through the physical structures of energy and energy's manifest matter. The emergence concept asserts that everything existent culminates into material substances that both emerge from and superimposes upon constituent physical properties. This notion, therefore, seeks to bridge the mind-matter explanatory gap by supposing that the brain's anatomical structure has evolved from more basic material systems. In fact, scientists submit that the advent of our cognitive capacity came into being by opportune probability: that is, an ideal result of emerging processes that have yielded integrative systems of self-replicating cells; moreover, scientists submit that these cells then evolved into greater anatomical structures that now adhere to the selective adaptations of fitness. And so, scientists seek to use this evolutionary elaboration of the emergence concept to discern how the brain's chemical, hormonal, and neuronal processes transform sense impressions into the intentional analogies of intuition; which are basically the implicit senses of material impressions.

As they shaped the current Standard Model of creation and as they gained a contemporary understanding of our nervous system, many scientists and philosophers roughly visualized the emergence concept as finely sequenced layered patterns. They envisioned layers that begin with chemical systems and then emerge as biological systems, anatomical systems, psychological states, and finally social relationships. Lastly, scientists concluded that all such layers superimpose upon energy's manifest matter.

With this initial layered pattern perspective, scientists came to believe that every mental attribute reduces to specific neuronal states. Nevertheless, scientists and philosophers eventually found that the patterned notion, in which material constituents create specific mental properties, has a significant problem: different arrangements of constituent properties, states, and elements often yield the same qualitative, mental sense. Likewise, they found that the same constituent states often render different mental senses. After they found that they could not reduce mental states to particular physical patterns, scientists termed their finding "multi-realization." In short, scientists and philosophers found the belief that material phenomena emerge unto predictive mental states to be false. For this reason, they found that the patterned notion of emergence does not apprehend, predict, or explain necessary or contingent outcomes.

To overcome these inconsistencies, philosophers and scientists are now beginning to accept two more fluid understandings of the emergence concept. One understanding necessarily entails the realization that constituent, fundamental properties are differential and virtual rather than singular and rigidly specific. With this first understanding, philosophers and scientists believe that the primary forces of nature are at first virtual before they effect the formation of assemblages and invariant consistencies; where consolidating heterogeneous parts relate as the wholes that our minds recognize. As we shall see further below in our description of the Standard Model, scientists now submit that fundamental constituents exist as virtual properties, before they actualize into observable identities.

In addition to their belief that virtual constituents sufficiently explain the unique rise of macroscopic properties, philosophers and scientists conceive a second popular approach to the emergence concept as follows: thinkers hold the assumption that unobservable varieties of distinct physical things necessarily collapse many of their unseen attributes to relate to other observable things. As a result, they believe that observable identities superimpose upon the former unobservable attributes.

The more fluid notions of the emergence concept seem to encourage naturalist explanations for the rise of our qualitative minds; however, the scientists continue to forgo any explanations for the natural-force-laws that precede and facilitate the supposed virtual relationships and collapsed states. Also, scientists do not explain how the perspective values for these laws determine whether a state is virtual or collapsed without the prejudice of intelligent perspective. We shall see that scientists' Big Bang theory is an emergence concept that purportedly explains the existence of the creation; however, the theory does not offer an explanation for the natural-force-laws or other conventions that precede the "Big Bang." Essentially, although the concept is formidable, the emergence concept does not entirely reconcile creation's asymmetric natural-force-laws.

Let us summarize the shortfall of the emergence concept in the subsequent way: as scientists seek to forgo the oppressions of metaphysical speculation and religious dogma, they seek natural explanations, such as the emergence concept, to explain and accommodate the seemingly "disembodied" qualitative mind. To accomplish this, they seek to close the explanatory gap by grounding our ghostly psychological states into neuronal states. And so, they apply the emergence concept to bridge the explanatory gap between the brain's emerging cognitive structures and the mind's intentional contingencies. Nevertheless, though the emergence concept asserts that all things emerge from physical constituents, the emergence concept does not truly explain how the qualitative mind holds transcendent thoughts that its constituent, material nervous system in no way exemplifies.

After we roughly detail the brain's workings below, we shall find that the emergence concept fails to identify how the mind remains contingently dependent upon the brain, even though the mind's concepts transcend what the brain's anatomical structure exemplifies. This contingent relationship, in fact, gives evidence that the appearing mind is a result of a metaphysical force law that consigns the mind's identity to be contingently dependent upon its constituent brain, instead of being the result of evolved anatomical structures. To be specific, scientists and philosophers have not convincingly explained what thinkers identify as the mind's topic neutral aspects, which do not have a material correspondent: the emergence concept does not definitively shed light on the brain's neutral or spontaneous attributes. In fact, the emergence concept's disregard for metaphysical unity in favor of differential and virtual states does not further our understanding of the way that the mind transcends diverse physical substances unto a metaphysical truth.

To conclude, we must say that the challenge that the emergence concept presents for practitioners of the scientific method is that the concept cannot explain how our understanding physically ascends beyond what we observe. For sure, the concept does not explain how or why our mind's qualitative sense of life extend beyond material phenomena, as our minds seek the transcendent unity of thought, itself.

Thus, the following are the necessary questions that our orthodox judgment must eventually answer: what is the dynamic mental physicality that the brain obtains, even though the dynamic physicality does not result from the brain's aggregate structures? And, what metaphysical convention relates the brain's dynamic capacity to its material structure?

These questions, the emergent concept does not foresee. Hence, the concept falls short of securing scientific understanding.

Epiphenomenalism

When we survey science's current Standard Model, the unresolved mind-matter question will continuously come to mind as we wonder what emerging physicality constitutes the mind. Because the emergence concept does not solve the qualitative mind dilemma, two opposing choices present themselves: if one accepts the qualitative mind's existence, one must explain how the mind independently arises within emerging material processes and retains its self-sufficiency. When we are without such an explanation, we hold the inclination to think that the mind breaks certain laws of physics: specifically, to us, the mind appears to undermine energy conservation within systems, by its adding or removing energy.

On the other hand, if one does not accept the qualitative mind's existence, by saying that the mind is solely an outcome of evolved material processes, one loses the sense of self. If this perspective were valid, science would never unfetter true knowledge from the ceaseless slave labor of existential analysis. As a consequence, our knowledge would never stand in the liberty of being the intrinsic sense of all that we observe.

Thus, only one way exist to reconcile these two choices: one must close the explanatory gap by finding the transition point between our qualitative sense and neuronal activity, without breaking the energy conservation law of physics. In this manner, one will not only establish the physical correlate to consciousness; but also establish our reference frames from which we existentially employ the scientific method to perceive the creation and our mind's intrinsic relation to it.

Empirical scientists, however, disregard the need to pursue the transition point between our qualitative experience and neuronal activity. Since they do not understand how the qualitative mind actually affects neuronal behavior, scientists maintain that the qualitative mind is an epiphenomenon: that is, a psychological figment that results from material events, but the figment does not affect material events. Instead of their realizing the necessity of preserving the qualitative sense of self, without undermining physical laws, scientists hold that all mental events are actually cognitive events. In this way, they diminish the worth of humanity's qualitative experience.

Behaviorism

The secular scientists' motivation is not necessarily to defeat the human spirit: again, the scientists simply seek to liberate modern society from metaphysical speculations and unsubstantiated religious dogma. For this reason, scientists attribute all behavior to environmental stimuli and evolved cognitive structures. By holding this perspective, they seek to naturalize what appears to be a spontaneous, self-sufficient, and qualitative mind. To achieve their aims, the scientists specifically use behavioral psychology and cognitive neuroscience to predict and react to all forms of human behavior. Through these means, scientists seek to separate the subjective content of the mind from what they seek to observe, objectively, with the scientific method.

Scientists' first obvious step in grounding the appearance of the mind's ghostly self-sufficiency is to redefine the psychological discipline, as a discipline that categorizes and anticipates behavioral responses. They disregard the initial practices of what contemporary scientists term "folk" psychology, in which past psychologists merely observed the aberrations of mental thoughts. Now behavioral psychiatrists primarily explain behavior by referencing such material causes as associative-environmental stimuli, genetic traits, relational adaptations, automaticity, and customary (or 'priming') reinforcement. These material consequences, the behavioral psychiatrists cite, without their referencing a pre-existing psychological character. In this manner, they seek to close the mind-matter explanatory gap.

Cognitive Neuroscience

To understand how the brain and nervous system's neuronal structure actually correlates with consciousness, mid-twentieth century scientists developed the cognitive neuroscience discipline, as a successor to behavioral psychology. Furthermore, the procedural advances in computer science, biology, and neurology made the discipline of cognitive neuroscience possible.

In addition to their drawing inspiration from computer science's information processing models, cognitive neuroscientists draw inspiration from biologists' key practice: they esteem how biologists systematically correlate water, protein, nucleic acid, carbohydrate, metabolite, and lipid molecules to define the greater relationships between living cells. So like the biologists' systematic consideration of molecular building blocks to understand whole cell processes, cognitive neuroscientists seek to apply procedural and information processing descriptions to neuronal-cell operations, in order to understand how the whole neuronal process corresponds with consciousness. In this manner, cognitive neuroscientists pioneer science's functional approach to understanding the qualitative mind.

Thus, securing a description of the way that the brain's neuronal signals regulate bodily operations in correspondence with cognition is the fundamental goal of cognitive neuroscience. To achieve this objective, cognitive neuroscientists build their work upon the following understandings of the neuron cell: neurologists recognize that the neuron consist of a cell body, which they term a soma; an elongated tubular axon channel that conducts electro-chemical signals from the cell membrane; and a dendrite—a tree-like formation—that receives electro-chemical signals from other neurons. Neurologists, in fact, describe the signal transfer between neurons as the chemical release of inhibitor or exciter neurotransmitters over small synaptic gaps between neurons.

Curiously, the neuronal electro-chemical signals that emerge as both bodily commands and conscious cognitions have their basis in the polarized interactions between the charged atoms of sodium, potassium, chloride, calcium, and a variety of chemicals mechanisms. Neuroscientists do not have an explanation for the way that these polarizing and depolarizing, charged mechanisms amount to consciousness; however, by using brain imaging techniques to register neuronal firings, cognitive neuroscientists characterize the operations and concentrations of the neurons to describe the brain's cortical regions and lobes. Thereafter, by observing neuronal activity upon stimulation, cognitive neuroscientists identify the brain locations that are responsible for sensory inputs, such as hearing, sight, and olfaction; moreover, they identify the brain regions that are responsible for motor-cell outputs to muscle fibers.

In particular, as they gain an understanding of the chemical transfers that excite or inhibit neuronal signals, cognitive neuroscientists gain better understandings of which cortical regions are responsible for attention, memory, and spatial awareness. Roughly locating areas that actively correspond with awareness states, cognitive neuroscientists tentatively establish the neuronal correlate to consciousness (NCC) by distinguishing the brain areas that operate upon perceptual stimulation, while other areas operate, despite perceptual stimulation.

Indeed, because they discern that much of the brain's operational commands occur despite conscious perception; cognitive neuroscientists attribute human and animal consciousness to being a recent evolutionary modification: they believe that this evolutionary modification merely came into being in a way that allows the brain to acquire a flexible capacity that adapts to multiple-choice situations. The neuroscientists, also, believe that the automated processes, which prime us to make expectant responses, precede this more 'flexible' conscious capacity. For instance, the manner in which the brain attains short-term and long-term memory from a variety of brain regions seemingly gives evidence of the brain's recent adaptability. Some brain regions, such as the hippocampus, experience increased neuronal activity, during novel events; while other regions, such as the temporal lobes, experience increased activity during ongoing or reoccurring events. Due to these facts, cognitive neuroscientists recognize the reality that consciousness involves a distributed process.

Many cognitive neuroscientists believe that the greatest mark of consciousness' flexible emergence, from other naturally occurring processes, is the manner in which consciousness flexibly forecasts or recalls moments of time: consciousness tentatively transcends the brain's neurological and other biological processes that adhere to circadian—that is, twenty four hour—periods of time. Contemporary neuroscientists understand that animal and human consciousness involves an apprehension of time that they describe as a magnitudinous outcome of many contributing factors. For instance, varying neuronal systems, of respective brain regions, entail different processing periods. As a result, the brain obtains an aggregate sense of time, ranging from brain regions that contribute to attention and arousal unto brain regions that host memory and emotional states. Concurrently, our conscious sense of time transcends millisecond periods, which we are not aware of; and our sense of time involves long periods that arrest our attention, tediously.

Cognitive neuroscientists find that human and primate brains have similar structures; however, scientists find that human brains have a far greater number of neuronal connections, which increase processing periods and, therefore, representational abstractions. To distinguish the superiority of human consciousness from animal consciousness, cognitive neuroscientists describe humanity's unique capacity to self-reflect, as a further evolved conscious capacity that flexibly adapts to changing environments. Cognitive neuroscientists, in fact, call this greater conscious capacity meta-cognition: the apprehension of semantic (meaningful) knowledge by generating visual and audio word representations of our experiences.

Despite their staunch belief in evolutionary explanations for the rise of human consciousness, cognitive neuroscientists have not explicitly identified material causes for our short-term, long-term memory; our brains' magnitudinous apprehension of time; and our capacity to unite many of the brain's material aspects to generate word representations of our life-experiences. Nonetheless, because the neuronal correlates of consciousness consistently arise from many brain regions, cognitive neuroscientists still confidently affix procedural schemes to the brain's neuronal activities in such a manner that the scientists seem to reduce our qualitative, self-conscious minds to automated subroutines.

In point of fact, many cognitive neuroscientists employ procedural schemes to describe how the brain encodes environmental stimuli and produce the appearing mind in the following way: they conclude that while the environment makes impressions upon us, the brain performs computational actions, which amount to 'if-then' algorithmic procedures, such as searching, specifying, and retrieval. They believe that these algorithmic procedures effectively describe how the brain redirects or interprets the environmental impressions in a way that the brain's procedural processes manifest the appearance of semantic (that is, meaningful) content. Cognitive neuroscientists believe that the brain's functional processes, in this way, produce the image of the self-sufficient mind. And so, to advance a natural understanding of the appearing mind, cognitive neuroscientists continue to employ their logic-based representations and procedural schemes. They persist in solely considering the brain in terms of information processing.

Though the accuracy of their observations is compelling, we must emphasize the fact that cognitive neuroscientists still have not bridged the mind-matter explanatory gap. Even as they handedly represent neuronal processes as procedural outcomes, cognitive neuroscientists do not realize that they are merely treating the brain as a computational organ: they essentially view the brain as an adaptive and computational product of our material environments.

As a matter of fact, cognitive neuroscientists seek to explain the brain's spontaneous cognitions by referring to the way that the brain's short-term and long-term memory anticipate ongoing experience with 'priming' and 'automated' analogies of past experiences; however, their efforts still do not effectively explain how the brain transforms the physicality of the neuronal networks into the unified senses and intentional concepts that produce consciousness. Mere computational explanations ignore the brain's generative capacity: a capability that assimilates, relates, and transforms the diverse neurological faculties, in such a manner that our cognitions are not merely passive effects of environmental stimuli, but rather active producers of novel outcomes. Essentially, cognitive neuroscientists fail to determine the manner in which the mind's unified senses and intentional concepts ascend from matter, as matter emerges from quantum elements.

In essence, the cognitive neuroscientists' computational and procedural approach cannot explain how such material processes, like the electro-chemical transfer between excitatory and inhibitory neurotransmitters, become unified mental properties. To be sure, the procedural approach cannot explain how the physicality of genes and hormones translate into behavior, emotions, learning, and the other states of awareness that the genes and hormones purportedly indicate. Like all practitioners of the emergence concept, cognitive neuroscientists cannot use procedural schemes to account for the mind's spontaneous generation of concepts: a generation that occurs regardless of environmental impressions.

Some critics have already recognized the fact that the cognitive neuroscientists' procedural scheme—which again holds that environmental stimuli initiate behavior, as computational systems project responses—cannot explain the mind's spontaneous queries. Still, critics realize that no other plausible theory stands to address the many unanswered questions. Overshadowing such issues as the unknown way that material genes, hormones, and neuronal actions induce awareness states; the general question, concerning the mind-matter explanatory gap, continues to puzzle all.

No current thinker has discerned a suitable explanation for the fact that mental concepts do not directly affect observable objects. Yet, the concepts somehow transform into our motor neurons' tangible signals, which command our bodies' interaction with the objects.

Some recent attempts to describe the mind as an aspect of the brain's localized electromagnetic fields show great promise in identifying the neuronal correlate of consciousness, as we shall see; however, current electromagnetic-consciousness theories fail to explain how or why some electromagnetic brain waves correlate with consciousness, while other electromagnetic waves, in the brain and throughout the body, do not. More importantly, current theories fail to explain how or why the electromagnetic brain waves' interface with motor neurons entail an intrinsic qualitative sense. The theories' current proponents merely retreat to tautological proclamations that assert that consciousness equals electromagnetic waves' interface with neurons, as though the building blocks that comprise this interface are veritable things-in-themselves that amount to consciousness.

Essentially, thinkers overlook the brain's dynamic capacity, which produces a mind whose conceptions excel its physical constituents and environment. As our pending orthodox judgment shall establish, the concepts of the mind do not affect the objects directly because the appearing mind is not solely the adaptive or computational product of environmental stimuli. Rather, the mind's spontaneous generation of concepts is synonymous with a heretofore undefined dynamic mechanism in the brain that transforms environmental impressions into tools that sustain the brain's dynamic capacity. As we shall later discover, this mechanism is the physical correlate of consciousness:

Eventually, when our judgment identifies consciousness' physical correlate, we will better understand how the mind dynamically translates the material workings of genes, neurons, and hormones into colors, odors, melodies, tastes, and textures: we will understand how these sensations solely stand in accordance to the mind's dynamic point of reference. Currently, we know that a particular gene, neuron, hormone, or even a region in the brain does not produce these sensations, without unifying the interworking of these supporting faculties, in relation to environmental impressions.

Of a truth, the mysterious way that our mental reference frames abstractly emerge to endow existing material realities, which even encourage our psychological and material well-being, puzzles all thinkers. The absence of a confirmable explanation that resolves this mystery continues to incite the conflicting assertions of theologians, philosophers, and scientists, alike.

Unmistakably, we conclude that to identify the brain's dynamic cognitive mechanism is to resolve the mystery of the physical correlate of consciousness; however, we cannot fully identify this mechanism, at this point. For now, we only seek to describe how secular scientists' naturalist approach to the mind-matter question produces a behavioral psychology and cognitive neuroscience that do not treat the dynamic function of the brain. As a result, the current scope of cognitive neuroscience actually confounds the dynamic structure of human knowledge.

The Epistemological Question

Many contemporary philosophers—who see that behavioral psychology and cognitive neuroscience fail to resolve the mind-matter explanatory gap—pursue a different approach. Instead of laboring over the actual anatomical or environmental physicality that produces consciousness and behavior, many contemporary philosophers wonder what the nature of knowledge, itself, demands. These philosophers essentially ask, "What are the necessary conventions of perceptual experience that justify our knowledge and beliefs as true?"

To satisfy their query, they further ask, "Does the structure and nature of knowledge demand the privilege of an anatomical structure that builds perceived experiences upon its internal sensed-based reference frame? Or does the structure and nature of knowledge demand the reliable aid of an external network of correlating material phenomena, which entail an invariant, environmental order that structures our thoughts?"

The unanswered questions lead philosophers to develop the discipline of epistemology: a naturalistic (and, therefore, existential) assessment of the conditions, possibility, and justified-true-belief of our knowledge. Essentially, epistemology's naturalist approach either seeks internal sources of justification (as one relies on what seems evident to one's senses) or seeks external sources of justification (as one ensures that one's beliefs have a high probability of being objectively true).

To ensure our knowledge's justification in either approach, epistemology seeks to determine the actual structure of justification, itself; because this sought-after structure respectively organizes our knowledge and justifies our beliefs. As we just indicated above, epistemology seeks to determine whether the structure of justification rest upon a privileged-belief foundation, upon which an overall superstructure of cognitive experience stands; or the structure of justification rest upon a network of reliable objective sources that coherently assimilate perceptual experiences.

Both viewpoints are inconclusive, however. On one hand, a continual dependency upon experience for validation undermines the privileged-belief-foundational approach: the continual experiences incline observers to reconsider whether any accepted 'privileged belief' is ontologically fundamental. Such questions thereby lead to ontology's infinite regress. On the other hand, a continual dependency upon experience for validation undermines the network of reliable-cognitive-sources approach, as observers initially question why some sources have more validity than others. This question afterward leaves observers to further question whether their coherent-network of cognitive sources is a true reflection of reality.

In the end, both approaches only assert that we have a probabilistic ability to apprehend justification from our perceptual experiences. Furthermore, the acceptance of justification's mere probability leads thinkers to conclude that we can only use perceptual experiences to refine our cognitive propositions, without settling upon a fundamental truth.

And so, as both approaches settle upon the chance-like apprehensions of justification from experience, they fail to answer the ultimate epistemological questions, which ask, "Why is perception a source of justification? How can we know that we correctly perceive the world?"

Epistemologists' inability to answer fundamental questions causes both approaches to fall short of apprehending ontological understanding. As a consequence, epistemology's naturalist pursuit of internal or external sources for justification ends in the infinite regress of never settling upon the essential worth of any perception.

The Rift between Science and Philosophy

Though the discipline fails to resolve the mind-matter explanatory gap, epistemology's chief aim is constructive: epistemology seeks to demonstrate that our knowledge is not autonomous but dependent upon either internal or external material structures. Nevertheless, agnostic and atheist practitioners wrongfully apply the discipline, because they hold the naturalist perspective that knowledge solely arises from specific material processes. In so doing, the naturalist practitioners miss the subtle but profound fact that the asymmetric creation metaphysically consigns our knowledge to be dependent upon internal and external material structures but not entirely produced by them.

To be sure, we have repeatedly noted that material compounds do not result from their constituents, even though the compounds' identities depend upon the compounds' constituents. Rather, material compounds result from the asymmetric natural-force-laws that govern the compounds' relationship with the compounds' constituents. In this vein, we have submitted that natural-force-laws also govern the manner in which the brain's dynamic capacity projects the physicality of our knowledge beyond the material world that the brain's identity depends upon. We, in fact, indicated that the brain's dynamic capacity accomplishes this by translating particular material impressions into analogous concepts that reflect the mind's perspective whole. Now, we may only add the subsequent crucial point: because both the brain's dynamic capacity and the material world adhere to creation's asymmetric natural-force-laws, the creation's material aspects, which correspond with our bodily senses, must exist in indicative states that exemplify universal wholes. In this way, the material world's asymmetric structure validates the dynamic mind's identity dependence upon the material world.

Of course, our orthodox judgment will define the brain's underlying dynamic capacity and how Y'haweh expresses the material world to us. For now, we must further underscore the conflict between empirical science and the rationalist trends of philosophy, as they struggle to understand the spontaneous cognitions that delineate the brain's dynamic character. Already, we have highlighted how behavioral psychology and cognitive neuroscience fail to encompass the brain's spontaneity. Now, let us further note how the epistemological discipline also fails to address the mind's spontaneity. In this fashion, we may identify the major schism between contemporary science and philosophy.

On the whole, epistemologists commit two major errors when they solely affix our knowledge-structure to either internal or external material processes, without their recognizing a metaphysical priority. First, epistemologists become likely to deem any cognitive activity, which occurs regardless of environmental impressions, as inconsequential. Thus, we may expose epistemology's first error as being the same fault that behavioral psychologists and cognitive neuroscientists commit: they dismissingly describe the brain's spontaneous cognitions as epiphenomena—that is, psychological figments that result from material events, even as the supposed figments do not affect the material events. Furthermore, while their naturalist approach causes them to disregard the brain's novel cognitions, epistemologists commit the second major error, which we may explain as follows: epistemology's very broad reliance upon either internal or external material sources for knowledge's justification is indeed a study that forgoes specific neurological or environmental causes; however, because the discipline relies upon material sources (howbeit undefined), epistemology's general approach still fails to consider whether our knowledge-structure relies upon incremental periods that establish a uniform basis for the brain's sense of time; or our knowledge-structure relies upon a network of emerging processes that encode the brain's sense of time.

We recall that cognitive neuroscientists established the fact that the necessary neurological contributors to consciousness—namely, short and long memory; language's visual and auditory word representations; and the molecular clock-like processes that contribute to our sense of time—hail from a network of many brain regions. We understood that many thoughtful cognitive neuroscientists have concluded that the brain's encoded sense of time especially hallmarks consciousness, because the brain's encoded sense is distinct from the normative cellular processes that obey such incremental conventions like circadian periods of time. Even so, we concluded that cognitive neuroscience's procedural approaches to our time-conscious sense (and consciousness in general) fall short of providing an explanation for the mind's ability to ascertain novel outcomes, despite material impressions.

As a result of what we have learned, concerning cognitive neuroscience's inability to address spontaneous (that is, novel) cognitions, we may finally conclude the following: even though epistemology does not seek particular material answers, the discipline must explain spontaneous cognitions in a way that coincides with the brain's distinct apprehension of spacetime. As epistemology considers internal or external source of justification, the discipline must explain why the spontaneous activities not only persist beyond one environmental impression, but also persist beyond a variety of impressions, in categorical sequence.

In truth, the brain's spontaneity occurs to the degree that the brain appears to anticipate and superimpose upon continued impressions. Summarily, we may recognize the fact that material explanations may explain how bodily functions correspond with one another; however, material explanations do not explain how cognitive functions correspond with hypothetical encounters. Even certain material impressions upon brain regions, which neurologists denote as memory centers, cannot explain how the dynamic mind forever holds passing impressions as impoverished to the unified sense that it seeks.

Indeed, under a unified sense, the qualitative mind categorically assimilates all things, by subjugating past and present impressions to the anticipated novelty of greater relationships. In this manner, the qualitative mind intentionally derives its relationship with distant things or things that it has not experienced.

Essentially, we must conclude that scientists and philosophers have not truly recognized or understood the fact that the brain necessarily obtains an independent cognizance of time, in order to produce all perceptions. This oversight is the second error that undermines philosophers' naturalist approach to epistemology. To be sure, as we view the brain's obtaining 'time-consciousness,' we witness thought processes transcend the material impressions.

Though most thinkers do not address how the brain uniquely gains time-consciousness, the increasing recognition that perceptions entail an independent time-conscious experience initiates a split between contemporary philosophy and science. Philosophia (the love of wisdom, inspiring the introspective quest to justify our beliefs) and scientia (the objective seeking of knowledge, in general) naturally seem to complement one another: both have united to seek natural explanations for the manner in which the mind ascends from, remains contingent to, and superimposes upon the quantum, electromagnetic, and gravitational forces that comprise the material world. Both have contributed their principles to a scientific method that entails logical postulations, mathematical descriptions, objective observations, and methodological analysis. As we have seen, science and philosophy have struggled together to hold a naturalist position that seeks to apprehend, predict, or explain all necessary or contingent outcomes, without resorting to theological dogma. In fact, until the 20th Century, philosophers and scientists both practiced natural philosophy, before secular scientists construed a physical-science discipline that they term *physics*.

Although philosophy and science have equally contributed to the principles of the scientific method, both disciplines have faced the shortcomings of applying the method in a naturalist vein. We have seen how philosophy's logical postulations—the basis of all hypotheses—cannot extend beyond themselves to justify themselves. Likewise, we have seen how science's mathematical systems cannot extend beyond themselves to justify themselves. Too, we have seen how science's emergence concept cannot use material explanations to explain the unique physicality of the mind. Along these lines, we have seen how behavioral psychology and cognitive neuroscience's respective existential and internal, material descriptions cannot explain the dynamic nature of the mind. Lastly, we have seen how philosophy's epistemological discipline fails to assess what knowledge's structure demands of internal or external material structures, within spacetime. Even as scientists and philosophers have faced challenges and maintained the principles of the scientific method together, their different stances on the relevance of our time-conscious experience have confused the scope and direction of the scientific method's application, as we shall shortly see:

Contemporary philosophers still recognize the necessity of answering the epistemological question: philosophers still realize the necessity of understanding whether our knowledge's justification arises from an internal privileged-belief foundation or an external network of reliable sources. So unlike scientists, contemporary philosophers continue to seek natural explanations for the brain's spontaneous cognitions, which traditional epistemology fails to encompass.

The contemporary philosophers chiefly recognize that the brain's independent time-conscious ability exemplifies how our knowledge's structure extends beyond the internal and external material sources, to the extent that the structure projects the senses of cause, effect, and purposefulness upon everything we perceive. Effectively, philosophers realize that our time-conscious experience translates our encounters with material objects into what philosophers call "lived experiences."

Notwithstanding, empirical scientists describe any further rationalist inquiries into our time-conscious experience as standing upon speculative ground, like theology. Even so, philosophers retort by asking what can we scientifically know or observe of the world without our time-conscious perspectives.

Phenomenal Experience

To address the fact that our sense of time physically obtains, regardless of specific internal or external material impressions, philosophers have recently developed the discipline of phenomenology: a discipline that simply seeks to describe how our time-conscious experience intentionally extends our knowledge-structure to the appearing material world. Like the discipline of epistemology, phenomenology does not seek to describe exactly how or why our conscious minds came into being; moreover, phenomenology does not seek to establish a cosmological theory that describes exactly how or why the physical world came into being. Phenomenology, in this manner, pursues a naturalist approach. Nevertheless, because phenomenology specifically treats our time-conscious experience, phenomenology seeks to ascertain how both our knowledge-structure and the material world relate within spacetime. Through these means, phenomenology ultimately seeks to close the mind-matter explanatory gap, by correlating the way we become cognizant of spacetime and the way material phenomena appear to us within spacetime. Phenomenology thereby holds science's pursuit of fully defining physical and material phenomena as secondary to phenomenology's quest for the necessary internal and external material conventions that facilitate our time-conscious experience.

We will here briefly describe why phenomenology's treatment of our time-conscious experience is a necessary discipline to understand, even though contemporary science ignores the discipline's relevance. We will realize phenomenology's worth, as we survey phenomenology's description of the way that our time-conscious experience enables us to ascertain all things per the sense of our own significance. At the same time, we will readily conclude the following: because phenomenology's naturalist approach neither identifies specific causality, nor explains and predicts our interactions in the world, phenomenology falls short of providing scientists with any critical understandings. Hence, we will certainly agree with contemporary scientists, who stress that phenomenology is not a suitable discipline that the public should consider as science. As a consequence, we will understand why physics assumes the role of social acceptability; especially as scientists downplay the crucial role that our time-conscious perspectives play in our interactions with the environment. Nonetheless, because contemporary scientists fail to recognize the conventional way that our time-cognizance enables our knowledge-structure to superimpose upon observed objects, we will recognize that phenomenologists rightly conclude that science, itself, is meaningless, unless its theorems regard the significant perspectives of our personal reference frames.

The early 19th Century philosopher Immanuel Kant pioneered the modern study of our time-conscious experience. Of course, Kant did not have a contemporary understanding of the brain's anatomy, and Kant did not have an understanding of how the brain dynamically obtains its time-conscious sense. Basically, Kant did not comprehend a physical explanation for the dynamic manner in which the brain translates perceptions of material phenomena into concepts that center upon the unity of spacetime. Kant, in fact, avoided the search for actual physical causes. Instead, he merely described our human sensibilities as the means through which our time-conscious sense enables us to perceive appearing objects, relating within space and time. And so, instead of discerning how our cognizance of time physically enables us to project our knowledge-structure upon the world, Kant merely described the functional convention under which our basic intuition of the self translates appearing objects into mental representations. Likewise, instead of discovering a dynamic, metaphysical, or cosmological cause for the appearing material world; Kant merely underscored the fact that appearing material objects must subsume under time's duration and succession. Furthermore, as we shall later detail, Kant concluded that all perceivable objects obey natural principles like the permanence and consistency of a material substance within spacetime. He also concluded that the material objects must obey the principles of cause, effect, and coexistence within time.

Kant perceived natural principles that enable our minds to form judgments by grounding all appearing objects into the cognitive categories of quantity, quality, relation, and modality. Upon these categories of judgment, Kant formulated what he termed a transcendental logic: a formulaic understanding that describes how our minds transcend immediate material perceptions to "imagine" such sublime ideals like the nature of the creator, metaphysical causality, and the meaning of the self.

The full significance of Immanuel Kant's work, we shall discover later. At this point, we may note the following: although many contemporary logicians mistakenly hold the view that Kant's transcendental logic stands upon a superficial precursor to their predicate calculus, Kant's transcendental logic actually attempts to describe how our rational judgments arise upon classical, Newtonian notions of a space and time.

Kant strongly identified with the Newtonian perspective that space and time stand prior to material objects; therefore, Kant held the view that our knowledge-structure, too, stands prior to the same mathematically describable material objects, which relate within spacetime. Essentially, Kant pioneered the conventional understanding that our unified time-conscious sense enables our *a priori* knowledge-structure to superimpose upon material impressions, which arise within spacetime. So by building our knowledge-structure upon an independent apprehension of space and time, Kant forged a way for phenomenology to ground the spontaneous concepts of the mind.

Though phenomenologists do not pursue physical causes like the naturalist approaches of the empirical scientists and other naturalist philosophers, phenomenology's rational descriptions continue to demonstrate the great promise of closing the mind-matter explanatory gap. Formal logic, the emergence concept, behavioral psychology, cognitive neuroscience, and epistemology fail to determine how the spontaneous predicates of our thoughts naturally reconcile with material objects and their properties: these disciplines primarily stand upon the belief that the qualitative mind is the resulting epiphenomenon of a material world that solely performs work upon us. In contrast, phenomenologists look beyond the current lack of scientific evidence for the brain's spontaneity. Rather than merely envisioning the world operating upon us, phenomenology finds the encouragement to envision how the mind reciprocally performs work upon the world. Clearly, phenomenology draws encouragement from the fact that the mind's independent time-cognizance enables it to impose concepts upon the material world, as the mind seeks its own significance.

Seeking to describe how the mind intentionally works upon the world, contemporary phenomenology expands upon Kant's initial description of our time-conscious capacity: instead of accepting Kant's assertion that our sensibility merely entails our cognizance of objects, relating within space and time; contemporary phenomenology expands Kant's notion of our sensibility. Phenomenology specifically draws attention to our innate cognizance of the inextricable relation between past, present, and pending material experiences. In this way, phenomenology discerns how our cognizance of a coherent spacetime gives evidence that our self-perspectives correlate with an inner, unified homogenous-background that physically merges past, present, and future experience, per our self-perspective reference frames. In other words, phenomenology acknowledges how we possess the operative, physical capacity to synthesize past, present, and future experience of the objects by translating them into retentive, intensive, and expectant analogues that garner the significance of our self-perspectives.

To further esteem our self-perspectives over our mere sensibility to the appearing objects, phenomenology builds upon Kant's description of the way material objects necessarily obey the same spacetime conventions that enable our time-conscious capacities. Contemporary phenomenology adapts Kant's observations, concerning how material objects necessarily adhere to the conventions of duration, succession, permanence, and consistency; as well as adhere to the principles of cause, effect, and coexistence. Then progressing beyond Kant's observations, phenomenology draws attention to the way the mind assimilates the emerging appearances that relating objects give voice to. In other words, phenomenology assesses how the emergent material appearances adhere to spacetime in a manner that invites the mind's intentional expectations. These expectations, again, fuse past, present, and future impressions to seek further emerging realities, in relation to the significant self. Hence, by assessing how objects and our thoughts adhere to spacetime, phenomenology observes how spacetime's coherence not only establishes the significance of our self-perspectives, but also suggests objective meanings for emerging material appearances.

So despite our inability to comprehend the ontological essence of every disjunctive (and often enigmatic) material object-in-itself, phenomenology recognizes the fact that our time-conscious capacity assures us that all material objects succumb to the uniformity of spacetime. In this way, phenomenology demonstrates our ability to assign relevance to all material objects, per our significant experience of the objects, within spacetime. While behavioral psychology and cognitive science only envision how the world works upon us, phenomenology finally describes how our minds perform work upon the world, through what we may describe as our self-will: even a will that we may define as our intentional attitudes that underscore the significance of our self-perspectives over what we observe.

The Crucial Cognitive Reality that Phenomenology Identifies

To understand the implications of phenomenology fully, we must first recognize that phenomenology's chief strength is its recognition of the subsequent cognitive reality: phenomenology recognizes the inextricable relationship between our finite, intelligent perspectives (of the observable world) and the manner in which the ordered creation unpacks our perspective understandings.

Instead of using specific material explanations to explain the cause, structure, and breadth of our finite minds; phenomenologists invoke the reality that the manner in which objects emerge into uniform spacetime facilitates the mind's dynamic nature. Though phenomenologists generally recognize the fact that spacetime is not a standalone empty void, existing by itself; an intelligent surveyor of the phenomenological discipline may readily glean the forgoing attitude that most phenomenologists maintain: they generally believe that the mind intuitively recognizes spacetime, as a culminating rationalization that holds appearing material properties as exemplifications of greater material relationships within spacetime.

And so, instead of considering material objects as existing unto themselves, enigmatically, with no sense of purposefulness; phenomenological writings merely treat the salient material relationships that instigate conscious perceptions. In his "Critique of Judgment," for instance, Immanuel Kant basically drew our knowledge-structure's limitations between, first, the sublime experiences that entail our inability to rationalize creation's awesome aspects and, second, the beatific experiences that entail creation's inspiring aspects that organize our thoughts in brilliant manners that we are unable to conceive.

We more perfectly liken a sublime experience to the secular notion of an overpowering, purposeless environment, existing unto itself; where our happenstance existence finds no utilitarian reference points that further our healthful vitality or even draw our understanding. Of course, we know that empirical scientists have this daunting view of creation: a perspective that leaves our very being facing the seemingly unbridgeable chasm between our qualitative minds and the material world.

Instead of viewing phenomena as sublime unknowable elements unto themselves, phenomenologists observe how no element exists unto itself at any past, present, or pending point in spacetime. Like so, they astutely surmise how asymmetric natural-force-laws maintain the continuity of identity. They envision how the natural-force-laws successively refer the element to macroscopic-properties; the material objects that the properties exemplify; the species of the objects; and the greater functional relationships that refer all to the conservation of forces, within spacetime as a whole.

Phenomenologists essentially envision all material objects as indicative of immaterial wholes, instead of the material objects' constituting the material wholes, themselves. Rationalizing all material things, phenomenologists observe how material phenomena successively stratify as either the appearance of complete disjunction;

the appearance of heterogeneous relationships; the appearance of slight variances; the appearance of gradation; or the appearance of complete homogeneity.

The jewel of phenomenology's recognition of the material world's indicative nature is the manner in which the recognition encourages phenomenologists to pursue explanations for our intentional minds' metaphysical stand upon the mind's being. Brilliantly, phenomenologists recognize how spacetime's referential nature allows us to translate contingent material objects into immaterial mental tools. The phenomenologists note that as stratified elements exemplify appearing materials that our finite minds can grasp, the mind then misrepresents what appears as we seek the utility that the appearing objects display.

Phenomenologists realize that material objects only infer or suggests outcomes, relationships, greater continuity, and even beatific meaning. Upon recognizing the world's 'ought' structure, phenomenologists observe how our self-perspective minds involuntarily unify the inferential appearances according to their similarity or correlation with one another. Phenomenologists note how we inexplicably synthesize the immediate impressions of the past, while we project analogous concepts upon the future. In this way, phenomenologists observe how we instinctively apprehend categories, kinship, and species. They note how we effectively liberate material objects not only unto their immaterial, mental horizons that the objects give voice to; but also unto the unified significance of our self-perspectives. Thereby, phenomenologists recognize that our encounter with natural beauty—a divine reflection within creation's referential continuity—induces our mental quests for meaning beyond our vulgar tastes and preferences.

After all, phenomenology's indicative description of creation does not only render science's sublime creation less alien. Phenomenologists also proceed to catalogue our degrees of awareness; from our sense of self within creation unto our sense of others. In this manner, phenomenologists unknowingly render the communal sense of beauty as thing that divinity confers, beyond our personal tastes and preferences.

On the whole, phenomenologists have ascertained rational means to describe our awareness and knowledge-structure as a continuous, time-conscious evaluation of our conceptions: they purport that creation's indicative nature rules out the notion that objects exist independently as things-in-themselves. As a result, phenomenologists conclude that we continuously evaluate our ongoing understandings of interrelating objects as true or false; satisfied or unsatisfied; and real or fictitious.

While phenomenology demonstrates great promise, the discipline still falls short of surmounting scientific scrutiny. Even though phenomenology's time-conscious descriptions do not have any mathematical limitations like empirical science, scientists still readily point out phenomenology's shortcomings. First, the discipline fails to close the mind-matter explanatory gap because the discipline fails to describe how the material brain takes a physical stand on its being. Fundamentally, phenomenology fails to provide a material explanation for the neurological mechanism that obtains an independent sense of time, regardless of specific impressions. Thus, phenomenology does not explain why our minds are not merely the epiphenomenal product of sequenced events. For this cause, the discipline actually fails to mark out the sentient, self-perspective from which our knowledge-structure arises to superimpose upon every appearing material phenomenon within spacetime.

Furthermore, scientists observe how phenomenology's description of creation's indicative nature does not predict, define, or establish the nature or meaning of the phenomenal world, beyond our personal taste and political purposes. Instead of examining our time-conscious experience to apprehend an epistemological understanding of our knowledge's internal and external justification, phenomenology only stresses how creation's rational network facilitates consciousness. Scientists, therefore, view phenomenology as an accumulation of unsubstantiated (tautological) statements, which are decidedly anthropocentric. As a consequence of empirical scientists' just denunciation of phenomenology, phenomenology leaves the scientific method to face the profound problem of saving creation's material phenomena beyond the centrality of human intelligence.

Notwithstanding, phenomenologists still dutifully ask what can science's scientific method ascertain or establish without regarding the significance of our qualitative, self-perspectives: phenomenologists wonder how can scientists apprehend an ontological understanding of material objects, without recognizing the imposing human perspective that colors our judgment. Because no object exists unto itself, they further ask how can scientists save the phenomena without establishing a metaphysical cause or epistemological explanation?

The striking discord between contemporary science and phenomenology is the latest break between natural philosophers who either stress the authority of empirical observations to justify their beliefs, or stress the authority of the rational mind to justify their beliefs. The earliest known philosophers who had critically stressed the authority of empirical observation where men like Thales of Miletus (c.625-c.545 B.C.), Anaximander of Miletus (c.610-c.545 B.C.), Parmenides of Elea (c. 480 B.C.), and Empedocles of Acragas (c. 440 B.C.). These prodigious thinkers pioneered today's scientific principles: they essentially held that natural philosophers can reduce all material bodies to elemental properties that operate mechanically without divine intervention. In contrast, antiquity's three major rationalist philosophers—Socrates, Plato, and Aristotle—sought to justify our beliefs by stressing the priority of comprehending the order of our thought processes, despite what we observe.

Now contemporary science's empiricist approach and phenomenology's more rationalist approach to our time-conscious experience seem destined to mark the irreconcilable split between scientists who stress the authority of empirical observation and contemporary philosophers who stress the necessity of our rational self-perspectives. Due to this impasse, our knowledge-structure still resides perilously aloft, not being able to rest upon a definitive truth for the material world.

As we shall here discover, science's inability to bridge the mind-matter explanatory gap continues to present tremendous social, cultural, religious, and political ramifications. Even so, our business is not to advance either the rational or empirical approach, precariously. Our pending judgment must reconcile both. In order for us to submit our judgment, let us now assess the shortcomings of science's scientific method and Standard Model, as we consider how scientists fail to answer phenomenology's crucial questions:

We must discover how scientists determine the functional operations of the creation, without their considering the supervening gauge of divine or human intelligence. Also, we must discover how scientists determine creation's universal functions by empirically observing the lesser constituents that they have on hand. Essentially, we must discover how scientists avoid functionally indeterminate conclusions when the asymmetric creation forever leaves them void of all the contingent factors.

The Scientific Method

To begin our survey of contemporary science, we must note that the first goal for any scientist is to distinguish an objective understanding of the world from the subjective mind's emotions and prejudices. Thus, scientists seek to replace religious dogma with scientifically acquired knowledge for the purpose of arbitrating public truths in the Western world.

To distinguish objective understanding from religious dogma, secular scientists view creation as a self-sufficient universe that entails an infinite number of mechanical processes that scientists hope to observe and quantify. The quest for critical observation is the inspiration for the scientific method: an empirical quest to establish methodologies that interpret all physical events as mechanical operations. By employing the scientific method, scientists advance our objective understanding of the world as they mechanically predict the cause, position, momentum, and other behavioral aspects of material phenomena.

Furthermore, by critically distinguishing the mechanical operations of the emerging world from the abstractions of the subjective mind, scientists seek to establish creation's basic structure. To achieve this end, scientists do not philosophically pursue the metaphysical essence or ontological identity of material things-in-themselves. Instead, scientists pursue the existential nature of matter: that is, they pursue the emergent properties that stand out in a manner that we can critically observe with our senses.

As we previously alluded to above, two key existential understandings of the natural-force-laws aid scientists in their establishing a scientific method: the first key understanding is their blunt acceptance that a non-intelligent, immanent, force stratifies into systems of emergent processes that natural-force-laws then qualify. Again, what is important to note from this first understanding is the fact that scientists do not accept a metaphysical or ontological identity for the pre-existing, natural forces, other than the forces' abstract capacities to perform or accept work. So instead of further inquiring into the essence and identity of the pre-existing forces, scientists existentially observe the dynamic manner in which the natural forces either amass or extend, in correspondence.

The second key understanding complements the first as follows: scientists implicitly observe the fact that our simple cognizance of the natural laws enables us to transcend our subjective perceptions, as we consciously seek such properties that fall under the natural laws. During these conscientious pursuits, scientists also recognize that we deny the immediate prejudice of our perceptions, as we fully expect rational emerging orders. Like so, we try to save (that is, possess a quintessential understanding of) the emerging appearances (or representations) of constituent and macroscopic phenomena. Having observed our mental access to the natural-force-laws, scientists expect all natural-force-laws to be mathematically definable and symmetrical—that is, immutable, uniform, constant, translational, and relevant to the observer. In this manner, scientists objectively deduce mechanical function and meaning.

To advance their mechanical understanding, scientists put forth mathematical relationships that correspond to their empirical observations, without their attempting to assert a subjective explanation for the mechanical relationships. Through these means, they try to forgo the mind's subjective predispositions as they evaluate phenomena: they try to understand phenomena without resorting to mere analogous pre-conceptions.

To grasp a comprehensive summary of what we have stated, we may conclude the following: the only cornerstone-principle that scientists intuitively deduce, prior to their empirical and methodological approach to understanding creation, is the expectation that they can mechanically quantify all knowable material operations under dynamic natural-force-laws; from which the scientists can ascertain causality and utility. For this cause, the practitioners of the scientific method employ the method as an open-ended, inductive analysis of newfound data, without a practitioner's regard for any metaphysical or anthropocentric truth. The method perennially engages an emergent universe, where all physical systems depend upon an array of fundamental forces.

Initially, using the scientific method, scientists characterize observations. Following, they form logical hypotheses, which entail critical suggestions, concerning the cause, effect, and mechanical function of the emergent properties that they observe. Next, they perform inductive experiments to test hypotheses. Lastly, they make predictions, using logical deductions and mathematical models: their finally being able to forgo prejudice, they methodologically predict future results by establishing theories that attempt to define further the natural laws that they observe.

As we begin our survey of scientists' employment of the scientific method, we first emphasize the subsequent crucial understanding: verifiable observation is contemporary science's foundation. Modernity's technological proliferation is a result of scientists' devising apparatuses to test predictions of what they empirically observe. Thus, the weakness of contemporary science is its increasing technological inability to devise devices that facilitate the testing of hypotheses. In the face of an asymmetric creation, scientists increasingly reach observational barriers that prevent them from vindicating their extension of the Standard Model to define a single cosmological cause.

The Rise of Newtonian Mechanics

The verifiable scientific discover, spanning from the 18th century late-classical-period unto the present, holds endless volumes of data and overawes. Even so, we will initiate a brief but critical survey of scientific discovery's chronicle: we will first recall the historical contributions of natural philosophers that gave rise to Newtonian mechanics' mechanical approach to the world. Then after we describe how classical physics failed to secure sufficient mechanical descriptions of heat, electricity, and light; we will finally describe the essential conventions, successes, and shortsightedness of contemporary physics, which attempts to secure classical physics' mechanical approach to the world.

Natural explanations for the world began when historical thinkers postulated that all material objects derive from the prolific elements that we readily observe; like fire, water, wind, and earth. As we mentioned briefly above, natural explanations matured as philosophers turned to logic and mathematical theorems to decide the hidden nature of the world.

We see a sure hallmark of the modern age's rise in the manner in which scientists began to evaluate their logical postulations and mathematical descriptions. They began to ascertain methodologies that predict and define empirical observations of what scientists deem as a world emerging under natural laws.

Once more, the effectiveness of scientists' establishing these methodologies has not only proliferated beneficial technologies. The effectiveness of scientists' establishing the scientific method has also validated the naturalist approach, to the extent that personal prejudice, superstition, and religious dogma have lost their preeminent place in official public discourse.

Though the critical investigations of pioneering philosophers like René Descartes incurred the scorn of the religious establishment; the unassailable methodology that Sir Isaac Newton (1642-1727) founded began secular science's usurpation of Church authority. Newton's methodological mechanics predicted, explained, and procured far reaching societal benefits: Newton vindicated scientists' natural approach to explaining the world. The resulting technological and intellectual advancement impacted Western civilization to the extent that the public at large began to dismiss the Church's religious prejudice against natural philosophy.

Ironically, Sir Isaac Newton, an unorthodox biblical enthusiast himself, was among the first successful scientific practitioners who publicly suppressed human subjectivity and religious dogma. Newton sought to obtain objective explanations that all cultures and creeds could universally agree upon. He championed the principles that pioneered the scientific method. He only recognized causes that sufficiently explain appearing material objects. Likewise, he held that all effects proceed from particular causes. Newton also recognized universal properties. Then he maintained the need to scrutinize all hypotheses with inductive analysis.

With these governing principles, Newton overlooked metaphysical and ontological speculation. Newton sought to apprehend only the phenomenal world that falls under universal forces: he pursued the existential identity of substantive matter. Newton secured his aim by characterizing a universal law of gravity, which corresponds with both celestial macroscopic bodies and terrestrial microscopic bodies. In regards to his inability to discover a mechanical cause for gravity, Newton undervalued the traditional preeminence of epistemological quests, by asserting that he "framed no hypothesis." In other words, he cut off the epistemological question, concerning what quintessential experience fundamentally justifies our knowledge of such things as gravity and the other fundamental forces.

Although his contemporaries criticized him for not defining a tertiary or substantial mechanism that generates gravitational forces, Newton merely substantiated the mechanical nature of the observable world that falls under his gravitational theory. He accomplished this by establishing axioms, entailing fundamental laws. Some of the laws—such as the notion of absolute space and time—he termed 'self-evident;' moreover, he postulated force laws to describe the interaction of phenomena within space and time.

In 1687, Isaac Newton published his mechanical methodology in his greatest published work, entitled Philosophiæ Naturalis Principia Mathematica ("mathematical principles of natural philosophy"). In the Principia Mathematica, Newton sought to describe the operative mechanisms of the material world by his constructing his mechanics as a geometry-based discipline. In order to represent creation's phenomenal aspects mechanically, Newton qualified all material phenomena under kinematics (the study of body motions, interactions, and changes in space and time) and dynamics (the corresponding study of causal forces).

Throughout the Principia, Newton defined the universal gravitational force as the dynamic-force attractions between two masses, which draw one another inversely proportional to their distance. Then under the universal gravitational force, Newton described the subsequent three fundamental force laws, which essentially describe how any object that experiences changes in motion, experiences forces that are acting upon it: first, Newton asserted that an object at rest or at a sustained velocity will remain in that state unless an external force acts upon it. Second, he asserted that such a force equals the object's mass multiplied by its velocity. Finally, he concluded that every action entails a reaction.

What proved to be one of Newton's greatest gifts to philosophical society is the fact that Newton used his gravitational and other force laws to rationalize the unobserved mechanical operations behind the astronomical observations of previous scientists. For example, while the kinematics of Galileo Galilei and Johannes Kepler had described planetary elliptical motions, Newton mathematically described gravity's dynamic forces that underlie the other scientists' celestial observations. Notwithstanding, Newton's mathematical descriptions stressed geometrical precepts, because Newton tried to evade his mathematical descriptions from being later overturned.

Above all, Newton's mechanical philosophy, which entails the characterization of creation's macroscopic material phenomena under fundamental forces, forever set the standard for all succeeding scientists. The success of Isaac Newton's mechanical approach to explaining the world advanced the scientific method from being a procedural expediency to being a public necessity: the success of Newtonian mechanics, in fact, transported Western civilization's standing upon blind religious faith unto Western civilization's standing upon scientific skepticism.

Because of Newton's successful work, scientists necessarily attempt to ascertain all material phenomena mechanically: in their sincere efforts to apprehend optimal, societal benefits from the environment; scientists try to describe the kinematical behavior of all material phenomena, under dynamic forces. Like Newton, they regularly utilize mathematical tools to explain and predict the ongoing behavior of the material phenomena. Being so armed, scientists commonly characterize emergent macroscopic properties, as abstract composites of microscopic constituents.

Two schools of thought, immediately, took up Newton's mechanical approach to understanding the world. The two groups reflect the empiricist and rationalist philosophers' respective inquiry into the relationship between microscopic and macroscopic phenomena: one empirical approach sought to ascertain the natural-force-laws that exhibit how microscopic relationships emerge as the macroscopic materials that comprise our environments. The other group, rationally, sought the natural-force-laws that describe visible macroscopic structures, despite their invisible, microscopic building blocks. Nonetheless, both groups sought to establish a mechanical understanding that methodologically describes all material phenomena in kinematical motion and trajectory, under dynamic forces.

How Newtonian Mechanics Failed to Describe the Immaterial Forces

Of course, technological advancement spurred Newton's successors the most. Newton's work further exemplified the fact that humankind can overcome nature's privations through mechanical means: Newton's mechanical approach to nature revealed ways for mankind to adapt such mechanisms and machinery that ease civilization's grievous labor.

Now technological advancement proves not only to be the driving force for scientific development, but also to be the ultimate confirmation for any given scientific theory. Effective technology proves that scientists possess an instructive working knowledge of the dynamics of natural systems that any given technology seeks to exploit.

19th Century natural philosophers, however, found that Newton's laws of motion sufficed to advance such things like non-automated engineering and navigation: Newtonian mechanics readily explained how terrestrial and celestial material objects adhere to gravitational forces, within Newton's conception of an absolute space and time. Nonetheless, the natural philosophers found that Newtonian mechanics did not absolutely define the dynamics of the immaterial forces like heat, electricity, and light: wrongfully, Newtonian mechanics conceived light as indestructible material particles. Soon after, some thinkers resorted to describing these immaterial forces as material fluids. They conceptualized heat as a fluid, which they termed caloric; however, empirical observations of heat's mechanical nature quickly proved this postulation wrong. For this cause, natural philosophers had to discover the true mechanical nature of immaterial phenomena like heat and electricity because these phenomena respectively powered the automated steam engines and chemical batteries that arose in the 19th Century's Industrial Revolution.

Mainly industrial incentives compelled natural philosophers to ascertain a mechanical understanding that predicts how immaterial heat, electricity, and light interface with material objects. Nevertheless, the sense of urgency that fueled their efforts was the poignant fact that their inability to describe and predict the behavior of heat, electricity, and light called into question the entire mechanical approach to nature. In effect, the mechanical approach had (by this period) become the very foundation of modern science.

How Natural Philosophers Employed the Scientific Method to Describe the Immaterial Forces

To be sure, the capacity to predict material behavior, by establishing the material phenomena's operative positions and momentum under dynamic forces, still constitutes the pursuit of science. Science's mechanical approach to the world continues to stand as a naturalists' bulwark against superstition and oppressive religious dogma.

The natural philosophers, therefore, struggled to envision how Newton's force laws of attraction, repulsion, position, and momentum apply to the hypothetical molecular objects that emerge as the immaterial heat, electric, and light phenomena that industry sought to exploit. In essence, classical philosophers wondered how to use scientific methods to extend mechanics in a way that encompasses the immaterial phenomena of heat, electricity, and light: they wondered how to conceive logical hypotheses, mathematical descriptions, and empirical observations in manners that establish such mechanical disciplines that methodologically predict and describe the dynamic causes, positions, and momentum of the immaterial forces.

An attempt to postulate the microscopic origin of heat was an obvious starting point for many natural philosophers who sought the mechanical properties of the immaterial forces. In his attempt to predict the microscopic relationships that amount to the observed macroscopic phenomena of heat, James Prescott Joule (1818-1889), for instance, conceived heat as a translational form of energy; moreover, his attempt to link heat with the motion of the hypothetical particles resulted from natural philosophers' efforts to apprehend an understanding of the inter-convertibility of forces. For example, Joule tried to establish the mechanical equivalent of work and force, by ascertaining conversion coefficients. Joule set up an apparatus that consisted of weights and pulleys that moved a paddle wheel, which struck water to the extent that Joule could employ empirical observations to reconcile levels of work and force with the increase in water temperature that resulted. Joule observed how the weights' particular lengths of travel corresponded with the specific heat that increased the independent temperature of the water. From this relationship, Joule discerned that the heat was the product of the potential (that is, the stored) energy of the weights and the kinetic energy (that is, the translating matter) of the paddle wheel that frictionally struck the water.

While natural philosophers recognized the great significance of ascertaining conversion coefficients that described the interconverting processes of work and force, some natural philosophers recognized the difficulty of describing the hypothetical motions of microscopic particles. Because Newton expressed his mechanics with geometrical descriptions, these rationalist philosophers recognized that they could not effectively use Newton's mechanics to treat immaterial forces like heat, electricity, and light. The rationalists forsook microscopic descriptions altogether. Then they solely tried to establish verifiable things. For example, the rationalists sought to establish the coefficients between, first, the force of material labor (which one exerts and receives from the work) and, second, the abstract measures of heat and electricity that result from material labor. In this way, they rationally extended the mathematics of mechanics beyond mere geometrical descriptions, unto the mathematical descriptions of the immaterial forces themselves:

With great confidence, thinkers like Hermann von Helmholtz (1821-1894) sought to work out mathematical formulations for the conversion forces. Through such means, the concept of energy arose among natural philosophers who sought to unite the phenomena of electricity and light as being manifestations of energy: the energy concept produced the expectation that natural philosophers could extend mechanics to describe and predict any material or immaterial behavior. The ability to use conversion coefficients, to define all immaterial forces as various manifestations of energy, secured this end.

Thermodynamics

Until they ascertained the requisite natural-force-laws, the natural philosophers could not establish their mechanical understanding of heat's being the product of energy transformations. The necessary apprehension of these laws then formed the basis for a methodological discipline that tentatively predicted the behavior of heat. First, the natural philosophers understood the necessity for a natural-force-law that ensures that energy is neither created nor destroyed, during energy transformations: without the existence of such a law, they reasoned, an ordered creation cannot exist. Second, they empirically observed how energy is lost to other processes, during the energy transformations of an observed material process; therefore, natural philosophers perceived a second natural-force-law: they perceived the entropy—that is, the unavailability—of relevant forms of energy to maintain any given process, perpetually. For them, this second law captured the ongoing linear process of material breakdown over time. At last, with these two natural-force-laws, the natural philosophers pioneered the contemporary discipline of thermodynamics: a discipline that quantifies and predicts energy conversions, especially in regards to heat.

The Laws of Thermodynamics

The recognition of thermodynamics' natural-force-laws brought about an unparalleled societal benefit: understanding thermodynamics' first and second laws enhanced humankind's ongoing effort to develop tools that facilitate civilization's perpetual well-being. An appreciation of the first law, which recognizes energy's conservation, during transformation, enhanced engineers' ability to produce automated machines that convert forms of energy, in manners that allow humanity to overcome the immediate privations of nature.

Further still, an acceptance of the reality of thermodynamics' second law had more far reaching social consequences, in ways that even prove disadvantageous to the Church today. With the second law, natural philosophers demonstrated the fact that no material system in creation perpetually reconstitutes itself. They demonstrated how the law suggests that all material systems break down unto less organized states. Holding this view, the natural philosophers promoted the technological, political, and social pursuit unending perfectibility. As an unforeseen consequence, societies at large increasingly dismiss the religious aspiration for perpetual satisfaction in a heavenly utopia.

In point of fact, we presently witness the curious inverse relationship between, first, society's achieving of short-term satisfaction through technological advancement and, second, society's falling away from the sound orthodox Church doctrines that underscore human nature's need for perpetual meaning and satisfaction within creation, as a whole. In the last chapter of this volume, we shall briefly detail how Western civilization has moved from the static provincial sensibilities of Protestant Christendom, which created self-determination within agricultural and early capitalist economics, unto modernity's never-ending quests for social evolution; where self-determination is uncertain.

Indeed, while Sir Isaac Newton's mechanics demonstrated the effectiveness of explaining creation's workings, mechanically; the 19th Century natural philosophers' understanding of thermodynamics' first and second laws furthered mechanical invention. In this way, the natural philosophers began to solidify secularism's public usurpation of Church authority.

To acquire a mechanical understanding of a self-sufficient mechanical universe, the 19th Century natural philosophers only needed to ascertain how electricity and light are manifestations of energy, like heat. And so, in order to obtain a full mechanical understanding of creation, the natural philosophers sought a methodological discipline that describes and predicts the behavior of electricity and light. The further employment of scientific method to obtain this end became an apparent necessity.

Electrodynamics

In their initial attempt to capture the mechanical nature of the electrical force, post Newtonian natural philosophers postulated that electricity is a fluid: they found that the equations that they used to describe fluids are similarly useful for mathematical descriptions of electricity. A noteworthy founder of the United States, Benjamin Franklin (1706-1790), empirically observed that the supposed "electrical fluid" had positive and negative charges that obeyed an inverse relationship between attracting opposite charges and repulsing like charges. Afterward, Charles Coulomb (1736-1806) observed the following natural-force-law: he understood that attracting or repulsing forces between two electric charges are proportional to the product of their charges and inversely proportional to the square of the space between them. The initial use of the fluid paradigm to describe electricity and light's physical behavior, not only helped natural philosophers to make these early critical observations; but also fostered a more mature stance from which natural philosophers could ascertain a better mechanical paradigm: that is, they could ascertain a model that actually identified the dynamic cause and kinematical behavior of electricity and light.

Soon the natural philosophers' understanding even advanced beyond their initial use of the "electric fluid" concept. They discovered the contemporary understanding of immaterial fields, which mechanically convey the dynamic exchange of electrical and gravitational forces over distances. In 1820, Hans Christian Ørsted (1777-1851)—a Danish Chemist—observed that an electric current in a wire diverted a nearby compass needle from pointing to magnetic North. To substantiate Ørsted's observations, André-Marie Ampère (1775-1836)—a devout Christian—discovered the natural-force-law that governs the way electric currents produce magnetic fields. Ampère postulated that magnets were microscopic electrical currents when he discerned that a wire holding an electric current not only affected magnetic fields, but also modified the space around the current, in a manner that affected other wires.

In a short time, the natural philosophers Michael Faraday (1791-1867) and John Henry established the fact that while electric currents produce magnetic fields, changing magnetic fields produce electrical currents. Natural philosophers even observed how electric fields run at right angles to magnetic fields. Eventually as Faraday further substantiated the reality that fields modify the space around charges, he postulated that fields are regions in space that give directions to objects.

Faraday's work helped advance a unified understanding. Yet, James Clerk Maxwell (1831-1879)—a British natural philosopher—finally made a critical observation that unified all the working theories that had attempted to describe the mechanics of electricity, magnetism, and light. Maxwell's observation even led to a working methodological discipline that universally employs mechanics: for sure, this methodology is what the above 19th Century natural philosophers had always pursued. Studying the work of those who preceded him, Maxwell observed how electric fields produce magnetic fields, and he observed how changing magnetic fields produce electrical currents. Intuitively discerning a natural symmetry, Maxwell postulated that changing electric fields produce magnetic fields, as well. He, therefore, manipulated Ampère's equations only to discover that accelerating electric fields produce electromagnetic radiation, traveling in waves corresponding to the speed of light. In this way, Maxwell not only discovered that light is an electromagnetic wave; but also established the indelible link between electricity, magnetism, and light.

Like the natural philosophers of his time, however, Maxwell could not conceptualize immaterial fields modifying space; therefore, Maxwell sought material descriptions of the fields. Because he and other natural philosophers could not conceptualize light's traveling through the empty vacuum of space, Maxwell envisioned light as a right-angle, transverse, electromagnetic wave that travels through a material ether with fluid-like vortices that constantly restore light's wave to its form.

After working out the mathematical descriptions, nonetheless, Maxwell kept his predictive equations. Then he did away with his conceptual postulations.

With his equations, Maxwell at last established a methodological discipline that he called electrodynamics. His equations—detailing how generating charges produce uncharged magnetic fields; how changing magnetic fields produce electric currents; and how changing electric currents produce electromagnetic waves of light—still stand today.

In point of fact, the renowned physicist Richard P. Feynman believed that from the distant future of human history, thinkers will judge Maxwell's discovery of the laws of electrodynamics as the most significant event of the 19th century. Feynman declared that "the American Civil War will fade into provincial insignificance in comparison with this important scientific event of the same decade."

Electricity's Effect upon Western Culture

As Franklin, Coulomb, Ampère, Faraday, and Maxwell apprehended the natural-force-laws that gave rise to Maxwell's electrodynamics, the entrepreneurial beneficiaries of their work spurred the technological innovation that transformed Western civilization. Remarkably, before Maxwell and his predecessors finished their queries into the nature of electricity, magnetism, and light; inventors readily introduced and perfected the incandescent light bulb, the electric generator, and the telegraph.

Curiously, such inventions revolutionized civilization and increasingly disenfranchised the established Church in the subsequent way: first, the incandescent light bulb expanded working hours and social interaction. Second, the telegraph united dissimilar global regions with instantaneous communication. As a result, the public interests progressively concentrated on advancing an understanding of the interdependence of the burgeoning industrial economy: an economy that reconciled material processes for temporary societal benefits. Finally, the increasing awareness of creation's interdependent operations rendered the social effect of the population's reliance upon natural answers, instead of the divine. Thus, the changing public interest progressively rendered the West's cultural quest for the Christ—the gift of the heavenly unblemished lamb of humanity's good conscience—as an abstract personal pursuit, in the face of the ever-present secular wants for socio-economic well-being.

The Consolidation of Classical Physics

Soon secular institutes outwardly proclaimed that the Church's spiritual doctrines are of immaterial consequence for society as a whole. Natural philosophers reveled in the fact that they could use Newtonian mechanics to explain the dynamic cause and kinematical motions of macroscopic material objects under gravitational forces. Furthermore, they found great confidence in the fact that they could use thermodynamics and electrodynamics to explain heat, interconverting forces, and electromagnetism, respectively. As other natural philosophers successfully classified all known elemental weights and other properties in a periodic table (which then predicted elements that they had not discovered), 19th Century natural philosophers seemingly secured natural explanations for all known material phenomena.

Unparalleled was the manner in which scientific proofs and technological innovations validated natural approaches to creation. Technological validation inspired natural philosophers to consolidate all scientific practices under the discipline of physics: a discipline that uses the scientific method, the concept of energy, and mathematics to reconcile all scientific domains, under natural causes. To be sure, at the end of the 19th Century, natural philosophers considered themselves physicists. As physicists, they stood upon the belief that the creation is in fact a universe of interrelating processes; moreover, they believed that they could reduce these processes to simple explanations. The new physicists saw their sole aim as using the scientific method to save the material phenomena with verifiable theories.

In the face of these dramatic challenges to their public authority, Church leaders and other influential Christians could only make tautological—that is, repetitive—proclamations, decrying the fact that the 19th Century physicists did not establish an ultimate cause or purpose for their observations. Likewise, the Church decried the fact that the physicists did not have an explanation for the qualitative experience of the human soul: they helplessly understood the fact that the new physicists had failed to answer the mind-body question.

Even so, the new physicists remained undaunted by the Church's criticisms. When oil and mineral mining industries discovered fossils dispersed in land stratifications, representing various geological eras; the fossil findings inspired another naturalist theory. Charles Robert Darwin championed the geological discoveries as being supporting evidence for his late 19th Century Theory of Evolution: a theory that held the promise of using natural explanations to explain how humankind had evolved to possess our sophisticated cognitive experience.

The Deficiency of Classical Physics

Notwithstanding, before the new physicists could rest on their laurels, they, themselves, realized the shortcomings of what contemporary physicists now call pre-20th Century "classical physics." As we have seen, classical physics essentially stood upon the early physicists' misconception that a one-to-one symmetrical correspondence exists between, first, a material phenomenon's position and momentum within spacetime and, second, the dynamic forces that the material behavior adheres to. Like contemporary physicists, the classical physicists principally sought a closed universal system of self-sustaining, symmetrical processes. We observed how their belief in this one-to-one correspondence enabled the classical physicists to escape the Church's dogmatic claim that divine power necessarily sustains the worlds. Like so, the scientists' belief in a self-sufficient universe allowed the physicists to overlook philosophical questions, concerning the asymmetric nature of creation and the necessity for an ultimate intelligent perspective. For sure, natural philosophers and classical physicists built Newtonian mechanics, electrodynamics, and thermodynamics upon the understanding that physicists could achieve specificity as they mechanically described all material behavior at any given point within space and time. In this vein, we saw how classical physicists like James Joule and James Maxwell thought that they had successfully applied mechanical descriptions to define heat and light's radiation. In addition, we observed how the proliferation of machinery seemed to prove that classical physicists had an intuitive understanding that predicts the behavior of moving bodies under gravitational and other forces. We even noted how early electronics demonstrated the fact that classical electrodynamics successfully predicted the macroscopic behavior of electrical currents.

Despite these technological successes, classical physicists soon realized that they had utterly failed to achieve a full mechanical understanding of the world. They began to recognize their shortcomings as they further studied heated objects. The physicists readily understood that the objects' distinct discoloration patterns represent the intensity of energy levels; moreover, their earlier employment of classical electrodynamics, to describe light's emission spectra, captured the fact that higher energies emanate in large frequencies and short wavelengths; while lower energies emanate in small frequencies and long (that is, less concentrated) wavelengths. Also, their thermodynamics practices even captured a basic measure of the power that the material object emits: the physicists had simply measured the amount of energy emitted each second, for every square meter of the object's surface. Yet, while conventional thinking led them to suppose that some material structures only accommodate increasingly higher frequencies, classical physicists surprisingly found that all materials emit the same energy proportions, despite the material objects' perspective compositions. To understand energy's universal and proportional emanation, classical physicists modeled energy's proportionality by envisioning perfectly absorbing bodies—black bodies. Like this, they studied how materials emit the same proportional graphs, despite the energy levels of the light.

Even as classical physicists made this startling observation, they began to recognize the fact that an unknown microscopic link exists between electromagnetism (as represented by the discoloration) and thermodynamics (as represented by radiated heat). Along these lines, classical physicists realized that they had failed to determine the microscopic origin of entropy, in regards to the energy that physical processes lose, in the form of heat and other radiation. For this cause, the physicists had further reason to explain why the radiated energy conformed to the universal "black body" emission spectra.

Mysteriously, the spectra universally adhered to radiating material objects that emit and absorb radiation, despite the specific energy levels and properties of the objects.

Of a truth, the recognition of a universal pattern of emission and absorption (that is, the universal black body graph) confounded the early physicists. Many classical physicists, therefore, lost the conviction that they could utilize the supposed specificity of their classical disciplines to discover the microscopic link between electrodynamics and thermodynamics. The mechanical picture of a self-sufficient universe, instead of a divinity-depended creation, once again slipped their grasp. Essentially, the subsequent brutal reality became apparent to classical physicists: electrodynamics' conception of a one-to-one correspondence between light's traverse waves and a hypothetical ether's elastic restoring force could not predict or explain the universal proportions of emitted and absorbed energies. What is more, thermodynamics' conception of a one-to-one correspondence between microscopic friction and macroscopic heat radiation could not reconcile the manner in which light's emission and absorption seemed to break thermodynamics' second law: a law that states that all physical processes endure a state of entropy and, therefore, never reconstitute themselves, entirely.

Classical physics' failure to apprehend a universal world picture became even more apparent as scientists experimented on discharge—cathode ray—tubes: they ran electrical currents through sealed glass tubes, only to find strange "x-rays" emitting from an appearing phosphorescent glow. Later, as scientists experimented with uranium, to reproduce the phosphorescent emission of x-rays, they accidentally discovered the nuclear emission of positive alpha rays, negative beta rays, and uncharged gamma rays: these strange rays emitted without the external absorption of other rays, such as sunlight or electricity. Upon further inquiry into the nature of the radiation, classical physicists discovered that the materials that emitted the radiation actually transmuted into other materials.

As these strange observations continued to arise, classical physicists increasingly struggled to apprehend self-sufficient mechanical explanations for the way that material objects adhered to the newly observed natural-forces. The physicists knew that religious dogma still loomed to fill the asymmetric void with improvable divine explanations; therefore, they pressed ahead with the classical tools that they had to command.

The classical physicists managed to achieve some lasting advances, however. Despite the fact that classical physicists failed to apply the classical specificity of ascertaining the exact position, momentum, and force of microscopic objects; classical physicists managed to standardize the basic physical structure of the atom. They left modern physicists to devise a more mathematics based mechanics to describe subatomic and other forces, abstractly.

The Enduring Contributions of Classical Physics

We may briefly delineate the foundational achievements that classical physicists gained for our understanding of atomic structure, as follows: first, we may note that though they failed to use classical understandings to derive the microscopic origin of heat and the relationship between light and entropy (that is, a system's inability to reconstitute itself, fully), classical physicists managed to create a new statistical mechanics. They devised a probability analytics that now enables contemporary scientists to relate a myriad of microscopic operations to macroscopic effects:

As natural philosophers like James Joule formulated notions of heat as being the result of molecular motions, others like James Maxwell devised ways to calculate the hypothetical motions around a mien distribution value that purportedly corresponded to temperature values. From these observations, the classical physicists wrongfully postulated that our macroscopic experience of entropy is a statistical effect. Still, even as these postulations failed, their statistical speculations encouraged Ludwig Boltzmann (1884-1906) to create the new statistics based mechanics: he simply likened the entropy of a system's irreversible processes to mathematical outcomes that are greater than zero. Afterward, he produced a constant of proportionality by reconciling probable microscopic configurations with macroscopic configurations.

Having exhausted their efforts to explain the black body pattern of emitted electromagnetic radiation, as well as entropy's relationship to it; classical physicists had greater success in identifying the physical properties of the alpha, beta, and gamma radiation. This success enabled them to determine the basic structure of the atom: classical physicists established a fundamental structure that physicists build upon today. First, classical physicists determined that x-rays are merely light waves with short wavelengths that allow them to pass through materials that repel or absorb visible light. Next, by deflecting cathode rays with electric fields, physicist J.J. Thomas (1856-1940) determined that the rays consisted of negative particles. After determining the negative particles' charge to mass ratio, physicists discovered the electron: the initial proof of the atom's subatomic structure.

The discovery of the negatively charged electron then led physicists to discover the positively charged proton, which balanced the negatively charged electron. Also, to account for the missing atomic mass (besides the electron and proton masses), classical physicists soon postulated and then discovered an uncharged subatomic particle, which they termed the neutron. Later, they further figured the structure of the atom by bombarding gold foil with positive particles, only to have the foil repel very few particles. From these observations, classical physicists understood that the atom consisted of a densely packed positive core, leaving empty space between the core and the large orbits of the electrons.

With basic understandings of the electron, proton, and neutron; classical physicists then described the known elements by their proportional concentrations of electrons, protons, and neutrons. Instead of arranging elements on the periodic table by their atomic weights, they arranged the elements by the number of protons that the elements consisted of. In fact, the proton number became the element's number on the periodic table.

For example, hydrogen gas has one proton; therefore, hydrogen has the atomic number 1. Likewise, solid iron has the atomic number 26; therefore, iron has 26 protons.

Great are the foundational achievements of the pioneering classical physicists; however, we witness the classical physicists falter as we observe how they could not find an adequate explanation for the fact that any atom's overall atomic weight slightly differs from the aggregate weight of the electrons, protons, and neutrons that comprise the atom. The physicists found that the elemental configurations on the periodic table that precede iron have greater aggregate weights than the gross weights of the atoms, which they reside in. In contrast, they found that the elemental configurations that continue after iron have lesser aggregate weights than the gross weights of the atoms that they reside in. As a consequence, the classical physicists struggled to ascertain the nature of the nuclear binding energy that bound the protons and neutrons in the atomic nucleus: this energy, they discerned, accounted for the lesser or greater weights of the atom, besides its electron, proton, and neutron constituents.

The physicists eventually found that uranium releases its excess binding energy as alpha, beta, and gamma rays; moreover, the physicists successfully determined alpha particles to be helium nuclei; beta rays to be high energy electrons; and gamma rays to be extremely high frequency electromagnetic waves (light). Nevertheless, the unknown identity of the atom's nuclear binding force demonstrated the shortsightedness of classical physics, even as light's universal black body emission spectra confounded classical physics' quest for specificity.

The Rational Strength of Contemporary Science

Ironically, the strength of contemporary physics is the fact that contemporary physicists have retreated from seeking the mechanical specificity of microscopic objects: as we shall soon detail below, contemporary physicists do not seek the exact momentum and position of microscopic elements. Also, because they retreat from the belief that they can discover the exact measure of microscopic behavior, physicists not only advance modern science's predictive capacity; but also secure the advancement of technological innovation. As a result, human civilization now appreciates a greater capacity to distribute wealth; as advanced technologies now enable the upward mobility of all social classes.

So instead of tediously unpacking every abstract aspect of the Standard Model, we have but to describe modern science's brilliant, rational descriptions of the subatomic world: these descriptions are responsible for modernity's technological and medical revolutions. As an outcome, we must show how these inventions entice the public to believe in the secular scientists' ultimate conclusion that a self-sufficient universe derived from a single physical event. Decidedly, we shall finally show how this conclusion ultimately fails to establish secular science's complete mechanical understanding of the creation. In the context of the natural approach's ultimate failure, we will then be able to submit our orthodox judgment.

The Rise of Modern Physics

We may summarize our brief description of contemporary physics and the Standard Model's rational form as follows: contemporary physicists first employ mathematical formulas to capture rational descriptions of the atom's nuclear strong force, nuclear weak (mediating) force, and the extant electromagnetic force. Then the physicists seek to reconcile their rational descriptions with the specificity of our macroscopic experience of our environments. The success of their work establishes the disciplines of quantum mechanics (QM), quantum field theory (QFT), quantum electrodynamics (QED), and quantum chromo dynamics (QCD): each discipline respectively uses statistical descriptions to define the behavior of the atom, electromagnetic fields, and the nuclear strong force. Finally, the union of these disciplines comprises contemporary science's Standard Model of the creation.

Thus, before we describe how physicists misinterpret the behavior of the several forces as deriving from a single physical event, let us briefly describe how the following thinkers pioneered contemporary physics' quantum field theory and the Standard Model: we will discover how Max Planck discovered the discrete nature of energy; how Albert Einstein overturned our classical conceptions of a static material world; how Niels Bohr established the atom's basic structure; how Werner Heisenberg and others formulated mathematical matrices to describe the atom's electron shells; how Paul Dirac rationalized the electromagnetic force; and how Satyendra Bose and others defined the nuclear strong forces.

Planck's Dilemma

Interestingly, his incapacity to be anything other than a nominal Christian gave Max Karl Ernst Ludwig Planck (1858-1947) the unique disposition to explain the universal black body emission spectra. Planck, thereby, paved the way for contemporary physicists to unify the disciplines of electrodynamics and thermodynamics: classical physics' inability to achieve these ends hammered the final nail into classical physics' coffin. During his upbringing, Max Planck recognized how Christian values, like dutifulness and charity, substantively benefited society and culture. He, in fact, recognized divine charity in the natural laws' rational cohesion. Planck marveled over such principles like the conservation of energy. In the natural laws, he perceived benevolent expressions of a creator. Like the ancient Platonist, Planck charged that atheists only study representative "symbols" of the creator.

Notwithstanding, Planck's rich educational background compelled him to find institutional Church dogma grievous. He found that the Church's demand for unquestioned belief repelled the critical scrutiny of skepticism.

A more diligent Bible enthusiast may suppose that Planck should have relied upon his personal study and devotion. Thereby, he may have found comfort in the Apostle's Sha'ul's declaration that Y'haweh actually encourages our inquiry. Sha'ul declared that "Y'haweh . . . had predetermined the times and bounds of our habitation that we should seek the Lord, in the hope that we might [propositionally] feel after him and find him, though he be not far from every one of us (Acts 17:26-27)."

Max Planck, however, did have enough faith to believe that physicists could apprehend the rational means to explain the universal black body emission spectra. At the same time, Planck had enough skepticism to discredit previous attempts to derive the black body graph from hypothetical molecular motions. Instead of using the classical equations that sought to preconceive the nature of the black body emission spectra, Planck used an experimental apparatus to mimic the black body effect. He distributed charges on oscillating springs, and he found the coefficient between the springs' mechanical action and the electromagnetic properties of the charges. Through these means, Planck matched the best results of the classical predictions. At the same time, Planck demonstrated their overall error. Thereafter, he simply adapted his equations to the equilibrium that the oscillating system demanded. In so doing, Planck found a constant of proportionality that exhibits the system's entropy, because it reconciles the systems' energies and disallows the system to go to absolute zero.

In using statistical counting methods to explain the system, Planck found that the equilibrium of the system demanded discrete (that is, indivisible) energy quantities; therefore, Max Planck employed whole counting numbers to denote the discrete energies. At the last, he found that the system necessitated a highest energy level cutoff, in the same manner in which the system did not decrease to absolute zero.

To summarize Max Planck's brilliant finding, we have only to say that he discovered that energy only imparts itself in discrete quantities, which Planck represented with his newly discovered proportional constant $\hbar$: a constant that posterity has named Planck's constant in Planck's honor. Max Planck inaugurated a new era by essentially being the first to rationalize radiant energy: he statistically correlated energy's manifestations above the specificity of matter within space and time.

Even Planck did not fully comprehend the profundity of his discovery for some period. He marveled at its foundational use in the burgeoning quantum physics discipline. Yet, he lamented when his peers embraced uncertainty: they believed that science could not obtain exact physical determinations, due to the lack of material specificity that Planck's constant entailed. Instead of worrying about the physicists' incapacity to identify the exact properties of the fundamental elements, Max Planck stressed the universal rationalism that upholds the constant. With the prescience of an Old Testament prophet, Planck saw how his peers' only stressing creation's material aspects would degenerate the time-honored Judeo-Christian values that have upheld Western civilization.

Einstein's Search for "the Old One"

Albert Einstein (1879-1955), a later acquaintance of Max Planck, was the first physicists to recognize the profundity of Planck's constant. More than any other thinker, besides Planck, Einstein pioneered modern physics, like Sir Isaac Newton birthed classical physics. Einstein's work advanced profound scientific understandings of both the microscopic and macroscopic worlds.

Albert Einstein's brilliance lied in his agnostic belief in an impersonal creator: above all, Einstein's success stood upon his capacity to believe in an underlying divine simplicity that unites all things. Like Planck, Einstein believed that the Creator expressed himself in the harmony of all things; therefore, Einstein naturally sought to reconcile many disciplines in science, and for the most part, he achieved success.

Perhaps had Albert Einstein believed in a more personal divine expression of a savior—the Mashiach—governing human relationships, Einstein would have not only benefited the public with his intellectual gifts, but also benefited his highly gifted wives and fatherless children: all of whom Einstein grossly neglected as he pursued fame and multiple adulterous relationships.

All the same, as Albert Einstein pursued the divine expression of "the Old One," he unpacked the significance of Planck's constant and the resulting manner in which the material world and spacetime do not exist unto themselves. Instead, he defined how they are all relative manifestations of energy, as measured by light. Einstein began by determining that Planck's constant is more than a mathematical tool: presenting the equation $E=\hbar f$, he established the reality that energy, E, emits in rational proportions, per respective frequencies, f, as scaled by Planck's constant $\hbar$. With this equation, Einstein demonstrated how Planck's constant represents the fact that light itself exist as discrete—quantized—particles, which we now term "photons." At the same time, Einstein established that light retains wave-like properties.

To prove that Planck's constant exhibits light's quantized and wave-like properties, Einstein discovered the photoelectric effect by determining how light, in the form of particle quanta (that is, photons), interface with metallic surfaces: he demonstrated how the frequency of light causes various energy levels of electrons to emit, despite the intensity of the light that hits the surfaces.

After he established light's particle-wave, dual nature; Einstein produced two revolutionary papers that describe the macroscopic dual nature of energy and matter, as well as the dual nature's effect upon space and time. The papers, therefore, rationalized and transformed many of Sir Isaac Newton and James Maxwell's classical axioms.

Einstein had observed how James Maxwell's descriptions of, first, static electrons' correspondence with electron fields and, second, moving electrons' correspondence with magnetic fields are actually two manifestations of electromagnetism (light), depending upon the relative standing-position or momentum of the observer. Upon this observation, Einstein asserted two postulations in his first paper: a paper that posterity has named Special Relativity. Unlike Maxwell and other classical physicists, who held that light speed obtains in respect to a static preexisting ether, Einstein dismissed the ether as a fiction. He instead based his paper's first postulate on the fact that all Newtonian laws uniformly apply to any observer's respective reference frame when the observer is at a constant velocity. So as a result of his first postulate, Einstein based his paper's second postulate upon the understanding that light retains a constant speed, while nothing in nature exceeds light speed.

Before an astonished intelligentsia, Albert Einstein demonstrated the profound consequences of his two postulates: he defined how objects increase their mass as they increase speeds. He showed how increasing velocities effect a slowing of time; and he demonstrated how space and time indelibly relate as spacetime. He even determined that objects require infinite energy to obtain light speed. In this way, Einstein showed how force, mass, and gravity are related. He of course produced his famous equation, $E=mc^2$, demonstrating the indelible relationship between energy and matter: Einstein proved the fact that the energy, E, of a mass, m, equals the product of the mass times the speed of light, c^2.

Lastly, Einstein demonstrated in his second paper how acceleration and gravitational fields are the same phenomenon. Thereby, he demonstrated how light bends in gravitational fields. As a consequence of this second paper, he finally demonstrated the fact that spacetime, itself, does not exist as a thing unto itself, but warps under the forces of energy.

Quantum Mechanics

Because Max Planck and Albert Einstein wiped away classical physics' deterministic foundation, the foundation of modern physics stands upon the ensuing fact: the discrete proportional emission of energy (which Planck's constant observes) means that one can never reduce any subatomic manifestation of energy to a specific physicality within spacetime. For instance, Danish physicists Niels Hendrik David Bohr (1885-1962) noticed how classical understandings could not ascertain why electrons neither scatter away from the atom nor collapse into the subatomic nucleus, as the electrons radiate electromagnetic energy; therefore, Bohr simply declared that atoms only allow certain discrete electron orbits, which Bohr haphazardly defined using Planck's constant h. Niels Bohr even began the use of "quantum" descriptions as he described how electrons emit or absorb discrete quantities of light radiation. Bohr detailed how emittance and absorption correspond with electron jumps to allowed orbits.

Nonetheless, amongst other problems, Bohr's specified electron orbits and electron momentum failed to predict the energy intensities that the physicists observed as they study spectral lines. Learning from Bohr's failure to achieve specificity, the German theoretical physicists Werner Heisenberg (1901-1976) became the first to rationalize classical mechanics: Heisenberg founded a new atomic mechanics upon the basis that energy emits in the rational proportions that Planck's constant determines. As physicists like Louis de Broglie (1892-1987) demonstrated the fact that the electron is a particle-wave like the photon, Heisenberg established the fact that the electron and photon's dual particle-wave nature prevents physicists from determining the specific positions and momentums of the particles. Heisenberg observed that position and momentum essentially define one another; therefore, he built a revolutionary "quantum mechanics" (QM) that utilizes mathematical matrices and Planck's constant to generalize the position and momentum of subatomic particles.

To establish Heisenberg's theoretical matrices with visual descriptions and real-world values, German physicist Erwin Rudolf Josef Alexander Schrödinger (1887-1961) developed a wave mechanics, featuring a "wave function." Then German physicists Max Born (1882-1970) demonstrated how physicists could utilize Schrödinger's wave mechanics to determine probability locations for the electrons. Finally, Austrian physicists Wolfgang Pauli (1900-1958) made the most consequential observation that validated the use of quantum mechanics for real-world applications: when Pauli observed how multi-electron atoms, in magnetic fields, yield pairs of spectral lines, he concluded that atoms must have double electron configurations at each energy level, in order to emit the radiated pairs, during the electron jumps. So as a consequence of this observation, Wolfgang Pauli determined how multiple electron systems stack up in the atom, allowing only certain configurations per energy level. After Pauli's discovery, physicists birthed modern chemistry as they defined how atoms share or exchange electrons to create the compounds and mixtures that comprise our biological and material environment.

Though quantum mechanics initiated revolutions in chemistry and biology, the greatest proof of quantum mechanics' successful description of the atom is the computer revolution: a systemic innovation that benefits every aspect of contemporary society. After mathematicians, such as George Boole (1815-1864) and Claude Shannon (1916-2001), demonstrated how one can reduce all forms of mathematics to "on/off" signals, computer scientists envisioned ways to utilize the electron's allowed energy levels as switches. Using silicone, which has certain crystal formations that allow or disallow current flows, scientists invented the transistor: a device that essentially functions as a conduit or valve—that is, an "on" or "off" switch. The correlation of millions of these transistors now assumes the basis of computer programming, thanks to quantum mechanics.

The Standard Model

Albert Einstein thought that quantum mechanics and its use of statistical mechanics were impressive; however, he and other rationalists viewed the use of statistical mechanics as recognition of humankind's limitations; whereas numerous empirical scientists, who were atheists, believed that many aspects of the microscopic world were unknowable. The atheists believed that many microscopic attributes were the result of chance. Thus, Max Planck, Albert Einstein, and other agnostic scientists not only disliked how these practitioners of quantum mechanics intervened upon their observations with mathematical fixes; but also detested the atheists' belief that their employment of statistical based mathematics gained for them a complete representation of the world. Indeed, Einstein stated that his intuition compelled him to believe that quantum mechanics does not capture the full picture: he stated that the theory does not get us any closer to solving all the mysteries of "the Old One" [Y'haweh], whom he believed did not cast dice.

Unfortunately, like Max Planck's ecclesiastical skepticism and personal devotions overshadowed Planck's scientific contributions, Einstein's agnostic belief in the "Old One" failed to lend Einstein an epistemological understanding that would have unpacked his intuitions. Succeeding physicists mocked Max Planck for his having not recognized the profound consequences of his discovering the proportional constant. Nevertheless, we may observe that Planck had overlooked his discovery because his faith gave him the intuitive recognition of the fact that humankind can never grasp a full picture. What is more, Planck understood that the justification for his mathematical abstractions stood solely upon his ability to predict real world physical behavior. In like manner, we have seen how Albert Einstein's belief in a creator's benevolent design empowered Einstein to overturn classical understandings with his abstract theories, so long as his theories produced real world predictions. And, though atheists are primarily responsible for producing the mathematical abstractions that comprise quantum mechanics, quantum mechanics' validity stands upon its ability to secure real world predictions, as modern chemistry and computer science presently attest.

Now we may survey how the atheist troupe of physicists began their attempt to construct a Standard Model of a self-sufficient universe: we shall here see that their work began fruitfully as they reconciled their mathematical abstractions by predicting the behavior of real world phenomena. First, we shall discover how they successfully reconciled Einstein's theory of relativity with quantum mechanics. We will see that they accomplished this feat only because they validated their mathematical forms with specific measures of observable electromagnetic waves (light). Too, we shall see how the physicists successfully applied rationalized mathematical forms to describe the unobservable subatomic forces: we will find that they verified their subatomic understandings by the correlating unobservable subatomic forces with observable nuclear radiation.

In the end, we shall see how the scientists lose the legitimate application of the Standard Model as the scientists fail to predict their postulations. We shall see how their Standard Model ultimately falls apart as their Big Bang theory fails to predict the interrelationships of all cosmological and real world behavior.

As we roughly layout the successful conventions and ultimate shortfall of the Standard Model, we must recognize how the atheistic scientists overlook the subsequent reality: the atheists do not recognize that any valid application of mathematical forms stands upon the reality that the asymmetric creation withholds all pertinent information. This point we alluded to in our brief survey of phenomenology; moreover, in our former survey, detailing the limitations of mathematics and logic, we understood that mathematics cannot justify itself. Likewise, we understood that logic cannot define a qualitative sense of a thing-in-itself. From these understandings, we inferred that the simplest arithmetic of adding one plus one seems to yield the definitive product of two; however, the analytical product "two" does not qualitatively define two objects other than relating them numerically.

Strictly because we are incapable of ascertaining every mechanical contingency, we can only justify our mathematical models by their capacity to predict the specific numerical relationships that our qualitative senses experience within uniform spacetime. So as we survey the basic conventions of the Standard Model, we must distinguish the Model's mathematical abstractions that have validity because they predict the specific phenomenal relationships that we experience. Afterward we can observe how the atheistic physicists undermine the Standard Model's valid mathematical forms. Again, we know that mathematical forms only facilitate the ontological study of relations; therefore, we understand that a single event, without qualification, defies mathematics. In this vein, we will find that although physicists can adapt mathematical models to support their Big Bang hypothesis, the fictional character of the hypothesis becomes apparent, as the hypothesis eventually fails to reconcile with all the emergent aspects of creation, which we qualitatively experience.

As a whole, contemporary science's Standard Model of creation is a quantum field theory (QFT): that is, the Model mathematically considers particle-wave systems, which have infinite degrees of freedom as they transmit energy within the fields of spacetime. To this end, the Model mathematically seeks to quantify creation's electromagnetic force, which operates outside of the atom and thereby fills the vacuum of spacetime. Also, the model seeks to quantify the atom's nuclear strong force and weak (mediating) force, which respectively hold the atom together and radiate its energy.

Paul Adrien Maurice Dirac (1902-1984) took the initial step in extending quantum mechanics' statistical form beyond its employment in describing how the atom's electron orbits emit and absorb light quanta. Dirac sought to reconcile, first, quantum mechanics' quantification of electromagnetism within the atom with, second, the nature of light in general, which Albert Einstein had described. In this way, Paul Dirac recognized the centrality of Einstein's equation, $E=mc^2$. In deference to Einstein, Dirac readily understood that he had to adapt quantum mechanics' statistical form in such a way that the mathematics both describes light's particle-wave nature and describes the inextricable relationship between energy and matter and how one converts unto the other, at light speed. To accomplish these ends, Dirac and others formulated equations that describe the inverted relationship between the creation and annihilation of particles, as their respective waves oscillate. Dirac's equations envisioned positive and negative particles annihilating each other to produce pure energy. In regards to electromagnetism, Dirac described how electrons and their proposed anti-matter counterpart—the positron—annihilate one another to create the energy of the photon.

In this way, Dirac established the discipline, quantum electrodynamics (QED). Physicists later successfully validated the discipline with real world measures, after they determined the mathematical means to reconcile the polarizing effect of measuring charges in the midst of collecting charges.

The excellent fruit that physicists, like Satyendra Nath Bose (1894-1974), gleaned from Paul Dirac's work is that they discovered how certain particles, like the photon, result from the coupling of fields, during the creation and annihilation process. Through such means, they discovered how these particles transfer the forces of the coupled fields. The physicists termed the particles with such characteristics, "bosons," as a tribute to Satyendra Bose; moreover, the physicists termed the overall process that produces the force carrying particles, quantum field theory (QFT): a mathematical understanding of the manner in which forces translate over distances.

Using the mathematical forms that Paul Dirac, Satyendra Bose, and others employed to produce quantum field theory, physicists finally possessed the mathematical means to establish a Standard Model of creation's forces: these include not only the electromagnetic force, but also the weak and strong nuclear forces. Physicists initially noticed a mathematical symmetry—an invariance—that enabled them to invert their quantum electrodynamics equations. Then by employing these inverted equations, the physicists secured the means to gauge the properties of the converging weak and strong subatomic forces and their respective force carrier particles: all of which they could not directly observe.

Yet, because the inverted equations predicted that the subatomic force carrier particles (the new "bosons") have the same properties as the photon (boson), the physicists envisioned how to relate the new bosons to electromagnetic waves, which they readily observed. In this way, physicists gained the means to verify the existence of subatomic force carrier particles.

Among many other particles discovered in cosmic rays, the physicists predicted and detected a residual strong force boson—the pion—that is responsible for relating neutrons and protons. Also soon they built particles accelerators that smash particles together to produce artificial particles to study. Using the accelerators, they predicted and discovered the W and Z bosons that mediate the subatomic weak force.

With the newfound W and Z bosons, physicists demonstrated how the subatomic weak force is responsible for the decay rate of neutrons, which break down into protons, beta radiation, and antineutrinos. The new understandings led to real world revelations: physicists discovered the manner in which the weak force enables nuclei to fuse with other nuclei to produce the heat radiation and helium elements of the sun.

To complete the Standard Model, Murray Gell-Mann (b. 1929) mathematically conceived several more fundamental particles (quarks) to describe the properties of all particles. Though these foundational particles proved to be impossible to observe, physicists vindicated Gell-Mann's prediction by discovering that the proton has internal structure. Afterward, physicists further postulated the existence of an underlying Higgs field. Then the Standard Model took its current form, as physicists categorized the litany of particles according to their respective properties.

How the Big Bang Theory Fails to Establish a Self-sufficient Universe

Physicists recognize the fact that the Standard Model is incomplete. The Standard Model's continued validity rest upon the manner in which it incorporates Planck's constant into mathematical forms that decisively predict the material behavior that our senses qualitatively observe.

We see how Planck's constant of proportionality exposes the discrete radiation values that enable the uniformity of our macroscopic world within spacetime. We observe that Planck's constant demonstrates how the discrete values constrain and define energy levels, allowing the material things in our environment to relate mechanically. We recognize that one cannot physically observe the mechanical cause of the discrete values, and we recognize that one cannot intuitively observe the manner in which macroscopic phenomena derive from the discrete values. We see that Planck's constant is *a priori*.

Also, we recognize that quantum mechanics demonstrates that an observer cannot determine the exact position or momentum of the particle-waves that conform to the discrete constant: only mathematical forms model the rational order of energy's proportionality. Essentially, we conclude that because radiated energy conforms to Planck's constant, energy itself bears a rational nature, intrinsically. In this vein, we appreciate Albert Einstein's understanding, concerning how light exists as a quantum wave of discrete proportionality.

Overall, we may draw the subsequent conclusion: because our macroscopic experiences within spacetime derive from a rational priority that consigns energy to manifest itself proportionally, one cannot truly trace all of energy's manifestations to any specific physical event without discovering the motive cause of energy's rational nature. Since scientists pursue a single physical event, without having the means to explain either energy's discrete rational proportions or the natural-force-laws' metaphysical priority, scientists necessarily admit that known physics and mathematical relations cannot describe the initial moment of the single event. As a consequence, physicists fail to derive from their Big Bang event a mechanical explanation for the creation as a whole. Even so, scientists entice the public with convincing mathematical models of the secondary cosmological events that they can mathematically explain. At the last, they convince all that our human values and qualitative experience are inconsequential, in the face of a vast and mysterious universe.

Nevertheless, we cannot irresponsibly dismiss the theories of brilliant well-intentioned scientists, whose works have dramatically enriched the material welfare of billions of people. So to conclude our survey of science's scientific method and the resulting Standard Model, let us briefly survey the empirical observations that entice the scientists to champion a single physical origin for creation and our qualitative experience. Then after we show how their natural explanations dramatically fail to predict both creation's complexity and our qualitative experience, we can responsibly demonstrate how our orthodox judgment answers the great questions.

To begin, let us note that universalism—the physicists' continuous quest to reconcile all forces with mechanical explanations—psychologically compelled physicists to postulate the Big Bang theory, which describes how all things chronologically derive from an initial "Big Bang" event. Pursuing universalism, physicists began to postulate the Big Bang theory as follows:

First, as physicists observed how heavy particles decay into a host of light particles that fill creation, the physicists postulated that only an initial Big Bang event could produce enough energy to create the heavy particles. Then by applying the Doppler Effect to star light, scientists perceived an expanding universe.

Now scientists postulate that the pre-Big Bang creation had been a singularity, holding all sub-atomic particles and energy in an area smaller than an atom. As a consequence of their later projecting the motions of the galaxies backward, scientists estimate the universe to be 15 billion years old. And, as a result of their mapping micro waves, scientists theorize that all the sub-atomic building blocks of matter instantly came into being, following the Big Bang. Also, they believe that super-heated particles spread to comprise the known universe in a fraction of a second. Cosmologists, in addition, believe that the expanding universe cooled from a hotter early period.

Scientists' chronological theory indicates that the cooling universe formed hydrogen and other more massive particles. The scientists' theory then suggests that atoms continued to coalesce, forming gaseous densities, with increasingly massive forces that formed galaxies.

Scientists also theorize that nuclear fusion then began, as stars formed. In this manner, they believe that a mass of debris consolidated with a dense core that became our Sun, while the rest of the debris became the planets of our solar system. At some point during this episode, scientists believe that a nearby supernova occurred, producing the heavy particles in our solar system, which particles our Sun could not produce. These heavy particles proved to be necessary for life.

In fact, scientists believe that life fortuitously occurred upon Earth around 4.5 billion years ago, as the Earth's advantageous location to the cooling Sun had allowed Earth to possess all the materials necessary for life, such as carbon. Scientists further theorize that chemical reactions then took place, resulting in new chemical compounds such as amino acids: the building blocks of energy rich protein. Scientists conclude that sometime after life giving elements congealed into chains of amino acids, living cells eventually solidified in hot waters upon cooling rocks. Furthermore, scientists assert that once simple life forms became capable of synthesizing energy from inorganic material, like light from the sun, the evolutionary process began. As a final result, scientists submit that life progressed unto today's large variety of life-forms through a process that scientists call natural selection, which entails the endurance of a genetically mutated life-form's more environmentally advantageous traits in the successive generations of the life-form.

So without venturing to possess knowledge of a metaphysical cause or purpose, scientists submit that they can utilize their chronological theory of natural selection to explain how complex life forms exist and endure because of vibrant species' fitness. For example, scientists purport that cells first evolved by manifesting nuclei, possessing DNA molecules: these molecules possess specialized cell instructions that allow specific cells to relate to other types of specialized cells to form greater multiple-celled life forms.

Scientists believe that the central nervous system that features the brain came into being under the natural selection process, as increasingly sophisticated biological life-forms required more specialized cell structures to transfer targeted messages, other than the meandering, chemically dispersed reactions of simple life-forms. Because computational mechanisms persist without awareness or consciousness, scientists presume that consciousness is a recent unnecessary adaptation that merely bears some utility.

For instance, scientists observe how many animal species share in common an embryonic brain developmental process, as well as many major brain regions. In this light, the scientists contrast the inferiority of animal brains to the "newer" advanced regions of a "fully mature" human brain. As we noted in our cognitive neuroscience survey, scientists view regions in the brain that are responsible for basic motor skills (the cerebellum), as being an older region of the brain. Scientists further postulate that other regions of the brain that are responsible for the emotional drive that we share with mammals are further adaptations to the afore mentioned "primitive" brain. Lastly, scientists view the brain region (the neo-cortex), which enables abstract problem solving, as "the most recent" brain region that we share with mammals, especially primates. For this reason, scientists conclude that what sets us apart from other primates is our brains' excessive enlargement of this most "recent" region: an enlargement that enables our reasoning capabilities.

To secure natural explanations for consciousness, itself, many scientists hold that the most probable anatomical correlate of consciousness entails short term and long term memory: that is, the respective temporary and sustained store of neuronal memory traces. As the scientists conclude that short-term and long-term memory entails the sequencing of patterned neuron firings, they postulate that awareness is the encoding of unstructured sensory input. In the end, the scientists conclude that consciousness entails an evolved ability of an organism to sense the physical integrity of its body in relation to ongoing impressions.

Above all, the atheistic scientists' chronological approach to explaining creation and our origin is most instructive: cosmologists successfully characterize celestial bodies, while biologists successfully correlate animal diversity with animal adaptations to the animals' respective environments. Yet, unlike the Standard Model, which successfully employs valid mathematical forms and accurately predicts phenomenal behavior; the Big Bang theory initially confounds the use of mathematically relations. The physicists disregard the fact that mathematics cannot define the creation at the chronological point of absolute "time-zero." Likewise, the theory again fails to explain the cause of energy's discrete proportional manifestations in a mathematical form that uniformly predicts all of creation's emergent aspects. Instead, cosmologists chronologically construct a patchwork of events that ultimately prove to be functionally indeterminate.

For instance, often solid state physicists—who study such things as phase transitions between gases, liquids, and solids—readily perceive the fact that multiple materials adhere to the same phases, despite having different elemental properties. The physicists find that an individual element's bare nature, such as an individual electron's perceived properties, seem to assume a virtual existence when the physicists consider the manifest solid state properties that entail wholes systems of electrons. Because physicists can apply invariant forms of mathematics to either the microscopic or macroscopic states to define the nature of the elements, mathematics seem to render equal ontological status to either microscopic or macroscopic states. As a result, the physicists' cosmological explanation, which uses the Big Bang and particle decay to explain the emerging creation, does not predict, anticipate, or explain the phase transitions and the invariant manner in which mathematics equates them.

Unexplained phase transitions and mathematical invariance alarm contemporary physicists because the curious transitions now accompany existing challenges to their Big Bang theory. Void of mathematical or observational verification, cosmologists stand as opportunistic religious leaders—an exploitive position of drawing dogmatic conclusions that the general public cannot confirm.

The Question of Freewill

Contemporary physicists' mathematical inability to derive the observable creation from a single Big Bang event does not come as a surprise. We understand that physicists cannot extend mathematics to describe a single universal cause: we observe how physicists can only employ mathematics to correlate physical events with other physical events. And so, we understand that mathematicians cannot utilize mathematical systems to justify the selfsame systems. Decidedly, we affirm that primary causality is metaphysical.

More importantly, we observe that philosophers cannot employ formal logic to quantify our qualitative sense of the world. As a result, we note that one cannot analytically employ physical descriptions, alone, to define the unified sense that our conscious minds extend from. Our orthodox judgment bears the responsibility to demonstrate how our qualitative sense also has a metaphysical derivation that situates the mind's contingent correspondence with our physical experiences.

Scientists who champion the Big Bang theory mostly accept a paradoxical universe, entailing celestial mysteries that are inconsequential to everyday life. Howbeit, extreme societal breakdown results as scientists attempt to constrain our qualitative experience into being only a chance outcome of a self-sustaining and deterministic universe. Because their mathematical models fail to capture cosmological and personal meaning; scientists erroneously exalt their physical universe as being preeminent. At the same time, scientists deem our belief in purposeful causes as relics of what they consider to be our epiphenomenal minds.

We may recall that scientists merely consider our minds as illusionary mental shadows of organic neuronal processes. Unfortunately, as scientists hold our qualitative experience as dubious, scientists unknowingly undermine civilization's quest to secure the substantive integrity of human worth, freewill, personal liberty, and social justice.

To be sure, the true worshipping elect have handedly championed civilization's quest for human supremacy. The elect Church is the greatest proponent of humankind's supremacy over the creation. Central to orthodox Church doctrine is the understanding that humankind is preeminent over the creation because Y'haweh—the self-existent Spirit who created all things—made humanity in his spiritual image. For this purpose, orthodox Church doctrine holds that all creation ultimately conforms to the justice of Y'haweh's expression of himself in Lord Yehoshua the Mashiach.

Like modern phenomenology, orthodox Christian doctrine proclaims the reality that our perspective reference frames superimpose over what we observe. In fact, only the orthodox Christian doctrine of "unconditional grace through faith" recognizes our sole dependence upon a metaphysical power, regardless of religious rites, physical practices, or any other assertion of human prowess.

We persist in our work for no other reason than to secure orthodoxy. We recognize that despite the elect's fervent convictions, the Church, as a whole, has not objectively established orthodoxy: the Church has not objectively described how we physically relate to Y'haweh's metaphysical being.

Because established Church institutes fail to predict the ongoing scientific understandings that inform modern society, we appreciate why contemporary scientists disdain any Church effort to answer the hard questions, such as the mind-matter explanatory gap. To many, the holy scriptures do not seem to offer any clues to resolve the way in which a self-determinate mind superimposes its freewill upon a physical world, which reciprocally structures the mind. We recall scientists scorn the traditional Christian anthropocentric and dualist belief that a Creator, having human attributes, breathed or spoke creation and our accompanying spirits into existence. Also, we recognize that modern scientists hold in contempt ancient philosophical suggestions that the physical world is a shadow of ethereal, metaphysical forms.

Notwithstanding, we appreciate the reason why the Church clings to dogma: the Church not only seeks to preserve souls in the world to come, but also seeks to preserve freewill and self-determination for the good of Western civilization. Unfortunately, now ecclesiastical authorities stand helplessly by as scientists increasingly succeed in publically discounting the ghosts of the Holy Spirit and justified souls, whom the Church deem eternal.

We have discussed at length how scientists only seek physical explanations to resolve the mind-matter explanatory gap: in our brief description of behavioral psychology, we described how scientists have postulated ways in which our physical environments produce direct "identity-to-identity" perceptions of the world. Also, in our brief description of cognitive neuroscience, we assessed how scientists have postulated ways in which the neuronal processes of the brain produce mental representations that superimpose upon ongoing experiences. We essentially detailed the manner in which scientists initially attempted to describe our qualitative thoughts as strictly behavioral effects. Then we saw how their behavioral descriptions failed to capture the nuances of any given person's subjective perspective. Afterward we saw how scientists then tried to match mental states with specific neuronal states; however, we observed that a variety of neuronal states produce the same mental state, even as a variety of mental states share the same neuronal state. For this cause, we even saw how most cognitive neuroscientists have retreated to functionalism: a belief that essentially holds that our mental states follow an overall functional order instead of a specific physicality. At the last, we concluded that although their functionalist approach is compelling, scientists have failed to produce exact physical explanations to vindicate their functionalist stance.

Let us reemphasize that cognitive neuroscientists have only delineated how the procedural processes of the brain correlate with cognition. We must underscore that they have not discovered how the physicality of cells and chemicals actually become our qualitative senses. What we must take away from our surveys is the fact that behavioral psychology and cognitive neuroscience have not been able to describe the intrinsic "like-thisness" of one's personal perspective.

Now that we have just about completed our survey of contemporary scientists' natural approaches, we may finally conclude the following: though they have not resolved the mind-matter explanatory gap, most scientists simply settle upon the explanation that the mind is an adaptive outcome of emergent, physical processes. Sadly, we see that the theory of evolution still cannot address the dynamic aspects of our conscious minds. The evolutionary theory does not explain how we possess an independent sense of spacetime that enables us to combine a variety of impressions under one invariant precept. Basically, the theory has not effectively addressed the profound manner in which the brain's unknown dynamic mechanism combines billions of neuronal algorithmic sequences under single precepts, such as facial recognition. As an effect of the mind's dynamic binding of impressions, we achieve invariance in recognition as we correlate a multiplicity of impressions from the several senses: we reconcile spatial dimension, momentum, texture, and sound. The mind's dynamic binding, which correlates with consciousness, even occurs at a quantum level, far below the molecular processes of gene mutation, which are supposedly responsible for the evolutionary rise of consciousness.

The scientists' biological study of random gene mutations and the fitness of adaptable species cannot explain the profundity of the uniform dynamic brain. The theory of evolution cannot resolve the mind-matter explanatory gap.

As we remarked in our cognitive neuroscience survey, recent electromagnetic theories of consciousness come tantalizing close to describing the manner in which the brain binds the multiplicity of sensorial impressions. Though the electromagnetic-consciousness theories are not mainstream, many respectable scientists support further inquiry into their efficacy. The electromagnetic-consciousness theories convincingly detail deterministic ways through which the brain binds diverse operations to exhibit top-down decision making. The theories are provocative to the extent that the theories demonstrate that the questions of freewill and the supervening first-person hang upon the resolution of the theories.

The shortcomings of the current electromagnetic-consciousness theories are that they suggest cause-effect, deterministic ways in which the brain binds ongoing sensorial impressions. Yet, the theories cannot utilize deterministic descriptions to capture how the binding communicates its unique—that is, free—first person, supervening state.

In few words, we may categorize the respective deficiencies of the electromagnetic-consciousness theories as follows: some electromagnetic-consciousness theories describe the deterministic (cause-effect) physical schemes in which the brain binds the multiplicity of neuronal impressions. Even so, the theories fail to describe how the deterministic aspects physically assume indeterminate (or free) and supervening forms. In contrast, other electromagnetic-consciousness theories suggest distinct, free states that the brain possibly achieves. All the same, the other theories fail to reconcile with evolution's deterministic processes. Essentially, all electromagnetic-consciousness theories fail to close the mind-matter explanatory gap.

As an example, one electromagnetic-consciousness theory suggests that consciousness occurs when electromagnetic waves (residing around the cerebral cortex's language centers) download their states through the charged voltage-gated-ion channels of motor neurons. This theory fails because it does not effectively describe why the electromagnetic waves of the cerebral cortex are intelligent, while others outside the brain are not. Foolishly, the theory seems to postulate that all deterministic systems are intelligent; only lacking the means to communicate their states to us.

Other deterministic, electromagnetic-consciousness theories, which thinkers term resonance theories, consider consciousness as an emergent result of synchronous firing neurons. The "resonance theories" of consciousness suppose that the patterned firings of neurons attain standing waves that encode supervening spatial patterns in the brain. Like so, the patterns supposedly simplify and structure the initial sensorial impressions. The resonance theories, in this way, observe how upper level neurons only fire after lower level neurons. By envisioning the role that the standing waves play (as they encode spatial patterns and simplify sensorial impressions), the resonance theories ultimately seek to explain the mind's top-down decision-making capacity.

While the resonance theories of consciousness demonstrate some utility in describing the determinate manner in which we settle upon macroscopic (or simplified) perceptions, the resonance theories fail to explain the dexterity of our targeted decision making capacity. Thereby the theories fail to identify the physical correlate of our first person supervening sense. In the end, the resonance theories merely state that consciousness results from resonating neuronal patterns, without adequate justification.

As a final example of the electromagnetic-consciousness theories, let us note that some theorists deem the likeliest physical correlate of our supervening and free minds necessarily features light's unpredictable quantum properties. We recall that light's particle-field nature is the only known physicality that escapes deterministic description. Notwithstanding, though quantum-like aspects of consciousness seem reasonable, they do not demonstrate how consciousness emerges as a contingent effect of actual environmental experiences. In other words, though our qualitative experience gives evidence of the mind's free expressions, our minds still "fall" into an ordered world that enables our conscious states.

Phenomenologists accurately describe the critical balance between our supervening will and the manner in which our environments augment and foster it. Nonetheless, contemporary scientists disregard the need to address this delicate balance. Essentially, scientists cling to their evolutionary theory's cause-effect, adaptive scheme, even though this schema cannot address the questions that concern our freewill and the mind-matter explanatory gap. Again, contemporary scientists rather leave these profound questions unanswered.

After all, we must conclude that instead of truly apprehending a mechanical understanding of creation by reconciling all its contingencies, today's scientists embrace the idea that some questions are unknowable. Also, instead of their demonstrating the relationship between mind and matter, as well as the epistemological basis of our knowledge, contemporary scientists denigrate our very existence as being happenstance.

As a final outcome of our scientific survey, we must conclude that atheistic scientists actually undermine scientia: they undermine theology, philosophy, and science's objective quest to reconcile our cognitive experiences within creation. In other words, they fail to discover how the human experience—that is, consciousness, conscience, freewill, culture, society, and government—reconcile with the matter and forces that comprise the physical creation.

Now personal and cultural liberties flee before secular integrating economies. Increasingly, autocratic and impersonal regimes arise to force global conformity, unjustly.

The Church's Tumultuous Quest for Orthodoxy

To the amazement of the Church faithful, the general public's faith in secular science remains undaunted. Many in the general public recognize the fact that scientists have failed to define the essential cause of the Big Bang, and many recognize the fact that scientists have so far failed to reconcile many cosmological events with the Big Bang theory. In addition, many acknowledge the reality that scientists have utterly failed to explain how inanimate processes produced the first living cell (in all its mechanical complexity). Despite these manifold failures, the technological advances, which result from science's successful predictions, entice the public to accept the fact that scientists embrace a chaotic universe that does not entail absolute truth.

Though scientists only acknowledge a utilitarian understanding of truth as being mere predictability, the public does not care that scientists increasingly confound our anthropocentric perspective of the world. Ironically, human civilization stands upon our ascribing to our environmental experience such principles like justice, honor, and equity; however, scientists deem any psychological ascriptions to the workings of creation as inappropriate. Scientists disregard philosophical notions of the good and truth. As mentioned before, when the scientists dismiss the necessity of a creator, they only view truth as the utility of our being able to predict material and biological behavior under the fundamental forces. Thus, the scientists' austere perspective inclines the scientists to view personifications like justice, equity, and love as psychological apparitions. With their austere perspective, scientists bereave Western civilization's governing laws of their divine mandate. As an outcome, contemporary society possesses no righteous compass as society chaotically integrates international economies and cultures. As we mentioned in our introduction to our treatise, secularists only view morality as a stoic and disinterested appeal to duty, despite personal worth.

The Church may well lay claim to fostering Western Civilization's cultural and spiritual principles. Although the Church has civilized the Germanic tribes by upholding the belief that creation bends to the truths, concerning the glory, holiness, righteousness, justice, and love of God in the Mashiach; the Church has yet to assert its revelatory authority over other belief systems. Like scientists, philosophers, and world religions, the Church falters at the time-honored rationalist-empiricist debate: though the Holy Spirit confirms the faith of individual worshippers, the Church has not established its public standing over other belief systems because the Church has not objectively proved its doctrines by describing how Y'haweh creates the worlds and by resolving the mind-matter explanatory gap.

Being inspired by such scriptures that declare the fact that no one can see or approach the transcendent Y'haweh, Christian theologians only ascertain Y'haweh's metaphysical simplicity and wholeness (that is, Holiness). The theologians correctly discern that the very name YHWH—the Lord who is—indicates the reality that Y'haweh is Spirit who lacks temporal parts or any other compositional extension within spacetime; therefore, the theologians understand that Y'haweh is one with his attributes.

For example, the theologians discern that Y'haweh is omnipotent (all powerful). Also, holding all power, theologians recognize that Y'haweh is not an instance of power. Likewise, theologians observe that Y'haweh is omnipresent (present everywhere) and omniscient (all knowing); therefore, theologians consider that omnipotence, omnipresence, and omniscience only signify the being of Y'haweh. Thus, the theologians understand that because Y'haweh is all in all, he can only instantiate (that is, represent) himself within creation.

For sure, the Christian theologians' description of the way in which Y'haweh stands apart is complete; however, since Y'haweh stands apart from the creation that we can sense and verify, the theologians' understanding of Y'haweh's simplicity and uniformity is supersensible. As a consequence, the theologians fail to prove their scriptural understanding by grounding their supersensible understanding of the invisible creator within the intuitive and rational bounds of our cognitive experience. The proof continues to resists the theologians.

At present, Christian theologians only seek to prove their metaphysical understandings by making non-substantial, tautological statements, which again are statements that are only true because the statements redundantly proclaim themselves as true. For example, theologians reason that a necessary, perfect, and self-existent being, created us; however, their dogmatic proclamations contain no demonstrable proof: their proclamations are only unsubstantiated statements. Also, some theologians infer from the harmony and complexity of creation that a divine hand created reality; however, they still cannot arrive at a conclusive identity other than the logical assertions that the human mind psychologically makes, because the mind bears the predisposition to establish itself in the unity of a single cause. Lastly, theologians seek to answer the cosmological question by dogmatically proclaiming that they discern an ultimate cause as they empirically assess the endless stream of existence; however, while they try to ascertain an ultimate cause in their incremental assessments, they fail to confront the understanding that our finite minds cannot limit an infinite Supreme Being to humanity's incremental and finite conditions: rightly, the wise do proclaim "infinitum non capax infiniti (the finite cannot encompass the infinite)." For this cause, non-Spirit-filled theologians fail to demonstrate the wisdom of their claims; therefore, they remain relegated to make only unsubstantiated statements about a Supreme Being.

As we have said at the beginning of our surveys, the only way to establish an orthodox understanding of the scriptures is to establish the manner in which our temporal mind-matter relationships derive from Y'haweh's transcendent mind. The absence of orthodox understanding increases the strength of secularism and thereby hastens Western civilization's cultural decay.

Divine Fiat

So far we, too, have not established the orthodoxy of our definition of truth, which we hold to be the biblical Testaments' underlying thesis: we may very well equate truth with the will of Y'haweh, who reflects his fulfillment through his relationship with us through the Mashiach. Yet, as we underscore the fact that theologians have not determined how our mind-matter experiences proceed from Y'haweh, we must recognize the fact that our initial definition likewise has not described how Y'haweh's spiritual will physically manifest the world.

As we have mentioned before, scriptural ambiguity is the source of the theological dilemma. The biblical Testaments' creation accounts merely give narratives, describing how Y'haweh's three distinct natures manifest the creation and our souls. Even so, the creation narratives do not divulge any objective function or scheme from which we may derive the structure of our knowledge and a critical understanding of our minds' relationship to our world.

Our orthodox judgment obviously seeks to be the objective function that both unpacks the creation accounts and Y'haweh's will, as the judgment resolves the mind-matter explanatory gap. In this fashion, our orthodox judgment seeks to substantiate our definition of truth.

To give all true worshippers a foundational tool to secure sound doctrinal understanding, we shall present our orthodox judgment in the light of the scripture's three main creation accounts. We shall first refer to the Apostle Yochanan's brief account, and we shall refer to the spiritual orthodoxy that the Lord Yehoshua captures in his instructive prayer. Later, after we complete our orthodox judgment, we shall see how the judgment vindicates the renowned creation account that Moshe the Law giver authored.

We proceed by first acknowledging the quarrel over the meaning of the most consequential creation account that enigmatically implicates our sought after proof, which again concerns how the entire physical creation and our qualitative experience derive from Y'haweh's metaphysical state: a state that Y'haweh only expresses in the person of the Mashiach. The first creation account is actually the prologue to the New Testament book entitled the Gospel according to Yochanan (John); moreover, the exact interpretation of the prologue (which again describes the derivative operations of Y'haweh's creative work) has eluded scholars since its composition: scholars cannot discern whether certain elements in the prologue are poetic devices (such as metaphors and personifications) or indiscernible but logically formed statements. As an outcome, the interpretations of the prologue are often unsubstantiated assertions that derivatively correspond with neither the other scriptures nor our natural experience of the world; which experience our orthodox judgment must explain.

So in order for us to avoid such unsubstantial interpretations of the prologue, we demonstrate how our orthodox judgment is a sound derivation of the prologue's correct interpretation, especially in regard to how our interpretation defines our physical relation to Y'haweh's spiritual reality. The prologue is as follows:

> In the beginning was the Logos [Word], and the Logos was with God, and the Logos was God. The same was in the beginning with God. All things were made by him; and without him was not anything made that was made. In him was life; and the life was the light of men. And the light shined into darkness; and the darkness comprehended it not.[1]

Concerning the scholars' inability to determine the correct meaning of the prologue, the scholars' interpretational difficulty centers upon the Apostle Yochanan's intended meaning for his usage of the word *logos*. The word derives from the Greek verb *lego*, which means to count out and gather together an inward sense into words.

Historically, Greek thinkers have used the word logos in a functional way, to describe the transcending force of reason that both pervades and animates creation. In turn, some Christian scholars have poetically used the word logos in a personalized sense that merely portrays the Mashiach as Y'haweh's outwardly expressed personification unto us: unlike the Greeks, these scholars did not use the word logos as a description of Y'haweh's outwardly expressed capacity that maintains a rational creation, despite us.

Regardless of the conflicting viewpoints of Greek and Christian scholars, we discern certain validity in both perspectives. When we reflect upon our definition of truth, which we deduce to be the Holy Bible's underlying message, we with confidence conclude that the Greek's rational-cosmological usage of the word logos and the early Christian's divine-personified usage are two building blocks that serve the same system; moreover, our definition identifies the system as the outwardly expressed relationship between Y'haweh's three distinct natures whom Yochanan encapsulates in the prologue: first, we readily witness the Father's intensive will when the prologue states that the "Logos was with God" before the actual expression of the Logos. Next, we witness the distinct, outward expression of the Father's intensive will as we witness the expressed Logos' not only setting the bounds for our rational environment, but also inherently defining the purposefulness of the environment by assuming the

---

[1] John 1:1-5

Father's Spirit filled expressed person. While we hold this specific purpose in mind, we finally discern the distinct beatific nature of the Father's expressed Holy Spirit who consigns the perfection, universally-recognizable good humor, and meaningful beauty of the Father's expressed person: we witness this beatific nature being expressed when the prologue states, "In him was life; and the life was the light of men."

Of all, we assert that the correct interpretation of the prologue that agrees with our definition is that Y'haweh—the Father—quantified his intensive will. Then Y'haweh spoke out his inward sense to the intimacy of humankind, by uniting within Y'haweh's expressed person (Lord Yehoshua) our diverse experiences in a rational world.

And so, in order for our orthodox judgment to resolve the rationalist-empiricist disagreement, our judgment must define how we derivatively and physically observe the manifestation of Y'haweh's inward will, as we continually experience our environments throughout our life-experiences. To this end, our judgment must prove itself by identifying the physical correlate of our souls, as well as the manner in which this physicality stands independent but contingent to the world.

After we produce our orthodox judgment, we will then substantiate not only the creation accounts, but also our definition of truth as being more than just unsubstantiated propositions that arise from our inwardly held prejudices. Instead, our statement will justify all the accounts and our definition as the truth-functional-form of the outwardly expressed fiat of the divine will: indeed, with our judgment, we will establish a quintessential understanding of Y'haweh's light both metaphorically and physically shining into our propositional darkness.

The Lord's Prayer

We briefly turn to the Lord's Prayer to see how it wonderfully captures an orthodox understanding of the manner in which our life-experiences derive from Y'haweh's expressed will. We present our pending orthodox judgment in the light of the Lord's Prayer.

Having told his disciples that they could not pray effectively because they did not know Y'haweh's explicit will, Lord Yehoshua instructed his disciples to pray in regards to the following truthful order:

> Our Father who art in Heaven, Hallowed be thy name. Thy Kingdom come, thy will be done on earth, as it is in Heaven. Give us this day our daily bread. And forgive us our debts, as we forgive our debtors. And lead us not into temptation, but deliver us from evil: For thine is the kingdom, and the power, and the glory, forever. Amen.[1]

The majority of biblical students would agree that the Lord's Prayer does not appear to be a creation account. Nonetheless, we deem the prayer to be so because it holds critical clues that exemplify how Y'haweh expressed his will to create our physical experiences within a creation that adheres to his glory.

At this point, we will not submit a traditional exegesis for the prayer. We, in fact, will not realize the full spiritual significance of the Lord's Prayer until we conclude our doctrinal treatise.

A dutiful student may readily perceive, from the Lord's Prayer, foundational Christian doctrines, concerning Y'haweh's holiness; the fallen state of humankind; and our redemption through grace by faith in the salvation and divinity of Lord Yehoshua and the Holy Spirit. Even so, our task again is not to reiterate sound, traditional doctrine: our only task is to establish the orthodoxy—the right belief—of Christian doctrine. Our goal is to refer to the prayer as we lay the groundwork for our orthodox judgment, which shall demonstrate how the structure of knowledge, the physical world, and our corresponding mind-matter experience derives from Y'haweh's will and extends within Y'haweh's two distinct extensions of himself: namely, the Mashiach and the Holy Spirit, the culmination of Y'haweh's Logos expression.

---

[1] Matthew 6:9-13

Reflecting upon our definition of truth, we may make a cursory observation and say that the Lord's Prayer adheres to truth's landscape in the subsequent way: the prayer initially reflects how the very structure of knowledge stands upon Y'haweh's intrinsic beauty and holiness. Then the prayer indicates that our mortal experience can only experience Y'haweh's transcending beauty as a Kingdom filled with his benevolence and good humor: the Kingdom entails a prevailing peace that we true worshippers receive and that human civilization's ingenuity and religious works cannot secure.

Foremost, when the prayer states "Our Father who art in Heaven, Hallowed be thy name," the prayer actually recognizes the fact that Y'haweh transcends all physical localities. The prayer adheres to the reality that Y'haweh's pure synthesis of spirit stands upon Y'haweh's intrinsic possession of all power, presence, beauty, and therefore satisfaction: the prayer signifies that Y'haweh stands at rest.

Essentially, the Prayer recognizes that Y'haweh is omnipotent; therefore, his eternal being is a synthesis with acute power, transcending the physical manifestations of energy that comprise our existence; moreover, Y'haweh's omnipotence means that Y'haweh is complete, requiring no existential work within spacetime. Likewise, the prayer recognizes that Y'haweh's omnipresence means that Y'haweh's infinite power does not have any physical or spatial boundaries to withstand: rather all things translate unto his spiritual synthesis. To this end, the prayer recognizes that Y'haweh is omniscient—even perfectly fulfilled aesthetic will. Thus, in the extension of all possible worlds, the prayer recognizes that Y'haweh is beatifically omnipresent, consigning every possible and analytically extendable world to fulfill Y'haweh's infinite sense of beauty, which again transcends spacetime.

Furthermore, when the prayer states, "Thy Kingdom come, thy will be done on earth, as it is in Heaven," the prayer recognizes the relationship between Y'haweh's infinite supervening power and our finite being. Likewise, the prayer indicates that Y'haweh's prevailing beatific will mediates values to us.

We may illustrate the asymmetric relationship that the prayer captures by first drawing the following comparisons: in contrast to

Y'haweh's being omnipotent, our finite strength corresponds to physical boundaries, degrees, and durations. In contrast to Y'haweh's being omnipresent, our finite consciousness stands upon points of reference, within spacetime. Thus, our finite understanding is not omniscient (even a self-being, spiritual synthesis who transcends any possible physicality, by possessing absolute beauty, intrinsically). Instead, our finite understanding is a contingent spiritual synthesis that is existent: namely, existere—a standing upon or out of the physical and social environments that complete our precarious identity. Hence, our contingent standing ultimately depends upon how Y'haweh beatifically arrays creation for our existential life-experience. Meanwhile, our finite knowledge fleetingly rests upon analysis, subjective propositions, prejudices, taste, and preferences.

To be sure, our limited mental abilities may suffice to secure our immediate wants; however, our self-centered limitations never entirely secure communal satisfaction. In fact, our inability to secure social agreement undermines our minds' interdependency upon other edifying perspectives. Soon we shall see that communal satisfaction is a final contingency that relies upon the manner in which Y'haweh beatifically reveals the universal peace of Lord Yehoshua's Kingdom to us.

So far, we see how the Lord's Prayer brilliantly recognizes the translation of Y'haweh's prevailing will into the charitable judgments of the Lord's heavenly Kingdom. In this vein, we may observe that our relating to the world and others for our completeness essentially translates Y'haweh's omniscience into the existential structure of quintessential knowledge; through which we experience Y'haweh's fulfillment as a beatific judgment upon our shortsighted understandings. Decidedly, we see that Y'haweh's prevailing right judgment proves to be the substance of the Kingdom.

From our finite vantage point, the structure of knowledge is uncertain. As we have seen, natural philosophy's epistemological discipline has yet to ascertain knowledge's structure. At best, we may consider our finite-knowledge-structure to be a mental state of the brain that has limited scope, like any other physical construction;

however, when we consider the structure of knowledge, itself, as deriving from Y'haweh's omniscient state, the structure of knowledge becomes equivalent to Y'haweh's Logos: knowledge becomes a universal construct that all things obey, including our conscious mind's ability to exist by standing out and upon our physical environments. Essentially, to consider knowledge as deriving from Y'haweh is to consider the essential nature of knowledge: even the Logos' prevailing right judgment—the orthodox right belief—that transcends our finite circumstance.

Remember, when we seek the Logos' prevalence, we are not merely seeking the standing of physical things. We are seeking the liberty and standing of human being over the physical world.

We see a reflection of human liberty in human relationships; especially in regards to industrial civilization's ability to produce such technology that overcomes nature's physical challenges. Though the natural marvels of the world are terrific, our finite being prevails upon them and manipulates them, for human benefit.

Albeit, our volatile personal and political relationships demonstrate that our standing above the physical world does not only depend upon the existence of Y'haweh whose beauty transcends the temporal world. The biblical Testaments demonstrate that our liberty especially depends upon how Y'haweh mediates his beauty to us, as a Kingdom that embodies the good judgment of our reconciled consciences, in the body of the Mashiach.

Having invoked the truthful order of the Lord's Prayer, we now turn to our orthodox judgment to prove the biblical Testaments' orthodoxy. We now turn to establish how Y'haweh expresses his beauty, unto our liberty in Lord Yehoshua's Kingdom.

The Introduction and Purpose of Immanuel's Law

Without further ado, we will call our orthodox judgment Immanuel's Law. By using the Hebrew word Immanuel, which means "God is with us," we will imply in the title of our judgment that it seeks to establish the following self-evident cosmological law: nothing exists without the transcending reality of Y'haweh, the self-existent Spirit, because everything is a product of his beatific expression of himself. In this respect, we will complement the abiding theme of the Lord's Prayer, which suggests that the cosmological order directly results from Y'haweh's beatific expression.

Though we appreciate the profundity of the Lord's Prayer, our simply agreeing with the prayer's implication that everything results from Y'haweh's beatific expression does not objectively predict or derivatively prove any critical or purposeful understanding of our physical experiences. Our dogmatic belief that Y'haweh beatifically created all things merely repeats the insufficient theological arguments that rationalize that a perfect creator is the necessary cause of the creation.

For some time, we have assessed how scientists fare no better in their attempt to establish cosmological understandings of our world. We have seen how scientists employ mathematical models to predict physical behavior. Yet, because mathematical systems cannot substantiate themselves, we found that scientists cannot mathematically derive cosmological understanding from observable physical systems. We have observed that the mathematical barrier relegates scientists to observing the world, empirically, without fully comprehending the world.

At present, neither Christian theologians and rationalist philosophers nor empirical scientists establish the certainty of our knowledge. Establishing a physical proof for the manner in which our cognitive judgments derive from Y'haweh's beatific expression shall, therefore, establish our orthodox judgment's worth, especially as our orthodox judgment overcomes science's mathematical limitations.

Before long, we shall not only demonstrate how our orthodox judgment's establishment is of the greatest significance to theologians, who merely rationalize our physical experiences through unsubstantiated dogma. We shall also demonstrate how our orthodox judgment's establishment is of the greatest significance to scientists, who merely observe the physical world to establish tentative truths upon what they can empirically predict.

As we alluded to at the beginning of our survey, scientists are right to denounce theologians and historical philosophers who wrongfully attribute teleological purposefulness to physical operations. Scientists commonly ascertain alternative explanations for the physical behavior that the theologians deem to be the physicality's sole purposeful design. At the same time, theologians are correct when they point out that scientists, themselves, necessarily frame all theories from the perspective values of intelligible designs, even though the scientists deny the need to admit the reality of an intelligent creator.

Let us present the following as a pertinent example of secular science and theology's conflicting stances: most theologians and teleological philosophers hold that the purpose of plant-life's ability to turn toward light sources is for plant-life to gain energy through photosynthesis. In contrast, scientists do not consider plant-life's phototrophic ability (to bend toward light sources) as a purposeful design feature. Scientists simply assert that surviving plant-life have acquired the adaptive ability to increase growth hormones on the sides of plants that the light does not directly stimulate. Denying any design intent, the scientists hold that this adaptive ability now allows evolved plants to gain energy from the sun more efficiently.

Notwithstanding, as we noted at the beginning of our survey, the scientists' evolutionary approach is not entirely objective. The scientists' simple recognition of adaption is a perspective value that forecasts an intelligent observer's rational dispositions upon inanimate matter, which cannot conscientiously seek adaptive stability. Rather, all matter succumbs to entropy's disorder, instead of increasing in order and complexity, per natural laws that only rational observers ascertain.

In consideration of creation's trend toward entropy, many Christians find it incredible that scientists believe that long-term adaptive processes can explain spectacular biological phenomena such as a caterpillar's rapid metamorphosis into an entirely novel winged creature—the butterfly. Yet, scientists retort by noting that the caterpillar possesses the genetic code that enables its rapid transformation; whereas other creatures, which endure metamorphosis, terminate their adaptive transformation toward adulthood in other ways.

Though the empirical scientists triumph over the dogmatic rationale of the theologians, scientists still cannot entirely escape humanity's shortsighted perspective values. Thus, scientists fail to render a total comprehensive and objective understanding of our physical experiences: necessarily, they expect some degree of order, measure, and repeatability as they seek causes for biological and non-biological material behavior. Evidently, the only pure objective understanding of creation that our orthodox judgment can establish is the knowledge of how Y'haweh physically posits our *a priori* perspectives of the world.

The "*A priori* Synthetic" Basis of Immanuel's Law

As promised, our orthodox judgment—Immanuel's Law—will establish the certainty of our knowledge, as our judgment escapes the shortcomings of the rationalist and empiricist arguments. As we have repeatedly said, our judgment will accomplish this by demonstrating the possibility and necessity of our apprehending metaphysical understanding: Immanuel's Law will establish physical proof of how our interdependent relationship with the world derives from Y'haweh's beatific expression, in a manner that transcends science's mathematical barrier.

The most appropriate way to begin Immanuel's Law is to touch upon how 19th Century natural philosophers easily undermined the Church's dominance over Western thought. Thinkers like Immanuel Kant pointed out that Church dogma and tradition do not suffice as a proof for orthodoxy's right and certain perspectives of the world.

We indicated above that Immanuel Kant came closest to resolving the rationalist-empiricist conflict: after he noticed how both rationalist and empiricist philosophers could not establish the certainty of our knowledge, Kant presented revolutionary understandings that almost resolved the rationalist-empiricists debate. First, Kant observed how theologians and rationalist philosophers dubiously held that their doctrines apprehended truths that stand prior to all physical occurrences. Indeed, Kant observed the problematic manner in which the rationalists held that their propositions were *a priori* and, therefore, necessary understandings: he saw that the rationalists resolved that their propositions appealed to universal laws, which do not require the validation of experience or observation. Despite their convictions, Kant observed how the theologians and the rationalists only base their understandings upon tautological and non-contradictory reassertions of their propositions, without their deriving informative, original, and predictive outcomes. Kant understood that the rationalists' trivial propositions resulted from the rationalists' failure to reconcile their propositions with established principles that are distinct from the propositions.

Finally after recognizing the contrast between scientific advancement and the unremarkable claims of the theologians and rationalists, Immanuel Kant also detected the shortcomings of the natural philosophers' empirical approach. Readily, Kant perceived how the natural philosophers' rudimentary employment of the scientific method managed to yield substantial knowledge: he appreciated how natural philosophers managed to derive novel understandings of what they observed by their reconciling their observations with the existing body of scientific knowledge. Even so, Kant perceived the subsequent weakness in science's empirical approach: he understood that because natural philosophers only embrace empirical observations that occur post (that is, after) an experience, the natural philosophers unavoidably embrace partial understandings that a given experience's particularity further limits. As an outcome, Kant ascertained that the empiricists can only obtain a finite knowledge: a myopic understanding that solely stands upon our contingent and impoverished sense experiences. Immanuel Kant essentially understood that the *a posteriori* understandings of empirical philosophers (and contemporary scientists) cannot truly transcend experience to establish universal understanding.

With the hope of resolving the rationalist and empiricist conflict, Immanuel Kant deduced that the certainty of knowledge stands upon our ability to perceive and cogitate mathematical relationships prior to physical experiences. Kant understood that our inherent mathematical ability spans the rational and empirical extension of our knowledge. Specifically, Kant noted how variables in simple arithmetic sequences, such as "7 + 5," are wholly distinct from the sequences' sum, e.g., "7 + 5 = 12." In other words, Kant understood that no aspect of the whole number "7" or "5" signifies the whole number "12." Only the synthesis of the whole numbers "7" and "5" with the independent principle of arithmetic derives the whole number "12," as the sum.

Immanuel Kant maintained that we intuitively cogitate such simple mathematical relationships prior to experience. What is more, Kant maintained that the entire rational basis of human intelligence stands upon our innate, mathematical ability to execute these "*a priori* synthetic judgments." Kant knew that the judgments not only fulfill the rationalists' quest for our knowledge's necessity and universal validity; but also fulfill the empiricists' quest for our knowledge's empirical objectivity.

In order to realize the full societal consequence of Immanuel Kant's work, we must resolve a crucial misunderstanding. We must realize that Kant's foremost theories relied upon false Newtonian notions of an absolute space and time, which purportedly stand regardless of a creator.

Contemporary scientists and philosophers disregard the balance of Kant's work, because early 20th Century physicists demonstrated that spacetime is not absolute. As a result of this disregard, contemporary thinkers overlook the profundity of Immanuel Kant's insight into the necessary structure of our knowledge: a structure that apprehends knowledge's universal validity and thereby derives our knowledge's empirical substantiation during experience.

Unfortunately, many contemporary logicians mistakenly think that Immanuel Kant's "*a priori*-synthetic" categorizations are imaginary: they hold that we only possess our mathematical preconceptions after previous empirical learning experiences; therefore, they believe that Kant imagined a fanciful metaphysical paradigm and then used rudimentary forms of predicate calculus to exhibit the supposed scheme of knowledge during experience.

Tragically, contemporary thinkers fail to understand that Immanuel Kant did not seek to apprehend knowledge's universality by merely pursuing the particularity of mathematical forms; which again scientists can only employ to describe and predict contingent events. Rather, Kant sought metaphysical certainty: he sought our cognitive connection to the underlying physical convention that gives us access to mathematics' universality. He knew that our knowledge's justification and centrality stands upon this connection. Since we instinctively expect the laws of nature and mathematics to apply universally, Kant perceived that our intuitive sense-perception of space and time must first demark our mathematical consciousness of the objects' adhering to space and time.

Though he based his work on an obsolete understanding of space and time, Immanuel Kant identified the necessary metaphysical relationship that both the physicality of our knowledge-structure and the material world must adhere to. To wit, as he sought to establish our knowledge-structure upon archaic space and time notions, Immanuel Kant demonstrated that our knowledge-structure never apprehends material phenomena in and of themselves. To the contrary, Kant demonstrated how our knowledge-structure intuitively apprehends the conventional totality that all material relationships conform to.

Hence, instead of apprehending particular things-in-themselves, Immanuel Kant demonstrated how we intuitively apprehend such physical conventions like the permanence of substances; the succession of cause-effect relationships in time; the coexistence of community and reciprocity of species-kind within a greater environment; and lastly the universal functionality of mathematics, itself—all of which stand prior to our actual experience of material objects.

Immanuel Kant presented the chief of his theories in his major work, the Critique of Pure Reason. In the first part of the Critique, Kant describes how our so-called "apperceptive" sense of space and time grounds concepts of understanding that the schematization of the world confers upon us. As he emphasized this unified and apperceptive sense, Immanuel Kant stressed that our understanding only adheres by categorizing similarity and difference from an underlying sense of space and time's whole.

Indeed, long before the advent of Darwin's evolutionary theory, Kant demonstrated how our understanding only obtains when the conventional scheme of creation arrays the diversity of species from a unified identity. Through these means, Kant demonstrated how our knowledge necessarily progresses from the similitude of material or biological species-kind unto increasing diversity.

For the reader, we may finally summarize the significance of Immanuel Kant's Critique as follows: first, Immanuel Kant found fault with the theologians and rationalists' unsubstantiated declarations that purported to be universal understandings. Likewise, Kant found fault with the empirical scientists' inability to apprehend universal understanding from incremental and particular observations. Then by envisioning how we forecast our unified "apperception" of space and time upon all perceived things, Immanuel Kant anticipated how we apprehend the symmetry and totality of any event prior to actual experience. Like so, Kant envisioned how to confirm our knowledge's structure with metaphysical certainty, despite his faulty notions of space and time. To be sure, without relying upon unsubstantial declarations or incremental observations, Kant demonstrated the promise of *a prior*—universal—understanding. He showed how our unified, *a priori* connection with creation's underlying physical conventions, renders our consciousness as unique but interdependently connected to the material world's unfolding structure; in a way that enables us to abstract and apprehend functional conventions that transcend what we immediately perceive.

Furthermore, Kant's false notion of absolute space and time compelled him to believe in a self-sufficient universe that stands, despite a creator. In the second half of the Critique, Kant described how the faculty of reason transcends the physical world, as our apperceptive sense of the whole psychologically encourages us to seek the totality of pure ideas, such as a creator and ourselves. As an outcome, Kant defied the dogmatism of the theologians by demonstrating that one cannot use empirically observed phenomena or tautological schemes of reasoning to prove the existence of a creator. Instead, Kant regrettably held that one's belief in a creator is only useful as a psychological aid when one seeks to interpret creation as a design. In fact, rather than invoking religious edicts to encourage public virtue, Kant adapted his universalist beliefs to construct secular notions of ethics and morality: he professed that individuals should "act only according to that maxim whereby one can objectively attest that his or her action invokes a universal law." The lasting consequence of Immanuel Kant's work is that Kant greatly contributed to the public's reliance upon secular-science's authority instead of Church authority.

Notwithstanding, any astute student of Kant's work cannot say that Immanuel Kant would have embraced the naturalists' understanding that the emergent cosmological order and earth's biological diversity, respectively, results from cosmological evolution and natural selection. A sensible student of Kant's work can only attest that Kant would have recognized the poignant fact that creation's schematized order and the gradual differentiation of material and biological species are critical facilitators for our knowledge's generation of conceptual analogues that seek a unified whole.

Immanuel Kant's theories that describe the *a priori*-synthetic structure of our knowledge may have even paved the way for modern cognitive neuroscience and phenomenology. Yet, because Kant did not possess a contemporary understanding of spacetime and neurology, he did not have the means to substantiate what he discovered to be the necessary structure of our finite knowledge: a structure that stands interdependently with the schematized world.

Immanuel's Law – Orthodox Judgment

We must initially present our orthodox judgment—Immanuel's Law—as a response to the inability of Immanuel Kant to vindicate his understandings of our finite-knowledge-structure. We have to begin by replacing Kant's notion that the unity of an absolute space and time gives rise to our knowledge-structure after we are cognizant of this unity. Our judgment will not rely upon the supposed manners that spacetime, the natural-force-laws, or any other indifferent process exclusively give rise to our consciousness. Instead, we will define how our finite-knowledge-structure derives from the Logos of Y'haweh's ineffable will, which purposefully manifests the physical world and our concurring mind-body experience. We will soon establish that only Y'haweh's personal extensions fulfill our mind-matter experience with right judgment.

To secure Immanuel's Law, we must basically apply a reconstruction of Immanuel Kant's *a priori*-synthetic judgment, in order to resolve the rationalist-empiricist debate. We must resolve the debate because the shortcomings of both rationalists and empiricists' methodology impede society from resolving the mind-matter explanatory gap. Similar to Kant's efforts, we must seek metaphysical certitude: we must reconcile the rational philosophers and theologians' insubstantial, universal claims with empirical scientists' inability employ our impoverished sense experience to grasp universal understanding from material particularity.

Not basing our judgment on antiquated notions of absolute space and time, Immanuel's Law must be what Kant and other thinkers thought impossible. Our orthodox judgment must be an *a priori*-synthetic judgment of Y'haweh—a judgment that is universally true and a judgment that adapts observable principles to derive conclusions that further our understanding during our impoverished experience.

To render our judgment, we must structure Immanuel's Law as the derivative and novel outcome of a concise series of theological statements that we have married to a supporting series of empirical-science statements. First, our theological statements must consist of the biblical Testaments' underlining truths, which we have gleaned from the Lord's Prayer and our definition of truth. The theological statements must fundamentally hold that the essence of the material world and our interdependent relationship with it result from Y'haweh's Logos' beatific expression: the statements must in this way describe how Y'haweh's expressed Logos entails an ontological order that we temporally apprehend to constitute the basis of our finite-knowledge-structure, which only Y'haweh's personal extensions complete.

Next, our empirical-science statements must consist of tentative, physical evidence for the manner in which the world and our knowledge-structure physically derive from Y'haweh's beatific expression. At the same time, the empirical-science statements must consider the fact that scientists' empirical methodology cannot corroborate the purposefulness of the divine directives that our theological proclamations suggest. Even so, our empirical-science statements must forecast how our judgment will overcome the scientists' shortcomings: the statements must suggest how divine intent and purposefulness drive the necessary physical convention that manifests the sense of beauty as our finite-knowledge-structure's foundation. In consequential order, the empirical-science statements must suggest how our knowledge-structure's unique physicality apprehends the uniform conventions that undergird the emergent world; even as our knowledge-structure remains inextricably interdependent upon the world.

Finally, our derivative statements must constitute Immanuel's Law. The derivative statements must substantially and derivatively demonstrate the possibility and necessity of our obtaining metaphysical knowledge to establish orthodoxy's right-belief. Like so, the derivative statements must resolve the rationalist-empiricist debate and close the mind-matter explanatory gap: the statements must establish the physical correlate of consciousness and the Logos' functional order that our knowledge-structure and the material world conform to. At the last, our derivative statements must establish the orthodoxy of the biblical Testaments: our statements must derivatively describe how Y'haweh's personal extensions necessarily complete our finite knowledge-structures.

Immanuel's Law - Theological Statements

Immanuel's Law's theological statements are as follows: because Y'haweh—the Lord who is—is by definition a pure and, therefore, inextricable spiritual synthesis of omnipotence, omnipresence, and omniscience, and so requiring no existential physicality or temporal convention to complete him; one cannot possibly use any analogy to describe and thereby apprehend indefinitely his subjective sense of beauty and holiness. One can only say that Y'haweh, of himself, is ineffable: Y'haweh's totality is an indwelling holiness—a consummate completeness within—that prevails upon any-possible-world without.

Thus, Y'haweh's Logos—Y'haweh's quintessential expression of knowledge—manifests the schematized creation as being merely an indicative sense of Y'haweh's whole; even as creation's indicative structure interdependently facilitates our temporal and contingent senses of Y'haweh's totality.

As a consequence, only Y'haweh's personal extensions can beatifically manifest Y'haweh's totality as lasting senses of right judgment, which Y'haweh extends after the following order: first, because we possess the basic unified sense that Kant described, we share with the animals an initial intuition of our environments' totality. From this unified intuition, we mark out our intelligent perspectives by prevailing upon creation's indicative structures with analogous concepts that enlarge our unified sense of self-worth over our environment. Furthermore, we humans produce greater mental abstractions that seek the totality of being, itself. Our temporal knowledge-structure does not only analogize gradational environments and successive animal species to facilitate the totality of our unified perspective. Our temporal knowledge-structure also analogizes interpersonal thoughts, as we seek an interpersonal sense of conscience, from intimate relationships unto complex public relationships.

Essentially, human nature intuitively seeks the totality of fulfilled human relationships over the creation, as a whole; however, because our finite judgments result in conflicting self-perspectives, we fall short of achieving this universal felicity. Thereby, Y'haweh's sublime capacity to demonstrate the integrity of conscience and impart judgment through election—despite class, creed, or individual religious prowess—qualifies Y'haweh's personal extension of himself, as the Mashiach and the reconciling Holy Spirit, respectively.

Wonderfully, through the Mashiach, Y'haweh extends himself in a personal form that he may analogously instill in us as lasting personal integrity. Likewise, through the Holy Spirit, Y'haweh extends himself in a personal form that he may analogously reconcile us communally. Like so, Y'haweh beatifically mediates a sense of his totality to us by sustaining our temporal knowledge-structure with impressions of an indwelling righteousness that eternally reconciles community over the world.

Immanuel's Law - Empirical Statements

Our theological statement basically maintains that Y'haweh beatifically expresses the creation as an indicative sense of his whole. The statement further concludes that Y'haweh's personal and communal extensions of himself, respectively, enable us individually and mutually to experience Y'haweh's totality as the eternal prevailing of Y'haweh's right judgment above our finite judgment.

Before we present our empirical-science statements, which seek empirical evidence for our theological statements, let us recall the following: by themselves, our theological statements are merely a rationalization of the biblical Testaments' underlying truths. Left alone, the statements stand without objective confirmation. Similar to the rationalist philosophers who make insubstantial claims, our statements merely assert that we have grasped the purpose for Y'haweh's expression. Yet, our statements do not objectively predict physical outcomes to establish the certainty of our finite knowledge, during physical experience.

We have seen how scientists do not recognize the validity of any theological assertions; because theologians have failed to demonstrate how purposeful directives proceed from Y'haweh to govern the creation's workings. Also, we have explained how scientists' ability to predict material behavior has enabled scientists to ascribe utilitarian values per the particular needs of society; albeit scientists' empirical methods have not ascertained a greater cosmological cause or purpose.

As they appreciate how quantum physics has advanced computer science, modern biology, and chemistry; physicists merely appreciate our ability to overcome what the physicists consider to be creation's purposeless processes. Essentially, physicists hold particle behavior and macroscopic solid-state behavior to be of equal ontological value, having no metaphysical directive to inform their status.

In our survey of cognitive neuroscience, we observed the ultimate illustration, concerning how scientists distinguish our human sensibilities from what they deem to be purposeless processes: we observed how cognitive neuroscientists actively reduce our qualitative affections unto being an epiphenomenon of neurological sequences. We in fact indicated that the dumbfounding of humankind occurs as secular governments misapply the social sciences merely to characterize civil justice without their actually accepting the supremacy of the human qualitative experience over the material world.

So, since contemporary scientists require proof of how a divine directive governs creation and how our qualitative senses superimpose upon the environment; our empirical-science statements must tentatively identify the physical conventions that support our theological statements, in the subsequent a way: first, we must suggest the physical convention that demarcates the divine derivation of our finite knowledge-structure. Also, we must suggest the physical convention that reflects how a divine directive qualifies the interdependent relationship between the world and our finite knowledge-structure. After we propose physical evidence for Y'haweh's divine directive, we must describe the limitations of employing the scientists' empirical methods to confirm Y'haweh's purposeful directives. Then in lieu of our empirical limitations, we must not only propose the physicality of our brain's dynamic mechanism, which equates consciousness. We must also suggest how the dynamic mechanism necessarily relies upon a metaphysical order. Through these means, we can anticipate how our pending derivative statements will further define the dynamic mechanism, not only to determine our finite knowledge-structure's breadth and justification; but also to prove how Y'haweh's right judgment predominates and superimposes the like form of our finite knowledge-structure over any-possible-world.

To suggest the physical convention that demarcates our finite knowledge-structure's divine derivation, let us begin our empirical-science statements by recalling the following lessons learned from our scientific surveys: in our earlier discussion on logic and mathematics, we saw that scientists postulate that an ultimate power-set of all sets must exist to transcend instances of energy. We, consequently, understood that scientists postulate the existence of the power-set because the scientists' mathematical pursuit of a singular power source invariable leads to an infinite regress. As an outcome, we saw how an asymmetric relationship exists between the power-set and the manifestations of energy that form the creation. We then later discussed how scientists quantify this asymmetry with the second law of thermodynamics; which observes the unavailability of energy to maintain particular processes, perpetually.

Though our empirical statements will not here present a proof for the cosmological sense of purposefulness that our previous theological statements describe, we shall take the liberty to say that we equate Y'haweh's pure synthesis of omniscient, omnipresent, and omnipotent Spirit with the power-set because Y'haweh is one with his attribute of being absolute power: we may readily liken the power-set's being other than any particular instance of energy or physicality to Y'haweh's being the only independent and intrinsically fulfilled, pure synthesis of Spirit. In our derivative statements, we shall see that the understanding that Y'haweh is the power-set is an objective principle that we may employ to demarcate his metaphysical standing, as we observe how his Logos' purposeful directive physically manifests in our life-experience. Also, we shall see that the notion of Y'haweh's metaphysical state's being equated to the power-set satisfies traditional Church orthodoxy, which concludes that Y'haweh must stand apart from the imperfect world that he created.

Furthermore, in addition to our assertion that Y'haweh's transcendent state equates the power-set, we must advance by specifically reflecting upon our previous consideration of the thermodynamics laws. In this way, we can spy a physical way to identify how the interdependent relationship between our finite-knowledge-structure and the material world stands upon Y'haweh's command and directive.

From the first and second thermodynamics laws, we understood that no material process disproportionately creates energy out of nothing or disproportionately destroys energy into nothing, during material transformations. At the same time, we understood that energy is unavailable to maintain particular processes, indefinitely. To be sure, from our survey of contemporary science, we observed how scientists have proved the second thermodynamics law in their macroscopic observations of energy loss, during machine processes. Likewise, we saw how contemporary physicists observe entropy's directedness on the microscopic levels of specific, allowable quantum energies: we observed the existence of specified energy levels that enable the measured degrees of the observable world.

And so, having witnessed the vindication of the thermodynamics laws, we may safely conclude that most scientists tacitly agree that the laws adhere to the ensuing natural directive: effectively, under a metaphysical power-set, no emerging material physicality conserves energy unto itself, to reconstitute itself and exists in and of itself. Instead, all material phenomena adhere to interrelationships, symmetry, and direction, during energy's perennial transformations.

Though many scientists subconsciously acknowledge a natural directive for the thermodynamic laws, other scientists justly oppose our unqualified employment of the term "directive." Our particular usage of the term not only denotes a sense of purposefulness, but also connotes an *a priori* sense of intention that the scientific method's empirical assessments cannot analytically recommend: principally, scientists cannot employ our trivial sense of the term to predict further observations.

It follows that science's analytical barrier seems insurmountable to most theologians and rationalist philosophers, who seek to establish universal directives. In spite of other theologians' dismay, we remain encouraged that we will bridge the seemingly irreconcilable chasm between our analytical limitations and creation's heretofore unfathomable directive. The uncanny way in which the enigmatic barrier reconciles with our theological conclusions actually encourages us to continue across truth's landscape. The scientists' incapacity to establish a purposeful directive for the thermodynamics laws corroborates our theological description of the world's being an indicative sense of Y'haweh's ineffable totality, which no audible dimension, instance, or attribute completely defines.

While we have yet to prove our theological assertions, we step ahead by further highlighting what distinguishes our theological descriptions from the scientists' analytical limitations. Our theological statements basically profess to translate creation's ineffable directives into an expressible orthodoxy: our statements champion their ability to grasp the purposefulness of a cosmological directive because the statements do not solely rely upon the scientists' analytical descriptions of the world, as though one can express the entire world as a self-sufficient and predictable state. On the contrary, because our theological descriptions recognize the asymmetric relationship between Y'haweh's ineffable, pure spiritual synthesis and the existential world that only indicates Y'haweh's totality; our descriptions recognize the need to observe the Kantian synthetic-analytic distinction.

We in fact may more perfectly observe how our theological statements grasp an expressible orthodoxy by observing how Y'haweh translates his ineffable state into expressible directives, as follows: first, when our theological statement asserts that Y'haweh's Logos constitutes the world order as an inexpressible sense of Y'haweh's whole; the statement infers that Y'haweh's pure spiritual synthesis holds the integral values of any-possible-world as insubstantial. Our statement essentially recognizes the reality that the possible worlds alone cannot constitute Y'haweh's whole; therefore, our statement concludes that the extended values of any emergent world are only substantial—that is, ontologically expressible—as the emergent structures enable and encourage such abstractions of thought that culminate into contingent senses of Y'haweh's whole. Similar to Immanuel Kant's suggestions, our theological statements propose that the world only maintains its expressible integrity as its basic physicality coincides with the basic physicality of our synthetic-analytic knowledge-structure.

For instance, when our statement infers that our finite-knowledge-structure's physical mechanism is interdependently contingent to creation's emergent structure; our statement infers that the mechanism becomes sentient as it seeks its healthful and unified perspective, through the abstract generation of intentional analogues that are expressible. Like so, our statement concludes that the intentional analogues unpack and substantiate the world's healthful values; even as the world's emergent schemes foster our unified self-perspective, within the totality of personal and social experience.

In short, our statement determines that the ineffable Y'haweh, the omnipotent, cannot expressively substantiate any-possible-world, as though anything can exist apart from him. Instead, our statement determines that Y'haweh can expressively substantiate our interdependent relationship to the emergent world, as his personal extensions secure the integrity of our mental abstractions, which seek his totality.

As a consequence, our theological statement's ultimate conclusion is that Y'haweh beatifically imparts our individual senses of his totality, as Y'haweh solely manifests the world to translate his ineffable whole into the expressible senses of his right-orthodox-judgment, which Y'haweh exhibits in the Mashiach and the Holy Spirit. Unfortunately, however, our theological descriptions scarcely secure objective evidence to support our conclusion. The descriptions fail to prove how Y'haweh's prevailing right judgment and beneficence unite as the expressible directive—the Logos—that governs the physical world. Our theological descriptions merely conjecture that we objectively witness the purposeful directive's physical reflection when our disinterested sense of beauty ascertains how all physical events adhere to the symmetrical conventions that facilitate our unified thoughts. With this conjecture, our theological descriptions merely assume that our disinterested experience of beauty corresponds to the spiritual manner in which Y'haweh transcends social standing and religious work to impart, beatifically, his right judgment, which again entails the Mashiach's good conscience and the communal Holy Spirit.

And so, because we have not secured more substantial evidence for our theological descriptions, our initial assertion that Y'haweh is the power-set may only intrigue a few theologians. Some rationalist philosophers may even empathize with our description of how our knowledge-structure must substantiate the emergent world, especially as our knowledge-structure and the world derive from an ineffable, metaphysical directive. Albeit, critical scientists may unjustly ridicule our citing the sense of beauty as objective evidence for a purposeful directive: likely, cynical scientists will assume that we believe that a representational sense of beauty indicates creation's purposeful directive. For sure, they will know that our simply observing a disinterested sense of beauty, which is merely a representational fiction of something more complex, does not predict or anticipate the nature of our ongoing environmental experiences.

So, before we proceed to identify other tentative empirical evidence for our theological statement, let us emphasize that we are not relying upon a common representational sense of beauty, as being physical evidence for a divine directive. Rather, we infer a dynamic sense, which we may quickly call attention to from the following perspective:

We, with scientists, must not only observe the fact that the thermodynamics laws permit the invariant emergence of the stratified creation; wherein we witness energy conservation and entropy on the microscopic quantum levels along with the macroscopic observable levels. Equally, we, with scientists, must recognize the trivial fact that the *a priori* thermodynamics laws permit the dynamic way in which the brain generates mental abstractions, which the conscious mind contingently binds as it maintains its unified, perspective sense.

Both the physicality of the brain's dynamic binding mechanism and the physicality of the actual abstractions adhere to the thermodynamics laws, like the emergent world; however, what distinguishes the physicality of brain's bound and unified abstractions is that the physicality of the brain's mental systems actively enable the appearing conscious mind to apprehend the emergent world's microscopic and macroscopic relationship, despite the specificity of material experience. In this way, the physical abstractions enable the conscious mind to apprehend the invariant conventions of energy's conservation and directedness, involuntarily.

The stratified creation's invariant order so brilliantly complements the unity of the material brain's emergent mind that the stratified creation seems to draw and facilitate the unity of our conscious perspectives; to the degree that the conscious mind appears to transcend, predict, and manipulate ongoing material experiences for personalized satisfaction. For sure, our discerning the manner in which creation's invariant order empowers the conscious mind is a non-trivial and disinterested sense of beauty that is not a mere representational fiction.

When our derivative statement closes the mind-matter gap between our knowledge-structure's physicality and the conscious mind, we will obviously conclude that the thermodynamics laws do not merely permit the way in which the material brain dynamically generates mental abstractions. Instead, we will hold true to the purposeful cause for which the Logos procures an expressible creation through our finite knowledge-structure. We will conclude the following: because the thermodynamics laws not only permit the brain's physical abstractions, but also permit the conscious mind's transcendent apprehension of uniformity and beauty, despite specific material experiences; the divine mediating of beauty is the transcending purposefulness of all such natural-force-laws, which govern the world's specific material interactions. In other words, we will conclude that Y'haweh's Logos ultimately directs the thermodynamics laws to establish our knowledge-structure upon *a priori* senses of uniformity and beauty, despite the specific material experiences that contingently gives rise to our senses.

Of course, from our lessons-learned, we know that behavioral psychologists refer to environmental conditioning as a natural explanation for our supposed ability to transcend specific experiences and predict events. Particularly, behaviorists observe how we perform learned-experiences subconsciously, in ways that give us the psychological impression that we transcend events. Likewise, from our lessons-learned, we know that cognitive neuroscientists dismiss our disinterested observations of a world investing qualitative senses of beauty. Many cognitive scientists reject the invested senses of beauty as an epiphenomenon of unconscious neurological impressions that render pleasant senses of novelty after we become conscious of them.

To answer the dismissive scientists, our derivative statement must decisively demonstrate that our transcendent sense of beauty is not merely an effect of environmental conditioning or any other fortuitous outcome of natural selection. Likewise, our derivative statement must conclusively demonstrate that our qualitative sense of beauty is not an epiphenomenon of the neuronal network's chemical impressions.

Our derivative statement must demonstrate the following: in the same manner that we distinguish the physical attributes of a candlestick from the flame that one kindles upon it, we must distinguish the neuronal network from the physicality of the mind that it apprehends. We shall see that the neuronal network apprehends a unique and dynamic physicality: the true worshipper shall discover that the dynamic mechanism binds complexes of neurons, as it forecasts its unified state. Specifically, we shall confirm that the physicality translates neuronal resonance as analogues of the emerging world's invariant order. In this manner, we shall see how the dynamic mechanism transcends material specificity and apprehends the conventional uniformity of emerging symmetries, all to secure its uniform state. Indeed, we will confirm that the dynamic mechanism's maintenance of its uniform state, by contingently integrating complexes of neuronal signals, translates as our qualitative sense of beauty.

While our derivative statement demonstrates the foregoing realities of the mind's dynamic physicality, the statement will particularly establish the critical fact that an invariant order's rational priority purposefully precedes the specificity of any-possible-world. Like so, the statement will demonstrate how the Logos lays creation's systematized landscape, which induces the mind's dynamic mechanism to transcend particular circumstances. Essentially, the statement will show that the metaphysical order induces intentionality: the order facilitates the mind's continuous, analytical query for the uniform totality of experience. Chiefly, we shall find the following: as the Logos enables our dynamic mechanism's abstract capacity to forecast and so communicate its states, the Logos enables the union of the intentional mind and matter. In other words, the Logos enables a fundamental and uniform physicality that inescapably translates as our qualitative sense of beauty; especially as the physicality dynamically regulates environmental circumstances by translating neuronal sequences as analogous values that reconcile with its uniform state.

In short, we may say that we are far from considering our qualitative sense of beauty as the outcome of environmental conditioning or a neurological epiphenomenon. To the contrary, we ultimately hold that our sense of beauty is the basis of our finite knowledge-structure. Unlike contemporary scientists, we hold our finite knowledge-structure to be equally substantial with the emergent world; because we appreciate the fact that our conscious minds' unique physicality independently apprehends the Logos' metaphysical order that the material world adheres to.

To be sure, scientists can only employ the scientific method to describe, with analytical specificity, the neurological network that facilitates our finite knowledge-structure. Yet, scientists cannot use empirical means to describe and justify our knowledge-structure's breadth and free, supervening qualifications. As we have seen, scientists can describe and predict physical events by mathematically ascribing temporal values to constituents of a function in ways that depict how physical events adhere to natural-force-laws. All the same, scientists' empirical approach can only qualify a necessary mode of free universality (over any-possible-world) to the natural-force-laws. Nevertheless, scientists cannot recognize the purposeful directive that invests the necessary status of the laws. As we have seen in the philosophical debate over the perceived purposefulness of plant-life's turning toward sunlight, scientists cannot qualify any emerging physical system with purposefulness or priority. Rather, they hold that all existential things have equal ontological value. Hence, as they hold our souls' qualitative experience to be an epiphenomenon, scientists render all aspects of the observable world to be functionally indeterminate; in regards to the qualifying sense of meaningfulness that we psychologically ascribe to any observed functional operation.

By contrast, our empirical statements thus far support our theological statement by observing how the natural-force-laws allow our finite knowledge-structure's physicality to transcend the material specificity and apprehend the priority of the Logos' uniform order. For this cause, our empirical statements now further observe that our knowledge-structure's physicality also bears the universal and free mode of necessity, in part. Only, in this way, can our knowledge-structure bear the qualitative capacity to make decisions, though our propositions are finite and, therefore, sometimes faulty. Even so, our empirical statements can conclude that our finite-knowledge-structure stands upon universal conventions, which scientists unfortunately confuse and conflate with the contingent and adaptable factors of the present world.

Thus, in order for our derivative statement to prove that our finite-knowledge-structure is equally substantial with the emergent world, we must demonstrate how our knowledge-structure uniquely relies upon the Logos' uniform priority that precedes and so metaphysically transcends any possible emerging, physical system. After our derivative statement demonstrates how our knowledge-structure's physicality derives from the power-set of Y'haweh's spiritual synthesis, we can substantively affirm the reality of our transcending knowledge-structure in a way that assimilates scientists' functionally indeterminate attempts to observe the neuronal correlates of consciousness (NCC). To pave the way toward this end, let us quickly adapt the scientists' indeterminate observations as our empirical statement's final physical evidence for our theological statement:

As we have seen, cognitive neuroscientists observe how chemical reactions within neurons either excite or inhibit neuronal signals. We briefly noted how neuroscientists observe the manner in which complexes of these excitatory and inhibitory neurological interfaces make up the cortical regions of the brain. We soon discovered that the cognitive neuroscientists never quite apprehend the absolute neuronal correlate of consciousness. Albeit, we have seen that they grasp the attributes of consciousness, as they delineate how specific cortical regions are responsible for exciting or inhibiting neuronal complexes in ways that render attention, spatial awareness, auditory and visual imaging, sleep, and memory. To this end, we found that because priming and other neuronal procedures occur before actual states of consciousness, cognitive neuroscientists comfortably consign consciousness to be a fortuitous after-effect of determinate processes.

In spite of the cognitive neuroscientists' confidence, we discovered that the mainstream neuroscientists' functional description of consciousness does not address the manner in which the dynamic mind binds neuronal impressions. Likewise, we described that mainstream neuroscientists do not address how the mind freely makes intentional choices that prevail upon ongoing environmental impressions. As a consequence, we ultimately found that the undiscovered physical correlate of consciousness and personal freedom depends upon recent unconventional attempts to define our free and peculiar states of consciousness:

We briefly noted how recent electromagnetic theories of consciousness purport to resolve the manner in which the mind binds neuronal impressions; however, we saw that the electromagnetic theories fail to differentiate themselves from other electromagnetic systems that occur throughout the body. In addition, we saw how harmonic resonance theories of consciousness claim that neuronal resonance creates the mind's unique and bound state. All the same, we understood that neuronal resonances patterns cannot alone produce the targeted decision making processes that the mind effects.

Before long, we finally saw how quantum theories of the mind suggest that the freedom of consciousness necessarily entail quantum aspects, such as quantum entanglement and the unpredictable collapse of wave functions: we observed that the wave function's unpredictable collapse aptly addresses the mind's free capacity to bind neuronal impressions and render decisions, despite the causal directions that the macroscopic world impresses upon us.

Notwithstanding, in order for our derivative statements to adapt the electromagnetism and quantum theories of consciousness, we must recognize that the quantum mind theorists do not explain how the free quantum components of the mind reconcile with the aspects of the mind that are the necessary result of neuronal determinateness, as well as ongoing environmental impressions. After all, we must essentially recognize that cognitive neuroscientists cannot decisively apprehend the neuronal correlate of consciousness, unless they explain exactly how neuronal action potentials amount to qualitative consciousness. Once more, the scientists' empirical method only yields functionally indeterminate answers. As an outcome, empirical scientists do not convincingly dissuade rationalist philosophers and theologians from holding the Cartesian dualist view of spirits and souls hovering over their respective bodies.

To span the mind-matter explanatory gap, Immanuel's Law must apprehend metaphysical orthodoxy, in order to adapt the contemporary conscious-mind theories: our derivative statement must distinguish the expressible manner in which the free quantum aspects of the mind derive from Y'haweh's being one with the power-set over any possible creation. Likewise, as we distinguish how our knowledge-structure's physicality and the material world interdependently extend from Y'haweh's power-set, we must establish the necessary relationship between the mind's free aspects and the contingently determined, neuronal aspects. Also, as we unfold our knowledge-structure's physicality from Y'haweh's power-set, we must even draw inspiration from a literal interpretation of the scriptural metaphor that the Apostles Yochanan and Sha'ul used when they described us as being children of light. To this end, we must distinguish what necessary aspects of the electromagnetic-consciousness theories constitute our knowledge-structures breadth and universality over any-possible-world.

To determine and establish Immanuel's Law, let us now turn to our derivative statements. Our having tentatively demonstrated how science's empirical observations support our theological statements, we have only to conclude our empirical statements by saying that we are far from believing that securing the metaphysical orthodoxy of Y'haweh's eternal truth is impossible. To the contrary, Immanuel's Law derivative statements shall now prove that metaphysical understanding is necessary for both theology and science.

Immanuel's Law - Derivative Statements Introduction

To begin Immanuel's Law's derivative statements, let us summarily reiterate the challenge of reconciling secular science with Christian orthodoxy, as we seek to close the mind-matter explanatory gap: we have just detailed how contemporary scientists and Christian theologians cannot distinguish the neuronal correlate of consciousness, which enables the mind to prevail upon and transcend physical events. We saw that scientists cannot metaphysically transcend mathematical barriers to qualify a purposeful directive and ontological priority for both the emergent world and consciousness' neuronal correlate. Near the end of our contemporary science survey, we saw how scientists successfully identify natural-force-laws to predict such physical events like nuclear decay, light wavelength changes, and gene mutation. Even so, we understood that as scientists extrapolate, from these predictions, concepts like cosmological and biological evolution; they cannot establish the ontological or epistemological basis of what scientists conclude to be a continuum of natural processes.

We have repeatedly mentioned the negative social consequences of the scientists' austere belief that our qualitative minds are epiphenomenal effects of the brains' automated sequences: we have noted that the scientists' inability to distinguish the mind's liberty diminishes the critical values that secure personal liberty within Christian civilization.

At the same time, we detailed how Christian theologians have failed to substantiate the orthodoxy of their dogmatic proclamations, concerning how Y'haweh gives human consciousness preeminent standing above the world, though we remain dependent upon the manner in which Y'haweh's Logos ontologically structures the world. Even as we saw how scientists have not grasped ontological understanding, we observed how the Church has not established the justification for the way our knowledge-structure spiritually affirms the emergent world's ontological order. As an outcome, we noted how scientists discern that the theologians' spiritual proclamations are not falsifiable. We appreciate why the scientists decry the fact that religious institutes effortlessly use their spiritual pronouncements to exploit and manipulate the uneducated masses.

Essentially, we have described two opposing approaches that both fail to resolve the mind-matter explanatory gap: theologians' dogmatic proclamations of the way that spiritual realities command the appearing world are inconclusive, because theologians fail to produce verifiable proofs. Likewise, scientists' successful predictions of material behavior fail to establish the epistemological justification for an observer's seemingly arbitrary and ephemeral points of reference. Though scientists effectively observe physical phenomena's adherence to natural-force-laws; scientists forgo any attempt to determine a metaphysical or epistemological understanding of the necessary physical convention that constitutes the observer's reference frame, which bears the dynamic capacity to distinguish the natural-force-laws' ontological values.

In consideration of the Christian theologians and secular scientists' shortcomings, Immanuel's Law must now identify the falsifiable and derivative way that Y'haweh physically expresses his ineffable directive, through which he creates and fulfills our finite knowledge-structures, as well as the world's ontological order. Only in this way, can we establish the orthodoxy of the biblical Testaments by closing the mind-matter explanatory gap as a proof.

Thus far, we have only reproduced the most common insubstantial arguments for a creator's existence. In our empirical statements, we only reproduced the ontological argument for a perfect being: we simply stated that Y'haweh is omnipotent, omnipresent, and omniscient and that Y'haweh does not require any possible physicality to complete him. As well, our empirical statements only rephrased the cosmological argument for a divine originator, when we described Y'haweh as being one with the power-set over any-possible-world. Finally, our empirical statements merely enhanced the insubstantial teleological arguments for an intelligent designer, when we described how the world only exists to facilitate and augment our sense of beauty.

Admittedly, Immanuel's Law will uphold the anthropocentric — human centered — arguments for a creator. Yet, as Immanuel's Law upholds the anthropocentric perspective, our derivative statements will vindicate our human centered stance when our derivative statements produce a falsifiable proof. Like so, we will uphold our theological and empirical statements.

With our proof, our derivative statements must essentially establish the following claims of the theological and empirical statements: though the world (and even most neurological processes) exists despite our consciousness, the world cannot exist, despite Y'haweh, who alone is complete, in and of himself. For this reason, the extension of any-possible-world is only a beatific extension that establishes our personhood: that is, Y'haweh's extension of our finite standing as an expressible extension of Y'haweh's infinite standing.

To establish our finite-knowledge-structure's physical basis and the manner in which Y'haweh's Logos expresses the world's ontological order, we have said that we will adapt the necessary aspects of the existing electromagnetic, quantum field, and neuronal resonance theories of consciousness. We, in effect, inferred that we will describe the subsequent relationship as being a consequence of the world's extension from Y'haweh's power-set: we suggested that light uniquely assumes the regulatory basis of our finite knowledge-structure, in the same way that light assumes the physical catalyst for the extended creation.

By our describing how light factors into consciousness, we will grasp a falsifiable proof that will enable theologians to demonstrate the metaphysical standing of Y'haweh. Likewise, our proof will enable scientists to qualify their predictions, ontologically, under a metaphysical directive. In this way, we will finally close the mind-matter explanatory gap.

As we demonstrate how light serves and the unique basis of our knowledge-structure, we must avoid the enticing ways that past and contemporary theologians present the insubstantial ontological, cosmological, and teleological arguments for the existence of a creator. As we described, these arguments merely proclaim the existence of a necessary creator who expressed the complex creation. For instance, we find inspiration from the fact that Moshe's creation account identifies light as the underlining physicality that Y'haweh's Logos expressed the creation with; however, our finding inspiration from Moshe's account does not demonstrably reveal any scientific understanding. Also, we find that our consideration of light as the physical basis of our knowledge-structure even reconciles with Immanuel Kant's reasoning that humanity's knowledge-structure must stand upon the underlining manifold of space and time. Even so, our agreement with Kant does not substantially close the mind-matter explanatory gap.

Enticing is the fact that the characteristics of light reconcile with the correlating free and contingent aspects of our minds. Indeed, we especially find comfort from the fact that the Apostles Yochanan and Sha'ul used a metaphorical sense light to describe how the elects' souls become purified, freed, and, therefore, set apart from the corrupt world. Nevertheless, our judgment must look beyond these enticements and stand upon falsifiable and derivative evidence.

We may begin to find a more critical reason, for our identifying light as the physical basis for our knowledge-structure, as we recall the following: from our natural science survey, we know that the macroscopic beams of light, which we partially observe, exist microscopically as both a wave and a particle, carrying quantized energies of varying wavelengths and frequencies. Also, we may recall that light invariantly shares its force carrying properties with a subatomic family of force carrying particle-waves, which we cannot directly observe.

Consequently, we saw that scientists mathematically employ light's properties to rationalize the unobservable subatomic properties. For example, we witnessed how scientists use a proportional constant to produce mathematical equations that quantify how light's particle-waves exchange forces. At the same time, we observed how scientists use the same constant to quantify light's energy by the manner in which an atom's electron orbits, of complementing quantized energies, emit and absorb light. Lastly, we recognized how scientists invert the quantum force-exchange equations to describe the inner most subatomic forces, which share behavioral properties with light. In a word, our recollection of how scientists readily use light's properties to describe the unseen irresistibly compels us to demonstrate that the dynamic mechanism of our minds constitutes a unique configuration of light that enables the conscious mind to rationalize and transcend the particularity of physical experience; as the intentional gaze of consciousness abstracts and anticipates ongoing events.

Immanuel's Law - Derivative Statements Illustration

In order for our derivative statements to define the mind's dynamic mechanism, let us first relate a detailed example of the way the conscious mind maintains its qualitative standing from which it rationalizes a multiplicity of material and biochemical processes; only to obtain the exactitude of emerging relationships that the determinant processes ontologically conform to. Let us illustrate how we literally move mountains of determinant and automated processes that we are unconscious of, as we consciously adhere to abstract senses like triumph and liberty. We must briefly illustrate how we adhere to aesthetic values from which we cannot empirically garner scientific predictions. To be sure, though the aesthetic values seem to be of no material worth, let us see how the world, residing under our feet, adheres to the values.

For instance, Cristina Daniela, an Olympic swimmer, may be unaware that an intricate system of muscles—tied to a complex of nerve cells, residing at the center of her brain—causes her eyes to blink at an average of 5 second intervals, in order to moisturize and irrigate her eyes; moreover, she may be unaware of how her sympathetic nervous system causes tiny muscles to contract at the base of her hair follicles, in response to the chill that she feels as she approaches the pool. Nonetheless, she has the intentional capacity to rationalize the chill and commandeer the automated systems of her eyes to wink at her cheering family, friends, and husband. As she winks, she instantly communicates affection and reassurance in a uniform and synthetic way that claims the exactitude of their hope that she masters trillions of unseen automated processes to fulfill her abstract purpose and goal of winning a gold medal: a highly vaunted prize that only has symbolic value.

We readily agree with the cognitive neuroscientists' descriptions of the biological systems that facilitate experiences like Cristina's. Nonetheless, we must further illustrate how the scientists' empirical descriptions cannot grasp the way Cristina qualifies her body and environment's determinant and automated processes. To be specific, we must decisively illustrate how empirical scientists' linear cause-effect descriptions cannot metaphysically grasps the epistemological structure of Cristina's finite knowledge. In other words, we must show how the natural scientists cannot grasp the epistemological structure that tentatively qualifies the emergent world's ontological standing.

Hence, soon after we conclude our brief illustration, our derivative statements will detail how Y'haweh's Logos metaphysically enables the brain to obtain a unique dynamic mechanism of light. Like so, we will detail how Cristina's ontological qualifications derive from Y'haweh's metaphysical standing.

To set up our illustration, let us quickly recall the methodological process that enables scientists to predict and define the human physiology that enables Cristina's behavior. Let us recollect how we observed the way scientists successfully employ the scientific method to refine ongoing hypothetical understandings that seek to envision a telos—that is, a purposeful totality—of the physical systems that make up Cristina, though the scientists do not actually accept the reality of an intelligent designer.

As we have seen, scientists can verify their hypotheses of Cristina's physical behavior, by successfully establishing natural-force-laws that determine the derivation, continuation, and effect of the observed physical systems that facilitate Cristina's intentional perspectives. We have seen how they can seemingly accomplish this without their determining an ultimate metaphysical or divine purpose to explain Cristina's conscious experience.

By only recognizing the ontological standing of physical systems that they can quantify to make behavioral predictions; scientists can categorize Cristina's behavioral systems to be a multi-cellular, sophisticated advancement of the most fundamental unicellular system that they deem to be life. Essentially, scientists can consider her to be a derivation of the smallest measure of an observable self-replicating system that endures metabolic processes to adapt and persist in a greater environment. Hence, scientists can readily conclude that she, like all living organisms, possesses hereditary traits and adapts to her environment through a complex metabolic growth and development system; moreover, they can observe that her complex metabolic system comprises a range of biochemical, charged circuits; which break down molecular structures for energy sources, as well as use energy sources for cellular development.

In point of fact, by using the scientific method to identify Cristina as an metabolic system of observable, self-replicating, biochemical circuits; scientists can establish the essential building blocks of the biochemical systems that gives rise to Cristina's behavioral experience: scientists can determine that out of creation's known 92 naturally occurring elements, 99% of Cristina's person result from molecular compositions that entail oxygen, nitrogen, phosphorous, carbon, sulfur, and hydrogen. Also, because 70% of Cristina's molecular composition are charged water molecules, scientists can capture the causal operations of Cristina's biochemical circuits by classifying all other molecular structures as hydrophilic (that is, reactive and soluble in water) or hydrophobic (that is, unreactive and insoluble in water).

As a further consequence, scientists can identify Cristina's hydrophilic molecules as proteins (which contain amino acids as building blocks); carbohydrates (which contain sugars and starches as building blocks); and DNA and RNA, nucleic acids (which contain nucleotides as building blocks). In the same fashion, scientists can identify Cristina's hydrophobic molecules as lipids, which contain such things as fatty acids and glycerol molecules as building blocks.

Roughly, from these categorizations, scientists can even establish that lipid molecules, containing traces of phosphor, comprise the cellular membranes of the trillion cells that constitute Cristina's body. Furthermore, scientists can observe how protein cellular walls, with ports, contain charged sodium and potassium pumps that allow the entrance of certain molecules into the cells.

By recognizing how charged molecular building blocks constitute the metabolic systems of life, scientists can ultimately qualify Cristina's metabolic systems as thermodynamic states that distinguish a given species by the way the species adapt, translate, and so impose their identities upon their respective environments. With this understanding, scientists can quantify the simplest unicellular thermodynamic states that adapt and translate microscopic environments. Likewise, scientists can quantify the most sophisticated multicellular systems: scientists can consider them as specialized systems that enable Cristina to rationalize and thereby transcend her environments.

In regards to the way that scientists consider Cristina as a specialized multicellular system, we emphasize that scientists only seek to reduce Cristina's cognitive capacity to being an epiphenomenon of the human nervous system's increasingly specialized biochemical processes. Too, we emphasize that the scientists seek to translate Cristina's conscious experience into the human nervous system and greater metabolic system's predictable thermodynamic states: that is, circumstances in which scientists can match Cristina's behavior with the observable biochemical energy conversions that constitute Cristina's metabolic system.

Still, before we continue with our brief description, concerning how the scientists' empirical descriptions accurately account for the biochemical systems that enable Cristina's behavior, let us also underscore the subsequent oversight that the scientists make. Let us note that although the scientists recognize the thermodynamic states that distinguish Cristina, they fail to recognize the significance of two principles that we gleaned from our empirical statements.

First, we observed that under Y'haweh's power-set, no physical phenomenon entirely reconstitutes itself to exist unto itself; therefore, we recognized that the thermodynamics laws reflect the temporal nature of the emergent world. Second, we understood that the thermodynamics laws ironically allow the mind to generate physical abstractions that transcend the world's temporal standing. Essentially, we found that because scientists disregard or fail to ascertain the implications of these two principles, the scientists' appeal to temporal biochemical processes cannot entirely explain Cristina's supervening understanding.

Nonetheless, although they fail to distinguish the principles that our empirical statements acknowledge, let us recognize that scientists correctly discern the basic thermodynamic operation of an intelligent life-form's charged metabolic system. Albeit, we must keep in mind that they cannot entirely grasp the physical correlate of the life-form's consciousness.

As we have said, they spy a thermodynamic process as they observe how cells adapt and break down molecular energy sources to build up the cellular structures that comprise the life-form's body, within a greater environment. Brilliantly, scientists observe how special hydrophilic molecules, which scientists term the deoxyribonucleic acids (DNA), play a critical, role in securing the thermodynamic states of life's metabolic processes. For instance, scientists note how the DNA molecules reside at the center of all cells; as the DNA molecules relate to other cellular molecules as the governors and schema for life's metabolic and, therefore, thermodynamic processes. Essentially, scientists observe that the DNA molecules hold the purposeful instruction for the building and maintenance of all cells.

Immanuel's Law 187

Thus, to complete our brief synopsis of how scientists ascertain the biochemical systems that enable Cristina's behavior, we have only to relate the subsequent examples, featuring DNA's critical role: we have only to summarize how a simplified DNA molecule governs the thermodynamic processes of a single-cell life-form's metabolic system. Afterward, we may summarize how a complex DNA molecule governs Cristina's trillion cell metabolic systems.

The DNA molecule of unicellular—that is, prokaryotic—organisms consists of a single chromosome of genetic material; and the molecule rests in the cell's water based cytoplasm. Like all DNA molecules, the unicellular DNA molecule transcribes its genetic material into a complementary ribonucleic acid (RNA) molecule, which then yields a messenger RNA molecule. After metabolic processes break down complex sugars into simpler sugar molecules, such as glucose; the processes produce the energy enzyme adenosine triphosphate (ATP). The ATP enzyme then assists the messenger RNA molecule to bind to cellular ribosomes, which are protein-RNA complexes. Following, the ribosomes produce polypeptide sequences, in accordance to the messenger RNA sequence. Next, the polypeptide sequences fold into new protein molecules, which are the critical building blocks of the cell. Finally, the production of special proteins enables the duplication of the DNA molecule's genetic material, as the prokaryotic cells divide into new prokaryotic cells. In this manner, the unicellular thermodynamic process realizes its completion.

In general, the cellular metabolism of Cristina's multicellular—that is, eukaryotic—system is similar to the cellular metabolism of the unicellular system; however, special characteristics of Cristina's DNA and ensuing cellular structures enable her multicellular system to achieve thermodynamic states that transcend the mere cellular division of prokaryotic cellular systems. The thermodynamic states of multicellular metabolism realize completion as entire, emerging organisms maintain homeostasis—that is, internal regulation—as the organisms adapt to greater respective environments.

The DNA molecules of multicellular—eukaryotic—organisms consist of multiple chromosomes; and the molecules reside chiefly in a double-membrane, cellular nucleus. Also residing in the nucleus are RNA molecules, which replicate the DNA sequence, during transcription. Like other multicellular organisms, Cristina's cellular organization entails important structures—specifically "organelles"—such as mitochondria. The multicellular organelles give Cristina's cells a variety of capabilities, which differentiate each cell's metabolic process from another's. Similar to other animals, for instance, Cristina's mitochondria employ oxygen to process sugars for the production the energy enzyme ATP.

Again, the breakdown of complex sugars to produce the energy enzyme ATP is a necessary metabolic process that all organisms share. Only the specialized DNA molecules differentiate, multicellular plants, animals, and human beings from unicellular organisms: the more specialized DNA molecules govern the advanced thermodynamic states that multicellular life achieve, as their metabolic systems translate environmental foodstuff into energy. Furthermore, to a greater extent than all animal species, Cristina possesses operative capacities to effect strategic motions in response to changing environments. Thus, her 23 chromosome DNA molecule enables her to achieve thermodynamic states far beyond plant-life's mere achieving of homeostasis, under the plant-life's stationary conditions.

For example, plants adapt to their static environments by using energy from the sun to convert atmospheric carbon dioxide and water into simple sugars. Through such means, plants produce ATP to facilitate the building of plant cells. Also, plants extract water and nutrients from the soil. So, in order to secure homeostasis, thermodynamically, within their set environments; plants finally employ integrative networks of specialized cells to signal the correspondence of the plants' varied metabolic states.

Cristina, likewise, requires integrated systems that progressively regulate her bodily operations to maintain homeostasis; however, she requires increased biochemical integration to enable the central processing and coordination of her mobile, strategic, and automated operations, which all respond to her progressive environments. Categorically, Cristina requires a diffused circulatory system that distributes nutrients and oxygen to her cells; moreover, in association with her circulatory system, Cristina requires complementing lymphatic and endocrine systems; which respectively process waste and diffuse hormonal signals to regulate cellular operations. Lastly, she requires peripheral and central nervous systems that directly and instantaneously communicate bodily states in association with the greater environment.

Above all, Cristina's circulatory systems maintain the integrity of Cristina's body, while Cristina's nervous systems maintain the integrity of Cristina's body, during its mobile operations in the greater environment. Firstly, to maintain the integrity of Cristina's body, Cristina's circulatory system consists of 90% water-concentrated blood plasma and red blood cells, which possess oxygen rich hemoglobin molecules. The water concentrated blood plasma dissolves glucose, fatty acids, and amino acid molecules, as the circulatory system distributes the nutrient molecules, along with the red blood cells' oxygen.

Secondly, to understand how Cristina's nervous system maintains her bodily integrity in motion, let us recall that the heart of Cristina's nervous system is the neuronal cell, which we described in our cognitive neuroscience discussion. Let us remember that the tree-like neurons instantly exchange a myriad of electrochemical, neurotransmitter signals that thermodynamically translate bodily and environmental states into the encoded electrochemical signals.

Simple radiata (that is, radially symmetrical) animals, such as jelly fish, have diffused neuronal networks; while sophisticated animals have centralized neuronal networks. For instance, bilateria (that is, linearly symmetrical) animals, like Cristina, all have a central processing brain and central spinal cord, which entails complexes of soma. The soma, in fact, act as relays that rationalize the signals of sensory neurons to relay the signaling of motor neurons, which initiate the body's physical responses.

In our cognitive neuroscience discussion, we observed that cognitive neuroscientists cannot precisely identify how the sophisticated, bilateria nervous systems enable animal cognition and human reasoning. At the same time, we also recognized that the nervous systems' analytical structure entices cognitive neuroscientists to reduce qualitative experiences, like Cristina's, to being the mere effect of biochemical and electrochemical causes.

Thus, at this juncture, we understand that scientists emphasize the mathematical logic of their procedural models without their grasping every peculiar biological particularity. Like so, they hope to capture the full thermodynamic translation of Cristina's environmental experience unto being the biochemical and electrochemical systems that scientists can analytically observe.

Essentially, scientists observe how the neuronal connections are capable of universal computation. They recognize that the nervous systems retain the capacity to generate patterned signals, intrinsically, despite external stimuli. Above a hundred types of synapses, receptors, and neurotransmitters yield an infinite variety of signaling responses to the environment. At the same time, long lasting effects of synaptic signaling produces memory traces: the nervous systems' very adaptation to the environment.

And so, we see that cognitive neuroscientists cannot ascertain the full mechanical scope of the nervous systems' complexity. Even so, we recognize that cognitive neuroscientists can tentatively produce mathematical models of the neuronal signaling and neuronal nets' adaptive plasticity.

As we also noted in our cognitive neuroscience discussion, scientists can mathematically understand Cristina's brain and nervous systems in terms of information processing. Short of their grasping the explicit neuronal correlate of consciousness, cognitive neuroscientists can dissect Cristina's person into being the sole effect of individual brain regions' neuronal architecture.

For example, we shall observe the fact that without any further mechanical qualifications other than mere observational designations, they can recognize how Cristina's pons is responsible for Cristina's respiration and facial expression detection. In the same way, we shall soon see that cognitive neuroscientists can recognize how Cristina's thalamus plays an active role in Cristina's wakefulness; even as Cristina's hippocampus plays a role in Cristina's memory.

By assessing the functioning of Cristina's nervous systems in terms of information processing, cognitive neuroscientists can essentially grasp the entirety of the biochemical systems that enable Cristina's behavior. For this reason, they confidently think that they grasp the entirety of souls like Cristina.

Notwithstanding, because they confound the liberty of Cristina's qualitative experience unto being the determinant effect of biochemical circuits, we shall here observe how the scientists' behavioral descriptions fail to explain our brief illustration that features Cristina's story. Afterward, in response to our rough description of how scientists define Cristina's physiology, we may more critically submit our derivative statements, which shall substantively explain how Y'haweh's Logos manifests the emergent world, organic life, and the brain's dynamic mechanism that corresponds with Cristina's consciousness.

Cristina, wearing a towel because of the unusual chill, proceeds to touch her toe in the pool's water. She is unaware of the multiplicity of biological systems that enable her actions, like the way her brain's cerebellum enhances her ability to balance on one foot as she extends the other. Too, she is not consciously aware of the hereditary frown on her brow, which her cheering mother recognizes to be the same distinguishing expression that Cristina's father had when he focused.

As she dips her toe into the water, Cristina instantly experiences a simple stimulus-response circuit, which neurologists term a reflex arc: the extreme temperature difference between the cold water and Cristina's warm body causes the electrical field across her skin cells' membranes to change. In response, an action potential fires a signal from the sensory neurons in her toe. Interconnecting neurons in her spinal cord eventually transmit a complementing signal to her leg muscles' motor neurons. Following, the firing motor neurons cause her leg to contract; even as inhibitory neurotransmitters diffuse in her brain. While a simple circuit seemingly defines Cristina's reflex response to the cold water, Cristina's entire experience requires more than simple cause-effect circuits as an explanation.

Though Cristina bears only a slight awareness of the inhibiting mechanisms that cause her to withdraw from diving into the pool, she immediately masters her inhibitions as she aspires to win the women's 200 meter freestyle race. In a split second, she visualizes the race: her attention falls upon the efficiency of her stroke, among other critical lessons-learned from her training.

After the race starts, much of Cristina's physical exertion falls into Cristina's subconscious background: Cristina's strict diet, rest, fitness, and sheer adrenalin suffice to meet the race's physical requirements. So, Cristina only becomes consciously aware of the unexpected ways in which her body responds to her intentions. Also, she becomes aware of the relative strengths of her competitors.

At the last, Cristina wins the race. As she stands on the platform to receive a gold medal, a host of conflicting thoughts and emotions constitute her mind. Above all, Cristina feels fantastic exhilaration as she praises the Lord for her success; however, these delightful feelings become bitter-sweet, as she feels the absence of her recently deceased Father, who taught her to swim in her hometown lake. Even as she laments over her absent Father, her country's anthem reminds her of the privilege she has in representing the liberties and triumphs of her countrymen. Still, Cristina also reigns in these triumphal feelings, as she recognizes the value of upholding Christian prudence to assuage the feelings of loss that her worthy competitors must suffer. Looking at her family and friends' raucous behavior, Cristina finally satisfies her want to exclaim, as she briefly finds comfort in her loved ones' hilarity. Then again, these comforts quickly fail when she broods over her husband's seemingly unaffected demeanor. Though she notices an amiable expression on his face, she observes how his looks are rather solemn. Unfortunately, what Cristina always fails to realize and what her husband always fails to communicate is the fact that Cristina has been a champion in her husband's eyes long before she dipped her toe into the Olympic pool's cold water.

Our brief illustration, featuring Cristina's story, basically portrays the manifold complexities of the human experience. Hence, in appreciation of our human complexities, the very basis of cognitive neuroscience stands upon the recognition that human qualitative experiences, such as Cristina's, entail more than simple-circuit explanations. Although cognitive neuroscientists have not explicitly ascertained the biological correlate of Cristina's consciousness, they remain confident that they can reduce Cristina's qualitative experience to such natural explanations that they can empirically observe: once more, the cognitive neuroscientists' ability to capture the basic aspects of Cristina's conscious experience, in terms of information-processing models of the brain, encourages the scientists in their attempt to reduce the human experience to the self-sufficient, determinant processes of complex biochemical circuits.

For us to demonstrate the reasons why the scientists actually fail to grasp qualitative experiences like Cristina's, let us hypothetically continue to delineate the way in which empirical scientists would proceed to describe Cristina's Olympics experience. We can demonstrate how scientists come tantalizingly close to proving their convictions that self-sufficient physiological systems solely enable Cristina's experience.

In an attempt to describe Cristina's experience, physiologically, scientists would roughly proceed as follows: first, neurologists would employ simple cause-effect circuit interpretations to describe how Cristina's spinal cord and brain stem structures, like the pons, control the Cristina's autonomic—involuntary—systems, such as Cristina's bladder and respiratory functions. Then, under the guise of evolutionary adaptation, scientists would extrapolate from the straightforward cause-effect interpretations of the autonomic systems; and they would increasingly employ information processing models to describe the brain structures that they roughly observe to be responsible for Cristina's arousal, reasoning, and voluntary motions:

Indeed, to describe the systems that enable Cristina's voluntary motions, cognitive neuroscientists would first observe how Cristina's thalamic, neuronal nuclei perform seminal roles that contribute to the rise of Cristina's arousal states, such as Cristina's sleep and wake periods. Next, as they empirically observe how Cristina's thalamic systems are active, during conscious states; cognitive neuroscientists would observe how Cristina's thalamic-cortical-resonance patterns assist in connecting the thalamus to major brain regions, such as the cerebellum and cerebrum, which entails the basal ganglia, neocortex, and the limbic system's anterior-thalamic nuclei and hippocampus.

While they would essentially consider Cristina's thalamus to be a biochemical-circuit relay, cognitive neuroscientists would proceed in their overall attempt to reduce Cristina's conscious states to Cristina's brain's multifaceted neuronal circuitry. To achieve this end, they would consider how particular brain regions, which functionally associate with Cristina's thalamus, maintain and assemble the building blocks of Cristina's consciousness. For example, cognitive neuroscientists would consider how an inhibiting and augmenting complex of neurons comprise the brain's hippocampus, which relates to the thalamus and other systems, to function as Cristina's episodic and spatial memory centers. Likewise, they would observe how the cerebellum's neuronal complex relates to the thalamus and other brain regions to function as the refiner of Cristina's voluntary movements.

Most notably, cognitive neuroscientists would consider how the neuronal systems that comprise Cristina's cerebrum relate to Cristina's thalamus in a way that renders Cristina's cerebral-cortex—the cerebrum's outer layer—as an executive decision maker. At once, the scientists would observe how Cristina's cerebral cortex isolates and maps the sensory regions of Cristina's body. Afterward, they would observe how the neuronal complexes that comprise Cristina's basal ganglia filter the cortex's motor signals back to the thalamic systems. In this manner, the cognitive neuroscientists would assess how the basal ganglia operate as processors that enable Cristina's cerebral cortex to execute such hierarchical functions like error detection and attention control.

Lastly, as the final attempt to reduce Cristina's consciousness to mere neuronal circuitry, cognitive neuroscientists would spy how the visual and audio representation centers of Cristina's cerebral cortex relates to the brain's episodic, spatial, and emotional memory centers: specifically, the hippocampus and amygdala. By means of such considerations, cognitive neuroscientists would essentially deem Cristina's consciousness to be the evolved capacity for Cristina to render a "meta-cognitive," self-narrative and coherent perception of her behavior within a greater environment, namely the Olympics event.

In short, we may say that scientists can brilliantly demonstrate how Cristina's consciousness depends upon the biochemical and electro-chemical systems that make up Cristina's body and respective nervous systems. Nonetheless, as we have noted in our cognitive neuroscience discussion, scientists cannot entirely reduce Cristina's consciousness to being the sole product of Cristina's nervous systems because neuronal states do not entirely correspond to conscious states; therefore, Cristina's intentional experience transcends Cristina's body's thermodynamic states, which translates Cristina's immediate environment. Clearly, the incongruity between Cristina's conscious states and Cristina's neuronal states demonstrates that Cristina's thermodynamic states cannot account for the way Cristina's intentionally qualifies and transcends trillions of determinate processes that Cristina assimilates with abstract paradigms of kindred relationships, patriotism, and spiritual salvation. Ironically, Cristina's mental abstractions often subject her physiological homeostasis to peril, as Cristina subjects her body to such mental abstractions as heroism and self-sacrifice. Hence, the empirical scientists' naturalist paradigm is insufficient, because the paradigm fails to predict Cristina's conscious experience with observational exactitude.

For sure, the cognitive neuroscientists can wonderfully describe how the brain retains such mechanisms as unifying resonance patterns and excitatory and inhibitory systems; however, they cannot explicitly apprehend the dynamic mechanism that enables Cristina to exercise free qualifying choices, in a manner that overrides her excitatory, inhibitory circuits. In sum, cognitive neuroscientists fail to determine the physical convention that gives Cristina the haecceity — that is, the transcending "like-thisness" — of the first person perspective: even the transcendent viewpoint that enables her to qualify the ever changing world's ontological status with a communicable exactitude that others, like her husband, intuitively perceive. Unfortunately, this epistemological understanding still eludes empirical scientists.

To conclude our detailed illustration (of the manner in which physiological descriptions cannot entirely account for human behavior), we have only to repeat that we empathize with contemporary theorists who presume that humanity's qualitative experiences, like Cristina's, necessarily entail electromagnetic and quantum explanations. With the theorists, we recognize how aggregate electrical currents rationalize the multiplicity of neuronal, electro-chemical reactions, which entail very low currents: that is to say, we recognize that the manifold currents assume a free and particular character, as the neuronal, electro-chemical reactions fuse, amplify, stop, and divert the aggregate electrical currents. Likewise, we understand how EM waves further rationalize the aggregate electrical currents, in turn. And so, in the end, we must agree with contemporary theorists who suggest that the quantum binding of the EM waves is an ultimate and free rationalization that enables the free qualifications of Cristina's consciousness.

Although we agree with them in several respects, we can only proceed so far in our agreement with contemporary electromagnetic and quantum theories of consciousness because the theorists' naturalist approach prevents the theories from establishing sure ontological ends. In other words, with their naturalist approach, the contemporary theorists cannot possible demonstrate how Cristina makes *a priori* judgments that apprehend the totality of materials systems: a totality that the thermodynamic, natural-force-laws disallow the systems' constituents from apprehending in and of themselves.

Immanuel's Law – the Critical Context of the Logos' Truth Functional Form

Unmistakably, a chief aim of our putting forth our illustration, portraying Cristina's story, is to highlight how secular scientists' physiological descriptions fall short of reducing our qualitative experience to biochemical circuits. As we have mentioned earlier, secular scientists' successful employment of the scientific method proves to be the scientists' greatest bane as modern science's dramatic achievements overshadow empirical science's shortcomings. By and large, science's great achievements cause the empirical scientists to ignore the crucial fact that they have not resolved the every-present rationalist-empiricist debate: a resolution that is the gateway to closing the mind-matter explanatory gap.

For instance, we noted at the beginning of our surveys that scientists necessarily appeal to preexisting nature-force-laws without their determining why a natural order exists instead of chaos. Once more, the scientists do not make an epistemological determination that addresses how they can establish the emergent order's ontological end, which the natural-force-laws facilitate. Essentially, like rationalist philosophers and Christian theologians, the scientists appeal to the universality of laws and principles without their demonstrably answering the utmost ontological question "why ('to what ultimate conclusion')?"

The greatest effect of our illustrating how the scientists' natural explanations fail to explain humanity's qualitative experiences is that we have secured a more critical context to present our derivative statements. We introduced our orthodox judgment's theological and empirical statements by recognizing how the 19th Century philosopher Immanuel Kant aptly identified and almost resolved the rationalist-empiricists debate. We described how Kant roughly captured an epistemological understanding of our finite-knowledge-structure: first, we saw how he objectively employed independent principles to establish many universal claims of the rationalist philosophers and Christian theologians. In particular, we observed the way Kant demonstrated how our supposed apperception of space and time gives us the judgment to apprehend the metaphysical order that all physical phenomena conform to. Along these lines, we then saw the way Kant described how our universal grasp of space and time presents the metaphysical context in which scientists can empirically observe physical objects emerge under such natural-force-laws like the permanence of substance, within successions of cause and effect. In a word, we understood how Kant's appeal to our purported capacity to apprehend an absolute space and time gives us the qualitative freedom to rationalize objects; though determinant principals and laws govern the emergent world and thereby structure our perceptions. In this manner, we appreciated how Kant employed independent principles to describe qualitative experiences, like Cristina's.

Having appreciated the way Kant grasped the rationalist-empiricist disparity, the initial context of our orthodox judgment stands upon our recognition of Immanuel Kant's brilliant epistemological descriptions of our supervening and free finite-knowledge-structure. At the same time, the very necessity of Immanuel's Law is recognition of the shortsightedness of Kant and other succeeding philosophers: our judgment necessarily responds to the fact that rationalist theories fail before empirical scientists because Kant, like contemporary phenomenologists, held matter-of-fact views of spacetime and the natural-force-laws.

We have seen how current understandings of general relativity and quantum physics have handedly repudiated Kant's Newtonian notions of absolute space and time. Also, we have extensively detailed how cognitive neuroscientists dismiss the free and supervening mind as a mere fortuitous epiphenomenon of evolutionary adaptation.

So, despite the audacity of our initial quest, our illustration has presented an even more critical context for the manner in which Immanuel's Law shall define how our qualitative freedom derives from Y'haweh. Our illustration has demonstrably demarcated the determinant bio-chemical systems, which enable the mind, from the unidentified dynamic mechanism that substantively constitute the qualitative and supervening freedom of the mind, itself. Our illustration has demonstrated how the mind's dynamic mechanism retains the acute capacity to apprehend universal physical conventions, in a way that enables the mind to abstract and prevail upon an untold number of determinant physical systems; as the mind achieves its purposeful ends. Like so, our illustration has demonstrated that the body's material systems are insufficient to account for the mind's dynamic capacity. As an outcome, our illustration has justified our pursuit of a metaphysical explanation that addresses the means through which the undiscovered dynamic mechanism entails unique quantum and electromagnetic aspects, other than the quantum and electromagnetic, determinant systems that comprise our environment. Principally, the critical context that our illustration sets for Immanuel's Law is that the illustration compels us to seek objective explanations for our interdependent relationship with an asymmetric world: namely, a world that Immanuel Kant could not grasp with Newtonian understandings of a self-sufficient creation.

As Immanuel's Law, our derivative statements, seeks to rationalize our theological and empirical statements with independent principles; we may now list three critical aims that our illustration secures for Immanuel's Law as follows: our first statement's critical aim is to resolve the conflicting domains of the rationalist approach to justifying our knowledge and the empiricist approach to justifying our knowledge, respectively. In particular, our first statement's critical aim is to establish how the observable world derives from Y'haweh's free ontological standing; while our second statement's critical aim is to establish an epistemological understanding of our finite-knowledge-structure's temporally free ontological standing; especially in regards to the structure's supervening physicality, as well as the structure's interdependence upon the existential world.

Rest assured, our resolving the rationalist and empiricist domains to reconcile our theological and empirical statements will afford us tremendous abilities: we will not only be able to assess how the worlds' determinate systems derive from Y'haweh's free ontological standing. We will also be able to distinguish our minds' temporally free physicality from the worlds' determinate cause-effect, physical systems. Following, we will be able to determine how all things derive from Y'haweh's absolute. In this way, we will then be able to realize our third derivative statement's critical aim: we will be capable of securing the objective means to corroborate biblical orthodoxy beyond the tautological and dogmatic proclamations of the Church's creeds. In effect, once we affirm our third derivative statement, we will effectively unite rational philosophy and empirical science with biblical orthodoxy.

Immanuel's Law – Normalizing a World of Tropes

The aforementioned aims that we have set for our orthodox judgment, Immanuel's Law, can bear no greater significance, because Immanuel's Law's realizing the critical aims advances us down the Landscape of Truth. In other words, we conclude that neither rationalist philosophers and empirical scientists nor theologians can obtain an ontological understanding of truth unless they resolve the successive aims of Immanuel's Law's derivative statements.

Curiously, we cannot resolve our first statement's critical aim until we resolve the time-honored question of the trope: a word that derives from the Greek word tropos, which means to alter or turn. Intriguing is the fact that the problem of the trope concept proves to be a key example of how rationalist philosophers, empirical scientists, and theologians fail to establish a true ontological understanding of the world and our relation to it.

All realizing varying degrees of success, the respective practitioners of many disciplines, ranging from the arts to the natural sciences, employ the term trope to describe slight changes to concepts that enjoy normal—that is, universal—recognition. For instance, scholars of literature easily recognize the change of a phrase from its original meaning as a metaphorical trope. Howbeit, practitioners of the natural sciences find the employment of the trope concept more challenging: empirical scientists, who employ the trope concept to denote particular instances of a property, wrestle with the concept because the acceptance of a phenomenon's ontological standing as an instance of a property suggests the preexistence of universal properties that the scientists cannot empirically corroborate.

In response to empirical scientists' denial of our encountering instances of preexisting, universal designs; rationalist philosophers and theologians maintain that critical thought cannot emerge unless one accepts *a priori* categorizations, unconditionally. As we have noted above, Immanuel Kant, himself, held that our imagining a creator's preexisting design intent is useful, even though Kant denied the possibility of our proving the creator's existence.

We have repeatedly observed why empirical scientists ignore the theologians' admonitions. We have seen the ways in which scientists have demonstrated how Christian theologians do not have an objective proof for the way Y'haweh rationally expresses the world and its interdependent relationship with our finite-knowledge-structure. All the same, we have also discussed, in our scientific survey, how modern physics is the sole result of 20th Century physicists' necessary acceptance that a quantum-based rational order has a universal standing that enables the ordered boundaries and degrees of the observable world. To be specific, we observed the great dilemma that classical physicists faced when their insufficient empirical observations of the microscopic world ultimately yielded incalculable, infinite-sum measurements. Further still, we even saw the crossroads that classical physicists faced when the Christian Max Planck and the agnostic Albert Einstein resolved the infinite-sum measurements after they discovered how energy universally comes in a discrete constant of proportionality, *a priori*. At that juncture, we then noted how contemporary physicists faced a choice: as one alternative, we recognized how physicists could choose to make more accurate—even normalized—predictions by mathematically reconciling empirical observations with Planck's proportional constant. As the other alternative, we saw how physicists could choose to heed the classical physicists' concerns that the new quantum physicists' observations were not purely objective; because the quantum physicists' rationalizing empirical observations with Planck's constant, effectively incorporated the rational observer into all empirical observations.

To the chagrin of the classical physicists, we later observed how quantum physicists have successfully employed Planck's constant to establish the rational conventions of the microscopic world that one cannot directly observe: we saw how quantum physicists have not only employed Planck's constant to establish an objective understanding of the atom's subatomic structure; but also employed Planck's constant to establish the mathematical form that reconciles fields of force with Albert Einstein's macroscopic, natural-force-law, $E=mc^2$.

All told, we surveyed how quantum physicists have secured a Standard Model of the creation by extrapolating from Planck's constant such mathematical forms that accurately predict the expanding and converging fields of force that relate to the atom. Yet, as soon as we detailed the shortfall of contemporary scientists' Standard Model, we finally appreciated the classical physicists' concern that the quantum physicists' reckless incorporating of the rational observer would undermine science's objective perspective of the world. In point of fact, we observed the way in which contemporary physicists fail to comprehend the ontological standing of macroscopic solid states that assume such unique qualities that seemingly render microscopic particles as virtual. And so, though we regarded the brilliance of the contemporary science's Standard Model of creation, we finally understood that empirical scientists' naturalist approach renders their conceptions of a Standard Model as functionally indeterminate.

As a consequence of modern science's shortfall, our orthodox judgment, Immanuel's law, must not only recognize the necessity of contemporary physicists' reconciling of their observations with energy's proportional constant: indeed, we must not only recognize the manner in which the physicists seek normalized assessments of the macroscopic world that we experience. Immanuel's Law, must also satisfy classical physicists' position that we must secure objectivity beyond human invention.

To achieve science's sought-after objectivity, we must also secure Immanuel's Law's second critical aim of closing the mind-matter explanatory gap like so: we must cast the quantum and electromagnetic theories of consciousness in a way that explains how the Logos enables our mind's dynamic mechanism to normalize microscopic elements into the macroscopic world that further instigates the stream of our conscious thoughts. In this manner, we can forgo the mere tautological statements of the theologians and rationalist philosophers. Likewise, we can forgo empirical scientists' ridiculous macroscopic explanations for consciousness, such as consciousness' being the sole outcome evolutionary fitness: we can demonstrate how evolutionary explanations cannot possibly explain how the mind possesses quantum states that render a normalized macroscopic world.

In particular, we will apprehend how our quantum and electromagnetic based finite-knowledge-structure derives from Y'haweh's power-set, in a way that distinguishes creation's underlining physical convention that the mind's dynamic mechanism employs to translate contingent perceptions under universal conceptions. Then once we grasp the physical convention that enables us to grasp universals, we will possess the objective means to qualify the ontological standing of contingent events as representational tropes; especially as we objectively recognize how contingent events enable the haecceity of our first-person perspective, within a normalized world. Finally, after we objectively establish the manner in which the Logos enables our mind's dynamic mechanism to render a normalized world, we will establish the justified-true-belief of our finite-knowledge-structure; especially as we distinguish how the Logos confers universal concepts that encourage the analogues of humanity's first-person, perspective.

Our empirical science surveys and subsequent introductions to our orthodox judgment may have seemed tedious to the reader. Even so, we have only sought to demonstrate the important fact that theological, philosophical, and scientific understandings are incomplete without an objective determination that concerns how we apprehend the ontological standing of all contingent things under the Logos' necessary (*a priori*) universal conventions.

As we just discussed above, the unavoidable mind-matter question leads to the questions of universals and tropes. For instance, if we, like scientists, employ the concept "renormalization" to state that our mind's dynamic mechanism normalizes energy's microscopic manifestations to render the observable, macroscopic world; we, like scientists, will psychologically rely upon the "pure (even spirited) idea" of preexisting archetypes, which we psychologically deem to be ontologically normative: we will unavoidably consider the appearing phenomena to be representational tropes of the psychological archetypes.

We saw how Christian theologians consider the world to be in a fallen state that contrasts the spiritual richness of the world's material archetype, the Garden Eden. Likewise, we noted how rationalist philosophers, like Plato and Aristotle, have categorically accepted the preexistence of necessary conventions; whereby the philosophers have conceived conceptual terms, such as potentiality and energeia, to describe how physical phenomena come into possible states of being. In this manner, we saw how the rationalist philosophers set the conceptual framework of modern physics.

In point of fact, in our empirical science statements, we recognize how both theologians and philosophers often find encouragement from the fact that the thermodynamics, natural-force-laws reinforce the understanding that creation has an asymmetric nature. Because thermodynamics' second law captures the way material systems never fully reconstitute themselves, Christian theologians readily view the second law as being indicative of a fallen world from a more perfect state. Similarly, because rationalist philosophers have historically framed or inspired the concepts that empirical scientists use to describe thermodynamic systems; most rationalist philosophers continue to deem their deductive reasoning method as the necessary approach to critical knowledge.

Notwithstanding, we also recognize that because the theologians do not submit an objective explanation, concerning how our spiritual downfall materially manifests into the current world's physical conventions, scientists disdain any religious interpretations of the natural-force-laws, like the thermodynamics laws. To be sure, we understand that instead of viewing the world in terms of a sin induced downfall, scientists more practically observe the world's thermodynamic systems in terms of states of stability verses states of instability.

Also from our lessons-learned, we observe the fact that though rationalist philosophers have framed most of modern science's conceptual models, empirical scientists necessarily question the scope of rationalist theories. Empirical scientists understand that the weakness of rationalism is that rationalists inherently consign all things under teleological perspectives. In other words, scientists understand that rationalists (either consciously or unconsciously) conclude all things under purposeful ends. Resolutely holding true to the very basis of empiricism, empirical scientists maintain that one cannot bind purposefulness to any particular observed cause; although we bear the disposition to conflate our sense of purposefulness to perceived causes.

So, at large, we must recognize the accountability and intellectual sobriety that science's methodical investigation demands of theology and philosophy. We must satisfy empirical scientists' want for objectivity. As we now pursue the critical aims of Immanuel's Law, our derivative statements must particularly show how Y'haweh's Logos enables us to apprehend a normalized material world; as the Logos enables us to reconcile representational tropes under the truth-functional-form's universals.

Immanuel's Law – First Derivative Statement

Now, we begin Immanuel's Law's first derivative statement: we proceed in the critical context of our adapting independent principles to detail how the Logos' truth-functional-form expresses and supervenes upon the observable world. In this manner, we advance to resolve the rationalist-empiricist debate. Pursuant to the first statement's critical context is our employing axiomatic, *a priori*-synthetic judgments to establish, first, the syntactical causality of the Logos' truth-functional-form; second, the impossibility of a Big Bang event; and, third, the manner in which the Logos expresses ontological relationships over the impoverished world.

To instigate our description, concerning how the Logos' truth-functional-form speaks out Y'haweh's absolute and ineffable being, we cast our theological descriptions of Y'haweh's spiritual synthesis with the power-set in the appreciable terms of independent principles. In our theological statements, we conclude that Y'haweh is a spiritual synthesis of omnipotence, omnipresence, and omniscience. In few words, we conclude that Y'haweh's state of being omnipotent means that Y'haweh is all power without physical constraints. Hence, we conclude that he is omnipresent—that is, Y'haweh is all present intrinsic being, without dependence upon existential dimensions. Then we conclude that Y'haweh is omniscient—that is, Y'haweh is the sentient, centrality of judgment, constituting all knowledge, without existential dependency upon analysis or concept. Ultimately, we conclude that Y'haweh's omniscience signifies the infinite union of mind with power. At once, we resolve that the absolute abstraction of Y'haweh's spiritual synthesis is substantive in regards to Y'haweh's encompassing all the existential attributes of any-possible-world. At the same time, we determine that the absolute abstraction of Y'haweh's spiritual synthesis is metaphysically free; in regards to the appearance of Y'haweh's intrinsic will as a metaphysical priority: namely, an absolute causal priority that one may readily observe as one witnesses how the existential physicality of any-possible-world adheres to Y'haweh's absolute state. All told, in our theological statements, we conclude that the intrinsic—self-sufficient—nature of Y'haweh's totality is both of any-possible-world and other than any-possible-world; as Y'haweh's metaphysical totality constitutes the only free state of ontological being in itself.

To cast further Y'haweh's totality in appreciable terms, we appreciate Y'haweh's omniscience, omnipresence, and omnipotence as the absolute positional perspective, momentum, and potentiality that transcend any sensible correlation with the world's determinate, physical systems. Hence, we comprehend Y'haweh's synthesis with the power-set as pure spirit (that is, the prevalent first-person possessive sense—I AM—that equates will); in the sense that Y'haweh metaphysically transcends and prevails upon any-possible-world's physical correlations.

To begin an understanding of the syntactical causality of Y'haweh's Logos, we begin to consider how the Logos' truth-functional-form expresses Y'haweh's absolute being as follows: first, we understand that to express YHWH—even absolute positional perspective, momentum, and potentiality (transcending any effable or sensible correlation)—is the mitigate ontological identity; which we sensibly appreciate as the transfer of temporal states across specific physical conventions to maintenance temporal perspectives. Thus, to *lego* (that is, to count out Y'haweh's intrinsic sense)—is to exist (that is, to stand out, to come into being over specific states) wherein we witness the Logos' truth-functional-form when the impoverished physical systems of any-possible-world come into syntactically allowed states under greater ontological relationships that reflect YHWH's absolute.

Since Y'haweh's absolute ontological being is one with the power-set, the asymmetric extension of any-possible-world's impoverished energies is the extension of the Logos expression of Y'haweh's person—an expression who, like energy's inextricable relation to the power-set, is of Y'haweh's totality but other than Y'haweh's absolute. We, therefore, understand that the Logos is a synthetic-analytic truth-functional-form: we understand that the Logos is a synthesis because the Logos substantively speaks out Y'haweh's power-set; moreover, we comprehend that the Logos is a synthesis in respect to the Logos' being a free physicality because the Logos' expressive form transcends any specific determinant physical system. At the same time, we consider that the Logos is analytical: we consider that the Logos extends as the inextricable union of the qualifying, quantifying, relating, and modulating natural laws with any possible force; even as Y'haweh is one with the power-set. And so, we further see the Logos' truth-functional-form as the Logos adapts energy's manifestations as operatives that express Y'haweh's first-person ontological identity.

Essentially, we understand that all natural-force-laws constitute the syntax of the Logos' truth-functional-form. We hold that the laws have their substantive being in the Logos' mitigating of the continuity of ontological relationships that reflect Y'haweh's absolute being. To be specific, we recognize that in order for the Logos to express Y'haweh's free, possessive standing above the world's determinant systems; the Logos' assumes a free, spirited physicality that both physically and syntactically regulate the world's determinant systems. We so recognize that as the Logos speaks out

Y'haweh's spiritual synthesis, the Logos speaks out an asymmetric creation: the Logos' synthetic-analytic order correlates specific relationships between physical phenomena and their attributes. In this way, we observe that the Logos maintains the continuity of ontological identity over the creation's impoverished properties that voice perspectives as the properties universalize under the schema of the Logos truth-functional-form.

Furthermore, while we recognize how the Logos' synthetic-analytic order consigns creation's determinant physical systems to subsume under Y'haweh's power-set and while we recognize how the Logos comprises the natural-force-laws as the dynamic syntax that governs any-possible-force to mitigate unto us the continuity of ontological identity; we proceed with the capacity to transcend rational philosophers and empirical scientists' mathematical limitations. Similar to Immanuel Kant's employment of spatiotemporal descriptions of our finite-knowledge-structure (instead of Kant's employment of insufficient predicate calculus, which reduces our finite-knowledge-structure's transcendence to impoverished variables); we recognize that we cannot use mathematics alone to justify our knowledge-structure's perceptions of the world. We appreciate the generally acknowledged understanding that mathematicians cannot employ mathematical variables to justify the mathematical systems that utilize the variables; moreover, we recognize the well-known understanding that mathematicians cannot analytically describe the power-set as merely the analytical set of all sets.

Transcending the scientists' mathematical limitations, we proceed to detail the basis upon which the Logos' truth-functional-form syntactically causes the extended creation: we start by reemphasizing the understanding that Y'haweh's totality—that is, Y'haweh's first-person and absolute being's synthesis with the power-set—is both of and transcends not only the dynamics of all forces, but also the emergent ontological relationships that the natural-force-laws syntactically effect. In this manner, we advance our judgment by detailing how the world's causality is equally dependent upon the

Logos' substantive expression of Y'haweh's power-set as well as the Logos' syntactical expression of the natural-force-laws.

Thus, because contemporary physics demonstrates that creation's energies extend in discrete proportions that relegate matter's magnitudes to stand relative to light speed; we describe energy's adherence to the Logos' truth-functional-form by describing how energy's quantized and relative aspects adhere to the rationalists' metaphysical categories—quality, quantity, relation, and modality. By adapting quantum physics and relativity principles, we proceed to describe how the rationalists' categories are the syntactical attributes of the natural-force-laws: once more, we understand that the laws, themselves, constitute the actual syntax of the Logos' truth-functional-form; which again expresses Y'haweh's absolute being and power-set. In particular, we assess how the energy's quantized and relative extensions adhere to the syntactical conventions of the categories, to the effect that energy's manifestations are not the consequences of linear causality, though creation linearly manifests as an effect.

To demonstrate how the categories syntactically effect energy's manifestations, we proceed to substantiate and redefine the philosophers' metaphysical categories like so: to begin, we make some passing observations concerning the categories that the rationalists identify as quantity and quality. To gauge how the Logos reconciles energy's quantifications with Y'haweh's power-set, we simply recall that the Christian physicist Max Planck empirically observed that the creation's scaled quantities of energy are possible because energy exists under a discrete constant of proportionality that modulates and so mitigates energy. In the same manner in which the ancient Greek philosopher Thales understood the logos as a measure of proportionality, we distinguish energy's proportionality as a syntactical attribute of the Logos' truth-functional-form.

In regards to the philosophers' metaphysical category of quality, we appreciate that the synthetic qualification of energy's discrete manifestations is possible because energy's discrete proportionality projects the unified power-set that is spirited as the power-set transcends any specific physicality; even as the power-set is of energy's analytical manifestations, while synthetically transcending energy's manifestations. For example, we distinguish the qualifying syntactical relationship between discrete manifestations of energy and Y'haweh's power-set. We recognize that from Y'haweh's free possessive being, the Logos syntactically qualifies the creation's determinant physical systems with the subsequent natural-force-law: creation's converging and expanding exchanges of force syntactically relate to light's photon to the extent that creation's energies stand in analytical measure to the absolute and synthetic power necessary for the physical systems to breach light-speed.

Besides our recognizing the syntactical character of the quantity-quality categories, we determine that the syntactical character of the relation-modality categories particularly render creation's linear effects. The relation-modality categories capture the way the laws project potential and allowed states beyond the impoverished world; to the end that the laws exemplify how the Logos mitigates the continuity of ontological identity through the regularity of interdependent relationships that emerge, despite specific magnitudinous events, within spacetime.

For instance, we recognize that essence of all natural-force-laws is a functional relation between distinct quantitative things; in which case the modality of the law is syntactical because the law's modality governs the expression of alternative operational values that the law's functional relation allows. As a consequence, the potentiality of the law transcends the circumstance of the world's impoverished events.

Exhibiting the reality that the Logos' natural-force-laws instantly unite with and freely transcend all possible manifestations of energy that extend from Y'haweh's power-set, we begin to see the modal syntax of the Logos' expression in the fact that energy's emitting under a proportional constant prohibits us from isolating any magnitudinous event to a single point within spacetime. In our classical and contemporary science surveys we note how scientists observe incomprehensible measurements, such as infinite magnitudes of compiled charges, when they attempt to reduce a causal force to a single point within spacetime. For this cause, we understand that no magnitudinous event within spacetime can be the sole causal force of an observable effect. Like so, we understand that true substantive causality is metaphysically syntactical, even a free physicality.

Furthermore, we see that measured instances of magnitudes in spacetime have equal ontological standing with the potential quantum states that the proportional constant allocates. For this reason, we employ the proportional constant to rationalize the events that we spy to be either a converging exchange of subatomic forces or an expanding exchange of force between fields of space.

We even see the modal syntax of the Logos' expression in the fact that subatomic exchanges of force occur as a consequence of allowed digital-like relations between specific quantum states of no certain position and momentum within spacetime. For instance, rather than the classical notion that force exchanges result from certain levels of volume, rapidity, or intensity; we understand that the subatomic exchanges of force result from the discrete energy frequencies. Our scientific surveys detail the way in which atoms absorb light, according to discrete light frequencies, regardless of the light's volume or intensity. With this understanding, we conclude that the governing law that digitally relates the quantum states is spirited; in the sense that the law is a syntactical supervenience that is a free physicality because the law is not an effect of the determinate systems within spacetime. In the end, we recognize that natural-force-laws digitally supervene upon the world, as they syntactically structure the Logos' truth-functional-form as it mitigates Y'haweh absolute being.

We finally glean the *a priori*-synthetic judgment that summarizes how the syntactical causality of the Logos' truth-functional-form extends the creation: because causality is syntactical and only metaphysically unified and dynamic within Y'haweh's power-set, we understand that the world's linear progression is an identity-dependent, modal, and effectual appearance of causality. We, in fact, comprehend that the progressive world is an asymmetric condition of impoverished physical systems' adapting to the *a priori* quantum states that the syntactical natural-force-laws digitally allocate and not linearly allocate at any one instance in spacetime. We essentially recognize that because the Logos' synthetic-analytic order consigns the natural-force-laws to bear syntactical, causal priority with the Logos' dynamic expression of the power-set; the advent of impoverished world is not entirely a linear event. Instead, to some extent, the advent is an appearance of correlating operations. Afterward, the creation's linear progression ensues as the impoverished world continually adapts to allotted states.

In the light of our establishing that the Logos syntactically causes the extended creation, we proceed to describe why the scientists' naturalist conception of the Big Bang event is impossible: first, from our science surveys, we recollect how scientists quantify the four forces that comprise the creation. We recall that our surveys roughly describe how the scientists distinguish the attracting gravitational force; the repulsive electromagnetic force; the strong subatomic converging force (which converts subatomic particle-fields into simpler and more stable particle-fields); and the weak subatomic force (which mediates subatomic decay).

Describing the mathematical structure in which the forces interact within spacetime, our surveys also detail how physicists categorize the respective force-exchanges between particles fields: the repulsive electron particle-field among other particle-fields that share similar properties, the physicists categorize as leptons; while the converging fields like those that compose the atomic nuclei's neutrons and protons, the physicists categories as hadrons, which entail baryons and mesons, depending upon the quark configurations.

In regards to the actual exchange of force between particle-fields, our surveys detail how the physicists categorize the particle-fields, themselves, as fermions to denote that fermion particle-fields do not at once occupy the same quantum state. Then to describe the manner in which the particle-fields affect one another over distances, our survey notes how physicists categorize each particle-field type as having an accompanying force-carrier particle that the physicists term a boson: that is, a particle that groups with other bosons to occupy the same quantum states.

Furthermore, our survey notes how physicists distinguish the force-carrier particle that translates the electromagnetic forces as the photon, and our survey distinguishes the other force-carrier particles that translate the strong subatomic force that holds the atoms together, as well as the weak force-carrier particles that govern atomic decay. Finally, our surveys conclude by describing how scientists make the dubious postulation that a singular Big Bang event necessarily occurred, having enough energy to produce the heavy particle-fields that the strong forces disallow our direct observance of.

Though we recognize that greater energies are necessary to produce the heavy particle-fields, we find the scientists' conception of the Big Bang event to be problematic because the scientists recklessly ignore the precedence of the natural-force-laws' syntactical and analytical qualifications. The scientists' conception of the Big Bang is that of an unparalleled expansion of energy that is nevertheless not an infinite expansion of energy. Like so, they unknowingly retain a classical physics world view in their conceptions of the Big Bang event: psychologically retaining the prejudice that physical systems are self-sufficient unto themselves, the scientists run afoul of their recognition that any finite amount of energy entails mathematical symmetries that natural explanations fail to explain the origin, thereof. As they consider the singular Big Bang event as a massive (though not infinite) expansion of energy, the scientists immediately face the question of infinite regress: finite quantities of things that are mathematically appreciable become mathematical variables that physicists cannot employ to describe a variable set of all variable sets. The Big Bang's quantitative set becomes yet another quantity. Then, instantly, the mathematics compels physicists to postulate preceding universes and numerous dimensions, among other conclusions that are impossible to substantiate. In this way, the physicists' conception of a Big Bang event is functionally indeterminate, in respect to the event's being inappreciable. As a consequence, the physicists' reckoning of the creation as issuing from the Big Bang event is functionally indeterminate though the creation seemingly appears to derive from the event and though the physicists can mathematically interpret the behavior of some phenomena under the Big Bang model. Still, the scientists' categorical regard for the Big Bang event turns into functionally indeterminate dogma as their conception fails to answer such questions as the cause for energy's emission under a constant of proportionality, as well as the emergence of macroscopic phase transitions regardless of variable quantum states.

We avoid the folly of the empirical scientists' envisioning a finite—though massive—Big Bang event. Unlike the scientists, we do not accept the functionally indeterminate mathematical models that suggest an untold number of preceding universes, to the end that the mathematical models that quantify the progressive world, in respect to the event, are also functionally indeterminate.

We draw a stark contrast to the scientists' dubious conception as we advance the Logos' truth-functional-form. Specifically, we recognize the syntactical causality of the Logos' expression.

A detailed example of the way that the Logos expresses energy's manifestations to convey the ontological relationships that reflect Y'haweh's being is as follows: we understand that all creation's energies that particle-field decays emit cannot capture the infinite energy of the power-set. In addition, we appreciate that the actual strong hadron force exchanges between converging fermion particle-fields and the lepton force exchanges between expanding fermion particle-fields do not occur within normalized spacetime; therefore, we understand that all force exchanges, which yield observable and normal manifestations of energy, are syntactical: the force exchanges merely demarcate and mitigate absolute power without equating it at any period within spacetime. As a result, we understand that no single event in spacetime bears causality unto itself. For instance, all boson force-carrier particle-fields invariantly relate to the photon force-carrier particle-fields to form the normal and periodic relationships of spacetime. Thus, only the general syntactical form of correlating force exchanges projects the power-set's infinite energy and so unite the spacetime schema; to wit, we see that infinite energy is necessary to increase the momentum of the aggregate lepton and hadron particle-field masses beyond light speed.

Because we cannot reduce the atomic structure's converging forces and the atomic structure's absorption and emission of radiation to exact points within spacetime; we understand the atomic converging-expanding force structure to be nested mathematical properties that interdependently project the power-set's ontological being. By understanding the atomic converging-expanding forces as nested mathematical properties and by understanding the atom's absorption and emission of radiation as nested mathematical properties; we proceed to detail how the atom's mathematical properties effect a normalized world, whilst the properties universalize in their projection of the power-set. Forgoing further descriptions of the particle decay and force exchanges that constitute the strong conversion forces within the atomic nuclei's protons and neutrons; we more importantly consider the following: we observe that the strong forces' mathematical properties relate to the expanding electrons' photon force-exchanges in such a way that the electrons maintain syntactically structured orbits around the nuclear protons and neutrons. The syntactical structuring of the electrons consists of specific quantized energy levels; quantized shapes of spacetime that electrons occupy; magnitudinous orientation of spacetime zones in which allotted force-exchanges occur; and finally quantized allowances for electron pairing within shared energy levels. The significance of the syntactical structuring of electron orbits is the fact that the structuring dictates how atoms unite with other atoms to form composite ionic compounds, molecules, and compound molecules; to the effect that the compounds, molecules, and compound molecules stand upon syntactical causes rather than classical notions of linear causality within spacetime.

We, therefore, observe how the mathematical properties of the atoms, compounds, and molecules universalize in their projecting of the power-set, as the atomic structure emits and absorbs specific energy levels of photons. What is of the utmost importance is that we observe how the photon's specific energy levels rationalize the quantum states of the atoms, compounds, and molecules. We then see that regular magnitudinous relationships emerge that often transcend the syntactical specificity of atoms, compounds, and molecules. We in fact observe these transcendent magnitudinous relationships to be the atomic properties that we catalogue in the periodic table of the fundamental elements. Too, we observe that the transcendent magnitudinous relationships enable scientists, philosophers, and Christian theologians to generalize the relationships with classical mechanics, determinant judgments, and even orthodox doctrine, respectively.

So rather than repeating the mistake of regarding the emergent properties as the result of classical notions of causality, we observe how each property that results from ongoing force-exchanges is a trope of a myriad of potential quantum states and subsequent macroscopic events that the Logos truth-functional-form syntactically allots; even as the form mitigates the continuity of ontological identity over the specificity of quantized, syntactical structures. To be specific, we observe that because every atomic, compound, and molecular state is a trope of potential and allotted quantized states; the atomic, compound, and molecular states perennially exist in states of entropy: that is, they exist in directed states that perennially subsume under *a priori* allotted, electron orbital energies, volumes, and pairings. And so, despite the atomic, compound, and molecular entropic states; we observe that prevailing magnitudinous, relationships persist over the syntactical specificity of the atom, as the photon force-exchange registers the atomic, compound, and molecular entropic states with the photon energy level shifts; which are not entropic, because the shifts adhere to discrete light frequencies, instead of adhering to a classical notion of linear energy loss. In the end, the emergent magnitudinous relationships and requisite properties flicker the Shekinah of Y'haweh's absolute ontological standing over the specificities of any possible-world.

In fact, we see the Logos' supervening expression as the existential creation's essence: the essential and intelligible relationship between phenomena and their respective properties, despite the specific syntactical identities that emerge at each instance in spacetime. In choice words, we see the Logos' supervening expression as the rational continuity of atomic, conventional, geometric, and mechanical identities arises within space-time, despite the fact that the material conventions inescapably possess variant quantum states at variant energy levels.

The Logos' synthetic-analytic order—enabling, first, the proportional quantum states that the Logos' syntactical structure allows and, second, the impoverished material systems with energies that the Logos scales by the power-set—is the extension of an asymmetric creation. The asymmetric relationship between the potential quantum states and the normalized world is a rationalizing relationship: a relationship in which the Logos' syntactical structure supervenes upon the impoverished world as the synthetic force of law.

Having used our theological understanding of the Logos' truth-functional-form to unite the rationalists' categories with empirical science's quantum physics and relativity, we confidently proceed to distinguish another *a priori*-synthetic understanding that exemplifies that we have reconciled the rationalists and empiricists' functionally indeterminate understandings. We now consider that instead of just accepting the existence of the thermodynamic laws of energy's conservation and physical systems' inability to reconstitute themselves, we conclude that the laws do not only apply to the material nature of physical systems. We conclude that the thermodynamics laws equally apply to the syntactical expression of physical systems, as the systems uphold the continuity of identity from Y'haweh's absolute power-set. We derive this synthetic conclusion as we reaffirm that true causality is metaphysical:

In reference to the thermodynamics laws, we reemphasize that subatomic exchanges of force are syntactical as the forces statistically allocate the unique, transferable macroscopic states that normalize, despite variable quantum states. What follows is that a syntactical understanding of thermodynamics' first law of energy's conservation recognizes the reality that each material instance in spacetime is a synthesis of a myriad of invariantly related conventions that subatomic forces digitally allocate, though the potential conventions are not proportionally present at that instance; therefore, the syntactical understanding of energy's conservation equates the notion of conservation with the mathematical invariance that effects the emergence of a normalized world.

As a direct consequence of thermodynamics' first law, a syntactical understanding of thermodynamics' second law recognizes the reality that each material instance is not a self-sufficient system: the instance is a trope, entailing particular quantum states and subsequent properties that universalize and so speak out the instance's particular perspective, which exemplifies the myriad of potential conventions. Thus, the syntactical understanding of entropy recognizes that the impoverishment of each physical event, as every event subsumes under a greater functional form.

We are finally confident that we have achieved the primary aims of Immanuel's Law first derivative statement. Our first statement objectively demonstrates that rational philosophers cannot establish the justification for their belief in a metaphysical reality unless they distinguish how the categories' derive from Y'haweh's power-set, in a manner that allows the philosophers to make predictions. Likewise, our first statement objectively demonstrates that empirical scientists cannot establish the justification for their belief that they can discern how a self-sufficient world obeys natural-force-laws, in a manner enables them to establish how all things derive from purposeless processes. Intriguingly, the statement demonstrates that the proportioned exchange of forces, appearing within spacetime, disallows single events to derive the modal alternatives that preceding or succeeding exchanges of force adhere to, beyond the spacetime's continuum. While the statement recognizes a progressive world that evolves through energy transformations (such as the modal breakdown of heavy particles), the statement comprehends that the transformations necessarily adhere to the digital states that the Logos' syntactical form allocates.

As we acknowledge the reality of the Logos' truth-functional-form, we view the world as it is in truth. Where naturalists see purposeless, self-sufficient processes enigmatically manifesting from an inexplicable event, we see operative elements adhering to the greater functional expression of absolute being, YHWH. Where naturalists merely see the utility of scientific knowledge for invention, we see the Logos' mitigating transferable states that we abstractly utilize to establish our finite perspectives, despite the scarcities of our environments. Where scientists see nature's false-starts and accidents, we see an impoverished world that incites the ascension of human knowledge unto the liberty of Y'haweh's absolute. Where they see science, we see Logos.

The ultimate consequence of Immanuel's Law's first statement is the necessity of the second derivative statement's critical aim of closing the mind-matter explanatory gap. By definition, our finite-knowledge-structure is not able to grasp an infinite understanding of creation. Nevertheless, Immanuel's Law's second derivative statement now proceeds to ascertain how the Logos derives the minds temporal freedom, which enables the mind to transcend creation's determinant systems and grasp the Logos' essential, beatific order that the thermodynamics laws and creation's ontological values express. Specifically, at this juncture, the second statement now proceeds to establish how the Logos employs creation's determinate physical systems to derive the free physicality of our mind's dynamic mechanism: a mechanism that is identity dependent upon the world, even as it temporally transcends the world to maintenance its temporally free possessive sense.

Immanuel's Law – Second Derivative Statement

We begin Immanuel's Law second derivative statement as an outcome of Immanuel's Law's first derivative statement. The first statement reconciles the rationalist-empiricist debate. The first statement demonstrates how creation's determinant systems adhere to the Logos' truth-functional-form's synthetic-analytic order: an order through which the Logos proportionally mitigates energy and so expresses the continuity of identity by rationalizing all under Y'haweh's power-set and absolute being. Thus, to secure the second statement, we continue in the critical context of adapting independent principles. With the principles, we detail how the Logos syntactically constructs the creation's determinate systems as truth functional operatives that beatifically derive the free physicality of our identity dependent, finite-knowledge-structure. Pursuant to the second statement's critical context is our employing axiomatic, *a priori* synthetic judgments to distinguish the free physicality that not only correlates with the most basic intentional supervenience of sentient animals; but also correlates with the more sophisticated intentional supervenience of our rational knowledge structures: a knowledge structure that entails, first, the intentional supervenience of kindred relationships and, second, the rational relationships of contractual associations that a citizenry's constitutional rights ensure.

Our detailing how the Logos employs the creation's determinant physical systems to derive the mind's temporally free physicality resolves the mind-matter explanatory gap by satisfying the following scheme: we first hold to our understanding that the Logos' free physicality rationally governs the determinant world's allowed contingencies, in order to express the continuity of identity from Y'haweh's absolute. Then being so fortified, we detail how the mind's temporally free physicality constitutes a unique translation of light that progressively grasps the normalized world as an operational construct of the Logos' rationalizing truth-functional-form.

We begin to detail how the mind's free physicality grasps a normalized the world as an effect of the Logos' syntactic structure as follows: we proceed by referencing the Logos' synthetic-analytic order as the context to unite and redefine the principles of the sundry disciplines that attempt to define the physical correlate to consciousness. We unite, first, quantum field, electromagnetics, and harmonic resonance theories of consciousness with, second, cognitive neuroscience and phenomenology's epistemological descriptions of our finite-knowledge-structure.

To set the context for our uniting the principles of the varied disciplines, we recollect empirical science's insufficient explanations for our illustration of an Olympic swimmer's intentional experience. Recall that our illustration particularly demonstrates how empirical scientists fail to reduce consciousness to being an epiphenomenon of thermodynamic states. Our illustration, in spirit, recognizes that thermodynamics defines the way energy remains constant as it converts from state to state. In this way, our illustration describes how scientists, first, distinguish unicellular life forms as the smallest measure of an observable self-replicating system that endures thermodynamic states during metabolic processes. The illustrations also notes how scientists then comprehend that the metabolic processes impose the self-replicating system's identity upon the system's environment as the system's charged circuits break down molecular structures for energy sources for the cell's development.

Next, our illustration describes how the concept of homeostasis especially encourages scientists to reduce our intentional experience to being an epiphenomenon of thermodynamic states. The illustration initially describes scientists' understanding of homeostasis as the internal regulation of a unicellular life-form during its complete metabolic process. Following, our illustration describes how scientists' recognition of homeostasis ultimately allows them to understand how multicellular life-forms translate their greater environments:

In some detail, the illustration at first notes the way scientists observe how plant-life achieves homeostasis through the integrative networks of specialized cells that signal the plant-life's metabolic states in a stationary environment. Afterward, the illustration notes how scientists believe that animals and humans have evolved the mobile capacity to maintain homeostasis as we translate transitioning environments. In explicit terms, the illustration even notes how mobile animal life achieve homeostasis as a consequence of increased biochemical integration to enable central processing and coordination through, first, a diffused circulatory system; second, complementing lymphatic and endocrine systems; and, lastly, peripheral and central nervous systems.

Finally after describing how scientists successfully capture all biological systems as the thermodynamic states of metabolic processes, our illustration poignantly describes how scientists fail to capture the swimmer's intentional experience as being the sole effect of the increasingly integrative biological systems. To be specific, the illustration describes how scientists fail to apprehend our conscious experience with a procedural, information-processing interpretation of the brain's functionality. At the same time, the illustration notes that the scientists manage to identify brain regions' requisite procedures that facilitate the properties of consciousness, such as memory, reasoning, and wakefulness.

The resulting axiomatic principles that we glean from our illustration, as well as our classical and modern physics survey, are the following: we understand that thermodynamic states are by definition entropic. In other words, we understand that thermodynamic states equally entail a uniform trend toward disorder. For this reason, we conclude that cognitive neuroscientists cannot distinguish consciousness in the brain, by employing information-processing interpretations that envision consciousness as an epiphenomenon of increasingly integrated thermodynamic states. We find that the scientists' interpretations do not grasp how consciousness' intentional experience necessarily transcends the entropy of the material systems that the conscious mind's identity depends upon.

From our classical and modern physics surveys, we gather a summary understanding of the entropy of physical systems that the consciousness mind must transcend: we gather that discrete force-exchanges between converging or expanding fields of space are syntactical consequences of energy's proportional manifestation; to the effect that apparent force exchanges are impoverished tropes of the potential exchange states that energy's proportional constant digitally allows. We understand that all emergent physical systems, therefore, endure the appearance of entropy—that is, the unavailability of energy to reconstitute a physical system—ultimately because of energy's proportionality. We also recognize that the proportional exchange of subatomic converging forces and the proportional exchange of expanding forces, between atomic elements, syntactically cause emergent physical systems to experience the appearance of entropy through the dissipation of useful energy in the form of subatomic and atomic radiation.

Even more significant is our conclusion that the invariant structure of converging and expanding forces in relation to light's photon force-exchange normalizes emergent physical systems' adherence to allowed states. We then witness the world's normalization as the continual (and yet entropic) coming into being of uniform physical conventions within spacetime. As the photoelectric effect demonstrates, we observe that light digitally interfaces with and registers the increasing or decreasing magnitudes of a physical system's force-exchange; however, we understand that light only respectively increases or decreases in its syntactically allotted frequencies, without acquiring magnitudinous changes, even as light maintains its constant speed. Like so, we see that the unchanging syntactical structure of force-exchanges, which culminate with light, normalizes all physical systems' states of entropy relative to light. And so, light endures entropy in the sense of the directedness of energy's proportional constant, though light does not endure the physical systems' entropic disorder.

Clearly, we see that Immanuel's Law's first derivative statement demonstrates how the normalizing of entropic physical systems adheres to the Logos' truth-functional-form's synthetic-analytic order: the statement describes how the synthetic-analytic order consigns invariant force-exchanges to mitigate the regularity of magnitudinous relationships as the continuity of identity from Y'haweh's absolute standing and power-set. We, therefore, have the understanding that the Logos' truth-functional-form relegates our finite-knowledge-structure to be totally dependent upon how the Logos' synthetic-analytic order mitigates the continuity of identity. Thereby, we understand that we are merely identity dependent upon the appearing world and our brain's entropic physical structures.

With the understandings that we glean from our first statement, we step ahead to distinguish the way the Logos' truth-functional-form consigns the world to enable our brain's unique apprehension of light's force-exchange: we venture to understand how our unique apprehension translates the naturally occurring force-exchanges' normalizing processes. We proceed to see how our unique translation is a unique normalizing process that is the free physicality of consciousness.

Since our illustration demonstrates that we cannot reduce our qualitative minds to evolved thermodynamic states, we confidently advance to reconcile and unite the major theories of consciousness that are incomplete because they do not distinguish how consciousness is the brain's unique capturing of force-exchanges' normalizing processes. Rather than solely relying upon shortsighted procedural, information processing interpretations; our second derivative statement advances by also relying upon such *a priori*-synthetic determinations that reveal how the brain's unique apprehension of light is a unique apprehension of the potential states of energy: an apprehension that normalizes the entropic physical systems. Our second statement, in this way, proceeds with determinations that establish how the brain's unique apprehension of light translates certain neuronal systems (which cognitive neuroscientists designate as memory and wakefulness centers) into the dynamic facilitators of force-exchanges' normalizing processes.

To advance Immanuel's Law's second derivative statement, we once more advance the critical distinction that our mind's finite-knowledge-structure is merely identity dependent upon the normalized working of our bodies and environment; while the mind ultimately depends upon the syntactical form that the world adheres to in the normalization of its impoverished states. We again emphasize that the scientists of course do not make this critical distinction.

In regards to our finite-knowledge-structure's identity dependence upon the brain's material systems, we celebrate the cognitive neuroscientists' ability to map the constituents of consciousness to respective neuronal complexes; however, we hold that though the neuronal networks demarcate consciousness' syntactical structure, the neuronal systems together fall short of equating consciousness because each material system is entropic. We recognize that cognitive neuroscientists agree that no single neuronal system is responsible for consciousness. Even so, we also recognize that the scientists do not acknowledge the need to understand how the mind transcends the entropic material systems.

To secure understanding, we observe the necessity to present further details, concerning the error of the scientists' consideration of consciousness as an epiphenomenal effect of the brain's autonomic (involuntary) neuronal systems; which again the scientists seek to appreciate in terms of information processing. We see the need to demonstrate that the reason that cognitive neuroscientists possess the methodological ability to describe consciousness as an epiphenomenal effect of neuronal systems is because of the way the systems' entropic breakdown—that is, the systems' pathologies—diminish consciousness' constituents.

Of the upmost importance is our further describing the shortfall of the scientists' description of consciousness as an epiphenomenon of an increasingly integrated nervous system. Our continued description of the scientists' shortfall gives our second statement the sound basis to describe how our qualitative mind's physicality ultimately depend upon the way the Logos mitigates the continuity of identity from Y'haweh's absolute.

As we roughly described in our illustration (as well as our cognitive neuroscience survey), the neuron cells' integrative operations are the chief inspirations for scientists to consider consciousness as an epiphenomenon of neuronal activity. As we have seen, neurons achieve a range of specialized configurations, which center upon the neurons' digital-like exchange of various excitatory and inhibitory electro-chemical signals throughout the body. For this purpose, cognitive neuroscientists appropriately designate the specialized operations of particular neuronal complexes with the rule-based terms that we usually employ to describe the syntactical elements of consciousness.

For instance, scientists first distinguish how afferent (sensory) neurons transmit bodily organ states into the spinal cord's dorsal route of the nervous system. At the same time, scientists observe how efferent (motor) neurons transmit information through the spinal cord's ventral pathways to regulate the organs. Scientists then observe how the spinal cord terminates at the brainstem, which features the medulla oblongata and Pons: neuronal complexes that scientists describe as the governors of autonomic processes like respiration, heart rate, sleep, and bladder control. Later when scientists observe the neuronal operations of the midbrain, resting upon the brainstem, scientists make the initial characterization of consciousness' being an epiphenomenal effect: the scientists recognize how the midbrain's ventral tegmental area entails dopaminergic neurons that operate as a reward system, effecting motivation and avoidance. Thus, as the neuronal complexes become increasingly specialized and integrative upon the brainstem and the midbrain, scientists progressively use syntactical terms to characterize other neuronal systems.

For example, upon the midbrain sets the thalamus nuclei, which neuroscientists necessarily describe as a motivating relay that plays a key role in conscious states: the thalamic nuclei have reciprocal circuits that convey sub-cortical, sensory signals to the cerebral cortex. Also, scientists detect that a subsystem of the thalamus is the hypothalamus, which releases stimulating or inhibiting hormones. Observing the hypothalamus' secreting of stimulating or inhibiting hormones enables scientists to make the determination that the hypothalamus controls body temperature, sleep, and wake cycles. In particular, scientists understand that the hypothalamus entails the suprachiasmatic nucleus, which operates as a biological clock that communicates through the reticular neurons to moderate brain states. In fact, scientists observe that severe injury of the reticular formation often results in a coma.

Before we continue, we remind the true worshipper that the security of Immanuel's Law's second derivative statement rest upon our establishing the statement upon axiomatic principles, which have the objectivity of *a priori*-synthetic understanding. Thus, we refrain from any daunting attempt to present a detailed survey of the brain's neuronal circuit: we merely present a description that demonstrates the cognitive neuroscientists' shortsightedness in their purporting that consciousness is an epiphenomenal effect of the neuronal circuits. To conclude our description of how the scientists derive the understanding that consciousness is an epiphenomenon, we have but to consider how the cerebral cortex reconciles sensory input and motor output in a way that rationalizes the neuronal input from other brain regions; to the extent that sensory input and motor output through the brain stem becomes more than an autonomic reflex arch.

We continue by recollecting that scientists believe that the epiphenomenon of consciousness' executive decisions occurs as a consequence of the way that the cerebral cortex employs the basal nuclei to rationalize sensory input and motor output, as the cortex relates to the thalamus; moreover, we understand that scientists conclude that the complementing epiphenomenon of consciousness' personhood occurs because of the way that the hippocampus and the amygdale, respectively, facilitate new impressions that the cerebral cortex and thalamic circuits process.

The scientists initially observe that the cerebral cortex is the brain's outer most sheath and is approximately two to four millimeters thick, consisting of six specialized neuronal layers of varying somatic densities. Furthermore, the scientists discern that the cortex entails two hemispheres, each entailing primary cortices and associating cortices; which employ the stratified neuronal structures to encode sensory input. Particularly, scientists observe that the stratified neuronal complexes (comprising the layers of the primary cortices) encode vision, hearing, and touch, amongst other sensations. In addition, they note that the primary cortices execute purposeful bodily movements. Too, scientists observe that the stratified neuronal complexes (comprising the layers of the associating cortices) rationalize the primary cortices' impressions. All told, the scientists witness that the associating cortices facilitate memory, language, abstraction, awareness, and executive decision making, that is, judgment.

In due course, scientists distinguish an epiphenomenon of consciousness' decision making, as the scientists observe how the basal nuclei's GABAergic neuronal cells inhibit the excitation of motor neurons in the cerebral cortex. Like so, the scientists observe how the basal nuclei ultimately render the effect of refining behavior and purposeful choice. In fact, as a confirmation of their conclusions, scientists observe how Parkinson's disease is an outcome of damage to the basal nuclei.

In regards to the actual personhood of consciousness, the scientists deem the sense of personhood to be the epiphenomenal effect of the way that the hippocampus and the amygdale support the ongoing operations of an important neuronal circuit that entails the cerebral cortex, basal nuclei, and thalamus. First, scientists observe how the hippocampus possesses stratified neuronal complexes that entail a variety of neurons, such as neurons that endure long-term potentiation, as well as place-cell neurons, which fire in response to positions in space. The epiphenomenal effect that scientists glean from the hippocampus' neuronal structure is that the scientists can employ syntactical terms to describe the hippocampus as supporting the cerebral cortex's long-term memory centers with episodic memory. Similarly, scientists observe how the amygdale entails specialized inhibiting and excitation neurons that relate to the thalamic nuclei by firing as a reward system. The epiphenomenal effect that scientists glean from the amygdale is that the scientists can employ syntactical terms to describe the amygdale as enunciating episodic experiences with emotional memory.

Though scientists have come tantalizingly close to reducing consciousness to being the product of neuronal circuitry, they stand at an impasse in their efforts to establish mathematical descriptions of intracranial neuronal activity. Still, scientists remain confident that consciousness is an epiphenomenon. Again, the scientists' confidence arises from the fact that neuronal circuits persist prior to, during, and after consciousness' emergence as a result of the neuronal activity.

In spite of their confidence, we still see the tragic end of the scientists' reducing consciousness to being a mere epiphenomenal effect of physical systems' priming and automaticity. We recognize that when scientists consider consciousness as an epiphenomenon, they fail to justify and establish a universally agreed upon physical structure that assumes the epistemological identity of the mind's finite-knowledge-structure. We in fact see that scientists fail to determine a necessary anatomical structure that equates consciousness because the neuronal systems that correspond with the mind's constituents are in a state of entropy (as the brain's sundry pathologies witness). In this regard, we understand that when the scientists reduce the mind to being an epiphenomenon of entropic neuronal systems, the scientists do not grasp the mind that freely transcends and qualifies the determinant and entropic systems. In the end, we grieve over the fact that scientists unknowingly confound our capacity to transcend physical events and establish our justified-true-beliefs.

We stand far from considering our qualitative minds as mere epiphenomena. We advance Immanuel's Law's second derivative statement by demonstrating how the brain apprehends our supervening and temporally free mind as a unique translation of light that temporally normalizes the world's entropic physical systems. We now approach the brains neuronal systems by gauging the manner in which they uniquely apprehend light and so establish the haecceity of consciousness' first-person perspective. Similar to the way in which computer engineers use processed silicon crystals to isolate the potential states of light frequencies, the cerebral cortex's specialized neuronal layers isolate and encode the electromagnetic waves that are present in the brain. Perennially processing sensory neurons, the specialized regions of the cortex respectively encode existing light waves to simulate physical conventions such as sound, among other magnitudinous relationships. Like so, the cortex's layers encode scaled relationships between the light, sound, and material densities as a reflection of real world relationships between other light frequencies that normalize entropic physical systems. As the cerebral cortex subtly adapts the light waves present in the brain to simulate the greater environmental contingencies, the cortex simulates the orders of succession, magnitude, and duration in accordance with the allowed magnitudinous, macroscopic states that energy's proportional constant allows.

When the encoded electromagnetic waves fill the circuit that relates the cerebral cortex to the thalamic nuclei, the encoded waves bind with the naturally occurring electromagnetic waves that accompany the circuits that connect the brainstem to the thalamus. At that instance, a perturbation occurs that is not merely a deviation from the naturally occurring electromagnetic frequencies that accompany simple neuronal circuits. Rather, a perturbation occurs that is a sustained deviation from the totality of the allowed frequencies that energy's proportional constant projects.

At long last, we determine that the binding of encoded electromagnetic waves with the naturally occurring electromagnetic waves results in the closing of the mind-matter explanatory gap. The resulting and sustained perturbation becomes the temporally free physicality of consciousness' possessive sense: the perturbation maintains its unified proportionality, despite the specific physical circuits that contribute to it. Also, since the sustained perturbation is a unique proportional outcome of the encoded electromagnetic waves' rationalization of a multiplicity of neuronal circuits; the perturbation becomes a free physicality that is the mind's dynamic mechanism. Like this, the perturbation entails the dynamic capacity to forecast a myriad of magnitudinous relationships beyond its immediate experience.

At the same time, the sustained perturbation's free standing is temporal because it does depend upon the encoded electromagnetic waves' capacity to signify the states of an untold number of automated circuits in relation to a normalized environment. In other words, the perturbation depends upon the encoded waves' finite capacity to portray the enabling automated systems, from the DNA molecule of a single cell's thermodynamic states; to the diffused circulatory systems of multi-cellular thermodynamic states; and ultimately unto the integrated signaling of nervous systems that maintain homeostasis for mobile animals.

We now detail how our distinguishing the sustained perturbation proves that we have closed the mind-matter explanatory gap. We present *a priori*-synthetic determinations to establish an epistemological understanding of the way that the Logos' truth-functional-form establishes the reliable environmental network and basic physical convention that fashion our finite-knowledge-structure. Indeed, to prove that we have closed the mind-matter explanatory gap and thereby substantiated the justified-true-belief that our finite-knowledge-structure accesses, we present *a priori*-synthetic determinations that surpass the categorical understandings of rational philosophers and empirical scientists. For example, unlike rational philosophers, we do not categorically take for granted that a rational order enables our metaphysical rationalization of the physical world. Instead, we comprehend that the philosophers' sought for rational order is actually the product of the way the Logos' truth-functional-form's synthetic-analytic order governs the normalization of magnitudinous relationships that emerge, despite the subatomic world's syntactical specificity. Also, unlike empirical scientists, we do not categorically take for granted that we possess an innate rational capacity to observe how physical events adhere to natural-force-laws. Instead, we hold that the mind's sustained perturbation dynamically synthesizes neuronal circuits to generate magnitudinous and qualitative representations to match and query the normalized environmental network that incites ongoing neuronal signals. In this manner, we understand that the mind's dynamic mechanism seeks to maintain its perturbation's unified and temporally free standing; moreover, in this way, we glean an epistemological understanding, concerning how the mind's dynamic mechanism substantively manifests spirited will and intentionality.

To present *a priori*-synthetic determinations, regarding how the Logos' truth-functional-form extends a reliable environmental network that gives rise to and facilitates our finite-knowledge-structure, we proceed to establish the ontological meaning that the Logos expresses. We recall that Immanuel's Law's first derivative statement leaves the question, concerning how to substantiate ontological meaning, for the second derivative statement to answer:

To frame the significance of the question that the first statement leaves, we quickly recall the subsequent understandings: in our first statement, we establish that causality is the syntactical force of the Logos' natural-force-laws, which express the absolute ontological standing of Y'haweh's power-set. And so, because it concludes that causal force is syntactical and thus necessitating appearing operational relationships; our first statement finds fault with the scientists' Big Bang conception: the statement recognizes that the Big Bang is a functionally indeterminate conception of a single, originating event. Also, our first statement observes that scientists wrongfully conclude that strong-force particle-decay results from the singular Big Bang event: only in the context of the Big Bang's creating the strong-force particle fields, the scientists conclude that the strong-force particle decay is responsible for the emergent creation, as it stands presently.

In response, our first statement rightly cast the particle-fields as mathematical operatives that universalize upon the invariant force-exchanges, under light speed. The first statement thereby concludes that the syntactical system as a whole projects the power-set's ontological standing; especially when emergent magnitudinous relationships arise, despite the specificity of this world's syntactical structure.

In some detail, Immanuel's Law's first statement describes how subatomic, strong, converging forces syntactically relate to expanding electron forces in a manner that syntactically structures ionic compounds and molecules; which then assume macroscopic, normalized properties as light's photon force-exchange maintains magnitudinous relationships, despite specific quantum states. Too, the first statement demonstrates that the emergent regularity of universal properties, which invariant force-exchanges effect, enables us to form rational and predictive understandings—even scientific, philosophical, and theological assessments—of the creation.

Nevertheless, seeing that each observable state persists in a non-self-sufficient state of entropy, we find that the question that the first statement leaves is the following: how do our scientific, philosophical, and theological assessments forgo human centered categorical conclusions, in order to establish a causal purpose for the non-self-sufficient and emergent systems that we observe?

As we noted at outset of our natural science surveys, even the most ardent naturalists who champion the theory of evolution necessarily employ utilitarian, anthropocentric terms when they describe evolutionary theory. They essentially coin biological evolution as an organism's capacity to adapt to environmental changes, as gene mutations fortuitously render the organism to be better fitted to survive the environmental changes. Whilst the naturalists imagine evolutionary theory, they overlook the fact that their use of the fitness concept is entirely utilitarian and so anthropocentric: standing without a qualification beyond the human perspective.

To grasp the inherent ontological being of creation's emergent physical systems that the Logos syntactically expresses, we reemphasize the previously discussed dispute between theologians, teleological philosophers, and empirical scientists over whether plant-life's turning to light sources is purposeful. We reemphasize that theologians and teleological philosophers deem plant-life's turning to light sources as purposeful; while natural scientists deem the plant-life's turning to light sources as the consequence of heliotropism: an outcome of the plant-life's evolved capacity to increase growth hormones on the side of plants that do not come into direct contact with the light sources.

To resolve this dispute, we grasp the purposeful expression of the Logos by distinguishing how individual states adhere to the Logos' form, which in turn uniquely expresses Y'haweh's absolute standing: we observe the unique standing and interdependency that the Logos' truth-functional-form renders to, first, energy's quantized mathematical properties that syntactically yield the plant-life and Sun's atomic force-exchange configurations; second, the emerging magnitudinous relationships under light that the invariant structure of force-exchange synthetically yields; and, third, the perturbation of the brain's encoded light that constitutes our minds' dynamic mechanisms. Already, our first statement recognizes that the atomic structure and photon force-exchange that constitute the sun's emitting of light results from a syntactical cause. Likewise, our first statement recognizes that the ionic compounds and molecules, which constitute the plant-life, entail adaptive features that result from syntactical allotments. For this reason, we extrapolate from our first statement's conclusions and discern that the plant-life's turning to the sun is at least an allotment that the Logos' nested mathematical properties syntactically anticipate. In other words, we see that the nested mathematical properties, which the quantized subatomic forces comprise, have a multiplicity of derivations that the Logos syntactically expresses when the Logos synthetically employs force-exchange to render atoms, ionic compounds, molecules, and the prevailing magnitudinous relationships that we apprehend with classical mechanics, phenomenology, and spiritedness. Yet, to distinguish the actual purposefulness of the Logos' syntactical expression, we consider the way our mind's dynamic mechanism arises as an outcome of the unique standing and truth-functional relationship between energy's syntactically expressed mathematical properties and the magnitudinous relationships that emerge:

Since all worlds fall short of Y'haweh's power-set, we recognize that any-possible-world has unique mathematical properties that syntactically universalize to express the greater magnitudinous relationships of any-possible-world; therefore, we recognize that the syntactical elements and the emergent magnitudinous relationships both bear their own unique standing, while both are identity dependent upon the Logos' truth-functional-form. Likewise, we gauge the mind's dynamic mechanism's perturbation of light as a unique derivation of the Logos' truth-functional-form because the perturbation is not the sole consequence of an evolutionary adaption to energy's syntactically allotted atomic states. Rather, the dynamic mechanism's perturbation adapts the cortical regions' layers to mimic energy's proportionally allotted magnitudes under light speed. With this understanding, we grasp the transient ontological being of the normalized creation by the manner in which the prevailing magnitudinous relationships incite the mind's dynamic mechanism's ability to project scaled magnitudinous relationships per the mechanism's state of being. In other words, because the dynamic mechanism depends upon its capacity to model emergent magnitudinous relationships and not the specificity of atomic states, we confirm that the mind's dynamic mechanism is a functional derivation of the normalized world's ontological relationships and energy's syntactical structure: all of which are totally dependent upon the Logos' prevailing truth-functional-form, while being identity dependent upon one another.

All told, in order for us to grasp the purposeful and ontological inherence of the Logos' expression, we avoid the mistake of categorically agreeing with the rational philosophers that our finite-knowledge-structure relies upon a network of reliable sources.

Instead, by our understanding that causality results from energy's mathematical properties' adherence to the Logos' syntactical expression, we secure the objective—the *a priori*-synthetic—means to confirm the rational philosophers' categorical assertion. We exhibit our objectivity as we distinguish the emergent ontological relationships as uniquely substantial and, therefore, purposeful by the way that the magnitudinous relationships sustain brain-waves' encoded perturbation; apart from the perturbation's identity dependence upon the actual syntax of the perturbation's supporting atomic structures. Of most import, we conclude that the invariant force-exchanges typify relational categories—such as, cause and effect succession; universals and property exemplars; and species kind. Then we observe how these relational categories have their transient being in their facilitating the unified being of the mind's perturbation; which exists by dynamically generating magnitudinous analogues per its state of being.

What follows is that no single physical state incites the mind's dynamic mechanism to generate scaled analogues that rationalize the normalized environment per its state. Rather, a succession of nested and interrelating magnitudinous symmetries unpacks the dynamic mechanism's capacity to rationalize sensory input and recreate magnitudinous relationships, per the subjective binding of the mind's perturbation. For instance, the dynamic mechanism first apprehends the regularity of plant-life's turning to sunlight in a determinate—that is, subconscious—manner, because of the way that the brain's neuronal structure uses light waves to adapt neuronal densities and then match scaled perturbation magnitudes with environmental magnitudes within spacetime. At such an instance, the appearing environmental network further arrays other magnitudinous periods of succession; similitude; and species-kind that are not necessarily associated atomically; however, the appearing relationships incite and facilitate the dynamic mechanism's growing inquiry. The regularity of the unfolding symmetries so engage and surpass the brain's capacity to encode and reconcile the relational symmetries that consciousness, itself, becomes a quest to match new magnitudinous analogues with what appears.

As a final reflection upon the way the Logos expresses the reliable environmental network to form our finite-knowledge-structure, we appreciate that scientists convincingly qualify every physical eventuality with a quantum field theory of spacetime; however, we spy the profoundest mistake in their reducing the cascade of potential magnitudinous relationships to a linear succession of physical events. Yet again, we decry the fact that they fail to observe the syntactical precedent that defies the notion of linear causality. We of course conclude that the Logos syntactically causes the magnitudinous interrelationships to facilitate our finite-knowledge structure's dynamic mechanism. Even as we inferred in Immanuel's Law's theological and empirical statements, we understand that the Logos' expression of creation's appearing operations is beatific unto the fulfilling of the human experience within Y'haweh's expressed person.

Having secured the objective—*a priori*-synthetic—means to demonstrate how the Logos syntactically causes a reliable network of ontological relationships that incite and facilitate our intentional experience; we now present an *a priori*-synthetic understanding of the basic physical convention that constitutes the haecceity—that is, the like-*thisness*—of our first-person experience. In a straight forward manner, we have but to distinguish the brain's neuronal functions that either contribute to our mind's dynamic mechanism's sustained electromagnetic perturbation; or respond to the mind's dynamic mechanism.

To repeat, we have the general understanding that sensory input from the body runs through the brainstem and thalamic regions unto the cerebral cortex's stratified neuronal layers. We understand that the stratified somatic densities of the cortex encode present electromagnetic waves, matching the present electromagnetic waves' magnitudes with the greater magnitudes that bodily states encounter. We spy that an electromagnetic perturbation then occurs as the encoded electromagnetic waves fill the circuit of the cortex and the thalamic regions, where naturally occurring electromagnetic waves are present.

To comprehend the awareness threshold of our first-person experience, we chiefly distinguish the neuronal structure of brain regions that cognitive neuroscientists identify as episodic and long term memory centers. Of particular note is the fact that the neuronal complexes, such as the hippocampus, possess stratified somatic densities like the cerebral cortex. Cognitive neuroscientists unfortunately hold classical prejudices when they assess the functionality of the memory centers: as we have said, they conceive memory to be the outcome of automaticity and priming. So to correct the scientists' naturalist error, we consider that the memory centers become active in response to the dynamic mechanism's perturbation: that is, the perturbation that enjoins the encoded electromagnetic waves that are present in the cerebral cortex with the electromagnetic waves that accompany ongoing sensory signaling, running through the brainstem.

Like the initial encoding of light at the cerebral cortex, the memory centers' somatic layers receive the encoded light waves after the perturbation. As a result, the memory centers personalize ongoing experience when the memory centers' stratified layers effect memory retention by forecasting and chemically recording potential states of the magnitudinous relationships that the cerebral cortex initially encode. In this manner, the memory centers and other brain regions that sustain the perturbation generate magnitudinous concepts to the effect that the awareness sensation occurs when ongoing sensory impressions do not subsume under existing chemical impressions. Upon such instances, the memory and awareness centers generate new neuronal pathways for the maintenance of the perturbation's binding of the encoded electromagnetic waves.

From our consideration of the manner in which the dynamic mechanism's perturbation adapts the memory centers' stratified layers, we spy three notable *a priori*-synthetic understandings. The understandings demonstrate that human and animal's finite-knowledge-structures share a basic physical convention that is free and qualitative and not an epiphenomenal result of evolutionary processes. Our first *a priori*-synthetic understanding is that we agree that automaticity and priming play a key role in memory (especially, in regards to producing chemical impressions); however, we understand the memory centers' further encoding of electromagnetic waves to be spirited. For example, we first recall that the regularity of force-exchanges between subatomic elements normalize the syntactical expression of the elements in a way that yields the worlds' emergent magnitudinous relationships. Then we observe that the emergent magnitudinous relationships enable the mind's dynamic mechanism to adapt the memory centers, in order to personalize the cortex's initial rationalizations of the normalized environment. For this reason, we understand that the perturbation of the mind's dynamic mechanism is spirited because it does not respond to single events or corresponding neurological circuits. Instead, the perturbation responds to the invariant scales of magnitudinous relationships that appear, despite the specific atomic structures that give rise to the relationships.

By responding to the digital nature of quantum mechanics, the memory centers generate magnitudinous circuits that model the magnitudinous relationships that appear in the emergent macroscopic world. The circuits then portray our body and mental states within the greater, normalized environment; which the brain's cortex initially portrays, as it continuously integrates sensorial input by recreating the emergent worlds' magnitudinous relationships.

Our second *a priori*-synthetic understanding is our recognition that the ongoing relationship between the cortex's initial encoding of electromagnetic waves and the memory centers' personalized encoding means that the mind's dynamic mechanism is actually a dynamic reference frame that constitutes the basic physical convention of our first-person experience. In point of fact, our understanding of our mind's dynamic reference frame is an objective understanding of the scientists' insubstantial conception of Cartesian reference frames, which they use to describe an observer's perspective. Unlike the Cartesian reference frame, our dynamic reference frame is an actual dynamis, marking the mind's magnitudinous supervenience, sentience, and temporal freedom: even the liberty of sentient personhood that arises from the moment that human and animal fetuses develop the capacity to encode light waves and sustain the resulting perturbation of light.

What follows is our third and last *a priori*-synthetic understanding: we comprehend the haecceity of our first person experience to be a rationalizing magnitudinous sense that is temporally free as it projects the totality of the magnitudinous relationships under light. Indeed, we understand that the perturbation's apprehension of totality is a synthetic and free dynamis that the contributing bodily faculties of the mind's perturbation do not equate. Like so, we recognize that the first-person magnitudinous sense transcends the particularities of any given experience. For example, we witness the vindication of rational philosophers' epistemological descriptions, as we observe that the brain's memory and awareness centers further translate magnitudinous relationships into concepts that the memory and awareness centers' necessarily reconcile with the dynamic mechanism's perturbation. In other terms, we witness a process that rational philosophers define as the systematic binding of concepts with the intuition of selfhood—that is, the self-image, centrality of judgment.

In sum, we see that human and animal dynamic reference frames reconcile the memory centers' analogues of magnitudinous relationships with the synthetic basicality of the mind's perturbation of light. In other terms, the neuronal nuclei of the brain's memory-awareness centers encode magnitudinous relationships, in reference to the brain's sustained perturbation of electromagnetic waves. The referencing of the perturbation then becomes the neuronal correlate of the mind's centrality of judgment. Thus, after assuming the centrality of judgment, the dynamic reference frames determinately respond to the normalized world by synthetically reconciling existence with instinctive essence; indeterminacy with the giveness of determinacy; abstractions with the concrete; and contingent particulars with necessary universals.

For the completion of Immanuel's Law's second derivative statement, we now consider the neocortex's relationship to the dynamic mechanism's perturbation of encoded electromagnetic waves and the cerebral cortex's initial encoding of the electromagnetic waves. In this context, we distinguish the contrast between the physicality of human dynamic reference frames and animal dynamic reference frames. We particularly distinguish the neurological structure that facilitates humanity's dynamic reference frame's ontological standing that temporally transcends the world. Like this, we draw a contrast to the animal's dynamic reference frames that only produce determinant apprehensions of their perspective environs; though the determinate apprehensions are qualitative.

First, our pronouncing the profundity of the neocortex's simultaneous relationship with, first, the cerebral cortex's initial encoding of light and, second, the memory-awareness centers' encoding of light (in reference to light's perturbation) necessitates our further denouncing of the naturalists' shortsighted approach to the evolutionary concept. We know that the naturalists conceive the survival of fit species that adapt to their environments as being responsible for the increasing diversity of animal species that nevertheless share artifact traits; moreover, we know that the naturalists use the evolutionary model to explain ineffective species' traits that seem to be genetic relics of pre-evolved states. In this light, we see that naturalists conceive the human neocortex as an evolutionary adaptation to the primate brain, which bears a physiological structure that is strikingly similar to human physiology, even unto DNA cell similarities.

Though evolutionary theory is enticing, we grasp an *a prior-synthetic* understanding of the actual functioning of the human neocortex: initially, we consider the neocortex's operation as a response to the dynamic mechanism's perturbation, which mimics energy's proportional allotments. In this way, we know that the perturbation's quantum effects cannot be the consequence of evolutionary adaptation. Next, we hold to the understanding that invariant force-exchanges normalize the world's magnitudinous relationships and so typify species categorizations in a way that enables human and animal memory-awareness centers to produce determinate, magnitudinous analogues of their relative body states and sentient perspectives within an environment. With these understandings, we proceed to detail how the emergence of species types and artifact adumbrations produce the necessary ought—suggestive—structure that enable humanity's neocortex to produce reflective and abstract judgments, which transcend the environment, as follows:

Whereas the cerebral cortex encodes magnitudinous relationships of body states within the environment and whereas the memory-awareness centers encode personalized magnitudinous relationships, in reference to light's perturbation; humanity's neocortex encodes the actual acts of the cerebral cortex and memory-awareness center's generating of magnitudinous relationships that capture our sentient perspectives within the environment. The effect is that rather than the determinate encoding of particular body or sentient states in association with particular environmental events, the neocortex abstractly encodes and captures the magnitudinous relationship between an objective convention and a personal perspective.

For example, the neocortex's reconciling the respective magnitudinous relationships of the cerebral cortex and the memory-awareness centers unites all objective environmental experience under the magnitudinous concept of "the"; which concept rationally assimilates any object, state, or action. Correspondingly, the neocortex captures possessive senses under the magnitudinous concept of "my"; which concept rationally assimilates any individual perspective or aspiration that associates with any object, state, or action. In between, the neocortex generates other magnitudinous abstractions such as the conjoining magnitudinous relation "and" or the contrasting magnitudinous relation "or." Essentially, the neocortex's distinguishing of objective and subjective states defines human being upon a language capacity: a magnitudinous capacity to objectify comprehension and thereby ascribe the phonological and visual representations of the cerebral cortex, in a way that constitute the meta-cognitive self-narratives of all human experiences. More importantly, the capacity to objectify comprehension (O.C.) affords each human the ability to ascribe his or her self-narratives to other persons' environmental experiences. In a word, the neocortex enables humanity to grasp the profoundest abstraction of all: conscience.

Though the neocortex gives humankind a profound capacity to transcend and define environmental experiences, we understand that the cerebral cortex and memory-awareness centers' initial generation of determinant judgments ground the neocortex's abstractions. In other words, we understand that the determinate analogues that the dynamic mechanism initially effects, secure our abstract concepts of the world with a natural jurisprudence:

Determinately maintaining an awareness of our wellbeing during experience, as well as our maintenance of conscience for others, we determinately grasp the world through possessive senses of kindred relationships before we rationalize an objective world of formal relationships and environments. We also determinately gauge our communal standing in relation to the progressive capacities of animal species, even unto the primates and their respective environments.

Notwithstanding, unlike animals, we gauge human freedom by humanity's capacity to conceptualize greater purposes and so forgo immediate pleasure, during circumstances in which the cerebral cortex and memory-awareness centers effectively associate body states to the normalized environment. Also, we gauge human freedom by humanity's capacity to endure pain, during circumstances in which the cerebral cortex and memory-awareness centers cannot reconcile body states to the normalized environment.

Essentially, the magnitudinous abstractions of the neocortex are physical, though free; therefore, our obtaining the justified-true-belief of the physical world entails our reconciling the physical world with the fulfilling of the free physicality of our finite-knowledge-structure. The mind's physical abstractions demonstrate that the universal ideals of righteousness, truth, and justice are in fact substantive conventions that the impoverished world adheres to as the Logos' truth-functional-form mitigates Y'haweh's ontological being. The universal ideals substantively reconcile all mental states, enabling humanity to prevail over the environment. Hence, the governmental, bureaucratic, contractual, and social relationships that humanity enjoins only secure universal justification when these abstract relationships reconcile the aspects of kindred relationships that humanity determinately apprehends.

Our illustration of the Olympic swimmer details how the swimmer instantly captures the Olympic event under the magnitudinous rationalizations of her self-narrative relationships. The illustration details how the Olympic swimmer reconciles an untold number of physical events under the conception of gaining an international prize, which she embraces in reference to her kindred relationships; her formal relationships that invoke national pride; and finally her Christian sensibility that usurps all her affections.

Now that Immanuel's Law's second derivative statement has secured its aim of closing the mind-matter explanatory gap, we see the necessity of Immanuel's Law's third derivative statement. We now turn to the third statement to substantiate the manner in which the Logos' truth-functional-form completes the justified-true-belief of humanity's mental abstractions. In this way, we look for the third statement to substantiate the orthodoxy of the biblical Testaments, which detail how the Logos reconciles humanity's relationships, from the early patriarchic societies unto today's international community. We now proceed to our third statement in order to set the context for the remainder of our journey down truth's landscape.

Immanuel's Law – Third Derivative Statement

We begin Immanuel's Law's third and final derivative statement. We begin the third statement as the culmination of Immanuel's Law's first and second derivative statements. We proceed in the critical context of demonstrating that the independent principles that substantiate the first and second statements also secure a critical understanding of our definition of truth, which we hold to be the underlining thesis that captures the biblical Testaments' orthodoxy: that is, the Testaments' right belief that Y'haweh's expressed will extends Y'haweh's holiness as the prevailing of right judgment that we witness in the Testator's pure conscience, which redeems our faith and condemns the unjust world's compromise of conscience.

We begin to describe how the Testaments demonstrate their orthodoxy as they foreshadow the first and second statements' independent principles throughout the Testaments' revelatory narratives. In this manner, the third statement vindicates the Church's key Trinitarian Creed—the Athanasian Creed—without relying upon dogmatic tautological assertions.

Pursuant to the third statement's critical context is our employing axiomatic, *a priori*-synthetic judgments to establish how the existential world—consisting of syntactical subatomic structures; emergent physical properties; regular magnitudinous relationships; and human and animal dynamic perspectives—adheres to the orthodoxy that the biblical Testaments relate. To wit, the third statement's critical context requires the demonstration of how the physical world adheres to the anthropomorphic convention of the creator's being a Father over his expressed person, a suffering Son, who as a testator and King elects some to become kindred beneficiaries of an eternal Kingdom of salvation from a fallen world of sin: namely, a world in which humankind fails to apprehend the substantive, universal conventions of salvation's truth and justice—even the expressed rightness of Y'haweh's totality.

As an ultimate outcome, the third statement's use of the previous statements' independent principles, to substantiate the biblical Testaments, also provides us with the critical context to unfold the remainder of the truth's landscape; in which we detail the application of the Testaments. We see that using the independent power-set principle, the first derivative statement substantiates Y'haweh's set-apart and absolute ontological being. Also, we observe that using quantum physics and relativity principles, the first statement substantiates the unique ontological standing of Y'haweh's Logos. Subsequently, we recall that the second derivative statement uses the principles of quantum field, electromagnetic, and harmonic resonance theories of consciousness to substantiate the temporally free physicality of our finite-knowledge-structure. By this means, we remember that our finite-knowledge-structure persists as a dynamic reference frame that the world's appearing magnitudinous relationships facilitate. Thus, in order to use the first and second statements' independent principles to substantiate the anthropocentric—human centered—biblical Testaments, the third derivative statement now proceeds to substantiate the Logos' extension as the Son and the Holy Spirit in subsequent context: the third statement proceeds to describe how the Logos' truth-functional-form syntactically expresses the emergent world's magnitudinous relationships ultimately unto the completion of human personhood and interpersonal community. Like so, the third statement correlates the Logos' beatific expression of Y'haweh's first-person, absolute being with the biblical Testaments' revelation of Y'haweh's Holiness; unto which the Logos, as the Mashiach and Holy Spirit, reconciles our souls.

By pronouncing humanity's inability to reconcile our intersubjective perspectives, the third statement sets the context for the rest of Landscape's treatment of biblical orthodoxy, concerning our redemption and salvation from the inequitable nations that result from humanity's inability to secure conscience. Yet, presently, for the completion of Immanuel's Law's third statement, we briefly venture to describe the actual free physicality of the redemptive work: the third statement ventures to describe how the physical world adheres to the Logos' substantive prevailing as the redeeming Son and communal Holy Spirit.

In order to substantiate the redemptive work that the biblical Testaments record, we proceed to build upon the lessons-learned from our first and second derivative statements. We describe the actual physicality of our spirits and souls as follows: first, we identify the brain's dynamic reference frame to be spiritedness, in regards to the way the post-perturbation neuronal circuits arrest the brain's memory-awareness centers' magnitudinous relationships to maintenance the brain's dynamic mechanism's perturbation of light. Chiefly, we deem the dynamic reference frame's ongoing reconciling of the cerebral cortex's initial encoding of light with the memory-awareness centers' personalized encoding of light to be spirited because the reference frame adapts itself to match the world's appearing magnitudinous relationships that transcend any specific physical event, as well as any specific sensory neuron's reaction to the event.

Of course, we remember that empirical scientists observe a multiplicity of physical factors that determinately affect human and animal behavior; however, we observe that the litany of behavioral factors do not amount to the quantum basicality of the dynamic mechanism's perturbation of light. We, therefore, recognize that the mind's dynamic reference frame has an asymmetric relationship with the nervous system and reliable environmental network that the mind's identity depends upon.

For instance, the haecceity—the like thisness—of our dynamic reference frame enables us to draw symmetrical distinctions between our greater perceptions of magnitudinous relationships and our impoverished sensations of particular events. During our cognitive processes, we instinctively become aware when our reference frame's symmetrical rationalizations of greater magnitudinous relationships are present. Essentially, we quantify our perceptions around the bounds of a unit after we establish a central point of the unit, and then our inquisitive sensations occur if our perceptions fail to affix themselves to any boundary or relation of parts. When we assess our sensorial faculties, we find that our cognizance of symmetry qualifies our retentive perceptions. And so, when we cannot ascertain any symmetrical value, we find that our intentional perceptions transform into the inquiry of contingent sensations. Our mental ability to appreciate symmetrical values is our response to the greater truth-functional-order that the creation's appearing magnitudinous relationships subsume under.

In sight, sound, and touch, symmetry persists: in sight, the eye draws the distinctions of parts; in sound, the ear ascertains the origins of sound; and in touch, the hands understand the boundaries of an object. In taste and smell, however, symmetry is less determined. We can ascertain differing taste upon the palate, but the origin of the taste upon the palate often remains undetermined. As well, the origin of an odor can have a symmetrical value in the odor's emanation. Yet, we fail to determine the odor's boundary when we are in the midst of the vapor itself; therefore, the sensorial faculties of taste and smell seem to lie on the frontier between perception and sensation because these faculties are sometimes void of a symmetrical value.

Nevertheless, when we derive pleasure from a perception that has no symmetrical value, we experience a retentive cognition that has a spiritual value, in respect of our being aware of the centrality of oneself. For this cause, we cannot indefinitely ascribe such pleasure upon a single object of perception. Furthermore, when our perception of the object is itself pleasurable, we deem the object to be beautiful after we ascribe our feelings of pleasure upon the object. Once again, we deem the appreciative sense of beauty to be an intellectual cast, because when we experience the sense of beauty, our dynamic reference frames succinctly identify an object of perception within a greater environmental order, in a way that facilitates our perspectives.

In the end, we understand that our senses of beauty and the sublime are hallmarks of the Logos' respective cultivation and confounding of our dynamic reference frames' free possessive senses. Our encounter with beauty is a disinterested and effortless encounter with the syntactical causality that gives rise to the interdependent relationships that sustain our perceptions. Furthermore, our reflective tastes are a consequence of our memory-awareness centers' intentional efforts to reconcile the impoverished world's contingencies, disjunctions, and incongruities that incite our thoughts. At the same time, our encounters with sublime environmental experiences, which our concepts cannot assail, humble our possessive sense.

We, therefore, qualify the animal and human spirit by its appreciative sense of beauty. Because the dynamic reference frame is greater than the impoverished events that its identity depends upon, we gauge the temporal freedom of the spirit's possessive sense by its willingness to exert efforts to reconcile its place in the impoverished environment. Hence, the nominal temperament of an intelligent being, during the being's response or reaction to its environment, defines its spirit. As an outcome, we define a spirit as self: the inherent intellectual, common basis of one's propensities.

Having used our lessons-learned from Immanuel's Law's first and second derivative statements to substantiate the existence of our spirits, we swiftly proceed to substantiate the existence of our souls. As well, we quickly substantiate the orthodoxy of the Testaments, which record the Logos' redemptive work upon the soul. To be sure, from the first and second derivative statements, we glean our sought-after *a priori*-synthetic understanding of the Logos' extension as the Mashiach, unto the completion of our personhood. Likewise, we glean our sought-after understanding of the Logos' extension as the Holy Spirit, unto the completion of our interpersonal relationships.

We equate the human soul with our self-narrative capacity—our mega-cognitive sense—that objectifies the very act of cognition; to the end that our sense of our personal perspectives rationalizes not only the environment, but also rationalizes the act of perceiving the environment. We appreciate the soul as unique and at the same time identity dependent upon the spirited dynamic reference frame.

In point of fact, we continue to appreciate that our spirit's possessive standing is an outcome of the asymmetric relationship between our dynamic reference frame and our sense of the impoverished environment. In view of that, we observe that our spirit's disinterested sense of beauty, within our physical environment, does not always prevail upon our soul: the human neocortex's auxiliary magnitudinous relationships operate as self-narratives that give us the capacity to withstand immediate pleasure for greater conceptions of satisfaction.

Thus, because humanity's self-narrative capacity reaches its zenith upon achieving interpersonal experiences, we observe that the Logos extends unto the soul as the integrity of conscience, which is the divine power and substantive cognitive state of the Mashiach; whose truth, humility, charity, and empathy our souls disinterestedly recognize as beauty. Also, we observe the inextricable accompaniment of the Logos' extension as the savior of conscience, the Mashiach: we recognize the Logos' corresponding extension as the communal Holy Spirit, in regards to the Mashiach's prevalent

Kingdom of reconciled souls. Decidedly, the extension of the Holy Spirit persists upon the beatific election and sublime judgment of our shortsighted interpersonal relationships. To this end, the Kingdom appears as beatific salvation; which human ingenuity—that is, religious works and the succession of human governments—cannot secure.

Above all, Immanuel's Law's third derivative statement concludes the following: the neocortex produces magnitudinous relationships that enable our interpersonal relationships to prevail upon the determinant world; therefore, the integrity of Lord Yehoshua's conscience is a universal state, expressing that any-possible-physical world subsumes under substantive and yet ontologically free spiritual purposefulness, namely Y'haweh's absolute pure synthesis of spirit with power. Like physical progression manifests strata and disjunction in order to incite our propositions, civilization's emerging governments forecast the state of righteous judgment of Lord Yehoshua's Kingdom.

To be sure, we have the orthodox context that unfolds the biblical Testaments. To the true worshiping reader's dismay, however, we withhold a description of the substantive manner in which Lord Yehoshua's Shekinah both confounds and liberates a worshipper in the sublime glory of the Lord's grace. Also, we withhold a description of the Kingdom and communion of the saints, until the end of our work.

For now, we see that Immanuel's Law's third derivative statement achieves its goal of demonstrating how the physical world adheres to the anthropocentric conventions of the biblical Testaments. What is more, its being the culmination of the first and second derivative statements, our third derivative statement completes Immanuel's Law, itself.

Realizing its goals, our orthodox judgment—Immanuel's Law—secures a critical understanding of the way the Logos expresses truth, as the Logos extends any-possible-world under Y'haweh. Thus, Immanuel's Law establishes a critical understanding of our definition of truth and even demonstrates objective proofs for the Church's Creeds: our orthodox judgment substantively establishes the set-apart holiness of Y'haweh; moreover, our judgment establishes how the Logos extends the world in a way that incites humanity's interpersonal experience, which the Mashiach and the Spirit completes. Of a truth, Immanuel's Law vindicates human freedom under the Lord.

Rejoice! Immanuel's Law is complete.

"In the Beginning"

Anxious are we to flee from the unrelenting complexity of our orthodox judgment: a complexity that denies the impatient reader any mastery. The true worshipper who gives his or her best effort to attend to Immanuel's Law's daunting details at least takes away the understanding that Immanuel's Law gives us a critical understanding of our initial definition of Y'haweh's expressed truth. Thereby, our orthodox judgment gives us license to continue down truth's landscape. Unmistakably, our orthodox judgment establishes the first revelation that we glean from the biblical Testaments: Immanuel's Law determines that Y'haweh is our creator, with whom is our fulfillment—even our meaning and purpose.

Later, we shall complete our first revelation, as we discuss Y'haweh's covenant with Adam, whose downfall, because of disobedience, requires reconciliation through the Mashiach, the new Adam, whose obedience sustains eternal fulfillment. At present, we can reflect upon the critical understandings of Y'haweh's expressed truth. We can swiftly describe the context of Moshe the law giver's creation account: an account that ultimately alludes to the fact that the Logos beatifically expresses the world, in order to express Y'haweh's absolute being and fulfillment, which we true worshippers experience, while Y'haweh's expressed persons fulfill our personhood within an interpersonal community.

To grasp an orthodox understanding of Moshe's creation account, we must first keep in mind that invisible Y'haweh does not need any appearing, existential physicality to complete him. Thus, the appearing creation extends to our benefit, in regards to our complete ontological being in him. Also, from Immanuel's Law, we recognize that the Logos' causality is syntactical; therefore, we recognize the fact that the appearing world's progression is for the cultivation of our dynamic reference frames' capacity to generate personalized magnitudinous analogues that maintenance our temporal ontological being.

Furthermore, we conclude that invisible Y'haweh does not need six days to bring about the appearing creation. The New Testament' speaks of the instant regeneration of the present creation into a new creation in a moment[1] in time—"in the twinkling of an eye"[2].

We understand that Y'haweh's Logos expressed the appearing creation in six days for our advantage: the six days magnify our rest from this world upon Shabbat—the seventh day of completion, that is, after the spiritual prevailing of Y'haweh's judgment completes our personhood and interpersonal community in Y'haweh's expressed persons, the Mashiach and the Holy Spirit, respectively. Upon the Shabbat, that is Heaven's Kingdom, we see invisible Y'haweh clothed in Lord Yehoshua's securing of our praises.

We must also keep in mind that Moshe the Law giver did not have our contemporary scientific understandings to describe the truths that the Holy Spirit conveyed to him: Moshe could not possibly perceive that the Earth maintains an elliptical orbit like other planets that orbit our Sun, which is one among innumerable stars within countless galaxies. Nevertheless, Moshe sufficiently related the truth-functional-form that the present creation abides by: Moshe's account essentially records how the Logos systematizes the creation to sustain our dynamic reference frames. Likewise, the account foreshadows the spiritual work that Y'haweh's expressed persons will effect upon Shabbat.

In simplicity, Moshe begins the creation account with a prologue that summarizes the whole account by saying, "In the beginning, Elohim [Y'haweh] created the heaven and the earth."

Afterwards, Moshe begins the body of his account by writing the following:

---

[1] Taken from the Greek word *atomos,* which means the smallest unit of a measure.
[2] 1 Corinthians 15:42

And the earth was without form, and void; and darkness was upon the face of the deep. And the Spirit of Elohim moved upon the face of the waters. And Elohim said, let there be light: and there was light.[1]

Unknowingly, when Moshe recorded how light precedes the forming of the worlds, Moshe related how the extension of the ordered worlds stands upon the regularity of converging force-exchanges that syntactically relates to the regularity of expanding force-exchanges, that is, light. With a critical eye, we observe that Moshe's creation account does not contradict the fact that the appearance of physical properties and magnitudinous relationships constitutes the appearing world, despite varying and specific quantum properties. Acknowledging the Logos' truth-functional-form, Moshe's account then describes the appearance of syntactically integrated biological systems, from single cell systems unto multicellular systems — that is, systems whose seed are in themselves.

Afterward, Moshe's account describes the appearance of mobile animals. In integrative — "evolutionary" — order, Moshe describes the appearance of marine life, fowls, reptiles, mammals, and lastly humankind. Finally, Moshe's creation account describes invisible Y'haweh's rest, foreshadowing the eternal Shabbat of the Mashiach in the Kingdom of Heaven.

The Choir of Angels

In Heaven's Kingdom, each soul that the Holy Spirit cleanses of the soul's profane value systems will give varying distinctions to invisible Y'haweh by appreciating Y'haweh's expressed person in Lord Yehoshua from the disposition of the soul's life-experience. Each soul will experience varying sensations in the brilliance of life by clothing Y'haweh in a glorious body of their praise and adoration, and then "the earth shall be filled with the knowledge of the glory of the Lord, as the waters cover the sea."[2]

---

[1] Genesis 1:1-3
[2] Habakkuk 2:14

Still, while we marvel at the coming Kingdom of Heaven, we still must contend with the present world. Since we understand that Y'haweh beatifically expresses the world to establish our temporal ontological being with his completing of our personhood and interpersonal community; we understand the context in which the biblical Testaments record the existence of another body of souls that immediately receive Y'haweh's beatific expression: the Testaments record that another body proves to be an affirming witness to the appearing world's subsuming under Y'haweh's universally expressed holiness, which the Logos' truth-functional-form expresses as orthodoxy's rightness unto our salvation and justice.

Remarkably, the Testaments record the creation of the souls of the angels as an addendum to Moshe's creation account. The Old Testament reports that the angelic souls witnessed the beginning of creation as follows:

> When the morning stars sang together . . . all the sons of God shouted for joy."[1]

One may interpret the metaphorical singing of the morning stars, in this scripture, as light and the invariant force exchanges' producing the normalized world and appearing relationships that reflect Y'haweh's glory. One may conclude that the angels witnessed this light in their souls; therefore, they perceived Y'haweh's ordinances from their inception.

Fittingly, throughout the Holy Bible we find evidence of Y'haweh's use of the angels as witnesses to his creative work. For example, *elohim* is a Hebrew term that the Testaments employ more than 2,500 times: the word means be strong or be in front, as we have said. Being plural in form, the Testaments use the name *elohim* for the biblical judges and angels; their bearing the oracles of Y'haweh's truth and the expression of Y'haweh's glory, respectively. More importantly, the Testaments also use this plural word as a designation for YHWH, because the word captures Y'haweh's use of

---

[1] Job 38:7

the angelic souls to witness his creative work. Basically, the plurality of the word *elohim* apprehends the multifaceted nature of Y'haweh, who assumes a glorious body (within the innumerable company of angels who give witness to his being within creation) until he fully expresses his body in the esteem of his true worshippers—that is, the Choir of Saints.

The biblical Testaments, therefore, describe the angels to be "ministering spirits"[1], because they prove to be the temporary witness that Y'haweh uses to receive his beatific expression of creation, while he procures humankind's adulation. The angels' witness of Y'haweh's expression affirms the existence of all things' adherence to Y'haweh's expressed truth; whether humanity perceives the truth or not.

What is more, because they are the first to esteem Y'haweh, the companies of angels are as a well-fitted garment to his being, and he inhabits their praises, continually. To this end, because their praises are assents of Y'haweh's truth and equity, Y'haweh uses the angels (and ultimately Lord Yehoshua) to proclaim Y'haweh's goodness unto humankind.

Furthermore, the angels are a species without precedent, because Y'haweh revealed his glory to them at the beginning of creation. And, because they witness creation's coming into being, the angels maintain a selfless knowledge of Y'haweh's expressed truth. For this cause, the elect angels do not possess the same faculty of choice and conviction as humankind because they measure the choice between good and evil by the precedence of condemnation that Y'haweh set upon the angels who were in discord with his truth at the beginning of creation. As a result, the angels are not subject to the same intellectual deprivations of humankind. On the contrary, the angelic soul stands in perfect order: their orderly souls perceive the Logos' expressed beauty.

Although the angels are a species without precedence, the biblical Testaments indicate that a precedence exists within their intellectual order. For example, we find that the cherubim are first in the order of

---

[1] Hebrews 1:14

comprehension of Y'haweh's glory. Bearing the designation as the guardians of Eden, the cherubim[1] guard the Holiness of Y'haweh. For this cause, the Old Testament often portrays Y'haweh as standing between two cherubim: his instruction for Moshe to place two cherubim[2] above the mercy seat, upon which the ark of his Covenant rests, witnesses this truth.

Effectively, the two cherubim serve as a symbolic depiction of the expressed person of Y'haweh that he affirms in a body of souls, which the body of angels temporarily composes. Interestingly enough, we see at the end of the biblical Testaments (in the Book of Revelations) that Y'haweh replaces his two cherubs with two anointed ones—Moshe and Eliyahu—who symbolically represent the Church body of true worshippers that will ultimately embody Y'haweh, in the Mashiach. Until such a time, the cherubim, along with the other angelic orders, happily perform their service.

Following the privileged status of the cherubim, all the remaining angels fall into order. There are seraphim[3] who conduct the perennial worship of Y'haweh, and there are archangels who execute Y'haweh's judgments. As well, there are territorial angels who are set over provinces. And lastly, we see guardian angels who watch over Y'haweh's chosen elect. All told, the angels serve the purpose of being witnesses of an incomprehensible, eternal self-existent Spirit to limited, very mortal human beings.

Although the angels are wonderful and superior to humanity at present, the angelic soul will not attain the primacy of a true worshipper's soul at the end of time, because the depravity that a worshipper will have been liberated from, by Y'haweh's expressed persons, heightens the worshipper's soul. Accordingly, the Apostle Sha'ul writes about the future primacy of the true worshippers over the angels by saying to his followers, "Do you not know that we shall judge angels?"[4]

---

[1] Genesis 3:24
[2] Exodus 25
[3] Isaiah 6:1-3
[4] 1 Corinthians 6:3

So, despite Y'haweh's angelic body, we understand that creation has a tentative existence until Lord Yehoshua fully manifests the totality of Y'haweh's truth and righteousness within the souls of his true worshippers. Even though the fruit of the tree in the garden requires the integration of our dynamic reference frames to appreciate the nourishment that we gain from the fruit; only the souls of the true worshippers can add true life to the tree when the tree is no longer misunderstood by the imperfect values of the human soul. And so, when the true worshippers apprehend the salvation knowledge of the risen Lord Yehoshua's pure conscience, which the Holy Spirit redeems the worshippers with; the tree will, itself, proclaim the equity of the overall good that we shall experience in communion with Y'haweh. At such a time, we will clearly understand that Y'haweh made the tree of life in love: a love that the tree exemplifies as it replenishes the air with oxygen, gives shade from the heat of the sun, yields fruit of no bitterness, and dazzles the eye with colors. Truly, such is the love of Y'haweh, and such will the value of the tree of life be to those who receive his love.

Chapter 4

Son of the Morning

"I form the light, and create darkness: I make peace, and create evil: I Y'haweh do all these things."

—Isaiah 45:7

Eden

Heretofore, we understand that truth is the Logos' expression of Y'haweh's good: the expression of the prevailing of right judgment that we see in the unblemished conscience of Lord Yehoshua, the Testator. Furthermore, we understand that we experience Y'haweh's truth as the Holy Spirit instills faith in us, the Testator's beneficiaries, whom the Holy Spirit empowers to turn away from humanity's unjust civilizations unto the Testator's eternal Kingdom. And so, we understand that by the grace of Y'haweh through the faith that the Holy Spirit instills within us, we accept that Y'haweh is existent and our creator; moreover, we accept that with him is our purpose and salvation—the immeasurable gift of his grace in Heaven.

Nevertheless, to understand and appreciate fully Y'haweh's truth and respond fully to Y'haweh's grace, we must further contemplate Y'haweh's enduring good in Heaven, in order for us to relinquish the temporal goods that we acquire through our own efforts. Let us, therefore, begin to contemplate Y'haweh's glory in Heaven by asking ourselves what conception of our salvation in Heaven must Y'haweh's Holy Spirit instill within us that will endow our faith and embolden us to seek the Testator's eternal reward? Likewise, we must ask ourselves what conception of our salvation must the Holy Spirit instill within us that will motivate us to resist the temptation that seeks only the temporary benefits of this world? Also, let us ask ourselves what overwhelming sense of beauty must persist in our souls? And, what sense of beauty reflects our appreciation of the ordinances of Y'haweh's Holy Spirit? In sum, we must ask ourselves what was the conception that the merchantman had of truth's priceless pearl that will likewise endow our faith with optimism and hope for "a better country, that is, a heavenly country?"[1]

If we were skillful artists, what image could we use to depict the heavenly state of felicity that our souls' conceptions must possess? What symmetrical values could we harmonize with whatever physical environment that would sustain our souls in a state where they perceive perennial beauty without, while they experience the bliss of a perennial state of serenity within? Moreover, how could we capture such a state in an image where our several senses are being continuously stimulated and gratified?

For sure, anyone would aspire to be in such a profound state of heavenly felicity forever if one could leave the tumult of life behind with all its ingratitude, strife, violence, loneliness, and the other misfortunes that chase happiness away: this generality must our image capture to do justice to a depiction of the true heavenly felicity that endows faith's hope.

Yet, with or without a skilled artist's painting, our souls can only possess an inner state of felicity when they comprehend what is or could be pleasant. For instance, a person may patiently maintain inner peace, while physical discomfiture strangles him or her; however, what fuels the inner peace within the person is a greater perceptional understanding of what an equilibrium of health and happiness should be.

Still, a picturesque state of felicity may be different from person to person, depending upon the discomfiture, as we shall see, but let us for now begin by painting a biblical model of such a state of tranquility. In this way, we will attempt to describe the common ground that all would readily agree a depiction of happiness should be. We may start by asking ourselves the subsequent questions: let us ask who would not readily agree with us if we say that envisioning

---

[1] Hebrews 11:16

rolling hills of foliage drenched fertile lands that greet the horizon is a pleasant thought? And who would not readily agree with us if we say that seeing a splendid variation of colors that warm and temperament sunlight fume from the fertile grounds is pleasant to the eyes? Could anyone say that a melody of sounds from an abundance of animal life of no savagery is not pleasant to the ears? Or would sweet fruit from trees that yield produce without stint offend anyone's taste? Perhaps if the vines that yield the fruit were bereft of its thorns, the fruit would be more agreeable. Moreover, a bed of soft grass sprinkled with sweet smelling flowers cannot fail to comfort a weary soul, could it? And would one wish for the anxiety of old age in a place where tranquility blends the seasons into timelessness and the heavenly angels give protection against the hazards of the elements?

Yet, to define, truly, our conception of tranquility, we must chase away political orders by apprehending an abundance of necessities; we must chase away vanity by apprehending a universal understanding of manifold beauty in every creature; and we must apprehend health's vitality by making the body impervious to age and disease. As well, we must assure ourselves with corporate benevolence, and perhaps we should even dismiss jealousy by building a community around a single pair—husband and wife—who are in love, having no challenge in their child rearing or no volitions that part one from another. Finally, we must ask ourselves one last question to apprehend a conception of Heaven: if we removed all the impediments of life from our minds, would we conceive a picture of Heaven?

It may be shocking to say that if we removed human history from our minds, our conception of a tranquil place would actually be a conception of a place where the spirit of the animal is at its zenith and the soul of man is perfectly stunted: our tranquil place continuously stimulates the spirit of the animal, while the soul of man, which seeks meaning and value, remains retarded because there is no understanding of want. Indeed, without the privilege of history's inconveniences, the souls of humankind in our place of tranquility remain dormant with no hope of fulfillment, because the soul stands upon an appreciative sense of those sublime understandings that ascribe meaning and value to all things existent, by weighing what is beneficial against what is detrimental. For this reason, the soul's appreciation of our place of tranquility cannot exist unless the soul endures a history of deprivation.

The hazards, which life is privy to, define by contrast our conceptions of felicity; therefore, we shall certainly not call a place that has not endured the grief of life Heaven. Perhaps our tranquil place would be Heaven if its inhabitants appreciated it as a place where they may rest from a life that has burdened them with sickness, lonesomeness, weariness, and fear.

More perfectly, Heaven is a place that proclaims justice to the souls who seek relief from oppression. It is a place of triumph over downfall. Heaven is a place where knowledge proclaims the purposes of the Creator to those who seek a reason for life's disparity. It is a place where time stands still on the answers, because the expectations of the faithful receive the certain knowledge of the Testator's liberty. In fact, Heaven is the expression of Y'haweh and the residence of salvation; therefore, without the privilege of human history's inconveniences, from which the Testator liberates us, we must give a place of tranquility another name. We must identify this place as Eden, because in Eden Y'haweh begins to fulfill the knowledge structure of the human soul, and in Eden, Y'haweh begins to express his own fulfilled soul.

Increasing Value by Increasing the Sense of Beauty

Both sharing the same physical disposition, Eden and Heaven only differ by the measure of value that the soul ascribes to Heaven after Y'haweh delivers the soul from states of detriment: the gifts and endowments that mark a suitors love cannot exist when a suitor and his beloved are in a timeless state of luxury, which luxury is not birthed by want. In Eden, therefore, Y'haweh's love was unknown because in Eden, there had been no want. In fact, one cannot appreciate Y'haweh's glory, which creation's uniformity expresses, when one esteems all things equally. Accordingly, in Eden,

Y'haweh's angelic body, which is splendid and beautiful, had no complementary sense of appreciation in humanity to invoke the sense of beauty, which is the perception of his glory.

We have concluded, therefore, that Y'haweh reflects his glory in Heaven by pronouncing his glory before our shortsightedness. The hazard-free state of Eden simply serves as the perfect model of the felicity that exists for those who seek Y'haweh; moreover, the hazard-free state of Eden verifies that Y'haweh reflects his glory and perfection from the beginning, despite our imperfections.

To appreciate our loss of Eden, let us ask ourselves what detriment defines by contrast the polar extreme of Y'haweh's glory in Heaven. What detriment do we apply to Eden, from which we may interpret all things with salvation knowledge of Y'haweh's glory? Also what detriment must we endure that defines by contrast what the soul must value to realize its fullness, in which the soul affirms Y'haweh's heavenly glory?

Maybe if we only made the soul ignorant of the many facets of nature's intricate design, which produces an array of dazzlingly geometry and elegant motions, nature's marvels would intrigue and compel the soul to find its fulfillment in the delight of satisfying curiosity. For example, the curious silent flutter of the butterfly's wings seems amazingly graceful when one contrasts them with the harsh and determined flap of the black crow. The butterfly's wings massage the eye with soft symmetrically patterned colors, while the black crow only delineates color variation when its harsh black void arrests the eye's attention from other colors. The black colorless wing of the crow, we may relatively describe as a detriment when our senses capture a sense of beauty when perceiving the colorful pattern of the butterfly. Perhaps if the soul's encounter with the colorful butterfly were more infrequent, each encounter would prove to be more delightful, and the sense of beauty that one derives from his or her gaze upon the beautiful butterfly might give the soul a surer sense of fulfillment.

Can one recognize Y'haweh's glory upon such personal fulfillment? Is this sense of fulfillment a heavenly quality?

Again, we must say no, because a person's subjective sense of satisfaction governs the person's appreciative sense that he or she derives from his or her encounter with the beautiful butterfly; therefore, another may or may not appreciate the person's subjective sense of beauty. Thus, the knowledge that the person identifies through what he or she values may or may not agree with another's understanding. And so, only a salvation knowledge that arrays itself around the most appreciable thing, which all value, apprehends Y'haweh's glory, which defines the essence of all things, including the beauty of the butterfly and, above all, the nature of Heaven.

In our continuing quest to unfold truth's landscape by apprehending the salvation knowledge, let us raise our base comprehension of such things as the beauty of the butterfly by raising their value by contrasting them to whatever detriment that we need to meet this end. Let us, therefore, proceed to step outside of Eden by adding mortality to ourselves, because mortality will necessitate a myriad of volitions to acquire the things necessary for our health and vitality. By adding mortality to ourselves, we will find that contemplating the beauty of the butterfly, apart from the toil of labor, will make us consider our butterfly contemplations as a recreational activity or a mark of rest, which we will consider a luxury: a thing of value. Likewise, if we further added detriment to ourselves by making our personal volitions conflict with another's, thus causing our conscience to be birthed by gauging self-gain without realizing another's harm, the strife and conflict that result from conscience's compromise would by contrast magnify our butterfly contemplation as being a heavenly state of an amiable mind. In addition, if we apply eternal suffering beyond the grave, we would identify such butterfly contemplation as the laurels and emblems of heavenly felicity: the evidence of Y'haweh's love, and the salvation of an eternal joyous life.

What is more, if we caused a minister to come graciously with good tidings that showed us how to resolve conscience's compromise, and the hazards thereof, everyone would forecast corporately upon him their subjective feelings of beauty through their common appreciation; and then the acquired salvation knowledge, which their common adoration defines, would invest Eden with the esteem of Heaven and him who bore the tidings with the name *King Eternal*; and upon such a king, we would define Y'haweh's glory and our concurring perception of felicity. Indeed, if the bearer of the good tidings were to have a single truth, he must invariably possess the same truth that we have before laid out.

Invariably, the bearer of good tidings must hold within his message the understanding that the detriment that Y'haweh allows to besmirch Eden, in order to appreciate its value and turn it into Heaven, is evil's mortality (its fatigue, sickness, and disease); and evil's strife (its fear, malice, and violence); and, of all, evil's ignorance, which invokes intelligence, self-determination, and government. All these seek to escape the bane of evil and gain heavenly felicity. In sum, the message of truth that the bearer has in his tidings must ultimately describe Y'haweh's Totality—his three expressions of himself to humanity that comprise not only the natures of both Eden and Heaven, but also the nature of the current world that stands between them.

Redemption (The Act of Grace)

Conclusively, we may say that the world that dwells between the glory of Heaven and the vagueness of Eden is a world that the spiritual disparity of evil initiated: evil transformed the physical comforts of Eden into whatever harsh environments that highlight the soul's discontent when the soul seeks another good other than Y'haweh's. Still, while we witness the bane of evil, in the world that dwells between Heaven and Eden, we also see the growth of the soul; indeed, we see the soul seeking its own fulfillment: we see a mirage of self-determination—the soul's intelligent ability to choose between two or more temporal goods, in an attempt to escape the bane of evil, to realize its own welfare.

Correspondingly, we see in the six day world, which dwells between Heaven and Eden, the establishment of Y'haweh's grace upon the soul's pursuit of its welfare: we see Y'haweh proclaiming, to the soul, that he will provide a salvation that equitably sustains human welfare, around him. In the interim world, the grace of Y'haweh affirms him as the eternal good and origin of truth: a truth that contrasts the detrimental and intellectually chaotic state of evil. So while humanity's communal choices produce temporary pleasures that they accept as the only good, which results from human invention, the manifestation of Y'haweh's truth endows the faith of Y'haweh's worshippers; thereafter, they perceive and strive for his true good in the seventh day world that is Heaven.

And so, while evil pronounces truth by contrast, Y'haweh's grace affirms truth by establishing his good in Heaven. At best, evil creates a world of temporary fulfillment inequitably, while Y'haweh's grace secures an eternal fulfillment that defies evil's everlasting pain.

In view of that, we must underscore the fact that the communal choices of humanity that seek to escape evil's bane cannot apprehend the salvation knowledge of Y'haweh without his revealing the truth, because the choices that humanity make invariably esteem someone or something above Y'haweh. As a result, Y'haweh must condemn the uninformed choices, because the knowledge that the soul gleans from the choices is faulty, given that Y'haweh arrays all things in Eden around his esteem. In particular, any faulty understanding of creation and its concurring temporary satisfaction (like evil) are chaotic and fleeting in time.

We whom Y'haweh elects must, therefore, appreciate the light of Y'haweh that allows us to peer beyond evil's distortions. By his grace, we behold (through faith) a corporately agreed upon place of tranquility. In this way, we disallow evil's misrepresentations, which cloak Heaven's true splendor.

In fact, we may metaphorically say that evil serves as an undercurrent to the river of truth, which runs through a world that stands between Eden and Heaven. As the biblical Testaments describe, the souls of the true worshippers are essentially the seeds that Y'haweh plants in evil's soil of corruption.[1] The water from Y'haweh's river of truth nourishes the seeds; from the kindred relationships that comprise marriages, families, and lower-level

---

[1] This analogy is a loose interpretation of 1st Corinthians Chapter 15: 35-50.

civilizations unto the complex relationships that comprise higher-level civilizations. Following, Y'haweh harvests the seeds with his grace, only to display them in his salvation as the fruit of Heaven's glory, after the fall of civilization. So, through his grace, Y'haweh harvests the corrupted seed of the soul by endowing them with the faith to see his greater good, which abides beyond human invention.

In detail, we find in the Holy Bible the understanding that Y'haweh, through acts of grace, affirms his imminence in Heaven by providing more of life's sustenance than that which the true worshippers have sacrificed of their own sustenance. Equally important, we find in the Holy Bible the understanding that Y'haweh's grace affirms his imminence in Heaven before humankind by even providing a far more valuable life than any life that one consumes with religious ambition: in the Holy Bible, we find that the heavenly good is vastly superior to that which religious hypocrites acquire through their seeking of self-renown through public acts of piety, in which they tediously observe religious law, without observing charity. So when we truly consider Y'haweh's priceless provisions, we interpret his grace as an act of redemption, because when he provides an eternal life that is of greater value than our earthly lives, he essentially redeems his worshippers, who have sacrificed their worldly volitions: he essentially buys back the lives of his worshippers from his condemnation of evil. Correspondingly, because Lord Yehoshua possesses the greater valued life in Heaven, which Y'haweh uses to redeem the lesser-sacrificed lives of the true worshippers, Y'haweh's redemption bolsters his grace by precluding that no religious deed that a worshipper accomplishes is worthy of his provision. Y'haweh's grace is, therefore, a free gift of an eternal life. And so, we may say that any performances of religious deeds that do not seek the vanity of public acclaim characteristically denotes those who only seek to commune with Y'haweh through faith.

What is most important for us to know, therefore, is that the Holy Bible declares that Y'haweh's only provision that redeems his worshippers is the life, death, and resurrection of Lord Yehoshua, whose life serves as a catalyst of redemption to secure the true worshippers from evil, in order for them to witness Y'haweh's glory in Heaven. Essentially, Lord Yehoshua is the bearer of Y'haweh's good tidings: in life, Lord Yehoshua lived selflessly unto Y'haweh by not regarding his own welfare; thereby he delivered the tidings of truth for the welfare of Y'haweh's true worshippers. In death, Lord Yehoshua suffered evil's condemnation in the place of Y'haweh's worshippers, even though he himself walked in perfect fidelity with Y'haweh's Law. Finally, in his resurrection, Lord Yehoshua lives forever as the consummate expression of Y'haweh's love for them whom Y'haweh eternally rewards for following the deeds of Lord Yehoshua, who gives the wealth of his eternal life to those who have given theirs.

We now begin to see the breadth of truth's landscape in Y'haweh's redemptive work: truth's landscape unfolds like a river that runs within the world that serves as a conduit between Eden and Heaven. The landscape begins at Y'haweh's allowance of evil, and then it unfolds unto the breadth of our redemption. Within the landscape, we see humanity's being confounded by evil's deprivation from which we seek Y'haweh's eminence.

Growing in Grace

What is left for us to do is to "grow in the grace"[1] of Y'haweh by strengthening our faith. We must experience the full richness of Y'haweh's grace by growing in the salvation knowledge of his truth, which initiated this world's quarrel between good and evil: the argument that is the respective subject matter for human history's poetry of ode and lamentation. Surely, by "having [our] loins gird about with truth"[2], we may briefly inspect evil (even the thing that binds and confounds our souls) to better understand and appreciate the good (even the liberty of our souls in Y'haweh's exultation).

Let us, therefore, not discourage ourselves with the temporary grief of this world because we know that our liberty is sure: we know that Y'haweh confounded chaotic darkness with the order of his

---

[1] 2 Peter 3:18
[2] Ephesians 6:14

light. Besides, we know from the scriptures and our concurring understanding of truth that Y'haweh pronounced his good and our salvation over evil's disparity. And so, we know that, for us, evil only serves as a necessary trial from which Y'haweh matures our knowledge structure, which the Mashiach and the Holy Spirit complete. This fact the scriptures allude to by saying, "My son, despise not the chastening of Y'haweh; and do not loathe his correction; for whom Y'haweh loves he corrects, even as a father the son he loves."[1]

The Golden Cities of the "Bright One"

We confidently expect to find our place of peace in Y'haweh's great redemptive work, which forms the expanse of truth. For sure, this place of peace we will find after we gain a better understanding of the spiritual states of both evil and good; because from the state of evil, Y'haweh redeems us by his grace through which he instills in us a perfect conception of his good, which witnesses his fullness as the utmost thing of value: that is, his being the true worshippers' salvation, which again is the single value that turns Eden into Heaven.

To arrest a definitive understanding of evil, let us briefly inspect two poignant Old Testament scriptures that show the coactive relationship between the satanic nature of evil and the mortal nature of sin, which is evil's derivative in the souls of humankind. Thus, by gaining an understanding of these two poignant Old Testament scriptures, which we find in the prophetic books of Ezekiel (Yechezkel) and Isaiah (Yesha'yahu), we may begin to understand how the spiritual natures of good and evil manifest themselves in this world as righteousness (which redemption affords) and sin (which Y'haweh's condemnation affirms as evil), respectively. The two scriptures are as follows:

> The word of the Y'haweh came to me [Yechezkel] again, saying "Son of man, say to the prince of Tyre, 'Thus says the Lord Y'haweh: Because

---

[1] Proverbs 3:11

your heart is lifted up, and you say, "I am a god, I sit in the seat of gods, in the midst of the seas," Yet you are a man, and not a god, though you set your heart as the heart of a god . . . With your wisdom and your understanding you have gained riches for yourself, and gathered gold and silver into your treasuries; by your great wisdom in trade you have increased your riches, and your heart is lifted up because of your riches. Therefore, thus says the Lord Y'haweh: because you have set your heart as the heart of a god, behold, therefore, I will bring strangers against you, the most terrible of the nations; and they shall draw their swords against the beauty of your wisdom, and defile your splendor. They shall throw you down into the pit . . .'

Moreover, the word of Y'haweh came to me saying, "Son of man, take up a lamentation for the king of Tyre, and say to him, thus says the Lord Y'haweh, You have been in Eden the garden of God; every precious stone was your covering, the ruby, the topaz, and the diamond, the beryl, the onyx, and the jasper . . . . The workmanship of your timbrels and pipes was prepared for you the day you were created. You were the anointed cherub that covers, and I had put you in the Holy height of God, where you were. You walked up and down in the midst of the stones of fire. You were perfect in your ways from the day you were created, until iniquity was found in you. By the abundance of your trading you became filled with violence within, and you sinned; therefore, I cast you profaned from the height of God, and I destroyed you, O covering cherub, from among the stones of fire. Your heart was lifted up because of your splendor. I have cast you to the ground."[1]

O shining star, son of the morning, how you have fallen from the heavens! . . . you are cut down to the ground. For you have said in your heart, "I will go up to the heavens; I will raise my throne above the stars of God, and I will sit in the mount of meeting . . . I will rise over the heights of the clouds; I will be compared to the Most High." Yet you shall be brought out to Sheol, to the sides of the pit.[2]

From the satirical elements that we find in Yechezkel's above lamentation, which he wrote to relay Y'haweh's word to the king of

---

[1] Ezekiel 28:1-17
[2] Isaiah 14:12-15

Tyre, we glean an understanding of the spiritual disorder that both constitutes evil and manifests the state of inequity that perennially oppresses humankind. Essentially, we qualify the spiritual meaning behind Yechezkel's lamentation by assessing how the lamentation retains parallel messages, within the satire and the lamentation's main body, respectively: first, the lamentation's satire describes the satanic actions that created the chaotic perceptions of evil's angelic soul. Next, the lamentation's main body describes the concurring inequitable actions of sin that prevent a lasting happiness for humankind. In other words, the satire of Yechezkel's lamentation alludes to the fact that evil has its origin in angelic pride and manifests itself as any misconception of value that is in discord with the true perceptions of the ordinances that delineate Y'haweh's glory as the ultimate value.

Within the satire of his lamentation, Yechezkel speaks of Y'haweh's necessary condemnation of evil, as Y'haweh affirms his glory. Afterward, in the main body, Yechezkel speaks directly of Y'haweh's pending judgment against the pride of the ancient king, to vindicate ultimately the faith of those who humbly look for the glory of Y'haweh by observing his covenants, which the social conscience of the king's people reflects. In the main body of the lamentation, we find that the king's pride cloaked Y'haweh's glory and good for all, because the king's wealth and prowess made his people esteem his unjust deeds as the most favorable way for them to acquire happiness. Regrettably, the people lusted for the riches of the king's city, despite the unjust means that the king used to acquire the riches. In this way, the people compromised their social conscience.

What is more, the king's knowledge of how to acquire gold and silver for the city's treasuries, through violent and other unjust means, caused the king to reach the height of narcissism: he esteemed himself as being god-like. So, it was necessary for Y'haweh to "defile [the king's] brightness" (the king's esteem in other people's eyes). Thus, Y'haweh judged the king harshly to make an example of the king. In this way, Y'haweh made the king's unjust deeds seem repugnant before the people. At the same time, Y'haweh justified the faith of the true worshippers, who pursue the true and lasting knowledge, unlike the fleeting knowledge of the corrupt king.

As we consider the vindication of the saints, which occurred when Y'haweh judged the king, we must note the greater design (behind Y'haweh's judgment and subsequent vindication) that the satire of the lamentation reflects. We ultimately glean from the above scriptural satire the understanding that Y'haweh's condemnation of the king of Tyre's pride is part of Y'haweh's eternal condemnation of a proud cherub who is ultimately behind the pride of the ancient king. In the beginning of the satire when Y'haweh says, "You have been in Eden the garden of God", we find that Y'haweh asserts that the king's pride began when he was a cherub in the Garden of Eden; moreover, at the end of the satire, we observe that Y'haweh finally condemns the cherub's pride by saying, "Your heart was lifted up because of your splendor. I have cast you to the ground."

Effectively, Yechezkel's satire continues by presenting the understanding that the pride of the cherub resulted from his exulted position in Y'haweh's angelic body: Yechezkel writes that the cherub was first in a body of angels who comprehend Y'haweh's glory, in Eden. From the scripture, we glean the fact that the proud cherub comprehended the elements of creation succinctly and, therefore, was the foremost to receive Y'haweh's expression of himself. It follows that the proud cherub (as well as the other cherubs) became the catalyst that Y'haweh used to witness creation's coming into being: the cherub "walked up and down in the midst of the stones of fire", bearing witness to the hot and formless state of the elements congealing into their present forms.

In effect, the proud cherub comprehended the precious stones, which rare aesthetic qualities draw distinction when one's gaze juxtapositions them to the prolific, opaque qualities of the more common elemental compounds; moreover, these stones (among other things) became the cherub's covering, which covering bears witness to the fact that all cherubs are the first to receive Y'haweh's expression of himself within creation. Too, his having been covered in a priestly garment of decorative stone, the proud cherub was ultimately a covering for Y'haweh himself. And so, the cherub in his priestly garment stood between Y'haweh and all others who ventured to perceive Y'haweh's beauty.

Nevertheless, the ministry of the cherub was short lived, because it was necessary for Y'haweh to ascribe iniquity to the cherub when the cherub had stopped complementing Y'haweh's person by the cherub's esteeming himself above every other creature. At that instance, the pride of the cherub dismissed him from the angelic body of Y'haweh, since Y'haweh orders all things in creation around his own esteem (to the proud cherub's dismay).

What is more, because Y'haweh casts the cherub out of his angelic body over Eden, the proud cherub no longer wears a priestly gown decorated with Eden's fine and precious stones, but the cherub wears the garment of a harlot: the worldly garments of the unjust gold gilded cities of Babylon. So instead of reflecting the glory of Y'haweh, the fallen cherub became *Satan*, which means *adversary*: and he is now the adversary of all who solely look to Y'haweh for their good, and he is presently a friend of those who seek his false good of self-aggrandizement, which false good Y'haweh condemns as evil for all time.

In addition, we see Satan's fall described in the satire of our second scripture, *Isaiah 14:12-15*, as well. The prophet Yesha'yahu satirically describes the ancient king of Babylon's downfall by describing Satan's downfall. Yesha'yahu describes the brilliant royal splendor that was the pride of the Babylonian king as being bright and shining—a lust for men's eyes; however, Yesha'yahu concludes that Y'haweh would casts down the king's splendor, as Y'haweh casts down the proud cherub.

In all, we glean the overall understanding from both of the scriptural satires: we glean that Y'haweh originally named the proud cherub *son of the morning*, which means bright beginning. So, we may conclude from our lessons learned heretofore that the positive name, which Y'haweh gave to a cherub who bears such negative qualities, forecasts the good that will come for those whom Y'haweh redeems from the cherub's downfall: although Y'haweh initiated the soul by allowing despair, he at the same time created the faculty of hope from the despair. In point of fact, Sha'ul the Apostle ultimately alludes to the truth of Y'haweh's good coming from despair when Sha'ul wrote to the Corinthians (concerning the Mosaic Law's condemnation of evil) by saying, "If the ministration of condemnation be glorious, the administration of righteousness exceeds in glory, for even that which was created in glory had no glory in this respect, by reason of the glory that excels. For if that which was done away was glorious, much more that which remains is glorious."[1]

Lastly, when we consider the truths that the prophets revealed in their satires, we may draw the conclusion that Y'haweh ultimately redeems us true worshippers from the unjust state of the soul, which exists in the chaotic state of evil, unto the just state of his glorious soul. In fact, we may glean the following understanding, of the circumstances of our redemption, from Yechezkel's lamentation: we may conclude that Y'haweh's redemption works in tandem with his condemnation of evil, because his condemnation of evil vindicates the faith of us true worshippers who look for his good in Heaven by not succumbing to this world's enticements, which follow after evil devices.

Summarily, when we join our interpretations of the above scriptures with our lessons learned heretofore, we have the understanding that Y'haweh created the necessary disparity that initiated the faculty of choice in the soul of humankind when Y'haweh created the attributes that gave the proud cherub the inclination for pride. Humankind's succeeding downfall after Satan's downfall is the beginning of humanity's journey to reach a sustained peace, which peace Y'haweh's grace truly fulfills. Hence, the downfall of humankind, which Satan's error initiated, created the fertile ground from which Y'haweh cultivates the fullness of his true worshippers' souls. And this fullness occurs when we true worshippers achieve an appreciation of his person in Eden by turning away from Satan's error, thus turning Eden into Heaven above.

---

[1] 2 Corinthians 3:9-11

Evil

Y'haweh's severe judgment upon the proud cherub sets a precedence of disparity upon the souls who do not fulfill Y'haweh's Law, while Y'haweh's judgment upon the proud cherub sets a precedence of peace and harmony upon the souls who obtain Y'haweh's grace: Y'haweh's benevolence is upon those whom he empowers to follow him. The disparity that Y'haweh casts upon those who are in discord with his ordinance is necessary because it is impossible for Y'haweh to reflect his eminence when a soul seeks its own imminence apart from Y'haweh's good. In effect, the disparity that Y'haweh casts upon Satan contrasts the good of Y'haweh that he casts upon the angelic body, which did not succumb to Satan's corruption. For that reason, the souls of the angels reflect Y'haweh's existence and good for humanity, while the souls of devils reflect the bane of evil that exists for those who fall under Y'haweh's condemnation. Overall, Y'haweh's judgment upon Satan's discord is the creation of good and evil: two polarized spiritual realities that are eternal (though not absolute) because the nature of the angels, from which Y'haweh defines good and evil, is eternal. Categorically, the eternal state of evil is irreconcilable with Y'haweh's glory because it pronounces Y'haweh's everlasting good by contrast.

As we accept this understanding, we interpret evil as a spiritual reality that the discord of Satan solely initiates and defines. Surely, Satan embodies evil because he turned away from the truth that Y'haweh had made known to him. As a result, Satan's discord determines evil to be a chaotic spiritual state of being. Essentially, Satan's angelic soul did not retain an intimacy with Y'haweh that does not need a law to mandate or describe, empirically. To be sure, because Y'haweh eternally condemned Satan, Satan's evil now manifests itself as the false perceptions of things, actions, or events that occur when one derives a false sense of a good from such things. Thus, while one entertains false perceptions, he or she undermines the true perceptions of the good of Y'haweh's being as a whole.

To be more specific, we understand evil's false perceptions to be chaotic because the false perceptions accept an understanding of a good that is detrimental to another's wellbeing under Y'haweh's good as a whole; therefore, within the false perceptions is where we find the heart of evil's detriment. We may, therefore, conclude that evil's dominion endures unto the breadth of Y'haweh's redemptive work, through which Y'haweh redeems the faith of those who are in the human quest for a peace that realizes his equitable good for all. These people of faith find no justice in evil's advances; and so they look for a state of justice that stands beyond human means, while others like the above ancient kings accept conscience's compromise by believing that there is no better way. Indeed, the children of faith believe that Y'haweh has preserved the absolute purity of conscience for humanity; and so, through faith, they deny themselves and seek for it. In contrast, the faithless children do not believe in absolutes, and they do not believe that Y'haweh has manifested himself unto humankind in a pure form; therefore, the faithless accept diverse corruption in society, unto no certain end. Y'haweh's vindication is, therefore, upon the people of faith who look for his glory, while his judgment is upon the faithless who do not; even as the scriptures proclaim by saying, "The righteous shall live by faith, for the wrath of God is revealed from Heaven against all ungodliness and unrighteousness of men, who hinder the truth in unrighteousness."[1]

Consequently, Y'haweh's vindication pronounces the good, while his judgment pronounces evil's disparity. Furthermore, for the duration of evil's dominion, there are temporary states of both pleasure and pain, because Y'haweh's condemnation of evil concludes that evil manifests itself as a temporary state of pleasure that a person derives from his or her conscience's compromise, even though Y'haweh's condemnation ultimately changes the temporary state of pleasure into eternal pain. Correspondingly, Y'haweh's vindication of the faithful elect concludes the good to be the salvation of those who have endured temporary pain to uphold their conscience for Y'haweh's everlasting pleasure. The ancient roman statesman Marcus Tullius Cicero affirmed this relationship between good and evil in one of his many writings when he wrote, "If you

---

[1] Romans 1:17-18

pursue evil with pleasure, the pleasure passes away and evil remains. If you pursue good with labor, labor passes away but the good remains."

The temporary pleasures that accept conscience's compromise are of such things that physically gratify the body like sexual or culinary satisfaction; moreover, one often derives these temporary pleasures from his or her relief from the following: the physical confinements of physical exertion, the impediments of the harsh elements, and the ills of the body. Summarily, one may say that the most baneful relief from which he or she derives temporary pleasure is his or her break with personal and social conscience to undermine another's good, while he or she realizes some temporary advantage for himself or herself. In contrast, the temporary pain that one endures to realize everlasting pleasure is the suffering of whatever discomfiture (without relief), while one seeks to uphold conscience, in order to prevent the harm of one's fellow. In this way, the everlasting pleasure of all becomes a gift that is salvation, instead of something that he or she has realized by his or her own invention. In short, one would be justified by saying that evil is a love for the temporary pleasures of the body that undermine the eternal wellbeing of the soul.

The Holy Bible describes the pinnacle of evil's everlasting disparity as the spiritual states of death and hell, which states exist to define Y'haweh's condemnation of Satan's discord. We may describe the spiritual sense of death as a separation from Y'haweh's good, and we may define the spiritual sense of hell as the chaotic state of the soul that exists when the soul is separated from any consolation. Then both death and hell joined together defines Y'haweh's eternal condemnation of evil. Accordingly, the Apostle Yochanan wrote of the condemned state of death and hell in the Book of Revelation saying, "Death and hell were cast into the lake of fire."[1]

In fact, the lake of fire, which Yochanan wrote of, is the pit of eternal punishment that the prophet Yesha'yahu described as the place where the proud cherub will be casts. Altogether, we may say

---

[1] Revelations 20:14

that the chaotic state of a soul that resides in death and hell polarizes the ordered state of a soul that resides in heavenly felicity. When the soul is in accordance with Y'haweh's ordinance, which delineates the order of Lord Yehoshua's heavenly Soul, the soul is in a perfect state of justice: no soul infringes upon another's good. In contrast, evil produces states of inequality for any soul that is in its dominion, because evil is borne of false perceptions of a thing, which thing one perceives out of its natural order.

The Veil of Sin

When we consider the horror of evil, the ensuing question comes to mind: we must ask ourselves what spiritual disposition caused the proud cherub to venture upon such a destructive path?

We may surely answer this question by considering the spiritual state of the angels that had existed before Y'haweh condemned Satan: we must consider the fact that there had been no detriment to portend Satan's downfall before Y'haweh condemned him. As well, there had been no detriment that defined by contrast the fullness of the angelic soul, before the condemnation of Satan. By considering such, we may conclude that temptation (an inclination to gain a benefit by resisting conscience) persists within souls who have not found fulfillment. In effect, let us say that if one cannot find contentment by imaging his or her station in life as the resting-place of his or her liberation from some disparity or the place where one earnestly quests to find liberty from present despair, one bears the inclination to appreciate one's station in life by gauging his or her station to another's inferior position; or one endlessly bears the inclination to seek untoward satisfactions.

Satan, therefore, filled his spiritual void with pride to appreciate his exalted position in the angelic body. Indeed, the proud cherub could only draw intellectual distinctions by relatively identifying an intellectual disparity in the other angels whose measured intellect had contrasted his own intellectual prowess. Altogether, the souls of the angels could not appreciate their intellectual order (which witnessed Y'haweh's expressed person within the creation that they saw come into being) because they did not possess a conception of disparity before Satan's fall; however, to sanctify some cherubim among other angels to himself, Y'haweh necessarily condemned Satan's pride to render to the sanctified angels the necessary sense of appreciation that confirms his glory.

The angels' eternal sense of appreciation, therefore, renders to them a surer understanding of all things in creation around Y'haweh's glory and esteem. For this cause, the angels find their health in exalting the person, will, and order of Y'haweh above themselves and all else: certainly, here is where we find the eternal salvation in which the angelic souls find fulfillment.

Notwithstanding, Satan's temptation forebodingly stands before the unfulfilled soul of the Adam (the beginning) of humanity who dwells in the vagueness of Eden, while Y'haweh's glorious light of salvation stands beyond evil's veil. Hence, the eternal condemnation of *Satan's yield to temptation* (evil) can only have a precarious hold upon the soul of humankind, while Y'haweh's redemptive work persists, because humanity (unlike Satan) had no certain knowledge of the eternal essence of elements of creation; therefore, Y'haweh does not eternally hold humanity culpable for Satan's misdeed. In fact, Y'haweh did not create the human soul to witness creation's coming into being (unlike Satan's angelic soul): he created the human soul to establish creation with the salvation knowledge of his goodly person (even with the utmost sense of his glory). In all, Y'haweh's glory in creation, which the angels affirm, stands within humanity's appreciation of his grace, which shines the light of salvation into the dark lives of them whom evil's bane binds.

To give a further explanation of humankind's temporary bondage under evil, let us note the following: when Satan succumbed to temptation, he entertained a desire to gain a corrupt understanding of existence by envisioning all things around his person. For this cause, he immediately incurred Y'haweh's eternal judgment to defy his eternally corrupt angelic soul. In contrast, when humankind succumbs to like temptation, their not having certain knowledge of good or evil, Y'haweh does not condemn the whole of humanity like he condemned Satan. Instead, some incur Y'haweh's grace, while Y'haweh allows others to fall under Satan's eternal condemnation. In this way, Y'haweh advertises his truth to his sanctified as salvation in the unblemished conscience of Lord Yehoshua. The dominion of evil and its concurring temptation, therefore, exist together as the necessary detriment that Y'haweh applies to Adam's Eden. Following, Y'haweh pronounces his grace, which changes Eden into his heavenly glory, as we have said.

As Satan's unfulfilled soul succumbed to temptation and then initiated the darkness of evil, which Y'haweh's light of salvation shines beyond, humanity's like succumbing to temptation incurred evil's mortal manifestation—*sin,* which is a false perception of one's good that actively compromises another's good and shrouds the light of Y'haweh's overall good. In other words, sin—the active faculty of evil—brought humankind into evil's dominion by disallowing a sustained perception of the true good of Y'haweh in the following way:

The veil of evil imputes sin upon humanity by causing them to strive for falsely perceived goods that are primarily borne of sensorial gratification. With their senses, humanity misnomer things in creation by gauging them for self benefit and not unto Y'haweh's glory and good for all. As a result, any gratification that humanity procures from their senses does not apprehend the lasting felicity of the true good: always contention arises between those who have opposing understandings of what is good. Following, scarcity exasperates social strife by disallowing perpetual satisfaction in health, resources, temperate climates, and wealth. For this cause, we see that the human soul, under sin, is unsound, because the soul ceaselessly exacerbates the hardships of life by interpreting life's obstacles with the false perceptions of jealousy, envy, fear, anger, doubt, and apprehension; even as the ancient Yisra'elite King David wrote of his soul's discontent under sin, by saying, "There is no soundness in my flesh . . . neither is there any rest in my bones because of my sin."[1]

---

[1] Psalms 38:3

As a whole, evil's imputed sin is the cause of humanity's inability to apprehend a correct value system that glorifies Y'haweh's person above all else; therefore, humanity's sinful value systems create inequality. Also, because of gross inequality, senses of insecurity ceaselessly arise among members of any given community.

People then pursue self-preservation, which is the most baneful manifestation of sin. In point of fact, one may justifiably conclude that the state of evil ultimately qualifies sin as an individual's self-esteem that is a detriment to another's esteem. Fundamentally, self-preservation causes an individual to devalue another's welfare to realize his or her own welfare; moreover, when one considers his or her own preservation above another's, he or she bears the inclination to commit a sin of conscience: a purposeful infringement upon another's good.

For instance, when one consciously commits sin, he or she chooses temporary satisfaction for himself or herself, while he or she acknowledges the injury that the sin afflicts upon another. Considering this, we may further define the sin of conscience as the purposeful choosing of what is detrimental to self or another over what is good to self without infringing upon another's good. In effect, the sin of conscience is a selfish act committed by an individual against another individual, robbing the offended person's soul of a state of justice.

In closing, let us say that the sin of conscience results from temptation, which is one's natural inclination to acquire some satisfaction for his or her unfulfilled soul without considering the greater and more equitable good of Y'haweh. The outcome of temptation is a blind pursuit of individualism apart from Y'haweh's angelic body. Without a doubt, the individualism is of Satan because Satan succumbed to temptation: he consciously committed sin and so set himself apart from Y'haweh's angelic body. Following, he initiated evil's darkness, and now the shroud of evil, which came into being after Satan's original sin, cloaks the true good and turns truth into a thing sublime—a thing that seems unattainable.

Patience—the Endowment of the Soul

Despite the veil of sin, let us encourage ourselves, since we know that our liberty is sure; therefore, let us rest assured that our patience is the redeeming quality of our souls, because it is the hallmark of virtue, and virtue is the thing that forgoes temptation's momentary aspirations for a conception of an everlasting good. Thus, patience is the measure of the soul's intellectual fulfillment, because it bears evidence that the soul has knowledge of a good that stands beyond its immediate grasp.

We must allow the fact, however, that evil has a strong hold on an unredeemed soul even if patience has endowed the soul, because evil distorts the ideal of what the unredeemed soul is to be patient for. Nonetheless, we who obtain the grace of Y'haweh must encourage ourselves because Y'haweh's Holy Spirit instills within us a conception of the true salvation that justifies the patience of us whom he redeems.

Patience is the natural outcome of the soul's ability to objectify its comprehension, because when the soul objectifies its comprehension and aesthetically seeks to know the variables of the overall good, patience withstands the immediate, sensorial satisfactions, since the soul has determined a greater and more enduring source of healthful vitality. Through patience, the soul's ability to value comprehension aesthetically identifies the benefits of sobriety over drunkenness; affability over malice; and restraint over compulsion.

In sum, patience qualifies virtue as the soul's ability to withstand the temptation of compromising conscience for immediate satisfaction by striving for a supreme and enduring good for all who uphold conscience's preservation. In fact, because the soul's virtue is predisposed to seek knowledge of whatever societal patterns that effect a corporate peace, the soul through common and familiar virtues stands predisposed to apprehend the glory of Y'haweh, as seen in creation's uniformity: that is, the very expression of Y'haweh's love and the enduring equitable good for all.

Once more, we must allow the fact that evil's veil distorts a corporate perception of the true good of Y'haweh: the very good that human civilization must patiently strive for. As a result, the human soul's constitution impatiently accepts the false goods that sundry temptations display: the frail human constitution betimes cannot perceive the faults of such things as over indulgence, lust, greed, and the like. For this cause, human government under evil's dominion accepts an inequity that we may define as the inability to reconcile personal virtue with the stalemate that exists between political injustice and the civil constitutions that seek to quell the injustice inequitably, within the cultures at large.

Despite the tempestuous veil that blinds the soul's virtue, Y'haweh redeems our personal virtue by giving us a conception of his ideal habitation, where personal righteousness dwells in a corporate state of justice. The fruits of his Holy Spirit, which the life of Lord Yehoshua makes manifest, redeems our personal virtue with the Lord Yehoshua's own: Y'haweh's Holy Spirit redeems our faith with Lord Yehoshua's longsuffering, love, patience, and all righteousness that strive for Y'haweh's Rest on the eternal Shabbat. Summarily, Y'haweh's Holy Spirit redeems our soul's virtue with a righteousness that he defines in Lord Yehoshua and imputes upon us his elect who faithfully follow after the equitable deeds of Lord Yehoshua, instead of the sinful deeds of this world. We can only say that because of the righteousness of the redeemer, Lord Yehoshua, our soul's virtue is "strengthened with all might, according to Lord Yehoshua's glorious power, unto all patience and longsuffering with joyfulness"[1]: the greater perceptional understanding of Y'haweh's good, as the equilibrium of health and happiness, gives our souls an inner peace that patience endows, while our souls resist evil's temptations.

Shadow of the Good

"In your patience possess ye your souls"[2], said Lord Yehoshua to proclaim the truth that the soul should strive for the true good and not the false goods of temptation, because the precarious spurts of

---

[1] Colossians 1:11
[2] Luke 21:19

integrity in the human soul are but the shadows of the veiled everlasting fulfillment that exists within Y'haweh's Holy Spirit. For our purposes, we will here identify these shadows as *virtue*, and we will define virtue as a reflection of Y'haweh's good in the environs of evil. Albeit, we must note that virtue is something other than righteousness, because it is impossible for Y'haweh's good to coexist with evil: righteousness is the unblemished conscience, which reflects the just, self-sacrificing, peaceable, and happy communion that the risen Lord Yehoshua has with Y'haweh his Father; and this righteousness redeems the virtuous faith of those who seek the same communion with Lord Yehoshua; whereas virtue, without faith, is only a behavioral response (which a person's conscience initiates) that pacifies the soul and allows it to sustain peaceable communions with others to acquire that which the soul thinks will gratify its senses, in this world. Thus, when we observe a person's virtues, we see those qualities of him or her that are beneficial for society; however, when we observe a person's virtues that seek to reconcile himself or herself with Y'haweh through faith, we observe the fruits of Lord Yehoshua's Holy Spirit: we see Y'haweh imputing Lord Yehoshua's righteousness unto the person; and then we observe "the spirits of just men made perfect."[1]

Because of sin, people have different opinions on what personal action might best sustain self-fulfillment. In other words, people have different opinions of what is virtuous: the idea of a picturesque state of felicity varies from individual to individual, as we have said. To some, virtue is sobriety in the midst of incessant lust; or courage in the midst of fear; or even conformity to social convention by denying self-indulgence. Yet, to others, virtue is industry in the midst of poverty; or great military prowess in the face of powerful enemies; or better yet, some deem virtue to be the convenience of wealth, affluence, and luxury over nature's scarcity.

Evil's dominion gives virtue a relative nature, because the sins of evil compromise that which all souls have in common: sin compromises conscience—the certain knowledge of what is harmful

---

[1] Hebrews 12:23

to self and others. Without the faculty of faith, humanity considers it impossible to avoid conscience's compromise, because they have no knowledge of Y'haweh's truth. For that reason, people erroneously weigh good and evil differently, because they weigh the outcomes of what they deem to be virtuous choices differently. For example, to some gluttony may be soothing to the senses; however, gluttony is a detriment to a person's overall health. Besides, where there is want for food among many, a person's gluttony is not only a detriment to the person's individual health, but also a detriment to the health of the overall company; therefore, one should not consider gluttony, in this vein, as virtuous. In addition, lethargy at times may be healthful to the body; however, when lethargy exists in the midst of some corporate and physical venture, lethargy is a social detriment. What is more, nudity may forecast the beauty of a person's form; however, when nudity steals the sentiments and affections away from a person's social obligations of fidelity, one should not consider nudity as virtuous.

Virtue stands on the horizon between good and evil: when one's virtue reconciles himself or herself with Y'haweh's ordinances through faith, Lord Yehoshua redeems his or her virtue with his righteousness; however, when one's virtue reconciles himself or herself with humanity apart from Y'haweh's glory, Lord Yehoshua condemns his or her virtue as the epitome of evil, because the consummate form of evil is a misinterpretation of something as being good when it actually leads to everlasting despair. In effect, there is no cultural or social convention that alone can produce the lasting good of Y'haweh, for the soul; therefore, a soul that ascribes its virtue to any human endeavor, apart from Y'haweh, falls into perdition.

With thanksgivings, we must always acknowledge the gifts of Y'haweh, especially the simple knowledge of him, which is our greatest gift. When we consider our wealth in understanding, we must be patient with those who have not obtained our intellectual gift. When we acknowledge the fact that some identify things as virtuous apart from Y'haweh's glory, we must also acknowledge the fact that no one would willingly destroy himself or herself: a person of sound mind would not willingly set himself or herself apart from the good of Y'haweh's Spirit, only to follow a course that leads to eternal pain, if the person had knowledge of what is truly good and evil in the eye of faith.

We then understand that our intellectual disparities beget the faculty of choice, which begets the complexities of our very souls; therefore, the disparities are necessary, until we find the fullness of our souls within the simple but brilliant Totality of Y'haweh. Surely, all intuitively seek peace, even though evil concludes the means to seek peace unto destruction when some seek peace apart from Y'haweh. Satan manifests his temptations through the unjust gold gilded cities, like ancient Tyre and Babylon, to beguile humanity into succumbing to evil's devices. Within his cities, Satan portrays himself as a political solution; a technological innovation; a sexual enticement; a novel social movement; a reason to seek self-aggrandizement; and, of all, a sure social panacea: at such a time, "Satan himself is transformed into an angel of light."[1]

The Faithful Body—the Temple of Y'haweh

We, who through faith seek the true light, must not fall prey to Satan's enticements, because we now know that the choices that we make are hazardous in the long run when sin turns the choices into selfish acts. Without the mercy of Y'haweh, our only respites from our bad choices spring from what we may call familiar virtues: that is, such virtue that we corporately pursue. We find brief respites in civility, morality, decency, and the public assents. Essentially, we find rays of hope in public agreement, because when familiar virtue bolsters a choice, the choice is not entirely selfish: familiar virtue determines all its choices to be acts of endearment, which are expressions of one's benevolence to another for the betterment of all.

In effect, virtuous choices often lead to the behavioral patterns that we recognize as devotion, duty, fidelity, allegiance, affection, obligation, and all that we identify as faithfulness within social relationships: evident is the fact that within communal betterment is individual betterment. We will here ascribe the name *faithfulness* to

---

[1] 2 Corinthians 11:14

the whole of the virtuous choices, because one is faithful to what he or she deems to be virtuous.

Even so, we now know that evil undermines virtue by putting forth the false goods of the golden cities of Babylon: perpetually, evil prevents humanity's devotions from seeing what is eternally good. In operation, evil confounds virtue, rendering its ideals unfulfilled, because the false goods that virtue grasps in evil's dominion only bear utility temporarily.

To see past the veil of sin, we have only to accept the fact that Y'haweh is the only one who must be entirely selfish in his aspiration because he is the bench mark of the truth and salvation that ultimately sustain creation to benefit all who devote themselves to him, through Lord Yehoshua. Y'haweh's selfishness (even his jealousy) benefits all whom he elects. In fact, Y'haweh redeems the virtue of his elect (whose virtue is sometimes self-serving) with the truly selfless and faithful righteousness of Lord Yehoshua, whom Y'haweh begot for Y'haweh's fulfillment.

As we have said, Y'haweh expresses his true good in the pure conscience of Lord Yehoshua; therefore, the good that holds Lord Yehoshua's devotions empowers him to be entirely selfless. In this way, the Lord overcomes evil's temptations to become the standard of truth for us. So, we must ascribe the name *righteousness* to Lord Yehoshua's virtue, because his is eternal fulfillment, while we only experience the shadow of such a rest.

Furthermore, when we consider the selfless devotion of Lord Yehoshua juxtaposed to jealous Y'haweh who expresses the Lord as the only true benefactor of the faithful, we begin to ascertain the fact that the purest form of faithfulness assumes a body composed of two, because it is impossible for an individual to be truly faithful, in all things, to more than one. When two devote themselves to one another, they assume this body; however, only Y'haweh through Lord Yehoshua and his body of true worshippers can assume the natural body of faithfulness that endures eternally.

For example, Y'haweh allowed the existence of evil that he might be the only one who is able to assume the form of being truly faithful to those who devote themselves to him through Lord Yehoshua.

Y'haweh is as the scriptures testify by saying, "Faithful is He who calls you."[1]

Y'haweh is certain to bring deliverance to those who invoke his benevolence with the higher knowledge of his glory that we find in our exultation of him. And so, while evil's sin disallows true faithfulness within humanity and the angels find harmony only when they center their devotions upon Y'haweh, we true worshippers will find our salvation by singularly devoting ourselves to Y'haweh's good through faithful Lord Yehoshua.

In view of that, we may say that Lord Yehoshua and all the souls who worship Y'haweh through Lord Yehoshua paradoxically define the natural body of faithfulness, which body Y'haweh composes of two: the like-minded souls of the true worshippers, whom Y'haweh redeems with the righteousness of Lord Yehoshua, are one body in spirit, while Y'haweh who expresses himself in three natures is one, even as the following scripture says, "Hear, O Yisra'el: Y'haweh our God is one Lord."[2]

The Lord Yehoshua's body of true worshippers bears a singular admiration for Y'haweh and affirms Y'haweh's fullness. In return, Y'haweh's Holy Spirit gives Y'haweh's worshippers the eternal felicity that their souls value as salvation, which is the thing that virtue's devotion strives for, in faithfulness.

All things considered, the body of faithfulness establishes the truth of Y'haweh, which is for all his worshippers to come to perfect knowledge of him as their benefactor who is faithful through and through. And because the body of faithfulness establishes his truth, the body of faithfulness is the eternal temple of Y'haweh. Furthermore, because Y'haweh realizes his Holy Temple by expressing himself to humanity through the faithfulness of Lord Yehoshua, we must call the body of faithfulness the Body of Lord Yehoshua, even the Body of Christ.

---

[1] 2 Thessalonians 5:24
[2] Deuteronomy 6:4

Marriage in the Holy City of the Kingdom of Heaven

In truth, our place of salvation can be no other place than in the Body of Lord Yehoshua, where we are sure to find the felicity of our souls. Certainly, in this place, Y'haweh possesses our eternal devotion, for no greater love can we have than our very own souls' salvation. In essence, the Body of Faithfulness is a Holy Marriage where two hearts beat as one. Thus, the conception that will hone our understanding of our place of salvation and prevent us from yielding to the temptation to seek false, immediate goods is a conception of an eternal Holy Marriage, in which we become one with Y'haweh to gain that which completes our souls.

What better conception of felicity can we have other than an image of a place where our wishes agree with Y'haweh's grants? And what better way to define salvation than to define it as our faithful marriage to Y'haweh's Soul?

Truly, the value that transforms Eden into Heaven is the salvation of this Holy Marriage, since no greater fulfillment can we seek. The breadth of truth that persists through Y'haweh's redemptive work concludes in the joyous life of this holy matrimony. In fact, the Holy Bible itself concludes with a description of the Holy Marriage between Lord Yehoshua and his true worshippers.

Because it is the fulfillment of truth, the Holy Marriage is where the state of justice resides: within the Holy Marriage, personal fulfillment exists in such a way that one's personal aspirations do not conflict with another's, for all appreciate his or her station in life as a place of salvation from unjust cities like Tyre and Babylon. So while others acquire wealth by defying conscience and enslaving those who dwell in Babylon, we true worshippers look beyond evil's enslavement to the liberty of our souls that will exists in a Holy Marriage. We expect to see a city that our hands have not made, because its riches are an expression of Y'haweh's grace. We seek the riches of a city that Y'haweh gives us freely; therefore, we do not have to rob others, because his love eternally provides our needs.

Essentially, we who seek the Holy Marriage seek to abide in New Yerushalayim[1], the *City of Our Peace*.

Unlike evil, which makes virtue assume a social state of objectivity that does not reconcile itself with the soul's subjective sense of beauty, the Holy Marriage will reconcile everyone's subjective senses with the sentiments of the Body of Lord Yehoshua, as a whole. Within the Body of Lord Yehoshua, Y'haweh's Holy Spirit will reconcile the subjective taste and preferences of the soul with humanity's sought for equity in social communion: the subjective sense of beauty in a true worshipper's soul will become married to the objective understanding that the members of the entire true worshipping Body of Lord Yehoshua possess. Effectively, the true worshippers' objective senses of beauty will apprehend the glory of Y'haweh, which the worshippers ultimately find in his holy matrimony.

In the end, when social doctrines run their course and fall short of rendering an equitable common good, Y'haweh will continue to reveal himself to those who seek him in faith, and when human progression seems more virtuous than Y'haweh's revealed true good, he will conclude history by judging the unfaithful with hell's condemnation, and rewarding the faithful with the blessings of his love in the harmony of his Holy Marriage. Then such will be the fullness of time.

Wellspring of Everlasting Life

We safely conclude that within Lord Yehoshua we find both the experience of creation's finite reign of evil unto the everlasting reign of Y'haweh's goodly Holy Spirit. A worshipper, then, has only to accept Lord Yehoshua's life's sacrifice in place of his or her own, and

---

[1] The name *Yerushalayim* derives from the pre 14th Century BC Semitic name *Urusalim*. The name contains the Semitic root words, *uru* (city) and *salim* (a name of a divinity), which words join together to give the name *Urusalim* the following meaning: "the city of the god Salim." *Salim* is thought to be a derivation of the name of the Akkadian god Shulmanu; however, the word *salim* eventually took its current Hebrew connotation (peace) to define the name *Urusalim* as "the city of peace."

a worshipper has only to accept Lord Yehoshua's devotion to Y'haweh's everlasting good in place of his or her own selfish aspirations.

In fact, one may justifiably ask how could a true worshipper devote himself or herself to the temporary benefits of evil, only to suffer its eternal consequences, if he or she has certain knowledge of the everlasting joy of Y'haweh's glory, which Lord Yehoshua embraced patience for? How could the merchantman give away truth's priceless pearl if he were certain of its value?

Let us not lose the pearl of salvation that Y'haweh has graciously given us in the Body of Lord Yehoshua, for now we know its measure and value, but let us here delineate the landscape of the pearl of wisdom, which we have unfolded, to secure within our souls the bond of Y'haweh's love: we clearly see now that the landscape of the pearl of truth runs like a river, emanating from the Holy City New Yerushalayim—the city of peace that beckons our souls' devotion. Moreover, we clearly see now that the river that springs from the City's fruit bearing tree of life is the Holy Spirit of Y'haweh, whose glory the City celebrates. The waters of the river revive our souls with hope, longsuffering, patience, love, and all such qualities that defy our compulsion to seek only temporary satisfaction. Thus, we can but respond to the Holy Spirit with love, standing wedded to our salvation.

Chapter 5

Adam

"What is man, that you are mindful of him? And the son of man, that you visit him? For you have made him a little lower than the angels, and have crowned him with glory and honor. You made him to have dominion over the works of your hands, and you have put all things under his feet."

—Psalms 8:4-6

Scriptural Misconceptions

A common error that non-Christians and some Christians make when interpreting the scriptures is that they make the assumption that Y'haweh miscalculated the actions that humanity would take. People assume that Y'haweh hastily provided a Mashiach in a haphazard attempt to become the panacea for humanity's spiritual and societal ills: they think that through such a provision Y'haweh sought to recover his suzerainty over humankind, at the last minute.

Common interpretation errors are unavoidable because the Church has not objectively established biblical orthodoxy in the manner that our orthodox judgment—Immanuel's Law—establishes orthodoxy: Immanuel's Law renders a critical understanding of Y'haweh's expressed truth, which inspired the scriptures. Immanuel's Law uses independent principles to demonstrate how the creation and our human experience adhere to the orthodoxy that the biblical Testaments entail—that is, that Y'haweh's expressed will translates Y'haweh's holiness as the prevailing right judgment that we see in the unblemished conscience of Lord Yehoshua, the Mashiach; unto whom the Holy Spirit redeems our faith and so fulfills human understanding, while condemning human civilizations' shortsighted judgments.

Because the Church lacks an understanding of the expressed truth that inspired the scriptures and the manner in which the Holy Spirit cultivates and completes human understanding, in respect to the prevailing of Lord Yehoshua's right judgment; non-Christians and the Church commonly entertain the subsequent misconceptions as they study the scriptures: not recognizing how Y'haweh cultivates and fulfills humanity's knowledge structure, the Church wonders to what extent that Y'haweh infused grace into Adam, enabling him to make moral choices. Not grasping orthodoxy, theologians fail to recognize that Adam only had a sense of Y'haweh's grace as Adam understood his physical and healthful dependency upon Y'haweh: the theologians ignore the fact that the scriptures relate that Adam did not have our moral aptitude before he ate from the tree of the knowledge of good and evil.

Without a systematic and orthodox understanding of Y'haweh's expressed truth, modern scholars readily misinterpret certain paradoxical statements in the scriptures and consider the ambiguous texts to be the result of translation errors. Often modern scholars overlook certain scriptural truth by considering some scriptures to be copy errors or even unnecessary rhetoric. And so, they perceive incongruities in the scriptures and render inaccurate translations. What is most unfortunate is that modern scholars even mistake gender terms (which the biblical authors purposely used) as a lack of sensitivity to the modern notions of political correctness.

We may say that there are many scriptures that testify to Y'haweh's foreknowledge of the course of humankind and the fulfilling of his pleasure, and these scriptures render accurate accounts of his will. We only have to consider the scriptures in the light of our orthodox judgment.

Translation obstacles arise at the very beginning of the scriptures. The accounts of humankind's beginning, in the first and second chapters of the book of Genesis, do not seem to correlate; moreover, the primary message of these chapters do not seem to give evidence of Y'haweh's sovereignty or Y'haweh's revealed person in Lord Yehoshua.

At the outset, Moshe, the author of the book, repeatedly used (in the first chapter) the term *elohim*—the plural Hebrew word for *god*—instead of using the term *eloi*, the singular form of the word. Then, to make matters more confusing, Moshe recorded Y'haweh speaking to a company when he decided to create humanity, Y'haweh's saying, "Let us make man in our image, after our likeness: and let them have dominion over the fish of the sea, and over the fowl of the air, and over the cattle, and over all the earth, and over every creeping thing that creeps upon the earth."[1]

Following, after Moshe recorded how Y'haweh gave man dominion over the earth, he recorded how Y'haweh not only made man after his image. Moshe also recorded how Y'haweh made a female counterpart of man, as well.

When a contemporary person considers how things transpired in Moshe's initial account of humankind's origin, he or she might be tempted to interpret Moshe's use of the word *man*—the term that Moshe used to describe both male and female—as a misnomer that Moshe should not have used. A contemporary person would likely assume that Moshe should have used more politically correct terms, such as *people* or *the human race*.

Even so, in the second chapter of Genesis, Moshe's account is less vague, by far. First, we see that Moshe affixed the Tetragrammaton *YHWH* to the plural word *elohim* to describe the self-existent Spirit. Secondly, we find out that Y'haweh provisionally allotted Adam dominion over the earth, on the condition that Adam not eat from a tree of knowledge: Y'haweh said, "The tree of the knowledge of good and evil, you shall not eat of it: for in the day that you eat of it you will surely die."

In addition, we find out that Y'haweh did not arbitrarily create Adam's female counter part: Y'haweh miraculously birthed her from Adam's body to fulfill him with her companionship. Also in the second chapter, we even find that Y'haweh gave Adam the responsibility of naming his female companion, in the same manner in which he had given Adam the responsibility of naming earth's

---

[1] Genesis 1:26

animal life. To wit, Adam named her Havah, meaning *Mother of the Living*.

The differences between the two accounts, in each respective chapter, are evident. Because the second chapter renders to Havah a far more submissive role than what a reader witnesses in the first chapter, scholars often assume that the second chapter is an illegitimate version that Moshe or other authors added to an unknown author's earlier account, which comprises the first chapter. To make matters worse, the third chapter seems to be incongruous with the first as well. In the third chapter, Y'haweh deprives Adam and Havah of the dominion that he had given them because the couple succumbed to the intrigue of a serpent, which they should have had dominion over: the serpent seduced them to eat from the prohibited tree of knowledge, even though they should have been wiser than he. In addition, the third chapter seems to paint the picture that the actions of the couple surprised Y'haweh: the chapter seems to indicate that Y'haweh hurried the couple out of the garden before they could grasp hold of his eternal life; moreover, the third chapter presents Y'haweh as hastily clothing the couple with animal skins to cover their shame.

To reconcile these interpretational issues, we must first trust in the scriptural integrity, and then with patience, we must expect the truth to become more obvious. To begin, let us state that Lord Yehoshua himself quoted the above scriptures, testifying to their validity. In addition, a multiplicity of manuscripts throughout the ages is consistent with the above content. Secondly, let us consider the fact that Moshe knew better than anyone that every layperson or scribe must not take the sacred name of Y'haweh in vein, even when writing. In fact, the scribes, who assumed Moshe's role of chronicling the sayings of Y'haweh, reverenced his sacred name, like Moshe: they applied the Tetragrammaton so well that they forgot its pronunciation.

And so, when we consider these particulars, we must recognize the fact that it is hardly possible that Moshe and the editors of the book of Genesis would arbitrarily use the term *elohim* instead of YHWH. Surely, if they adapted an earlier account to their own, they would have replaced the word *elohim* with the Tetragrammaton. It is evident that whatever scriptural conventions that the authors, scribal chroniclers, and priests passed down to us have significant meaning, even if the scriptures seem ambiguous or paradoxical.

Of course, the business of this work is to shed light on some of the scriptural ambiguities. We recall that we have put forth an explanation for Moshe's use of the term *elohim*: we recollect that we described how and why Y'haweh's body of angels where present to witness his creative work.

Although Moshe noticeably fails to implicate the angels in this way, other scriptures do. For instance, Moshe himself mentions their presence in the same book of Genesis: he calls the angels *the sons of God*—an appellation given to them in other scriptures.

We realized in our last chapter that the angels assume a body to cover invisible Y'haweh, their being expressions of him. We understood that the angels who did not succumb to Satan's temptation ascribed salvation to Y'haweh, their seeing and reflecting his Glory throughout creation.

From our lessons, we may interpret the above scriptures in the following way: when Y'haweh said, "Let us make man in our image, after our likeness: and let them have dominion . . . male and female made he them", he was speaking to the angels who ascribed salvation to him. And because he was speaking to the body of angels, we may assume that the image that he sought to mimic, by creating Adam and Havah, is not only his personal image—that is, his Spirit—but also the image of him and his wedded angelic body: a body that foreshadows the Body of Christ. To this end, Y'haweh created Adam to become the benefactor of his wife, as he is the benefactor of the angels, his worshippers, and all creation.

If we accept this understanding, we would readily understand the sentiments behind a curious doctrine of the Apostle Sha'ul, who taught that a man praying, seeking to associate himself with Lord Yehoshua, must pray with his head uncovered, in recognition of the fact that Y'haweh made him in his image. At the same time, Sha'ul taught that a woman must pray with her head covered, because Y'haweh made her in the image of the man; therefore, her covering recognizes that the male and female's relationship reflects Y'haweh's faithful angelic body's foreshadowing the Holy Marriage of the Body of Christ. Thus, the infidelities of male and female relationships offend the faithful and obedient angels, even as Sha'ul rights, "For this cause ought the woman to have authority on her head because of the angels."[1]

Adam's Lost Dominion

If our assertion that Adam and Havah reflect the Holy Marriage is true, one may wonder how does Y'haweh glorify himself in such an indirect relationship with Adam: the only thing that subdued Adam and his companion to Y'haweh was their obedience to his prohibition from their eating of the tree of knowledge. Furthermore, because Adam and Havah never really seemed to retain dominion over Eden, one may wonder if Y'haweh could not have foreseen their downfall when he proclaimed to the angels "Let them have dominion over all the earth": without a doubt, it would seem that Y'haweh did not perceive the rise of evil's dominion when he looked for Adam's dominion.

Again, we must commend the scriptural integrity, for the scriptures retain definitive answers to these questions. If we quickly interpret a regularly mistranslated statement that Sha'ul the Apostle made in a letter to the Hebrews, we will reconcile the interpretational difficulties of the above scriptures. The passage of scripture, which we have retranslated into English (remaining as true to the original Greek as possible), is as follows:

> In many times and in many ways of old, God spoke to the fathers by the prophets. In the last days, God spoke to us within the Son, whom He appointed heir of all, through whom indeed He made the ages; who being the radiance of His glory and the express image of His essence, upholding all things by the word of the His power, through his cleansing of our sins. [He] sat down on (the) right of the Majesty on

---

[1] 1 Corinthians 11:10

high, having become so much better than the angels, because he inherited a more excellent name than they.[1]

The latter half of the second sentence in this passage of scripture seems rhetorical to some; moreover, modern translators cannot ascertain which sentence the last prepositional phrase—"through his cleansing of our sins"—modifies, for it seems to modify both the second sentence and the third sentence, which has a contracted subject. Because the statement, which the prepositional phrase makes, seems to be unrelated to the statement of the second sentence, translators unfortunately use the phrase as a beginning modifier of the third sentence. And so, they usually omit a very important Greek preposition, *dia* (which translates as the word "through") in their attempt to augment the third sentence. In this manner, they lose the author's poignant statement, which describes how Y'haweh fulfills his dominion over all things through a new Holy Spirit filled Adam, whom the author proclaims is the essence of Y'haweh and who upholds all things *through* his cleansing of the very sins that caused Adam to lose his dominion. Essentially, the translators usually omit the Greek preposition because they wonder how exactly Lord Yehoshua physically upholds creation by purging our sins. Yet, now having a more perfect understanding, we know that the physical creation is only an expression of Y'haweh: an expression that will console us if we accept him who retains Adam's lost dominion and delivers all power and authority to Y'haweh. In other words, because he gains our appreciation through his sacrifice, Lord Yehoshua gains our singular perception of Y'haweh's glory in creation, after the evolution and fall of human government at the conclusion of the ages that the above scripture notes. In this way, Lord Yehoshua upholds creation by purging our sins.

In addition, by considering Sha'ul's closing statement in the above scripture, we are more able to grapple with Moshe's Genesis account: again, Sha'ul writes that after Lord Yehoshua upheld the creation by purging our sins, the Lord sat down next to the Majesty

---

[1] Hebrews 1:3-4

of Y'haweh, having inherited a far better name and station than the heavenly angels.

In consideration of the above scripture, we see that Y'haweh gave mankind dominion over the earth, even though he used the angels as a catalyst that witnesses the earth and the whole of creation's coming into being; therefore, we see that although Y'haweh gave the angels less physical limitations than that of humankind, Y'haweh blessed humankind through Lord Yehoshua without limitation, giving them dominion. Even though Y'haweh savored the appreciative senses of the angels, who did not fall with Satan, Y'haweh gained his truest sense of fulfillment from humanity upon the sacrifice of Lord Yehoshua.

For us to recall our understanding of truth is for us to know that Y'haweh expresses his fulfillment. For the purpose of affirming his fulfillment, Y'haweh does not esteem any angel to be the expression of his Word—that is, an expression of his mind. Likewise, he does not esteem Adam to be the expression of his Word: he only determined Adam and Havah to be a fleshly image of him, and not his actual Son, who has his mind.

Only Lord Yehoshua inherited the appellation, *the Word of Y'haweh*. Although he walked in the flesh, he held the mind of Y'haweh, as his obedience exemplified. After Y'haweh resurrected him, he regained Adam's dominion for himself and all those whom Y'haweh has empowered to follow him by walking in the higher knowledge of the Holy Spirit, even in accordance with the following saying of the Apostle:

> The first man is of the earth, earthy: the second man is the Lord from heaven. As is the earthy, such are they also that are earthy: and as is the heavenly, such are they also that are heavenly. And as we have borne the image of the earthy, we shall also bear the image of the heavenly. Now this I say, brethren, that flesh and blood cannot inherit the kingdom of God; neither doth corruption inherit incorruption.[1]

---

[1] 1 Corinthians 15:47-50

It is evident that Y'haweh planted the soul of humanity in an environment that he did not intellectually equip them to appreciate. For instance, seeking the reciprocity of his love, Y'haweh planted Adam in the paradise of Eden, but Adam could not identify Y'haweh's consolation. Likewise, Y'haweh created Havah from the flesh of her husband's bosom, but Havah found no fulfillment in her own flesh (that is, her husband's body); therefore, she became the prey of temptation. In short, Y'haweh planted the souls of humankind in spiritual corruption; however, Lord Yehoshua raised them in spiritual incorruption:

> And so it is written, the first man Adam was made a living soul; the last Adam was made a quickening spirit.[1]

Creating the Knowledge of Good and Evil

A closer inspection of the symbolism that Y'haweh used when he created mankind and a closer inspection of the metaphor that Moshe used when he recorded the creation of mankind will reveal the fact that Y'haweh necessarily created an untenable condition for Adam that would ultimately require the sacrifice of Lord Yehoshua; who would then uphold all the things that the angles merely witnessed coming into being. Knowing that he did not instill an appreciative sense of fulfillment into Adam (for Adam never experienced deprivation), Y'haweh prohibited Adam from eating from a symbolic tree of knowledge that Y'haweh beautified and placed in the very center of the Garden of Eden. As a consequence, because Adam did not have an appreciative sense that would allow him to ascribe a salvation knowledge to the purposes of Y'haweh, Adam could only attribute his lack of fulfillment unto the physical thing that he thought was the only thing that he lacked: he thought that he only lacked the fruit of the tree of knowledge when what he truly lacked was the appreciative sense of the benevolence of Y'haweh. In effect, Adam lacked the salvation knowledge of *God*.

---

[1] 1 Corinthians 15:45

In Adam's story, we see the curious disposition of the human soul: we see that the soul determines wealth by what environment that it can afford where the soul is intellectually stimulated by such actions or articles that gratifies its senses. In other words, one determines wealth by what lasting sense of fulfillment that he or she possesses. In consideration of his carefree life, many would say that Adam was wealthy because we deal with scarcity on a day-to-day basis. Yet, one must consider the following: while a sense of fulfillment derives from a sense of appreciation that one acquires because he or she has obtained that which gratifies his or her senses, intellectual stimulation occurs when the soul assesses its gain over detriment: Adam could not make such an assessment; therefore, Adam did not consider himself to be wealthy because he was not intellectually fulfilled.

Strikingly, we see in Adam's story that Y'haweh physically enfranchised Adam in the vast riches of the Garden of Eden: a garden that symbolizes paradise to agricultural cultures—that is, cultures that are the hallmark of human civilization's kindred relationships. Nevertheless, Adam could not spiritually appreciate the wealth; therefore, Adam could not perceive the consolation of Y'haweh. Y'haweh, in fact, gave Adam all the physical trappings that we will enjoy in the Holy Marriage, but Adam had no spiritual sense of devotion to the marriage, because he could not perceive an eternal good to devote his soul to. Adam and his wife did not have any notions of animosity between them, for they gained and shared all things in common. The couple did not suffer any deprivation that would foster any sense of apprehension in their relating to one another. Too, the couple did not have any notion of infidelity between them that would impede their sexual expressions of affection toward one another: Adam and his wife laid bare their souls and bodies before Y'haweh and one another. Still, unfortunately Adam and Havah could not appreciate this supreme relationship as the salvation that we all lack.

In the bosom of Y'haweh, Adam and Havah dwelt in suspended time, despite the momentary actions of life that peaceably radiated Y'haweh's glory around him. Even so, Adam could not appreciate the fact that having a fulfilling relationship with Y'haweh, who alone is eternal, is the only eternal good.

As Y'haweh had expected when he warned the couple not to eat from the prominent tree in the midst of the garden, Satan easily tempted the unfulfilled couple to pursue their own good despite Y'haweh's prohibition. Satan easily tempted the couple because he presented to them a reflection of Y'haweh's truth, even though he actually knew that Y'haweh would confound the couple with Y'haweh's condemnation of Satan's eternal lie. The serpent said the following to them:

> God knows that in the day you eat thereof, then your eyes shall be opened, and you shall be as gods, knowing good and evil.[1]

Satan's statement is true, for the knowledge that appreciates Y'haweh's good as salvation invests Eden with heavenly attributes; and such knowledge fulfills the purposes of Y'haweh, who seeks such glory. In such a way, those whom Y'haweh empowers to pursue his fulfillment in fact possess his mind; and in this way they become the sons and daughters of *God*, being *strong ones*.

Still, although Satan presented the couple with an actuality, he actually enticed the couple to ignore Y'haweh's prohibition. As a consequence, the couple did not become children of Y'haweh because they defied his will: lusting for self-endowment, the couple did not realize the fact that to step outside a covenant relationship with Y'haweh is to experience death. Satan encouraged their lusts and blinded them from seeing the truth: they could not see that instead of gaining the dominion of gods, they would incur Y'haweh's necessary condemnation; because immediately after the couple chose another course of action other than that which Y'haweh chose for them, they devalued Y'haweh's truth by ascribing a greater value to their own purposes. As a result, Y'haweh gave them a world of dire scarcity to establish his place of habitation as the only good.

---

[1] Genesis 3:5

As an outcome, instead of gaining the dominion of gods, Adam and Havah suffered under the dominion of evil: and so, instead of Adam's being enfranchised within Eden's fertile grounds that yield fruit without stint; evil's dominion disenfranchised Adam in alienating environments where thorns and thistles display scarcity; moreover, instead of rest, evil's dominion offered labor and strife. Also, instead of eternal life, evil's dominion offered sickness and mortality. Thus, instead of rendering unto them the sure self-fulfillment that Satan's temptation wrongfully promised, evil's dominion confounded Adam and Havah in depravity and prevented them from returning to the peace of Eden and its tree of life, which the cherub now guards with the flaming sword of Y'haweh's wrath and judgment. In the end, instead of Adam's having dominion over all things, Adam found himself bound to Satan in darkness, fearing the elements and gasping for the breath of life that Y'haweh had once freely breathed into his nostrils.

Despite the fact that Adam certainly fell from grace, he could now appreciate the consolation of Eden with his newfound knowledge. Adam's sin not only alienated him from Y'haweh, but also alienated him from the wife of his bosom, for they no longer saw a world that guaranteed them equal fulfillment. Immediately, when Adam and Havah broke Y'haweh's law and stepped away from the peace of Y'haweh's angelic body, they identified themselves as individuals, with individual aspirations:

> The eyes of both of them were opened, and they knew that they were naked; and they sewed fig leaves together and made themselves coverings. And they heard the sound of Y'haweh [their] God walking in the garden in the cool of the day, and Adam and his wife hid themselves from the presence of Y'haweh [their] God.[1]

When Y'haweh gave the couple over to selfishness, he necessarily cursed the foundation of society to magnify further his salvation. Y'haweh withheld the full complement of his Holy Spirit from the

---

[1] Genesis 3:7-8

woman, allowing her to suffer under a malicious desire to usurp the authority of her husband, in whose bosom she had been ironically nourished in. Accordingly, Y'haweh withheld the full complement of his Holy Spirit from the man, disallowing him to appreciate his wife, perennially: for his own gain, he often exploited her weaknesses. Finally, the man perceived the earth as an unforgiving taskmaster, while the woman perceived the man as an oppressor; and lastly the children, who had sought nourishment from their parents, inherited their parent's bad value systems. Thus, they bore the inclination to separate themselves from the love of Y'haweh, even further. In essence, when Adam and Havah sinned and, thereby, stepped outside of Eden (because they could not appreciate the charity of Y'haweh), they stepped outside of the true peace of Y'haweh's fulfilling and peaceable Holy Spirit.

Praying for the Kingdom

We can imagine that Adam had a keen sense of awareness of the paradise that he had lost, when he saw the strife and hardship of his children who suffered because of his sin. Surely, Adam mourned when he saw animal life turn to savagery, leaving the visage of death everywhere. Adam certainly longed for the land that he could now appreciate.

Let us not lament for Adam, nonetheless. We know that Adam shared our hope in Lord Yehoshua. We see in Moshe's record that Y'haweh cursed the serpent, saying that Havah's seed would bruise the serpent's head. Thus, we comfort ourselves by considering the fact that the well-educated Moshe knew that the serpent in his writings served as a metaphor for Satan; therefore, we conclude from Moshe's writings that Adam's descendant will confound the works of Satan by both conquering death and evil's dominion. We know that Adam foresaw the Savior, because he knew that the woman's seed, who would confound Satan, would not be of Adam's progeny who shared Adam's fallen state. With this understanding, we know that Adam acknowledged the necessity of Christ.

When Adam reconciled himself with Y'haweh, he did not expect to return to Eden: Adam understood that he was unable to gain the perennial peace of Y'haweh's charitable and meek Holy Spirit, which the cherub continues to guard with a flaming sword. The only hope that Adam had for him and his children was the birth of a new Adam from the woman alone: he hoped for one to arise and gain the knowledge of Y'haweh after he first suffers Adam's death and then rises again with the spiritual body of an angel and the sense of appreciation for Y'haweh's Eden.

It may seem that Moshe's account does not exhibit the fact that Adam had salvation knowledge of Lord Yehoshua, but if one takes note of the fact that Y'haweh clothed the couple's shame with animal skins, one should understand that Adam knew that the animals died for his transgression. Y'haweh could have clothed the couple with wool, cotton, or silk; but he symbolically clothed them in the skins of the animals, whose sacrificed lives were symbolic propitiations for the lives of the couple.

What is more, although Adam wore the skins of the animals, he certainly knew that the animals could not return him to paradise: the skins of the animals could not clear his conscience, which he often compromised when confronting the scarcity of life. You see, Adam and his descendants found it hard to sustain justice, when people valued personal aspirations over the common good of all. How could Adam continually deny himself of immediate pleasure by considering the happiness of all?

Repeatedly, Adam saw that people chose their own good despite an opportunity cost for all. Adam knew that only a new Adam would forgo the temptations of life by continually ascribing equity to Eden when he confronted injustice; moreover, the new Adam would gladly ascribe plenty and good to Eden when he confronted the destitute. Of all, Adam knew that his religious works or the superficialities of his people's moral virtue would not respectively earn his or their admittance back into Eden: he knew that the aspirations of his heart through faith imputed the righteousness of the new Adam upon him; because the new Adam alone retains an unblemished conscience. Naturally, Adam knew that the seed of the woman whom Y'haweh would not condemn to death would regenerate the fallen world and restore the paradise that Adam lost. Adam, therefore, wedded himself to the Savior, knowing that he would be of the Savior's spiritual flesh, in an eternal marriage that will endure.

The Power of Prayer

We understand that prayer is essential for the descendants of Adam who seek the new Adam's paradise. Through prayer, Lord Yehoshua put on the mind of Y'haweh, despite the temporary strife of this world.

So if we are to model ourselves after the Lord, we must understand that through prayer, one affixes his or her mind on the true and lasting consolation of the coming Holy Marriage. In fact, one may determine the measure of his or her best efforts by the sense of fulfillment and satisfaction that he or she gains from Y'haweh's truth, in order to withstand the temptation of pursuing the fleeting satisfactions of this world.

To be sure, through prayer, we the elect encounter the truthful expressions of Y'haweh's Word, who admonishes us to forgo the sins of this world, while we claim the salvation that he empowers us to fulfill. After all, the prayers of the heart for the Kingdom simply exhibit the election of us whom Y'haweh empowers to seek his Kingdom; therefore, Y'haweh answers our prayers to encourage us to fulfill his desires that he has already established.

The Two Adams

We may conclude our assessment of the scriptural accounts of our beginning by identifying how our covenant relationship had begun with Adam and ultimately found its fulfillment in Lord Yehoshua. If we consider the fact that Y'haweh affirms his fulfillment by being glorified before Adam and his progeny in the person of Lord Yehoshua, we should readily grasp the fact that Y'haweh's first covenant (or promise) to humanity is a covenant of condemnation upon those who do not observe his law. By recalling our understanding of truth, we may readily understand that Y'haweh's first covenant must initially conclude all under the despair of evil in order for Y'haweh to establish the succeeding covenants, which confirm the revelations of his being the creator, redeemer, and the salvation of his worshippers. We may witness Y'haweh's first covenant when Y'haweh prohibited Adam and Havah from eating from the tree of knowledge, and we may see the resolution of the covenant when Lord Yehoshua remained obedient and so retained the knowledge of Y'haweh.

When Y'haweh said unto the angels, "Let man have dominion", Y'haweh realized his own dominion by assuming the person of Lord Yehoshua, after Adam's fall. Likewise, when Y'haweh said unto the angels, "Let us make man after our image", Y'haweh predestined the empowerment of humankind to reflect his image when Lord Yehoshua secures a new spiritual body with the redeemed—that is, a Holy Marriage and temple for Y'haweh to dwell in. So in this way, Y'haweh reflects his glory over all.

Essentially, Y'haweh uses two Adams to fulfill his truth: the first Adam falls under his condemnation, and the second Adam reflects his glory. The first Adam finds no fulfillment in his marriage to his wife who issues from his flesh; while the new Adam achieves the utmost fulfillment with his wife, the Church, who issues from his spiritual flesh. Finally, the first Adam loses his dominion because he cannot appreciate the creation that the angels witness, while the second Adam assumes dominion over all things, including the angels, because he regenerates creation anew with his salvation knowledge of Y'haweh's glory.

Hence, we find in Adam's story the beginning of evil's dominion over humanity. As well, we find the beginning of Y'haweh's redemptive work unto his Holy Marriage. In regards to the true heavenly marriage, we note that after their fall, Adam and Havah's renewed fidelity in their marriage before Y'haweh served as a bulwark from evil and an innate counselor to their consciences: their healthy marriage functioned as an ideal conception of the heavenly place of rest for their souls, its benefits being tangible before their eyes. Thus, having lost the intimacy of Eden, where trust was intuitive and natural agreement between us under God was evident, Adam and Havah's progeny now contend with isolation, fear, penal law, animosity, and at best tentative social agreements. For now, the only visage that we have of Adam's lost paradise in the human environment are healthy, loving marriages, where we lay our souls bare before those whom we devote ourselves to, as we seek the intimate consolation of Eden.

Chapter 6

The Golden Cities of the Prodigious

"For the poor will never cease from the land; therefore, I command you, saying, 'You shall open your hand wide to your brother, to your poor and your needy, in your land.'"

—Deuteronomy 15:11

A Glimpse behind the Veil

When we hold a conception of the fruits of fidelity that our marriages bear, we by the grace of Y'haweh peek behind the veil that we cast between ourselves and Y'haweh as we continually break his first covenant, which states that we must be obedient to his will, for with him is our purpose. Surely, we see that the veil not only prevents us from achieving a true intimacy with Y'haweh, but also prevents us from achieving a true intimacy between ourselves; whereas Y'haweh, by his grace, gives us the opportunity to see behind the veil by giving us the salvation knowledge of his good, through faith in Lord Yehoshua the Mashiach. And so, by his grace, Y'haweh allows us to acquire a true intimate relationship with him. In this way, his love gains its eternal reciprocity. In effect, because Y'haweh allows us to peer within his very Holy Spirit, we elect and redeemed true worshippers achieve an intimacy with him that other relationships cannot replicate, even "as it is written, 'the eye has not seen, nor has the ear heard, nor have it entered into the heart of man, the things which God has prepared for those who love Him.' But God has revealed them to us through His Spirit. For the Spirit searches all things, yes, the deep things of God. For what man knows the things of a man except the spirit of the man which is in him? Even so no one knows the things of God except the Spirit of God. Now we have received, not the spirit of the world, but the Spirit who is from God, that we might know the things that have been freely given to us by God."[1]

In contrast to our supreme spiritual union with Y'haweh, the unfaithful and unredeemed do not enjoy the benefit of our intimate true worshipping relationship with Y'haweh. As the scripture says, "For he has set the world in their heart, so that no man can find out the work that God makes from the beginning to the end."[2]

Now we are sure that there will be no salient convention behind the veil that we will need to augment our oneness with Y'haweh. Indeed, behind the veil, we will not need the conventions of moral law to mitigate social contentions. Likewise, our intimate knowledge of Y'haweh, which we will possess behind the veil, will not need any language conventions to augment our understanding of Y'haweh; therefore, we will not need any grammatical or other communicable conventions that haphazardly attempt to affix our subjective and erroneous understandings to Y'haweh, because we will all be of his Spirit, love, and passion, in the Holy Marriage. To this end, there will only stand the single convention of his love and our adoration for him, behind the veil.

For this reason, when we consider the grace of Y'haweh and our concurring appreciation of it, we must declare that the essence of the Holy Marriage is a perfect system to govern the union between the beneficence of the strong (elohim) and the appreciation, admiration, devotion, and support of the weak who thus augment the strong. As well, we must acknowledge that only Lord Yehoshua and his Church can establish this perfect union that exists behind the veil, while here on earth, we must accept its shadow in the natural relationship that sustains the devotion between a male and a female.

At length, we hold within this glorious conception of our relationship with Y'haweh that we see through faith, while the veil

---

[1] 1 Corinthians 2:9-11
[2] Ecclesiastes 3:11

blinds us. Within the lamp of our souls is the oil of the Holy Spirit that fuels the light of our faith through which we wait and devote ourselves to our true love and benefactor. For this cause, Lord Yehoshua says to us that "the Kingdom of *God* is within you"[1], because within we devote ourselves to our coming liberation that Lord Yehoshua establishes in Heaven's just Kingdom, while without we withstand the thorns of the inequity that enslave us in this current world. Effectively, within our hearts we hold a covenant relationship with Y'haweh that reflects our future, heavenly marriage with him and contrasts this present strife amongst ourselves. Like Sha'ul the Apostle who had seen the heavenly vision of Y'haweh's glory but bore the thorns[2] of condemnation that the glory would be of Y'haweh and not of himself, we too must bear the thorns of deprivation, while keeping the covenant of faith and obedience, until Y'haweh manifests himself as the strong who alone gives us the glorious salvation that presently stands behind the veil.

The Thorns of Conscience

In effect, the thorns that hold us captive are the sins of conscience that we endlessly commit against each other and ourselves, due to the fact that the breaking of the Covenant imputed this burden upon us. As a consequence, the burden comprises the veil that blinds those who are unfaithful from seeing the truth of Y'haweh's Holy Spirit whom Lord Yehoshua possesses. It follows that Lord Yehoshua is he who only upholds conscience and prevents conscience from being compromised. In this manner, he establishes justice: the ability for an individual to exercise and be satisfied by his or her natural gifts, after acquiring truth's equitable fulfillment within that he or she might not infringe upon another's volition without, thus culminating in the felicity of equitable social communions.

---

[1] Luke 17:21

[2] Sha'ul was given Satan's thorn of the flesh that the trying of his soul might make him perfect, by maintaining his dependency on Lord Yehoshua, thus making Lord Yehoshua's strength his own and all to uphold the heavenly vision.

Consequently, when the Holy Spirit fosters our consciences, our consciences mature with human government as the natural, unwritten, and only true constitutions and counselors, condemning the unjust and encouraging us the just to seek Y'haweh's salvation by faith, when we find no justice in the earth. For that reason, the scriptures even affirm that "[we] the just shall live by faith."[1]

To this end, our true benefactor Y'haweh justifies us by giving us faith in his Yehoshua. Then after we suffer evil's deprivation, which puts forth scarcity that contradictory volitions might necessitate governments of good conscience, we understand that of all the crafts that aim at the good, the one that is subordinate to no other, but rather directs them is governing.[2] Thus, good government is the form of salvation that we ascribe to Eden to turn it into the Heaven that the Holy Marriage between Lord Yehoshua and the true worshippers will reign over, behind the veil.

Yet, when the rest of humankind accept the inequitable status quo set before them by not looking by faith for Y'haweh's New Yerushalayim, they defile their consciences and render the thorns of deprivation to be of no worth, because the unfaithful no longer have valued the salvation that contrasts the inequity of the thorns. Thus, when their denial of Lord Yehoshua is complete, Y'haweh will take the grace of his Holy Spirit from the earth. Following Satan will lead the nations into perdition, and lastly the judgment: Y'haweh will gather the wheat of his faithful harvest into his stores, while his angels gather the thorns of the contentious to be burned without.

The Heart of Government

Nonetheless, when we consider that Y'haweh reaps the souls of his faithful to reflect his fulfillment in a Holy Marriage with them, it should become apparent that marriage is the heart of his heavenly government in the new Yerushalayim. While we consider this, it should also become apparent that the maintenance of marriage

---

[1] Hebrews 10:38
[2] The above statement is inspired by the opening thesis of Aristotle's Nicomachean Ethics.

should be the heart of any government in this present age as well; since human marriage not only tentatively upholds conscience, but also actively seeks a beloved's greater good.

Resting upon the bond of love, a married couple's shared devotion begets the attributes of Y'haweh's ordinance that conscience apprehends and patience secures, such as selflessness, sobriety, modesty, humility, order, wisdom, and manifold beauty, even serenity within and perceptional harmony without. Truly, the government of New Yerushalayim is after these eternal qualities of Y'haweh's righteous Holy Spirit.

Even as deprivation casts need upon all and initiates everyone's pursuit for his or her personal satisfaction, marriage assumes the only form of human government that reconciles one's sensual and subjective satisfactions with the objective understandings of conscience, which involves such virtues as commitment, trust, love, and (above all) faithfulness. Indeed, since we consider government as the enforcement or maintenance of an agreed upon course of conduct through which individuals seek to uphold their shared constitution (especially while they reconcile their needs and aspirations with their physical and social environment), we proclaim marriage as the ultimate form of government, because marriage's constitution is of the heart; therefore, marriage's government does not necessarily need codified law. Marriage then is that social convention that seamlessly reconciles intimacy with common civility, because it is the optimal (socially sustainable) system that governs the beneficence of the strong with the admiration, devotion, and support of the weak (and that without the necessities of whatever legal measures that mitigate social strife). To this end, the married couple readily appreciate each other's physical environment and, therefore, ascribe a singular affection for the world or even a single aesthetic value that is not a reflection of perverse political or social idiosyncrasies: a married couple's single affection for their temporary environment directly reflects the single eternal love between Lord Yehoshua and the Church, which defines the salvation knowledge of a creation that displays Y'haweh's glory.

Furthermore, in this life, a fulfilled married couple can as well agree upon a single aspiration and resist those satanic temptations in society that seek to destroy holy matrimony. The greater society will then benefit from the fulfilled marriage and avoid the societal breakdown that unfulfilled marriages create.

We have noted that Satan easily tempted Havah because she did not find fulfillment in Adam, who likewise did not initially find fulfillment in being obedient to Y'haweh. So, we have seen the societal chaos that spoiled marriages create.

It follows that, each partner's endowed conscience, which has some knowledge of Y'haweh's good, puts limitations on the other partner's sensual aspirations. Thus, the married couple ascribes greater values to the things that conscience allows. In this manner, they inhibit conscience's compromise. As a result, the married couple innately witnesses the ordinance within their souls: the selfsame limitations that their mutual affection placed upon them emanate from the limitations of the natural laws that reflect Y'haweh's ultimate value that is his glory.

Hence, the values of trust and fidelity have no better caretaker than the marriage unit. Basically, the married couple experiences between themselves a sort of liberty from the enslaving perversions of society. Thereupon, the couple's marriage becomes the optimal and natural medium for child bearing: marriage assumes the foundation for all kindred relationships as it provides an intuitive jurisprudence in the transfer of property, skills, and tradition to the married couple's progeny. Essentially, the married couple passes on the values, which they gleaned from marriage's liberty, to their children who then produce other healthy marriages to benefit the greater society at large with the ideals of marriage's eternal truth.

Furthermore, when longevity pursues a marriage, happiness persists. Nonetheless, when longevity exhausts itself and abruptly dismisses itself (thus greeting the marriage unit with the mortality of a partner) or when whatever social perversion undermines a nuptial, biting grief assumes the place of happiness:

There can be no lasting fulfillment under evil's dominion that stands apart from the good of Y'haweh, who resides behind the veil.

The institute of marriage can only foreshadow the culmination of truth that the Holy Marriage realizes: only the enduring marriage between the Lord and the faithful reconciles this world's unfaithfulness. So, even as deprivation casts conflicting needs upon the families of a given society, it is with the truth of the Holy Marriage's actuality (and thereby with everyone's personal satisfaction) that families only reconcile themselves: a civil constitution's obedience or disobedience to conscience respectively produces the pros or cons of cultural values, which infiltrate the hearts and minds of those in the founding marriage units. The voluntary maintenance of conscience mimics the glory of the Holy Marriage, while the denial of conscience manifests chaos.

The Strife between Kayin and Hevel

When a people center their cultural values on marriage's preservation, they refine their personal consciences; however, when a people do not regard the preservation of marriage, they encourage those contentious tempers in society that are the veritable thorns of conscience. In fact, we see the thorns in the relationships that immediately follow the intimacy of the marriage unit (if not within the marriage itself): people decreasingly adhere to the same measure of conscience that marriage dictates as social obligations grow distant from the marriage unit.

One may justly asks the following: how can our weak grasp of the virtues of fidelity and selflessness (which we vicariously see in the best marriages) subdue human frailty's sin imputed compulsion to secure personal necessities or desires, despite conscience? Or how can distant relations secure an intimacy that mitigates everyone's fleshly vice, as well as the Holy Marriage?

Even sibling rivalries come to bear after the marriage unit. Consider the biblical story of Kayin and Hevel, the sons of Adam and Havah: Kayin and Hevel's strife initiated the history of intimacy lacking civilizations, where civility corporately reconciles people just enough to overcome scarcity. While Kayin and Hevel's professions readily sufficed for not only their individual needs, but also the needs of each other as well as their community, their inability to relate affably to one another undermined their prosperity, even as such social discord continues to rob contemporary society of like prosperity.

We must take note of how Y'haweh did not predestine Kayin, the crop grower of the community, to have the same measure of faith as his brother Hevel, the shepherd of the community. So, unlike his father Adam, whom the Lord did not impute inequity (but he had elected Adam to receive salvation by grace), Kayin, not having the measure of grace, fell under evil's condemnation (Kayin's being predisposed to sin); and still "Y'haweh is justified when he speaks and clear when he judges"[1], for all fall under condemnation, while Y'haweh retains the liberty to free whom he wills to define himself as salvation. To this end, Y'haweh left Kayin under the burden of sin to cause Kayin to become Hevel's burden as well, because through their eternal strife, Hevel's conscience, faith, and desire for Y'haweh's *yasha*[2] would strengthen. As a result, Hevel would reciprocate the love of Y'haweh by wedding himself to Lord Yehoshua, the only salvation, forever.

To secure this outcome, Y'haweh had given Hevel a constitution that conforms to the Holy Marriage's government in New Yerushalayim. Being fulfilled with the truth of Y'haweh, Hevel's soul observed the fruits of conscience, such as sobriety, charity, wisdom, and patience. Consequently, Hevel (whose name means *temporary*) offered the best of his flocks in gratitude to Y'haweh. Indeed, through faith he offered the blood sacrifice of redemption that ultimately points to the sacrifice of Lord Yehoshua, whose salvation for Hevel's encumbered faith is eternal (unlike this world's temporal benefits of sin that Kayin fleetingly enjoyed).

To be sure, the faithless acts of sin—such as jealousy, animosity, envy, fear, and covetousness—will Y'haweh judge, as Y'haweh

---

[1] Psalm 51:4

[2] The word *yasha* is a primitive, verb root of the Hebrew word *yeshua*, which means salvation. The word *yasha* in particular, however, suggests the meaning *to open wide*, *to save*, *to rescue*, or *to be delivered*.

justifies Lord Yehoshua's faithfulness, compassion, humility, and love. Y'haweh will judge those whom he left under condemnation, like Kayin, whose faithless heart had pursued temporary gain.

One may clearly see that Kayin did not appreciate the covenants of the Lord. Unlike the liberal sacrifice offered by selfless Hevel, Kayin offered a grudging sacrifice from his crops. What is more, Kayin (not seeking the eternal good behind the veil) sinned further by murdering his brother Hevel out of jealousy. Afterwards, when he irreverently asked the question, "Am I my brother's keeper?" Y'haweh answered the question with a resounding yes by punishing Kayin for his unjust deed, with harsher environments: Y'haweh made Kayin's labor more arduous, in order to refine the consciences of the righteous when they witness the social ills that Kayin's unjust economic choices create.

Thus, "Blessed is he whose transgression is forgiven, whose sin is covered. Blessed is the man unto whom the Lord does not impute iniquity and in whose spirit there is no guile."[1] Also, cursed is he whose transgression is not forgiven and whose soul Y'haweh leaves under evil's condemnation. Cursed is he whom the Lord leaves faithless, being blinded by the veil.

The condemned now cultivate perverse ideologies for the self-gain of the industrious and strong. The condemned are they who undermine the Holy Marriage and inspire Y'haweh's worshippers (like Hevel) to appreciate the Marriage when Lord Yehoshua gives it to them as the salvation that stands behind the veil.

Being blinded by the veil, Kayin went from the presence of Adonai into the land of *Nod*[2] and characteristically sought his own salvation in a city that he named after his first-born son Enoch, whose name means *initiation*. Although Kayin initiated his government to secure his welfare and that of his progeny, by seeking fulfillment despite the will of Y'haweh, his ambition failed from the

---

[1] Psalm 32:1-2
[2] *Nod* is a Hebrew proper noun that means, "wandering."

start, because he had named the city after his son[1]—his own volition: Kayin did not have the faith to center his wealth and prosperity on him who stands behind the veil and who seeks equitable volitions for all.

The Rights of the Mighty

When we consider the downfall of Kayin, we deduce that his curse was to measure creation by his own accomplishments and not by the needs and fulfillment of all, unto the glory of Y'haweh. Kayin set the precedent that the unjust of the industrious—the "mighty men"[2]— would follow, for they in strife proceed to litter every civilization with their temporal accomplishments. In this way, they cloak the eternal splendor and peace of New Yerushalayim. Instead of perceiving the charity of Y'haweh to establish understanding, Kayin's progeny misinterpret creation, because their insatiable lusts withhold from them the simple sense of appreciation for Y'haweh. As a result, their corrupt understandings create their own calamity. Accordingly, the Apostle Sha'ul writes the following to describe the social turmoil that they bring to civilization, because they cannot appreciate Y'haweh's simple charity:

> . . . because that, when they knew God, they glorified him not as God, neither were they thankful; but they became vain in their imaginations, and their foolish heart was darkened . . . and even as they did not like to retain God in their knowledge, God gave them over to a reprobate mind, to do those things which are not convenient; being filled with all unrighteousness, fornication, wickedness, covetousness, maliciousness; full of envy, murder, debate, deceit, malignity; whisperers, backbiters, haters of God, despiteful, proud, boasters, inventors of evil things, disobedient to parents, without understanding, covenant-breakers, without natural affection, implacable, and unmerciful.[3]

---

[1] Notably, Y'haweh commanded the children of Yisra'el to offer their first born to the Lord's ministry that the product of Yisra'el's labor would be attributed unto Y'haweh.
[2] Genesis 6:4
[3] Romans 1:21-31

Essentially, those of Kayin's ilk, upon whom Y'haweh imputes sin's condemnation, esteem those who are best able to manipulate the dual force of innovation and integration for immediate satisfaction, even as they undermine a common equity for all: the deeds of unjust prodigies prove to be the unjust standards that direct the tumultuous course of human history. In point of fact, throughout history, as Kayin's faithless cities forsake conscience for immediate gain, the unjust of the industrious appear to be seemingly virtuous to the faithless, despite conscience's compromise. At the same time, oppressed peoples appear to be culpable for their downcasts state, in the eyes of the unjust. It is even necessary for the righteous, themselves, to scorn the sluggards who further incite the industrious to deem the poor blame worthy.

To draw distinctions between the just and the unjust, let us conclude the following: the unjust sum up virtue by the vitality of a state that provides personal gain, while the just sum up virtue by a sublime equality—a faith in the purposes of a higher power. Thus, while the unjust seek fulfillment in industry and sensuality, the just, who have faith in Y'haweh's equitable New Yerushalayim, forsake the temporal pleasures that do not reflect the enduring good of Y'haweh. So, the unjust ever fill the void of insecurity by idolizing and questing for the wealth and power of the prodigious. In so doing, they blindly wander after inequity. Even so, the just quest for the true peace of all: their souls become more refined as they become selfless, and they begin to appreciate the eternal laws of Y'haweh. Subsequently, the just advance the human constitution that ultimately finds its rest in Y'haweh's good. In the end, the just readily empathize with the physically oppressed, under-classed, politically castigated, and impoverished, who slave, merely, to acquire the staple needs of life.

It follows that the faithful find no true and enduring good in this age of iniquity: they consider that salvation is impossible for those who dwell amongst the goyim (the unredeemed) who stand apart from Y'haweh's truth. Even though it is evident that "man cannot live by bread alone, but by the word that flows from the mouth of

Y'haweh"[1], the unfaithful accept injustice in their cities, thus causing the poor to be always present.

Y'haweh's selective acts of grace are, therefore, necessary. It is necessary for Y'haweh to justify the virtue of some, in order to establish an eternal reward that surpasses the societal rewards of them who conform to the whimsical, social conventions of the mighty, who rule in this temporary age.

If the eternal reward for Lord Yehoshua did not exist for those who model their virtue after him, all would forever see a chaotic and mysterious universe through the prism of the prodigious' moral shortcomings. Indeed, we ourselves would not see the true creation that Y'haweh has ordered by one truth and one good, which stands behind the veil as everlasting fulfillment.

Thus, it is necessary for the salvation of the Holy Marriage to be a gift of redemption from Y'haweh to those like Adam and Hevel who only order their virtue after the righteousness of Lord Yehoshua. Surely, there can be no pride in one's personal virtue, because all things are for Y'haweh's good. Fundamentally, it is necessary for judgment to be exacted upon all that do not receive the gift, while Y'haweh's gift makes Lord Yehoshua the justifier.

The Fraternal Orders

From here, it is for us to build our hopes and lives on the eternal gift of wedded bliss that Lord Yehoshua holds behind the veil, for his faithful. In this life, the faithless, who do not hold our heavenly conception of husband and wife, can only possess the perishable bonds of fraternity with its fleeting lesser friendships, even after the bond of brother and sister fail.

Essentially, we will here identify the world's fraternities as the fellowships of those who agree upon social values. Then they commune together, politically, to secure the economic needs of their society or immediate communion. Fundamentally, a civilization's fraternities initially organize to secure the three primary needs of all: they first secure provisions for food, shelter from the elements, and

---

[1] Deuteronomy 8:3

raiment for the body. Accordingly, the founding crafts of any community are farmers for the provisions of food, carpenters for the provision of shelter, and craftspeople for the provision of apparel and storage utensils.

In addition, a fraternal order, which seeks to benefit a community with a good or resource, immediately exercises power or influence over competing fraternal orders or individuals within a community. As a result, the exercise of power by a fraternal order redefines that fraternal order as a political order to those without. In this way, politics becomes an exercise of power and influence over competing powers or influences. To all intents and purposes, the social systems that result from the political balance of power between the fraternal orders not only manipulate and secure scarce resources to be distributed to the general populace as goods and services, but also become the culture's veritable economic system, in which all the members of the society seek their own benefit, in a haphazard pursuit of happiness. Consequently, members of the populace acquire these goods and services by the measure of their political aptitude.

All told, when fraternities function together to secure the primary needs of a people of equal social status, elements of what we identify as a communal economic system exists, which is what current thinkers identify as a rudimentary form of communism. In addition, when those prodigies of a burgeoning culture retain wealth and resources through political acumen and innovative thinking to influence others politically, these prodigies capitalize from their social standing and, therefore, influence the economy of the culture. Thus, we identify the economic outcome from the political balance of this system, as a form of capitalism.

Even so, as needs are met or not met equitably between the two fundamental economic systems and new needs arise, fraternities often fail: fraternal orders only ascribe to creation aesthetic values of such temporal things as ownership, wealth, advantage, power, penalty, reprisal, and compensation. Yet, humanity seeks to discover a government that relates to a world in such a way that there is freedom from want; to the extent that the human pursuit of happiness seeks to secure everyone's advantage.

So when we consider that the prodigious only establish understandings of creation that render satisfaction inequitably (because of sin) and then other eventualities uproot the understandings, we are confident in our understanding that salvation is a gift that realizes our utmost devotion to Lord Yehoshua through whom Y'haweh gives the gift of truth. Therein lays our eternal devotion to the Holy Marriage.

The Three Natural Forms of Human Government

Foreseeing our good end in the government of the Holy Marriage, we do not have to be amazed at the curious vicissitudes of human government. Instead, we can further appreciate Y'haweh's grace after we inspect the brief triumphs and enduring downfalls of civilization: unlike the faithless who covet their affluence or fear when they are in want, we do not have to fear the loss of economic success when necessity compels us to give charitable, because we know that our true wealth stands in the heavens; moreover, we do not have to despair when economic calamity arises because we know that certain benevolence is at hand.

Knowing that our happiness is sure, let us now ponder over the fact that throughout humanity's pursuit of happiness, three fundamental forms of government arise to govern the degrees of both economic systems: there is the government of one, the government of the privileged, and the government of the majority. Furthermore, these three governmental forms bear both the brief semblance of marriage's liberty and the enduring entanglements of sin's oppression.

For example, we may identify a semblance of liberty in a government when the power of the strong complements the advantage of the weak, like a caring husband seeks to please his adoring wife. Likewise, we may identify oppression in a government when the power of the strong exploits the disadvantage of the weak, like an abusive husband disregards the welfare of his humbled wife.

To understand the liberating and oppressive qualities of the several governments, let us first consider and redefine the ancient Hebrew term *yasha*. We will modify the word's original meaning—*to open wide* or *to liberate*—by expanding the meaning of the word to express the true source of our liberation, and that is the liberal open hand of Y'haweh, the beneficent strong. Thus, we will define *yasha* as a noun that means *Y'haweh's open hand*. Thus, in any case, we can clearly see that Y'haweh extends an open hand to us through the risen Lord Yehoshua whose righteous soul Y'haweh sacrificed and delivered in order for Lord Yehoshua to become our redeemer. We can see that Y'haweh has reserved his yasha (the salvation that we seek to experience in our everyday lives) for those who by faith bear a love for Y'haweh and their fellows, with a mind to conduct their lives as servants to Lord Yehoshua: fulfilling the love of the Lord, these true worshippers model their charitable dealings within their community after Y'haweh's benevolent deed, which we define as his yasha—his open hand in the Mashiach.

While holding Y'haweh's opened hand in mind, we may conclude that when the government of a people acknowledges its human frailty by identifying its need to invoke even a semblance of the Creator's benevolence, shadows of liberty exist in the community of the people, because the government seeks a charitable end for them through its laws and effects. Correspondingly, let us further conclude that when a people do not acknowledge or seek the open hand of Y'haweh in their decision making, the whole of the people are in spiritual bondage, whether they are the oppressors or the oppressed. Truly, in such a case, the strong, "whose god is their belly [and] who mind earthly things"[1], hold the weak subject to their whims and desires. In addition, the blind rulers of such governments are ultimately the greatest obstacles of the lasting happiness that the faithless seek, because these rulers falsely portray themselves as the ultimate human good by "having the form of godliness, but denying

---

[1] Philippians 3:19

the power thereof."[1] In this manner, they mask the true good of Y'haweh that benefits all.

In short, we observe that when liberty stands, Y'haweh's justice harmonizes the aspirations of the weak with that of the strong. Likewise, we observe that when oppression abides, the strong compromise their conscience and portray a false sense of justice that meets their desired end, despite the weak. In either case, the best of a culture's social prodigies always portray justice inequitably, because true justice stands behind the veil within Lord Yehoshua's unblemished conscience; therefore, the best forms of human government can only inhibit injustice in this world.

To this end, the excesses and limitations of injustice not only obstruct personal liberty, but also draw distinctions between the three categories of government, respectively: there are, at times, fewer safeguards that grapple with the injustices that the government of one commits than there are safeguards that the government of the privileged retain. In other words, the government of a few retains some measure of accountability, in contrast to the government of one. On the other hand, some of the privileged authorities are occasionally more covetous than a liberal, self-ruling sovereign; therefore, these covetous rulers often produce more social factors that undermine a good sovereign's charitable hands. Correspondingly, there are, at times, fewer social safeguards that labor against the injustices that the government of the privileged commits than there are safeguards that fight for the maintenance of liberty in the government of the majority. Yet, in contrast, there are, at times, many social obstacles to justice that result from a chaotic government of the people, which ultimately defy personal liberty itself.

Finally, if Y'haweh opens his hand upon the several governments, the people enjoy the fruits of liberty. In contrast, if Y'haweh closes his hand, the people continue under sin's condemnation. Hence, a sovereign who has found the grace of Y'haweh is like a savior to his people, while a sovereign who denies

---

[1] 2 Timothy 3:5

Y'haweh's glory bears the inclination of being his people's greatest tyrant. Likewise, those governments of shared power may only maintenance liberty according to the measure of grace that Y'haweh gives to individual rulers who must buttress their consciences against the excesses that other unjust rulers commit. As a consequence, the measures of liberty or oppression that shared power governments manifest are often less profound than the measures that the government of a single sovereign manifests.

The ancient Yisra'elite King David noted the above dichotomy when he spoke of his government's shortcomings, as compared to the salvation of Lord Yehoshua's coming Kingdom. David said the following:

> The Spirit of Y'haweh has spoken by me, and his word was on my tongue. The God of Yisra'el said, the rock of Yisra'el said, "he who rules over man righteously, rules in the fear of God: as the morning light, he rises, even as a morning sun with no clouds. Then [his] shining after the rain [of oppression] springs the tender grass [of liberty] from the earth."
>
> Although my house is not so with God, he has made me a covenant for the age [of Lord Yehoshua] to come, ordered in all things and kept; for this is all my salvation and all my desire, for God has not caused it yet to spring up.
>
> [Yet] as for the unjust, they all shall be driven away as worthless thorns [of contention] . . . with fire, they shall be utterly burned in the cessation.[1]

It is sure then that Y'haweh does not extend his full measure of grace upon any government except the government of New Yerushalayim, which the Holy Marriage comprises and the Lord Yehoshua eternally reigns over. This fact the following scripture affirms when it speaks of Y'haweh's profound grace that he confers upon Lord Yehoshua by saying, "My glory will I not give to another."[2]

---

[1] 2 Samuel 23:2-7
[2] Isaiah 42:8

In the light of this truth, we may conclude the following: as virtue is but a shadow of righteousness, the brief semblances of liberty that the several governments enjoy are but shadows of Lord Yehoshua's Holy Marriage with his true worshippers.

By keeping the glory of the Holy Marriage in mind, we determine the degree of liberty that exists in a culture by the degree of social affection and camaraderie that exist between the culture's governors and governed, like Lord Yehoshua's affection for his Church. In turn, we determine this degree by what measure the camaraderie meets the fruits of fidelity that exists between a caring husband and doting wife; because the affectionate relationship of the husband and wife naturally models the Holy Marriage that Y'haweh establishes by extending an open hand to us.

Correspondingly, the attributes of a given culture's social structure that do not reflect the fruits of marriage's fidelity are signs of humanity's struggle with their continual compromise of conscience. One such sign is a culture's creation of penal laws, which do not merely serve to encourage morality but reflect the necessity to combat the crime and lawlessness that exist in the people's community. In addition, we see another sign of conscience's compromise manifested in a culture when we see signs of economic inequality, which results when the uncharitable behavior of the strong creates noticeable chasms between those who dwell in affluence and those who dwell in poverty.

All told, when a culture tacitly indoctrinates a general sense of camaraderie into their society by legally binding good social conduct into their law codes, the socially indoctrinated spirit of camaraderie becomes civility. And so, those cultures that bear constitutions that seek a happy fellowship between all its members retain such civility that depends upon the social constitution's effectiveness. In contrast, those cultures under peoples who thwart the civil trust, by seeking only the advantage of the industrious and strong (to the chagrin of the weak) are uncivil and bear not a constitution of conscience. Finally, we, therefore, determine the height of any given civilization by the degree the civilization meets everyone's satisfaction equitably, by upholding the conscience and justice that truly find their haunt in Lord Yehoshua's government in New Yerushalayim.

Notwithstanding, the degrees of injustice that the several governments respectively commit or avoid are somewhat indistinguishable in lower-level civilizations, where the human mind cannot encompass the profundity of the Mashiach. In lower-level civilizations, there is no sophisticated administration commenced to draw together specialized talents to gain the mastery over nature in such a way that liberty becomes a creature of leisure and, therefore, aesthetic satisfaction. Likewise, there is no tyranny, in these civilizations, that politically dominates the cultural institutes in such a way that social oppression is geographically far reaching, as well as institutionalized. For this cause, there is no appreciative sense—the salvation-knowledge—of a just one who rules "like a god among men"[1] and in such a way that all, in the human endeavor, find salvation in creation's marvels and requisite beauty.

Notwithstanding, unlike the lower-civilizations, the excesses and limitations of injustice are evident in all three categories of government that preside over higher-level civilizations: in the higher-level civilizations, the triumphs and downfalls of human government are salient. Yet, at the same time, the true worshippers' reverence for Lord Yehoshua's enduring throne is all the more steadfast, because the worshippers seek something other than the fleeting liberties and constant oppression that they endure under the worldly governments.

From the inception of the lowest levels of civilization unto the culmination of the highest levels of human development, the prodigious continually find new ways to gain temporary satisfaction, while the faithful and disaffected, having no sense of fulfillment in the cities of the prodigious, continually march the human constitution forward: having faith, they look for eternal satisfaction beyond. The historical quarrel between faithless Kayin and faithful Hevel repeats itself throughout history in this way.

---

[1] Plato's *Statesman*

The Prodigious

To further our understanding of the thorns of conscience, which give rise to injustice and then curiously endow our faith, we must first look quickly into the nature of lower-level civilizations, where is the inception of the injustice. Afterwards, we will understand, completely, how the continual compromise of conscience matures the selfsame injustice, which then corrupts the higher-level civilizations that Lord Yehoshua redeems us from.

To begin, let us understand that the degrees of liberty and oppression are less evident in lower-level civilizations, because the degrees of power and influence are less pronounced between the fraternal orders. Too, in lower-level civilizations, where sophisticated governments and economies are absent, people realize their need for one another. Often they realize their need for a beneficent creator who reflects his fulfillment in their love for one another and him.

Communes of peoples who are of equal social status create lower-level civilizations to overcome scarcity by merely producing the staple needs of life. The majority of the populace of these communities comprise the labor force that produce the staple needs; therefore, the common income and property of the populace does not incite the political animosities that foster social strife among influential social forces that do rudimentarily exist in the community.

Consequentially, it is apparent that more sophisticated civilizations require greater social consciousness. In actual fact, the leaders—the socially prodigious of the people—require the greatest sense of conscience, if not only the sense of Y'haweh's truth.

Despite the common social status of the lower-level civilization populaces, social prodigies arise at the heart of every civilization: these prodigies influence or inspire the cultural values of the common people, through their industry and mental fortitude. The prodigious seize upon and advance the scarce opportunities that their physical or social environment offers. Following, they direct the affairs of others who seek like prosperity. In this manner, a prodigious person may help or hurt others in his or her personal pursuits.

If a social prodigy obtains the grace of Y'haweh and understands by faith the necessity to escape the eternal judgment of Y'haweh, the prodigious person will by faith seek the salvation of Y'haweh. To be sure, he or she will then esteem the equity of Y'haweh's Holy Spirit and justly inspire all whom he or she has influence over. However, if Y'haweh leaves a social prodigy under sin's condemnation, like he left Kayin, he or she will not consider the judgment of Y'haweh, even as Noach's generation did not consider and even as the unredeemed still do not consider today. Furthermore, in such a case, the social prodigy will not seek the truth of the Holy Marriage, but he will only seek what satisfaction that comes from the works of his hands: worldly articles and vices will always enamor him, despite social consciousness. Besides, he will inspire others to follow his unjust conduct.

Of all, an unjust, prodigious man always has to contend with the disaffected who do not find satisfaction from his slightly opened hand. The people who suffer under an unjust social prodigy look for novel ways to unfetter their lives, even upon the pains of strife.

In actual fact, when we look here upon Kayin and Hevel's contention, we find that all social prodigies mark the growth of human understanding in the human experience: some look unto the coming kingdom for the inspiration to find new and inventive ways to better themselves and their neighbors, while others only seek satisfaction for themselves in this world, despite their neighbors. In other words, at times, the volition of a social prodigy is just, when he or she complements the eternal truth of the Holy Marriage; and at other times, the volition of a social prodigy is unjust, when he or she seeks his or her own benefit, despite the truth of Y'haweh.

The Patriarch

At the outset of the human experience, social prodigies begin to lead the people by assuming the roles of patriarchs and elders: the seminal social figures of communities who even inspire other social prodigies and their succeeding generations, who in turn create the governments and fraternal orders that preside over higher-level civilizations. Furthermore, the social prodigies who assume the form of patriarchs or elders usually preside over communal economic systems, effectively functioning as the capitalists of their cultures, while the rest of the community function under a common, economic, social status. In patriarchic communities, individuals do not enjoy a significant legal status apart from the individual's identity within the kindred group. The patriarch's oracular determinations stand as the law, while cultural tradition stands as legislation.

It follows that a common person's reverence for a patriarch is the person's first step toward finding the same communal quality of liberty that he or she innately understands to be the heart of the marriage unit, where a beneficent husband cares for a reverent wife. Thus, if the patriarch seeks the justice of the Holy Marriage, after the patriarch obtains the grace of Y'haweh, the patriarch will eternally stand as a beacon to the common peoples whom he inspires. Indeed, he and they who follow him will endure the thorns of strife and scarcity and, thereby, gain the salvation knowledge of Y'haweh's Totality, through a profound sense of appreciation for Y'haweh's yasha, in the Mashiach. Conversely, if the patriarch does not obtain the favor of Y'haweh, the natural human frailties that haunt those, whom sin's imputation binds, will corrupt the virtue of the patriarch and render him as an imperfect role model to the nations, which already bear the inclination to be unreliable caretakers of liberty. In such a case, these faithless patriarchs will not perceive the glory of Y'haweh within creation, because they cannot see past the veil of their greed and understand the equity of Y'haweh's Holy Spirit.

The notable patriarchs in history, whose virtue is of this world's order, are men like Remus and Romulus, the legendary founders of ancient Rome. As well, there is the fabled Theseus, the founder of ancient Athens. Also, in modernity, there are such men like George Washington, Thomas Jefferson, and Benjamin Franklin who are among the American *Fathers* who founded the United States of the American republic.

Yet, apart from these, there are the patriarchs of Yisra'el who have obtained Y'haweh's favor and whom Y'haweh uses to build the

Kingdom that he, in the person of Lord Yehoshua, will reign over eternally. Y'haweh's grace is upon the Yisra'elite patriarchs, while his grace is not upon the worldly patriarchs. So, you see, he establishes a covenant relationship with the Yisra'elite patriarchs, like a faithful covenant between a husband and wife; moreover, Lord Yehoshua fulfills the Covenant so that the common people who enter into the covenant relationship might inherit the blessings that the Yisra'elite patriarchs quest for. To this end, Y'haweh denies the worldly patriarchs of a true fellowship with him, in order to establish his grace upon Yisra'el. In effect, he withholds true liberty from the worldly patriarchs and the nations that follow them, while he allows the patriarchs of Yisra'el and his worshippers to gain access to the city New Yerushalayim: that is, the City that stands beyond the highest level of any worldly civilization, because in New Yerushalayim, a worshipper's relationship with Lord Yehoshua and other worshippers is not merely civil but so affectionate that the relationship bears the fullest bloom of a loving marriage.

Shadows of the Holy Marriage

Undeniably, we see that the best social agreements and political settlements (which respectively comprise the societies and civilizations that the worldly patriarchs initiate) cannot render the eternal liberty that we will enjoy in the Holy Marriage. Even so, we may see qualities of liberty in the worldly relationships that stand upon natural affection instead of social obligation. In view of that, we understand that liberty is uncertain as social relationships grow distant from the marriage unit; therefore, we expect to see the natural hallmarks of the Holy Marriage's liberty more manifest in a marriage between a loving husband and wife who reside in patriarchic societies, than in a marriage between a loving husband and wife who reside in higher-level societies because of the following: in lower-level civilizations, the natural dispositions of a respective male and female must optimally manifest their utility within the marriage and family units to overcome the privations of nature that lower-level civilizations cannot overcome. In other words, the married couple and family unit must rely upon their natural skills to benefit one another, instead of relying upon the artificial aids that contractual relationships create; even such aids that mask the utility of amiable male and female kindred companionships.

To illustrate further our point, let us concede the following: the sum disposition of the mental faculties that comprise the spirit of the male usually prompts him to perceive creation logically, sequentially, rationally, analytically, and of all objectively; therefore, the male quantifies whatever he perceives into identifiable parts. In contrast to the male's mental disposition, the female's mental disposition usually prompts her to perceive creation holistically, intuitively, synthetically, and of all subjectively; therefore, the female qualifies things that she perceives as parts of a whole. Unmistakably, females are usually more able to be in touch with their feelings, because of their uncanny ability to perceive things introspectively. So when a male reconciles his aspirations with those of the female, the female further civilizes the male by considering not only the physical needs of the family, but also the psychological needs of having the best sociable environment for the family's mental health.

As a consequence, it is apparent that while the male may be more suited for drawing conclusions that he bases on reason or fact and, thereby, identifying the variables that constitute the whole, the female may readily relate things as they are in their present state, by patiently suspending judgment to consider things in the context of the selfsame whole. Thus, while the male may be, at times more able to form a task to realize a certain end, the female may be, at times, more able to understand and sustain the process that leads to the end.

Overall, the qualities of liberty that we see in an affable marriage between a male and female stands as a shadowy silhouette[1] that the light of Holy Marriage casts upon the male and female's mental dispositions, respectively. We may further see these reflections of Y'haweh's glorious light of truth by observing how the enlightened offspring of the married couple may either assume the *masculine*

---

[1] The metaphor draws a theological parallel to Plato's Republic, Book VI.

social positions of being honorable prodigious leaders or assume the *feminine* social positions of being the dutiful supporters and civilizing forces that culture the social prodigies. What is more, we may see a direct reflection of Y'haweh's glory when a society sustains a harmonious relationship between its leaders and supporting peoples, because the city that the leaders and the people enjoin may assume a feminine form that seeks the blessings and yasha of Y'haweh, as a dutiful wife expects the loving care of a honorable husband. To this end, we true worshippers will see the glory of Y'haweh, itself, when Y'haweh's expressed person, Lord Yehoshua, assumes the form of a husband who gives an eternal reward to the only faithful bride, the city New Yerushalayim—the City of our peace.

The Hallmarks of Liberty

As we proceed, in our consideration of the lower-level civilizations, unto our goal of understanding our redemption from the unjust higher-level civilizations, let us quantify the glints of liberty in this world's order by observing the contrast between the depraved worldly civilizations and the excellent Holy Marriage of New Yerushalayim. If we begin by recalling our lessons learned, we should readily attest that the several hallmarks of Heaven's liberty, which we fleetingly witness in this world, are as follows: first, we may observe a source of liberty in a culture when the culture fosters the fidelity of the marriage unit that fulfills both male and female partners; and, second, we may note the preservation of liberty in a culture when the members of the community share a kindred sense of family and belonging, not only between the common people, but also between the governors and governed, as has been said. Also, we may qualify a more involved third hallmark of liberty in a culture if we quantify the aesthetic values that the culture exhibits, which attempt to approximate the true manifest beauty and fidelity of creation that the Holy Marriage dutifully displays in New Yerushalayim.

For example, the aesthetic sense of appreciation that work offers to a people's leisure time is a microcosm of the salvation knowledge that Lord Yehoshua offers to those who will dwell in the Shabbat peace of New Yerushalayim, after the labor of this life. So, if we consider that we will advertise our happiness in the heavenly City by devoting ourselves to him who has not only delivered us from scarcity, but also fulfilled us with the good of his Holy Spirit eternally, we may determine the measure of a civilization's happiness by the measure of the civilization's work-effort that centers upon charity, art, and recreation.

To discover our comparison between our heavenly rest that Lord Yehoshua secures and the leisurely activities that temporary affluence affords in this life, let us consider the following: initially, one must understand that that which propels us to seek felicitous actions that are satisfying in and of themselves is the fear of slavery—the most degrading condition of the human soul, in which the niggardliness of the earth coupled with the severity of heaven holds us captive with a closed iron hand. Following, one must also understand that that which oppresses mankind is not a physical actuality but a spiritual actuality: the unjust oppress the humble and the unjust are uncharitable because the unjust are ignorant of the spiritual good of Y'haweh whose opened hand freely supplies all things to the obedient. Thus, after one understands that true bondage derives from spiritual bondage, he or she will understand that one should not merely seek to free himself or herself from physical oppressors, simply to enjoy recreational activities, but one should seek the eternal freedom of his or her body, spirit, and soul, ultimately in Heaven's Kingdom.

It is sure that the unjust neither oppress, steal, nor kill for physical things, in and of themselves. Likewise, it is sure that the enslaved neither labor, resists, nor decry only to free themselves, physically, from their shackles: essentially, we all labor for inner fulfillment, in and of itself. In this vein, one may conclude that a man has no liberty when he only labors to overcome scarcity and when no time remains for leisure and joyful reflection.

Only, we must consider the fact that "every craft and every investigation, and likewise every action and decision, seems to aim at some good"[1]; to wit, every action that we take to escape the labors of life are not satisfying in and of themselves. One merely labors to escape life's bondage to acquire an existence that is satisfying in and of itself, which is ultimately the true good—even the value of the Pearl of Great Price, which value is a salvation and fulfillment in Y'haweh's Totality: a Holy Marriage. To this end, recreational play—the pleasurable deeds that we leisurely perform for their intrinsic utility—reflect our future, joyful existence in New Yerushalayim's Holy Marriage.

Our third quality of the Holy Marriage's liberty, which we may at times witness in a culture, can only be the culture's selfless pursuit for the mental and spiritual vitality of its people: that is, the vitality of the people's souls who are free from anxiety and free to appreciate the environment, aesthetically. We, in fact, may readily observe the greatest measure of this third hallmark of liberty in a culture when the rich foster such industry that affords charitable abilities to the greater populace, as a whole; not only to give the excesses of their wealth to the down trodden whose labor generates no wealth, but also to create such technologies that overcome natural hazards and generates more leisure time for all to enjoy. In this spirit of mutual benefit, the Apostle Sha'ul wrote the following: "For the gift bestowed upon us by the means of many persons, thanks [for our liberty] may be given by many on our behalf."[2]

In addition, we may see further manifestations of our third hallmark of liberty in a culture when the members of the culture patiently reconcile life's natural hazards with the culture's concept of creation. For instance, if the culture tacitly communicates the shared aesthetic values of the community's members, the people may well qualify the modes of life artistically, either through pictures, architecture, or various forms of symbolism. Then, within these aesthetic conventions, the people may also find new utility in scientific systems that facilitate their interaction with creation, either to acquire the sustenance of life or to explore recreational activities.

---

[1] Aristotle's Nicomachean Ethics
[2] 2 Corinthians 1:11

And, of all, the people may possibly identify an agreed upon lifestyle that is for the good of all and a complement to a creator's design intent. Lastly, such would be the cultural ideology that seeks to approximate the salvation knowledge of Y'haweh, which informs New Yerushalayim of his glory.

As a final point, let us take note of the fact that a culture that retains our third hallmark of liberty retains the necessary sociable environment where we would even find a fourth hallmark of liberty, and that is a civil constitution that reconciles social equity with personal justice, by rendering to everyone his or her due, with satisfaction. To be sure, if a culture possesses our third hallmark of liberty, the culture would possess a civil constitution that treats the eternal good in its injunctions and not the temporal vulgarities of life.

Even so, only the luster and manifold beauty of a culture that has the countenance of our fourth hallmark of liberty would contest New Yerushalayim, herself, if the culture also possessed a subsequent fifth hallmark of liberty: we can only ascribe this fifth hallmark to a culture that assimilates willful peoples from lesser cultures into its way of life by paying due regard to its alien citizens as though they were naturally born into the culture. We must be certain that the apex of any culture is charity for the down trodden, in such a way that all ascend to prosperity.

Hitherto, these liberties we may begin to witness in patriarchic lower-level civilizations, when we witness how the equal status of the major populace does not exacerbate the envies and lusts of sin but rather encourage harmony and a profound sense of family, belonging, and community. As well, we may note that because patriarchic kindred groups have simplistic understandings of their physical environment, they are free from the industrial and commercial burdens of greed and consumption, ownership, debt, and the like: they understand nature in a staple needs only way. Also, we may observe that because their hard-work ethic produces their staple needs from the regularities of nature, their understanding of creation is aesthetically uniform and meaningful: these people team with their environment, having a constitution that remains unwritten but understood by all through tradition and custom.

Having no need for codified law, the people of these cultures accept each other's words as their bonds.

In a timely manner, patriarchic cultures celebrate the cycles of the seasons ritually, by patiently sowing and reaping the fruits of their labor in concert with circuit of nature. Thus, for them, the wonders of a creator are evident, so they conduct their social economic endeavors with reverence, hoping that they might enjoy a creator's goodwill.

The Burden of the Patriarchs

Nevertheless, the liberties that the patriarchic lower-level civilizations enjoy are fleeting because Y'haweh does not extend his open hand to the whole of the populace, as we have noted above. Instead, he withholds his open hand by not giving everyone the measure of faith, in order for him to establish his grace upon his elect who receive his gift of faith. As a consequence, the faithless peoples cannot forge a personal and social constitution after the true liberty that exists behind the veil. As it happens, sin's imputation blinds the people from seeing the common good for all and withholds the patience that the soul needs to overcome the temptation to seek self-advantage. Hence, the population as a whole cannot safeguard all the above listed qualities of liberty, because their souls cannot perceive the greater good that we see in the Holy Marriage's fidelity.

Above all, the absence of the several qualities of liberty mark the lawlessness, oppression, and general depravity that cause the social turmoil that we see throughout the history of both lower and higher-level civilizations. In fact, vital marriage, the first hallmark of liberty that we listed above, is usually the first quality of liberty that we see corrupted in the civilizations. For example, in the fourth generation after Kayin, we see Kayin's descendants in the midst of social corruption: Kayin's descendant, Lamech, defiled his conscience by greedily marrying two wives, instead of marrying one, as the fidelity of the Holy Marriage dictates. After which, Lamech, being blinded by his own selfish aspirations, further defiled his conscience by killing a fellow man: a deed done that undermines our second hallmark of liberty, which is general social camaraderie.

Lamech's sin exemplifies the following fact: at the very beginning of the human experience, the patriarchic societies, which did not perceive the love of Y'haweh or the truth of the Holy Marriage, could not effectively bolster the institute of marriage in their culture as the cornerstone of their society or a reflection of Y'haweh's good. As a result, they could not retain a true sense of community. At best, the people's leisure time had only afforded them thoughts of a virtuous marriage as being the bond between a strong providing male and a dutiful female who preserves the income of the male and nurtures the children.

The patriarchic societies' shortsighted understanding of marriage is unfortunate. The people should have considered their rest from their labor as the product of a communal affection that creates liberty and becomes Y'haweh's espoused love.

What is more, because sin's imputation inhibits them from experiencing the love of Y'haweh, as that which fulfills their love for one another, the worldly patriarchic cultures cannot perceive the coming salvation of Y'haweh in the City of peace, New Yerushalayim. Essentially, these lower-level civilizations cannot overcome sin's selfishness to form communities for the sake of neighborly love, but they form the communities because of physical necessity. Likewise, these lower-level civilizations do not seek the favor of Y'haweh out of love for him, but they seek the favor of a creator because of the selfsame physical necessity.

Unfortunately, worldly patriarchic societies often perceive Y'haweh as a god who stands aloof and indifferent. The final outcome is that they ascribe such false identities to him that their technological grasp and rudimentary understandings of creation afford.

It follows that without a true understanding of their creator and the requisite sense of his fidelity, which informs their marriages and healthy relations, the unredeemed patriarchic societies are unable to retain our third hallmark of liberty, as well: they are unable to corporately reconcile life's natural hazards with everyone's satisfaction; therefore, they further alienate each individual's aspirations from another's. If at all possible, these unredeemed peoples can only surrender such things that are without their understanding to the dominion of "the unknown god," whose favor they seek through their perverse observance of superstitious rites and rituals that psychologically help them to withstand the ominous vicissitudes of life, by haphazardly noting life's depravity. For this cause, the peoples of lower-level civilizations invariably form fertility cults that desperately seek to invoke the favor of a god through ritualistic ceremonies that purport to ensure the fertility of the people and their agricultural economy.

Consequently, because the patriarchic societies have not acquired the first three hallmarks, the societies cannot realize our fourth hallmark of liberty, which we defined as a civil constitution that reconciles social equity with personal justice: invariably the patriarchic lower-level civilizations that do not have the example of the open hand of Y'haweh have corrupt value systems that misallocate value inequitably. For example, women and less industrious people fall prey to slander, disdain, and scorn, undeservedly. In the meantime, the rest of the populace, excessively, afford gross honors to the industrious (that is, the patriarch and elders) to the chagrin of others. And so, the true *yeshua* of Y'haweh the populace cannot perceive because the imperfect patriarch is the only model for virtue. In fact, great hardship confronts the patriarchic culture when a patriarch denies the needs of his people and the due honor to his creator, because (in such times) the patriarch seeks his own personal gain and satisfaction. Even so, a greater evil confronts the patriarchic culture when the people do not appreciate a just patriarch.

Furthermore, as the true brilliance of creation, who sits enthroned as salvation, remains unknown in patriarchic cultures (for the cultures' minor economic needs necessitate no further inquiry into creation's wonders), the patriarchic society's lack of scientific understanding leaves its people prey to a verity of natural hazards. For this reason, in their best states, patriarchic cultures invariably fail in the face of technological innovation or civil integration:

First, new political realities undermine the social status of the patriarch or elders. Following, the new realities afford new powers to challengers who usurp the power of the patriarchs, either through military strength or through peaceful political transition.

Social Disorder and Unrest

Usually, the beginning of innovation is surplus labor: over production affords to the industrious the leisure time to become specialists. In this manner, they maintain or augment their economic viability by increasing their wealth and political influence. Also, the afforded leisure time allows the industrious to become patrons of the arts for personal pleasure or gain. In this way, they strongly influence the cultural values of the people, as a whole: they begin to qualify and ascribe aesthetic values to the personal triumphs, downfalls, and aspirations of the people. Through art, therefore, the values of the human soul decide the course of human history, unto humankind's eventual dominion over the earth. We must essentially conclude that the leisure time of the industrious affords them the opportunity to question or redefine established societal conventions.

For example, the sons of Lamech initiated trends that changed the earliest society by creating new lifestyles that redefined the culture that they lived in: Lamech's son "Yaval was the father of those who dwell in tents and have cattle. [Yaval's] brother's name was Yuval, who was the father of all who handle the harp and pipe . . . [And their half brother, Tuval-Kayin, was] the forger of every cutting instrument of brass and iron."[1]

Typically, the industrious begin their careers by exchanging their goods and services for the now cheap staple goods, at a price that depends on the aesthetic value (or sense of utility) that a patron ascribes to the industrious person's good or service. Like so, these prodigies of culture amass stores of wealth (capital), and then they spend a part of their wealth on materials to produce more goods and services. Through these means, they direct the course of civilization by cornering markets, zoning land, forming guilds, producing

---

[1] Genesis 4:20-22

apprenticeships, and proliferating monetary exchange systems. Thus, the end result of their work is population skill dependencies: the common people become less self-sufficient and more dependent on the fleeting benevolence of the strong.

Nonetheless, when the industrious, who have overshadowed the patriarchic authorities, cannot inhale or exhale in harmony with the common people or themselves, they birth new political bodies that vie for their perspective interests. Under such circumstances, the people, as a whole, do not merely lose civility, but lose the sense of Y'haweh's Holy Spirit, which liberates Yerushalayim with the several liberating qualities that we cited above, that is, fidelity, friendship, beauty, social consciousness, and charity.

In actual fact, when the people are without a harmonious governing system that fosters affable relations between all segments of their society, the culture of the people not only loses the several hallmarks of liberty that we cited above, but also manifests the hallmarks of social strife: instead of kindred fidelity, there is adultery, fornication, lasciviousness, and irreverent offspring. Instead of brotherly love and friendship, there is the dishonored pledge, oppression, envy, deceit, malice, and violence. And instead of the manifold beauty of the Creator, there is idolatry, wantonness, and confusion, because the people value the golden wares of the prodigious above the maintenance of conscience and even above the love of their fellow man. To be sure, under the ideals of such capitalistic influences, the spiritual values that interpret creation become misnomers.

Finally, when the people are without government, the civil constitution that conscience bears flees before the will of the mighty, and then the rulers even become adversaries to weaker alien peoples who stand in the way of their avarice. One can easily assess the measure of affliction that the alien peoples encounter by the lack of liberty in the culture: when there is absolutely no liberty, the alien peoples encounter genocide or slavery; and when there is some semblance of liberty, the alien peoples encounter segregation or forced assimilation. In the end, all cultures eventually succumb to the hostility of war, as they confront alien civilizations.

Higher-level Civilizations

In the face of social tumult, one may justly asks the following question: what semblance of liberty can the higher-level civilizations possibly wrest from their specialized economies, which they create to govern the technological innovations and economical integrations that have uprooted the shared output and income of the lower-level civilization's communal economies? What weights and measures could they establish that all would justly recognize, or what landmarks would both the weak and the strong honor? Moreover, what code of conduct should a civil authority bring to bear, which would secure everyone's respect?

To answer these questions, we must consider the people's very notion of civility: that is, the politeness or courtesy that must permeate the social relations of sophisticated cultures. To consider general civility, let us ask ourselves another question: is the people's notion of civility agreeable with a mind that seeks through faith the greater good of all, even a mind being redeemed by Lord Yehoshua's unblemished conscience unto Y'haweh's Glory; or is the people's notion of civility agreeable with a mind that seeks the best advantage of the privileged or many, despite ever present injustices?

In any case, civility falls short of the righteousness of New Yerushalayim, which liberally renders to everyone satisfaction unto the glory of Y'haweh. In this vein, the Apostle Sha'ul once wrote, "The kingdom of God is not meat and drink; but righteousness and peace, and joy in the Holy Spirit."[1]

In other words, the Kingdom of Heaven does not stand upon the lesser friendships that only seek personal sustenance or fleeting pleasure, but the Kingdom stands upon the righteous and eternal friendship of the Holy Marriage. Accordingly, Sha'ul also wrote, "The Lord is that Spirit: and where the Spirit of the Lord is, there is liberty."[2]

---

[1] Romans 14:17
[2] 2 Corinthians 3:17

That which defines a higher-level civilization is the way in which a government recognizes some form of a constitutional relationship with individuals to the extent that the population's legal status extends beyond a group—for example, a tribe or kindred family that corporately secures scarce resources. Rather, higher-level civilizations extend legal status to individuals who retain abstract constitutional relationships with the government that allows the individuals to obtain personal property, depending upon individuals' contribution to the specialized economy that the government oversees.

Thus, unnatural is the peoples' move from the natural legal status of kindred group, which psychologically and economically enfranchises the people, depending upon regularity of the agricultural economy. In the contractual relationships with higher-level civilizations' constitutional governments, the peoples' enfranchisement is volatile and at best progressive, as the constitution continuously evolves to meet new economic conditions and political realities: as we shall see, the legal status of individuals continually change as higher-level civilizations' constitutions continually evolve through a process of, first, legal fictions (that is, cultural attitude changes, despite the law); second, equity (that is, the continued quest for general consensus); and, third, legislation (that is, forced political consensus).[1]

We shall now see how the three forms of government fleetingly uphold their respective constitutions as they reconcile the constitutions with the hallmarks of liberty; in regards to the governments' incorporating the kindred relationships of marriage and brotherhood, which reflect Heaven's Holy Marriage. We shall

---

[1] Henry James Summer Maine (1822-1888) was a British historical jurist who notably captured the manner in which legal history stands upon how civilization developed from considering respective societies' legal status in terms of groups unto considering respective societies' legal status in terms of individual merits. Maine observed that humankind's natural state of nature is a communal group; therefore, Maine decried the unnatural notions of socialist governments that hold that individualism must be protected at the cost of the protection of historical kindred groups.

also see that when the governments do not secure the hallmarks of liberty, concerning marriage and kindred brotherhood, the people become disenfranchised, isolated, with no social or cultural redress, as they vicariously stand subject to the whims of an impersonal, centralized, and autocratic regime. To this end, in our subsequent chapter, we shall see that only the orthodox Church justly reconciles kindred relationships to effect global higher-level-civilizations, as the Church seeks the gift of the Testator, regardless of class, ethnicity, social status, or male or female sex.

Essentially, it suffices us to say that whatever constitution that either of the perspective three forms of government engender, the constitution must codify the above several hallmarks of liberty to bear even a semblance of Heaven's glory. For instance, a monarch must selflessly seek the will and benevolence of Y'haweh, if he is to be a true servant and deliverer of the people; otherwise he will prove to be a tyrannical anti-savior, an "anti-Christ," who is the people's greatest bane. As well, the aristocracy, who are the prodigious and industrious of the people, must liberally share their luxuries with the weak (who must in turn surrender due regard) that all might enjoy such a mastery over their environment that they will attain freedom from want. Indeed, if the aristocrats are covetous, they will become oligarchs that terrorize and exploit the disadvantaged and, ultimately, defeat themselves. Additionally, a democratic people must cultivate a formal constitution that all willingly adheres to. They must delineate just rules for everyone's advantage, despite class or creed; because if they do not, strife and affliction will continually defeat every civil action.

Finally, the aesthetic arts that leisure time affords must celebrate the societal liberties that all the above governments foster, in such a way that architecture, painting, literature, sculpture, music, doctrine, and science reflect the perspective government's constitution in spiritual grandeur. In this manner, the aesthetic arts must inspire succeeding generations to observe the constitution.

All three forms of government claim that their respective constitutions secure the peoples' liberties: the constitution of a monarch determines that divine providence dictates the rule of a monarch; therefore, the constitution assumes that the monarch is the natural guide for the people (like the patriarch): the monarch's constitution, therefore, censures any dissent by the governed against the monarch's eminence, despite conscience's compromise. Next, the aristocratic constitution determines that a group of rulers (like the elders) are naturally endowed to guide the people; therefore, their constitution derides any contrary social dissent by those that they deem to be of less social worth. Lastly, the constitution of democracy determines that individuals can naturally benefit one another; therefore, the democratic constitution guards against the excesses of the domineering: democracy seeks to reconcile everyone's social aspiration, even in times when it is apparent that true justice does not stand, because the people give the base and the worth the same acclaim, in order to establish their democracy.

The Gold of the Priestly King's City

Usually, of the three governmental systems, monarchies first arise to quell the excesses of sin and ply a course for human history, as the other two governmental systems—aristocracies and democracies—succeed the monarchies, respectively. Among the prodigious of the society, a monarch arises by accruing wealth and land through his industry, and then he distributes somewhat of his wealth to loyal relatives, friends, and allied associates. Following, he sets the self-same close relations in key places of his administration, while in the meantime he hires a police force to enforce his law and collect tribute and rent from the lower class of his society. Lastly, he proclaims that he is the savior of the people, while he suppresses his rivals in the upper class. The monarch then initiates the first legal fiction that separates the people from their kindred groups to become subjects under the king's rule. The monarch fashions himself as the father of many kindred groups. Also, to further establish his government, the monarch and his supporters usually purport that the divine mandates his rule. For this cause, the monarch correlates his rule with a complementary religious institution. He, in fact, often assumes the role of being the high priest of the people. In this vein, the monarch is a natural image of a *god*, for the monarch brings law, direction, and order to his people.

Albeit, the monarch can only be a true high priest if he obtains the grace of Y'haweh. He and his administration must effectively retain the several hallmarks of liberty if the monarch is to be Y'haweh's true servant and ambassador to the people. In point of fact, the qualities of liberty, which monarchs enjoy from the open hand of Y'haweh, flow from the marriage and immediate family unit of the monarch. We readily witness our first hallmark of liberty in monarchies when the common people (who hold the patriarchic marriage and family unit as sacred) receive a monarch's house by perceiving the monarch to be a heightened patriarch and his family as the first family, even the royal family of the society at hand.

Because of the common people's acceptance of a monarch's social status, monarchies may as well uphold our second quality of liberty—general, social camaraderie—despite the fact that there is a noticeable amount of social disparity between the monarchic ruling class and the common people. The king, his house, and administrators effectively function as the capitalists of the culture, thus establishing their elite status, while the peoples of the lower class typically gain their subsistence communally; though a subsequent merchant class arises and pays the king tribute. Even so, the law of conscience has a faculty that garners its adherents in a strong monarchy because the rigid class structure causes the people to be more accepting of their lot in life and less envious of their upper-class neighbors.

As it happens, the nature of the monarch's administrative city further harmonizes the privileged status of the monarch with the lesser status of the general populace. The city of the monarch readily qualifies the aesthetic values of the people (which values seek to reconcile creation's beauty with the people's cultural modes of life). In this manner, the monarchic government retains our third hallmark of liberty: communal aesthetic affections that interpret Y'haweh's fidelity within creation and foster mental health. As a result, the political intercourse between the various administrative bodies, guilds, and other fraternal orders necessitates a code of conduct that gives rise to an increasingly urbane upper class. In this way, the industrious of the lower-level civilizations become urbanites: they move from the rustic countryside environments of the agricultural economy into the city where they, as civil authorities, conduct business in such a way that work involves contractual transactions of a kind that requires no husbandry or shepherding. The elitists' code of conduct then transfers to the lower class of the populace to instill a single cultural identity upon both classes.

Initially, the monarch and his administration begin to establish his city by establishing measures of value for mediums of exchange. In other words, the monarch establishes a currency that proves to be a necessary medium for those industrious people who seek to exchange their goods and services for other goods and services. So, instead of producing goods and services to exchange in a bartering market where a trading partner's goods or services are not necessarily available or of dubious value, industrious individuals produce their goods and services to acquire the monarch's mediums of exchange; because they recognize the fact that the accepted value of the king's currency will allow them to purchase other goods and services when they are available and of a sure value.

To this end, gold becomes the most popular universally accepted medium of exchange because of its physical properties; moreover, its value often holds because it is scarcely found in nature. Gold does not corrode, and it is pliable, and to the earliest civilizations, gold seemed to have miraculous properties. Thus, a strong king's marked gold retained the greatest value throughout civilization.

During such times of prosperity, it becomes apparent that as a monarch's industry increases, established weights and measures become necessary; therefore, scribes who utilize mathematics and grammar for bookkeeping proliferate. Consequently, banking systems ensue to allow people to amass savings or borrow money with interest loans to finance great building construction or other public works such as sewage and water utilities. As well, due to the greater division of labor, the other arts and sciences become more refined and culturally distinct under the monarch's realm: painting and architecture usually become uniform and easily appreciable by all. So, in this manner, the art of the monarchy further defines the society's cultural identity. Conclusively, a united city that stands happily under the identity of a charitable monarch naturally produces cultural wealth and enjoys economic prosperity.

The Shipmaster's Law in Action

Without question, long lasting culture and traditions usually form under monarchies. The people project the best of their cultural values upon the monarch and his family: they ascribe great ceremony to the monarch's throne. In turn, the monarch's throne portrays the people's religious and moral consciousness. Because he is the embodiment of his society's cultural identity, the king himself becomes our fourth hallmark of liberty: a living breathing constitution unto his people.

For all intents and purposes, if the king obtains the yasha of Y'haweh, the anointed king will with great foresight perceive the eternal attributes of Y'haweh's Holy Spirit, and then the king will rationally apply pure directives to govern his people. With great political sagacity, the king will clearly outline the most fruitful enterprises for the people to embark upon: he will point to the greatest good for all whom he shelters under the stability of his government. First, he will find out the sincerest values of the people by gauging what personal labor they are willing to offer, in order to gain that which they deem to be of an eternal value. Afterwards, he will prevent the masks of "wages, profit, and rent . . . the three original sources of all revenue"[1] from covering Heaven's enduring wealth. Finally, he will teach his people to labor after the true eternal riches above: having salvation knowledge, he will clearly see that the natural price and market price of goods and contractual services continually change upon supply and demand, causing currency values and legal status to fluctuate, continually; while the Holy Spirit of Truth remains priceless forever, over all. Staying true to this understanding, the king will continually remind his people that it is impossible to affix a currency price upon our pearl of truth.

---

[1] Adam Smith: *An Inquiry into the Nature and Causes of the Wealth of Nations*

For this cause, those who do not have the salvation knowledge, which appreciates Y'haweh's truth, ascribe the greatest value to the worldly idols that they can affix currency values upon. Fittingly the Apostle Sha'ul, therefore, proclaims, "The love of money is the root of all evil."[1]

So, in order for us to escape certain evil, we have only to observe the following saying of the only true King and Savior, Lord Yehoshua:

> Labor not for the meat, which perishes, but for that meat which endures unto everlasting life, which the Son of man shall give unto you: for him has God the Father sealed.[2]

When one considers the above, one may begin to understand that while an anointed king enjoys the privilege of singularly deciding the best course of action, it is actually the king's people who possess the greater benefit: their economy flourishes because of the political solidarity that the king secures for his administrators. As a result, the people pursue greater enterprises unto the king's glory, their not having any dissenting, political inhibitors. In point of fact, whenever Lord Yehoshua underrated the miracles that he performed, Lord Yehoshua esteemed the greater benefits that his followers will enjoy by saying, "Indeed, I tell you truly, he that believes in me, the works which I do that one shall also do, and greater than these he will do, because I go to my Father."[3]

In all honesty, we may conclude, therefore, that it is not for the king to do the work; it is only for the king to inspire the work. Like a shipmaster, the anointed king will look past the passing tempest of life and affix his eyes upon the stars that brilliantly array themselves around the eternal beauty of the Father of all creation. The king will not guide his ship by written enactments, which fail to traverse the vicissitudes of life's storm, but he will observe a law in action "by

---

[1] 1 Timothy 6:10
[2] John 6:27
[3] John 14:12

useful application of his knowledge of seamanship . . . It is in this way that he will preserve the lives of his ship."[1]

We may only add once more that such justice that a good king upholds begets insurmountable wealth, which actually is a result of the general sense of fairness that unites the king's people. In few words, one ancient writer commends the prosperity of a just king, who returns the riches of Eden, as follows:

> A good king, who reigns . . . upholds justice and right, and the black earth renders him her foison, barely, and wheat, and his trees are laden and weighted with fair fruits, growth comes to his flocks and the ocean is abundant with fishes.[2]

Our noting the obvious utility of such a monarch begs for us to ask the following question: would not foreign peoples gladly assimilate into such a monarch's realm? Surely, they would readily see the wisdom of his reign and come and add their strengths to his kingdom, only to establish the kingdom's fifth hallmark of liberty, and that is the willful assimilation of alien peoples, who pay due homage to his throne.

"The Death of Kings"

When we consider the nature of viable monarchies, we cannot hinder ourselves from considering how remarkable the monarch's throne is. The monarch's throne safeguards our several liberties, as the people acclaim the throne saying, "Upon the king! Let us our lives, our souls, our debts, our careful wives, our children and our sins lay on the king!"[3]

Yet, when we consider that liberty demands a natural affection between the beneficent strong and their appreciative beneficiaries (in a marriage of mutual satisfaction) and when we subsequently consider that liberty salutes the celebrity of a just monarch before his loyal and cared for subjects (both common and industrious), it

---

[1] Plato's Statesman
[2] Homer's Odyssey
[3] Shakespeare's Henry V: Act IV Scene I

should not surprise us that the nations naturally coalesce into political systems that seek a centralized authority, having a sovereign that shares powers, by degrees, with both common and industrious peoples. The mortality of justice in human monarchies necessitates this political concession: although people prefer the embodiment of a god among men, the lack of such godly qualities among men or the lack of the Holy Spirit given faith, which allows the elect to see the true *yeshua* of Y'haweh, causes the people to acclaim a lesser government that stands upon shared power between classes. Indeed, while the earth writhes and grows toward a centralized authority that political compromises realize and notions of civility brook, a multiplicity of insubstantial cultures and traditions fail in the river of truth until Lord Yehoshua rips the veil that blinds the nations and we — his faithful — see him as the true figure of Y'haweh sitting justly upon his throne, having casts down the false images of himself. As the Apostle Sha'ul wrote, "Having stripped the principalities and authorities, he [Lord Yehoshua] made a show of them openly, having triumphed over them in it."[1]

Thus, on the sound ground of the Holy Marriage, which weds our eternal appreciations with Y'haweh's open hand, we will stand. Through faith we will seek Lord Yehoshua's government of New Yerushalayim, the eternal solid rock that stands in contrast to the temporary governments of the higher-level civilizations, which the industrious build upon political compromises.

To be sure, not only are the governments of this world like delightfully inflated balloons that rise upon the core of good conscience only to be blown by conscience's compromise; but also are the worldly governments' bonds of civility feeble. Thus, they cannot grasp hold onto the eternal bond of love. Nevertheless, we rest assured that New Yerushalayim's Holy Marriage establishes the eternal bond of Y'haweh's love, because in Yerushalayim the grants of Y'haweh (the beneficent strong) agree with the wishes of his appreciative elect true worshippers; therefore, only in such a hallowed marriage can conscience find its preservation.

---

[1] Colossians 2:15

We, in fact, see the frailty of civilization's civility in the fleeting celebrity of a worldly king. Even as some monarchs, like those who obtain Y'haweh's grace, find humility in the fact that graves, worms, and epitaphs not only encompass the common people, but also encompass them too (thus they give place to justice); other monarchs, who do not find Y'haweh's open hand, fall into the snare of Satan's conceit; therefore, they forget that pomp and circumstance not only are unable to impede injustice, but also are unable to ensure the popularity of the monarch, the health of the state, or the individual health of the people.

In other words, social etiquette and protocol are without merit when they illegitimately mask injustice with the appearance of virtue. For this cause, righteous indignation has an infinitesimally greater value when it stands juxtaposed to such hypocrisy. To be sure, even the general populace, whom a mere sense of civility suffices, despair when an empty crown is not filled with integrity. Indeed, they seek to place their dearest affections and allegiances upon a sovereign who is true, their hearts crying out "may the king reign forever!"

The eternal reign of Y'haweh's ambassador is the hope of the wise, for who would chance to dwell under the burden of a liege whom flatteries intoxicate and whose boundless lust holds good conscience in contempt, to the chagrin of the people. What is more, the darkness of sin that entices a pompous king is not his private possession, since the darkness entices the industrious to seek their own advantage; therefore, they lay in wait searching for an opportunity to exploit the frailties of the monarch. Hence, an ancient playwright rights as follows:

> [T]here the antic sits,
> Scoffing his state and grinning at his pomp,
> Allowing him a breath, a little scene,
> To monarchize, be fear'd and kill with looks,
> Infusing him with self and vain conceit,
> As if this flesh which walls about our life,
> Were brass impregnable, and humour'd thus

Comes at the last and with a little pin
Bores through his castle wall, and farewell king!
[In this manner] some have been deposed; some slain in war,
Some haunted by the ghosts they have deposed;
Some poisn'd by their wives: some sleeping kill'd;
All murder'd...[1]

The Codified Penal Law of the Aristocrats

Summarily, we conclude that while the law of conscience may find the strongest ally in a just monarch who submits to Y'haweh's glory, the law of conscience may find the greatest foe in a monarch who becomes a tyrant by seeking his own self-will despite the good of his people or the glory of Y'haweh. Even if a monarch is in his best form, his natural imperfections distort the perceptions of creation that those who are under his rule possess; moreover, an imperfect monarch consigns the idea of a perfect monarch—that is, a savior—to dwell only in the minds of the people of faith.

Seldom seen is a righteous king among men; therefore, do the privileged class of the industrious (the aristocracy) seek to quell the power of one by advertising the fact that the virtues of industry and morality are not of a single person's private possessions. As an alternative, they purport that their privileged status issues from an inherent superiority that qualifies them to be the natural rulers of the people. Instead of forecasting the manifold virtues that reflect the qualities of the divine upon a single person, the aristocrats perceive such virtues more abstractly: they qualify distinctions of virtue in a more spiritual way, as an alternative to affixing the appellation of virtue haphazardly on a single individual. The aristocrats are, therefore, those leaders that have the foresight to perceive somewhat of the eternal qualities of Y'haweh: they, partially, perceive Y'haweh's righteous state of being immutable and unchangeable. Following, they attempt to replicate the qualities of the state of righteousness, by pursuing virtuous actions that benefit their society at hand. In other words, they try to encourage virtue's integrity,

---

[1] William Shakespeare's Richard II: Act III Scene II

truthfulness, work ethic, camaraderie, and the general sense of industry that secures physical prosperity.

In the place of the monarch whose throne formerly endeavored to portray itself as a state of virtue that reflects Y'haweh's eternal state of righteousness (the monarch's having the law in hand), the aristocracy endeavor to compel the people to practice virtue in action, by confronting them with static penal law codes, which list the many offenses that are intolerable for a society that seeks to be virtuous, perennially. In its most idealistic form, the law code of the aristocracy seeks the greatest benefit of the many and not only the benefit of a single person. Using the code of law, the aristocratic government tries to capture the fading glory of the ancient, unwritten, patriarchic, and self-evident laws of conscience that once inspired the culture and former king (who once jealously fortified them, in a figure of majesty, when he was in his best form).

When the aristocratic government upholds conscience in their society, the several hallmarks of liberty manifest themselves in the following way: first, their having the foresight to see the greater good for all in their political and industrial pursuits, the aristocracy become the natural leaders of the people: they take the spiritual form of the benevolent husband in a loving marriage with those who are best able to effect that which the husbandmen foresee. Subsequently, the beneficiaries of the husbandmen become natural servants: they assume the form of the appreciative, obedient wife whose obedience can truly be a complement to the glory of Y'haweh, if the husbandmen are themselves servants of Y'haweh, in righteousness. Accordingly, the natural marriage between a male and female best exhibits the above relationship between the aristocratic ruling class and the common people: the love and affection that binds the marriage reflects the state of righteousness that the aristocratic law code seeks to proclaim as that which is most virtuous in their culture.

Furthermore, the political affinity between an aristocrat and other aristocrats consigns the subservient population, who are under the aristocrats, to conform to the social order that the aristocratic law codes dictate. In point of fact, the conformity of an aristocrat with other aristocrats, along with their respective subservient populations, necessitates some level of camaraderie, which we have identified to be our second hallmark of liberty.

Additionally, the above marriage (between the government of a few and the governed) houses our third hallmark of liberty—that is, spiritual vitality within common aesthetic values—in a city-state that is synonymous with an ancient Greek *polis*[1], a word from which we derive the word *politics*. We have the understanding that the polis is an extension of the former monarch's administrative city, because it comprises not only the business of one sovereign entity, but also the business of several sovereign entities, which relate to one another through whatever political compromise that their law code establishes. To be sure, the law code itself is the very constitution that we identify as our fourth hallmark of liberty. Also, in point of fact, having such a constitution to govern their political relationships, the aristocrats at times become business *companions*: in this way, their business *companionships* form the first commercial *companies*.

Essentially, we have the understanding that the polis is a city-state, because an aristocratic polis is in actuality a rudimentary representational form of government: even though the commoners who reside in strict aristocracies have no political autonomy, a virtuous aristocratic overlord will dutifully consider the health and welfare of his people in his political dealings with other aristocrats who plead the cause of their own estates in the governmental arenas of the city. In fact, the political deliberation that the ruling class enjoins necessitates greater inquiry into social consciousness, among the ever increasing sizes of the ruling class's respective constituencies: in their deliberations, the ministers of state rationally seek to secure virtue over vice for the good of the city-state, which the law code presides over. And so, because of its deliberative processes, the city-state not only possesses the ability to uphold conscience among a greater group of people, but also possesses the ability to bolster an even more specialized economy. Also, because of the level of civility that aristocrats achieve through their deliberative inquiry into conscience, the aristocratic society has the ability to

---

[1] An ancient Greek urbanized political center, comprising a city.

bring together an increasingly diverse culture: the city-state relates a dissimilar people one unto another, in such a way that more people acquire personal wealth, which wealth was the sole possession of the former king, the king's ministers, and the king's family. In the place of the monarch, the aristocrats function as the capitalists of their community, while their subservient peoples generally function under communal or merchant orders.

In addition, while a marriage between the benevolent government of a few and the appreciative, supporting body of the common people implicates the above city-state, where there may be deliberative inquiries into constitutions of conscience, the institute of marriage itself ultimately serves as an optimal medium that secures our fifth hallmark of liberty: the willful assimilation of alien peoples. Aristocracies usually rely upon marriage alignments to retain wealth and quell hostility between competing aristocratic families. When competing aristocratic families align themselves through marriage, the subservient aliens of their populations usually conform under the alignments, agreeably.

The Covetous Oligarchs Who Initiate the Rise of Secularism

When we consider all the hallmarks of liberty that an aristocratic government may retain, we can ascertain that the chief benefit of their government is that their government, in measure, impedes the rise of tyranny. An aristocracy is more likely to avoid the horrors of tyrannical power, such as the total enslavement of a people. The aristocratic government contains a measure of redress in its shared power, where aristocrats check the power of other aristocrats. The aristocracy's natural inquiry into the eternal qualities of virtue, instead of the virtuous actions of a single individual, generally inspires those within and under their government not to trust in the total power of one. Like so, they avoid the rise of the tyrant.

Yet, when an aristocratic government does not, as a whole, receive Y'haweh's open hand, they cannot through faith perceive the salvation knowledge that exists in the fidelity of the Holy Marriage.

Without faith, the unredeemed aristocrats observe the natural laws of creation and perceive an eternal dimension beyond the brevity of life's labor; however, they cannot entirely perceive the unchanging, righteous state of Y'haweh himself; moreover, they cannot selflessly conform their lives to him. In fact, the unredeemed aristocrats cannot possibly understand that their political law code cannot ensure the same mutual affection that exists between Lord Yehoshua and his body of true worshippers; especially when there is no sense of fidelity between all who fall under the code of law. What is more, without faith, they cannot understand that the virtuous actions that their law codes foster are fleeting because such actions are momentary; therefore, the law codes do not of themselves reflect the Mashiach's unblemished conscience, which redeems a person's virtuous actions. In a word, the virtuous actions that the true worshippers commit by faith are redeemable because they seek to associate themselves to the eternal, righteous state of the Holy Marriage, instead of merely seeking the fleeting worldly satisfaction that is due under the law.

We might note as well that even though law codes bear precious fruit as they reconcile competing fraternities, the law itself may at best aspire unto what is merely due under its injunctions, instead of what is mutually fulfilling for all: the law only finds a compromise that may be tentatively agreeable to all. Categorically, we must assert that "it is impossible for something invariable and unqualified to handle satisfactorily with what is never uniform and constant"[1]: namely, a code of law cannot be uniquely applied to benefit each individual's ever-changing taste and preferences, neither satisfactorily nor eternally. Even so, the free gift of salvation—the Holy Marriage of Lord Yehoshua's Body—reconciled by the Holy Spirit, which changes individual appetite to conform gratefully to the Lord's Body, delivers a satisfaction to the individual that law cannot approach: indeed, even the law of conscience, itself, merely points to such a state of felicity.

---

[1] Plato's *Statesman*

In sum, the aristocracy's inclination to observe their codified laws without faith leaves the aristocracy to be even less likely to seek an intimate relationship with Y'haweh than the former, fallen monarch. Although the aristocracy's understanding of Y'haweh may be more rational than that of the former monarch, the aristocrats are less likely to inquire into the righteousness of the Mashiach: they are more likely to seek the eternal qualities that the Mashiach's righteous Spirit manifests (such as wisdom, sobriety, and justice), not knowing that they cannot retain these qualities unless they associate themselves with the Mashiach.

In contrast, the sole rule of the monarch inclines the monarch to seek the favor of the very person of a deity, above all else. It is certain that even in cultures that observe many deities, monarchs usually single out one deity as their patron.

We may further illustrate our comparison by noting that the natural sciences—the knowledge of immutable, physical reality, a knowledge that secures a benefit for everyday life—enamors the aristocrats, while the prospect of inspiring the people, by becoming an image of all eternity's majesty, rouses the king. For this cause, the king is more likely to have monotheistic inclinations, because his legal injunctions must be decisive and binding upon the whole of his people like a sovereign *god*, while the aristocracy is more likely to have agnostic, deistic, or pantheistic inclinations, because their administrative system must, in order, govern the city-state like what they assume to be a supernatural administrative system that governors the mechanisms of creation.

All the same, when we consider that both governments' deliberative processes aim at some good, we understand that both governments equally seek to make rational choices that secure virtue over vice. The sins of conscience that both governments commit are usually involuntary. And so, it is evident that without the benefit of Y'haweh's open hand, no people can resist the seducing spirits that cloak the true and eternal good, when devils (in the form of greed) put forth temporal satisfaction. Despite the fact that the aristocracy endeavor to affix their laws upon the eternal attributes of the divine (like wisdom, sobriety, honor, and charity), sin eventually consigns them to affix their laws upon the fleshly frailties (like health, wealth, and comeliness).

To be more specific, we may conclusively say that without the salvation knowledge that the Holy Marriage's eternal satisfaction affords to creation, the aristocracy becomes a mere oligarchy—a term that as well designates the government of a few. Yet, instead of giving the term *oligarchy* a positive connotation like the term *aristocracy*, we must give the term a negative connotation. We must say that unlike the term *aristocracy* (a term that denotes the privileged class of leaders, whom Y'haweh endows), the term *oligarchy* merely denotes the worldlier rule of the few people who are politically sagacious, economically industrious, or affluently born.

We see the beginning of the government of a few's change from an aristocracy to an oligarchy when nepotism fails to birth the wise and charitable. The aristocracy begins to fall when deficient rulers arise who fail to perceive the good that the established code of law points to. In contrast to the aristocrats who attempt to affix their law codes on a perceived eternal good for the people, the oligarchs affix their law codes on such things that they believe will afford to them immediate benefits. The oligarchs, having inherited the wealth of the former aristocrats, often compromise conscience to retain their rule and wealth.

Not having the foresight to see past sin's veil and comprehend the eternal good, the oligarchs not only relax the social stigmas that denounce incontinence, but also disdain the faithful who hold the eternal good above the oligarchs' worldly lusts. In truth, these secular oligarchs hold the religious as ignorant. In the oligarchs' eyes, the religious not only spend wasteful energy on uneconomically productive efforts, but also chide the excesses of pleasure, which the oligarchs count as wealth and gain.

The oligarchs never accept fundamental truth: they continuously chase after novelty. They consign the world system to follow a linear thought process: they are always ready to exploit some new innovation.

The oligarchs deny the worth of faith because they believe that they can work out their own purpose for existence through rational calculation. They only accept the existence of the natural laws to describe the workings of creation. As a result, they falsely perceive the creation as a universe that stands devoid of Y'haweh's purposes.

We may identify the oligarch's belief system as secularism: the belief that one may approach a greater good in civilized societies using scientific studies and rational philosophies to explain the natural world without any necessity to believe in supernatural deities or spiritual entities. Thus, the secular oligarchs' only conception of the good is the advancement of scientific knowledge to control and make amiable human environment, by advancing commerce unto the greater distribution of goods and services. To wit, they believe that growing an economy through technological innovation is the only source of human wellbeing. Effectively, their secular form prevents them from seeing past sin's veil of temporary pleasure and acknowledging the fact that "every craft and every investigation, and likewise every action and decision seems to aim at some [eternal] good"[1]

The Loss of the True Friendship

We essentially conclude that when oligarchs do not by faith receive the open hand of Y'haweh, the several hallmarks of liberty flee before their midst. Then suddenly sin's imputation bolsters the nescient cloud that veils the Holy Marriage: the very state in which Lord Yehoshua establishes the elect upon the core of his good conscience.

As it happens, we further define the foreboding veil of sin by surmising not only the government of a few's feeble grasps onto the friendship of Y'haweh's love, but also the other two governments' feeble grasp, as well. As we noted above, the necessary investment that all higher-level civilizations must ascribe to creation's eternal attributes is the very fidelity that only Y'haweh's eternal love exhibits as an uncompromising friendship to the elect, who shall eternally dwell within his Son, his beloved.

To qualify the higher-level civilization's loss of this true friendship, we have only to observe the fall of the aristocracy into an

---

[1] Aristotle's Nicomachean Ethics

oligarchy in particular. At the same time, we may qualify the aristocracy's loss of the several liberties.

First, if we quickly define friendship as two or more people's individual pursuits for each other's good (that is, a relationship where each member in turn assumes the complementary roles of being both the benefactor and beneficiary of the friendship), we may say that the only true and eternal friendship is the Holy Marriage, while the mortal friendships of this age are those relationships that pleasure or necessity enjoins, despite the true necessity for each member to complement another member for the true and eternal good of all.

The first and true friendship, we define as righteousness. It is the friendship between Y'haweh and Lord Yehoshua, who is (of course) Y'haweh's expression of himself as the salvation of his beneficiaries, the true worshippers. In the first friendship, Y'haweh's Holy Spirit delivers unto his Yehoshua the truest sense of appreciation of Y'haweh's glory in creation, which includes not only Lord Yehoshua's felicitous place in the creation, but also the true worshippers' felicitous place in the creation. Being so completely satisfied, in such a way that novelty cannot approach him with its enticements, Lord Yehoshua inescapably becomes an expression of Y'haweh's love to the true worshippers:

It follows that Lord Yehoshua cannot seek a greater benefit other than that which he already possesses within; therefore, he can only seek to become the benefactor and justifier of others, while he does not seek anything for himself. Essentially, he only seeks the glory of Y'haweh. Standing in the gap between the jealous love of Y'haweh and the selfishness of humankind, Lord Yehoshua's selfless service unto Y'haweh empowers him to be a spiritual, *female-like*, civilizing force that pacifies the very masculine and jealously wrathful Spirit of Y'haweh, who seeks satisfaction in the justice of his truth. And so, being satisfied with the good of Y'haweh, Lord Yehoshua qualifies the righteousness of Y'haweh as an internal satisfaction that allows one to seek actively the benefit of others without the expectation of any reward except the justice of the Holy Marriage, where justice stands to benefit all whose faith Lord Yehoshua redeems.

In our current state of social and personal discontent, however, we can only perceive the fruits of the first friendship through faith. Truly, when we are without faith and a true conception of the justice of the first friendship, sin's imputation consigns us to endure only the other two manifestations of friendship, which do not have the salvation knowledge of the Lord: there are, again, the friendships of pleasure, which people enjoin despite the eternal good for all, and there are the friendships of necessity or expediency, which people enjoin for self-preservation. Without salvation knowledge, people's varying notions of what their immediate pleasures or necessities are will undermine the relationship between benefactors and beneficiaries. For example, instead of being truly charitable to render lasting services to the needy, sin often consigns wealthy benefactors to exploit those who are in their care. Also, instead of fully appreciating the deeds of philanthropists, sin often consigns debtors to begrudge the privileged state of their benefactors whom they are indebted to.

As we have said above, only the shadow of righteousness, that is, virtue, reigns in this world. Nevertheless, we who through faith and refined consciences intuitively begin to perceive fidelity within creation, and finally we begin to seek something other than our own benefit. After all, our virtue becomes righteousness when Y'haweh's Holy Spirit invests a subjective sense of satisfaction within us in concert with the objective sense of satisfaction that his Holy Spirit invests within our fellows. Truly, we all then acquire measures of the sense of appreciation from Y'haweh's benevolence, as seen in the resurrection of us whom he justifies in the risen Lord Yehoshua. When he thus satisfies us with our due, justice reigns. Then we all seek each other's advantage without expectation. Indeed, we all become a "body nourished and knit together by joints and ligaments, [grown] with the increase that is from Y'haweh."[1]

Through the friendship of Y'haweh, we—who will dwell in heavenly New Yerushalayim—escape this volatile age, the saeculum, where true friendship falls before social division, anxiety, and all

---

[1] Colossians 2:19

such things that the political strife of the covetous allow. The greed of the oligarchs themselves bears witness to civilization's loss of the true friendship amid the loss of civilization's several hallmarks of liberty.

Of course, the first hallmark of liberty that the oligarchs lose is the quintessential friendship of the institute of marriage, which points to the righteous and holy marriage of Y'haweh. At best the oligarchs might uphold marriage to establish an elite code of conduct that reinforces familial inheritance.

Often in more capitalist economic systems, when technological advancement still requires manual labor but entrepreneurship may afford an industrious person the ability to set off labor to his or her employed, leisure time might only afford such understandings of a virtuous marriage as being a bond between, first, a talented and industrious man who secures goods and services for his household and, second, a talented and principled woman of good social standing who educates her children and advances the cause of her husband.

The oligarchs' myopic understanding of marriage's fidelity demoralizes their society, because the oligarchs do not portray the gains of their wealth as that which they have acquired through charitable and fair dealings with the underprivileged. And so, they (like the ancient king of Tyre) set an evil example when they acquire gain, even as they do not empathize with the plight of the downcast. Consequentially, the people of the culture cannot observe the law of conscience when they do not possess a sense of empathy for the plight of their neighbors. What follows is this: instead having fidelity's foresight to see the greater good for all, lust becomes their natural guide to overruling conscience. Greed then enslaves the helpless and treats them as inanimate tools. Indeed, our second hallmark of liberty, which invokes brotherly love, is in this way broken.

Besides, people begin to become less self-sufficient under oligarchies: the guarantor of the people's subsistence is no more the regularity of the earth's agricultural yield; instead the guarantor is the fleeting industry and charity of the wealthy; therefore, the reaping and sowing of the people's industry does not necessarily harmonize with the new moons, but the people's industry invariably must harmonize with the whims of the overlord's rapaciousness. Essentially, the oligarchs undermine the former cultural marriage between the former monarch or aristocracy (who had portrayed the benevolent capitalists of the culture) and the general populace (who in turn had portrayed the appreciative and charitable communists of the culture).

The oligarchs' lusts for power and prestige further pollute creation with their capitalistic signs of power: the art of the oligarchic state is less rural or natural. Only symbols of power and personal license arise to display the boasts of the oligarchs before those who are less fortunate. As a consequence, their culture loses our third hallmark of liberty, which aesthetically celebrates creation's fidelity under Y'haweh.

Also, the loss of the culture's civil constitution of conscience (liberty's fourth hallmark) quickly follows the above cultural breakdowns. In such a plight, the oppressed find no social redress in the government. Instead, to find legal help, they at best must pay exorbitant sums of money to professional students of law who pervert the law for gain, despite the law's original intent to uphold some appearance of a social consciousness.

The Quarrel between Secularists and the People of Faith that Necessitates the Common Wealth of Democracy

Even though their privileged status seems well established, the covetous oligarchs cannot acquire any enduring satisfaction from their ill-gotten gains. Nothing in evil's dominion endures forever, except deprivation. The same innovative and integrative economic forces that provide the oligarchs the opportunities to gain more capital are the forces that provide the oppressed populace with new industrial realities, which in turn afford unto them windows of opportunity to liberate themselves from their oligarchic oppressors: the downcasts essentially find opportunities to advance their lot in life, through increased skills and entrepreneurial services. While the oligarchs establish new capital investments in such industries that garner them fixed profits (ultimately to establish such wealth that they measure in comfort, novelty, and leisure), individual contractual arrangements enable the lower class to transform their lively hoods from the kindred group status of personally growing and manufacturing their own staple needs into a lively hood of their becoming human capital: they become floating labor forces that work for specified time periods at fixed wages.

In effect, many from the lower class arise from a surplus of agricultural labor forces and become specialists, such as merchants and artisans. These flow from the rural lands into the cities and proceed to grow the former aristocratic polis into something other than a city-state that preserves the wealth of a few. The new specialized work forces become new urbanites. Under a democratic constitution, individuals sale their skills to exercise their right to property. Interestingly, the new property owners add an aesthetic sense of nationality to the city-state. In this way, they incorporate the welfare of their former lower class kindred groups, which heretofore comprised 90% of the populace. Thus, the product of a new specialized labor force is a new urban middle class, which for the first time in history renders to individual commoners some fleeting public distinction or validation outside of their immediate kindred relationships: indeed, for the first time in history, common individuals affect the course of their social-economic environment.

While we take note of the fact that a society with a strong middle class invariably signals its prosperity, we must also take note of the fact that the wide spread prosperity that contractual arrangements incur among all classes often blurs the societal roles that define the friendships between social benefactors and beneficiaries. Obvious is one's inclination to ask the following questions when new social realities often make the poor rich and the rich poor: how can the rich empathize with the plight of the poor when economic opportunity may transform the poor into rich competitors? And how can the prodigious entrepreneur empathize with the disenfranchised when the entrepreneur thinks that he or she has pulled himself or herself up by the same bootstraps that the poor presently wear?

Furthermore, how can the poor house within their sentiments for the privileged the conflicting feelings of both envy and appreciation?

For sure, even the principal ideals that arise from the fractured interests of the people come in to conflict. Overall, we note two primary ideals that the people's belief systems foster, and these two ideals naturally create a threatening social dichotomy within the community:

One of the two primary idealisms is secular humanism. The humanist casts are the people who appreciate the social and physical benefits that science has provided their new middle class society; therefore, these forsake the fanciful idea that humankind's only place of felicity is in the hereafter. Accordingly, they look for pragmatic examples of virtue throughout human history, and then they form public institutes that implore the people to value only such things like personal judgment, duty to society, and above all the free will of humankind. In this way, the humanists despise the dogmas of organized religion, surmising that for political gain, religious institutes coerce the people with the fear of spiritual condemnation. So the humanists believe that religious institutes impede the people's natural quests for physical and intellectual freedom.

Seeing that the secular humanist cast assumes such a prevalent role in a new middle-classed society, it is inescapable that the other of the two primary idealistic casts in the society is the very institutionalized religious faith that the humanists abhor. After encountering other belief systems, the peoples of faith critically study their own established beliefs. While they have more control and responsibility over their own lively hoods and while they critically surmise new societal ills, the people of faith seek to endow their institutes, ensuring the institutes' central place in their society, in opposition to the secularist institutes.

The only agreements between these two incongruous factions of society are that both groups deplore the oppression of a tyranny or an oligarchy and both groups value a political and economic stability that upholds a social sense of liberty. With these two values in mind, the people of the new middle classed society agree upon a social constitution to govern both their lively hoods. It follows that when the means of productivity and prosperity reside in the many hands of a diverse people, a majority government is usually the strongly middle-classed people's preferred government, where all may democratically elect their leaders. Thus, democracy[1] is often an effect of common people's liberation from oppression. The chief aim of democracy is to secure freedom and autonomy for the commoner in this current age, while respecting varying doctrinaire based ideologies that purport to hold true to absolutes. When ideological faith and secular ideologies come into conflict in democracies, the central idea of personal liberty from the former oppressive regimes becomes the potent rallying point for both ideological forms. In this vein, a democratic people consider themselves to be the law of conscience's best host, in spite of the fact that democracy places unnatural obstacles before conscience, because democracy's political compromise falls short of the Holy Marriage's true love.

Hence, for the faithful, the advent of a democratic government usually denotes the unfortunate fact that the downfall of the former monarchy and/or aristocracy have finally veiled civilization's commonly shared idea that divinity inspires virtue in select individuals to guide the common people into a salvation of plenty and freedom from political or personal strife. Invariably, in the place of such fabled people of virtue, arises in the hearts and minds of the secularists the idea of a virtuous state, which meets the immediate economic needs of all people, despite class, familial lineage, or even a faith in the pending advent of a heavenly realm.

The Treasures of Increasing Social Consciousness

Notwithstanding, when Y'haweh opens his hand upon a democratic people, the people through faith envision and hold true to his absolutes. In this manner, when the people have a social understanding of a common good, the people overcome the social, political contentions that varying interests create.

---

[1] The word *democracy* is derivation of the ancient Greek word *demos*, which means "the crowd."

For example, because democracy's liberal nature often presents all segments of the democratic society with the opportunity to play both roles in the society's relationship between social benefactors and beneficiaries, a democratic government must foster greater social consciousness in its laws and effects, if it is to govern its people affably. A lawmaker must reassure his or her constituency that he or she is zealously addressing the constituency's needs. At the same time, the lawmaker must reassure other lawmakers that his or her interests are in agreement with their interests, because other lawmakers plead the causes of their constituencies, in kind.

We qualify our first hallmark of liberty (which extols the sanctity of marriage) by identifying a democracy's genial relationship between its benefactors and beneficiaries—a relationship that reflects the Holy Marriage's friendship in the following way: in a democratic majority government that views all its citizens to be of an equal social status, we attest that one who guards another's liberty and lively hood is the benefactor of the person whom he or she guards. Correspondingly, one who receives such benefits and seeks to return such favors is the beneficiary who is soon to be the formers benefactor. In this vein, spoke Solon the ancient Athenian statesman when someone asked him which city he considered the best governed; he replied, "The city where those who have not been wronged show themselves just as ready to punish the offender as those who have been [offended]."[1]

It is needless for us to detail our second hallmark of liberty—the brotherly love that quickly follows the above social friendship, but liberty's third hallmark, which we may find in a healthy democracy, we here more brilliantly describe. To begin, let us recall that we

---

[1] Solon, the Athenian lawgiver and reformer (c.639-c.559 B.C.), lived during a time of political and economic turmoil in ancient Athens. He was elected chief archon in 594, and he was best known for his defense of the peasant lower-classed peoples who were increasingly losing their lands to rapacious nobles (oligarchs). Of most importance, Solon outlawed such loans that indebted a commoner's very liberty for payment. Solon annulled debts, as well as mortgages, and he even put limitations on land holdings. Finally, regulating trade to benefit the rise of new artisans, Solon created a new middle class, like the one we have described above.

defined our third hallmark of liberty as an aesthetic sense of social fidelity that celebrates the beauty of creation, under the glory of Y'haweh. We concluded that the appreciative sense that work offers to leisure time, in which one pursues activities for the joy of the activity itself, is the selfsame sense of fidelity that one has for Heaven's Kingdom, which one seeks to dwell in for the joy of the glory of Y'haweh, himself. Finally, we concluded that when the wealthy become charitable benefactors like a loving husband to his beloved wife, the poor experience more leisure time to enjoy and investigate creation's wonders; and so, they appreciate the world together with their benefactors. Following, we observed that all perform such work through science and lawful acts to fulfill these ends.

We readily witness our third hallmark of liberty among a democratic people, who obtains Y'haweh's yasha, in the following way: after being freed from their oligarchic oppressors, the people color creation with a profound sense of liberty and personal empowerment. Among the people, we hear in the public discourse such words like *res publica*[1] — things common to the public, describing "a fair government of several households and of what they hold in common, with the power of sovereignty."[2]

No longer do the people identify with a dynasty or nationality, but the people identify with a state that commits itself to the cause of preserving personal liberty. Facilitating these aims are more sophisticated financial systems that extend to all segments of the citizen body. Greater currency circulation, therefore, replaces barter systems. More private companies come into being, along with greater business investment. As well, rented property and mortgages replace vassalage.

Essentially, opportunity greets the basest of the people. So it is not surprising that democratic people are always innovators being always competitive, unlike their former oligarchic oppressors who never venture to risk their gains. Quite the opposite, the democratic

---

[1] *Res publica* are Latin words that mean "thing" and "public," respectively.
[2] Spoken by Jean Bodin, a 16th Century French jurist and natural law philosopher.

people encourage themselves, even when they exhaust all their resources, for they imagine that some new enterprise will replenish their wealth. Sufficiently capturing the democratic spirit, an ancient thinker writes the following:

> They will take chances against their better judgment, and still, in the midst of danger, remain resolute . . . . for they think that the farther they go the more they will gain. If they aim at something and do not acquire it, they think that they have been robbed of what belonged to them already; whereas, if their effort is successful, they regard that success as nothing compared to what they will accomplish next . . . . Of them alone it may be said that they possess a thing almost as soon as they desire it, so swiftly does their actions follow upon their decisions.[1]

To the above, we may only add that the monuments of personal achievement litter democratic cities. One may observe their public works in grandeur.

Of all, the democratic constitution is magnanimous; it usually invokes God's favor upon all people, equally. Many foreign peoples find refuge under its wings.

The Terrors of Anarchy

Wealth exists for a people of like minds who share the same vision of Y'haweh's good; however, by in large, a diverse people seldom realize any political agreement. An individual so easily compromises conscience. Then others further undermine conscience in response. Suffice it to say that without a sure corporate appreciation of the salvation knowledge of Y'haweh's open hand, manifesting greater social consciousness, a majority government will inevitably fail after it runs its lifespan.

Usually, the end of a viable democracy occurs when the people become so enthralled with personal progress in accruing possessions that they lose the sense of appreciation for their past liberation from oppression. Instead of seeking the common good, people pursue personal liberty, even despite the personal liberty of others.

---

[1] *Thucydides.*

Essentially, sin's selfishness saliently reveals itself in all the peoples' aspirations: first the people lose an appreciation for the institute of marriage. Afterwards, all social friendships fail.

As an example, let us here note the following phenomenon: in capitalist economic systems, when technology is so prolific that the measure of manual labor does not discriminate between the respective physical aptitudes of males and females to become income providers and when the government is that of a democracy, leisure time might only afford the people thoughts of a virtuous marriage as being the bond between those whose incomes or professions brook no jealously and whose political persuasions are in harmony. As well, leisure time might only afford them thoughts of a virtuous marriage as a condition where society does not discriminate between an individual's role of being the provider or nurturer for his or her children within the marriage unit, despite his or her sex. Of a truth, these superficial understandings of marriage do many in such cultures possess, because the sense of appreciation and reason for life (which a viable marriage between a well-defined benefactor and beneficiary create) are lost. People in such cultures have a tendency to govern their sense of fidelity for their partner by convenience, social standing, or personal pleasure.

In contrast, we true worshippers govern our sense of fidelity for the Holy Marriage (between Lord Yehoshua and us) by a profound sense of appreciation for Lord Yehoshua who is the benefactor of our souls. With our salvation knowledge, we stay all creation on the Sabbath day of eternal thanksgivings.

Unlike those who have not found any lasting satisfaction in their pursuit of happiness in this world, we have spiritual satisfaction within the Holy Spirit; therefore, our sense of satisfaction inhibits us from beguiling socially prodigious persons of their honors when such prodigies offer social benefits to us. Likewise, when we ourselves assume the role of being social benefactors, our spiritual appreciation prevents us from becoming narcissists who oppress the humble.

In the Holy Marriage's state of justice, we will only seek each other's good. We will only find satisfaction with our inheritance whether we have the opportunity to benefit another or we receive a gift as that which is ultimately from the charitable opened hand of Y'haweh.

Thus, when a people do not rest their own personal aspirations to work out the natural marriage roles between the social benefactors and beneficiaries, the husband and wife marriage unit falters. Then the greater societal units such as employer and employee relations falter, as well. In actual fact, as the society loses the significance of its kindred identities, the societies' standing upon the individual welfare, under temporal contractual professions, falters as the economy falters. After that, we see a complete social breakdown: first, we see increasing instances of adultery, fornication, and all manner of sexual lasciviousness. Quickly following are family breakdowns, which create many instances of orphaned children. Additionally, we see increasing instances of homosexuality[1] becoming a socially acceptable practice:

In confusion, the contract based societies first do not differentiate the legal standing of individuals, who contribute to the specialized economy, from the natural legal standing of kindred groups that maintained agricultural economies. Then the societies equate homosexual and lesbian unions with the natural union between the male and female sex: the homosexual and lesbian unions thereby result from legal fictions that the specialized contract economy affords. Finally, using legal fictions, the contract societies erroneously equate homosexual and lesbian families with naturally occurring

---

[1] It is the author's opinion that there are several causes of homosexuality or lesbianism: firstly, let us note that relatively few males and females have genetic or other physical abnormalities that cause them to manifest effeminate or masculine qualities, respectively. Secondly, some males and females are never socially educated to feel comfortable in mature relationships with the opposite sex; therefore, they act out their sexuality with the same sex with which they feel comfortable. Next, some people of both sexes have suffered from long-term sexual abuse; therefore, they psychologically question whether they have become complacent in the abusive acts after they lose the will to resist. Like so, they thus confuse their sexuality. Lastly, some individuals have no moral aversion to satisfying their sexual desires with either sex, even if they are primarily attracted to one sex.

families: the homosexual and lesbian families stand upon the states' contract-based allowance of the adoption of children rather than the natural child birth between male and female parents.

Next, we see that the society esteems both people of virtue and the basest nature to be alike: the laborer does not feel any aversion to esteem himself above his master, and the child does not feel any necessity to pay homage to his or her parent. As well, the alien feels that he or she is of greater worth than the free and naturally born citizen. Effectively, pride and lust usurp all power from wisdom and prudence. The people excessively pursue perverse notions of liberty, for every person thinks that he or she has the right to entertain any profane act that he or she likes, saying "whatever rises to our lips [we will speak]."[1]

At last, we may list the hallmarks of utter societal collapse. Initially, the lusts for worldly gain inform misguided business ventures, which fail as other businesses pursue other ventures, haphazardly. Afterwards, political and business corruption causes all manner of social upheaval: bank fraud and currency fluctuations cause many to lose their fortunes and livelihoods. Endemic unemployment results because business revenues significantly decrease. Excessively high prices confound the poor. Finally, the people, who fleetingly gain social identity and enfranchisement due to their professions under contracts, become disenfranchised and socially isolated, having lost the strength of kindred relationships.

What is more, even the religious institutes become corrupt in the societal collapse. People seeking wealth, political power, and fame assume leading roles in religious circles after they have manipulated the weak minded with a collage of rituals and pageantry that cloak the covetous natures of the deceitful leaders. In fact, these corrupt religious leaders seek self-renown through the appearance of pious works. For this cause, they become proud and unthankful for the charitable hand of Y'haweh: they cloak Y'haweh's simple expression of charity (which we see in Y'haweh's outstretched hand in the Mashiach) with esoteric religious scholasticism, their seeking to

---

[1] Quoted from Plato's Republic, Book VIII

secure their elite status over the common congregant, whom Y'haweh seeks to redeem. Thus, instead of showing the love of Y'haweh through patience and quiet admonitions, they become judgmental, condemning all who do not follow their religious works. For this reason, they make their religious institutes seem even more onerous to the secularists than before.

In summary, we can safely conclude the following after listing the above societal disorders: a democratic state that loses sight of the grace of Y'haweh is a broken state that thirsts for political change. For sure, the cries of revolution can be heard in the city streets.

The Indifferent Spirit of the Anti-Savior and His Hybrid Governmental Beast

At the downfall of their democratic society, the people realize that the greatest bane to happiness is not a tyrannical or an oligarchic animal, which has a temperament that we may readily predict and act upon; but the people realize that the greatest bane to their happiness is an unnatural animal—the beast of sin, which dwells within the human soul and gives rise to unjust people in every realm of society. Of a truth, this beast is unpredictable. An earthly power cannot tame it, since such a beast even gives rise to corruption in the institutes of faith—the very institutes that purport to invoke a power that stands beyond human frailty.

As a result of the corruption in the religious institutes, many of the people lose faith in their being any true idealistic answers from the heavens. Hence, they in despair join the secularist cast. Unwilling, the former people of faith refrain from seeking any divinely inspired societal goodwill, as though some perverted spirit seduced them with never ending forecasts of calamity.

Being jaded by religious quarrels, people increasingly make prominent the doctrines of the secular humanists, who seek only an earthly government that brooks humankind's imperfection, as long as a majority realizes some tentative degree of prosperity. Because religious strife dulls the people's religious sensibilities, the secular humanists convince the people to pursue religion as a private matter, while they teach the people to pursue cultural and social solidarity as the greatest good among all classes. With such arguments, the humanists teach the people that a religion of the state is the immediate source of stability and order; therefore, humanists essentially assert that a secular religion of the state must assume the responsibility of governing public actions, instead of any faith-based religion of the heavens. In the end, they convince the people that civil and secular authorities have more immediate burdens that warrant everyone's devotions, despite faith.

The secular humanists usually begin their quest to influence society when they encounter other cultures. At that time, they begin to compare and contrast; they begin to reason by association: they observe some utility in alien modes of life and, therefore, begin to question all cultural concepts of eternity. Then after leisure time affords them the opportunity to make systematic cultural inquiries into history, the humanists house all belief systems under the banner of cultural relativism: a comparative study of philosophy and religion. As an outcome, they believe that experience and experiment should usurp the authority of faith and belief. They begin to teach others to observe only the product of scientific studies, instead of faith.

Consequently, the main driving forces behind the secular humanists are the new entrepreneurial, wealthy powers that the specialized currency economy created. These secular entrepreneurs seek to create an industrialized nation state, which increasingly turns the poor, who bartered their goods and services in the former agricultural economy, into consumers who earn wages to consume other goods and services.

Because of the necessity for commoners to acquire further skills to have purchasing power in the new economy, the wealthy fund public educational systems that give rise to an intelligent citizen body, as a whole. Subsequently, scholarships from the higher institutes of learning begin to be obtainable for the lower classes, and afterward the former three societal levels of upper, middle, and lower classes of society transform into several levels of society, such as the upper class, the lower-upper class, the middle class, the working class, and the working poor of society.

In addition, because the lower classes of society play vital economic roles in rendering services and becoming consumers, the people of the lower classes often find opportunities to amass political clout. Instead of merely accepting a lesser lot in life, the lower classes readily create such political instruments as labor movements, through which they organize against exploitation and combat the extreme poverty of the economically disenfranchised.

Essentially, we may say that the lower classes of the people feel a sense of prosperity when they feel less socially marginalized. They even start to harbor nationalist feelings about their localities, so they pursue greater roles in their local governments.

The result of their labor is not only more social reform, but also the creation of a popular culture—a new social phenomenon—that does not usually celebrate the liberties that marriage's fidelity allow, in good conscience, but usually celebrate personal license, that is, the abandoned ability to titillate one's senses despite good conscience. For example, at first the people usually become patrons of government sponsored arts and religious expression. Then when they acquire prosperity's leisure time, the people glamorize national sports personalities. Following, popular musicians arise, along with other artists. In the end, people pursue whatever artful expression that reflects their shortsighted sense of value. Interestingly, at such a point in human history, we may witness the brief triumph of Kayin, the son of Adam, because not only do the prodigious seemingly prosper in secular life, but also do the common people begin to experience a like sense of tentative prosperity.

It is not difficult to list the successes of a secular society; however, it is a chore to find a government that will preserve the secularists' gains. So in order to house the newly endowed secular economy, the secular humanists search throughout history to discover the strengths of all three fundamental forms of government, while they sensor the depravities of the same. From their labor arises a hybrid government that incorporates all three fundamental forms of government.

For instance, in parliamentary or federal governments, we often find a prime minister or a president who governs with one or more representative bodies: political parties that represent all segments of society comprise these representative bodies. The prime minister or president functions as a constitutionally sanctioned king who, under the code of law, serves the people. Accordingly, one of the representative bodies that governs along with the prime minister takes the form of a senate or even a house of lords to address the needs of the privileged class, while the other representative body come into being merely to plead the cause of the common people, while standing in opposition to the elitists' representative body.

Though it would seem that everyone would be happy with a hybrid government that represents every segment of society, the fact is that no government can completely satisfy everyone's subjective desires, equally. As we have seen, a myriad of lusts and temptations, which forever plague civilizations, springs from humankind's selfish nature. In reality, we conclude, again, that although scarcity has provoked further inquiry into creation's design, human frailty prevents humankind from seeing the true and eternal good. In other words, although people may secure scarce resources by benefiting from the gathered intelligence of the workings of creation, their lack of the higher knowledge of the things that they have intelligently perceived prevents them from gleaning the best benefit for all from the intelligence. Thus, the worldly respite that technology gives to their bodies does not give the same spiritual satisfaction to their souls.

In consideration of the above dilemma, the secularists seek to fill the void that the sense of religious obligation left. They realize impart that the sense of religious duty, only, placates the whims of human selfishness. In the place of religious faith, the hybrid government tries to foster a sense of patriotism—a secular religion of the state. In this manner, the secularists hope that the people might agree upon a sense of reverence for the state constitution regardless of their own desires.

If we were asked to define the fundamental qualities of the secular state religion, we would only have to borrow the connotations of a few ancient Latin words, which defined the social consciousness that many ancient Imperial Roman citizens possessed. To begin, let us adapt for our purposes the very word *religio* from which we derive our contemporary word *religion*. Let us slightly expand the word religio's ancient denotation, and say that religio is the good of the state that binds all peoples together. We may understand that the notion of religio encompasses not only the physical welfare of the people, but also the spiritual welfare of the people.

In addition to religio, let us add the sense of *hubris*—an exaggerated sense of pride or self-confidence, which invariably issues from the state's economic productivity and military strength and from the greatly distributed wealth among the state's citizens. Also, while we consider the state's prosperity, let us consider the ministers of the state who strive for the state's welfare. Upon their upright conduct, we can only affix the word *pietas*: a word that describes a sense of duty for the social good and a word from which our contemporary word *piety* derives itself.

Truly, we see that to govern such a sophisticated state in political harmony, the state's ministers must despise corruption, believing in the gravity of the state's cause, and that cause is to prevent the ruin of men. And so, in conclusion, we understand that the state must imbue all its citizens with a sense of *gravitus*—a weighty and sober seriousness, considering that the state has within its possession the welfare of all.

Altogether, we may note that the people whom a secular power governs can only experience virtue by being true to one's responsibilities, while they stoically suppress any personal and contrary lusts. For certain, we may qualify this public sense of responsibility as the people's notion of civility. Indeed, with this notion of civility, the secular powers attempt to subdue the myriad of human subjective thoughts that have no bases in scientific inquiry. In other words, the secularists determine all the people's personal proclamations of truth to be assumptions, prejudices, beliefs, and opinion: the intangible ghosts of subjective thought, which may only materialize for corporate inspection when artists somehow capture the thought in poetry and paintings. Hence, the humanists readily put forth public anthems that sing odes to the country's ability to bring so many diverse peoples together in strength.

Nevertheless, even though the hybrid government may be more resilient than the other forms of government, the same social passions that afflict other governments afflict the multifaceted government. For this reason, it is evident that the hybrid government can never be truly good: it merely can provide some tentative refuge from the overt acts of evil that human lusts instigate.

To be more specific, we may note two reoccurring social problems that are somewhat endemic for three tier secularized governments, and both social problems issue from social progression and physical novelties, respectively: we may define the first social problem as the government's inability to be sensitive to the needs of all people when it pursues social progression. And, we may witness an example of the government's inability to be always sensitive to the needs of all when *majoritarian politics* (that is, the active political engagement of a majority of the citizen body) loses its effectiveness: bureaucracies, corporations, media moguls, military leaders, special interest groups, and religious organizations become the social elite by taking an active interest in overseeing the details of government policy, while the citizen body stands intellectually aloof, even disenfranchised. In the end, the government increasingly becomes autocratic and centralized: bureaucracies proliferate, making people dependent on the bureaucracies' impersonal transactions, as the people become increasingly less self-sufficient.

What is more, we may witness another example of the government's inability to be sensitive to the needs of all when the economic policies of the government naturally foster innovation and integration to create new markets and wealth, even if people are chronically disenfranchised. The secular government's economists look for future benefits for the state, while they willing accept the human cost of upsetting the welfare of a minority group of people whose antiquated livelihoods fail before the state's prosperity. In fact, the secular culture accepts the social anxieties that business competition create as normative behavior.

Subsequently, the second social problem exasperates the insensitivities of the government. The problem arises when perverted tastes and preferences arise that have no grounding in the true appreciative knowledge of liberty; therefore, these lusts lead the people to entertain further activities that waste the time and resources that would better the welfare of the people, as a whole. Furthermore, these whimsical desires divide the people in such a way that they endanger general civility.

Having no true sense of good conscience, because the leaders do not seek a single truth, which the prophetic shipmaster-King once sought, the people regard only temporary pleasure and personal welfare, their knowing that civil leaders and politicians unfailingly compromise the good for all. For sure, instead of seeking the single truth of Y'haweh, which all inherently respond to, the faithless politicians only try to tame the beast of human lusts in the subsequent manner:

> [Politicians only gather] the opinion of the multitude . . . as if a man were acquiring the knowledge of the affections and desires of a mighty strong beast, which he had under his command: [he seeks to understand] how it is to be approached and touched, and in what way it is made most savage or calm. He gathers a mastery of the sounds it makes, in respect to whether it is pacified or violent. Knowing nothing in reality about which of these sounded opinions and desires is honorable or sordid, good or evil, just or unjust . . . [he then determines his best advantage].[1]

Seeing how the secularist happily grasp the veil of evil's dominion, in such a manner, the true worshippers must patiently invoke the truth of Y'haweh's Yehoshua, even though the secular humanists invariably seek a more earthly savior who can galvanize some form of public solidarity in the midst of a diverse and contrary people. More likely than not, to save the welfare of the secular state, the secular humanists will adore a lawyer or legislator who is proficient in the social morays of the global culture. In fact, this

---

[1] Plato's Republic Book VI

prodigious man will not necessarily come from a wealthy family; indeed, his first love will be the ideology of the humanist, global state and not his personal estate. What is more, through might and political acumen this prodigious man will reconcile all segments of society, by force if necessary.

At the last, he will fashion himself to be a sort of secular savior, since such a personality must he become to inspire so many diverse peoples: the diverse population will fail to agree upon penal laws that express the public's indignation at sundry corruption. Instead, minor restitutive laws will mask corruption. The government will become centralized, bureaucratized, and autocratic. Likewise the hybrid government will become suspicious of institutes and groups that claim kindred solidarity around spiritual truths; therefore, the government will censor the power of Church to protect the perverted passions of individuals.

In this manner, the anti-savior and his state will become the epitome of evil, finally giving Satan an individualist's body, while the anti-savior and his bestial government suppress the true worship of Y'haweh, to benefit the secular state. Following, the people as a whole will not notice their own depravity, because upon the ascension of the anti-savior, the secular society will proclaim "peace and safety"[1], their coveting their worldly articles and personal perversions. They will then become an unnatural beast—an unnatural animal that merrily seeks its own destruction. The godless peoples will joyfully harbor sentiments of indifference to a divine truth. At the last, the beast will incur Y'haweh's judgment.

Vindication of the Faithful unto the Glory of Y'haweh

It is unquestionable that from the appreciative sense of personal fulfillment, which the Lord's people possess, comes the charitable deeds that do not need the injunctions of the law or the superficialities of civility. Instead, the charitable deeds only need the eternal injunctions of the heart. Here we are speaking of the charity and sense of appreciation between faithful spouses. As well, we are

---

[1] 1 Thessalonians 5:3

speaking of the love of a parent for his or her dutiful child, the good neighbor, and the hospitable host who cares for the needy. In essence, we are speaking the community of the Church—the members of Lord Yehoshua's body who observe good conscience, while they commune with the Holy Spirit.

It is the eternal Holy Spirit of Y'haweh that gives a satisfaction to his true worshippers that will color the earth with the knowledge of his good and glory. And so, it remains evident that the sovereign Lord cannot tolerate the totalitarianism of a global government that conceals pride, self-interests, public contention, inequity, violence, lusts, and all such evil that issues from defiled consciences; who cry, "Let us eat and drink; for tomorrow we shall die."[1]

As one ancient thinker says, "How indeed my friends can there be the barest particle of wisdom where there is no agreement?"[2]

In other words, we may ask how can the earth attain the Lord's Shabbat—his Rest—when disagreement and corruption hold the earth bound? For this cause, the grieved Spirit of Truth, Y'haweh, initially judged the earth by destroying all living things, except Noach and his family, whom the Lord redeemed to carry the knowledge of his glory unto the generations of faithful true worshippers to come: we find that Y'haweh's judgment upon the generation that began with Adam and concluded upon the deliverance of Noach is a corporate extension of his judgment upon Adam and Havah's original sin. It was necessary for Y'haweh to demonstrate his full displeasure upon humanity's corporate and complete rebellion (from the individual sins of Adam and Havah unto the complete sin of human civilization); thereby, Y'haweh could demonstrate his full measure of grace upon our generation, both individually and corporately. Hence, we are certain that our next chapter will demonstrably conclude truth's landscape. The chapter will detail how the biblical Testaments overcome the perdition of the nations; as the Testaments record how Y'haweh's right judgment prevails over the nations' political impasse, from which Lord

---

[1] Isaiah 22:13
[2] Plato's *Laws*, Book III

Yehoshua—the Testator—redeems the faith of his elect true worshippers.

Chapter 7

The Kingdom of Heaven

"The earth shall be filled with the knowledge of the glory of Y'haweh, as the waters cover the sea."

—Habakkuk 2:14

Optimism

It seems to some that Y'haweh's judgment upon Noach's generation was severe, especially when one thinks of the thousands of children that had perished in the global flood. Nonetheless, one must consider the fact that Y'haweh takes no joy in the downfall of the faithless for he asks, "Have I any pleasure at all that the wicked should die? says Y'haweh: and not that he should turn from his ways and live?"[1] As well, he says, "I have no pleasure in the death of him that dies[2]; therefore, turn yourselves and live."[3]

On the other hand, we must note that Y'haweh takes no pleasure in the confused ideologies of the higher-level civilizations, which invariably turn the faithless away from the true worship of him. It is, therefore, necessary for Y'haweh to validate the faith that he bequeathed to the elect, by redeeming their virtue. At the same time, he condemns the same virtue in the unfaithful, which virtue does not actually apprehend his truth, because of humanity's selfish

---

[1] Ezekiel 18:23
[2] We must here underscore the point that Y'haweh spoke these words to Yisra'el, his elect nation: one may even venture to interpret the statement of the scripture, as "Y'haweh has no pleasure in the death of any; however, he must punctuate his grace upon the faithful elect of Yisra'el." In other words, while he extends his hand to the faithful of Yisra'el, it is necessary for him to judge other nations. In this way, Y'haweh further underscores his grace upon the elect of Yisra'el.
[3] Ezekiel 18:32

predisposition to lack true faith in him. In this manner, the Lord testifies of the one good that resides in his Holy Spirit; and, simultaneously, he condemns those unfaithful volitions that do not augment his person, as being truly evil. In essence, the Father first loved some by giving them his Holy Spirit, while he despises the evil works of others who walk contrarily to his Spirit. Once more, he empowers some to reciprocate his love through faith, even as the scripture says, "God so loved the world"[1] that he redeemed the faithful virtue of some with the righteousness of Lord Yehoshua, to establish all creation in his eternal Rest.

Thus, the consequence of Y'haweh's choice love for the elect is that Y'haweh of necessity condemns the misguided virtue of the faithless, and thereby he establishes the true knowledge of creation upon his grace, his extended hand in the Mashiach. So, what more can we say other than the following: his grace is necessary "for all have sinned, and come short of the glory of God."[2] In this vein, Y'haweh spoke through the prophet Yesha'yahu saying the following:

> For I will not strive throughout the age, nor will I always be wrathful, for the spirit, [of humankind that came] from [me and stands] before me, is feeble and the souls that I have made.[3]

To appreciate further the grace of Y'haweh, we have to consider what our condition would be like in the cities of the strong, if Y'haweh did not validate our faith. In the eyes of secularists, our faith should be vanquished from society; therefore, if Y'haweh's grace lingered, we would end up as poor field peasants who lost their resolve to journey abroad and capture the wealth of a city:

Indeed, even though they had been minded to cross the ocean, their ship was without a sail. And even though they had been minded to climb the tallest mountain, the air was far too thin at the top: they fainted. Though the peasants had prepared themselves to

---

[1] John 3:16 (loosely quoted)
[2] Romans 3:23
[3] Isaiah 57:16

fight a war, having rallied their troops and promised them the unseen riches of a golden city, the walls of the city proved to be too awful for them to climb. Who could imagine, anyway, how poor field peasants could manage to negotiate those towering edifices?

A wise old sage[1] once said that one should not laud too many praises on an object of desire; because when one finds that he or she is unable to acquire the object, one realizes that he or she has only published with his or her praises a great loss! So the peasant army withdrew itself from the city feeling this great loss. Even so, they were satisfied in the evening when they were lying in their tents in the open fields, after the fever of the commotion of the day had been broken.

For you see, the boundless stars are abundant and particularly brilliant when seen away from the city glow. Well, if we were forced to depict such a sight in a word, we should choose the word optimism: a word that encourages our faith. And faith indeed must we true worshippers have, because if we cannot capture a golden city here on earth, how can we expect to capture the real golden city that stands presently beyond the stars?

The sin of humanity that vanquished us out of the secular cities is the same sin that veils the heavenly good. All the same, we may find a sure answer to our question in the ministry of Lord Yehoshua, who answered our question when he answered his disciples who asked, "Who then can be saved?"

Lord Yehoshua replied, "With man, it is impossible, but with God, all things are possible."[2]

The Tree of Life

To reassure ourselves, we have only to recall the following fact: by grace, Y'haweh maintains a tree of life in the middle of heavenly Yerushalayim. From the tree flows the water of his Holy Spirit, empowering us through Lord Yehoshua to one-day dwell there.

---

[1] Socrates
[2] Matthew 19:25-26

To fulfill all things that he created, Y'haweh not only planted the same tree of life in the beginning of creation, but also planted a tree of the knowledge of good and evil. As had been said, these trees he first planted in the Garden of Eden: we saw that the tree of knowledge possesses the forbidden fruit, while the tree of life possesses the fruit of the Holy Spirit that some of humankind have yet to partake of. Together, the two trees serve us, allegorically, because of the following: we know that knowledge invariable manifests from our sense of appreciation; therefore, we know that for us to possess a true knowledge of creation that entails our having a sense of fulfillment that prevents us from compromising the will of Y'haweh, we must first experience the disparity that comes upon us after we break his commandment by eating the forbidden fruit. Afterwards, we will appreciate his commandments that harmonize all creation when we obtain his grace—his giving us the knowledge of his equitable good, in order for us to repent of our selfishness through the power of him who alone is sinless. In effect, we may only obtain salvation knowledge of what is truly good by the grace of Y'haweh, because we first broke his prohibition. By his grace alone, therefore, we will in repentance learn to appreciate Y'haweh's salvation and devote ourselves to him, happily. In the end, when Y'haweh secures our devotion in this way, he will resurrect us, and then we will partake upon the tree of life.

And so, to truly repent that we may eat off the eternal tree of life, Y'haweh must empower us to heed the words of Lord Yehoshua who said, "Except a man be born of the water [of repentance, being cleansed outside the city of corruption] and of the Holy Spirit [even being empowered to perceive and mimic the charity of the risen Lord], he cannot enter into the Kingdom of God."[1]

Lord Yehoshua's statement is one of the primary messages of Lord Yehoshua. In addition, we see that he declared to his disciples that through him only can a person obtain eternal life, by being imbued with a sense of appreciation for his salvation: an appreciation that he defined in the tree of knowledge, which in turn points to his

---

[1] John 3:5

glory, as seen in our eating from the tree of an eternal life of holy matrimony.

To wit, we may say that the tree of the knowledge of good and evil grows within us: when the fruit of our souls is evil, the Lord casts our tree into the eternal fire. And, when the fruit of our souls reflects his good, Y'haweh reaps our souls and grafts us into the tree of life, which stands only in the Holy Marriage's Kingdom of Heaven.

Predestination

The most important observation of the tree of life that we must note is that the tree existed in Eden, yields the fruit of the Holy Spirit within us true worshippers presently, and abides in the coming Kingdom of Heaven. To further qualify this observation, we must note that Y'haweh had planted the tree of life before he rested from his work on the Sabbath day; therefore, despite the present distress of humankind's rebellion against him, we must know that Y'haweh has already predestined our eternal life, in the Holy Marriage, to be the conclusion of all things. In other words, we must know that he has already preordained[1] our very participation in the Holy Marriage, as the fruits of the Holy Spirit within us, presently, witness.

The essential point that we must conclude from our above understanding is that Y'haweh—self-existent-being—is intrinsically the state of the good, while we (through our acquiring knowledge)

---

[1] Many Christian scholars do not retain a sound understanding of the biblical doctrines of predestination and election. Ignorantly, they make the claim that Y'haweh does not pre-engineer the unfolding of all things, because they claim that "a production of human robots cannot glorify him." What the scholars fail to understand is that the self-existent Y'haweh has fulfillment intrinsically: he does not possess satisfaction because of the whims of human choice. Instead, he freely places his Spirit in those whom he intellectually enlightens to appreciate the Body of Christ. What scholars must understand is that although Y'haweh predetermine our destinies, he (being the husband of the Holy Marriage through Lord Yehoshua) does not possess fulfillment because of the linear state of human frailty in this life; but the husband will eternally possesses fulfillment in a transcendent wife who appreciates the gifts of the husband holistically, intuitively, synthetically, and of all subjectively, as we described above (see *Shadows of the Holy Marriage* in chapter 6).

can only practice virtue in such actions that seek our soul's pending, eternal rest in his good. Essentially, we taste the fruits of the eternal good (even the tree of life) when the Holy Spirit sprinkles our consciences, turning them away from our selfish and temporal deeds, to be obedient to Y'haweh's good.

Nonetheless, we may ask how can we have knowledge of such an eternal satisfaction, unless one (who intrinsically possesses salvation knowledge) experiences our temptations and then empowers us to seek Y'haweh's good? Likewise, we may ask how can one be a friend to Y'haweh unless Y'haweh manifests himself in a comprehensible way to befriend us first?

Herein lays the ministry of Lord Yehoshua, our consolation: Y'haweh predestined Lord Yehoshua to become our benefactor. At the same time, he predetermined our destiny by giving us the hearts that receive his gift.

Because Y'haweh's Logos culminates in the Holy Spirit filled Lord Yehoshua, Lord Yehoshua dwells in a state of righteousness. He cannot succumb to the state of evil or the temporality of sin.

Also, he walked among us (who do not exist in a state of righteousness) to suffer the deprivations of our daily life unto death. Yet, because his state of righteousness is eternal, he rose again for us, being even more filled with the knowledge of Y'haweh. In this manner, the Spirit of Truth foreknew us by preordaining our hearts and minds to trust and respond to the Lord, through whom Y'haweh makes it possible for us to dwell eternally in his state of righteousness.

The Second Revelation of Y'haweh: He is the Supplier of Truth and Justice

To aid our understanding, let us list a second revelation of Y'haweh, which we may glean from another biblical covenant that he made with Noach after the global flood. To fulfill the grace that we are speaking of, Y'haweh countered his first covenant by making another covenant with Noach and his descendants: the first covenant (which we defined as his being the creator who holds our purpose for life) forecasts our disparity when we walk contrary to his good; however, the second covenant speaks of the necessity for Y'haweh to exhibit his grace to establish his good in the world. The scripture reports Y'haweh's Covenant as follows:

> And God said: "This is the sign of the covenant which I make between me and you, and every living creature that is with you, for perpetual generations: I set my rainbow in the cloud, and it shall be for the sign of the covenant between me and the earth. It shall be, when I bring a cloud over the earth, that the rainbow shall be seen in the cloud; and I will remember my covenant which is between me and you and every living creature of all flesh; the waters shall never again become a flood to destroy *all* flesh. The rainbow shall be in the cloud, and I will look on it to remember the everlasting covenant between God and every living creature of all flesh that is on the earth." And God said to Noach, "This is the sign of the covenant which I have established between me and all flesh that is on the earth."[1]

Let us note that the compassion of Y'haweh, which we see being expressed in his covenant with Noach, is not an admission by Y'haweh that he did not justly execute the judgmental, global flood. On the contrary, Y'haweh's covenant with Noach indicates the fact that Y'haweh shows his grace upon some to establish his truth and justice. In fact, Y'haweh merely said that he would no longer judge all flesh by a flood, despite the fact that his pending judgment upon the faithless unto the justification of the faithful is necessary. Y'haweh will only relent from seeking judgment until he grows his desired fruit of appreciation in those who will glorify him in spirit and truth. Until such a time, we only witness the fact that he alone is the supplier of truth and justice, in the above manner: this truth is our second revelation of him.

Our second revelation, therefore, stands upon the suzerain covenant that Y'haweh concluded with Noach and thereby us, the elect: the covenant is a treaty between a greater power and an inferior vassal, who adheres to the covenant to avoid hostility.

---

[1] Genesis 9:12-17

The most important thing for us to understand, in regards to Y'haweh's suzerain covenants that comprise the biblical Testaments, is that the covenants are grants of the Testator's reconciliation of our inter-subjective perspectives, which the human dynamic reference frames obtain. The covenants are thus imputations of Lord Yehoshua's unblemished conscience, to the extent that the suzerain grant is an indictment upon the efficacy of the vassals' self-serving religious efforts to secure justice with compromised consciences.

The New Adam

When we consider our life journey unto the *Rest* of Heaven, we must know that while Y'haweh grows the fruit of his Holy Spirit within us individually, he grows the fruit of his Holy Spirit in an assembly of saints that will comprise the heavenly City's bride, as a whole. Like the secular nations, the heavenly City's roots begin with the lives of its patriarchs: these Y'haweh makes suzerain covenants with. And so, because the deeds of the first Adam put us under condemnation (meaning we lost the friendship of Y'haweh that ensured our wellbeing), the heavenly City's patriarchs looked for a new Adam who is not under our fleshly condemnation but is one who has dominion over all things, including the souls who glorify Y'haweh. To this end, New Yerushalayim's patriarchs looked for this new Adam who not only holds the wealth and welfare of the tree of life, but also identifies with our human plight, to overcome it.

As we follow the example of the patriarchs, looking for a savior, we must overcome scarcity through the strength of our love for Y'haweh: a love that appreciates the power of the new Adam, who is Lord Yehoshua the Mashiach. He alone can bequeath to us the riches of the tree of life, which will give us such a sense of satisfaction that will empower us to stop valuing vain things, inappropriately.

In this way, the Lord's Holy Spirit will overcome the temptations that incline us to devalue our neighbors' welfare, when we selfishly seek our own gain. When we have the fulfillment of the Lord's Holy Spirit within, we will lend ourselves to charity, honest labor, fair business practices, and above all prayer and supplication, in true worship of him who will vindicate us with new resurrected bodies that are not under sin's condemnation. For sure, at that time will be our rejoicing.

Seeking Righteousness

To appreciate the savior fully, we must first understand his lordship over our personal lives by considering his personal relationship with the patriarchs of New Yerushalayim. Following, we must consider his lordship as it relates to this world's political quagmires, by considering his civil relationship with the people of Yisra'el. After we consider these relationships, we may begin to reach spiritual maturity and complete our understanding of the landscape of Y'haweh's truth, which concludes in Y'haweh's ultimate fulfillment: that is, the totality that he realizes in the Holy Marriage between Lord Yehoshua and his true worshippers.

Let us proceed by first noting the fact that Y'haweh proclaims the following, about the eventual reign of the Mashiach, through the prophet Yesha`yahu:

> In mercy shall the throne be established: and he [Lord Yehoshua] shall sit upon it in truth . . . judging, and seeking judgment, and hasting righteousness.[1]

We may readily interpret this scripture by keeping our definition of truth in mind. Indeed, we have only to recall the fact that the veil of sin prevents us from relating to Y'haweh; therefore, Y'haweh necessarily shows mercy by miraculously revealing himself to us in the righteous form of Lord Yehoshua, who establishes the above merciful throne of Y'haweh in the following way: initially, Lord Yehoshua becomes the most appreciable thing by holding the keys to eternal life, after he suffers death in our place. Afterwards, Lord Yehoshua becomes esteemed in the minds of those who receive Y'haweh's Holy Spirit; thereby, he realizes for Y'haweh the

---

[1] Isaiah 16:5

reciprocity of Y'haweh's love, which in turn is the realization of truth and the eternal establishment of Y'haweh's throne.

Even so, the latter half of Yesha`yahu's scripture (that is, *judging, and seeking judgment, and hasting righteousness*) we have yet to define here. Let us understand that the prophet proclaims above that Lord Yehoshua will not only judge the actions of humanity, but also empower his true worshippers to judge the actions of humanity. The Lord Yehoshua makes this possible by enduring and overcoming the same afflictions of those whom he seeks to redeem. For this cause, Y'haweh, himself, proclaimed the following through Yesha`yahu:

> He [the Lord Yehoshua] shall see the travail of his soul, and shall be satisfied [after he is resurrected in vindication]: by his knowledge shall my righteous servant justify many; for he shall bear their iniquities.[1]

All of such is to say that it is not enough for Lord Yehoshua to condemn the world. Instead, he must empathize with our daily activities by empowering us to overcome life's temptation with our knowledge of his justice. To this end, Y'haweh seeks to publish his just laws throughout civilization by extracting the people Yisra'el from humanity and defining Yisra'el by their observance of his laws that instruct humanity to turn away from selfishness and seek the goodwill and favor of Y'haweh, corporately.

In fact, using codified law, Y'haweh encourages acts of charity until the King of Righteousness (the new Adam) comes to redeem those who (through faith in the spiritual blessings of the new Adam) forsake worldly lusts and fulfill the law through their brotherly love. What is more, their being empowered by the fact that the new Adam arises unto eternal life after suffering the worst of the human condition, which is undeserved persecution and death, the elect people of faith forsake their former disobedient lifestyles, which separated them from the good of Y'haweh. Afterwards, they gladly offer their personal sacrifices and spiritual gifts, while invoking the lordship and power of the new Adam over their heavenly destiny.

---

[1] Isaiah 53:11

At the last, during the time when Lord Yehoshua shall rule over us in the Kingdom of Heaven, our salvation knowledge of him, through appreciation, will result from our internalized understanding of his righteous judgment. It is then that we will dwell in the state of righteousness that the above scripture indicates that Lord Yehoshua will hasten.

Hence, we must patiently endure the frets of life until Lord Yehoshua casts down the worldwide secular power that seeks to suppress his Church body. At such a time, the Lord will casts down all worldly dominion, and then he will be gracious to us who will exalt him, as the following scripture indicates:

> And therefore will the Lord wait, that he may be gracious unto you, and therefore will he be exalted, that he may have mercy upon you: for the Lord is a *God* of judgment: blessed are all they that wait for him.[1]

The Course of the Gentile Nations

Obvious is the fact that we should bolster our patience by knowing that there is a course for human history that leads to a good end for us who seek the love of Y'haweh. This fact the Apostle Sha'ul affirmed when he wrote saying, "All things work for good to them that love God, to them who are the called according to his purpose."[2]

In essence, we may configure all human history that occurs after the judgmental flood into stages that exemplify Y'haweh's developing friendship with us, the true worshippers, whom Y'haweh shall marry. To this end, Y'haweh must overcome sin's selfishness, which veils his truth from our wondering eyes and causes us to seek contrary pursuits of happiness in our personal relationships, as well as our communal relationships.

As we have delineated above, sin is that which first causes the relationship between husband and wife to fail. Following, sin also causes other relationships to fail, such as the relationship between a parent and his or her child. Following are the failed relationships

---

[1] Isaiah 30:18
[2] Romans 8:28

between siblings and friends. In sequence, the major social relationships between the governors and the governed fail, such as the failure of a patriarch's rule over his people; the unfortunate transformation of a king into a tyrant; the rise of an oligarchy, as an aristocracy falls; and, lastly, the political compromise of democracy that finally gives rise to the hybrid beast, which an anti-savior esteems, as he seduces the people away from the true worship of Y'haweh.

The culmination of an evil state, which governs humanity and alienates them from the truth of Y'haweh, is inevitable. Notwithstanding, the realization of Y'haweh's glory over the earth, after he judges the same evil state and thereby vindicates the redeemed, is inevitable as well.

Let us here consider the fact that soon after the judgmental flood, all peoples first settled in Mesopotamia—*the Land between Two Rivers* (the Tigris and Euphrates rivers). This land comprises the major part of a vast stretch of fertile plains that begins in the city states of ancient Sumer[1] (the lower region of early 21th Century Iraq). In a crescent ark that juts forth to the left, the land ends in the fertile plains of the Nile River valley of Egypt. Hence, the fertile plains when joined together comprise the lands that modern scholars call the Fertile Crescent.

After the peoples settled in the region of ancient Sumer, they formed a single totalitarian government with a single leader, Nimrod, as their guide. To further solidify all peoples, the people under Nimrod built a tower that they purported to be their link with the wealth of Heaven. Figuratively, like the field peasants, they tried to seize the riches of the heavenly, golden city through their own

---

[1] Arno Poebel briefly postulated on the origin of the Sumerian people. His comments are recorded in an article that is published in the *American Journal of Semitic Languages* (LVIII [1941], 20-26). Poebel noted that the actual name of *Sumer*, as recorded in cuneiform, is pronounced *Shumer*, and he noted that the word is written as *Shumi*. He went on to point out that the ending vowels of Sumerian words are often left off unless the word is followed by a particle that contains a vowel; therefore, in its base form, the word *Shumi* is actually *Shum*: a word that directly translates into Hebrew as Shem, who is Noach's son.

power instead of humbly and obediently seeking the grace of Y'haweh. For sure, we know that it was necessary for Y'haweh to bring down this global government that arose at the dawn of this current age. He, in fact, confounded the language of the people, destroyed their tower, and scattered the people over the globe to create a myriad of conflicting cultures. In fact, one of the few things that the cultures retained from their common Sumerian heritage is the idea that there was a judgmental flood[1]; therefore, from this knowledge they retained some reverence for a creator.

At best we may say that even though these conflicting cultures will one day coalesce again into one evil totalitarian state, Y'haweh began to form his faithful bride from those whom he has given the inspiration to seek a new Adam who solely holds Heaven's blessings. As we shall see, Y'hawch began to cultivate his bride by befriending the heavenly City's patriarch, who lived in the land of Sumer.

We find that Y'haweh befriended the patriarch of our faith in Sumer, because the Sumerian city-states were the beginning of the nations. These city-states inherited the immediate technology, craft, and governmental systems of Nimrod's state. Sumerian government even retained semblances of a bi-cameral legislature, which they enjoined to plead the cause of a multi-classed society. Also, having reached the status of higher-level civilization, the Sumerians even initialized social reforms: the common Sumerian was aware of his or her personal rights; therefore, they guarded their social freedoms against those powers that might attempt to infringe upon those rights. The most notable reformer of the Sumerians was King Urukagina[2] of the Sumerian city-state Lagash. This King fought corruption in such a way that the peasants thought that his laws were divinely inspired. His is the first example of judicial reform.

For sure, it follows that the rudiments of democracy were first reached in Sumer, because the competitive spirit that existed

---

[1] There are more than 500 historical deluge accounts that have arose around the world. It can be said that a little less than 100 of them have origins that are independent of the biblical account of the flood or the Mesopotamian accounts.
[2] Circa 2350 BC

between the sometimes warring city-states often created political compromises that necessitated forms of representation, in order to represent the vying interests of private citizens. Essentially, Sumer's city-states agreed culturally but opposed the political dominance of one Sumerian city-state over another.

Still, the greatest contributions of Sumerian culture to the world are not only their legal and technological systems, but also their analytical understandings of cosmology. Even though they had lost the truth of Y'haweh, the Sumerians possessed the most sophisticated understanding of the Heavens among other prehistoric peoples. They believed in a pantheon of gods, in which each god had some responsibility for ensuring the harmony of the creation. They believed that everything that existed resulted from the gods' speaking order over primeval waters. Also, the Sumerians dissected every cosmic entity into a corresponding cultural entity, each being held together by a set of rules and regulations that they called *Me*. The Sumerians then held sacred such idols that they created to represent the *Me*'s of the cosmos.

Versions of the Sumerian pantheon took root in other cultures that arose within and around the Fertile Crescent and specifically around the coastal regions of the Mediterranean Sea: that is, the Western lands that bank Mesopotamian lands. The Egyptian pantheon of gods possessed similar functions as the Sumerian; and by way of the island of Crete, the ancient Minoan culture past elements of the Egyptian pantheon to the Greek isles, where strong democracies took root. At the last, Greek culture then spread to the Italian peninsula giving rise to the power of Imperial Rome, which exploited the political quagmires of the warlike Greek states, adapted the strengths of Mesopotamian cultures, and then rose to dominate the Mediterranean world.

As a matter of fact, the Roman government out of necessity became a hybrid government to meet the needs of the vast people under its rule: at the head of Rome's government was the Emperor who held absolute power. Next, in line were two consuls who ordered the armies and decided tax law among other ordinances. As well, there was the senate, which represented the well to do and influential. Also, to counter the power of the senate, there arose an assembly of free citizen men who elected tribunes to plead their case before the senate. The Roman government was so sophisticated that many of the existing governments in our contemporary era are derivations of the ancient Roman government. For sure, the anti-savior himself will seek to assume the emperor's seat over a newly constituted contemporary Rome.

Notwithstanding, the nations that we have been speaking of comprise areas of the globe that we call the West and the Middle East, respectively. The land of Yisra'el lies in the midst of these areas, being flanked by the Mediterranean Sea on its western border and the major lands of the Fertile Crescent on the other surrounding borders.

We will not treat the other cultures that have settled in other parts of the globe. The human societal equations adequately play themselves out for our inspection in the geo-political interplay between the West and Middle East.

For instance, the geography of the Western and Middle Eastern lands creates conflicting cultures. As a result, sophisticated governmental systems arise to manage conscience's compromise, while Yisra'el tenuously stands by clinging to Y'haweh's revelations.

The Third Revelation of Y'haweh: He is a Friend to His Faithful Elect

When we consider the myriads of peoples that have resided in ancient civilizations and when we consider their foundational achievements that still remain the corner stone of our modern world, the following questions arise: can we say that Y'haweh has not opened his gracious hand upon all cultures in some way, by showing them reflections of himself? Or can we say that individuals who do not necessarily know of the Savior do not seek some form of a personal relationship with Y'haweh?

These questions have been at the heart of religious strife since the dawn of this age. And so, it is right for us to ascertain definitively that which makes our relationship with Y'haweh eternal and not just for this current age, this saeculum.

To answer these questions, we have but to consider the fact that any true relationship with Y'haweh entails an everlasting satisfaction that sin cannot encumber. Heretofore, no person or government enjoys uninhibited tranquility or immortality; therefore, according to our understanding, no person truly possesses a relationship with Y'haweh. As a consequence, we may say that the hallmarks of liberty that we see among the ancients can be attributed to Y'haweh's benevolence, while the fall of the ancient societies can be attributed to the societies' inability to relate to the peace of the only sovereign Lord.

Even the members of the Church suffer from this inability; therefore, we are sure that the only thing that justifies our claim of being the beneficiaries of the truth is not our personal relationship with Y'haweh but Lord Yehoshua's personal relationship with Y'haweh; wherein Lord Yehoshua's unblemished conscience is an existential expression of Y'haweh's eternal good as right judgment: only through the Lord may we aspire to possess eternal satisfaction. Furthermore, we know that we cannot ensure the truth of Y'haweh; only Y'haweh ensures his truth as witnessed by the tree of life that stands in Heaven and bears the fruit of Y'haweh's Holy Spirit in us. Thus, the agreement between the Holy Marriage's benefactor (Lord Yehoshua) and beneficiary (the Church Bride), Y'haweh secures by extending his grace unto us, to mature our sense of appreciation for his new Adam who directly glorifies him.

The Lord Yehoshua is of course the only one whom the fleshly pursuits cannot captivate. He only pursues the heavenly good unabatedly, while he identifies with our disparity by enduring our temptation and suffering death undeservedly in our place. Thus, through death and resurrection, Lord Yehoshua not only becomes a new Adam (who is born of the Holy Spirit instead of the flesh), but also becomes a testator (who has died and left the wealth of Heaven to us his appreciative beneficiaries). What is more, Lord Yehoshua's sacrifice makes it possible for us to have a friendship with Y'haweh by allowing us to invoke Lord Yehoshua's Testament, in which he leaves us the fruit of the Holy Spirit, who seals our eternal relationship with Y'haweh.

Furthermore, we cannot even love Lord Yehoshua or appreciate his throne unless Y'haweh befriends us first, by planting the seeds of faith and trust in us, who will then yield the fruits of his Holy Spirit. Lord Yehoshua affirms these facts by saying the following:

> All that the Father gives me shall come to me; and him that comes to me I will in no way cast out; for I came down from heaven, not to do mine own will, but the will of him that sent me. And this is the Father's will who has sent me, that of all which he has given me I should lose nothing, but should raise it up again at the last day . . . No man can come to me, except the Father who has sent me draws him: and I will raise him up at the last day.[1]

Let us qualify the fact that Y'haweh first befriends us (whom he has elected to receive salvation) as the third of our seven revelations of Y'haweh, which we are noting to mature our relationship with him. Once more, because he not only befriends us personally, but also befriends us corporately, Y'haweh defines our friendship with him through his friendship with the patriarch of the faithful City: Y'haweh's covenant with Avraham, the Patriarch of our faith in Lord Yehoshua, therefore, witnesses our third revelation of Y'haweh.

The Seed of Avraham That Y'haweh Plants in an Unassuming Promised Land

To understand the nature of Y'haweh's relationship with the patriarch of our faith, we have only to consider the fulfillment of the Holy Marriage's truth, which the relationship between Y'haweh and the Patriarch Avraham leads us to. We know that the personal sense of fulfillment that comes from a healthy marriage involves each member's denying of their own aspirations, while both members actively seek the others satisfaction and advantage. Likewise, Y'haweh ultimately expressed his love for the patriarch and us by

---

[1] John 6:37-44

sacrificing his only son as a response to the faith of Avraham who offered to sacrifice his only son and heir as Avraham pursued the glory of Y'haweh. So must we also sacrifice our own worldly aspirations to fulfill the love of Y'haweh by being thankful for the eternal wealth of his grace.

By grace, Y'haweh first loved Avraham by befriending him in the Mesopotamian city-state of Ur.[1] In glory, Y'haweh appeared to Avraham (whose name was then Abram) and told him to leave his father's house, brethren, and kindred and depart from Ur, in order to go into the land of Canaan[2], a land that Y'haweh would give to Avraham's descendants and make Abram a Father and a blessing to many other nations.

Y'haweh began to cultivate Abram's faith when he gloriously appeared to him: Y'haweh not only asked Abram to leave the worldly prosperity of the backslidden societies, but also asked him to leave the cultic Mesopotamian pantheon of gods that his father Terah worshipped. Abram was a 75-year-old childless man when he departed to follow the glory of Y'haweh; moreover, he then became a stranger in the land of Canaan, which had many pagan city-states. Through faith Abram began to understand the necessity of Lord Yehoshua's ministry, since Abram knew that only Y'haweh could break the power of darkness by birthing a new Adam to see past the veil of sin, which shrouded the land of Canaan: historically, the most volatile political region in the world. Abram knew that neither he nor an earthly descendant could inspire the people of Canaan or the peoples of the world to pursue the good will of all and so unveil the glory of Y'haweh.

The land of Canaan is a natural corridor between the civilization bearing river valleys of the Fertile Crescent, which valleys (again) reside on two separate continents—Asia and Africa. Canaan is 130 kilometers at its widest point. The Mediterranean Sea flanks

---

[1] Avraham was more than likely born in the Third Dynasty of Ur around the year 2165 BC.
[2] Canaan (Kana'an) is the grandson of Noach. Kana'an's name means "lowland." Noach cursed Kana'an for his father Ham's misbehavior: Noach foretold that Kana'an would be a slave to his neighbors.

Canaan's western border, and the Arabian Desert flanks Canaan's southeastern border. To the North, lay the nations of Syria and Lebanon of Mesopotamia and to the South lay Egypt of the Nile River valley. Furthermore, Canaan serves as a widow to three continents: to the Northwest lay Greece, Rome, and Europe proper; to the South lay Egypt and the rest of Africa, laying adjacent to the Red Sea, which is a passage way to the Indian Ocean and the remainder of the orient. In the other surrounding regions lay Russia to the North and the remainder of Asia.

The land of Canaan, therefore, served as an area of transit to these regions. A host of merchantmen and caravans have plied a complex network of roads through Canaan to foster trade between the nations. For example, Lebanon to the North sold its vast reserves of cedar trees to Egypt, and Canaan itself produced barely, grapes, wheat, pomegranates, figs, and olives to trade.

When the local power centers (within each respective continent) tried to grow outside their natural boundaries to become international powers, they first sought to subdue the land of Canaan to gain access to its trade routes before they exercised hegemony over other power centers. For this cause, Canaan has proven to be the most conquered and exploited land in the world: Canaan has proven to be the world's greatest international battleground. Its history is a record of never-ending social turmoil and political upheaval, only having few periods of peace or sovereignty. As a result, the land has been ruled and conquered by all the fundamental forms of government, bringing these governments into conflict with the succeeding tabernacles of Yisra'el.

What is more, while the external, geographic situation of Canaan casts such political threats upon it from outside forces, Canaan's internal geographic features greatly hindered any cultural solidarity: the settlers found that the topography of the country bred social conflict. To make matters worse, a myriad of foreign peoples from the northern countries poured into Canaan's conflicting landscapes, which litter the countryside; moreover, these foreigners brought with them a host of fertility cults: the foreigners worshiped various deities from the pantheon of gods from more advanced cultures. Fertile plains composed the area that lays adjacent to the western Mediterranean border of the country; these plains laid exposed to invaders and foreign influences, such as the Amorites, Indo-Aryan peoples, and the Hurrians, all ancient peoples. Forests lands composed the northern section of the country, and these lands were, for the most, economically unproductive; nonetheless, the northern kingdom of the Hittites often settled its people in these regions.

Mountain and highlands comprise the eastern area of the country. This area is a more remote region; therefore, the area fostered political solidarity, it's being less privy to foreign influences. The Jordan valley, which is below sea level, flanks the mountain area on the far eastern border of the country, and the desert plains of Arabia runs adjacent to the Jordan valley to the South at notably higher elevations.

When he considered the complexity of the land, Abram looked past the great difficulties that he saw with his eyes and believed in the promises of Y'haweh. He believed that Y'haweh would judge the Canaanite city-states and give the land to his descendants and the other redeemed peoples of the nations who would become the blessed of the world.

It is evident that Y'haweh first preached the gospel of Lord Yehoshua to Abram when Y'haweh told Abram that his descendant would become a blessing not only to such a tumultuous land, but also to the world. Abram knew that he had no power of his own to foster such a blessing other than his obedience to Y'haweh's will. As we have noted above, only the new Adam could secure Y'haweh's eternal friendship with humankind. In effect, Y'haweh's promise to Abram was that Abram's descendant would be Lord Yehoshua, Abram's own redeemer unto eternal life. Consequently, Abram invariably knew that the only true blessing for the world that his descendant could bring is the removal of sin's condemnation of death to unite all peoples eternally in love, under Y'haweh.

If one should ask us what virtue did Abram have to secure the favor of Y'haweh not only on him but also on his descendants, we would have to say that Abram's virtue was not of himself, but the faith that Y'haweh cultivated in Abram to believe in the promise of the new Adam's blessings imputed the righteousness of Lord Yehoshua upon Abram. For twenty-four years, Abram wondered in the land of Canaan and Egypt anxiously waiting for the promise, even though he was childless: Abram's wife Sarah could not bear children, so in desperation she used her maid to bear Abram a son. Nevertheless, Y'haweh declared that the promised child would be a descendant of his barren wife Sarah and that the name of her child would be *Yitzchak*, a name that means *laughter*. As a token of the promise of salvation through the new Adam (who was to be a descendant of Sarah's child), Y'haweh initiated the practice of circumcision among Abram's descendants.

In addition, Y'haweh officially changed Abram's name to *Avraham*, a name that means *father of many*. Y'haweh then told Avraham to stand before him and be perfect, by upholding such conscience that the promised new Adam will redeem. Hence, when Avraham's descendants uphold the law of conscience, in the hope of obtaining Avraham's promised blessing, their mark of circumcision becomes a mark of the faith that Y'haweh instilled in their hearts[1]; moreover, when some of Avraham's descendants walk disorderly, while we directly follow Avraham's walk of faith, we actually uphold Y'haweh's covenant with Avraham, while his descendants circumcise themselves in vain.

During the twenty-five years before the birth of Yitzchak, Y'haweh continued to increase Avraham's faith. For example, Y'haweh empowered Avraham to rescue his nephew Lot whom three warlike Canaanite kings held captive. Avraham rescued Lot by using three hundred men who were born in the household that the Lord had given him. Upon his return, the Lord inspired an ancient, priestly king Malki-Tzedek of Yerushalayim (the city of peace) to greet Avraham with the provisions of bread and wine for Avraham and his men. The Holy Spirit then inspired King Malki-Tzedek to

---

[1] The Apostle Sha'ul writes about the purpose of circumcision in his epistle to the Romans (2:29).

bless Avraham by calling him a servant of the highest *god*[1], whom the King continually aspired to worship. In response to the witness of the Holy Spirit who encouraged the words of King Malki-Tzedek, Avraham paid tithes to King Malki-Tzedek.

By paying tithes to Malki-Tzedek, Avraham recognized the fact that Y'haweh gave him victory. Essentially, Avraham looked past the ancient King and saw the figure of the true priestly King Yehoshua who will truly bring the Heavenly City of Peace to the land and thus make Avraham's eternal prosperity possible.

Finally, after Avraham's promised son Yitzchak was born, Y'haweh procured the faithful act from Avraham that stands as an ensample of the love and commitment that Y'haweh seeks from us all. Knowing that he would one-day sacrifice Lord Yehoshua for Avraham, Y'haweh asked Avraham to sacrifice his promised son Yitzchak whom Avraham had waited so long for. But when Avraham had begun to sacrifice his son, Y'haweh prevented him, because Y'haweh was satisfied because Avraham had proven that he loved Y'haweh more than Avraham loved himself. Because of Avraham's faith and love, Y'haweh provided an unblemished ram to replace Avraham's sacrifice.

Thus, what we must conclude from Avraham's attempted sacrifice is that Y'haweh does not accept religious acts of self-justification, such as suicide, human sacrifice, and the other forms of self-affliction, because we do not have anything that we may sacrifice that is remotely equivalent to the sacrifice of his lamb, our Lord Yehoshua. Instead, Y'haweh only seeks the sacrifice of our obedient hearts, which desire him above our selfish aspirations.

Thus, we must know that Y'haweh's suzerain covenant with Avraham entails the imputing of the first friendship of Lord Yehoshua's unblemished conscience, which manifests Y'haweh's good and glory. Y'haweh's covenant with Avraham is a poignant

---

[1] We cannot definitively ascertain whether Malki-Tzedek had a true knowledge of Y'haweh, by foreseeing the new Adam. Quite possibly, Malki-Tzedek worshipped the highest pagan deity of a pagan pantheon of gods. Nevertheless, Y'haweh used Malki-Tzedek to comfort Avraham by making Malki-Tzedek a figure of Lord Yehoshua's future priestly ministry unto Avraham and us all.

example of the biblical Testaments' indictment upon the efficacy of self-serving religious works, social status, and the other inequitable forms of human self-renown.

Because of the faith that Y'haweh matured in Avraham, we have an example of what fruit of the Lord's Holy Spirit will manifest in our life when we patiently trust in the revealed word of Y'haweh. As well, we know what deeds of a faithful life, in us, are met by the sacrifice of Y'haweh's son. Accordingly, the scripture affirms our blessings in Y'haweh's relationship with faithful Avraham as follows:

> And the angel of the Y'haweh called unto him out of heaven, and said, "Avraham, Avraham": and he said, "Here *am* I." And he said, "lay not your hand upon the lad, neither do thou anything unto him: for now I know that you fear God, seeing you have not withheld your son, your only *son* from me." And Avraham lifted up his eyes, and looked, and behold behind *him* a ram caught in a thicket by his horns: and Avraham went and took the ram, and offered him up for a burnt offering in the stead of his son. And Avraham called the name of that place Y'haweh-yireh: as it is said *to* this day, "in the mount of the Y'haweh it shall be seen." And the angel of Y'haweh called unto Avraham out of heaven the second time, And said, "By myself have I sworn, says Y'haweh, for because thou hast done this thing, and has not withheld your son, your only *son*: That in blessing I will bless thee, and in multiplying I will multiply your seed as the stars of the heaven, and as the sand which *is* upon the sea shore; and your seed shall possess the gate of his enemies; And in your seed shall all the nations of the earth be blessed; because thou hast obeyed my voice."[1]

Ya`akov's Apology

Despite the great faith that Avraham exhibited in his life, we must reaffirm that there is neither any virtue that we may find in Avraham that can ensure the eternal prosperity of our souls, nor any ability that we may find in him that enables him to single handedly turn the pagan nations from their false ideologies. Avraham now sleeps with his fathers and can no longer do any deeds that may directly affect us

---

[1] Genesis 22:11-18

now, for better or worse. In the same manner, his descendants cannot secure salvation for us or even themselves. These facts unquestionable affirm the truth that the Lord's sacrifice is our only true hope; we must, therefore, affix our hope on the sacrifice that the Lord provided for Avraham to replace the sacrifices of Avraham and his mortal sons. Indeed, Y'haweh provides us his own sacrifice in Lord Yehoshua who rose from death to minister to our souls eternally, in response to the faith of Avraham. In this vein, we may glean from the above scripture that Y'haweh necessarily swore by himself and not by frail, mortal Avraham who could not fulfill any oath eternally, unlike Lord Yehoshua who can.

We can only study Y'haweh's relationship with Avraham's fleshly descendants who inherited Avraham's Promised Land, even though they could not maintain a faithful relationship with Y'haweh to make the land the place of salvation. Knowing that they alone could not transform the land into the paradise of Eden, we may learn from their downfalls to further appreciate the grace that Y'haweh extends to us, because it is our appreciation and adoration of Y'haweh that secures his benevolence. In effect, we may rightly conclude that wherever we enjoy a friendship with Y'haweh is the actual place of salvation. Only in such a place of peace, may we truly worship him.

To this end, when Avraham's son Yitzchak and grandson Ya`akov inherited the promise of Avraham, they inherited Avraham's friendship with Y'haweh. First, Y'haweh appeared unto Yitzchak, like he appeared to his father Avraham, and affirmed Avraham's suzerain covenant with him by saying, "In thy seed shall all the nations of the earth be blessed."[1]

Second, Y'haweh further refined his covenant with Avraham through his friendship with Avraham's grandson Ya`akov: before Ya`akov's mother gave birth to him and his twin brother Esav (who became the first born of the two), Y'haweh loved and befriended Ya`akov by endowing him with the sense to trust and to have faith in

---

[1] Genesis 26:4

his truth. In contrast, Y'haweh hated Esav by not extending to him the same measure of faith.

To fulfill the truth of the Holy Marriage, it was necessary for Y'haweh to appear, unabashedly, as the benefactor of the Patriarchs. So by loving the second born, who traditionally did not inherit the wealth of his father, Y'haweh secured the appreciation from Ya`akov that fulfills the reciprocity of Y'haweh's love. In this way, Y'haweh demonstrated that his gift of faith in him is by his grace alone: the fact that Esav, the first born, did not fully appreciate the blessing of Y'haweh when he grew up, even though Ya`akov did, justifies this fact. Thus, when Y'haweh elected Ya`akov to receive Lord Yehoshua's salvation, Y'haweh exhibited his power and glory through his grace.

Ya`akov's parents even gave Ya`akov the name *Ya`akov*, which means supplanter, because his very first action was an attempt to supplant his brother and become the first-born: the infant Ya`akov grabbed the heel of his twin brother Esav's foot at birth. As a consequence, Y'haweh eventually redeemed Ya`akov's faith, despite the fact that Ya`akov unjustly succeeded in stealing his brother's blessing and birth right: Y'haweh appeared to the fugitive Ya`akov in a vision showing him that the Promised Land of Avraham is a land that Y'haweh loves, because of his friendship with Avraham and because Y'haweh would exhibit his power and glory by changing this most contentious place in the world into a place of eternal peace. Furthermore, in appreciation of Ya`akov's faith, Y'haweh then told Ya`akov that he would give the Promised Land to him and his descendants, who strive for the blessings and glory of the Lord.

To effect such a blessing, Y'haweh instilled within Ya`akov the true understanding that Ya`akov's wealth and happiness is the product of Y'haweh's grace, alone. Also, to prevent Ya`akov from striving with his neighbors for the temporal things of this world, like the Canaanites who corrupted the Promised Land, Y'haweh gave Ya`akov a heart that valued his covenant relationship above all else. In faith, therefore, Ya`akov responded to the grace of Y'haweh by promising Y'haweh that such wealth that Y'haweh gives to him who (at the time) possessed nothing, he Ya`akov will give a tenth to uphold the worship of Y'haweh before men. In his actions, Ya`akov testified to the fact that observing a covenant relationship with Y'haweh is of more value than silver or gold.

Y'haweh was so delighted in the fact that Ya`akov possessed such a certainty of Y'haweh's power that Y'haweh gave him a new name, which even defines us who follow Ya`akov's zeal. You see, having feared the reprisal of his brother Esav, Ya`akov wrestled an angel of Y'haweh, demanding the blessing of the Lord. Then Y'haweh, being pleasantly amused at Ya`akov's faith and foresight, blessed Ya`akov and changed his name to *Yisra'el*, a name that means *he who strives with God and prevails*.

In other words, through striving to be obedient to Y'haweh's will, those who obtain the name *Yisra'el* with the Patriarch Ya`akov, will regain the dominion of the earth that the first Adam lost but the new Adam regains. Of all, we may say that Ya`akov-Yisra'el pursued the good of Y'haweh from his birth until his death, despite the frailties of his flesh.

As Ya`akov-Yisra'el's life began with an act of faith, his life ended with an act of faith, as well. When Yisra'el considered how the grace of Y'haweh gave him a life of triumph, Yisra'el knew not to confirm the blessing of Avraham on any particular one of his twelve sons. Instead, Yisra'el conferred blessings on the works that they perform in obedience to Y'haweh, and at the same time he cursed their unrighteous deeds, knowing that the true, obedient seed of Avraham, who will inherit the promise, will arise to bless whomever the Lord chose to strive with him in faith. For instance, when Yisra'el foretold that the Kings of the Promise Land would arise from the descendants of his son Yehudah, he also foretold that the monarchy would not stand until Shiloh comes—that is, *until he comes whose right it is*.[1] In other words, Ya'akov foresaw that Lord Yehoshua, who figuratively springs from the tribe of Yehudah, only will gather the elect around Y'haweh's glory, making peace in the name of Y'haweh throughout the world.

---

[1] Ezekiel 21:27

The Power of the Holy Spirit Establishing our Personhood within the Elect Community

When we consider the blessing and curse that Ya`akov conferred upon his sons, who faced the challenge of overcoming the sinful land of Canaan, we become all the more certain of the following: for Y'haweh to transform us into "the Yisra'el of God"[1], he must first subdue our selfish natures by using the power of Lord Yehoshua's Holy Spirit. Following, we must strive for his good by forsaking our own volitions for the good of Y'haweh and others whom he relates to; because though we find sure satisfaction in our personal relationships with Y'haweh, we must recognize the fact that he requires us to relate to him in communal relationships, as well.

We feel his pleasure when he generously gives us the sustenance and social wellbeing, in order for us to benefit others with like generosity. Also, we feel his compassion when the charitable hands of others supply our most pressing needs. We partake in Y'haweh's Holy Marriage in every aspect of our godly communities, whether we are formerly married or not. At times, we assume the role of being another's benefactor, and at other times, we become the beneficiaries of another's labor. From our family members and associates, we gain friendship's approval, encouragement, inspiration, and love. And when we find no constant friend, we have the truest friendship of Y'haweh that we see directly manifested in his sacrifice of Lord Yehoshua on the cross. Hence, the scriptures comfort us by saying, "There is a friend that sticks closer than a brother."[2]

Still, while we recognize the benefit of Y'haweh's love, it should be all the more obvious to us that humankind's inability to see past sin's veil of selfishness to perceive Y'haweh's love gives rise to all life's problems. For instance, we witness a striking phenomenon when we observe how the pollutions of a single, covetous individual can withhold the green rolling hills, lush forests, and crystal springs of Eden from everyone's enjoyment. Moreover, we witness an even

---

[1] Galatians 6:16
[2] Proverbs 18:24

more amazing phenomenon when we observe how the disaffected consciences of others cause them to disregard the injuries to the earth because personal cares and desires present to them more private concerns. At best, these disaffected people consider the sundry corruptions of the earth to be the necessary cost that they must afford for their own personal opportunities. In this way, sin causes people to devalue the beauty of Y'haweh that the earth readily advertises.

One may justly ask how can humanity retain satisfaction without knowing the love and beauty of their creator. As well, one may ask how can humanity conquer the evil that blinds them if they cannot agree upon what evil is. And lastly, one may asks how can humanity possess the good if they cannot agree upon what is good for all.

The ever present contentions in human relationships, therefore, justify our assertion that a right value of creation must be given to us by the Spirit of Y'haweh, in order to pacify the tastes and preferences of the human self-will. To this end, the salvation knowledge's appreciative sense, of Y'haweh's mercy upon us, gains for us this right value, after we strive with Y'haweh in his judgment upon the very human self-will that pollutes creation. Again, our appreciation of Y'haweh's mercy is a reception of his love—the fulfillment of all things. As we shall further see below, Y'haweh's marrying of our corporate and individual senses of appreciation, unto him, is the sincerest exercise of his power.

In view of that, let us reaffirm the prophet Yesha`yahu's statement—"In mercy shall [Lord Yehoshua's] throne be established"—because now we may began to understand further how Y'haweh does not merely express his power in the physical wonders of creation. Instead, we see that Y'haweh expresses his true power through the wonders of his Holy Spirit, who through acts of mercy transforms our hearts to value the resurrected Lord and to be satisfied when his Spirit, corporately, resurrects us who follow him.

Essentially, to establish his throne, "Y'haweh has concluded all in unbelief that he might have mercy upon [us] all."[1] In this manner, he ensures the manifold reciprocity of his love.

---

[1] Romans 11:32

Let us continue together by affixing our eyes upon the risen Lord, and let us know that Y'haweh will redeem our faith with the Lord's righteousness. We may, therefore, take joy in tribulation, since in the midst of strife Lord Yehoshua consoles us by giving us knowledge through an appreciation of his righteous judgment and our future, eternal existence before his equitable throne. In fact, we may further glorify him by using our spiritual gifts to "comfort those who are in tribulation, by the comfort wherewith we ourselves are comforted of God."[1] And when we receive like benefit from those who share our faith, we find comfort in the social body of the Savior.

We whom Y'haweh elects to receive salvation must not despair when we consider the self-centered human condition; since we see our good end afar off. We must not despise the chastisement of Y'haweh; nor must we loath his correction, "for whom Y'haweh loves, he reprimands, even as a Father reproves the son that he loves."[2]

Y'haweh fulfills our souls through patience and obedience to allow us to appreciate the triumph of the obedient Lord and the vindication of the same Lord who loved selflessly, only to be unjustly persecuted. Let us take comfort in the fact that his burden is light upon us who are obedient to his glory, while his wrath is furious against those who rebel against his glory. The power of Y'haweh is a response to those actions that glorify him; therefore, let us be obedient to his will and be filled with the fruits that his power produces in his developing relationship with us.

The Burden of the Children of Yisra'el

We can only understand the stages of Y'haweh's developing relationship with us, which unfolds the enigmatic course of human history, if we definitively understand the blessing and cursing that Ya`akov conferred upon his sons, because Y'haweh impart withheld his Holy Spirit from them. From Y'haweh's developing relationship

---

[1] 2 Corinthians 1:4
[2] Proverbs 3:11, 12

with the children Yisra'el, we may quantify the rest of Y'haweh's several revelations that speaks directly to our needs.

For this cause, we must not foolishly mock the tumultuous history of the children of Yisra'el, because the burden that Y'haweh has placed upon them brings to fruition our redemption in Lord Yehoshua. Thus, we may conclude that Y'haweh did not necessarily give the seed of Ya`akov over to evil when he withheld his Holy Spirit from Yisra'el's sons, but he allowed part of the children of Yisra'el to pursue self-will only to scatter them from his glory.

Following, Y'haweh assembles a true Yisra'el among those children of Yisra'el who are obedient to the promised seed of Avraham who fulfills Y'haweh's law. As well, Y'haweh adopts us into his Assembly—his Ecclesia—of people who are likewise obedient to the new Adam: the Mashiach Yehoshua, our Lord.

After we all, who are elect, will have exhausted ourselves from seeking our own self-will, we will find ourselves assembled and relating to one another in appreciation of Y'haweh's love. Indeed, it is evident that Y'haweh reflects his fulfillment in personal relationships with some of Ya`akov's descendants and us true worshippers, who remain scattered throughout the world because of sin, for Y'haweh gathers and resurrects us together by the power of his love. In this way, Y'haweh (who manifests himself in Lord Yehoshua) will conquer evil's dominion over the world and so fulfill his truth.

With thanksgivings, let us acknowledge the fact that it is for our sakes that Y'haweh did not establish the friendship between him and Avraham (through the sacrifice of the Savior) with all Ya`akov's descendants. Y'haweh only established a relationship with the children of Yisra'el to fulfill his grace upon Avraham.

The same covenant relationship that gives him fulfillment with Avraham, Y'haweh seeks with others who assume the covenant relationship. To this end, Y'haweh impart extends his grace to Yisra'el, because his mercy cannot be appreciated by the children of Yisra'el who gain his benevolence by inheritance and not by an instilled desire for his Holy Spirit.

The Kingdom of Heaven

When Y'haweh delivered the children of Yisra'el from the bondage of Egypt to establish himself as salvation, he did not imbue all the Yisra'elites with an appreciation of the knowledge and lordship of the new Adam; moreover, he did not birth the new Adam among them. Instead, to pronounce his benevolence upon us who do not deserve the inheritance of the Patriarchs, Y'haweh withheld his Holy Spirit from the natural children of the Patriarchs. In the Spirit's place, he gave them a law that reflects the eternal state of his righteousness: he gave them a law that only the new Adam—the righteous King—can eternally uphold. As a result, the children of Yisra'el could not all perceive Y'haweh's good beyond the King's law; therefore, the Righteous King's Law now curses the disobedient of Yisra'el, while the Law matures the obedient with the righteous judgment of the King who will redeem our faith and virtue with his righteousness.

After fourteen generations[1] from the sacrifice of Avraham, Y'haweh only gave the children of Yisra'el a little comfort at the height of their civilization by giving them a monarch who possessed his Holy Spirit in part, to portray the reign of the true eternal King who will unite us all. Then after a determined fourteen more generations, Y'haweh allowed the Kingdom of Yisra'el to fall and the children of Yisra'el to be scattered abroad: Y'haweh allowed the volatile geo-political situation of Canaan to undermine the Kingdom of Yisra'el, which tentatively united the land under its sovereignty. Deliberately, Y'haweh used malicious foreign powers to persecute the corrupt rulers of Yisra'el, who had exploited his congregation for their self-interests. In this way, Y'haweh began to purge his congregation. Following, when Y'haweh gathered the children of Yisra'el together again to show the elect of Yisra'el his mercy, he did not fully extend his open hand to them. Instead, he allowed covetous rulers to gain power again for fourteen more generations; in which period, he subjected the children of Yisra'el under the succession of governments, until the dawn of the world power of Rome. At such an expedient time, Y'haweh placed the humble, obedient savior to

---

[1] The number of completion multiplied by two

minister to the height of this world's civilization, which in this age governs us all.

And so, because the covetous rulers of the Yisra'elites rejected the Savior, we whom Y'haweh empowers to accept the Mashiach as our Lord and savior appreciate the tender mercy of the Lord. Of a truth, the grace of Y'haweh has come to us, the Ecclesia of Y'haweh: his grace has come to us whom he calls from around the world to assemble around him in true worship. For sure, we must not disdain the plight of Ya`akov's children, but we must appreciate the fact that the truth of Y'haweh has come to us until he refreshes them again with his sweet Holy Spirit. In this light, we empathize with the lamentation of Moshe who said, "Oh, that all of Y'haweh's children were prophets and that Y'haweh would put his Spirit on them."[1]

Let us be glad, for the Spirit of Truth has come to us, even as the Apostle Sha'ul notes that the Church is the body and house of Y'haweh, "the pillar and ground of the truth."[2] We must know for sure that after we have preached the good news of Lord Yehoshua's sacrifice to the elect who have not heard and after the rest of the world will have rejected the true worship of Y'haweh, the Lord will conclude this age by redeeming us and judging the disobedient.

We may now freely rejoice before the works of Y'haweh who has given us knowledge of repentance through the Law that we have believed and the risen Lord who redeems us by fulfilling the same Law that condemns our disobedience. If we simply follow Lord Yehoshua our redeemer and forsake our own selfish aspirations, we may find peace with Y'haweh, instead of condemnation.

The Fourth Revelation of Y'haweh: He is the Governor of His Obedient and Repentant Assembly

We have said, definitively, that our love is that which Y'haweh procures above all else: he essentially fulfills our love in his Holy Marriage to us. As we have noted, Y'haweh procures our love by cultivating our sense of appreciation for his salvation and mercy.

---

[1] Numbers 11:27
[2] 1 Timothy 3:15

Then from our salvation knowledge of his good comes the patience that we need to withstand the myriad of temptations that incline us to seek lesser satisfactions by committing sins against ourselves and others. To wit, we may ask the following: how could our marriage with Y'haweh stand if we do not operate with him to fulfill one another's needs first? And what can be the measure of our cooperation with the will of Y'haweh other than our obedience? If patience is the measure of our knowledge of Y'haweh's good, then our obedience is the measure of our love for him who graciously supplies the good through the resurrected Lord. Furthermore, because we need the power of his Holy Spirit to be obedient, obedience is the sincerest mark of our eternal election.

We can only understand Y'haweh's covenant with the children of Yisra'el, which he delineates through a codified law, if we keep in mind that the thesis of the covenant is that they must be obedient to his word. Under the stipulation of obedience does the Law that defines the Covenant lists what virtuous actions that the children of Yisra'el must pursue in faith. For instance, in the manner that Avraham obediently offered to sacrifice his first born son, the children of Yisra'el must in obedience sacrifice their best possessions, which they invariably would have used to pursue whatever worldly volitions, instead of their pursuing the true eternal riches of the risen Lord whom Y'haweh sacrificed.

Furthermore, when we acknowledge the fact that the obedience that the Law seeks to invoke within us reflects our love for Y'haweh, we must understand that our love for our neighbors, friends, and family members (who are likewise obedient to Y'haweh's will) reflects our love for Y'haweh, as well. For this cause Lord Yehoshua proclaimed the following:

> "You shall love the Lord your God with all our heart, and with all your mind." This is the first and great commandment. And the second is like unto it. "You shall love your neighbor as yourself." On these two commandments hang all the law and the prophets.[1]

---

[1] Matthew 22: 37-40

Considering the profundity of this knowledge, it is expedient for us to quantify our fourth revelation of Y'haweh by saying that *he is the faithful Governor of his obedient and repentant assembly*, until the obedience of our hearts fulfill his Law. At such a time, he will become the husband of the same assembly. In other words, to form the Body of Lord Yehoshua, we must love one another unconditionally without the necessity of the law: only then will Lord Yehoshua find a true bride in us. The fulfillment of this truth is that which the Covenant seeks.

Hallowed Ground

With the understanding of our fourth revelation, we may conclude that the Law is holy to we elect whom Y'haweh matures to perceive and appreciate the wealth of the absent King who died and became a testator who will give us the wealth of his resurrection. Correspondingly, we may conclude, as well, that the Law is dreadful to the disobedient who do not obtain the grace of Y'haweh and, therefore, cannot through faith perceive the true eternal glory of Y'haweh. For this cause, they cling to the worldly ambitions that are an affront to him.

Consider the extent of Y'haweh's grace upon Moshe the lawgiver, who is a descendant of Ya`akov's son, Levi. First, Y'haweh rescued Moshe from the Egyptian King's murdering of the infants of Yisra'el. Then Y'haweh raised Moshe in the succeeding Pharaoh's household as an educated prince. Then when Moshe killed an Egyptian as Moshe tried to defend a fellow son of Yisra'el, Y'haweh delivered Moshe by guiding him safely into the mountains of Sinai, where Moshe raised a family and became a shepherd.

Having loss the wealth of the cities of the prodigious Pharaohs, Moshe could only cling to the wealth of a heretofore-unknown God; therefore, it was easy for Y'haweh to garner Moshe's obedience to relate to him. Y'haweh simply caught Moshe's attention with a simple miracle: Y'haweh kindled a fire upon a bush on Mount Sinai, but he did not allow the fire to consume the bush. When Moshe came to observe the burning bush, it was easy for Y'haweh to produce a right value system in Moshe: Y'haweh commanded Moshe to remove his shoes and consecrate the very dust on the ground, as a place of salvation (that is, any place beyond the pollutions of human society where Moshe looked past himself and appreciated the love and mercy of Y'haweh).

In truth, we can only describe the consecrated ground of salvation, which Moshe beheld, in the following way: when the conscience of the soul meets the ordinance of Y'haweh's Holy Spirit, the soul experiences shame, being aware of its sin, because it beholds the justice of the Holy Spirit that the soul's conscience formerly perceived through faith. Yet, when the embattled conscience of the soul realizes that Y'haweh has vindicated its conscience (by condemning the same manner of the soul's sin in others) and redeemed the soul's frail virtue with the obedience of the risen Lord Yehoshua (who died for our transgressions and arose as the new Adam), the soul experiences the profoundest sense of appreciation, being both forgiven and justified: the soul becomes born again into the new Adam's—the unblemished Lamb's—body. Following, the soul at last experiences Y'haweh's Rest because it relinquishes the never-ending labor of following those pursuits that have pricked its conscience when the soul coveted such things that it had known to be a detriment to itself and others. Essentially, when the soul experiences Y'haweh's Rest, its faith gives way to knowledge and excellence because it possesses the good that it formerly perceived. In other words, it gains the degrees of felicity and all that a pure conscience offers that is contentment, consolation, and forgiveness. Thereby, the soul's newfound knowledge gives the soul the perception of beauty throughout its environment, while appreciation gives the soul serenity within. Essentially, the soul finally captures the meek and simple peace of Y'haweh's Holy Spirit; therefore, we must conclude that this eternal felicity of the soul is the very temple of Y'haweh: the realization of his truth and the heart of his Holy Marriage. Thus, finally standing upon hallowed ground, the soul can look past sin's veil and see Y'haweh's benevolent hand, even the beauty of Y'haweh's grace, in all the wonders and actions of creation.

With this understanding of Y'haweh's holy place, we may further understand the seasons of Y'haweh's revelations to us, his elect, his beloved. We must understand that it is essential for Y'haweh to become the supreme benefactor of us who dare to tread upon sacred ground, if we are to hallow the place of his Soul's habitation. This ground the humbled Moshe walked upon, reverently; however, some of his brethren—the children of Yisra'el—could not, because they could not all perceive and appreciate Y'haweh's open hand, despite the fact that Y'haweh stretched out his hand to them. For this cause, Y'haweh did not totally destroy the Egyptians who had held his people captive for 430 years; moreover, for this cause, Y'haweh did not totally liberate his people when he gave them the Righteous King's law, which declares his benevolent hand to us (the obedient) and condemns those who like Esav disregard his grace. Y'haweh's covenant with the children of Yisra'el, in fact, initiated a period of reconciliation between him and his elect: in the period of reconciliation, his Law either condemns the faithless whom sin's veil confounds in darkness, or reconciles the faithful who see the light of Lord Yehoshua who fulfills the Law and so breaks the power of darkness.

The Salvation Knowledge of Lord Yehoshua the Mashiach

Let us first note the following to begin our survey of Y'haweh's Law: Y'haweh initiated his Covenant and subsequent Law between himself and the children of Yisra'el by first befriending Moshe the Levite, in consideration of his covenant with Avraham. Of a truth, we know that Y'haweh established his friendship with Moshe upon Y'haweh's friendship with Avraham, because at one point Y'haweh sought to punish Moshe for not circumcising his sons in observance of Avraham's covenant.

Whatever the case may be, we must note that while Moshe's relationship with Y'haweh is an extension of Y'haweh's friendship with Avraham, Moshe acquired a special friendship with Y'haweh.

The scriptures report that, "Y'haweh spoke unto Moshe face to face, as a man speaks unto his friend."[1]

In turn, Moshe thus served as a prophet (a spokesman) and a friend to the children of Yisra'el. To Moshe, Y'haweh gave the responsibility of becoming a steward of the Law of the absent King, who is our single eternal friend: Moshe comforted the Church—the Ecclesia—of Y'haweh and thus began the Church's edification of itself in love.

We may begin to understand the necessity of the Law of Moshe (that is, the King's Law), when we consider how we have alienated ourselves from Y'haweh by pursuing our own self-will. The very need for the Law simply advertises humanity's remoteness from Y'haweh, instead of their oneness with him in the Holy Marriage's first friendship.

For instance, while Moshe found the hallowed ground of the beautiful mountain of the Lord, the children of Yisra'el, whose consciences were alienated from Y'haweh, found quite a different mountain: they found a mountain that thundered and quaked—the trumpets of justice blaring against their pride, covetousness, jealousy, lusts, envy, malice, and all such sin that separate the unredeemed from the city of Y'haweh's glory. Indeed, the Cherub continued to guard Eden with his flaming sword. Even though Moshe had treaded upon holy ground and worshipped, the children of Yisra'el could not even touch the mountain with their fingertips. Moshe found forgiveness, because his heart searched for something beyond the world's strife; therefore, Y'haweh could readily appear to Moshe as Moshe's benefactor. Even so, the children of Yisra'el found a terrible mountain, because it was necessary for Y'haweh to show his power before them, in order to sanctify himself (that is, set himself apart) in their minds as the only true God. All in all, one may rightly conclude that even though the people readily beheld the mountain of Y'haweh just meters before them, their sin's alienated them from Y'haweh in such a way that the peace of Y'haweh still seemed to be trillions of kilometers beyond the stars.

---

[1] Exodus 33:11

Unfortunately, the children of Yisra'el merely sought an end to Pharaoh's oppression: often losing patience with Moshe, they repeatedly tried to return to Egypt or regain their worldly way of life. They could not perceive the true glory of Y'haweh that Moshe beheld. So while Moshe looked passed sin's veil through faith, the children of Yisra'el could not even behold the imputed countenance of Lord Yehoshua that Y'haweh had casts upon Moshe. In fact, Moshe even had to put a veil on his face when he appeared to minister to the people. Having been a prince in Pharaoh's house, Moshe had experienced the best that the worldly life had to offer. Nevertheless, he saw this world's continual compromise of conscience (especially the oppression of his people); therefore, he readily turned away from the world when Y'haweh gave him the salvation knowledge that Y'haweh conferred his sins upon another and justified him in the risen Lord Yehoshua. In contrast, the children of Yisra'el did not have the hearts to turn to the Lord, even though he had freed them from physical bondage.

What we may conclude is the following: it is a small matter for Y'haweh to exercise his power to overthrow Pharaoh's fertility cult, but it is a more tedious matter for Y'haweh to destroy the tyranny of sin, which secures its strength from the idols of the human heart; that is, the pride of selfish kings who become tyrants; the covetous and narcissistic spirits that transform aristocrats into oligarchs; and the incontinence of democrats who lust over the novelties and sensuality of popular culture. For this reason, Y'haweh must eternally judge the sins of this world and establish the eternal fidelity of the future world upon his grace. And so, we who gladly accept salvation knowledge (of our forgiveness and redemption in the Mashiach) look forward to dwelling in his Kingdom to come.

Like the Patriarchs of Heaven's Kingdom, Moshe invariably saw the riches of the Kingdom of Lord Yehoshua—the everlasting hallowed place that is not made with human hands. Still, we must recall that those who dwell in patriarchic lower-level civilizations cannot fully comprehend the splendor of all creation being enthroned as a savior; therefore, we cannot ascertain what degree of understanding the Patriarchs had of Lord Yehoshua's throne, because Y'haweh has only reserved excellent knowledge for us, his Church, who seek deliverance from the unjust higher-level civilizations. We do know, however, that the Patriarchs possessed the same salvation knowledge that we have inherited a better understanding of. They knew that "the wages of [Adam's] sin is death"[1], since they offered sacrifices hoping that Y'haweh would pass their sins unto others. To this end, they sought the eternal rest of their souls, because they understood that in this life there is only strife and labor, with only brief periods of rest; therefore, they sought a removal of the penalty of death that Y'haweh had conferred upon Adam. Besides, the Patriarchs knew that "Y'haweh is not a God of the dead, but of the living."[2] And so, seeking peace with Y'haweh, they sought the peace of a blessed new Adam.

After all, even the pagans, such as the ancient Egyptians, had knowledge of an afterlife; therefore, it should not come as a surprise to us that the Patriarchs shared an understanding of the resurrection through the promised seed of Avraham. Indeed, Avraham had certain knowledge of the blessed seed who would arise among his descendants and bless the families of the earth. Likewise, Ya`akov declared that unto Shiloh the people will be gathered. For this cause, the Patriarchs spoke of resting with their fathers upon their deathbeds, instead of speaking of death, itself. They all spoke of a hallowed ground: when they offered sacrifices in this life (their seeking eternal rest), they had some knowledge of eternal judgment and the corresponding eternal throne of the redeemer, our Lord. For example, Job the elder looked passed his own oppression and sickness and testified saying the following:

> For I know that my redeemer lives, and that he shall stand at the latter day upon the earth: and though after my skin worms destroy this body, yet in my flesh shall I see God: whom I shall see for myself, and mine eyes shall behold, and not another; though my heart be consumed within me.[3]

---

[1] Romans 6:23
[2] Matthew 22:32
[3] Job 19:25-27

Lastly, Moshe himself knew of the redeemer, since it was he who chronicled the lives and covenants of the Patriarchs: Moshe recorded Y'haweh's declaration that a new Adam will regain the old Adam's lost dominion and crush Satan under his feet. What is more, Moshe's record of the testimony of Bil`am the diviner speaks to Moshe's knowledge of Lord Yehoshua, because Moshe records that Bil`am foresaw the rise of a King from Yisra'el who would have dominion over all the earth.

The Law of Moshe: the Testator's Sanctification of the Church through the Commandment

Unlike Moshe, the children of Yisra'el did not have knowledge of their sins and the knowledge that Y'haweh extends to them his benevolent hand by forgiving their sins and giving them a redeemer who possesses eternal riches. When the people came to the mountain, their impure consciences, therefore, prevented them from seeing the benevolent gift of a heavenly testator. They could not see a glorious city descending from the heavens to reflect a righteous spirit that Y'haweh seeks to build up in them. They were too blind to see Y'haweh's good, because they could not appreciate Y'haweh's place of rest as all that they have strived for in righteous judgment with him. Nor could they appreciate the gift of Y'haweh as that which met all that they desired when they looked beyond personal temptations for the greater good of all: essentially, the Law seeks the liberty of Y'haweh's prevailing right judgment, which reconciles our intersubjective self-narratives in Lord Yehoshua's unblemished conscience.

For this cause, Y'haweh began to cultivate salvation knowledge within the children of Yisra'el: he exercised his power to overthrow their vanity, and he issued commandments to deliver salvation knowledge to the obedient. He first exercised his power to provoke the Egyptians to set the children of Yisra'el free, in the following way: Y'haweh commanded the Yisra'elites to kill a lamb for each of their families to feast upon in haste upon a determined night.

Because of their haste, he commanded them to bake unleavened bread, leaving no time to add the yeast that causes the bread to rise. More importantly, he ordered the children of Yisra'el to use the blood from the slaughtered lamb to cover the door posts and lintels of their houses: the blood of the lamb represented the condemnation of sin that Y'haweh passed unto others, and the innocence of the sinless lamb represented the unblemished conscience of Lord Yehoshua who would die and rise again to vindicate those who strove to be obedient to Y'haweh in faith.

And so, upon the determined night of the feast, an angelic destroyer passed over the houses of the redeemed and killed the first born of the Egyptians who did not have the Passover blood upon their houses. Then, in despair, the Egyptians let the children of Yisra'el go free.

To bring remembrance of their redemption from Egypt, Y'haweh commanded the children of Yisra'el to honor the month, in which he had delivered them, as the first of their months. In addition, Y'haweh commanded the Yisra'elites to initiate a Passover feast in the midst of the first month, featuring the lamb that Y'haweh had used to liberate them.

Now, it is important for us to understand that Y'haweh could have exercised his power by totally annihilating the Egyptians; however, Y'haweh only sought to give the Yisra'elites the following two understandings: first, because of their imputed sins, the Yisra'elites deserved the same judgment that the Egyptians had suffered; and, second, their liberty was the inheritance of the innocent redeemer who fulfilled their obedience, despite their imperfections. In other words, Y'haweh wanted to emphasize the fact that the blood that they struck over their doorpost was the blood of a testator whose liberty they inherited because they believed and obediently struck his blood upon their houses.

In addition, Y'haweh did not arbitrarily choose to kill the Egyptian first born, but he killed the best of the Egyptians to secure unto himself, for service, the lives of the Yisra'elite first born, because he had passed the judgment of the Yisra'elite first born onto the Egyptians. In fact, Y'haweh coveted the first born of the faithless children of Yisra'el to reflect the offering of the first born that Avraham willingly offered and Y'haweh redeemed by the blood of his ram, which he had held in the thicket. What is more, Y'haweh further showed his grace by replacing the Yisra'elite first born with Moshe's tribe (the Levites) to serve him. And this service was, itself, a blessing to the people as a whole, because when Y'haweh sanctified (set apart) the Levites for service, he began to inculcate the relationship of the Holy Marriage into their society. For example, when Y'haweh sanctified the Levites to conduct the worship of him by administering the Law and distributing sustenance to the poor, Y'haweh commanded the people to support the Levites, financially. In this way, he began to cultivate the roles of social benefactors and beneficiaries; moreover, these social roles correlated with Y'haweh's role of being the ultimate benefactor, because the Passover lamb—the same ram that Y'haweh had caught in the thicket—redeemed them all.

Because of their privileged status, the Levites should have appreciated the grace of Y'haweh that was upon them. In fact, Y'haweh had intended for them to find fulfillment in his Holy Spirit and, therefore, deliver honest judgments unto the people. In effect, Y'haweh had wanted the Levites to encourage the people to be faithful to the Covenant. To be sure, Y'haweh sought for justice and righteous judgment among the children of Yisra'el, as a whole, in order for them to overcome the scarcities that evil's dominion had laid before them, in the land of Canaan.

With this purpose in mind, Y'haweh began to build their trust in him by miraculously giving them sustenance in the midst of the desert, when they journeyed to Mount Sinai: he rained a bread-like substance from the heavens, which the children of Yisra'el named manna; moreover, he miraculously sprung water from a rock, exemplifying the fact that the true waters of life (that is, his Holy Spirit) springs forth from the rock of his truth and fulfillment, which New Yerushalayim dutifully displays. Y'haweh sought to gain the esteem of being their sole benefactor.

The redemption of the whole people through the blood of the sinless, Passover lamb and the redeeming of the Yisra'elite first born for service, ultimately affirms Y'haweh's esteem, in such a way that we ourselves fulfill the conventions of the Holy Marriage, because of Y'haweh's sacrifices: we first love Y'haweh who provides our redeemer; and, secondly, we love our neighbors through whom Y'haweh expresses his love, as we have said.

Thus, after Y'haweh brought the children of Yisra'el unto Mount Sinai to make himself a name and after he had made a covenant of obedience with them, he immediately instigated a law that perennially demands his esteem in their personal relationships with him (through the blood of the Passover lamb) and in their social relationships with one another, as his Passover lamb eternally redeemed them all.

In summation, when we consider the above along with our understanding of truth, we may conclude the following: Y'haweh's covenant relationship with the children of Yisra'el, ultimately, seeks his and our fulfillment in our personal relationships with him and in our communal relationships with each other; therefore, our appreciation for his providing our redeemer, who only fulfills the Covenant, brings Y'haweh and us fulfillment. Undeniably, one cannot possess a definitive understanding of the relationship between Y'haweh's sacrificed Lamb, the Covenant, and the Law, unless one understands that our observance of the Law does not uphold the Covenant nor establish justice among us. Instead, our desire for the righteousness of Y'haweh's Lamb upholds the Covenant and secures Y'haweh's grace among us all. Unquestionably, a true worshipper of Y'haweh must understand that Y'haweh's Lamb represents his righteous state of being; therefore, he establishes his Covenant upon our obedience, because our obedience reflects our desire for his righteous state, while the Law simply decries the inequitable actions that result from our ignorance. In addition, Y'haweh does not establish the Covenant upon our ability to fulfill the Law, because religious self-justification cloaks his benevolent hand and, thereby, shrouds his charity, which unites us. Instead, he establishes his Covenant upon our selfless desire for the Lamb's righteous state, which naturally fulfills the Law for us. In this manner, he empowers us to appreciate the justice of the Law: as we acknowledge our own misdeeds, our inability to fulfill the Law, humbly, compels us to accept the fruits of Lord Yehoshua's Holy Spirit; and then through a profound sense of appreciation, we naturally mature into Lord Yehoshua's righteous body, which the Law seeks. In the end, our purified bodies in the Lamb become the temple of Y'haweh's Soul, because Y'haweh ultimately seeks to fulfill the eternal desires of our hearts.

Essentially, what we must conclude is that when Y'haweh presented an unblemished lamb, a covenant of obedience, and a codified law, he both acknowledged our frailties and sought to mature us unto his transcendent state of fulfillment, by simply maturing our transcendent sense of appreciation for his charity. Accordingly, Moshe records the following words that Y'haweh said to him when Y'haweh began to seek the obedience of our hearts within his hearts fulfillment, as he initialized the covenant:

> "'You have seen what I did unto the Egyptians, and how I bare you on eagles' wings, and brought you unto myself. Now therefore, if you will obey my voice indeed, and keep my covenant, then you shall be a peculiar treasure unto me above all people: for all the earth is mine: And you shall be unto me a kingdom of priests, and a holy nation.' These are the words, which you shall speak unto the children of Yisra'el." And Moshe came and called for the elders of the people, and laid before their faces all these words, which Y'haweh commanded him. And all the people answered together, and said, "All that Y'haweh has spoken we will do." And Moshe returned the words of the people unto Y'haweh.[1]

Because we understand that Y'haweh has instilled in us the desire for the righteousness of Lord Yehoshua (which desire naturally compels us to fulfill the eternal righteous friendship that the Law seeks), we should not be surprised when human frailty often encumbers us from fulfilling the Law that Lord Yehoshua handedly fulfills for us. Likewise, we should not be surprised that even though the Yisra'elites had promised to be obedient and observe the

---

[1] Exodus 19:4-8

covenant, they could not possibly fulfill their promise, because they did not all have the salvation knowledge of the hallowed ground that Moshe had and that the Holy Spirit now gives us a better understanding of. We may rightly ask how could the people retain the knowledge of Y'haweh's holy place in their minds when life's temptations continually afflicted them with scarcity, despair, lusts, pride, fear, anger, and all the consequences of selfishness. Even Moshe struggled to retain the knowledge of the holy place of Y'haweh's Soul, because Y'haweh did not immerse him fully in his Holy Spirit like Y'haweh would fully immerse the new Adam. On the contrary, Y'haweh merely gave Moshe the knowledge of his salvation in the new, resurrected Adam, even as Y'haweh continued to condemn Moshe's flesh as being the figure of the old, disobedient Adam.

Too, we all, who love the appearing of the resurrected Lord Yehoshua, not only walk impart in the Holy Spirit, but also succumb to the temptations of the flesh, unwillingly; because our souls aspire to acquire Y'haweh's greater good, even though our flesh remains under Adam's condemnation, in this life. Essentially, the profound statement of Yeshua Bin Nun (who ruled immediately after Moshe) is true: Yeshua told the people, "You cannot serve Y'haweh; for he is a holy God; he is a jealous God; he will not forgive your transgressions nor your sins."[1]

Even now, like Moshe, we struggle to defy our fleshly lusts, while we continually repent to gain the riches of the risen Lord. In the end, we may readily assert the following fact: when Y'haweh made a Covenant with us, *the Yisra'el of Y'haweh*, he pronounced our disparity and made obvious our need for the redeemer that he provided to secure our desire, that is, our intuitive aspiration to reciprocate his love. For sure, the Law makes our frailties (and need to find completeness within him) evident. We may even agree with Sha'ul the Apostle who wrote the following:

---

[1] Joshua 24:19

I find then [in observing] the law, that, when I would do good, evil is present with me. For I delight in the law of God after the inward man: but I see another law [of condemnation] in my members, warring against the law of my [spirit filled] mind, and bringing me into captivity to the law of sin, which is in my members. O wretched man that I am! Who shall deliver me from the body of this death? I thank God through Yehoshua the Mashiach our Lord [who fulfills Y'haweh's Covenant and redeems us]. So then with the mind I, myself, serve the law of God; but with the flesh the law of sin.[1]

If we keep in mind the fact that we seek the just state of our souls (which we have no power to apprehend) and if we keep in mind the fact that Y'haweh expresses his equitable love that we cannot fully reciprocate, we may completely understand how Lord Yehoshua fulfills the Covenant for us. Basically, the Lord fully reciprocates the love of Y'haweh, because he is fully obedient; moreover, because Y'haweh raised him from death to reward his obedience, Y'haweh will raise us from death as well, because we pursue the Lord's justice in our hearts. At such a time, Y'haweh will clothe us with spiritual bodies, which Adam's condemnation can no longer hold captive.

We, therefore, must not despair at the true saying of Sha'ul the Apostle who said, "When the commandment came, sin revived, and I died"[2]; because Lord Yehoshua reconciles us with Y'haweh. No nation has approached the justice that the Covenant details; and no individual, like Moshe and the Patriarchs, have set his or her foot upon hallowed ground without first being obedient to Y'haweh, because of the salvation knowledge of Lord Yehoshua, who only upholds the first friendship with Y'haweh. Thus, we may likewise approach the hallowed ground, if we aspire to be obedient because of the salvation knowledge that Y'haweh instills within us.

To emphasize this truth, Y'haweh concluded his covenant with the children of Yisra'el by quantifying ten essential commandments: he quantified ten commandments to hone our perception of the just state of his first friendship; moreover, he quantified ten

---

[1] Romans 7:21-25
[2] Romans 7:9

commandments to demand that our communal relationships reflect the justice of the first friendship's esteem of him. He personally wrote the commandments upon stone tablets to show that they proceed from him, and he eventually sequestered the tablets away in a designated holy place among the children of Yisra'el to show that the true Promised Land of his fulfilled Soul has yet to be understood.

It is essential for us to understand that Y'haweh comprises his suzerain covenants with commandments and not laws, because his commands directly demand obedience. Our breaking his commandments does not only further condemn us, but also further condemn the constitutions of the nations that we observe in our lesser friendships, which entail social status and other forms self-aggrandizement. And so, the righteous Lord who fulfills the commandments (and, thereby Y'haweh's Soul) not only breaks the power of darkness in us who seek to be obedient, but also destroys the dominion of evil that covers the world.

With this understanding, let us now briefly look at the ten commandments of Y'haweh that seek the fulfilling of his love and foreshadow his justice in our communal relationships of this age: Y'haweh's qualifies the first commandment by indicating that he alone has delivered us from the oppressions of the Egypts of this world; therefore, he alone has provided our redeemer and forgiven our sins after he instills salvation knowledge in us to secure our obedience. Thus, he states his first commandment by saying, "You shall have no other gods before me", which is to say that we shall not worship anything other than him, because he alone is salvation.

To complement the first commandment, Y'haweh states his second commandment by saying, "You shall not make any graven image" of him or any other thing to worship; moreover, he qualifies this second commandment by saying that we shall not worship any other thing in the heavens, the earth, or under the earth, because he alone (who is justifiably jealous) fulfills all things. Additionally, he continues by saying that he shows mercy to whom he has empowered to fulfill his love, and he condemns others whom he has not. In essence, he prohibits the elect from quantifying him apart from the whole of creation, which expresses him: indeed, when we gain the salvation knowledge of him, his true beauty, fidelity, and glory pervade over the earth before our eyes.

With this object in mind, Y'haweh's third commandment—"You shall not take the name of the Lord your God in vain"—complements the first and second commandments, because we must esteem his name above everything, in order to reciprocate his love, which is our salvation in the Holy Marriage. What is more, being bolstered by the principal and leading three commandments, Y'haweh's fourth commandment is the first of the ten that directly commands us to observe such social behavior that reflects the eternal nature of his Rest in the Holy Marriage's first friendship: Y'haweh commanded the children of Yisra'el to "Remember the Sabbath day, to keep it Holy." Essentially, he wanted them to perform the labors of life in six days (as he labored for six days to create all things) only to rest on the seventh day with a fulfilled soul. By commanding them to hallow the seventh day of the week, he commanded them to seek the fullness of his Holy Spirit upon that day, perennially: he wanted them to be satisfied by the salvation that he had given them. So upon Shabbat[1], Y'haweh tacitly asked them to project all the enjoyable actions of their leisure time, to inspire them to seek and remember the true rest of his eternal Shabbat.

Expecting his elect to fulfill the reciprocity of his love, Y'haweh said that he "blessed Shabbat and hallowed it." In effect, Y'haweh related his delivering of the children of Yisra'el from Egypt with his delivering of us all from Adam's condemnation unto his actual Rest—his Shabbat.

It follows that the remaining six commandments, actively, reflect the justice of his Rest in our relationships, in this age. Y'haweh commands us to "honor our fathers and mothers," for they are those whom Y'haweh uses in his creative work. And so, they assume the role of being society's first nurturing agents, which reflect his role in the Holy Marriage of being our true benefactor. Next, Y'haweh commands us not to kill, saying "You shall not kill"; because when one murders, he or she not only murders a person whom Y'haweh

---

[1] The Sabbath

created in his spiritual image, but also figuratively robs Y'haweh of a relationship with the person in this life, even as Y'haweh perfects the relationship in the world to come.

Additionally, Y'haweh commands us not to commit adultery, because when we commit adultery, we defy the fidelity of our Holy Marriage to Y'haweh. As well, Y'haweh commands us not to steal; because in doing so, we deny the justice of the selfsame Holy Marriage. What is more, Y'haweh's ninth commandment seeks to uphold the justice of the Holy Marriage, as well: he prohibits us from bearing false witness against our fellows, for when we bear false witness, we assume the form of Satan who distorts the truth of Y'haweh's Holy Spirit.

Finally, Y'haweh's last commandment seeks to proclaim the essence of justice, itself, unto us whom he satisfies with salvation knowledge of him: even such knowledge that empowers us to look for his eternal salvation, even though we temporarily endure evil's scarcity in this life. Y'haweh commands us not to covet another's prosperity; he wants us to be satisfied with our life in him.

Evident is the necessity of the tenth commandment. From the unsatisfied soul proceed lusts, envy, malice, and all that temptation cultivates in the faithless who do not possess salvation knowledge of Y'haweh's good.

Our Obedience Seeking the Riches of the Holy Marriage

Although they are excellent and bear the utmost utility, the Ten Commandments cannot of themselves bring a person everlasting fulfillment simply by reading them. The commandments merely point to the excellence of the Holy Marriage in contrast to the defectiveness of the human condition that is due to disobedience. Of a truth, those whom Y'haweh fills with his Holy Spirit (after they gain his salvation knowledge and concurring education of the Law) do not need any commandments to fulfill the Covenant through obedience, since Y'haweh already weds their hearts to his beauty and justice. In contrast, those who eternally fall under the Law (which points out their perversions) display the absence of Y'haweh's fulfillment, within their souls, especially as they continuously embark upon disobedient and disorderly conduct.

By using the measure of our disobedience, we see that none of us who fall under Adam's condemnation truly possess the full complement of Y'haweh's Holy Spirit, in this age; therefore, all continuously break the commandments. None truly possess the knowledge of Y'haweh's glory over Eden. Only the new Adam, who has died, suffered, and remained obedient, inherits the full complement of Y'haweh's fulfillment in this age, as we have said.

We all fail to obey the first commandment daily, because we forget that Y'haweh is our only salvation in every aspect of our life. As we have noted, the human mind is unable to retain the glory of Y'haweh without the constant aid of his Holy Spirit. This inability is evident when we distress ourselves, longing after things and pursuits that bear no eternal fruit. In this manner, we compromise our consciences, being blinded by sin's selfishness. We then commit idolatry, disobeying the second commandment: we leave behind Y'haweh's true and eternal wealth, while we reach for such vanity that is fleeting and that we cannot possess eternally.

Here, we may know the gravity of taking Y'haweh's name in vain, because when we do not hallow his name as salvation, we fulfill his name when his law condemns us. In fact, Y'haweh made his truth evident to us when he defined his name to an inquisitive Moshe who asked to see his person. Answering, Y'haweh said the following:

> "I will make all my goodness pass before you, and I will proclaim the name of Y'haweh before you; and will be gracious to whom I will be gracious, and will show mercy on whom I will show mercy." And he said, "you cannot see my face: for there shall no man see me and live."
>
> And Y'haweh passed before his face, and proclaimed: "Y'haweh, Y'haweh God, merciful and gracious, slow to anger, and abundant in goodness and truth, keeping mercy for thousands, taking away iniquity, transgression, and sin, an not entirely leaving [sin] unpunished;

charging iniquity of the fathers on the children, and on the children's children, upon the third and fourth generations."[1]

By using our understanding of truth together with our lessons learned heretofore, we may readily understand the identity that Y'haweh proclaims of himself. First, let us understand that when Y'haweh said that he will make all his goodness to pass before Moshe, he naturally indicated that the completion of creation along with the redeemed actions of the elect ultimately celebrate Y'haweh's eternal fulfillment, which is the only true good. And because Y'haweh's expressed person in the Mashiach is the only unblemished conscience, Y'haweh only has the liberty to vindicate virtue or condemn all who fall under sin's vice; therefore, he proclaims, "I will show mercy on whom I will show mercy."

Accordingly, Y'haweh even says to Moshe that Moshe cannot see Y'haweh's face, since Moshe falls under sin, while Y'haweh chooses to show him mercy. Lastly, while we consider the fact that Y'haweh alone is good, we may now know why he proclaims his name to us in such a curious way: he is merciful, gracious, longsuffering, and abundant in goodness and truth to us whom he elects to find hallowed ground upon the whole of creation, during his eternal Shabbat. Yet, he is the judge of those whom he leaves under sin's condemnation, necessarily condemning the wicked actions that defy his eternal Rest.

Our life's aspiration should be our seeking the riches of Y'haweh's name as our salvation. Having salvation knowledge, we know that while Y'haweh possesses all the riches of creation, we gain such wealth according to the measure of knowledge and obedience that his Holy Spirit bequeaths to us, to fulfill his commandments like the Lord Yehoshua. For example, if we justly gain such earthly riches through industry that allows us to become benefactors of our fellows, we are rich with Y'haweh's charity. Also if we suffer earthly persecution unjustly, because we labor and remain true to Y'haweh's

---

[1] Exodus 33:19-34:7

just Holy Spirit, the light of our souls shines even brighter in the eternal Shabbat to come.

Here we may note the despair of the unredeemed nations, which stand outside "the commonwealth of Yisra'el"[1]: when an unredeemed person's conscience restrains him or her from committing some sinful acts and the person falls prey to abuse because of his or her passivity, he or she does not have redemption in the Mashiach because the person does not perceive the benefactor who raises the sinless, persecuted lamb to redeem the obedient acts of Yisra'el. Likewise, when the unredeemed nations secure wealth justly, they cannot retain the wealth, because the redeemed of Yisra'el who reside among them will offer the treasures of their life experiences to be redeemed by the King, who will then give them his inheritance of eternal life, even as the following scriptures proclaim:

> And it shall come to pass in the last days, that the mountain of the Lord's house shall be established in the top of the mountains, and shall be exalted above the hills; and all nations shall flow unto it.[2]
> And they shall bring your brethren for an offering unto Y'haweh out of all the nations.[3]

In particular, Y'haweh blesses and curses the nations throughout history, ultimately, to develop a relationship with us and build his relationship with Yisra'el, his Church bride. From his hardening of Pharaoh's heart (which afforded Y'haweh the opportunity to deliver Ya`akov's children) unto his giving the anti-savior over unto delusions (which will provoke Y'haweh to judge the higher-level civilizations of this world, as he delivers us), Y'haweh expresses his truth, having rested after he had predestined all things to fulfill his will.

It should not be a wonder to us that he elected Avraham to claim a tumultuous Promised Land as the place of the future capital of the Lord's peace. Also, it should not be a wonder to us that Y'haweh

---

[1] Ephesians 2:12
[2] Isaiah 2:2
[3] Isaiah 66:20

elected individuals and families that dwell in significant places throughout history (such as the world power of Rome) to establish the testimony of Lord Yehoshua throughout contemporary civilization.

We must, therefore, be eternally grateful that his salvation plan includes us in his work, as he draws out a Yisra'el of the Spirit, from all the nations, in order for them to worship him in truth. In addition, we must continually look past the temporal things of this world and hold true to his and our everlasting joy; since there are no greater riches than the love of Y'haweh who manifests himself as the faithful groom of the Church. When we are with him, we do not have to fear the darkness of life, because we possess the eternal light of his glory. As well, we do not have to suffer from hunger, because we possess the bread of life in the Christ; and neither do we thirst, because we are always replenished by the springs of the waters of his Holy Spirit, bursting forth in our hearts.

In the day of salvation, he will clothe us with spiritual bodies to prevent us from being tempted with the privations of the elements. He will feed us with the fruit from the tree of life.

Now we, having salvation knowledge of Y'haweh's true riches, must forever reconcile our activities with a mind that seeks a happy end with him, despite the temporary grieves and pleasures of this world. Unlike the unredeemed of this life, we must not judge our true wealth by the circumstances of this life. Instead, we must judge our wealth by the power and understanding that the Holy Spirit gives us to be obedient to Y'haweh's will, because our obedient souls seek the eternal riches of the Mashiach.

If we quickly consider the temporary poverty of the elder Job in comparison with the temporary wealth of the ancient Lydian King Croesus[1], the true wealth will bear itself out. An unredeemed person might regard the great misfortunes that temporarily plagued the life of Job as ill-fated and unfortunate; however, because Job remained reconciled with Y'haweh, we know that he actually increased his eternal riches because of his trust in the Lord. Equally, an

---

[1] Croesus reigned in the ancient Kingdom of Lydia around 568-554 BC.

unredeemed person might regard the affluence of the Lydian King as worthy of men's praise and something desirous; however, we know that an unredeemed person who possesses wealth in this life is truly unfortunate, since the shadow of temporary wealth tempts the person away from seeking true, eternal happiness. Furthermore, we may say that Job has a happy life, because he retains an eternal good, while King Croesus has an unhappy life, since although he tried to hold the phantom of happiness, he actually grasps eternal despair.

The brief accounts of these two men brilliantly attest to the nature of true happiness. For instance, King Croesus learned the hard way not to presume himself happy (in this life) until he had fulfilled the end of his days, happily. During the height of his reign, he boastfully showed the Athenian lawgiver, Solon, all his riches and asked Solon whom did Solon deem the happiest man of all whom Solon had met throughout his travels. To Croesus's dismay, the wise Solon answered saying that three others were the happiest men that he had known, since they had ended their lives in health, all having done great deeds for their perspective countries and families and having gained respect in the memories of those whose lives they have affected.

Wisely, Solon noted that many vicissitudes accompany a person in his or her seventy-year life span. More often than not, he noted, there is no measurable differences between the contentment of a wealthy person and a common person when they both possess their basic necessities without too much labor. For sure, the wealthy man is better suited to buffet life's physical calamities, Solon continued; however, sickness and disease affects all the same, and all have an equal chance to possess beauty.

Solon then began the conclusion to his answer by saying that scarcity prevents individuals from enjoying all of life's advantages, as no country possesses all its needs and wants: he even noted that "oftentimes *god* gives men a flicker of happiness, and then plunges them into destruction."[1] And so, he concluded that the country or

---

[1] Herodotus: the Histories, the first Book *Entitled Clio*

individual who retains the most advantages unto the end of his life span is the happiest.

Regrettably, at the time, Solon's reply annoyed Croesus. But, in the end, Croesus, himself, came to recognize the wisdom of Solon after Croesus had found himself defeated and about to be burned alive by his adversary, Cyrus, the great King of Persia. Woefully, Croesus even lost his beloved sons and fortune, and now at the last his life was in jeopardy. When his captors ignited the flames of the pyre that held him bound, Croesus in grief cried the name Solon three times, finally realizing the profundity of Solon's wisdom, in light of the ignominy that he was suffering. Yet, fortunately for Croesus, when Cyrus heard of Solon's prescience, he freed the defeated Croesus, hoping that he, himself, would not one day come to Croesus's end.

Like most who cherish the vanities of this life, Croesus was poor, indeed; however, Y'haweh has not bound us to his fate. Y'haweh has given us the understanding not to cherish those articles that we cannot truly keep, because vanity withers like spring flowers upon the winter season of lost prosperity.

The Elder Job had like understanding. He bore the same dramatic worldly losses of King Croesus, and still Job remained as wealthy as before, because his wealth remained constant in the heavens. We have noted his testimony that he knew that his redeemer lives; therefore, we know that Job had placed his hope on the eternal good and not on the fickle fortunes of humankind. Although he lost riches, children, and health, his testimony concerning the Lord remained the same: he said, "Y'haweh has given, and Y'haweh has taken away; [still] blessed is the name of Y'haweh."[1]

Truly, blessed are they who put their trust in him. So in like manner, let us affix our praise, poetry, art, song, and all acclamations on the eternal good of Y'haweh and not on the sundry lusts of human appetite. By committing to Y'haweh the celebrations of leisure time that our virtuous actions afford, we will reconcile our lives with him who is perfect and unchanging. Thereby, the darkness

---

[1] Job 1:21

of social chaos, which forever springs from insatiable lusts, will no longer hold us captive, because Y'haweh will perfect us in Lord Yehoshua who only fulfills the eternal state of righteousness for us. Likewise, Lord Yehoshua will judge the fleeting vanities of humanity, which vanities results from their disobedience to his Law, when the measure of our "obedience is fulfilled."[1]

The eternal riches that inspire our steadfast obedience to Y'haweh's will is that of a fulfilled bride who fully appreciates the beneficence of her husband, who provides her with love, appreciation, safety, and shelter. In fact, Y'haweh is he who not only gives us a husband who has died for us (allowing us to obtain his eternal wealth), but also gives us his Holy Spirit (surrendering to us the understanding to appreciate his sacrifice). Y'haweh, therefore, has set the supreme government of the Holy Marriage upon Lord Yehoshua's shoulders, because he enforces or upholds what Y'haweh's Holy Spirit determines to be the good for all unto the Totality of Y'haweh. Thereby, Lord Yehoshua reconciles all creation with our instilled desires and aspirations unto Y'haweh's Rest, that is, his fulfillment—his dwelling in a Holy Temple that comprises all creation.

The Four Phases of Y'haweh's Interim Government

We see how multifaceted our relationship with Y'haweh is as we journey through truth's landscape. We find that through Lord Yehoshua, Y'haweh is our Creator, Justifier, Friend, and Governor. Also, we have yet to find that through Lord Yehoshua Y'haweh is our Righteous King, High Priest, and the Husband of the entire true worshipping body of the faithful. To this end, let us understand that upon the realization of truth, Y'haweh's fulfillment comprises an eternal and holy temple in our Holy Marriage to Lord Yehoshua, the Savior; moreover, in the Holy Temple is the eternal splendor and wealth of our souls.

We take comfort in our happy end, even though we only see the evidence of Y'haweh's Holy Temple within our hearts. Still, we must

---

[1] 2 Corinthians 10:6

rest assured that the splendor of Y'haweh's presence will cover the world when Lord Yehoshua regains Adam and Havah's lost dominion. Unlike Adam and Havah who could not appreciate Eden as the Holy Spirit's prevalent habitation (by their appreciating Y'haweh's communion with them), we like Moshe will exult the Savior who has borne our sins and vindicated our faith: we will readily relinquish all the labors that compromise our consciences. Then we will rest in the "beauty of holiness"[1], having a salvation knowledge of Y'haweh, even dwelling upon hallowed ground.

Having joy in the Body of Lord Yehoshua, who fulfills the commandment, we will no longer suffer the condemnation of Havah, who issued forth from the flesh of her husband Adam and still fell prey to temptation because she found no fulfillment in Adam. On the contrary, we will find fulfillment in the salvation knowledge of our Lord Yehoshua, even the Immanuel who knows "to refuse evil and choose the good"[2]; because our spiritual, resurrected bodies will issue forth from the resurrected Lord Yehoshua—the new Adam.

For now, we may enjoy his lordship in our personal relationships with him, and we may feel his consolation when we commune with a believing assembly. Until all who are elect receive the salvation knowledge of the Savior, we must wait to experience Lord Yehoshua's future government over the earth. Indeed, we must wait to walk upon a new hallowed earth that our praises will fill because of our joy in the Holy Marriage—the very Temple and fulfillment of Y'haweh.

In this age, however, we can only witness an interim government of reconciliation that Y'haweh initiated when the children of Yisra'el accepted his Covenant but could not relate to him, directly. Fearing the thundering mountain, the children of Ya`akov asked Moshe to mediate between Y'haweh and them. Their not having the appreciative sense of the hallowed ground, the children of Yisra'el instinctively sought for someone who not only fulfilled the Law for

---

[1] Psalm 29:2
[2] Isaiah 7:15-16

them, but also instructed them patiently without immediately condemning their transgressions.

We must qualify our description of Y'haweh's interim government of reconciliation by citing the following fact: because Y'haweh exists in a state of eternal righteousness, it is obvious that he sought the same eternal state in his elect body of worshippers when he issued his Ten Commandments to the children of Yisra'el. In regards to the first commandment, we must say that it is not enough for the children of Yisra'el to remember him as salvation some of the time; and in regards to the tenth commandment, we must say that it is not enough for Yisra'el to be satisfied with the good of Y'haweh (and, therefore, not covet their neighbor's property) only some of the time. If we only consider the fact that Y'haweh seeks the fulfillment of his Law and Soul, perennially (and, therefore, eternally), we would comprehend the nature of the Holy Marriage that is Y'haweh's very Holy Temple: doubtless, Y'haweh wants us to know that he delivers us from the Egypts of this world all the time. Beyond question, he wants us to hallow his name as the quintessential beauty of creation in a perennial day of rest. Furthermore, he wants us to know that he is our Holy Father, who joys over our Holy Marriage to Lord Yehoshua; because in such a fulfilled marriage unto him, there is no hatred, and all share things in common. For this cause, there is honesty, for all find satisfaction in his good. Truly, such is the fulfillment of the Ten Commandments, and such is the Totality and Temple of Y'haweh.

In order for the children of Yisra'el to assume the form of being Y'haweh's Holy Temple, Y'haweh had to pronounce the disparity between his righteous state of being and the Yisra'elites' precarious hold upon virtue, through the Yisra'elites' momentary faithful actions. Thus, we may identify Y'haweh's interim government as that which governs the following relationship: first, through revelations and proclamations to the Yisra'elites, Y'haweh proclaims his righteousness through his commandments; and, second, the elect repentantly receive Y'haweh's revelations and proclamations, while they edify one another and gain an eternal appreciation for Lord Yehoshua, their righteous savior and heavenly husband. To this end, the appreciation of the elect for Y'haweh's savior personage is the very love that fulfills the Holy Marriage's righteous first friendship and eternal government; and it follows that such a government does not need any commandments, because the bride and groom reconcile themselves directly with conscience and, therefore, one another's hearts. And so, in this age, Y'haweh, by declaring his righteousness through the commandments, had consigned his worshippers to embark upon a perennial state of repentance until Lord Yehoshua secured for the elect Y'haweh's righteous state through, first, Lord Yehoshua's mortal death in the stead of the elect and, second, his subsequent resurrection to redeem the faith of the elect with his salvation.

We identify four distinct phases in Y'haweh's interim government, and all the phases accompany a tabernacle that symbolically draws a distinction between this age of reconciliation and the future eternal Kingdom of Heaven; moreover, each phase supersedes the preceding phase, as Y'haweh matures his worshippers. At the same time, a succeeding interim tabernacle inaugurates each new phase, until the eternal government of the Holy Marriage stands as Y'haweh's enduring Temple, upon the completion of the human experience.

We may quantify the four phases as follows: we identify the interim government's first phase as being comprised of the Levite Priesthood's administering of the Covenant unto the people, while the people supported the priesthood and tabernacle through their tithes and offerings. In this way, the social relationship between the Levites and the people simulated the Holy Marriage's benefactor-beneficiary relationship, at the inception of Yisra'el's lower-level, agrarian civilization. Then when the camaraderie of the Levites' relationship with the people had faltered and Y'haweh had found no hospitable dwelling place in the strife of the backslidden people, he began the second phase of the interim tabernacle.

It follows that we identify the second phase of Y'haweh's interim government as the House of David's rule over the children of Yisra'el. In this phase, Y'haweh issued a suzerain covenant with a Yisra'elite monarch to solidify Yisra'el's new higher-level civilization around the worship of Y'haweh, in accordance to his covenant relationship. Through his relationship with the obedient and god-fearing King David, Y'haweh further defined his Covenant with Yisra'el: Y'haweh proclaimed to King David that the new Adam would be a descendant of his; moreover, Y'haweh allowed King David to establish a permanent resting place for his tabernacle in the earthly city of Yerushalayim, upon the mountains of Tziyon, where Avraham had offered Yitzchak for sacrifice.

When the sons of King David did not uphold Y'haweh's covenant relationship between him and the children of Yisra'el, Y'haweh initiated the third phase of his interim government to purge his Kingdom and tabernacle, globally. We identify the third phase of Y'haweh's interim tabernacle government as the global priesthood of Lord Yehoshua, whose priesthood supersedes the Levite priesthood, because Lord Yehoshua fulfills the Covenant in such a way that (through the power of his resurrection) he empowers whom he wills to strive for the eternal good, within and outside of the Kingdom of Yisra'el. Indeed, Lord Yehoshua empowers whom he wills from all classes to become the sons and daughters of Y'haweh, despite the corruptions of his interim tabernacle and the secular, global beast that seeks to suppress the true worship of Y'haweh. And so, we understand that when the secular, global government will attempt to suppress the true worship of Y'haweh (after the true worshippers preach the good news of Lord Yehoshua's sacrifice), Y'haweh will begin to judge the world, and he subsequently will begin the fourth and last phase of his interim government.

At the last, we identify the fourth phase of Y'haweh's interim government as the reign of Lord Yehoshua—the King of Righteousness—who will reign for a thousand years, in which period he will vindicate the faith and righteous judgment of him and his elect before the conquered world of the unbelieving. Following, when humanity by nature rejects his reign, Y'haweh will eternally judge the guilty, while he consummates the Holy Marriage by giving us the gift of New Yerushalayim—his eternal tabernacle among men. In this way, we will find the loving husband that our souls seek.

The Interim Tabernacle of Testimony and Reconciliation

In its very first phase, Y'haweh's interim government begins to define the glory of the final government. Subsequently, throughout the successions of the governments and Y'haweh's concurring revelations of himself to us, we grow in appreciation of his beauty and love. In the first phase of the his interim government, Y'haweh sanctifies the children of Yisra'el unto himself, as we described above, to be the holy nation that Lord Yehoshua will eventually govern, eternally.

To show the disparity between him and the children of Yisra'el, Y'haweh instructed Moshe to construct a tabernacle—a transient tent that shelters wandering nomads—to characterize the unfulfilled relationship that he has with the children of Yisra'el, in this temporary world. To underscore the transitory nature of the tabernacle, Y'haweh instructed Moshe to separate the tabernacle into two separate compartments: one elongated, rectangular-prism compartment that begins at the doorway of the tabernacle and another equitable cube shaped compartment quarantined off at the rear of the tabernacle and separated from the first compartment by a veil. The first elongated compartment represents our growing relationship with Y'haweh through our repentance and appreciation of his good; and the cube shaped compartment represents our reconciled relationship with him in the Kingdom of Heaven, the Holy Place that is the first friendship of Lord Yehoshua's unblemished conscience, which reflects Y'haweh's good and holiness as the prevailing of right judgment over the inter-subjective perspectives of our lesser friendships. Most importantly, the veil that prevents our entering into the last compartment (even though we may readily enter into the first through repentance) is the veil of sin that only Lord Yehoshua rips open for us upon his sacrifice and subsequent resurrection.

To understand the function of the tabernacle definitively, we must understand the fact that Y'haweh designed it and its accompanying laws and sacraments to underscore the priceless value of his mercy and grace: it is through his mercy that Y'haweh gives us his Holy Spirit, which empowers us to appreciate the sacrifice of Lord Yehoshua; moreover, the sense of appreciation that the Holy Spirit gives empowers us to turn away from our selfish volitions and value the true good of the Holy Marriage. Essentially, we must understand that the Holy Place of Lord Yehoshua's unblemished conscience sanctifies the religious articles of the remainder of the tabernacle, which articles and acts fail to amount to the eternal value of the unblemished Lamb; therefore, the Holy Place sustains the orthodoxy of right belief rather than the orthodoxy of right practices.

Having this understanding, we should not be surprised that at the heart of the tabernacle is a symbol that expresses the following: to appreciate the mercy of Y'haweh through the sacrifice of him who is sinless is to gain the fulfilling Holy Spirit of Y'haweh's love—the only thing that fulfills the Law; therefore, to gain the redemption of the Savior is to gain access to the true Promised Land, and that is to dwell within Y'haweh's angelic body. For this cause, Y'haweh named the very symbol that expresses his coveted mercy, the *mercy seat*, which he positioned at the central point of the cubed shaped room that he in turn named the most holy place; that is the Holy of Holies.

The mercy seat is essentially a cover that Y'haweh told Moshe to place upon an ark that Y'haweh instructed Moshe and the children of Yisra'el to build for the purpose of sequestering the unfulfilled Ten Commandments. Interestingly enough, the main physical features of the mercy seat are the two cherubim that Y'haweh instructed Moshe to have sculptured on the top of the mercy seat, to cover the unfulfilled laws: this symbolic gesture betimes compels us to declare that until Lord Yehoshua sacrificed himself and so empowered us to worship Y'haweh in truth, the heavenly angels only witnessed Y'haweh's glory, because they are of his body: only the angels unabashedly witness the good of his Holy Spirit prevailing over the Eden that the cherub still guards with the flaming sword.

From this profound symbol, we know that in order for us to dwell in Y'haweh's Totality behind the veil, we too must be of the Lord's Body by denying our own bodies. Through Lord Yehoshua, we may see past the veil of sin that Y'haweh casts upon us when he imputed the sin of Adam upon us. Indeed, we may see past the veil because Lord Yehoshua frees us (the sometimes disobedient) by his being obedient. Essentially, we must understand that our hope then lies in the bosom of the Lord—Y'haweh's sacrifice—because through him we fulfill the commandments and, therefore, Y'haweh himself. In this way, we assume the place of the two cherubim by becoming a covering for invisible Y'haweh in the Body of Lord Yehoshua.

To this end, Y'haweh had instructed Moshe to place a golden incense altar immediately outside the veil that separates us from the most holy place, until Lord Yehoshua fulfilled his commandments and so freed us. Also, Y'haweh had commanded the Levites to burn special incense, continually, to represent the prayers of the elect who pray for the coming of Lord Yehoshua's Kingdom—the very Temple of Y'haweh upon earth.

In fact, as the golden incense altar symbolically represents our prayers and hope for the Kingdom, we the elect fervently pray for the mercy of Y'haweh to empower us through his Holy Spirit that we may flee from the committing of trespass. Likewise, we pray to overcome temptation, while we seek the Kingdom that resides behind the veil.

Even so, let us remind ourselves that we who turn away from the temporal pleasures of this world can only do so because Y'haweh empowered us from the beginning to find satisfaction in his Temple: he predestined us to partake upon the fruit of the tree of life that stood in Eden, bears fruit in us presently, and now forever abides on the other side of the veil of sin, until we appreciate the risen Lord who will give us the fruit of life, liberally.

With these thoughts in mind, we may appreciate and fully understand the remaining two symbols in the elongated room of the tabernacle, which symbols stand adjacent to the incense altar. In actual fact, the remaining two symbols define one another's function: the first symbol is a golden lamp stand that has one standing post with seven horizontal candle tops situated upon golden blossoms, which in turn rest upon what Y'haweh calls seven branches. Also, to light the candles, Y'haweh commanded Moshe to make special oil.

Next, the second symbol directly faces the tree-like lamp stand from the opposite side of the room. The symbol is a golden table that holds twelve fresh loaves of bread, representing the twelve tribes of the children of Yisra'el. Y'haweh, in fact, calls the bread, the bread of presence (that is, the Show Bread).

To understand the symbolism of the candlestick and table, let us first acknowledge the following fact: while Y'haweh provides the tree of life for us whom Lord Yehoshua empowers to uphold the commandments (through our love for Y'haweh and one another because of Y'haweh), Y'haweh will provide the sustenance of life in this world of scarcity, as well, especially when we forsake the lusts and inequitable deeds of the faithless. Also, knowing that the elongated room represents the interim period of our growth in the knowledge and righteous judgment of Lord Yehoshua the Savior, we may interpret the symbolism of the golden table and lamp stand in the following way: first, we see that Y'haweh instructed Moshe and the priests to display the bread of presence before him on this side of the veil to bear witness to the fact that Y'haweh ultimately provides the sustenance of life for Yisra'el, despite human industry; therefore, our recognizing that he is our provider (*Y'haweh-yireh*), we must strive always for his true riches that eternally stand behind the veil, whether we are physically prosperous in this life or not. Also, when we know that he is our provider, we hold within our hearts the right value system that sees the beauty of him in creation, even while sin shackles us to this backslidden world. Essentially, having knowledge of his mercy, we gain the purest form of knowledge and begin our approach unto the tree of life, as witnessed by the seven burning candles of the tree-like lamp stand.

It follows that the lamp stand, with seven candles upon seven blossoms and branches, represent our increasing knowledge and growth in the Holy Spirit. Also, the oil that lights the lamps is a symbolic representation of the Holy Spirit, himself: the seven candles exemplify the Holy Spirit's completeness. Too, the plant life sculptured on the lamp stand represents Y'haweh's glory, which nature expresses and which we have yet to perceive, fully.

Plus while we are speaking of the glory of Y'haweh, we must note the symbolism of the tabernacle covering. Knowing that that which is precious—the fulfillment of Y'haweh—is symbolically housed inside the most holy place and knowing that the mercy of Y'haweh allows us access into the holy place through the sacrifice of Lord Yehoshua, we may define the coverings of the tabernacle in the following way: the outer covering is that of seal skin, representing the Body of Lord Yehoshua. Next, within the outer covering is a covering of ram skin died red, representing the blood sacrifice of the Savior—the lamb of Y'haweh. Following is a covering of goat's hair—a covering that represents our sins, which the blood of the lamb takes away. Lastly, the covering that actually covers the wooden structure of the tabernacle (which covering, one may see inside) is an attractive tapestry of blue and scarlet, decorated with cherubim to represent the habitation of Y'haweh as that which is the most beautiful of all.

To complete our understanding of the King's Law—the Law of Moshe—and to summarize the myriad of laws that accompany the tabernacle and the Ten Commandments, we must first sum up the overall message in Y'haweh's building of the tabernacle. We may summarize the overall message of the tabernacle by citing what we have defined as truth itself: from our definition of truth, we understand that Y'haweh expresses his good in the Mashiach's unblemished conscience, and we understand that Y'haweh expresses his love by redeeming our faith in the Testator's fulfillment. Like so, we understand that Y'haweh's eternal good—truth's priceless pearl—inspires us to forsake the temporal goods that now hold our affections. And so, we see that the very good that we find in his mercy is the gift of an eternal, felicitous life: the reward of the obedient new Adam, who even died for us in obedience to Y'haweh's will. Thus, we may say that the whole purpose of the tabernacle is to grow our appreciation of the sacrifice and reward of Lord Yehoshua, since our appreciation for his salvation behind the veil affords us the ability to sacrifice our selfish lives, while we seek his redemption: that is, the testator's inheritance of Y'haweh's eternal joy.

So to inspire them to appreciate his mercy, through which he freely gives us the testator's inheritance upon our personal sacrifices, Y'haweh commanded the children of Yisra'el to observe such sacraments that reflect the eternal sacrifice of Lord Yehoshua. Using the sacraments, Y'haweh began to reconcile the world unto himself by, first, demanding the observance of his sacraments from the children of Yisra'el and, second, demanding repentance from the whole world after Lord Yehoshua fulfilled the Law through his sacrifice.

To begin with, Y'haweh commanded the children of Yisra'el to observe three sacramental feasts in recognition of his benevolence to them: he commanded them to observe the Feast of Unleavened Bread, through which they remembered their deliverance from Egypt. He commanded them to observe the Feast of the First Fruits, through which they recognized that he is the sole provider of their economy. Lastly, Y'haweh commanded them to observe the Feast of Harvest, through which they again observed his benevolence. More importantly, Y'haweh also commanded Moshe and the priests to build a brazen altar in front of the tabernacle to recognize the fact that the wealth of the children of Yisra'el is that of the innocent one whom Y'haweh sacrificed to bear their sins and gain his eternal reward; therefore, a symbolic understanding of the multiplicity of animal sacrifices that Y'haweh commanded the priests to offer upon the altar in the stead of the Savior will be the end of our survey of the Law:

While we recognize the fact that the heart of the heavenly government resides in the fulfilled Law of the heart behind the veil, under the cherubim, we must also recognize the fact that the heart of the interim government of Testimony and Reconciliation resides in the service of the altar, which reconciles the virtuous actions that we perform by faith with the righteous state of the Savior, who offered his blood upon the mercy seat and so ripped the veil of sin apart to vindicate our faith. To symbolize the state of his righteousness, Y'haweh commanded the Levite priests to offer certain sacrifices perennially, like he commanded them to burn the seven candles on the lamp stand and the incense on the incense altar, perennially. Seven days a week, they offered sacrifices in the morning and in the evening.

It was necessary for the priests to offer these sacrifices, perennially, because although the faithful seek redemption, sin's imputation inclines them to recommit the same sins, perennially, either because of ignorance or temptation. For this cause, their consciences are not always pure before Y'haweh who (through Lord Yehoshua) seeks to become the groom of a perennially pure bride.

Wonderfully, because all the people's sacrifices did not amount to the sacrifice of the Testator, the sacrificial system pointed to the fact that the people's upward social mobility stood upon faith and righteousness instead of material wealth or social standing. Thus, a worshipper must understand that only Lord Yehoshua the Savior can continually uphold a pure conscience for us. He only needs to sacrifice himself once. Because Y'haweh resurrected him again, he will resurrect us without Adam's burden. In this manner, Lord Yehoshua will forgive us and purify our consciences. Then we will gain his new Adam's body, and Y'haweh will have a perennially pure bride.

The wonder of the brazen altar is that we see the children of Yisra'el repenting of their personal sins that they have committed through faithless actions. At the same time, we see them gaining fellowship with him, whose eternal offering, the Levites seek to reflect in their perennial offerings. In point of fact, we see two worlds coming together, at the brazen altar.

To reconcile the people's actions with the equity of his enduring Kingdom, Y'haweh put forth certain casuistic (conditional) and certain apodictic (commanding) judgments that sought justice not only in the people's contemporaneous, economic relationships, but also in the people's perpetual communal relationships. To fulfill his good end, Y'haweh commanded the people to observe certain purity rites, in order for them to seek the pure riches of Heaven, despite whatever economic and social novelties that usually temp prosperous individuals away from the pursuit of his enduring equity. Y'haweh sought to instill an aesthetic sense of wholesomeness in them, in order for them to complement the natural order of his creation. In other words, he compelled the people not to pursue such perverse novelties of popular culture that have no bases in the salvation knowledge: that is, such knowledge that appreciates utility and comfort as blessings from Y'haweh, who alone relieves us from the labors of life. Y'haweh, in effect, prohibited those superficial pleasures that people covet when they do not seek an eternal good for all.

In his judgments, Y'haweh recognized the industry of those prodigious persons who gained wealth, honestly. He only expected them to foster the equitable distribution of goods and services to all: Y'haweh expected them not to covet earthly wealth above charity for the suppliant. For this reason, Y'haweh advertised the true wealth behind the veil, in order for them to desire fellowship with him over ill-gotten gains. Thereupon, Y'haweh forbade the oppression of workers and foreigners.

Furthermore, the offences that directly defied the glory of Y'haweh and his eternal Holy Marriage incurred the ultimate punishment of death: Y'haweh did not allow people who committed these crimes to offer the sacrifices at the altar that Lord Yehoshua redeems. The crimes committed against Y'haweh that incurred the death sentence are of such things like witchcraft, murder, enslavement, and blasphemy—the worship of other invented gods or the worship of oneself, in defiance of Y'haweh. As well, there are the sins of perverse sexuality and sensuality that defy the equity of the Holy Marriage, such as homosexual or lesbian intercourse, pedophilia, gross fornication, adultery, rape, and bestiality: these sins incurred Y'haweh's judgment.

The purity rites that Y'haweh instituted, to cultivate a sense of decency that would deter the people from pursuing sexual or other sins, were of such things that actually concern dietary habits or social and personal hygiene. Y'haweh prohibited the people from eating animal fat, scavenger animals, or animals that do not filtrate their waste well. Also, he prohibited the people from handling animal carcasses, unnecessarily.

In addition to the purity rights of the body, Y'haweh initiated sacraments to cleanse the people's perceptions of how they should relate to the natural order of the earth. For instance, to display his eternal charity, Y'haweh made allowances for the children of Yisra'el to retain the inheritance of their land. Correspondingly, he instituted seven year Sabbaths, in which he commanded the people not to farm the land, in order for the land to replenish itself. And so, in this period of time, Y'haweh expected creditors to relieve workers from their labors and debts, in order for the workers to rest in Y'haweh's good, as well. In like manner, Y'haweh instituted the year of Jubilee to be recognized after every 49 years: upon the year of Jubilee, people regained their family's inheritance, despite their debts.

Altogether, Y'haweh's Sabbaths foreshadow our enduring rest in the Kingdom of Heaven; moreover, the people's appreciation of the Sabbaths reflected their knowledge of the hallowed Spirit of Y'haweh—the essence of creation, itself. We may make such a claim, because when the people faithfully adhered to the Shabbat, they exhibited their knowledge of Y'haweh being their provider. In addition, they showed by their observing the Shabbat that they valued the good and rest of Y'haweh above their personal lusts.

Those who sought the eternal blessings of Y'haweh readily brought their offerings and tithes: they brought peace offerings, seeking fellowship with Y'haweh; they brought money to uphold the priesthood and worship of Y'haweh, at the tabernacle; they brought sin offerings, seeking to be cleared of their impurities; and they brought trespass offerings, seeking to be forgiven for the wounds that they inflicted upon their neighbors and the wounded Savior.

Y'haweh commanded the priests to receive certain offerings of the people, while he received the most significant offerings himself: the priests ate the offerings of the people and so satisfied themselves with the wealth of the people, as Y'haweh found satisfaction in their worship of him. Through their sense of appreciation for their privileged status, Y'haweh had intended for them to comprehend the beauty of his mercy seat.

In point of fact, we see the image of Lord Yehoshua in the High Priest of the Levites, whom Y'haweh dressed in a garment of precious stones, like the original adornment of the proud cherub, before his fall: for sure, the High Priest prefigured the eternal High Priest, Lord Yehoshua, whose cross fulfilled all the offerings on the Day of Atonement, that is, Yom Kippur. You see, Y'haweh commanded the High Priest of Yisra'el to acquire two goats, along with an ox, to sacrifice for the sins of both the priests and people upon the seventh month of the year. The High Priest sacrificed the ox for his sins and one of the goats for the people's sins, and he conferred all the sins that the children of Yisra'el committed upon the other goat, which he subsequently set free to wonder in the wilderness. Symbolically, the first goat died for the transgressions of the people, and the second goat carried their sins away. In this manner, Y'haweh finally allowed the High Priest to enter into the Holy of Holies on that single day to sprinkle the blood of the goat upon the mercy seat, simulating the finished work of the Savior, who forever proclaims, "It is accomplished."[1] Thus, as the odor of the animals and the scent of the incense ascended unto the heavens, Y'haweh affirmed his fulfillment by smelling the repentance of his people.

More importantly, it follows that he finds his eternal fulfillment, in this manner, when we repent by accepting the sacrifice of his only begotten son. There are many understandings that we may draw out from the Law of Moshe; however, the essential understanding that we must possess is that our Day of Atonement—the Day of Salvation—stands before us perennially in this age, because of the sacrifice of Lord Yehoshua. Essentially, the Law seeks to impress the understanding upon the children of Yisra'el that they should seek the true wealth that Y'haweh holds in the bosom of Lord Yehoshua, their husband. To this end, we may conclude our understanding of the Law by noting the fact that Y'haweh commanded the people not to have social or economic relationships with the surrounding cultures of Canaan, because the economic bonds of debt and service would invariably yield exploitation or the lusts for untoward lifestyles that betray the salvation knowledge of Y'haweh. It would then follow that the children of Yisra'el would commit adultery against the sovereign Lord. And then the people would lose the Sabbaths that clearly point to the heavenly Rest.

To prevent their fall, Y'haweh even commanded the kings of the people not to esteem themselves above the people. He wanted them to seek true wealth, while they benefited the people charitably with

---

[1] John 19:30

their *god* given talents. For this cause, Y'haweh prohibited the kings from pursuing their own glory.

Nevertheless, knowing that the Yisra'elite Kings would break his Covenant in the tumultuous land of Canaan, Y'haweh foretold the eventual establishment of his enduring tabernacle by having Moshe to say the following:

> Y'haweh your God will raise up unto you a Prophet from the midst you, of your brethren, like unto me; unto him you will listen; According to all that you desired of Y'haweh your God . . . saying, "Let me not hear again the voice of Y'haweh our God, neither let me see this great fire any more, that I die not." And Y'haweh said unto me, "They have well spoken that which they have spoken. I will raise them up a Prophet from among their brethren, like unto thee, and will put my words in his mouth; and he shall speak unto them all that I shall command him. And it shall come to pass, that whosoever will not hearken unto my words which he shall speak in my name, I will require it of him."[1]

When we consider the Prophet that Moshe spoke of in the above scripture, it becomes obvious to us that Moshe did not speak of any ordinary prophet, because he said that the people would revere the Prophet like they revered him: Moshe alone was the single ruler of Yisra'el who gathered the people before Y'haweh in solidarity; therefore, Moshe spoke of the Shiloh that Ya`akov spoke of. In addition, when Moshe made the above statement, he did not mention the people's adherence to the Law, which he had just laid before the people. Moshe, in this way, indicated that the words of the Prophet (that is, Lord Yehoshua) would reverberate in the hearts of the elect, not with the Law but with the Spirit.

Righteous Judgment

Our encounter with the commandments of Y'haweh, which include the Ten Commandments and the interim tabernacle sacraments, can be burdensome or liberating, depending upon how we value the sacrifice and eternal wealth of the redeemer. At times, we lust for

---

[1] Deuteronomy 18:15-19

another's spouse, visage, or material goods. Too, at times, we insult or injure another, being angry: we often seek to undermine another's welfare, because of bitterness or jealousy. When we are comely and industrious as social constraints bind us, we think that the Law robs us of what should be rightfully ours: being blinded, we think that the Law deprives us of the fleeting satisfaction of the lesser friendships, even though the Law points us to the eternal friendship of righteousness; therefore, the Law annoys us when it condemns our adulterous, covetous, and violent thoughts. Still, at other times the hypocrisy of our flesh is obvious when we seek the comfort of Y'haweh's Law after evil's dominion robs us of what makes us happy. When we are meek, persecuted, or suffer loss, we begin to see the charity of the Law, and finally the thoughts of our past sins become grievous to our newly endowed consciences. Then, wonderfully, Y'haweh empowers and purifies our souls, in order for us to empathize with others. Thereafter, we grasp humility and thankfulness, seeking only to stand upon the hallowed ground of Y'haweh's Temple, that is, within the sinless lamb—our Mashiach.

Knowing that our redeemer sits behind the veil, we eat the bread of presence because we realize that the heavenly City (where is the presence of Y'haweh) stands no longer beyond the stars. Instead, the truth of Y'haweh approaches our very hearts, even as the following scripture declares:

> For this commandment that I am commanding you today is not hidden from you, neither is it far off. It is not in Heaven that you should say, "Who shall go up for us to heaven, and bring it unto us, that we may hear it, and do it?" But the word is very near unto you, in your mouth, and in your heart, that you may do it.[1]

Upon the disposition of our hearts stands the righteous judgment of him whom Y'haweh enthrones upon the mercy seat of his Temple. Here, we may know the full quality of Y'haweh's mercy seat: Y'haweh calls it a mercy seat because Lord Yehoshua does not

---

[1] Deuteronomy 30:11-14

determine his righteous judgment simply by identifying the contrast between his perfect soul (which fulfills the Ten commandments under the mercy seat) and our imperfect souls (which defy the Law because of imputed sin); because if drawing such a contrast were the extent of his judgment, all would perish, except him; and there would not be a true appreciation for the world that is due to his mercy. Fortunately for us, Lord Yehoshua says, "God did not send his son into the world to condemn the world; but that the world through him might be saved."[1]

Essentially, Lord Yehoshua establishes his righteous judgment by identifying with the broken or unfulfilled souls whom Y'haweh has inspired to find satisfaction in the world to come. And so, they appreciate his grace, and then they reciprocate his love; as the scripture says, "The sacrifices of Y'haweh are a broken spirit: a broken and contrite heart, O Y'haweh, you will not despise."[2]

Y'haweh glorifies himself by showing mercy to the needy. It is evident that the humble who appreciate Y'haweh's grace are they whom Y'haweh elects, as the Apostle Sha'ul notes, "There are not many wise men according to the flesh, nor many mighty, not many well-born, that are called: for Y'haweh has chosen the foolish things of this world to confound the wise; and Y'haweh has chosen the weak things of the world to confound the things, which are mighty . . . that no flesh should boast in his presence."[3]

The proud find confidence in this world system, while the simple look beyond for the golden city in the sky. It follows that Lord Yehoshua's righteous judgment of private individuals is the same judgment that he uses for communal assemblies and nations, as a whole. When a nation is young and humble, the nation seeks the mercy of Y'haweh; and when the nation grows strong, it defies the laws of Y'haweh, even blotting his sacred name from its public circles.

---

[1] John 3:17
[2] Psalms 51:17
[3] 1 Corinthians 1:26-29

For this cause, Y'haweh severely punished the Kingdom of Yisra'el when she grew strong, prosperous, and ungodly. Y'haweh did not necessarily punish her for her sins, because she had always needed to appear before the brazen altar, perennially. On the contrary, Y'haweh needed to stricken her in order for her to appreciate the mercy seat of his power. In this manner, the landscape of truth unfolds to its good end:

As nations rise and fall, some individuals gain salvation knowledge and some seek satisfaction in the things that perish. In the end, Y'haweh fills his eternal Kingdom with us who seek mercy and consolation from him who is able to fulfill and administer the Law to our hearts. Overall, Y'haweh fulfills his statement, in which he said, "I will be gracious to whom I will be gracious, and will show mercy on whom I will show mercy."

Essentially, Y'haweh creates our souls (and subsequent life experiences) to become the vessels of his Holy Spirit, as the following scripture indicates:

> Willing to show his wrath, and to make his power known, [he] endured with much long suffering, the vessels of wrath fitted for destruction . . . that he might make known the riches of his glory on [us] the vessels of mercy, which he had before prepared unto glory.[1]

For sure, Y'haweh prepares our hearts to seek his forgiveness and comfort, while others do not seek redemption. Instead, they despise the Law and expect for him to accept the self-centered choices that they make.

The Fifth Revelation of Y'haweh: *He is the King of Righteousness*

We may make the above statement because we know that the meek of the children of Yisra'el, whom Y'haweh endowed to find their hope in the Law, certainly looked for the righteous opened hand of one who could enforce the Law, justly. They sought a governor who

---
[1] Romans 9:22-23

could empathize with their problems and watch over their interests like a husband cares for the welfare of his wife and a shepherd guards his flock.

Because of the successive backsliding of the children of Yisra'el, the elect of Yisra'el could not find social benefactors among the people. For this cause, the tenure of the interim tabernacle's first phase was not exhausted when some of the people could not appreciate Y'haweh's holy place and bring sacrifice. Instead, the tenure of the first phase was exhausted when the Levite priests—the first born of Yisra'el—could not appreciate the holy place and guide the people, justly.

Because of their weak rulers, the people continuously backslid from the worship of Y'haweh; moreover, the people no longer appreciated Y'haweh as their governor. Broken families, inequality, over farmed lands, oppression, crime, poverty, and a host of other social ills ensued. Then because of the societal chaos within Yisra'el, the neighboring powers, surrounding the land of Canaan, easily exploited the people and the land.

To make matters worse, the people valued the style of government of their oppressors over their own. They assumed that the foreign powers were stronger, solely because of the earthly gains of the greedy, warlike pagan kings. In essence, the people did not acknowledge the fact that their downfall resulted from a lack of protection from a very jealous Y'haweh, whom they failed to appreciate.

So to secure his name as the salvation of Yisra'el, Y'haweh brought the elect of the children of Yisra'el one step closer to appreciating fully the mercy seat of Lord Yehoshua: Y'haweh selected a king to shepherd his people, like the Savior. To appoint the king, Y'haweh cultivated the love of David ben Yishai[1]: Y'haweh expressed his love to David to ensure that King David valued the Law over personal volitions, in order to rule the people justly.

To mark him whom Y'haweh chose, Y'haweh used the oil that fuels the tabernacle's seven candlesticks to anoint David before the

---

[1] David the son of Jesse

people: as the seven candles upon the tree-like lamp stand represents the fullness of Y'haweh's Soul upon the Sabbath day of creation's rest, the oil that fuels the lamp represents the selfsame Holy Spirit that fulfills us and gives us rest. As an outcome, the true Savior, Lord Yehoshua bears the title of the anointed one—the Mashiach, whom Y'haweh chose to be the Savior of the world—because Lord Yehoshua, like a shipmaster, only perceives Y'haweh's glory in creation and retains eternal satisfaction for those whom he guides.

While keeping this understanding in mind, we realize that Y'haweh created an anointed king by anointing his heart with the Holy Spirit: Y'haweh cultivated a sense of appreciation in the king that he selects. To this end, Y'haweh did not choose anyone because of his or her personal qualities, since all fall short of his glory, except Lord Yehoshua. So he selected the person whom he endowed with an appreciative sense, which approaches the salvation knowledge of his good. Fulfilling his purposes, Y'haweh chose David over his older brothers, like he elected Ya`akov over Esav. In fact, David's family was humble among the families that descended from Yehuda, Ya`akov's son. Even so, Y'haweh endowed David with faith, and then Y'haweh gave him opportunities to advance in rank to inspire the people: Y'haweh gave him the faith and courage to overcome his personal enemies, as well as the enemies of the people.

Eventually, King David not only solidified a god-fearing nation to rule over the contentious Land of Canaan, but also subjected the surrounding nations to pay tribute to his kingdom's economy. What is most important, King David conquered Yerushalayim, the fortress city of the mountains of Tziyon,[1] and he made Yerushalayim the capital city of Yisra'el. David even brought the tabernacle there.

King David accomplished these things because he first loved Y'haweh above his own desires. He desired the riches behind the veil and, therefore, he found no fulfillment in robbing his people, as other rulers did. Instead, David found fulfillment in the righteous judgments sequestered behind the veil. Wonderfully, his testimony is as follows:

---

[1] Zion

> One thing have I desired of Y'haweh, that I will seek after; that I may dwell in the house of Y'haweh all the days of my life, to behold the beauty of the Y'haweh, and to inquire into his temple.[1]

King David loved Y'haweh so much that he aspired to build Y'haweh a permanent stone temple in Yerushalayim to replace the transient tabernacle; however, Y'haweh's answer to King David is most precious to us, as we will here note: Y'haweh told King David that David could not build a temple because David gained his kingdom by the sword, while the true Mashiach, Lord Yehoshua, will build Y'haweh's Kingdom and Temple by securing the devotions of the heart. In this way, Y'haweh's Temple will cover the earth.

Still, to honor the relationship that Y'haweh secured with his people through King David, Y'haweh made a covenant with David, declaring that David's immediate son would build an interim temple of stone and the Mashiach will be a descendant of King David; moreover, Y'haweh told David that the Mashiach will build an eternal Temple of the Holy Spirit: Y'haweh declared that the Mashiach will sit upon King David's throne, having built Y'haweh's eternal Temple of the heart that will endure. What is more, King David, himself, would come to understand that this messianic descendant of his is his own redeemer: after King David finally succumbed to temptation by committing adultery (and even murdering the husband to cover his adulterous relationship), King David realized the fact that if he could not remain a good shepherd of all his people all the time, a descendant of his would not be able to shepherd the people any better, unless Y'haweh filled the descendant with his Holy Spirit all the time, even from birth until death, like the sinless Lord. This David declared about the Mashiach:

> Your Kingdom is an everlasting Kingdom, and your dominion endures throughout the generations.[2]

---

[1] Psalm 27:4
[2] Psalm 145:13

In consideration of King David's profound insight, let us here note that the King of Righteousness, who is King David's Lord, qualifies our fifth revelation of Y'haweh. Of a truth, Y'haweh in the person of Lord Yehoshua is the only Righteousness King.

We must, therefore, admire the faith of David, despite his imperfections. Although David sinned greatly and bolstered the doubts of the faithless, King David's devotion to Y'haweh grew stronger, and he began to understand Y'haweh's profound election of the true worshippers. In his early days, David wondered why the Lord was so gracious to him: he asked, "Who am I, O Lord Y'haweh? And what is my house that you have brought me here? And this was but a small thing in your sight, O Lord Y'haweh, for you have spoken also of your servant's house for a great while to come."[1]

King David may have even supposed that only the integrity of his heart secured Y'haweh's blessings, because David was faithful beyond his peers. Yet, after he sinned so greatly (even above the same peers), King David knew that all men including himself needed a redeemer, despite his past walk of integrity; therefore, he sought redemption anxiously saying, "Create in me a clean heart, O God, and renew a right spirit within me. Cast me not away from your presence, and take not your Holy Spirit from me. Restore unto me the joy of your salvation, and uphold me with your free Spirit."[2]

At the last, King David realized that he had only obtained Y'haweh's grace, in order for Y'haweh to glorify himself by gaining David's appreciation and subsequent salvation knowledge in concert with the elect, whose sins Y'haweh blotted out, as he blotted out David's sins. So, instead of wondering why he obtained the grace of Y'haweh, King David declared, "Blessed is he whose transgression is forgiven, whose sin is covered. Blessed is the man unto whom the Lord does not impute iniquity, and in whose spirit there is no guile."[3]

---

[1] 2 Samuel 7:18-19
[2] Psalm 51:10-12
[3] Psalm 32:1-2

David finally realized the fact that the very temple in Yerushalayim, sitting upon mount Tziyon, will be an eternal Shabbat place. David recognized that the Temple will house those who obtain Y'haweh's grace from the mercy seat of the true Mashiach.

The Sixth Revelation of Y'haweh: He is the Priest who gives the Holy Spirit of Truth

After he gained a mature understanding of the tender mercies of Y'haweh, King David became so filled with Y'haweh's Holy Spirit that he began to see with clarity the nature of the throne of the true anointed one, whom Y'haweh fills with the Holy Spirit, always. David began to understand the true desire of Y'haweh's heart, which David then sought to fulfill. In the Spirit of the true Mashiach, King David wrote the following:

> Sacrifice and offerings you have not desired; ears have you prepared for me; burnt offerings and sin offerings you have not required; then said I, "Lo, I have come," in the volume of the scroll it is written of me. To do your will, my God, I have delighted; and your law is within my heart.[1]

In the early years of his rule, King David zealously sought to abide by Moshe's Law, which commanded the kings of Yisra'el to be students of the Law; however, when King David realized that he could not fulfill Y'haweh's desires completely, he began to perceive even more the glory of the true Mashiach's throne: David's reign hailed the beginning of Yisra'el's higher-level civilization, a civilization that could appreciate the splendor of creation being enthroned as salvation. And so, when David saw his own Kingdom's failures, he knew that Y'haweh truly opened his hand to Yisra'el, using the eternal King to come. As well, King David realized that Y'haweh would reconcile both the failure of the Levite priesthood and the backsliding of the children of Yisra'el in the following way: Y'haweh would accept the new Holy Spirit filled King as the only Priest of the people, and then this priestly King and Mashiach would

---

[1] Psalm 40:6-8

write the Law of Y'haweh on the backslidden people's hearts and so fulfill the eternal Temple.

David's own words testify of David's knowledge of these facts as follows:

> Y'haweh said unto my Lord, "Sit yourself at my right hand until I make your enemies your footstool. Y'haweh shall send the rod of your strength out of Tziyon: rule in the middle of your enemies. Your people shall be willing in the day of your supremacy, in the beauties of holiness from the womb of the morning: you have the dew of youth." Y'haweh has sworn and will not repent, "you are a priest forever after the order of Malki-Tzedek."[1]

In consideration of Y'haweh's oath to the Mashiach, we will qualify our sixth revelation of Y'haweh by recognizing the fact that, in the Mashiach, *He is the Priest who gives the Holy Spirit of Truth*. Thereby, Lord Yehoshua alone receives our prayers, and he alone mediates between our Father Y'haweh and us.

The Purge of the Tabernacle

King David's prescience hallmarked the prescience of others whom Y'haweh cultivated a relationship with, despite the fall of the subsequent generations of peoples and leaders. Upon a generational Shabbat (that is, fourteen, generations after Y'haweh made a covenant with Avraham), King David's devotion inspired an elect body from the children of Yisra'el to perceive the true benevolent form of Y'haweh in the foreseen Mashiach. In those whom Y'haweh endowed to appreciate the benevolent throne of the Mashiach, Y'haweh for the first time possessed a figure of the Holy Spirit filled Body of Christ that will comprise the bride of the Holy Marriage.

The new Spirit filled people often cried out against the children of Yisra'el when the Yisra'elites compromised the covenant relationship: the Spirit filled people found encouragement in the Holy Spirit's proclamation of the future consolation and vindication of their faith by the righteous King to come. Moreover, these Spirit

---
[1] Psalm 110:1-4

filled people exercised the gift of prophecy, which means to bubble forth the Holy Spirit that flows from the heavenly city. Essentially, they had great foresight, like King David: they perceived the hallowed ground of the coming Kingdom.

In fact, we would be remiss if we did not note that the foresight that Y'haweh cultivated in King David was extraordinary: David learned to value more the coming equity of the Mashiach than the worldly gains of popularity, sensuality, or riches. The fact that David found value in a seemingly theoretical, overall good (that he could not readily grasps) over the immediate pleasures of the flesh (that the people even had expected him to entertain) exhibited his salvation knowledge of the good behind the veil. What is more, the salvation knowledge that the tabernacle symbolically testified of seemed obscure to most, because the events of both the Exodus and the Passover had occurred above four hundred years prior to King David's era; therefore, the value of rigidly observing the seemingly arcane and unyielding religious laws seemed untenable to many Yisra'elites.

King David's peers probably thought that he should have spent his energy on enlarging his kingdom instead of seeking a heavenly Kingdom. What most historians fail to realize is that King David could have easily exploited the weaknesses of his neighbors: if he followed the manner of other kings, he could have committed genocide by killing all the elite males in the surrounding countries and possessed their lands. Truly, to a worldly king in David's situation, such an unjust deed would have seemed strategically advantageous, because David would have acquired more defensible lands for his people. Perhaps the succeeding Yisra'elite Kings, as a whole, could have maintained such unjust deeds to solidify an inequitably Yisra'elite empire. Fortunately for us King David was obedient to Y'haweh: he stayed within the bounds of the Promised Land, in order for Y'haweh to fulfill his purpose by subjecting the Yisra'elites to foreign influences, while Y'haweh both judged the children of Yisra'el and the foreign powers, to magnify his grace upon the elect.

For this cause, we must harbor a profound sense of appreciation for the children of Yisra'el, because Y'haweh could have birthed the promised messianic descendant of King David early, and Y'haweh could have concluded the Holy Marriage with the prophets of Yisra'el who dwelt in the Kingdom of Yisra'el with David's immediate descendants. Still, if Y'haweh would have birthed Lord Yehoshua early and opened the children of Yisra'el's hearts to accept him, we who were outside the commonwealth of Yisra'el would have perished in our sins without redemption, while Y'haweh vindicated his blessing on them. Fortunately for us, Y'haweh determined to birth the Mashiach at such a time when the world could receive him.

Y'haweh, himself, testifies to the fact that he sought to redeem the world through the Mashiach, instead of redeeming just the children of Yisra'el. Y'haweh said the following unto the Mashiach:

> It is a light thing that you should be my servant to raise up the tribes of Ya`akov, and restore the preserved of Yisra'el: I will also give you for a light of the Gentiles, that you may be my salvation unto the end of the earth.[1]

And so, it is for our sakes that Y'haweh did not immediately fulfill his promise to King David by allowing his successor, King Shlomo,[2] to build Y'haweh an everlasting temple. Instead, Y'haweh allowed King Shlomo to build a fixed, stone interim tabernacle in Yerushalayim to signify the fact that Lord Yehoshua will locate the capital of his Kingdom of Peace at the most contentious place in the world. In this way, he will magnify his mercy seat by changing the most contentious land into a place of tranquility that celebrates the glory of Y'haweh. Witnessing this fact, gold poured into Yerushalayim's strong economy from many parts of the Mediterranean and Middle East, during Shlomo's godly reign.

Despite this fact, it follows that Shlomo himself pondered the wisdom of trying to confine the glory of Y'haweh into a single place. He asked Y'haweh the following:

---

[1] Isaiah 49:6
[2] King Solomon the son of King David

> But will God indeed dwell on the earth? Behold, the Heaven and Heaven of heavens cannot contain you; how much less this house that I have built?[1]

Shlomo justifiably raised the question because the fact is that Y'haweh cannot dwell in any single place: he can only dwell in the love and appreciation of his worshippers, whom he gives the salvation knowledge that appreciates him throughout the world. In fact, Y'haweh's promise to Avraham that Avraham's seed would become a blessing unto the families of the whole earth still remained for Y'haweh to fulfill, even though Y'haweh fulfilled another promise to Avraham, by allowing Avraham's descendants to rule the land of Canaan: although the children of Yisra'el had worshipped him tentatively on mount Tziyon, he still needed to spread his tabernacle over the Earth.

Again, let us recall the fact that Y'haweh could not cultivate the sense of the eternal bride's appreciation for his benevolent form (in the Mashiach) among all the children of Yisra'el, if they expected his mercy by right of an earthly inheritance. Under such circumstances, the children of Yisra'el would have no need to value the Lord's righteous judgment, because they would have obtained salvation by inheritance. Unto the elect of the children of Yisra'el, Y'haweh adds many sons and daughters from all the families of the world, through the seed of Avraham who redeems them and, thereby, blesses the whole earth. Speaking to the redeemed of Yisra'el who will inhabit the Holy City of Tziyon, Y'haweh himself said, "The Gentiles shall come to your light, and the kings to the brightness of your rising."[2]

We have only to discover how Y'haweh obtains his glory over the earth, as he transforms the interim tabernacle into the Body of Lord Yehoshua: namely, the marriage that is Y'haweh's eternal tabernacle. To begin, let us first recall the transitory nature of the interim tabernacle: let us understand that the interim tabernacle initially

---

[1] 1 Kings 8:27
[2] Isaiah 60:3

stands in the midst of the children of Yisra'el and finally stands in the hearts of all who refer to its symbolism, while they are reconciling their lives with Y'haweh through Lord Yehoshua. We may underscore the transitory nature of the tabernacle by saying that the tabernacle does not establish righteousness: it only points to him who establishes righteousness, as he judges inequity and redeems those who Y'haweh empowers to appreciate his righteousness.

Y'haweh uses the Lamb's judgments of the tabernacle to vindicate the redeemed of Yisra'el or condemn the faithless of Yisra'el whom he left under sin's condemnation. At the same time, he forecasts his mercy upon the redeemed of the world through the Mashiach. In addition, he forecasts his judgment upon the faithless of the world through the Mashiach.

When the elect of Yisra'el, such as the prophets, had perceived the equity of the Holy Place and when the prophets sacrificed their best for its eternal riches, the elect of Yisra'el gained the same Holy Spirit that Lord Yehoshua gives to us who forsake our worldly aspirations, while we pursue the common good of the Body of the Lord. In like manner, when the faithless of Yisra'el compromise Y'haweh's Law by pursuing the vanities of popular culture, despite the staple needs of the poor and socially castigated, Y'haweh judges them like he will judge the inequitable higher-level civilizations of the world.

We may recall that because Adam broke Y'haweh's covenant and so subjected humanity to the mirage of self-determination, Y'haweh reserves the right to be gracious to whom he likes. By right, Y'haweh blessed some by giving them his Holy Spirit to secure their love for him; and by right Y'haweh withheld his Holy Spirit from others to establish his grace upon his elect, as we have said before. When he withholds the grace of his Holy Spirit, Y'haweh then purges his tabernacle by necessarily judging the unjust ruling bodies of humanity. At the same time, he purifies the elect with his Spirit: he does not withhold the Holy Spirit from us, because he does not withhold the Holy Spirit from the Mashiach whose body we abide in.

We witness unjust ruling bodies among the self-serving rulers of Yisra'el who did not regard the welfare of the common people, throughout the fourteen generations that Y'haweh allowed them (the descendants of Avraham) to rule. Correspondingly, we witness unjust ruling bodies among the self-serving rulers of the world, whom the leaders of Yisra'el imitate: these, too, Y'haweh judges because his true tabernacle is the whole of creation, which our souls perceive.

After the death of King David, the Yisra'elite rulers (whom Y'haweh did not fill with his Holy Spirit) lusted for the popular culture that manifested from the inequitable courts of foreign kings and aristocrats. First, Y'haweh withheld somewhat of his Holy Spirit from Shlomo: Y'haweh did not cultivate the same salvation knowledge in Shlomo like he did with David, Shlomo's Father. Afterwards, when foreign ties and relations seduced King Shlomo and the succeeding Kings of Yisra'el away from the worship of Y'haweh, the leaders stop benefiting the people, and the nation fell apart, having no vision of the glory of Y'haweh. The rulers valued worldly things more than they valued Y'haweh's salvation: they valued the vanities of prestige, class, privilege, and all such things that the Church tries to prevent among its congregation.

Because the Kings of Yisra'el idolized things above Y'haweh's salvation, they made horrible economical choices, which made the scarcity of the land even direr. The Yisra'elite rulers fancied sensual pleasures and status symbols over the common good. While they robbed people of their wealth, they wasted goods and resources, impoverishing the land. For instance, the rulers often forced the commoners to labor on expensive building projects. At the same time, they dispossessed the people of their inheritances. Also, the rulers often forced the people to turn out produce for foreign powers in order for a subjugated Kingdom of Yisra'el to pay tribute to its conquerors. As a result, the prices of the staple needs of the poor increased; therefore, disparity grew between the upper class and the impoverished.

While foolishly idolizing a popular culture that ignores the plight of the poor, the rulers ignored the Sabbaths of Y'haweh, which Sabbaths seek to liberate the selfsame poor and the land. The rulers defied the Sabbaths because they sought to gain money, in order to pay for their sensual vices or pay off debt.

Also, the daughters of Yisra'el forsook chastity and virtually began to prostitute themselves before the covetous rulers and foreign nobles. Basically, the whole land lost our third hallmark of liberty, as inequity colored the land with whoredom: the result of the people's self-serving decisions.

To make matters worse, false prophets ministered to the King's court for prestige and monetary gain, while the Levite priests continued to perform their religious sacraments, despite the upheaval of the Covenant that the sacraments pointed to. In the end, the twelve tribes of Yisra'el broke apart because they became weak: they became indifferent to the truth of the tabernacle, while the avarice of foreign powers grew strong. Initially, ten of Yisra'el's twelve tribes went into captivity, and then the tribes of Yehuda and Shim`on, which governed Mount Tziyon's Yerushalayim, went last.

And so, after the fourteen generations of the earthly sons of King David's rule, Y'haweh expelled the children of Yisra'el from the land to purge his tabernacle of the corrupt rulers and priests. He fulfilled his promise to condemn those who do not uphold his Law. At the same time, Y'haweh began to fulfill his promise to Avraham: Y'haweh began to bless the families of the earth with Avraham's elect descendants, whom Y'haweh spread around the world. Wonderfully, the children of Yisra'el whom Y'haweh dispersed across the region, brought to the nations the light of Y'haweh's Law and the knowledge of repentance unto one sovereign God—Y'haweh—who provides the means of redemption through his grace.

Furthermore, for us whom Y'haweh gifts with salvation knowledge to appreciate his benevolent form in Lord Yehoshua, the Yisra'elite Diaspora brought with them the writings of the prophets who not only cried out against the injustices of the Kings of Yisra'el and the rulers of this world, but also foretold the manner in which the Mashiach would appear to identify with the faithful and persecuted. The prophets declared the following manner in which Y'haweh would prune the vineyard that he planted, which did not yield the fruit of his Spirit's tree of life: they declared that Y'haweh would prune the corrupt leaders, priests, and false prophets from the elect, as Y'haweh only accepts his humble suffering servant who will bear the sins of many and then faithfully rule as a wonderful counselor.

We learn, in this manner, how the Savior will establish the devotions of the Holy Marriage; and we learn how he will purge the Temple of those who do not appreciate it. Essentially, the most important message that we glean from the prophetic proclamations concerning the Mashiach is the understanding that he will not rule over his people by force. Instead, he will become the ruler of the elected hearts. We find this understanding in the writings of the prophet Yirmeyahu[1] who records Y'haweh's declaration of a new covenant with his people, in which he would write his laws on their hearts. Correspondingly, the prophet Yesha`yahu declares that Y'haweh would effect the New Covenant by first putting the Mashiach on the earth in an humble form to undermine the covetous rulers and priests who would not receive the Savior as the Mashiach, because of his unpopular form.

As we shall detail further below, the prophets essentially declared the following in their writings concerning the Mashiach: because the rulers of Yisra'el persecuted and murdered Lord Yehoshua, the Lord now readily identifies with the lowliest of the people. In actual fact, he too was poor, impoverished, unattractive, and sorrowful. And so, because Y'haweh resurrected him and made him, eternally, more beautiful than any other creature (because of his righteousness), Lord Yehoshua now encourages the outcast and persecuted of civilization, whom Y'haweh empowers to seek his salvation in a renewed Holy City that sits upon Mount Tziyon. In this vein, Yesha`yahu writes the following:

> Out of Tziyon, the perfection of beauty, God has shined. Our God shall come, and shall not keep silence: a fire shall devour before him, and it shall be very tempestuous round about him. He shall call to the heavens from above, and to the earth, that he may judge his people. "Gather my

---

[1] Jeremiah

saints together unto me; those that have made a covenant with me by sacrifice." And the heavens shall declare his righteousness: for God is judge himself.[1]

The Diaspora, Hellenism, and Anti-Semitism

In the Spirit of the above scripture, let us say that in the vanguard of Y'haweh's light that shines out of Tziyon is the Law; moreover, what we may glean from the scripture is that the fire of Y'haweh's righteousness shall devour those who do not desire his judgments. Thus, we may rest assured that those who make a covenant with him through the Mashiach shall behold his light and beauty.

To describe how Y'haweh kindles his light out of Tziyon, let us first make the following statement: in the same manner in which the advent of the Law proved to be both a blessing and a curse to the children of Yisra'el, the Diaspora of the children of Yisra'el proves to be a blessing and curse to the higher-level civilizations of the world that receive the children of Yisra'el, whom Y'haweh expelled because they had broken his covenant. As Y'haweh had expelled Adam and Havah from his presence to gain ultimately their appreciation, Y'haweh expelled the Yisra'elites to gain ultimately their appreciation of the sacrifice of Lord Yehoshua, whose Spirit always abides in the heavenly manifestation of Eden.

We may describe the blessing that the Yisra'elites gained in the Diaspora, in the following way: instead of possessing a weak political identity as a nation among unredeemed nations, the children of Yisra'el established a reinvigorated spiritual identity within the nations by observing their faith; even while they were in the midst of foreign persecutors. The conquerors of the children of Yisra'el often had attempted to break Yisra'el's kindred family links; therefore, only the faith of the Yisra'elites firmly redefined and established their identity among their oppressors. Having their former corrupt, monarchic leaders replaced by foreign ones, teachers of the Law arose to prominence among the Diaspora communities. The leaders began to quantify the holy books and subsequent oral laws,

---

[1] Isaiah 50:1-6

systematically, to teach the remnant of the people. The end result was that the common people of the Yisra'elites became more knowledgeable in exile than the commoners had been in the former Kingdom: they began to contemplate the meanings behind the sacraments abstractly, without performing the sacraments themselves, due to the loss of the Temple. What we may conclude is that although foreign rulers persecuted them, the children of Yisra'el became even more blessed than they had been before, and the Gentiles who observed their prosperity came to the light of Y'haweh and became blessed as well.

Still, to identify further the blessings and cursing of the light of Y'haweh's Law that the children of Yisra'el carried with them into the Gentile nations, we must assess the order of the nations themselves: to realize this end, we must acknowledge the writings of the prophets who give us lucid detail of how the initial phase of Y'haweh's purge proceeded for another fourteen generations when the children of Yisra'el first brought the Law into the Mesopotamian and Mediterranean worlds.

First, if we keep in mind the natural process of innovation and integration (which process is an effect of the works of the prodigious who direct the course of history, either by benefiting others or by benefiting themselves), we may understand the proclamations of the prophets and the manner in which Y'haweh purges the nations. Too, we must keep in mind the fact that Y'haweh initially spreads the righteous judgments of his Law, and then he reconciles the elect through his suffering servant, who suffers at the hands of those who do not keep the Law.

Let us quickly refer to the writings of the prophet Daniel, to whom Y'haweh explained the order of the nations and his subsequent purge of the nations: Y'haweh gave Daniel a vision and an interpretation of the vision to record his purposes for our understanding. In the vision, Daniel saw a splendid statuesque idol that had the form of a man, who represents the course of the international, ideological powers that unfold human history: during the time periods that the idol symbolically depicts, Y'haweh reconciles his elect, while he completes his purge of the tabernacle.

Curiously, to portray the evolution of the nations and Y'haweh's subsequent purge, the idol that Daniel saw had a head of gold; breast and arms of silver; an abdomen and thighs of brass; legs and feet of iron; and toes of both iron and clay. Also, at the end of the vision, Daniel saw Y'haweh carving a rock out of a mountain, without the aid of human hands. Following, he saw Y'haweh using the rock to crush the idol, leaving no remnant of it. In the end, Daniel saw the rock grow into a large mountain that stood forever.

Adapting the prophet's own interpretation with our understanding of truth, we may interpret the vision as follows: the idol's head of gold represents the ancient Babylonian Empire, which consolidated the Mesopotamian countries under the monarchy of King Nebuchadnezzar, who ruled in the name of his *god* Marduk. Nebuchadnezzar's, in fact, was not the first empire; however, Nebuchadnezzar's was the first empire to claim sovereignty over mount Tziyon[1], where Y'haweh had recently placed his name by proclaiming it to be the future capital of his Kingdom (that is, the place of salvation). As a consequence, the Babylonian Empire is the first international power that caused the covenant bound elect to submit to an earthly authority, other than the Mashiach whom Y'haweh's covenant with King David promises.

Even so, Y'haweh depicted the Babylonian Empire as a head of gold to represent the uniformity of the integrated peoples and cultures under the Babylonian's monarchic government. The Babylonian monarchy readily gave a sense of commonality to the subjugated peoples, whose economies the monarchy integrated under its own.

Next, the silver breast and arms of the idol represent the Persian Empire. The kings of Persia were less autocratic than the Babylonian kings, because the Persian realm was less a monolithic, ideological entity than the Babylonian realm: aristocrats, known as satraps, rose to rule under the Persians. These aided the Persian Emperor in his

---

[1] The preceding Assyrian Empire did not conquer the southern tribes of Shim'on and Yehuda, which housed Yerushalayim and her Temple. Assyria only led the ten northern tribes of Yisra'el into captivity.

rule over the people. They had one codified law to join the nation together. The Persians tolerated other belief systems as long as the peoples paid homage to not only their god-like emperor, but also the Satraps and the Persian Law. Because of their social tolerance, the Persian Empire was more malleable to change; therefore, Y'haweh used a less precious (but more useful) metal to depict the Persians in Daniel's vision.

The empire that succeeded the Persian rule is the Hellenistic Empire of Alexander the Great. This empire comprises the brass belly and thighs of Daniel's idol. Although the Hellenistic Empire was even less an ideological monolith than the Persian Empire, the Greeks' more democratic ideals left a greater mark upon the peoples and cultures under their rule. In fact, there was even a period when the Yisra'elite identity seemed endangered of being diminished by Hellenism and its democratic tendencies.

The wars between competing Mediterranean and Mesopotamian civilizations and the succeeding wars between competing Greek city-states, which possessed different governmental systems, shaped Greek thought. First, the free peoples of Greece fought off the totalitarian Persian Empire. Following, the Greeks endured the Peloponnesian War among the Helens, themselves: the Peloponnesian War vied Monarchic, Aristocratic, and Democratic Greek city-states against each other. All the states appealed to the same pantheon of gods; however, the Greeks began to realize that their religious fervor did not decide the battles. Instead, as many Greek thinkers began to notice, the perspective governments and social orders often determined the victors of the continual struggles. As a result, Greek thought began to evolve out of the realm of superstition into the realm of abstract, rational thought: Greek thinkers began to dismiss the mythological realm of the capricious gods, whom they formerly sought help from. Instead, they embraced the practical observations of natural philosophy: the precursor to modern science.

In fact, we can summarize the evolution of Greek thought by stating the following: initially, the Greeks discovered the wealth of understanding that abstract thought achieves. Afterwards, the

Greeks discovered pragmatic ways to apply abstract concepts to the modes of existence. In this way, the Greek philosophers intellectually grounded abstract concepts to identify regularities in the vicissitudes of the creation and human life. At first, schools of thought arose among the Greek philosophers, such as the Ionian philosophers, who sought a material principle of such things that seemed to vanish and reappear. Following, other schools of thought arose and concluded that the essences of all things are in a perpetual state of flux. They figured that all things adhere to what they conceived to be *logos*[1] — 'word,' 'reason,' or 'logic' — which gives parallel structure to both the creation and the human soul: a universal order. Furthermore, a notable school of thought that succeeded the above schools of thought is the Eleatic school founded by Xenophanes. The Eleatic philosophers championed the doctrine of *One*: they tentatively looked past pantheism and declared that God is one eternal unity who upholds creation by his thought. To this end, the disciples of the Eleatic school of thought, such as Parmenides of Elea, purported that one unchanging existence can be perceived. Along these lines, Greek philosophers, like Empedocles of Agrigentum, maintained that there is an unchangeable nature to substance. Likewise, explicit materialistic notions arose in the teachings of Democritus who conceived the doctrine of atoms — the 'uncuttables' that are infinite in number, imperishable, and undividable. Still, because the Eleatic school could not identify practical applications of their metaphysical understandings, more rational schools of thought took root, such as the Sophists, and purported that our senses cannot gain access to one truth; therefore, they applied their dialectical applications (methods of logical arguments) to everyday life.

The most celebrated Greek philosopher, who reconciled the abstract thinkers with the Greek pragmatists, is Plato of Athens. His understanding even at times subtly paralleled the truth of Lord Yehoshua. Plato professed that there are ultimate forms of perfection that this world is a shadow of; however, he conceded that our senses

---

[1] The Greek concept of logos is the innate (but shadowy) sense of what we have identified as Y'haweh's expressed Word.

cannot directly apprehend the perfect forms: only our inner beings—our souls—can rationally relate to the forms by apprehending a sense of the good. Plato theorized a perfect government that enlightened men, who saw past the world of shadows, ruled. Plato conceptualized that under the enlightened men's government, a city would exist as a single body (like the Body of Christ). Furthermore, Plato fathomed the rule of an enlightened philosopher king who would rule his people, amicably.

Indeed, one may even venture to say that Plato would have rejoiced if one had preached to him the gospel of our Lord. Unfortunately, he could not possible perceive the reality that the elect can gain salvation knowledge through a common sense of appreciation of the Lord's sacrifice. If Plato had known the Gospel, he would have understood that all in the Body of Lord Yehoshua apprehend similar senses of appreciation as the Logos' truth-functional-form fulfills our dynamic perspectives by establishing our personhood in the Mashiach and our environmental community with the reconciling Holy Spirit. Following, Plato would have understood that the emergent forms of life that we perceive do not truly animate until the Logos fulfills our perspectives, allowing us to perceive the love and beauty of Y'haweh within: such renders the forms as being expressions of Y'haweh's good.

And so, without the grace of Y'haweh, it is no wonder that Plato's successors fell away from the pursuit of perfect forms. For example, although he acknowledged the concept of Plato's perfect forms, Aristotle—Plato's intellectual successor—did not acknowledge the actual existence of perfect forms beyond the material world. Aristotle sought the practical applications of Greek philosophy. Aristotle's school of thought, of course, was widely received by the multitude of diverse peoples that began to consolidate in the Hellenistic world and the succeeding Roman world: a world that forms the iron legs of Daniel's idol.

Notwithstanding, before we finish describing the symbolism behind Daniel's vision of the Idol that depicts the civilizations, let us briefly mention a complementary vision of Daniel that depicts the strength of each succeeding government in the vision: Y'haweh gave

Daniel a vision that depicted the more democratic King Alexander and his army as a one horned goat that charged a totalitarian Persian, two horned ram, without touching the ground. Prior to Alexander's time, the Persian despotic Kings tried to subdue the free Greek city-states, but they failed because the people of Greece fought more passionately for their freedom than the Persians fought to expand the rule of an unjust king. Thus, in Alexander's time, the Greek army easily destroyed the Persians, because the Greeks fought for their free lands, personal rights, and private property, while the Persians had no desire to uphold their despotic Emperor, who only sought to gain more power.

As to be expected, the free spirit of Hellenism even enamored many of the secular children of Yisra'el, who could not appreciate the true liberty behind the veil: they thought that the Law of Moshe robbed them of their personal aspirations. Fortunately, however, many of the elect of Yisra'el showed a greater worth than the Greeks when the Yisra'elites gave themselves freely to be executed rather than deny the worship of Y'haweh for personal gain, as some of the Gentile rulers had demanded.

In truth, we see like faith among the followers of Lord Yehoshua in the succeeding Roman era. We certainly applaud the faithful acts of the martyrs of Lord Yehoshua whom the Romans slew because the Christian martyrs would not deny Lord Yehoshua's hallowed name. International Rome retained all the facets of human government; therefore, only the faithful could look past Rome's cultural relativism and cling to Lord Yehoshua's truth.

Indeed, following the Hellenistic monarchs, the Roman Empire assumed the form of the iron legs and feet in Daniel's vision. With its three tier governmental body, the Roman Empire readily consolidated all the nations held under its rule.

Like we have said above, we expect to see a modern version of Imperial Rome consolidating the advanced civilizations of our time. With this thought in mind, let us consider the toes of Daniel's idol that Y'haweh depicts as being part clay and part iron: the iron toes represent the Roman power, while the clay toes represent the elect who cannot be swayed by Rome's ideology.

In this vein, we may qualify the following statement from the symbolism of the vision: a government that has most successfully bound all peoples under its ideology, despite Y'haweh, is not on sure footing because the government fulfills Satan's evil. Thus, in Daniel's vision, we finally see that a natural solid rock—the Kingdom of Heaven—will crush the idol, gather the clay, and become a mountain that human hands cannot carve; because we only obtain the Kingdom of Heaven by the grace of Y'haweh and not by our own efforts.

In Daniel's vision of the idol, we see human history unfold to serve Y'haweh's purposes, beginning with the Babylonian Empire and ending with a contemporary Roman-like Empire that tries to suppress the elect of Yisra'el and the Church. Firstly, under the Babylonian Empire, the captive children of Yisra'el developed a strong semi-autonomous population center in the city of Babylon, and they flourished. Under the Persian Empire, the children of Yisra'el enjoyed a degree of autonomy in their homeland: the Persian kings reconstituted the former land of the tribe of Yehuda by turning the land into a province named Judea; moreover, it follows that the term *Jew* means an inhabitant of Judea. From this point in our work, therefore, we will use the term *Jew* to describe the repatriated children of Yisra'el.

Furthermore, what is the most important event of the Persian era is the building of the third interim tabernacle (which is actually the second temple). After its construction, the Temple reclaimed its status of being the center of Jewish identity. Under the rule of the Greek dynasties that had succeeded the rule of Alexander the Great, the Jews enjoyed a degree of autonomy under the government of their Temple; however, the fighting that eventually occurred between opposing Greek dynasties led to turmoil in Judea, which was situated between the ruling dynasties. Prefiguring the anti-savior, the Greek King Antiochus Epiphanes sought to destroy the Temple altogether, in his attempt to consolidate his power by Hellenizing all the cultures under his dominion. Despite his efforts, the Jewish people survived and prospered under the Roman Empire.

Under the Roman era, the Jews planted Jewish communities throughout the Roman world. In so doing, they set the stage for the arrival and gospel of the Mashiach, whom the Gentiles could easily receive, instead of following the tedious oral laws and sacraments of the Jewish sages.

At this point, we may further qualify the blessing and curse that the Jewish people experienced in the Diaspora. Also, we may further qualify the blessing and curse that the Jewish Diaspora brought to the Gentiles.

To qualify the blessings upon the Diaspora, we have noted the reinvigorated personal modes of worship that the Jewish community observed to save their identity among the Gentiles. We may only add to this blessing, the advent of the Synagogue and the religious parties that arose and pioneered what has become modern day Judaism. One of the two major parties that arose is the party of the Perushim (Pharisees): the Perushim strictly observed the carefully handed down oral laws and written word of the scriptures. The other major religious party that arose is the party of the Tzedukim (Sadducees): the Tzedukim strictly observed the written Law of Moshe and the Temple sacraments, only. The Perushim were extremely popular with the common people because the Perushim believed in an afterlife where saints find their good deeds vindicated, while the Tzedukim did not believe in the afterlife; therefore, the rich favored them because the rich found satisfaction in this life only, like the Tzedukim.

To qualify the blessing that the Diaspora brought to the Gentiles, we have only to note the following: although the Mesopotamians cultivated sophisticated law codes that sought justice for the poor; prescribed sophisticated measures for commercial dealings; retained legal measures for divorce, inheritance, property rights, and the like; the Jewish faith greatly affected the Mesopotamians. Although the Romans retained the wealth of Greek rational thought and fostered the most sophisticated government that had been seen at the time, the Jewish faith had a profound impact on the Roman world, as well. What impacted the Gentile world is the Jewish understanding of one Supreme Being who encompasses all things and whom all must be accountable to, despite class or creed. The Jews brought the light of the Law that demanded reconciliation above piety or privilege. Essentially, the Gentile systems based their political, religious, and metaphysical understandings upon economic output, even imaging that they may observe the fertility cult gods' anger or appeasement by observing favorable or ill-fated environmental conditions, respectively. The Jews, on the other hand, brought the understanding that all the wealth of the earth is the property of one sovereign Creator who shares his wealth with equitable social bodies that reconcile themselves with him. In stark contrast to Gentile cultures, Jewish culture retained the most practical understanding of the nature of Y'haweh, by seamlessly correlating divine concepts with sensible ethical behavior and by finally securing an optimal relationship between religious precepts and civil law—a relationship that has enduringly ensured the viability of Jewish culture, beyond geographical bounds.

Nonetheless, like many false Christian leaders that arise in the prosperous days of the Church, false Jewish leaders proved to be ineffective cupbearers, even though Y'haweh had sought to exhibit his grace through them. For instance, political aspirations had colored the judgment of many Perushim, who began to esteem themselves above the common Yisra'elites. Often they only sought public standing, instead of seeking to aid the needy.

Consequently, we may now observe the curse upon the Diaspora by first noting the following social phenomenon: the superiority of the Jewish mode of life became evident to many in the Roman world. For instance, many Jewish converts multiplied from every region of the Roman dominion before the advent of Lord Yehoshua. As a consequence, the ruling Perushim in Yerushalayim increased in power and arrogance, their losing the light that once shined through their sincerity.

The Tzedukim, too, fell prey to corruption: they were satisfied with their political status and the political stability that the Temple provided for the nation, despite the poverty of the people. Unlike the Perushim, the Tzedukim did not look for the rewards of a resurrection; they were more secular in their beliefs than religious.

Frequently, Jews who had benefited greatly from their above average level of literacy (because of their traditional religious education) forsook the rigid observance of their faith. The secular Jews began to cultivate the secular societies that they flourished in.

Indeed, the secular societies naturally attract the secularized Jews because the societies fight against the national religions and dogmas of the Gentile cultures that the Jewish people are minorities in. For this cause, many Gentiles who do not prosper in the integrating multinational economies and cultures and who cherish their former belief systems, utterly despise the whole of the Jewish people, wrongfully thinking that the Jewish people are the sole cause of the liberal, progressive policies that have caused the down trodden Gentiles' economic disparity. Repeatedly, throughout the history of the Jewish Diaspora, unto the present day, unscrupulous Gentile rulers take advantage of the paranoia of such ill-tempered Gentiles and pass the blame of their shortcomings onto the Jewish people, as a whole. Finally, the end result is a nightmare that is a grief to any knowledgeable soul: the nightmare is the excesses of anti-Semitism.[1]

Obviously, we see the curse of the Diaspora manifested in the form of anti-Semitism; moreover, we see the same curse become a snare for the Gentiles who despise the Jewish people, because when an anti-Semite seeks to undermine the Jewish people, he or she denies the Holy Law that the Jews are caretakers of. Lord Yehoshua who came among the Jews to fulfill the Law is, therefore, an enemy to those who abuse the Jewish people. At the same time, he is an enemy to those secular Jews who seek to suppress his Law, because they harm their own brethren who are trying to comprehend the arrival of the Mashiach, who brings the liberty that the Law points to.

---

[1] Anti-Semitism is hostility or social prejudice against the Jewish people, who are of Semitic origins like the Arab, Hebrew, Amharic, and Aramaic peoples. These Semitic peoples are descendants of Noach's son Shem from whose name the word *Semite* derives itself. Although there are Semitic peoples other than Jewish people, anti-Semitism traditionally applies to hatred and social prejudices against Jewish people.

The Advents of Lord Yehoshua

While we are defining the curse of the Jewish Diaspora, let us definitively identify the sole blessing of the Diaspora, a blessing that shined past the darkness of secularism and anti-Semitism. Even though we have recognized the fact that Moshe's Law of redemption by one Lord does not regard social class but regards all people who seek the justice of the Lord's eternal Shabbat, we must still contend with the fact that the Gentiles not only perceived the ritualized Jewish observance of the Law as being tedious, but also perceived the injustices that the backslidden Perushim and Tzedukim had committed as being the belligerent aspiration of Jewish nationalism, which stood against Gentile ascendancy. And so, while we consider the unfortunate attitudes that both Jews and Gentiles cultivated against one another, we may understand the fact that the sole blessing that the Diaspora brought to the Gentiles was a geopolitical and social situation that necessitated the birth of the Mashiach whom Y'haweh uses to reconcile all nations with himself.

We may readily understand not only the advent of Lord Yehoshua, but also the appeal of the Lord, if we consider the disposition of the elect whom Y'haweh fulfills in both Jewish and Gentile worlds. We must note the fact that the political environment that necessitated the Lord's first advent, in which he calls us to repent, is similar to the geopolitical and social environment that necessitates the second advent of Lord Yehoshua, in which he comes, both to judge the faithless and vindicate his faithful.

We may call the geopolitical and social situation, which we are speaking of, *inequitable secular globalization*, which occurs under a single unjust political regime that an emperor type individual prefigures: secular globalization integrates all cultures and governmental systems and, unwittingly, provides a critical opportunity for Y'haweh to contrast his truth with the whole of human invention. The Prophet Daniel's writings describe this government that we are speaking of as a beast that is more unnaturally complex than the ram of autocracy or the one horned goat of democracy. Daniel envisioned a complex beast with the feet of a leopard, the body of a several-headed dragon, and the teeth of iron: indeed, the beast with its leopard feet, seven heads, and iron teeth quickly devours every ideology insight. Daniel's vision was that of a Roman type government, which will invariably rise again briefly to rule the earth. It is this unnatural beast that the fallen, chaotic cherub fills and uses to fight against the uniform natural body of Lord Yehoshua.

We refer to Rome as the model of the government of the anti-Christ because Rome proved to be the world's first attempt at secular globalization: the Roman government figuratively represented all classes of society, unlike the preceding governments. Rome adapted the best attributes of Greek Hellenism and subdued the Mediterranean world under Roman law and economy. As a result, the subdued nations grew under increased global integration and interdependency in trade, finance, technology, and investment. While a global class arose to consume higher levels of goods and services that the intellectual and technological exchange fostered, the global class ignored the superiority and inferiority of native cultures that respectively created and impeded the social environments from which the intellectual or technological innovations grew. Of course this social phenomenon is an injustice that even the current global class ignores: they think that integration is the greatest good despite the iniquities that various cultures allow.

Because of the global class's lack of insight, exploitation obviously occurs: often the global class accepts certain depravities in cultures as a lack of a comparative advantage that other nations enjoy. For this cause, new social classes arise between the industrious and the non-industrious. Following, unnatural feelings of superiority arise among the prosperous, or unnatural feelings of inadequacy arise among the socially castigated: it is no wonder that the Jewish Law of Moshe appealed to those who perceived the injustices of the Roman world. However, the Perushim could not fulfill their ministry and equitably receive the potential Roman converts, because the Perushim sought only to ensure their privileged status, even though they should have encouraged a ministry of reconciliation that points to him who will fulfill Y'haweh's Law and spread Y'haweh's tabernacle over the world. When the Roman era came into being, the spiritually poor of both Jew and Gentile had no hope.

We cannot blame the Perushim, particularly, for their downfall because no ministry can encompass the profound love of Y'haweh. As we have said, we break the Law every day and, therefore, we never completely apprehend the eternal fidelity of the Holy Marriage. The modern day spiritualists ignorantly point to the hypocrisies of such groups like the Perushim, saying that religious groups fail to apprehend the essence of love as they do; however, what the spiritualists fail to understand is that only Lord Yehoshua can love completely all the time, as we shall see. And because he retains the full complement of the Holy Spirit, Lord Yehoshua, alone, continuously values Y'haweh as salvation and hallows his name. As a result, only Lord Yehoshua seeks to ensure a Rest for Y'haweh. Also, because he is fulfilled in the Holy Spirit, he only seeks to fulfill the Father's glory in us whom the Father cultivates the sense of appreciation in.

Let us not foolishly disdain the Perushim for their fall, because they like many other Christian ministers began with integrity. There were many honest Perushim prior to the advent of the Lord, such as Hillel who, around the time when Lord Yehoshua the Mashiach was born, coined a saying for what we have identified as the law of conscience: Hillel said, "What is detestable to you, do not do to your neighbor. This is the whole of the Torah; all the rest is commentary. Go learn it."[1]

Like the Jewish ministries, many of the Gentile ministries started with good intentions. Among the Gentiles, who suffered from the injustices of the Roman world, many *mystery religions* gained popularity from those who sought the redemption and rebirth of the soul. The mystery religions acquired their name because they claimed that only *mystai*[2] could gain the secret wisdom of life by observing certain rites that magically produced ineffable understandings of the natural life, death, and rebirth cycle of life. The

---

[1] Talmud, Shabbat, 31a
[2] Mystai is a Greek word that means "initiates."

mystery religions taught that gaining the secret knowledge linked the mystai with some dying god who rose again from the dead.

The appeal of the mystery religions to the hopeless Romans is obvious. Yet, the mystery religions unfortunately exacerbated the state of sin that confounded the Romans in the following way: the mystai invariably felt an unnatural sense of self-worth over others; because the sacraments that the mystai performed, seemingly, had earned them the so-called secret wisdom that others could not have; moreover, the initiates forbade others to write down this wisdom because the mystai wanted to hold the wisdom for a select few. Such a practice directly contrasts the public proclamations of revealed religions.

Of course, many non-Christian scholars attempt to categorize Christianity as a mystery religion; however, such a categorization is grossly incorrect for the following reason: Y'haweh definitively intended for the message of the sacrifice and resurrection of Lord Yehoshua to be received publicly by every caste of society, unlike the mystery religions. First, Y'haweh used the symbols of the interim tabernacle to draw people from every strata of society to seek redemption, and then Y'haweh filled the prophets with his Holy Spirit, empowering them to proclaim the time and manner in which the Mashiach would by-pass the sacrifices of the corrupt priests by sacrificing himself to secure the redeemed for Y'haweh. For instance, the prophet Daniel even foretold how and when the Mashiach's life would be cut short for others.[1]

The Redemption of Both Jew and Gentile

All in all, the adherents to the mystery religions (who resemble the self-righteous Perushim) fail to see the significance of the mercy seat. The subsequent saying of Lord Yehoshua describes the quenching of Y'haweh's light by both Jew and Gentile who all had been exposed to the knowledge of Y'haweh's Law because of the Diaspora: Lord Yehoshua said, "The Kingdom of Heaven suffered violence"[2] until

---

[1] Daniel 9:26
[2] Matthew 11:12

the rise of Yochanan the Baptist. Essentially, Lord Yehoshua implied that until Yochanan baptized the people unto Lord Yehoshua, covetous rulers either tried to prevent the ministry of the tabernacle or twist its laws for the rulers' benefit. Lord Yehoshua on the other hand upheld the tabernacle, and he sacrificed himself upon its mercy seat to allow us to come into the Holy of Holies and worship Y'haweh, in spirit and in truth.

Yochanan was the last prophet before the ministry of Lord Yehoshua. Having camel's hair for his apparel and honey for his food, Yochanan forsook the pleasures of this world. He only sought the good pleasure of Y'haweh. Simply abiding in the wilderness, he stepped outside of the comforts of first century Roman Judea, to await the coming of the Lord. He cried, "Prepare the way of Y'haweh. Make straight in the desert a highway for our God. Every valley shall be exalted, and every mountain and hill shall be made low: and the crooked shall be made straight, and the rough places plain: and the glory of Y'haweh shall be revealed, and all flesh shall see it together."[1]

It is Y'haweh who filled Yochanan with his Holy Spirit. He, afterwards, used Yochanan to call all those who sought true redemption, by their not seeking the vain public shows of piety. Y'haweh, in fact, filled Yochanan with his Holy Spirit to show others how to repent and receive the redemption of the Mashiach. Thus, unto the repentant who heard Yochanan calling them to step outside of the golden cities of corruption, Y'haweh sent his Son.

What is even more remarkable than the manner in which Y'haweh cultivated a repentant people is the manner in which he refined their repentant hearts by empowering them to appreciate a humble Lord: instead of sending an attractive, industrious, high classed, wealthy Caesar, Y'haweh sent a poor working classed carpenter to identify with the common people. Also, instead of sending another privileged priest who sequesters himself from the unfortunate and disadvantaged, Y'haweh sent a salvation knowledge

---

[1] Isaiah 40:3-5

filled High Priest who directly identifies with the burdens of the oppressed.

To understand the true nature of Lord Yehoshua, may the reader lend his or her patience to hear a description of the humble Savior of the author's dreams, since words often cannot convey the Spirit of the Lord as well as visual images. Often contemporary films render a false image of the Lord, in an attempt to make the Lord more popular or appealing, when in fact his humility receives the full spiritual power of Y'haweh; defines the obedience needed to fulfill the Law; and even identifies with the lowliest of men. Let us, therefore, envision the humble form of the Lord:

Lord Yehoshua had an average height, ruddy skin color (he tanned easily), with dark golden brown hair. In fact, his straight hair extended slightly below his ears, being somewhat parted in the middle. His hair was somewhat oily, needed a wash; moreover, he twisted his hair inward around his temples to prevent his hair from falling into his face: a common hairstyle for observant Jews. The Lord had very muscular calves, and he walked very excitedly and harshly, tilting forward slightly when he stepped. He was lean and muscular, though not stocky. His mustache and beard were thin, and his forehead and hairline were small and full, respectively. He had a very normal face: he was neither handsome nor ugly. His cheekbones, however, where really pronounced, flaring out, and his nose protruded out in a slight hook. Although his nose was unattractive, it did draw attention to his very sincere (dark but noticeably brown) eyes, which lucidly expressed his sincerity and innocence. His cheeks added to his sincere expression, for they were slightly drawn in, only to pronounce his quaint mouth.

The Lord had a diligent and excited demeanor that the appearance of sadness never failed to check. For this cause, he seemed naive to those who did not know him. Still, while he hurried about enjoying fellowship with his disciples, the disciples always curiously looked on with slight frowns of concern on their brows: anxiously, they always tried to follow his lead. He briskly walked before them sporting a very nice red coat and a fine tan garment that stood out, for the clothes of his disciples and the crowd were not so well made. Thus, Y'haweh honored his son among proud men, as the following scripture records:

> [Lord Yehoshua] grew up before [Y'haweh] as a tender plant, and as a root out of dry ground. He has no form or attractiveness; and when we see him, there is no beauty that we should desire him.[1]

Although the Lord's form was lowly, his heart held more beauty and love than anyone can imagine. The humble, the meek, the thirsty for righteous will behold his true beauty behind the veil, when Y'haweh resurrects, within Lord Yehoshua, those who forsook the pride and other sins of this world, while holding true to Lord Yehoshua's faithful Soul.

While we consider the necessity of Lord Yehoshua's sacrifice for the world, let us lament over the fact that throughout history, many foolishly charge only the Jewish religious parties and people for killing Lord Yehoshua. Ignorantly, people think that the Jewish people, as a whole, are cursed; however, we must consider the fact that Lord Yehoshua came to defy the pride of evil's dominion, altogether, by selflessly offering himself for sacrifice.

One cannot say that Y'haweh cursed the whole of the Jewish people just because they endured a tumultuous history of persecution, since Christians endured a history of persecution, as well. The persecutors are they who persecute those who humbly bear Lord Yehoshua's cross. The difference between the respective causes of Jewish and Christian persecution is that the Jews observe the Covenant of the interim tabernacle that demands nationalist sentiments among the Jewish people. In fact, even those who do not settle in the Land of Yisra'el have strong kindred and cultural bonds that are exclusive; therefore, because their culture is exclusive, they incur animosity from the Gentile nations that they dwell among. In contrast, Christian exclusivity is more tolerable for unbelievers, because the true Christian observes a new covenant with Y'haweh that looks for an eternal tabernacle beyond the sky; therefore, the true

---

[1] Isaiah 53:2

humble Christian who only holds allegiance to the Kingdom of Heaven instead of the state usually does not cultivate any exclusive nationalist sentiments. For this cause, Christian persecution is less excessive because there are many Christians that span cultural, ethnic, and national boundaries. What both persecuted Jews and Christians do have in common, however, is that they suffer under political persecution by secular nations. Unfortunately, sometimes the persecutors figuratively assume the form of Jews or Christians, even though the persecutors undermine the Law of Moshe and the gospel of Lord Yehoshua that defines both Jews and Christians, respectively.

Knowing that Y'haweh seeks to redeem peoples from both Jew and Gentile worlds, we must understand why he allowed the Jewish people to endure such affliction. We must establish the fact that Y'haweh does not seek the destruction of the Jewish race in favor of the Gentiles, because Lord Yehoshua impart was a descendant of the Jewish King David. Lord Yehoshua's disciples, too, were Jewish: they came from every class of Jewish society. There were even some reformed Perushim in the body of believers. In fact, for these believing Jews, Lord Yehoshua could have easily returned after his resurrection to prevent the Jewish Temple from being destroyed: he could have easily established a Holy Marriage on earth with the believing Jews. But fortunately, he did not for our sakes.

Essentially, when the covetous Jewish rulers denied the rule of the humble Lord Yehoshua, other factions (who tried to establish an independent Jewish nation) arose to provoke the wrath of the Romans who subsequently destroyed Judea and her Temple, in the year 70 A.D. The catastrophe initiated a second Diaspora; and so, the Jewish people have confronted anti-Semitism for almost 2,000 years of exile, until a new world order recently reconstituted the Jewish people into their homeland.

While in exile, the successors of the Perushim preserved the Jewish people by expounding upon the Perushim's teachings. To

The Kingdom of Heaven

their credit, these Jewish sages pioneered Judaism: the Talmudic[1] approach to interpreting and applying Moshe's Law to everyday life. Judaism preserved Jewish culture, during a period of 2,000 years of social upheaval. We must note that even Lord Yehoshua, tentatively, upheld the Perushim's teachings of the Torah by saying the following to those Jews who were not chosen to follow him at the time:

> The scribes and Perushim sit in Moshe's seat: all therefore whatsoever they bid you to observe, that observe and do; but do not after their works: for they say and do not.[2]

Yet, it should remain clear to us that Lord Yehoshua despised the hypocritical stances of the Perushim who corrupted the Law. The Perushim withheld the liberty that the Law pointed to, while Lord Yehoshua came to fulfill the Law for the people, in order to set them free. It is no wonder that Lord Yehoshua's tentative support for the teachings of the backslidden Perushim have baffled many people who understand the obvious need for redemption only through Lord Yehoshua. But if we look a little closer at the Lord's tentative support for the Perushim, we would actually see the expression of his love for us, in the above enigmatic saying. Simply put, Lord Yehoshua upholds the Jewish leaders until he reconciles the world through the Gentile preaching of his sacrifice. Following, the Jews, themselves, will come to appreciate him as their savior when he reappears to save them from the terror of the global beast.

---

[1] The Talmud is a compilation of Jewish social and civil laws that scholarly interpretations of the Law of Moshe inspire. The Talmud consists of two parts: the *Mishnah* and the *Gemara*. The Mishnah is the written version of traditional oral Jewish law. Correspondingly, exhaustive explanations of the Mishnah comprise the Gemara. The fruit of the Talmud are the scholarly arguments that make up the foundation of the Gemara. As a result, the Talmud legalistically treats a variety of social and civil issues that arise in everyday life.

[2] Matthew 23:2-3

The Seventh Revelation of Y'haweh: He is the Husband of the Redeemed Assembly

One must know that Y'haweh does not establish his mercy seat only for the Jewish people: the six covenant related revelations, which we have listed thus far, universally speak to the innermost insecurities of all who seek a heavenly savior. Only, we must underscore the fact that those who profess to love and who do not accept Y'haweh's perfect expression of love, through the humility and selflessness of Lord Yehoshua, do not truly love, because they for selfish reasons reject the Mashiach, the embodiment of love. What is more, they who reject the true expression of love reject the six revelations that Lord Yehoshua typifies; therefore, they cannot become the loving wife of him, the heavenly husband whose form assumes our seventh and final revelation of Y'haweh, and that is that *He is the loving Husband of the Church, the Redeemed Assembly*, who is the heavenly wife. Besides, those who do not seek the heavenly husband do not seek the Holy Marriage, the very Temple of Y'haweh; therefore, it is no wonder that Y'haweh actively seeks to purge them out of his Temple (both Jews and Gentiles, alike).

Although some elect enthusiastically receive Y'haweh's seventh revelation, Lord Yehoshua continues to minister to all in the form of the sixth revelation, until he fully cultivates the elect with his Holy Spirit, in order to fulfill the Holy Marriage. In other words, the Lord continues to assume the ministry of Malki-Tzedek, in order to fulfill Y'haweh's promise to Avraham, in which Y'haweh declares that he will bless the earth through Avraham's descendant: invariably ministering to the bosom of Avraham by assuming an everlasting priesthood, Lord Yehoshua administers a New Covenant between Y'haweh and his elect, by instilling Y'haweh's Law in the heart of them whom he weds. Because of the gracious Lord, Y'haweh no longer sequesters the Law behind the veil of sin, which exhibits both our souls' imperfection and Y'haweh's perfection. Instead, he allows Lord Yehoshua to rip the veil of sin apart by redeeming us and, thereby, grafting us into his perfect spiritual body; where we find such satisfaction that we naturally fulfill the Law through our love for the Lord, the faithful husband.

In this world, Lord Yehoshua—our great High Priest—surrenders his perfect Holy Spirit, which reminds us of his example: the Spirit reminds us—his espoused—to forsake the corruption of this world, which the Law testifies against. Hence, naturally complementing the Law, we seek only the riches of Lord Yehoshua's Holy Marriage. As we mentioned briefly above, some think that the Law robs them of the vain liberty to exercise their power and vanity without a sincere regard for others. In contrast, we—the holy bride—who have Y'haweh's Law written upon our hearts (because of our love for the Lord) seek the justice, protection, consolation, and the overall goodness that the Law points to, even the ordinance of Y'haweh's Holy Spirit.

The difference between Lord Yehoshua's priesthood and the Levite priesthood is that Lord Yehoshua's priesthood is eternal because he does not fall under Adam's condemnation, like the Levites; therefore, Lord Yehoshua's heart retains Y'haweh's beauty in Eden always. When Lord Yehoshua tasted the burdens of the flesh, Y'haweh filled him with his Holy Spirit, which enabled him to forgo temptation and brook temporary depravity, ultimately, to serve Y'haweh's purposes. Unlike the often proud and covetous Levites and Perushim, Lord Yehoshua remains eternally faithful; and so, he liberally gives the Holy Spirit to those whom Y'haweh empowers to perceive his grace through the sacrifice and resurrection of Lord Yehoshua, his only son. Thus, knowing exactly who is repentant and who desires to reciprocate the love of Y'haweh, Lord Yehoshua separates the true worshippers from those who are merely religious for cultural reasons. In this way, Lord Yehoshua purges the Temple of Y'haweh and, thereby, eternally establishes the Temple in holy matrimony.

Finally, we may reconcile our understandings of, first, Y'haweh's ultimate revelation of himself as the eternal husband with, second, Lord Yehoshua's transitory priestly ministry if we keep in mind the fact that Y'haweh's preceding revelations are Y'haweh's transitory responses to our progressive life-experiences; which experiences result from Y'haweh's spiritual cultivation of us within Y'haweh's truth. In few words, the preceding revelations (which speak to the inner most needs of the elect who discover comfort in the Law) find their fulfillment in priestly ministry of Lord Yehoshua, who fulfills the Law and, thereby, seeks to comfort the elect, eternally, in the Holy Marriage: the Temple and fulfillment of Y'haweh's love. Looking toward this good end, Y'haweh himself notes the transitory nature of the Levite and Malki-Tzedek tabernacle ministries in the subsequent scripture; through which he expectantly calls his scattered elect unto the Holy Marriage that the New Testament of the heart establishes:

> Turn, O backsliding children, says Y'haweh; for I am married unto you: and I will take you one of a city, and two of a family, and I will bring you to Tziyon: . . . they shall say no more, "The Ark of the Covenant of Y'haweh": neither shall it come to mind: neither shall they remember it; neither shall they visit it; neither shall that be done anymore. At that time they shall call [New] Yerushalayim the throne of the Y'haweh; and all the nations shall be gathered unto it, to the name of Y'haweh.[1]

The Power of Lord Yehoshua's Baptism

To make a complete assessment of Lord Yehoshua's transitory earthly ministry and the succeeding transitory ministry of his Apostles, we have only to understand the following realities to assess both ministries without surveying the entirety of the New Testament: to begin, let us again acknowledge the fact that none, who falls under Adam's condemnation, dwells in a state of righteousness like Lord Yehoshua; because all who bear Adam's sin can only possess the Holy Spirit impart, while Lord Yehoshua possesses the mind of Y'haweh always: he only retains the first friendship of righteousness with Y'haweh, allowing him to appreciate the eternal good of Y'haweh, even from Y'haweh's power in creation unto the simplicity and meekness of Y'haweh's beauty. In contrast, we retain the lesser friendships of pleasure and necessity; therefore, sin's veil blinds us

---

[1] Jeremiah 3:14-17

with vanity. Even when we have the best intentions, our lack of faith causes us to seek solace only in such vanities as social class, forms of cultural acceptance, or economic status, among other forms of idolatry; therefore, social prejudice and covetousness resides in us all, to some degree.

Even Yochanan the Baptist briefly despaired, wondering if the humble Lord Yehoshua was actually the Savior: imprisoned and endangered of being martyred because of his ministry, Yochanan wondered how could the Lord make right committed wrongs, while the Lord maintained such a humble form. Fortunately, however, the Lord encouraged Yochanan not to look at the standing of a person by worldly values; instead, as the Holy Spirit now encourages us, Yochanan should have looked at the standing of a person according to the sense of Y'haweh's fidelity that the person has in his or her heart.

We have already noted the fact that human idolatry chaotically distorts the glory and power of Y'haweh, which creation expresses. Subsequently, we understood that the children of Yisra'el's idolatry caused Y'haweh to display his power by thundering upon the mountain against those of the Yisra'elites who did not forsake the idols of their hearts. We then recognized the fact that Y'haweh expelled the children of Yisra'el from the Promised Land because of their idolatry. As a result, the Jews now bear unto the world the Law that does not only decry the acts of injustice committed among the Jews, but also decry the acts of injustice committed throughout the Gentile world.

Another reality that we must reaffirm is how Y'haweh exercises his power: we elect who possess the Holy Spirit must reaffirm the fact that we may not only see the ultimate exercise of Y'haweh's power, merely, in the physical wonders of creation. Let us recall our understanding of truth and, thereby, we will know that we witness the sincerest exercise of Y'haweh's power when he enables us to fulfill his righteous friendship, which the Law seeks; because when Lord Yehoshua empowers us to fulfill Y'haweh's Law, we walk in harmony with him and each other and perceive Y'haweh's beauty in creation.

Strikingly, we see the ultimate exercise of Y'haweh's power in the unpopular, humble, and servile form of Lord Yehoshua. Directly contrasting the social idols of popular culture, which cause injustice, Lord Yehoshua secured the power of Y'haweh by denying himself, to honor Y'haweh's will only; therefore, Y'haweh showed his pleasure by delivering the keys of Heaven unto the Lord Yehoshua's faithful hands.

On earth, Lord Yehoshua came from humble origins; always sought the good of others who glorified the truth of Y'haweh; and finally gave his life even for those who forsook him. On earth, he was "despised and rejected of men; a man of sorrows; and acquainted with grief: and we hid as it were our faces from him; he was despised, and we esteemed him not."[1] But now, in our Holy Spirit filled hearts, he is triumphant and dutifully praised, eternally.

Any casual observer, however, would think that one who could perform miracles and not die of natural causes (unlike Adam's progeny) would be the happiest man of all. Still, Lord Yehoshua was unhappy in this world because he knew that the very people who crowned him with laurels (because of his miracles) would be the same people who would applaud the unjust actions of his persecutors, who crowned him with thorns. Even his disciples could not fully appreciate Lord Yehoshua, solely, because of the miracles that he performed, for they often lost faith when danger arose, and then they of necessity relied on their own talents and social conventions.

As we have noted before, the true source of Lord Yehoshua's wealth and power is his fulfillment in Y'haweh's Holy Spirit, which enables him to be obedient to Y'haweh's will. Thereby, the Lord can selflessly seek the good of others whom the Father loves and empowers to reciprocate his love. To understand how Y'haweh exercises his power in us, let us cite the following testimony of Lord Yehoshua, in which he declares that his power results from his obedience to Y'haweh's will:

---

[1] Isaiah 53:3

> The Son can do nothing of himself, but what he sees the Father doing: for the things the Father does, the Son does likewise. For the Father loves the Son and shows him all things . . . the Father judges no man, but has committed all judgment unto the Son, that all men should honor the Son, even as they honor the Father: he that does not honor the Son does not honor the Father that sent him.[1]

Lord Yehoshua continues by saying the following:

> I can of my own self do nothing: as I hear, I judge: and my judgment is just; because I do not seek my own will, but the Father's will who sent me.

It is obvious to us that Lord Yehoshua enjoys an exclusive relationship with Y'haweh that sin prevents us from enjoying. So if we note how the disciples, initially, lacked faith before Y'haweh gave them the Holy Spirit that Lord Yehoshua secured for them, we may begin to accept the fact that we can only obtain the power of Y'haweh after he mercifully instills within us the inspiration to wed ourselves to the Savior, whom the Spirit empowers, eternally. To qualify this understanding, let us acknowledge the following saying of Lord Yehoshua who proclaimed, "No man can come to me unless the Father who has sent me draws him."[2]

From this Statement, we may conclude that the best and sincerest person cannot reciprocate the love of Y'haweh unless he or she becomes a part of the Savior through the power of the Holy Spirit. In the same manner that the children of Yisra'el despaired at the slightest danger, even after Y'haweh performed many miracles to deliver them from Egypt; those who followed Lord Yehoshua fell away by seeking the security of the popular culture, even though Lord Yehoshua performed many miracles in their presence. For sure, without the power of Y'haweh, no person can come unto Lord Yehoshua unless the Father draws him.

---

[1] John 5:19-23
[2] John 6:44

Many virtuous individuals looked past the idols of society and came into the wilderness to be baptized by the nomadic Yochanan the Baptist: the meek came; those who wanted a clear conscience came; and all those who found no satisfaction in Roman Judea came. Out of love, Y'haweh inspired these repentant people to walk away from the idols of this world; however, Y'haweh necessarily gave his Holy Spirit to them only through Lord Yehoshua, because Y'haweh wanted the people to know that their liberty is a gift to the selfless savior, whom the true seeker of righteous becomes a part of when he or she mimics his love and accepts his lordship over his or her life.

If Y'haweh did not consign the people to become a part of the selfless Lord Yehoshua, the people would esteem their own virtue above another's; and then their disharmony would foster the sin that they sought deliverance from. For example, a rich man, who had figuratively obeyed all the Law, sought to esteem himself before Lord Yehoshua, asking what does it take to get into the Kingdom of Heaven. The Lord answered him by saying that if the rich man wanted to become perfect, the man would have to forsake his wealth and follow him. The rich man then lamented because he did not have the faith to do so. It is unfortunate that the rich man did not know that the worldly wealth that he inequitably coveted is a source of the injustice that the Law (which he had claimed to observe) decries.

Only after Lord Yehoshua made the ultimate sacrifice, could we, as a body, reciprocate the love of Y'haweh and receive the treasures of the Holy Spirit, together with the biblical Patriarchs and Prophets, who saw his sacrifice and accepted it long ago. In this manner, Y'haweh, who dwells within Lord Yehoshua, becomes the single benefactor of his Church bride.

In addition, it is important for us to understand the necessity of our election: that is, it is important for us to understand further why Y'haweh chooses some to receive salvation and not all. We remember the fact that it is necessary for Y'haweh to redeem the virtue of some, while he condemns the same virtue in others, as evil. We know that, in this way, Y'haweh establishes his grace and judgment, respectively. So if we apply Y'haweh's grace and judgment to the idolatrous ideologies of the world, we would bring to light the understanding that it is necessary for Y'haweh to require all types of people (who seek the consolation of his Law) to be redeemed by the sinless Savior, despite the people's heritage or creed: it is necessary for Y'haweh to establish the first friendship of true brotherly love, by overturning the vanity and superficiality of civility, which do not prevent idolatrous classist attitudes. For sure, because Y'haweh elects some and enables them to reciprocate his love through the humble Mashiach, their education, privileged status, comeliness, and other worldly talents are of no value to Y'haweh, other than causes for personal thanksgivings.

In short, all the elect, equally, require the humble life and wonderful resurrection of Lord Yehoshua: no one of any class or race lives a completely selfless life, only seeking the welfare of others, as Lord Yehoshua does. Also, no one inherits the Kingdom and power of Y'haweh, like the good Lord.

His not having been condemned to bear Adam's isolation from Y'haweh, Lord Yehoshua retained the passion, will, and consciousness of Y'haweh from birth. Also, because he did not have the guilt of sin upon him in his human experience, the Lord could endow his consciousness of the glory of Y'haweh by esteeming the peace of Y'haweh over the depravities that we are subject to.

Thus, to experience the Lord's peace, we must become a part of him by bearing his cross in this life. Then we will rejoice within his eternal body, that is, the Holy Marriage in the world to come.

The example that Lord Yehoshua left us is as follows: first, Lord Yehoshua retained the beauty of Y'haweh, which Eden exemplifies. Following, when he went into the dominion of evil, he prayed always, in order for him to retain the mind of the Father.

For us, he went outside of the golden cities of corruption to be baptized with the repentant people, in order to overcome the heavy burden of flesh that the people sought deliverance from: when he went into the baptismal waters, he did so praying, and the Father, being fulfilled with his love, proclaimed, "You are my beloved son, in whom I am well pleased."[1]

---

[1] Luke 3:22

And then Y'haweh said unto the people, "Hear him."[1]

And later Yochanan the Baptist, likewise, pointed the people to the Mashiach by saying, "Behold the lamb of God who takes away the sins of the world."[2]

Immediately after his baptism, Lord Yehoshua overcame Satan's temptation, by being submissive only to the will of the Father; gained popularity by healing the sick; reached out to the disenfranchised; and fed the poor, declaring that he is the bread of life, the very showbread of the temple. Unto the submissive true worshippers who sought the comfort of the King's just Law and not the heavy burden of the Law's condemnation, merciful Lord Yehoshua (upon the healing wings of forgiveness) called saying, "Come unto me, all you that labor and are heavy laden, and I will give you rest. Take my yoke upon you, and learn of me; for I am meek and lowly in heart: and you shall find rest unto your souls. For my yoke is easy, and my burden is light."[3]

To summarize the realities that we have noted, concerning our idolatrous inability to relate to Y'haweh without the humble sacrifice of the Mashiach, we can only conclude the following: one cannot possibly understand the profundity of Lord Yehoshua's earthly ministry in its correct context, unless one definitively understands how exactly Y'haweh extends his peace to us by planting Lord Yehoshua upon the earth in such a humble form. One must know that the humility and subjection of Lord Yehoshua is succinctly comprehensible to the most simple and vulnerable parts of our souls, which suffers from fear, anxiety, and foreboding: these are the human frailties that result from sin's imputation, which haphazardly causes us to protect those qualities of humility and subjection within us by our harboring sentiments of jealousy, anger, pride, greed, lust, and all of such sentiments that encourage the sins that we commit against good conscience. Even so, when Y'haweh humbled Lord Yehoshua, in such a manner, to experience the disparities of the

---

[1] Luke 9:35
[2] John 1:29
[3] Matthew 11:28-30

human condition, Y'haweh made Lord Yehoshua's meek form approachable and intelligible to us: our consciences directly identify with his humble form. As an outcome, we may joyfully note that after the resurrected Lord freely delivers his peaceable Holy Spirit unto us, we through faith will secure the conviction that that which is faintly pure in us will eternally endure within him; therefore, we will find rest in this life, as we let go of the vanities and fleeting aspirations of our insecure souls, which the Law had condemned. Letting go of our vanity, sophistication, and pride, we will become as gentle as little children, "for of such is the Kingdom of Heaven"[1], said Lord Yehoshua.

In these regards, Lord Yehoshua will dispense his humble Holy Spirit, endowing our patience with a uniform and inherent appreciation for the hallowed ground. In this vein, Y'haweh declares the following through the prophet Yesha'yahu, concerning Lord Yehoshua's humble experience on earth (as we have noted before):

> He shall see of the travail of his soul, and shall be satisfied: by his knowledge shall my righteous servant justify many; for he shall bear their iniquities.[2]

Depictions of Heaven

Summarily, the Lord openly taught the manner in which the humble seed of his Holy Spirit will spring forth in the elect to become the same Holy Spirit's tree of life. At the same time, he chastised those religious leaders who held sin over the people's heads, while the leaders sought to retain this world's vanity, wealth, and privilege. For this reason, the Lord withheld the true wealth of his understanding from the covetous leaders by speaking in front of them in parables, knowing that those whom Y'haweh empowered to seek the Lord would successfully unfold the Lord's pearls of wisdom.

---

[1] Matthew 19:14
[2] Isaiah 53:11

Using parables, the Lord described how the disciples' faith would receive his humble and peaceable Holy Spirit, allowing them to fulfill his love. The Lord described how the disciples would look past the vanities and selfish aspirations of Babylon and then grow, with salvation knowledge, from the humble mustard seed of Lord Yehoshua's sacrificed body, until they flourish in the Holy Marriage's Kingdom of Heaven.

The New Testament Book of Matthew records one of the Lord's parables that illustrate the salvation of those whose faith Y'haweh's grace cultivates by giving them a conception of his pending heavenly rewards in the Holy Marriage. Additionally, the parable records the condemnation of those who have not received Y'haweh's grace, their never seeing the wedding day. Paradoxically, Lord Yehoshua begins his parable by stating that the Kingdom of Heaven, in which Y'haweh consummates the Holy Marriage, is like the outcome of the actions that Lord Yehoshua describes in the parable. So to correctly interpret Lord Yehoshua's paradoxical statement, we must describe the nature of the Kingdom of Heaven as a just state that the resolution of the actions in the parable conceives: the parable describes the Kingdom of Heaven as a place of vindication for those who desire the eternal riches of Y'haweh in contrast to the condemnation incurred by those who solely desire the world's temporary pleasures.

That people should desire intimate fellowship with Y'haweh above all else, as one who through faith greatly anticipates his or her nuptial to his or her beloved is the primary message of the parable. The parable is as follows:

> The kingdom of Heaven shall be compared to ten virgins who took their lamps and went out to a meeting of the bridegroom. And five of them were wise, and five foolish. Those being foolish, taking their lamps did not take oil with them. But the wise took oil in their vessels with their lamps. But the bridegroom, delaying, all nodded and slept. And at midnight a cry occurred: "Behold the bridegroom comes! Go out to meet him." Then all those virgins rose up and prepared their lamps. And the foolish said to the wise, "Give us some of your oil, for our

lamps are going out." But the wise answered, saying, "No, lest there not be enough for us and you. But rather go to those who sell, and buy for yourselves." But they going away to buy, the bridegroom came. And those ready went in with him to the wedding feast; and the door was shut. And afterwards the rest of the virgins also came, saying, "Lord, Lord, open to us." But answering he said, "I do not know you!"[1]

For our purposes, let us render the following translation of the above parable: first, the parable describes two groups of people with contrary value systems, as two groups of virgins who await their wedding hour: one group has faith; therefore, their value system renders them wise (and these wise attain an award), while the other group has no faith; therefore, their value system renders them foolish (and these foolish find themselves condemned). Both groups of virgins wait long into the night: the wise group, being faithful, look past temporary pleasure and vanity and seek the eternal riches and fidelity of the bridegroom, whom they are to marry. In contrast, the unwise and unfaithful group, caring for the pleasures of this life, treats the truth and arrival of the bridegroom with indifference.

And so, the parable ultimately depicts those who earnestly seek to reconcile themselves with Y'haweh as the wise virgins: these possess Y'haweh's Holy Spirit, whom the parable depicts as the oil in the lamps that the faithful virgins carry to light the darkness of the night of life. Accordingly, the parable depicts those who hold Y'haweh's person in lesser esteem (because of their otherworldly cares) as the foolish virgins: these have no oil in their lamps; therefore, they do not possess Y'haweh's light of truth, which in fact emanates from the countenance of Lord Yehoshua the bridegroom.

Lastly, the parable concludes with the vindication of the wise virgins for their faithful deeds. They valued the meeting of their husband above all else, and they were ready to greet him at his arrival. Likewise, in the conclusion of the parable, we see the bridegroom condemning the actions of the unfaithful virgins when

---

[1] Matthew 25:1-12

the bridegroom alienates them from the eternal pleasures of the *great communion* upon the wedding day.

Furthermore, to correctly interpret the parable, we must describe the faithful virgins as us true worshippers of Y'haweh (whom we see in the person of Lord Yehoshua), and we must describe the bridegroom as Lord Yehoshua. Then correspondingly, the faithful virgins' wise choice to keep oil in their lamps bears a similitude to our choice to wait patiently for the Holy Marriage, which is the conception of our eminent salvation that the Holy Spirit has placed in our hearts. So, as the faithful virgins chose not to fall prey to the temptation to follow after temporary pleasures instead of waiting patiently for the enduring pleasure of the wedding day, we should steadfastly look beyond the vanities of this world by waiting on the eternal reward that the Lord has conceived in our souls for the self-same wedding day. This is the primary message of the Lord's parable.

Clearly, we can appreciate the profound wisdom of the Lord's parables and other sayings when we consider how the Lord simplified the complexities of truth's landscape by disseminating salvation knowledge into short stories for the simple to understand. Teaching his disciples to seek the true wealth and power of Y'haweh, he commanded his disciples to love and seek one another's good, in order to fulfill his eternal love, which the righteousness of the Law seeks: he both summed up the Law and qualified a law of conscience by saying, "All things, whatsoever, that you would like men to do to you, even so, you do to them: for this is the sum of the Law and the prophets."[1]

In essence, Lord Yehoshua put forth the saying because he knew that one's heart's desire to reconcile with others fulfills the Lord's love that does not need a penal law to encourage reconciliation. In like manner, our desire to assume the peaceable image of Lord Yehoshua fulfills our love for Y'haweh, who then fulfills all things with his Holy Spirit.

---

[1] Matthew 7:12

Consequently, Lord Yehoshua declared that he has come to fulfill the Law for the meek, "the pure in heart"[1], those "who hunger and thirst for righteousness"[2], and the unfulfilled in spirit. For this cause, he declared to Shim'on Kefa[3] that he would build his Kingdom upon those who have patient faith in him; moreover, he declared that he would give the faithful the abundance of life, through the simplicity of his salvation knowledge. To this end, he declared that those who observe his word build the houses of their souls upon the solid rock of his Word. In this manner, he becomes the corner stone of the Temple of Y'haweh, which the humble and obedient true worshippers fill. At the same time, the Lord declared that the storms of life would destroy the proud and covetous who cling to the selfish aspirations, political intrigue, and the other vanities of this world.

Agnus Dei, Lamb of God

Knowing what advantage he had by possessing the power of Y'haweh, Lord Yehoshua was patient with the human frailties of his disciples, who could not enjoy his advantages until Y'haweh gave them his power by making them members of Lord Yehoshua's resurrected body. Until the disciples gained the Holy Spirit, the Lord suffered the betrayals, the persecutions, and the doubting of those whom he came to free.

On the faithful Passover, in which Y'haweh predestined the Lord to assume the place of the Passover Lamb, who had redeemed Avraham, Yitzchak, Ya`akov, and the elect of the children of Yisra'el, Lord Yehoshua declared the truth of the Passover: he not only declared that he is the unleavened bread and the manna that descended from Heaven to be broken by those whom the bread nourished in the wilderness, but also declared that his sacrificed body is the broken bread, which will rise again and give life to all that observe his New Covenant that will reside in their hearts:

---

[1] Matthew 5:8
[2] Matthew 5:6
[3] Simon Peter

Yehoshua took bread, and blessed it, and broke it, and gave it to the disciples, and said, "Take, eat; this is my body. And he took the cup, and gave thanks, and gave it to them, saying, "Drink all of it; for this is my blood of the new testament, which is shed for many for the remission of sins.[1]

In essence, Lord Yehoshua declared that the Passover wine that the disciples were drinking represented his soon to be spilt blood, which in turn represented his death. And from his death, the Lord intended for them to inherit his resurrected eternal life that he sealed for them in his new testament: the gift of Lord Yehoshua's eternal, triumphant life, because the Lord did not have the condemnation of Adam upon him, as his disciples did. Hence, the Lord could not die because of sickness or disease. On the contrary, he had to be martyred, in order for the disciples (who had followed him in the Spirit) to be raised with him in his eternal spiritual body. In this vein, the prophet Yesha'yahu declared that the Lord "was wounded for our transgressions, he was bruised for our iniquities: the chastisement of our peace was upon him; and with his stripes we are healed."[2]

In essence, what we must conclude is that at the Lord's Great Communion, that is, our Passover, he pronounces his sacrifice and subsequent resurrection, which secures our life of fulfillment in him: he pronounces Y'haweh's grace to us, in order for us to appreciate the mercy seat of Y'haweh and, thereby, gain access to the first friendship of righteousness. When we aspire to the first friendship of Y'haweh by keeping the remembrance of Lord Yehoshua's sacrifice in mind, we fulfill the maturity of the New Testament by forgoing the lesser friendships, of the world's civilizations, to obtain an inheritance that will endure. Like Lord Yehoshua, we find an enduring fulfillment and then selflessly yield our talents to serve others who seek the friendship of the Father.

To be sure, the most anxious moments and the darkest hours of his life, Lord Yehoshua used for service. Having run out of time to teach his disciples, the Lord instead prayed before them unto the

---

[1] Matthew 26:26-30
[2] Isaiah 53:5

Father, saying, "I have manifested your name unto the men which you gave me out of the world . . . I pray not for the world, but for them which you have given me, for they are yours . . . Holy Father, keep through your own name those whom you have given me, that they may be one as we are one. . . . Neither pray I for these alone, but for them also which shall believe on me through their word; that they all may be one; as you, Father, are in me, and I in you, that they also may be one in us."[1]

By demonstrating the power of prayer, Lord Yehoshua had allowed his disciples to witness how he would overcome his most fearful moment by praying to the Father, to be inspired by the Father's will and good pleasure, despite Lord Yehoshua's temptation to give up. In actual fact, the Father Y'haweh wanted Lord Yehoshua to complete his ministry: the Lord had to continue to identify with the burdens of the people who had sought deliverance at Yochanan's baptismal ministry. To complete his ministry, the Lord had to identify with the lowliest state of the human condition: he had to be falsely accused and imprisoned; he had to be socially castigated; he had to suffer shame; he had to be ridiculed; he had to suffer dire physical discomfiture; and he had to be expelled from the golden city of corruption, as a cursed person, condemned of *God*.[2]

The Lord had to accomplish such a sacrifice, because our cries ascend up to our Heavenly Father when we suffer from such things in a world that originally advertised his beauty. King David, in fact, captured the spirit of our cries when he wrote, "My God, my God, why have you forsaken me? Why are you so far from helping me . . .

---

[1] John 17:6-21
[2] Here, we are speaking of the necessity of Lord Yehoshua's substitutionary atonement for the sins of the elect. Through his substitutionary atonement, Lord Yehoshua initially endures the imputation of Y'haweh's condemnation of our sins; afterwards, Y'haweh resurrects the Lord because of his righteousness, which Y'haweh imputes upon us, in response to the irresistible gift of faith that he elects us with. As an outcome, the personal sense of justification that the elect internally experience is actually the Holy Spirit's sanctification of the elect souls, solely because of the objective reality that Lord Yehoshua has justified them because of his righteousness that Y'haweh imputes upon the elect by faith.

O my God, I cry in the daytime, but you do not hear me, and in the night time, I am not silent."

In our groaning spirits that look for answers to life's miseries, we all cry out at Yochanan's baptism, "Agnus dei qui tollis peccata mundi Miserere nobis . . . Agnus dei qui tollis peccata mundi dona nobis pacem":

> Lamb of God, that takes away the sins of the world,
> Have mercy on us.
> Lamb of God, that takes away the sins of the world,
> Have mercy on us.
> Lamb of God, that takes away the sins of the world,
> Grant us peace.

A merciful Lord: even in his darkest hour, when his tormentors hung his afflicted body upon the cross, he thought first of others, asking the Father to forgive them, who persecuted him, ignorantly. Afterward, he gathered enough breath to utter the same prayer of King David, saying, "My God, my God, why have you forsaken me?"

Then, fortunately, for us, HalleluYah, Y'haweh instantly heard his prayer, and for us Lord Yehoshua rose again, after an unquestionable three days, that we might believe that he died and rose again to become and establish our hope. He is our peace!

The First Fruits of the Temple

We, therefore, who look for redemption, hoping "that the righteousness of the Law might be fulfilled in us"[1] who faithfully seek the liberty that the Law points to (and not its condemnation), may take comfort in Lord Yehoshua's last words to us. Concerning our atonement, Lord Yehoshua said, "It is accomplished."[2] In other words, Y'haweh resurrected Lord Yehoshua with an eternal reward, after Lord Yehoshua had fulfilled the Law by leading a completely sinless life (only to sacrifice his life for our sakes): Y'haweh made him the heavenly Testator who freely bequeaths to us his Holy Spirit. For

---

[1] Romans 8:4
[2] John 19:30

this cause, we must take comfort because the Holy Spirit now empowers us to fulfill the Law, intuitively, within our hearts. As a result, our hearts now naturally seek the eternal riches of the simple knowledge of Y'haweh's good and benevolence, instead of the vanities of this world.

At the moment of his death, as the scriptures record, "[Lord Yehoshua] bowed his head, and gave up the ghost."[1] Having identified with our burdens, he became our clear benefactor by becoming the testator for us, the elect, who seek to become ministers of his New Testament. Now our hearts naturally seek the eternal justice of the Law that the Testator died to fulfill in the harmony of his resurrected, spiritual body. For this cause, an earthquake ripped the veil of the Temple immediately after Lord Yehoshua died, because his offering upon the mercy seat eternally atoned for our sins and, thereby, comforts us with an eternal Sabbath day of peace within Y'haweh. In other words, upon his death and subsequent resurrection, Lord Yehoshua ripped the fleshly veil of our sins and mercifully began to incorporate us, the elect, into his new, eternal, resurrected body that abides in beauty and excellence for all time.

At present, he is the consummate leader, caregiver, friend, and husband; because he cares for us and seeks the best advantage for us who are essentially his flesh, the beloved temple of Y'haweh. In this vein, the Apostle Sha'ul declares, "So ought men to love their wives as their own bodies. He that loves his wife, loves himself, for no man ever yet hates his own flesh; but nourishes and cherishes it, even as the Lord the Church: for we are members of his body, of his flesh, and his bones."[2]

Keeping the love of Y'haweh in mind, let us understand that Lord Yehoshua inaugurated the Church by only giving the Holy Spirit to the Church on a day that highlighted the mercy and glory of Y'haweh. The Lord told his disciples to gather in the Temple until they received his Holy Spirit: the Lord then chose the feast day of the first fruits of Y'haweh's harvest to give them the Holy Spirit, since on

---

[1] John 19:30
[2] Ephesians 5:28-30

that day, devout Jewish pilgrims would fill the international city of Yerushalayim. The pilgrims would come from every social class of the Diaspora, arriving from every corner of the known world to participate in the celebration of the First Fruits: a day that not only commemorates the first fruits of Yisra'el's harvest, but also commemorates Y'haweh's giving of the Law to the children of Yisra'el, fifty days after their exodus from Egypt. And so, instead of celebrating the first fruits of Judea's produce and Yisra'el's receiving of the Law, Lord Yehoshua celebrated the first born of Y'haweh's Church: the ecclesia—the assemblage—of common Jews who hailed the experience of those whose seeds of faith Y'haweh cultivates.

We recall that to cultivate the seeds of faith, Y'haweh, first, proclaims the Law that cries out against Yisra'el's alienation from his Holy Place. Afterwards, Y'haweh gives the faithful an intuitive desire to become reconciled in the Holy Spirit filled Body of Lord Yehoshua, who intuitively fulfills the Law by being the expression of the self-existent Spirit, Y'haweh.

Although Lord Yehoshua initially appointed twelve Apostles to lay the spiritual foundation of the Church, he primarily used a few in whom he directly cultivated a profound sense of appreciation for his grace: Shim'on Kefa yielded much fruit for the Lord, because his soul grew from the profound sense of appreciation that he had gained after the Lord forgave him for denying the Lord. As well, Yochanan (not the Baptist) bore the fruit of the tree of life for Lord Yehoshua, because a profound sense of appreciation endowed his soul, as well: Yochanan appreciated the special friendship that the Lord had cultivated with him, above the other apostles. And so, being thankful, Yochanan especially taught of the profound love of the Lord. Next, Yehuda[1], the earthly brother of Lord Yehoshua, too, gained a profound sense of appreciation for the Lord's mercy that was upon him. The Lord forgave Yehuda for initially not believing in him, when the Lord had conducted his ministry on earth. Yehuda, eventually, became a main pillar of the first century Yerushalayim Church.

---

[1] James

All of these, who had experienced the love of the Lord, became faithful ministers of the New Testament: the enduring covenant and proclamation that declares that Lord Yehoshua has fulfilled the Law for those in whom Y'haweh has instilled an intuitive desire to seek, obediently, the righteousness of a first friendship with him. To this end, the Testament gives us access to the Holy Marriage between the Lord and Y'haweh's worshippers, in which is the liberation of all things unto the glory of Y'haweh, even unto Y'haweh's eternal Shabbat that the Law merely points to.

With the truth that we have unfolded, heretofore, we may begin to qualify the Apostles' ministry and writings by further understanding the situation in which Lord Yehoshua inaugurated the New Testament ministry of the Apostles: the Lord purposely baptized them corporately with his Holy Spirit, while they were in the midst of the devout Jews of the Diaspora. Again, the Jews had gathered from their dispersal throughout the Roman world, in order to observe the feast of the First Fruits—that is, Pentecost[1], as the following scripture describes:

> And when the day of Pentecost was fully come, they were all with one accord in one place. And suddenly there came a sound from Heaven as of a rushing mighty wind, and it filled all the house where they were sitting. And there appeared unto them cloven tongues like as of fire, and it sat upon each of them. And they were all filled with the Holy Spirit, and began to speak with other tongues, as the Spirit gave them utterance. And there were dwelling at Yerushalayim Jews, devout men, out of every nation under Heaven.[2]

By recalling our definition of truth, in regards to the Holy Spirit's indiscriminately redeeming the faith of the elect, despite social standing, we may begin to interpret the above scripture in the

---

[1] Pentecost is synonymous with the Old Testament mandated celebration of the feast of weeks, in which Y'haweh commanded the children of Yisra'el to observe a feast to commemorate Y'haweh's giving of the Law to the Yisra'elites approximately 50 days after their exodus from Egypt. Christians changed the name to Pentecost, meaning the fiftieth day, in Greek.
[2] Acts 2:1-5

subsequent manner: let us initially recall that Y'haweh's self-existent spiritual nature compels him to affirm his person by predetermining the reciprocity of his love from whom he, indiscriminately, elects to appreciate his benevolence. With this understanding in mind, we may observe that upon the day of Pentecost, Y'haweh for the first time since Adam's expulsion from Eden could extensively extend the Holy Spirit's first friendship of righteousness unto his purified assembly of people, without his quintessential act of benevolence being distorted by the veil of sin. In this manner, Y'haweh's creation of a new triumphant Adam, upon the resurrection of humble Lord Yehoshua at the dawn of Imperial Rome, allowed Y'haweh to cultivate the fruits of the Holy Spirit's tree of life by substantiating the faith of the elect whom he predestined to find fulfillment in his mercy, after he forgives their trespasses and sins. Decidedly, Y'haweh could begin to establish his glory upon our fulfilled sense of appreciation for his love: indeed, his gleaning the eternal reciprocity of his love, in this manner, is his harvesting the fruit of his Holy Spirit's tree of life.

We may recall, as well, that the sense of faith first arose in Adam when he saw his and his family's inability to recapture the peace of Eden, either through religion or the superficialities of moral virtue: we understood that Adam's sense of faith especially arose to seek a first friendship when he saw how the lack of faith in Y'haweh's benevolent purposes consigned the unfaithful to seek the lesser friendships of sensuality or necessity. Too, we understood that under such circumstances Adam invariably saw the frailties of the flesh (such as greed, incontinence, malice, and lasciviousness) cloak the peace of Eden. So as we considered how Adam lost Eden, we ultimately understood that Y'haweh's greatest gift to humankind is the revelatory salvation knowledge of the new, meek Adam, which knowledge Y'haweh freely gives to those whose faith he selectively endows to look past the unrighteousness and pride of the unfaithful, as he confers the righteousness of the new Adam upon them.[1]

---

[1] Here, we must underscore that fact that one cannot experience the sanctification (that is, the setting apart and reconciling peace) of the Holy Spirit by one's self-

Even so, beginning with Adam's generation, Y'haweh could not continually pour out his Holy Spirit jointly upon a large group of people, because either the temporal triumphs and aspirations of the prodigious obscured the gifts of Y'haweh, or the religious deeds of people made them think that they were deserving of Y'haweh's opened hand. For this cause, it was necessary for Y'haweh to judge the pre-Noach age, in order to pronounce his grace in this age, as we have said.

Even after the judgmental flood, Y'haweh could only extend the promise of his fulfilled Holy Spirit to individuals and small-scattered groups of people. Indeed, with these people, he could restrictively cultivate a sense of appreciation for his outstretched hand. After the flood, Y'haweh extended his grace by endowing the Patriarchs Avraham, Yitzhak, and Ya'akov's faith with the salvation knowledge of a new Adam. Y'haweh, in fact, could only demonstrate before the Patriarchs how the new Adam's Holy Spirit would eventually turn the contentious lands around Mount Tziyon into the eternal Kingdom of Heaven: the place where the Patriarchs and the faithful of Avraham's children would dwell in. Yet, when Y'haweh made a covenant of obedience with the children of the Patriarchs, requiring them to observe such laws that ordered their personal, communal, and economic activities with deference to the hidden new Adam's greater fulfillment, the selfish aspirations of the people either compromised the Covenant outright, or undermined the Covenant's objective, as the people esteemed personal vanity over the new Adam's greater good.

Only upon the ascendancy of an international, hybrid governmental power, such as the Roman Empire (which assimilated ancient Yisra'el and Yerushalayim's Mount Tziyon) could Y'haweh pronounce his grace and glory over the nations: Y'haweh could, indiscriminately, pour out his Holy Spirit among those whom he

---

justification through personal merit or religious works. Y'haweh must first express the full measure of his Holy Spirit in the selfless and atoning Christ, whom eternally fulfills Y'haweh's good pleasure. Following, Y'haweh imparts Christ's Holy Spirit unto us, in order to suppress our self-wills, as Y'haweh realizes his predetermined eternal justice in Christ.

elected to have their faith endowed with the salvation knowledge that looks beyond human nationality, race, class, ingenuity, personal prowess, inheritance, or religious rite to see the only humble Lord Yehoshua as salvation and the embodiment of Y'haweh's love. As the prophets inferred, only upon the latter days—that is, the culmination of a pervasive and conflicting international government—could Y'haweh indiscriminately pour out his Holy Spirit upon humankind, to secure the irresistible response of the heart that yields the fruits of his Holy Spirit's righteousness. Upon Pentecost, Y'haweh could freely reveal to all nations the mystery of his Holy Spirit's rest, "which was kept secret since the world began."[1]

From Canaan, the most tumultuous land, therefore, Y'haweh could demonstrate (through Lord Yehoshua's sacrifice) his love for the humble, the meek, and all whom his peaceable Holy Spirit inspires to seek his peace around the world. Thereby, upon Pentecost, Y'haweh could finally secure the devotion of the elect by securing "the obedience of faith"[2], as the elect began to appreciate the eternal riches of the Lord's Testament: the elect could, unabashedly, begin to appreciate the free gift of the risen Lord's Holy Spirit. At the same time, Y'haweh's Holy Spirit could freely cultivate the predestined seeds of faith by turning the elect from the old Adam's selfish aspirations, which the Law decries, to the free pursuit of the new Adam's salvation knowledge: the elect could freely pursue such knowledge that arises from the appreciative sense of Y'haweh's transcendent good, benevolence, and Shabbat Rest within a heavenly Eden that the old Adam could not appreciate.

Thus, Y'haweh (in the form of the great High Priest, Lord Yehoshua) bequeathed (in the Lord's Testament) the Holy Spirit, in the Holy Spirit's transitory form of a promise: an irresistible hope in the justification of the elect's faith upon the eternal judgment of the world, which will occur upon the totality of human government and humanity's subsequent rebellion against Y'haweh. So as the Holy

---

[1] Romans 16:25
[2] Romans 16:26

Spirit finally empowered the Apostles to peer behind the veil into the Holy of Holies, the Apostles acquired the irresistible sense to fulfill the love of Y'haweh piously among one another, despite the vanities of religious pride. In this manner, by becoming maturing extensions of Lord Yehoshua through love, the Apostles (through righteous judgment) began to fulfill the righteous, first friendship that the Law seeks. They began to appreciate the simple but brilliant treasures that their purified consciences allowed; and they began to detest the vane aspirations and fleeting sophistications that their former defiled consciences had tolerated, especially when they had tried to gain false senses of security in a world of scarcity. As an outcome, they could fully substantiate within their hearts the Law that cried out against not only their personal sins, but also the corporate sins of the worldly civilizations; moreover, at the same time, they surrendered the ultimate sense of appreciation to Y'haweh who redeemed their faith with the blood of the resurrected Mashiach. Indeed, when their hearts finally let go of their former, perverted aspirations, they displayed unto Y'haweh the first fruits of the Holy Spirit, as they devoted themselves to the coming Kingdom of Heaven. So, like Moshe, finally standing upon hallowed ground (even standing upon a transformed Mount Tziyon), the Apostles "received grace and apostleship, for obedience to the faith among all nations for Lord Yehoshua's name."[1]

Directly peering into the Holy of Holies by freely communing with the Holy Spirit now dwelling within them, the Apostles uninhibitedly saw that which their faith had inherently quested for: they, inherently, saw the fulfilled love of Lord Yehoshua's future Holy Marriage unto them. Having the righteousness of the new Adam conferred upon them, the Apostles began to perceive the word of truth, even the good news that is the gospel: they, inherently, understood the proclamation of the revealed mystery and truth of Y'haweh, which details how he (in self-affirmation) has freely instilled and cultivated the faith of the elect. In this manner, his Spirit irresistibly compelled them to seek, obediently, their predestined

---

[1] Romans 1:5

inheritance held in Lord Yehoshua's Testament, which symbolically assumes the form of a sevenfold sealed book that details the cultivation and redemption of the elect by the Lamb, who only opens the sealed Testament, unto their liberty. Through these means, the Lamb secured the glory of Y'haweh.

Even so, possessing the earnest of the new Adam's Holy Spirit as they peered behind the veil, the Apostles could at last look behind them upon the preceding Law and the accompanying interim tabernacle and see within the Law's tenets a spirit of expediency, expectancy, and constant deferment to what is truly valuable, as the Law and sacraments point to the true eternal riches behind the veil. The Apostles could readily see in the Law the necessity to turn away from self-esteem, while they meekly appreciate Y'haweh's shared gifts for all.

And so, being empowered by the Holy Spirit of the new Adam, the Apostles finally understood the Law in its correct context, seeing within the Law a reflection of the righteous Holy Marriage. Because of the sacrifice of the humble, obedient Mashiach, the Apostles knew that the elect do not have to observe the tabernacle's sacrificial sacraments and purity rights, which actually seek to reflect our reconciliation into the purified Body of Lord Yehoshua: they, certainly, understood that, now, our obedient faith in the Lord is our purity. Even so, the Apostles began to understand that the temptations of our dying flesh still fall under the Law, which only seeks to reconcile our consciences with one another, under Y'haweh. Notwithstanding, they knew that our liberated souls find eternal freedom beyond the Law, through having faith in the resurrected Body of the Mashiach.

Qualifying a full understanding of the gospel of the Mashiach, the Apostles could use the Law as a schoolmaster that decries sin's selfishness in every aspect of civilization. Thereby, they taught all to relinquish the fleeting wealth gotten from life's labor, by ascribing the aesthetic values of the soul only unto the enduring Kingdom of Heaven. In this way, they taught the new members of the Church to let go of their former aspirations, as they all proceeded with faith unto Heaven's tree of life.

Of all, we must note that Lord Yehoshua gave the Apostles their authority according to the measure of faith that his Holy Spirit instilled within them, making them obedient to Y'haweh's truth and purposes. In this regard, Y'haweh stretched out his hand to dispense freely the salvation knowledge and mystery of him, unto his glory. To this end, the Apostles manifested their authority by their earnest efforts to deliver the gospel of the Lord's Testament transparently, liberally, simplistically, and completely, knowing that all whom Y'haweh "ordained unto eternal life [would] believe."[1]

Being faithful stewards of the New Testament, the Apostles delivered the gospel without using esoteric and religious jargon. Instead, they used plain words that all congregants could readily understand. Essentially, the Apostles sought to ensure that the faith would not turn into another mystery religion, among elite priests, scholars, and doctors of religion: unfortunately, today many supposed ministers seek such elite status to the actual detriment of the gospel, which Y'haweh intended to be freely shared among the saints. To their credit, the Apostles sought to disseminate the gospel liberally, even as Lord Yehoshua looked past the religious elite—that is, the priests and religious doctors—to empower the working class to discover salvation knowledge. And so, carefully building the Temple of Y'haweh upon its corner stone (the humble Savior), the Apostles began to spread Y'haweh's tabernacle over the world, truly binding on earth what is bound in Heaven.

Invariably, laying down the foundational New Testament doctrines of the Church with great care, the Apostles, as a faithful bride to the Lord, raised the children of faith (whom the Lord had given them) with the selfless love of a doting mother: merely using the Law as an edifying spiritual guide, the Apostles always sought out the elect children of faith by gauging what fidelity their congregants had for the righteous Kingdom that the Old Covenant Law pointed to. Because of the Apostles' faithfulness, the spiritual offspring of the Apostles grew spiritually rich because of the Apostles' sacrifices of humility and poverty.

---

[1] Acts 13:48

The Apostles, furthermore, remained obedient to the Holy Spirit by only seeking those whom the Lord had elected to receive the grace of Y'haweh. Because of their obedience, the Church, for a time, remained pure, because the Apostles did not try to gain superficial congregants by watering down their message for popular culture's sake. Instead, the Apostles preached the gospel of Lord Yehoshua as they had received it from him. They knew that the Holy Spirit would inspire all classes of people whom Y'haweh had predestined to worship him. Thus, the Apostles preached with power and sincerity, again, delivering the good news of the Lord's Testament in simplicity: the fruit of their efforts is that they directly ministered to and gained the true children of the Lord and not merely self-serving religious people.

Lastly, because Y'haweh empowered them to deliver, faithfully, the gospel of Lord Yehoshua, he gave them the gifts of miracles to validate their testimony and establish the Church upon their teachings. For example, Y'haweh first gave them the miraculous ability to speak in unknown and foreign languages, which ability allowed them to transcend cultural barriers by speaking to the chosen in their native tongues. For sure, this miraculous ability evidenced the confirmation of the Holy Spirit upon the Apostles, as the day of Pentecost witnesses. Furthermore, the Apostles delivered the word of Y'haweh so carefully and faithfully that Y'haweh only gave his Holy Spirit to their hearers after the Apostles had laid their hands on the hearers. In this way, Y'haweh validated the Apostles' foundational teachings.

In their teachings, the Apostles often denounced any congregant or Church leader's lusts for unjust monetary gain. Instead of coveting resources to benefit themselves, the Apostles worked hard and shared all things in common, despite class or creed. What we may essentially conclude is that the Apostles were faithful ministers of the New Covenant of the heart: they remembered the communion of Y'haweh, the Lord, and the Holy Spirit, while they recalled the sacrifice and humility of Lord Yehoshua by breaking bread with one another, in love, always.

The Apostle Sha'ul's Ministry of Reconciliation

The last Apostle that we must note is Sha'ul: he is the primary Apostle that the Lord used to build his Church, because the Lord could use Sha'ul's background to demonstrate the full measure of his grace upon Sha'ul and future disciples, even surpassing the measure of grace that the Lord had dispensed upon the original Apostles. At one time in his life, Sha'ul was a Parush (one of the Perushim) who organized and instrumented the persecution of the early Church. Even so, Lord Yehoshua miraculously appeared to him, not in flesh as the humbled Suffering Servant but in the brilliant light of his eternal glory. The Lord then bequeathed unto Sha'ul the abundance of his grace, in order to convert the then blinded Apostle.

Sha'ul's conversion was necessary for the Church, because ignorant believers began to idolize the original Apostles just because the Apostles had walked with the Lord, while the Lord was on earth. In effect, the ignorant new disciples actually began to esteem the Apostles just for being Apostles, instead of esteeming only the message that the Apostles carried. And so, Sha'ul's conversion served as a poignant example to the early Church that none are worthy of Y'haweh's grace: on the contrary, anyone from any social background can experience the grace of Y'haweh, like the original Apostles, when Y'haweh opens his hand to him or her. In this regard, Sha'ul, himself, declared that the Lord forgave and used him as the chief Apostle to demonstrate his mercy for the generations of the elect who would arise after Sha'ul. He declared the following:

> I obtained mercy, that in me first Yehoshua Mashiach might exhibit all longsuffering as an example to them, who should hereafter believe on him to everlasting life.[1]

Undeniably, the Lord gave the Apostle Sha'ul greater spiritual understanding than he gave the other Apostles. Sha'ul, himself, even declared that they who do not receive the revelations that the Lord

---

[1] 1 Timothy 1:16

had given him, which the other Apostles affirmed, should be branded heretics.

Indeed, we accept Sha'ul's teachings because Shim'on Kefa, himself, acknowledged Sha'ul's superior apostleship by acknowledging the fact that Sha'ul's teachings are "hard to be understood"[1] for the newborn child of Y'haweh. Many scholars note that Sha'ul conveyed a more advanced New Testament message than the other disciples: although Sha'ul and the twelve Apostles before him commonly shared a profound revelatory understanding of Lord Yehoshua, we defer to the authority of Sha'ul, because Lord Yehoshua revealed himself to Sha'ul transcendently, allowing Sha'ul inherently to place into order the preceding transitional revelations of the Lord that speak to his elect, in this life. In other words, Sha'ul transcendently encountered the Totality of Y'haweh, while the other Apostles indirectly encountered the Totality of Y'haweh, progressively, through the priestly ministry of the Suffering Servant, who eventually cultivates all disciples unto a transcendent understanding of Y'haweh's fullness in him.

Understanding Sha'ul's doctrines concerning the scriptures is, therefore, a necessity for those who seek to become mature disciples of Lord Yehoshua. To some extent, the justification for our treatise is to expand and elaborate upon Sha'ul's doctrine, by considering his work in the light of other New Testament scriptures, which he may or may not have had access to. As well, we aspire to consider Sha'ul's work in the light of certain natural principles of conscience, which have inspired the three fundamental forms of secular government.

Sha'ul may not have possessed all the final copies of the epistles and gospel chronicles that the other Apostles composed[2]; moreover,

---

[1] 2 Peter 3:16
[2] One may establish the fact that the New Testament books were written before 70 AD, a year of significance in which the Romans destroyed the second Jewish Temple. First, we may establish an early date for the book of Acts, because the author, who identifies himself as Luke (an aid to Sha'ul), chronologically records the beginnings of the Church; however, he does not mention the martyrdom of the Apostles nor the destruction of the Temple, even though he had knowledge of the fact that Lord Yehoshua predicted the destruction. Beforehand, Luke had identified himself as the author of a preceding gospel record of the ministry of Lord

he did not correlate his revelatory understandings with the complementary revelations of Yochanan, the favorite of the Lord. Likewise, he may not have completely understood the Prophet Daniel's vision of the procession of the Gentile governments, which ultimately fulfill Y'haweh's will, in Y'haweh's condemnation of them as Y'haweh vindicates his faithful. In addition, the Apostle never found the time to assess and write a critical analysis of his own writings; because if the Lord had afforded him the opportunity, one would be inclined to assume that the Church would have been stronger. Although the Apostle Sha'ul experienced transcendent revelations of Y'haweh that empowered him with the inherent ability to assess the scriptures from his standpoint in human history, we can critically assess his transcendent understanding by considering his work in the light of the human history that has unfolded unto this critical global era.

In the light of the truth that we have unfolded heretofore, we may began to assess Sha'ul's doctrines by first considering his second transcendent experience, which occurred shortly after Sha'ul's original encounter with the brilliant emanation of Lord Yehoshua's light. In this second experience, Y'haweh allowed Sha'ul to see the full landscape of his truth unfold to reveal Y'haweh's fullness in Lord Yehoshua; who (as Sha'ul would then declare) "ascended up far beyond all heavens, that he might fill all things."[1] Y'haweh instantaneously produced Sha'ul's soul beyond the dimensions that Y'haweh's expressed light produces; Sha'ul, therefore, experienced the simplicity of true worship as he inherently saw beyond the physical and social impediments that Y'haweh uses to cultivate a sense of appreciation for the brilliant light of his benevolence. Thus, Sha'ul inherently saw past the vanities of temporary pleasure and necessity: he saw past the idolatry of the world that Y'haweh

---

Yehoshua. What is of most importance is that Luke's record of Lord Yehoshua parallels other accounts that the other Apostles wrote before him. Therefore, Luke's gospel establishes an even earlier date for the other gospels. Lastly, the epistles that the Apostles wrote quote the stories that the early gospel accounts record; in like manner, they reference one another and the contemporaneous events of the time.

[1] Ephesians 4:10

exercises his power against. Sha'ul then retained an understanding of the righteous friendship of Y'haweh, through which Y'haweh refines our souls by freely instilling within us an irresistible sense of appreciation for his Holy Spirit's, meekness, and the charity of his abiding love. In the end, Sha'ul began to see life as an experience through which we overcome deprivation by gaining the utmost appreciation for the love of Y'haweh "that mortality may be swallowed up with life."[1]

To some, Sha'ul's vision may seem esoteric; nevertheless, we must assert that his experience (of which he probably retained little rational memory of) gave him an uncanny ability to assess the unfolding will of Y'haweh. To this end, Sha'ul became the greatest Apostle, delivering the entire truth of Y'haweh in the Mashiach.

Having a transcendent understanding, the Apostle Sha'ul instinctively understood why Y'haweh revealed himself in the humble Mashiach and subsequently dispersed his Holy Spirit, during the culmination of classical history, which again occurred upon the rise of the international Roman Empire. Writing to the dispersed Hebrews of the Mediterranean Roman world, Sha'ul instinctively indicated that upon the last days of classical history, as the international Roman Empire assimilated so many conflicting governments and cultures, Y'haweh could finally make known his mystery to his elect, as his Holy Spirit freely instilled in them an inherent sense of appreciation for the humility and sacrifice of Lord Yehoshua. Essentially, because he transcendently saw how Y'haweh placed in Lord Yehoshua the fulfillment and purpose for all creation, Sha'ul could inherently understand the following more perfectly than the original Apostles:

At the dawn of the Roman Empire, Y'haweh could at last fully demonstrate his displeasure upon the multifaceted Roman world by demonstrating his full pleasure upon the only righteous Lord Yehoshua. To this end, Y'haweh could poignantly decry every aspect of human corruption that Rome concealed, as the Roman world ignorantly pursued the vain knowledge of pleasure and worldly

---

[1] 2 Corinthians 5:4

necessity. In reality, Rome's progressive pursuits began as they established unjust governments and shortsighted religious institutions; moreover, Rome's progressive pursuits persisted as they further condoned demented value systems, as displayed in their perverse art and irreconcilable personal behavior. Thereby, Y'haweh could wonderfully triumph over the unjust human civilizations by demonstrating that he in the form of the resurrected Lord Yehoshua is the savior of those qualities of the human soul that are pure, universally intelligible, and (therefore) directly responsive to Y'haweh's beauty, charity, and love. In other words, Y'haweh could make known the fact that Lord Yehoshua alone, eternally, preserves the universally intelligible qualities, such as meekness, selflessness, empathy, and submission: these qualities reside at the foundation of the human soul; moreover, these qualities we, unfortunately, pervert or suppress as we seek false senses of security in the fleeting vanities of this world, as we have said.

In essence, Sha'ul understood that when Y'haweh resurrected Lord Yehoshua's pure body and soul, Y'haweh could at last demonstrate the futility of vanity's shortsighted pursuits, which the self-serving nations continually engage in. Indeed, holding Lord Yehoshua's righteousness as the foundation of his Temple, Y'haweh could display the glorious reward of the Testament that he holds for the elect, whom he inspires to seek the dispersed riches of Lord Yehoshua's pure Holy Spirit. In this vein, Sha'ul wrote that Y'haweh could "[abound] to us in all wisdom and prudence"[1], as he resurrects the selfless Lord and graciously dispenses the Holy Spirit, of the Lord's universally intelligible nature; whereby his Spirit mitigates the corruptions of humankind with joy, patience, charity, eternal love.

To assess Sha'ul's doctrines, definitively, we must note how Sha'ul sought to preserve and disseminate the salvation knowledge by creating a laypeople based Church environment that empowers the elect, despite personal, social, or religious egotism.

---

[1] Ephesians 1:8

To begin, let us understand that the Apostle Sha'ul warned the Church not to seek the wisdom of humankind but to seek the true reconciling wisdom of Y'haweh in Lord Yehoshua. Sha'ul encouraged the Church to appreciate and pursue only the simple, intelligible, and benevolent expressions of Y'haweh, saying, "Lest as the serpent beguiled Havah through his subtlety, so your minds should be corrupted from the simplicity that is in Christ."[1]

Sha'ul endeavored to cultivate the peaceable fruits of Lord Yehoshua's Holy Spirit among all Church members, in order to mature the children of the Lord. Sha'ul created an environment of learning by noting how Lord Yehoshua dispensed spiritual gifts, in order for us to reconcile the world. Writing to the Church at the ancient city of Corinth, Sha'ul wrote, "When [Lord Yehoshua] ascended up on high, he led captivity captive, and gave gifts unto men."[2]

Reflecting upon the benefactor-beneficiary relationship of the Holy Marriage, the Apostle noted that some of Lord Yehoshua's followers receive the leadership gifts in the assembly of saints, such as apostles, prophets, evangelists, pastors, government, and teachers. Others received the service gifts, such as administrators, helps, tongues, counselors, care givers, the word of wisdom, charity, and stewardship. The Apostle further noted that the bond of Lord Yehoshua's love fosters all the gifts, "until we all come in the unity of the faith, and of the knowledge of the Son of God, unto a perfect man, unto the measure of the stature of the fullness of the Mashiach."[3] With this understanding, the Apostle noted that the Lord gave all the gifts to the elect, in order for them to rely upon one another and seek one another's good, as his body matures unto the eternal love of the Holy Marriage that will transcend all; therefore, the Apostle noted that the ability to love one another, selflessly, fulfills all the gifts and the will of Y'haweh. Thus, the Apostle declared, "Now abides faith, hope, and love, these three; but the

---

[1] 2 Corinthians 11:3
[2] Ephesians 4:8
[3] Ephesians 4:13

greatest of these is love [for it endures forever, as the other transitional gifts succumb to the fulfillment of Y'haweh's love]."[1]

To further understand how the Apostle further created an environment in which the Church could corporately retain the knowledge of Y'haweh, we must interpret the following scripture with our understanding of truth. In this way, we can easily assess how Sha'ul ordered the early Church:

> [Submit] yourselves one to another in the fear of God: wives, submit yourselves unto your own husbands, as unto the Lord. For the husband is the head of the wife, even as Christ is the head of the Church: and he is the savior of the body. Therefore, as the Church is subject unto Christ, so let the wives be to their own husbands in everything. Husbands, love your wives, even as Christ also loved the Church, and gave himself for it; that he might sanctify and cleanse it with the washing of water by the word, that he might present it to himself a glorious Church, not having spot, or wrinkle, or any such thing; but that it should be holy and without blemish . . . . For we are members of his body, of his flesh, and of his bones. For this cause shall a man leave his father and mother, and shall be joined unto his wife, and they two shall be one flesh. This is a great mystery: but I speak concerning Christ and the Church.[2]

Writing above to the Church members at the ancient Roman City of Ephesus, Sha'ul encouraged all the members of the Church to submit themselves to one another, in order for the whole Church to assume the form of a single healthy body that submits itself as a pure bride unto Lord Yehoshua, who sacrificed himself as the loving husband. By considering Sha'ul's above statement with our lessons learned heretofore, we may readily conclude that it is necessary for Church leaders and members to submit themselves one to another, holding one another accountable. In this way, the Church retains a healthy environment that preserves the knowledge of the Holy Spirit's charity and fidelity. What is more, the hallmark of liberty that exists within the Church's benefactor-beneficiary relationships

---

[1] 1 Corinthians 13:13
[2] Ephesians 5:21-32

assumes the countenance of the pure bride who waits for Lord Yehoshua, the true husband and liberator of the Church.

Essentially, while they portrayed the liberty of the Holy Marriage by equitably sharing in the benefactor-beneficiary roles among the saints, the early Church under Sha'ul's tutelage naturally conveyed the salvation knowledge that Y'haweh preserves for the true worshippers of him in Lord Yehoshua's Kingdom. In other words, keeping in mind the equity of the Holy Marriage that exists between Lord Yehoshua (the heavenly benefactor) and the Church (the spiritual beneficiary), we may even further draw out the direct reflection of the Holy Marriage from the themes of Sha'ul's teachings. As we further note from above how he taught wives to submit themselves to their husbands, as the Church submits to the Lord, we understand that ultimately both male and female worshippers will equally assume the form of the bride of the Mashiach in the Holy Marriage.[1] And so, when we note how Sha'ul taught the husbands to serve and love their wives, as Lord Yehoshua served his disciples, we must note how Church leaders must selflessly seek to render an accurate, intelligible, and clear account of the Word of Y'haweh, their knowing that Lord Yehoshua is the true leader of us all.

Holding the heavenly institute of marriage as the reward of the New Testament and, therefore, the foundation of the Church, Sha'ul forbade fornication, unnatural sex (that is, homosexuality), and adultery. Also, using the marriage model, Sha'ul encouraged employees to submit themselves to their employers, and he encouraged employers to care for and not exploit their employees, even as the Lord is a careful ruler of us. Likewise, Sha'ul encouraged citizens to submit to rulers, and he encouraged rulers to care for their subjects. Essentially, Sha'ul encouraged the Church to love and seek the good will of all, which includes those who are in political authority, knowing that the Lord elects and liberates people from every class, unto the salvation of matrimony in the single Body of Christ. To this effect, Sha'ul wrote as follows:

---

[1] See Galatians 3:28

For as many of you have been baptized into Christ have put on Christ. There is neither Jew nor Greek, there is neither bond nor free, there is neither male nor female: for you are all one in Christ Yehoshua.[1]

And so, while he kept in mind the eternal Holy Marriage model, the Apostle organized the whole transitory structure of the Church. Essentially, not seeking to renew the cold stone tablets of the Law, he only encouraged such tenets that reflect or foster a worshipper's desire to be reconciled with Y'haweh in the Lord's Holy Marriage; therefore, he did not allow women to assume leadership positions over men, and he encouraged the people of lesser gifts to submit themselves to those whom the Holy Spirit anointed with the pastoral, prophetic, teaching, and governmental gifts. Acknowledging the fidelity of the Holy Marriage, Sha'ul encouraged accountability among the congregants. In like manner, he encouraged the whole Church to retain orthodox doctrines, asking every believer to strive to be well versed in his or her faith: that is, the doctrine of grace in which our Savior redeems us by greeting our repentance with the remission of our sins upon our acceptance of his sacrificed and resurrected life, which is a life that allows us to become beneficiaries of his Testament through which we become eternally married to him, being one with the Savior of humankind through the prevailing of his Holy Spirit.

All told, Sha'ul encouraged the whole Church to pray patiently in the manner that Lord Yehoshua described, teaching all to seek patiently the riches and justice of the Lord's coming Kingdom, in order to prevent Church corruption. For this cause, he especially sought to encourage the Holy Marriage's fidelity between Church leaders and congregants: because the Church leaders assumed such significant roles over the Lord's people, Sha'ul instructed the people not to empower any novice to rule in the Church, and he encouraged the people to seek rulers who do not lust for the riches of popular culture: such as fancy apparel, luxurious houses, and public acclaim. Sha'ul knew that if a leader were truly inspired by the justice of the

---

[1] Galatians 3:28

coming Kingdom, he would not desire the fleeting vanities of this life, even as Yochanan the Baptist and Lord Yehoshua did not desire vanity, but they sought fulfillment, only, in the Holy Spirit. In this way, they sought to become sincere, humble benefactors of the people.

To conclude our assessment of the Apostle Sha'ul's doctrines, we must note that the major outcome, concerning Sha'ul's ordering of the Church, is the following: when Sha'ul taught the Church to seek the true riches that Lord Yehoshua's Testament held for his elect beneficiaries, in the justice of the Holy Marriage, Sha'ul realized that it was the Church's responsibility to seek the same justice of Y'haweh in the world, while the Church recovers the redeemed of Y'haweh (even the salt of the earth whom Y'haweh had scattered across the world). In essence, Sha'ul knew that it was the Church's job to enjoin the interim tabernacle's ministry of reconciliation. Now that all types of people could experience the true power of Y'haweh (after observing the humility of Lord Yehoshua and experiencing the charity of the Holy Spirit), the Church could purge the world of its violence, lusts, greed, and warfare by cultivating those whom Y'haweh redeems. To this end, Sha'ul encouraged the Church to seek the power of Y'haweh by being humble, forgiving, submissive, and patient; for through such fruits of the Holy Spirit's Tree of Life, the Church could pacify a barbarous world by gaining the benevolence of Y'haweh.

Seeking to conquer the world by manifesting the power of Y'haweh through the body of the risen Lord, Sha'ul taught the Church how to be clothed with the Lord's Holy Spirit by putting on the spiritual armor of truth. The Apostle was well aware of the state of evil that repelled the truth of Lord Yehoshua: he saw Satan's discord manifested in the confused ideologies of the Roman world. Like the other Apostles, Sha'ul understood that those who do not believe in or accept the purity of the resurrected Lord Yehoshua either lust after or accept the many subtle injustices and vanities of humankind. In the light of this understanding, Sha'ul witnessed the cultural relativism that readily took root under the multifaceted Roman government:

Rome assimilated so many peoples who had adhered to contrasting belief systems. Indeed, the early secular humanists of the Roman world, therefore, sought to secure the good of the state by suppressing any overt proclamations of truth, which they actually deemed to be relative.

The single truth that Sha'ul experienced through the New Covenant, Sha'ul taught the believers to be clothed in. In this manner, the believer would overcome the dominion of evil by seeking only the power of Lord Yehoshua's resurrection. Sha'ul wrote the following:

> Stand, therefore, having your loins girt about with truth, and having on the breastplate of righteousness; and your feet shod with the preparation of the gospel of peace; above all, taking the shield of faith, wherewith you shall be able to quench the fiery darts of the wicked. And take the helmet of salvation, and the sword of the spirit, which is the word of God: praying always with all prayer and supplication in the Spirit.[1]

As Lord Yehoshua increased Sha'ul's understanding of truth's landscape, Sha'ul increasingly understood the fact that the spiritual weapons, which believers gained in the Body of Lord Yehoshua, are infinitely more powerful than the worldly weapons that the faithless employ. In one respect, the Holy Spirit's patience, empathy, wisdom, longsuffering, hope, and the first friendship's unyielding love handedly win the friendship of those who have yet to believe. And in another respect, the anxious prayers of the elect who endure persecution because they assume the humble form of the Lord, invokes the benevolence of Y'haweh who is quick to deliver his children to vindicate their faith in him. Knowing that Y'haweh conquers the world by instilling his Holy Spirit into elected hearts (while he justly judges others, ultimately, to secure the appreciation of the elect), Sha'ul realized the profundity of the spiritual gifts that Lord Yehoshua freely gave the true worshippers, to secure and edify the hearts of those whom Y'haweh has chosen. And Sha'ul realized

---

[1] Ephesians 6:14-17

the awesome power of the prayers and supplications of the believers, who know that Y'haweh will respond to their prayers, in order to fulfill all things. Finally, having such a realization, Sha'ul testified of the profundity of our spiritual power by saying, "For the weapons of our warfare are not carnal, but mighty through God to the pulling down of strong holds; casting down imaginations, and every high thing that exalts itself against the knowledge of God, and bringing into captivity every thought to the obedience of Christ."[1]

The Death of Sha'ul

Realizing that the Church can only exercise the power of the Holy Spirit by appreciating the humility and selfless sacrifice of Lord Yehoshua, the Apostle Sha'ul first exercised his spiritual weapons against those who esteemed themselves in the Church, since they ignored the finished work of the Mashiach. Following, Sha'ul exercised his gifts to win the hearts of new converts, teaching them that Y'haweh extends his grace to those whom he empowers to fulfill his love in the humble Mashiach. Sha'ul realized that the false disciples could not put on the garment of truth; instead, they presented themselves to the unlearned as covetous wolves dressed in the sheep's clothing of public shows of piety. Thus, the Apostle went through great lengths to oppose those who observed the old Covenant sacraments only to justify themselves over others. Essentially, Sha'ul knew that those who honor themselves, in this manner, sew together again the veil of sin that Lord Yehoshua ripped apart for those whom Y'haweh will graft into Lord Yehoshua's sinless body. Thus, Sha'ul understood that Lord Yehoshua's body is free of the pride of rulers, the covetousness of the elite, and the wantonness of the commoner. For this cause, Sha'ul demonstrated that those who find temporary pleasure in vain shows of piety deny the priceless sacrifice of Lord Yehoshua, whose sinless body only inherits and reflects the internal rewards of Y'haweh.

We conclude that the greatest challenge that Sha'ul faced in executing his New Testament ministry of reconciliation was the

---

[1] 2 Corinthians 10:4-5

following: like Moshe who walked upon hallowed ground but could not impart his experience unto the children of Yisra'el, Sha'ul intuitively experienced the Totality of Y'haweh within, but he could not implant his experience into the souls of others. He, invariably, found that only the Holy Spirit could instill understanding in them whose hearts the Holy Spirit empowers to look past the fleeting conventions of this world unto the transcending world of the new Adam. Sha'ul could only reflect his experience in his systematic approach to the scriptures. And so, although Sha'ul could assess the transition of the old Testament's interim tabernacle into the new Testament's enduring tabernacle (that is, the Holy Marriage's Holy of Holies), Sha'ul could not functionally convey his systematic understanding in rational and pragmatic ways that would make the natural principles of the interim tabernacle and Holy Marriage less abstract and more intelligible to the disciples' souls. Sha'ul could not fully articulate his personal experience in a way that allowed other saints to discover, directly, the mystery of Y'haweh: a mystery that retains the reason and meaning of life that all can intellectually comprehend.

As we have noted, Sha'ul's experience afforded him the understanding to speak of predestination; the necessity of the Law; the free dispensation of grace and knowledge; and the perfecting of our souls in the new Adam, unto a Holy Marriage. Even so, during his time period, Sha'ul found it extremely difficult to pronounce those principles of the Law and tabernacle that transcend religious service and ritual, because some faithless disciples could only note how the expediency of the Law directly addressed the agrarian social, economic, and civil environment of the Roman world: undeniably, Rome had an agrarian based culture that was similar to the pre-Roman Mediterranean world in which the Law had been written.

Unlike Sha'ul's time period, in which the Law's economic aspects directly addressed Sha'ul's culture, the Law's transcending principles abstractly address our needs today. In fact, the transcending principles of the Law not only abstractly address the more complex issues that we intellectually wrestle with presently, but also abstractly point to the Holy Marriage, in which we do not need the Law. In essence, we can abstractly appreciate the transcending tenets of the Law, because the Law's treatment of the sins of the ancient agrarian world through animal sacrifice only underscores the necessity of Lord Yehoshua's enduring sacrifice that ministers to and rises above our more complex lives, today.

In his time period, Sha'ul could only use the symbolism of the interim tabernacle to demonstrate the means through which Lord Yehoshua assumed a prevailing Priesthood upon his sacrifice, which allowed him to administer a new and eternal covenant: Sha'ul's first century Church, which the Jewish Diaspora encompassed, still retained the inclination to seek justification in the actual rituals of the tabernacle that the priests still had performed. And so, Sha'ul found it hard to use the tabernacle symbolism to convey how the eternal Covenant does not merely instill a law that reconciles us with our fellow in the conventions of this world, but points us to a world where we only seek reconciliation with Y'haweh through the peace, meekness, simplicity, and affection of his prevailing Holy Spirit.

Once more, the Apostle Sha'ul did not want to renew the cold stone Law of the old Covenant: a covenant that had pointed to the sins of the people without removing the depraved condition of the people's consciences. Sha'ul, therefore, could at best draw out of the tabernacle's tenets the manner in which Lord Yehoshua continues to use the symbols of the tabernacle to convey how we should relinquish our vanities in this life and receive his eternal sacrifice upon the mercy seat.

Notwithstanding, because we benefit from the environment that the Lord empowered Sha'ul to lay down for us, we are more able to look past the seemingly antiquated social, economic, and civic principles of the Law and concentrate on the eternal glory that the symbolism of the interim tabernacle points us to. We are more able to see within the Law the reflection of an enduring world that transcends the circumstances of this life: we can easily glean from the symbolism of the tabernacle's most Holy Place the fact that we will replace "the cherubim of glory shadowing the mercy seat" of which Sha'ul said that he could not then "speak particularly."[1]

Despite Sha'ul's dilemma, we may affirmatively conclude at this junction in time that we can speak particularly: we may readily observe how the symbolism of the tabernacle reflects the landscape of truth that we have detailed thus far. First, to secure our Spirit-filled understanding of the tabernacle, we have only to observe how sin's imputation disallows the unfaithful from reconciling with the souls of others: we can surely understand why the old Covenant Law condemns such sins like lust, fear, violence, self-aggrandizement, religious pride, and envy; because these are the sins that the unfaithful commit when they haphazardly seek to secure a false sense of security, even though sin binds them in a state of alienation from one another and Y'haweh. Finally, being more able to perceive the eternal principles of the Law in this age, we may readily decry all forms of self-aggrandizement, as the Holy Spirit compels us to let go of the faithless values of our souls and corporately embrace the eternal values of Lord Yehoshua's meek Holy Spirit, which intelligible appeals to all.

Unlike the unfaithful, who remain alienated from one another, we may peer directly into Y'haweh's Holy Place and, thereby, each other's purified souls. To be sure, we may finally marry our souls to the Holy Spirit of Y'haweh. We may comprehend fully the mercy seat of Lord Yehoshua by embracing our election, which dictates that we cannot approach the eternal peace of Y'haweh through any physical, intellectual, or spiritual efforts of our own, because Y'haweh's self-esteem tolerates no other's self-esteem above his own. To humble ourselves appreciatively in the meek Body of Lord Yehoshua and reach spiritual maturity, we have only to understand that Y'haweh requires us to esteem the eternal good of his fullness, above any esteem of humankind, even as the Apostle Sha'ul says, "that no flesh should glory in his presence."[2]

---

[1] Hebrews 9:5
[2] 1Corinthians 1:29

This understanding Sha'ul inherently perceived in the Spirit; however, he was hard pressed to exemplify such a profound understanding to those who merely sought the utility of the Law for their self-preservation, in this life. What is more, because the Apostle fought hard against those who esteemed themselves in their perverse observance of the Law, Sha'ul found it hard to convey how the Lord, himself, in his Priesthood, still temporarily establishes the utility of the Law, in order to condemn those who continually succumb to temptation and ignorance:

The faithless seek fulfillment in this life, while they do not seek the lasting fulfillment in the enduring world. For this cause, we recognize why Lord Yehoshua clearly declared that "until heaven and earth pass, one jot or one tittle shall in no wise pass from the Law, until all be fulfilled."[1] In point of fact, we must underscore the truth that the Law continuously condemns the sins of humankind, while Lord Yehoshua only fulfills an eternal peace for those who seek the eternal righteousness that the Law points to.

To clarify, again, the temporary utility of the Law, we may only note that we must not observe the purity rites, sacrificial offerings, dietary prohibitions, and ritual services of the interim tabernacle, because these symbols point to the sacrifice of Y'haweh's unblemished lamb who fulfills the reciprocity of Y'haweh's love for us, who confess that he is our Lord and the redeemer of our faithful works. And so, to complement the love that Lord Yehoshua fulfills for us, we must seek fulfillment in his Holy Spirit. Thereby, we will fulfill the Law by overcoming the temptation to commit adultery, bear false witness, steal, murder, or covet another's good. What is more, when we make mistakes, we have no need to offer sacrifices, because Y'haweh judges our hearts by our desire to fulfill his will, even though we are not perfect. Indeed, we only find our perfection in the Lord who redeems our best efforts. Thus, during this interim period, the Law stands as a guide and not as a justifier.

In all, we may say that it is okay for a worshipper to acknowledge his or her harvest as a blessing from the Lord. Indeed,

---

[1] Matthew 5:18

it is okay for a worshipper to appreciate the symbolism of a Sabbath Day to acknowledge his or her leisure time as a manifestation of the beauty and Rest of Y'haweh. And it is okay for a worshipper to study the Law, in order to gain a complete understanding of the finished work of the Mashiach. Only, the worshippers of Y'haweh must know that despite their best efforts they may only obtain the salvation of Lord Yehoshua by accepting it as a free gift, which we have only to respond to through love.

Any true worshipper of Y'haweh must understand that the cornerstone of the Temple is that Lord Yehoshua alone fulfills that which the Law seeks: the law seeks a righteous friendship with Y'haweh, whom the two cherubim cover in the Holy Place. Thus, Lord Yehoshua alone empowers us to fulfill the Law, when we make him our Lord and corporately partake upon his humble and sacrificed body. The embattled Apostle Sha'ul tried to convey this fact throughout his ministry: a ministry that became the foundation of the Church that stands upon the solid rock of Lord Yehoshua's servility. Nevertheless, because he died a martyr, Sha'ul could not complete the course that he had embarked upon.

Knowing that his time was coming to an end, Sha'ul anxiously warned the Church about those who would come and "frustrate the grace of God"[1] by teaching false doctrines for personal gain. Remembering the teachings of Lord Yehoshua who said, "Beware of false prophets, which come to you in sheep's clothing, but inwardly they are ravening wolves"[2], Sha'ul called these false teachers wolves, for they prey upon the sheep of the Lord: calling themselves disciples, they flagrantly pursue the lusts of the world. As a result, the wolves incur the scorn of unbelievers; and, in this way, they turn the Church into just another political organization that often invites public animosity.

To be sure, the greatest of calamities occur within the Church, as a result of the death of Sha'ul and the other Apostles. After Sha'ul's death, many in the Church fell upon the stumbling block of Lord

---

[1] Galatians 2:21
[2] Matthew 7:15

Yehoshua's humility: even as the Apostle Sha'ul taught his students that some Jews stumbled[1] because they failed to appreciate the humility of the Lord's sacrifice (as these Jews exalted themselves through mere religious observances), many members of the Church still fall before the same stumbling block, as they likewise exult themselves before others. In this way, they cover the true beauty of Y'haweh that the Mashiach so readily displays through his servitude. Indeed, due to the death of the Apostle Sha'ul, Church leaders historically fail to understand the nature of Y'haweh's transcendent power, knowledge, and love, as he extends himself unto his fulfillment in Lord Yehoshua's meek, intelligible nature. In effect, they fail to see the culmination of the landscape of truth that the prophet Eliyahu saw, as the power of Y'haweh passed by him in a strong wind and earthquake that rent the mountains of vanity, shook the earth of unbelief, and finally purified the soul with the fire of righteousness, all to surrender the peaceable knowledge of Y'haweh in "a still small voice."[2] They fail to observe, from the ultimate exercise of Y'haweh's power, "that the Lord is very pitiful and of tender mercy."[3]

Essentially, upon the death of the Apostles, many in the Church, whom Y'haweh did not entirely fill with his Holy Spirit, lost a complete understanding of the full gospel-truth, which the Apostles had inherently possessed and tried to convey in their writings. If we recall that quintessential knowledge begins with an understanding of Y'haweh's benevolence, we must then understand that many in the Church fail to reach spiritual maturity because they do not understand the nature and complementing restrictions of Y'haweh's love; moreover, they do not fully understand the necessity of our election, in which Y'haweh secures his love through Christ, as we have described above.

We must keep in mind that Y'haweh only reflects his fulfillment by cultivating our eternal sense of fulfillment in the pure conscience

---

[1] Romans 9:32-33
[2] 1Kings 19:12
[3] James 5:11

of Lord Yehoshua; therefore, we must understand that when our Lord Yehoshua proclaimed that "God so loved the world, that he gave his only begotten Son, that whosoever believes in him should not perish, but have everlasting life"[1], Lord Yehoshua was stating that Y'haweh the Father seeks to save the pure qualities of humankind that can perceive and celebrate his loving expression in creation. For this single purpose, Y'haweh gave Lord Yehoshua to preserve, steadfastly, the fruits of the Spirit that directly reflect the righteousness of Y'haweh that intelligibly communicate to all the elect: as we have mentioned above, Lord Yehoshua eternally preserves selflessness, empathy, charity, and love; and these eternal qualities of his Holy Spirit communicates to all whom Y'haweh inspires to appreciate him. In this way, Y'haweh covers the earth that he loves with his pleasant and intelligible glory.

Possessing this salvation knowledge, eternal understanding, and reconciling wisdom of the Mashiach, we must know that Y'haweh does not accept humankind's chaotic and vain knowledge, into his most holy place: humankind's perverted understanding, again, continuously confounds them in the irreconcilable relationships that alienate them from Y'haweh and one another in sin; therefore, Y'haweh does not allow sin's self-aggrandizement among his elect. In this vein, the Apostle Yochanan said the following:

> For all that is in the world, the lust of the flesh, and the lust of the eyes, and the pride of life, is not of the Father, but is of the world. And the world passes away, and the lust thereof: but he that does the will of God abides forever.[2]

Ultimately, the true worshippers must understand from the symbolism of the interim tabernacle that Y'haweh strips away sin's jealousy, envy, malice, and lust, when he asked the people to sacrifice their best. Following, he builds his most holy place upon Lord Yehoshua's humility, empathy, charity, selflessness, and love, when he only accepts the eternal sacrifice of the Mashiach in the people's

---

[1] John 3:16
[2] 1 John 3:16

stead. And because we understand that Y'haweh strips away vanity before he incorporates us into his holy place, we must know that he disseminates the knowledge of him simplistically and liberally. For this reason, any just congregation of saints must acknowledge that Y'haweh has made his teaching and prophetic gifts accountable and intellectually measurable by the common Church body, as a whole. To this end, the shared understanding that is the cornerstone of any assemblage—that is, any ecclesia—of true worshippers must conform to the declaration of Yochanan the Apostle, who said, "Those who do not confess that Yehoshua the Mashiach has come into the world is not of God: and this is the spirit of the of anti-Christ."[1]

Without a doubt, we understand that the Apostle Yochanan's statement is vital because what Yochanan is actually saying is that those who do not believe that Y'haweh actually resurrected the purity of Lord Yehoshua's righteous body and Soul (and, thereby, invites us to seek his eternal life over the fleeting aspirations of this passing world) grasp the chaos of evil, which Y'haweh eternally condemns. In contrast to unbelievers, we find joy in our election, knowing that Y'haweh has instilled the knowledge of him within our hearts; moreover, we are certain that we have not come to the knowledge of the truth through our own intellectual or physical efforts. In this way, we finally find the maturity to comprehend, fully, the symbolism of the interim tabernacle: we first understand that the tabernacle initially encourages us to sacrifice the fleeting riches of this world. Following, we approach the wonderful mercy seat after we stop performing religious services for self-justification and social convenience; moreover, we approach the mercy seat after we recognize the fact that no religious service or ritual secures our fellowship with Y'haweh: we approach when we gain an eternal sense of appreciation for Y'haweh's love. With this knowledge, we directly fellowship with Y'haweh. At that time, we replace the cherubim who cover his mercy seat.

Due to the fact that many in the Church do not fully comprehend the landscape of the gospel-truth or understand their election in Lord

---

[1] 1 John 4:3

Yehoshua, they cannot understand the basic doctrines of the Apostles. They become confused over some simple statements of the Apostles, thinking that their statements contradict each other. For example, when Sha'ul wrote that "we trust in the living God, who is the savior of humankind, specially of those who believe"[1], many unlearned scholars of the Church ponder over the ultimate value of Christian faith as they erroneously assume that Sha'ul is saying that Y'haweh had intended to elect all people, despite their faith. To the contrary, the Apostle is actually inferring that Y'haweh used Lord Yehoshua to save individuals, despite their class, race, or sex.

Owing to the Church's uncertainties, the wolves of the Church readily arise and exploit the weakness of the Church by esteeming themselves through religious acts of piety. They often begin by falsely claiming that they possess prophetic gifts, which are hard for common congregants to hold accountable; moreover, they produce esoteric doctrines and schools of thought that are not readily accessible to the understanding of common congregants: instead of pursuing a transcendent approach to the scriptures that results from the Holy Spirit-inspired fidelity of the heart, the wolves only encourage scholastic approaches, under the guise of science, ultimately because they lack the faith to comprehend intuitively the hidden glory of Y'haweh. As a result, they esteem those who negotiate their shortsighted educational systems, instead of esteeming those who grow in pure knowledge through faith and love. To this end, the wolves become covetous leaders who shroud the simple, benevolent expressions of Y'haweh from his Church bride. Regularly, the wolves of the Church fool the simple of the Church because the simple cannot imagine how the false disciples can exercise such audacity.

Usually, the wolves of the Church undermine the sound doctrine of election: they teach people that believers earn their salvation through works. In this manner, they teach people to accept their perversions of the doctrine of grace.

---

[1] 1 Timothy 4:10

Solely because of such perversions of sound doctrine, ignorant Christians form unwarranted prejudices against unbelievers. The ignorant Christians begin to believe that they are inherently superior to others. Such perverted attitudes then give rise to the politicization of the Church and the subsequent persecution of non-Christians, which perpetuates anti-Semitism. Unfortunately, the ignorant do not understand that the sins of all peoples necessitated the sacrifice of the Mashiach, our Christ.

When we consider how the succeeding Churches, which have arisen after Sha'ul, could not assess the continuity between the physical and spiritual exercise of Y'haweh's power, which ultimately unfold the glory of Y'haweh within the peaceable knowledge of the Mashiach, we begin to understand the schisms that continue to arise within denominations of the Church, because blinded leaders still do not have a coherent approach unto the scriptures that all worshippers can readily appreciate: once more, the blind leaders cannot reconcile, first, the austere laws of the Old Testament (which laws Y'haweh actually designed to overcome the vanities of the nations, as he secured justice in an agrarian nation that did not enjoy modern conveniences) with, second, the spiritual maturity of the New Testament of the Lord's merciful heart (which seeks the first friendship of the Holy Marriage, that is, a friendship that transcends the lesser friendships of pleasure and necessity, which friendships corrupt all levels of economic and social progress). Indeed, some denominations ignorantly invoke some austere Old Testament scriptures that Y'haweh actually designed for the maintenance of the agrarian Kingdom of Yisra'el through the Levite Priesthood. The ignorant Christian leaders ignore the fact that Y'haweh necessarily put forth austere laws, in order to compel the economically unsophisticated people to look past personal necessity and abstractly identify with the needs of all. To this end, Y'haweh gave the universally intelligible Lord Yehoshua all judgment because his peaceable Holy Spirit alone fulfilled the Law; therefore, Lord Yehoshua, only, can execute whatever austere penalty, while we can only invoke austere measures when repeated unlawful behavior, measurably, endangers the ecclesia of law-abiding people, as a whole.

In the other extreme, some Christian denominations tolerate all manner of human perversion: they think that the sacrificed life of the Lord covers the sins of the unrepentant, even when the unrepentant zealously continue to sin. The blind leaders who champion such perverse understandings of Y'haweh's grace do not consider the fact that Y'haweh wrote austere Laws to show his displeasure with inequitable forms of personal, social, and civil conduct. The blind leaders fail to see that Y'haweh sent his son to be baptized and resurrected for those people whom the Holy Spirit empowers to step away from the golden city of corruption: he sent Lord Yehoshua to those whom he has inspired to abide outside the city by not committing adultery, thievery, blasphemy, and the other trespasses of the Law, which the nations endlessly commit.

The Christian and Secular Successors of Rome

Apparent is the Church's weakness and the greater societal fallout that occurs because of the Church's inability to establish orthodoxy. To address the Church's shortfall, our orthodox judgment—Immanuel's Law—enables us to establish a systematic understanding of Y'haweh's expressed truth, which the biblical Testaments entail. Immanuel's Law demonstrates how the Logos manifests as the free physicality of a pure conscience—the Christ—to present a unified analogue that our conflicting self-narratives and inter-personal perspectives can reconcile with, as the Logos likewise impresses upon us Y'haweh's Holy Spirit, in innumerable magnitudinous relationships that reconcile a community of inter-personal perspectives into one. Like so, Immanuel's Law substantively demonstrates how Y'haweh's right judgment prevails upon the conflicting belief systems that our shortsighted self-narratives and inter-personal perspectives create.

The implication of Immanuel's Law is that the Churches cannot properly assess the biblical Testaments or properly apply the Testaments' injunctions, unless they assess the scriptures from the reality of the orthodox judgment that Immanuel's Law entails. Furthermore, because our proof demonstrates how the Mashiach establishes the natural jurisprudence of conscience and how the Holy Spirit maintains a community by reconciling our consciences, per the Mashiach; the Churches who embrace the orthodox judgment that Immanuel's Law details can demonstrate how Church orthodoxy empowers the upward mobility of all social castes, whose conflicting self-narrative perspectives the Mashiach and the Holy Spirit reconcile.

Decidedly, if the Church ignores the manner in which Immanuel's Law establishes our personhood, secular society's agnostic and atheistic proponents will have no way to combat the anarchic and amoral whims of a self-serving democratic culture that champions the freedom of vice. Likewise, if the Church does not accept the way in which Immanuel's Law demonstrates how the Holy Spirit substantively reconciles our self-narrative perspectives, by maintaining the prevalent right judgment, magnitudinous analogue of the Mashiach's Holy Marriage and Kingdom; secular powers will progressively consider human social experiences as epiphenomena. Then they will champion a socialist, autocratic government that only brooks nihilism.

Thus, we see that the strength of today's secular authority stands upon the Church's inability to agree and establish orthodoxy; however, the existence and viability of today's secular culture is a consequence of how the orthodox and non-politicized Church provides upward mobility and, therefore, liberty for all its adherents, whose consciences and faith the Holy Spirit reconciles, despite social standing. The security of religious freedom and personal liberty depends upon the Church's ability to establish universal truth and personal autonomy: secular governments increasingly challenge universal truth and personal autonomy, as the secular governments attempt to integrate all under socialist ideologies.

Though the Apostles did not deliver orthodox doctrine in a way that would undermine heresy and predict social and cultural innovations, the Apostles did predict the social and cultural fallout that only the Last Days' socialist and autocratic government would incur; especially as the government disenfranchises the Church and private fraternities for the supposed freedom of the individual, who will ironically find him or herself disenfranchised from kindred group relationships. For example, in his second letter to his disciple Timothy, the Apostle Sha'ul seems to foresee that a multicultural society will arise in the Last Days and not tolerate sound doctrine. Also, Shim'on Kefa foresaw that members of kindred groups, such as sons and fathers, would turn against each other. The Apostles foresaw how an indifferent people would arise and not respect contracts and oaths, as the nihilistic people failed to agree upon what to disdain as amoral behavior.

To look toward the completion of our doctrinal treatise, we now detail the major causes, concerning how the non-politicized Church advanced liberty and thereby advanced European Christian culture's dominance over the world. As well, we proceed to draw themes from our last chapter, in order to detail how Church's lack of orthodoxy empowers the secular world order, which threatens the Church and individual liberty.

To present a brief chronicle, concerning how the Church empowered the West, we proceed by recalling that Roman society could not equally enfranchise and secure liberties for the German and other Mediterranean peoples that Rome conquered. The Roman class-based society initially centered on a patrician upper-class that served in chief government roles; a plebeian landowning middle-class that could afford to buy armament to serve in the military; and a proletariat lower-class that birthed children for the Roman society's labor force. As patrician generals conquered lands, turning the conquered into roman citizens, the generals eventually formed standing armies comprised of the proletariat instead of the land owning plebeians. The plebeians became further disenfranchised as large farms emerged, undercutting prices. As a consequence, more plebeians moved to the cities to become dependent upon the state.

As for the conquered peoples' legal status, Rome distinguished the conquered peoples under ius gentium, in which the Romans gleaned stoic principles of equality from which the Romans appreciated a natural law. In contrast, the Romans elevated the privileges of Roman citizens under a legal status that they identified as ius civile: under ius civile, the Romans introduced preferential inequalities for Roman citizens, despite their recognizing the natural equality of all foreign people. And so, later, ius gentium inspired secularists to pursue an international and socialist ideology that equates all civilizations and cultures.

The beginning of Rome's fall occurred when the landowners over taxed and over farmed lands, often upon ongoing outbreaks of malaria. The Roman legions diminished because of the loss of tax revenue, and German tribes increasingly invaded the country side as the nobles retreated to fortified enclaves. As a result, the regions of the Roman Empire began to foster nationalist sentiments. Following, international commerce dried up; the value of currency then deflated; and political cohesion finally faltered. The Empire separated into two distinct entities: the Western Empire, which comprised the lands of modern Western Europe, and the Eastern Empire (the Byzantine Empire), which comprised the lands of Modern Turkey and Lebanon.

The Church assumed universal power when the classist Roman Empire fell. Unlike Roman cultural practices, Church doctrine could reconcile the kindred groups of the German tribes, despite class, race, societal standing, and male or female sex. Initially, the Romans charged orthodox Christians with the crime of atheism because the Christians did not believe in the efficacy of the Romans' pagan rites and rituals, which sought the favor of a multiplicity of fertility cult gods; however, as the Church endured Roman persecution, Christians became popular for their charity, as Rome faced economic upheaval. Christians, for instance, rescued infants that Romans left out for exposure to the elements. The Christians also housed and fed the poor. They cried out against gladiator events that featured the slaughter of innocents and captive foreigners.

Unfortunately, we understand that as the Church became publically recognized, Church corruption ensued as cultural and self-serving adherents joined the Assembly—the ecclesia—of the elect. We witness the earliest example of corruption when Ananias and his wife pretended to sell all their belongings, while other members sold all to give to the needy. Trying to appear pious instead of being so, they lied to Shim'on Kefa. As a result, the Lord punished them to set an example.

Cultural Church adherents did not enter the Church when unbelievers persecuted it; however, corruption began after the Church had gained popularity by proving to be the healthiest institute in the politically tumultuous Roman Empire. Hence, when the Emperor Constantine oversaw the organization of the scriptures and made Christianity the state religion, many people soon after sought to gain political power through the Church.

The cultural and self-serving adherents to the Church began to challenge orthodox doctrine, concerning mankind's ability to justify himself, as well as concerning Lord Yehoshua's deity: their not recognizing how the Lord's unblemished conscience establishes our personhood, even as the Holy Spirit sustains our interpersonal community, the cultural and self-serving adherents plunged the Church back into the rationalist-empiricist debate, in regards to what self-sufficient physical conventions justify our knowledge. As we mentioned in our introduction, the Church, out of necessity, produced the famed Creeds of Christendom to define orthodoxy, despite the fact that the Creeds do not entail an objective proof.

The beginning of widespread political corruption occurred when the Bishop of Rome gained influence over the other bishops in the Mediterranean world. Soon after, Roman priests made laypeople depend upon them by conducting all religious services in Latin. What is more, they even went so far as to place the communion bread in the worshippers' mouths, instead of humbly breaking bread with the Body of the Lord in common. Committing all manner of sacrilege, they even sold entrances into Heaven, and likewise they pardoned people's sins upon monetary gain.

Furthermore, while the Byzantine and oriental empires continued unmolested, because of the political stability that their autocratic governments secured for them, the Western Roman Empire fragmented due to the relentless invasions by such peoples like the ancient Germans, Norwegians, and the peoples from the northern Slavic lands. As a result of Roman civilization's fall, large commercial cities deteriorated, while small-fortified fiefdoms arose and littered the lands. A dark age of robbery, rape, infidelity, disease, and starvation ensued: jealous mothers turned against their daughters, and greedy sons killed their elderly fathers, while no significant form of a transnational government remained to foster any sense of civility. Essentially, Europe lost civilization and had to begin again in a patriarchic age. Only the Roman Church remained as a coherent international body.

The Church, too, fell into more corruption, because worldly men used its infrastructure for their own purposes. Reports of Bishops engaging in elicit sexual orgies and drinking parties arose. Local people began to worship familiar deceased people and biblical personalities as their patron saints, unfortunately thinking that these alleged saints received prayers in concert with the great High Priest, Lord Yehoshua, himself.

Notwithstanding, the strong centralized Roman Church systematically organized and funded the evangelizing of Europe's Germanic tribes. Afterwards, Christian monarchies proliferated across Europe.

We will not detail the history of the East because the non-Christian Asian belief systems and prejudices continued to disenfranchise large segments of society, even until the current era. We can readily witness the fruit of the Church's blossom in the rise of modernity from the calamitous fall of the Western Roman Empire. While the succeeding oriental empires prospered (because they maintained the geo-political, social cohesion that they inherited from the Hellenic age and the Mesopotamian Empires of old), the Church essentially had to overcome the fall of civilization, itself: the Church had to nurture a myriad of conflicting barbaric kindred groups, until Christendom produced the most dynamic and sophisticated culture that the world has ever seen. After the West regained its footing under the tutelage of the Church, the Church could readily utilize the West's resources to preach the gospel unto the far reaches of the earth, wherever the prosperity of the West spread.

From this chaotic state, the natural stages of government, which we have delineated in the previous chapter, arose to advance solidarity and seek out liberty. Moreover, the Church played a key role in the development of these governments, unlike before. First, we may identify a patriarchic stage in the Church's organizing of Germanic kindred groups into the feudal orders that arose across Europe: the feudal order entailed a landowning feudal lord who bought mercenaries by allowing the mercenaries to govern plots of land that commoners labored upon. The commoners—serfs—worked the land for food and protection from the barbarous peoples around. Additionally, the Church had representatives within the dominions of the feudal lords to give a sense of order and hope to the people. In return, the feudal orders paid tithes to the Church, giving the priests their sustenance.

Secondly, we may identify the beginning of the monarchic stage in Europe upon the rise of Charlemagne—Charles the Great. As Christian monks converted pagan cultures, Charlemagne and his descendants began consolidating the feudal lords under their rule. Following, other European dynasties came into being, and the Catholic Church sanctioned their rule before the people.

The monarchic age that Charlemagne initiated hailed a period of relative peace: a period that historians define as a so-called Middle Age. In this period, the grand cathedrals of Europe arose: the hardships that continued to linger from the dark ages reminded a newly settled Christian Europe to seek, only, the eternal truths of the heavens. The Church solidified social norms, morality, and legal ethics; while the kings' courts permeated high cultural aesthetics, jurisprudence, and economical standards.

Next, we may identify an aristocratic phase of Europe in the period that followed the Middle Ages. This phase entailed an agricultural revolution in which agricultural output produced surplus labor and the beginnings of specialized professions. Thus, the aristocratic phase entailed an increased literacy among a new and growing middle class of merchants. While commerce and invention began again to proliferate because of the Christian peace, the people gained translations of the scriptures in their national tongues. Common parishioners became aware of the gross perversions of the Catholic Church. The end result was a Church schism between protestors of the Catholic Church (the Protestants) and the Catholic Church itself.[1]

In addition, unbelieving people (who left the fields of the feudal lords and gained wealth through commercial ventures) obviously despised the corrupt rulers of the Church, as well; mainly because the wolves of the Church—the Church's political exploiters—often tried to suppress scientific innovation, because the wolves feared the loss of political influence. Even so, the newly industrious people created a new class beyond the feudal system: these people came to be known as the bourgeoisie—members of the middle class. The bourgeoisie comprised a mixture of people: Catholic laypeople, Protestants, bankers, merchants, writers, and secularists.

The secular bourgeoisie used their newfound printing presses and translations to rediscover the writings of Greek thinkers. Unfortunately, the secularists ascribed a glorified image to the ancient world: they forgot Roman barbarity and romanticized everything that preceded the Christian world. Like contemporary secularists, these secularists did not understand that their wealth, leisure, and civil environment were the product of the honest lifestyles of the believing Christians who upheld oaths, respected personal property, pleaded the cause of the poor, and essentially provided a civil atmosphere for learning and commerce.

---

[1] In their liberation from the Catholic Church, Protestant reformers utilized the following five Latin slogans called the Five Solas, which summarized both the tenets of their beliefs and their opposition to the unbiblical teachings of the Catholic Church: 1) *Sola Fide*—faith alone—indicates that a worshipper is only justified by faith in Lord Yehoshua alone; 2) *Sola Scriptura*—scripture alone—indicates that the Bible is the only authoritative word of Y'haweh, which is completely accessible by all congregants, whereas the Catholic Church upholds that the scripture can only be substantiated by the Catholic traditions of the Pope and Bishops; 3) *Solas Christus*—Christ alone—indicates that Lord Yehoshua is the only mediator between Y'haweh and his worshippers, whose mediation, definitively, excludes false mediators such as the Virgin Mary, recognized saints, and priests; 4) *Sola Gratia*—grace alone—indicates that the grace of Y'haweh secures salvation and not the religious acts of worshippers; and 5) *Soli Deo Gloria*—glory to Y'haweh alone—indicates that Y'haweh is alone glorious, while worshippers are not worthy of his glory but receive it by grace.

Unfortunately, the secularists could not distinguish corrupt religious leaders from the righteous who salted the earth.

Furthermore, the continuing excesses of the European monarchies exasperated the secularists' disdain for the Christian monarchies. The kings of Europe upheld the mission of the Church for political gain: they Christianized the Americas by the sword, seeking to fill their coffers. In the name of the cross, they either enslaved or slaughtered all non-Christian and non-European peoples who opposed them. Also, in the name of the cross, they expelled Jewish populations from the whole of Western Europe, robbing the Jews of their land and material wealth. Finally, having committed all manner of evil, which the scriptures actually speak out against, the pseudo Christian monarchs and priests began to fight each other, continually: Catholic kings fought against Protestant kings, perennially. All told, the rulers of Europe put a greater cloak upon the mercy seat of the tabernacle than the cloak that Lord Yehoshua ripped in the days of the Perushim. It is no wonder that the secularists did not see any worth in the teachings of the Church because the rulers of Europe covered the Church in hypocrisy.

Modernity: "the Fullness of the Gentiles"

To establish our qualification of European Christendom's aristocratic stage, we must distinguish how the aristocratic stage gave rise to modernity. Once more, we observe how Europe's patriarchic stage occurred as the Church incorporated a myriad of Germanic kindred groups into a feudal agricultural order. Next, we observe how Europe's monarchic stage occurred as Charlemagne's Holy Roman Empire and other Christian dynasties consolidated under the Church to solidify cultural norms and jurisprudence across Europe. Now, we more explicitly qualify Europe's aristocratic stage by the manner in which new forms of commerce gave rise to an upper-middle class, whose livelihoods and legal standing did not rely upon the feudal order's agricultural economy. To qualify Europe's aristocratic stage definitively, we must definitively qualify our understanding of modernity and the subsequent post-modern era that we see emerging currently.

Secular thinkers roughly conceive modernity to be the era in which the general populace enjoys constitutional rights of private property and protection from the arbitrary seizure of property or the arbitrary seizure of one's person for forced labor. Furthermore, secular thinkers conceive modernity to be the era in which law enforcement, health care, economy, and social policy stand upon scientific investigation rather than religious doctrine. Secular thinkers finally see the industrial economy's apposing socialist and capitalist ideologies to be the surest sign of modernity in which an individual's welfare depends upon the individual's execution of the individual's contractual rights of employment rather than the individual's being subject to a lifetime of vassalage under a rapacious overlord or clergyman.

The secularists' general qualification of modernity seems unassailable until we consider how only the non-politicized orthodox Church enables our purest conception of modernity. The apostolic Church jurisprudence seeks the reconciliation of all classes, ethnicities, and male or female sex unto the Lord Yehoshua's righteous, unblemished conscience. True apostolic Church jurisprudence does not condemn unbelievers unto a lower social caste. Nor does apostolic Church jurisprudence regard holy places or any discriminatory factor that privileges any individual over another. In particular, apostolic Church jurisprudence does not hold women as second class citizens, preventing them from engaging in economic endeavors: only in religious service does apostolic Church jurisprudence discriminate, in order to portray the Church's espoused relationship to the bridegroom of Heaven's Holy Marriage.

Church orthodoxy seamlessly reconciles all social castes from natural kindred relationships (in which individuals retain enfranchisement by having an instinctive understanding of jurisprudence) unto sophisticated contractual organizations. Like so, the Church enfranchises all adherents, rendering to all a communal landscape of upward social mobility. Essentially, the Church secures liberty. Hence, the secularists rightly decry the grave instances when self-serving adherents used the Church for political means; however, the secularists cannot say that the New Testament, itself, incites the exploiters.

In regards to our qualifying the aristocracy that gives rise to a modernity in which the rights of property, governance, and legal standing also reside in the working class like the upper and middles classes, we note that only orthodox Christianity truly upholds modernity's democracy. In this current era, secularists, who rightfully decry Church corruption, seek to incorporate the non-Christian belief systems, which entail rites, traditions, and practices that are inherently discriminatory. As an effect, all peoples are becoming increasingly disenfranchised because no legal body has the means to justify any decision in a way that the entire populace agrees upon; therefore, autocracy forebodingly looms.

The Aristocratic stage of European Christendom solidified as merchants introduced new forms of commerce that cracked the feudal order. Under increasingly sophisticated contractual arrangements, merchants introduced notions of wage, profit, and time. Urban middle-classes arose in merchant towns: trading cities especially emerged along water corridors; where seafaring determined the commercial output and the resulting political power of the perspective state. Business speculators cornered markets and produced specialized farming, which caused peasants to become floating wage laborers. Finally, intellectuals endeavored to reestablish a universal order like the Roman Empire had under ius gentium; therefore, to counter the power of the Church, philosophers sought the patronage of enlightened Kings, such as Frederick the Great of Prussia and Catherine the Great of Russia. As the bourgeoisie observed that trade makes wealth and wealth favors freedom, the middle-class intellectuals concluded that the new distributions of wealth necessitated new distributions of power; therefore, philosophers conceived the notion of the social contract.

Being bereft of the austere balance of the feudal order—that is, the balance between the feudal lord, the knights, peasants, and clergy; the philosophers fell prey to the rationalist-empiricist debate, in regards to their consideration of the power of the state verses the power of the individual. To consider the balance between the state and the individual, two camps arose to argue on the behalf of either side.

We may briefly note two prime examples of Renaissance philosophers who championed the power of the state that a strong prince governs: Niccolò Machiavelli (1469-1527) and Thomas Hobbes (1588-1679) championed strong social contract governments under the power of a prince. In his work that we know as "the Prince," Machiavelli argued that the state could realize the fruits of social security and stability even when a culture accepts moral corruption: Machiavelli argued that the state should not concentrate on what makes a good person, but concentrate on what makes a good prince. Machiavelli, essentially, sought the virtues of strength and skill in a ruler. Thus, Machiavelli argued that a modern prince must distinguish between public and private morality. Machiavelli concluded that the prince must appear virtuous, even as the prince uses brute force, audacity, and ruthlessness to forward his cause over any opposition.

In his work that he entitled Leviathan, Thomas Hobbes prescribed the means to realize Machiavelli's prescriptions for the amoral prince. Hobbes held that the people in their natural state of nature are brutish, solitary, and given to strife; therefore, Hobbes opposed the classical idea that people innately retain a rational inclination that makes them political animals. Hobbes determined that political society is artificial; therefore, he held that the people must surrender their freedoms to a sovereign under a social contract in which the sovereign holds power over the government, military, and the Church.

Interestingly enough, Hobbes viewed the social organization as an artificial person that he called Leviathan; moreover, Hobbes purported that an effective king prefigures this Leviathan for the good of an assenting people.[1] Accordingly, Hobbes argued that the decisions of the monarch may be arbitrary and without merit (unlike

---

[1] Evidently, Thomas Hobbes's Leviathan is like a corrupt version of the Body of Lord Yehoshua: Hobbes' Leviathan actually describes the prophet Daniel's beast.

the true anointed shipmaster); however, Hobbes held that the social order that the monarch brings to the people is of the greatest worth.

Standing in opposition to Thomas Hobbes' view of a strong centralized government that rules the burgeoning middle and lower classes, John Locke (1632-1704) held that the legitimacy of any government rest upon the consent of the governed, who inherently seek property rights upon which their perspective work ethics add value. Locke believed that Y'haweh created the world to be cultivated; therefore, Locke believed that those whom Y'haweh bestowed gifts to cultivate the world are the people's natural benefactors. For the prosperity of the people who observe thrift, economy, diligence, and economy; Locke sought to retrain the government with checks and balances of power.

Despite the profundity of the strong centralized government arguments of Hobbes or the empowered citizen arguments of Locke, the enlightened European monarchs did not put into practice either philosophical notion to liberate the working classes unto being citizens of a free state, instead of being subjects of a despotic realm. The liberation of all classes of people occurred as a consequence of the Protestant Reformation; wherein biblical literacy extended to all castes, teaching them that all must seek reconciliation with the justice of the Mashiach.

English and German princes printed official Holy Bible translations in their respective native tongues. In this way, the princes united the dialects of a litany of English and German kindred groups around a universally recognized Christian culture.

The Christians Who United the States of America

We see the greatest example of the manner in which the Protestant Church seized democracy for the enfranchisement of the working class in the forming of the United States of America. Because the Church apprehended a Christian culture that reconciles kindred relationships with sophisticated contractual relationships, the American colonists retained a cultural mobility that mitigated the effects of European classism, to the end that the colonists enjoined a government that balanced the rights of the state with that of the citizenry.

An 1843 interview with Captain Levi Preston, a 91 year old Revolutionary War veteran, poignantly speaks to the fact that the aristocratic ideas of Hobbes, Locke, Thomas Jefferson, and James Madison could not come to fruition until the ideas stood upon the civility of the Protestant Church culture, which had enabled to people to self-govern. Mellen Chamberlain, who was researching the American War of Independence interviewed Captain Preston: Chamberlain asked Captain Preston, "what made you go to Concord to fight?"

"What did I go for?" Captain Preston replied.

"Were you oppressed by the Stamp Act?" Chamberlain further asked.

Captain Preston responded by saying, "I never saw any stamps and I always understood that none were ever sold!"

Incredulously, Chamberlain then asked, "Well, what about the Tea Tax?"

"Tea Tax?" Captain Preston scoffed.

He said, "I never drank a drop of that stuff. The boys threw it all overboard!"

Amazed, Chamberlain then quickly asked, "But I suppose you had been reading Harrington, Sydney, and Locke about the eternal principles of Liberty?"

Dismissingly, Captain Preston said, "I never heard of these men. The only books we had were the Bible, the catechism, Watt's Psalms, and hymns and the almanacs."

Finally yielding to his utter perplexity, Chamberlain exclaimed, "Well, then, what was the matter?"

Reflexively, Captain Preston stated, "Young man, what we meant in going for those Redcoats was this: we always had been free and we meant to be free always! They didn't mean that we should."

Recognizing the unifying power of a non-state sanctioned, non-politicized, and orthodox Church; the American Colonialists enjoined a restrained government, which John Locke envisioned; however, the colonialists recognized that a government that balanced the power of the people with the state could only stand by ensuring religious liberty, in regards to the manner in which the Church empowered the people to self-govern.

At the beginning of American colonial history, English puritans founded the Massachusetts Bay Colony: they sought to establish a laypeople Christian society that did not have the hierarchical structure that the wolves of the Church exploit. Thus, public literacy was a necessity, in order for people of all classes to live by a code of conduct. To prevent political exploitation, the people organized into autonomous congregations where the laypeople could vote on public issues. For this purpose, the Colony instituted town hall meetings for public deliberation. Eventually, the autonomous congregations essentially became miniature governments, having termed offices, administrations, and committees, all of which served the purpose of the active political engagement by the common people of society; moreover, such political engagement by everyday people fostered an American political culture of great citizen political participation that other countries fail to attain. Undeniably, the Christian American experience hallmarks the true beginning of the democratic stage of the West, after the fall of Rome.

Other American colonies organized under the idea of religious freedom, as well; however, we must note that the idea of religious freedom to the colonialists was the freedom to choose what Christian denomination one wanted. Still, Jewish people found a tenable peace among the colonialists: eventually, they built strong Jewish communities and complementing international Jewish organizations. Indeed, the Jewish people stood as equal citizens under an American Constitution that guaranteed religious liberty. Even so, while early Americans peacefully assimilated European and Russian Jews into the American cultural landscape, contemporary ideologies and non-Christian religions such as Hinduism, Atheism, and Buddhism were alien to the gross majority of early Americans.

Before the signing of Declaration of Independence, a religious revival called the Great Awakening crossed the Colonies, teaching that all people equally needed redemption in the Mashiach, despite class. The product of the revival was that the common adulation, which all the people from various states enjoyed, birthed a common American identity.

It is no wonder that the people resisted the English King and his hierarchical Church, by declaring their independence under God. While a significant minority of the founders were secularists or deists, the vast majority were devout Christians, who loved the Church but resisted the idea of a government ruling over the existing Christian denominations, like the English Crown ruled over its state sanctioned Church; therefore, what the founders shared in common is that they sought a government that only regulated commerce and guaranteed religious freedom. Notwithstanding, the framers of the Constitution recognized their need for the benevolence of the Mashiach when they ratified the Constitution: they only signed the document unanimously in deference to the year of Lord Yehoshua's birth, their writing "by the unanimous consent of the States present the Seventeenth day of September in the Year of our Lord one thousand seven hundred and Eighty seven and of the Independence of the United States of America."[1] As a result, the Americans formed a three tier federal government under God, reminiscent of the government of ancient Rome.

The Legal Fiction of Socialism

The profound manner in which Protestant Christians in America understood enough of orthodox doctrine to look past social standing and benefit from the rights that the newly enjoined American Constitution afforded them reduced the debilitating effects of commercial materialism: an effect that incites envy and greed amongst all classes. The American Protestants' more orthodox understanding of the biblical Testaments enabled them to reconcile their kindred relationships with the burgeoning contractual relationships of industry and commerce under the rights that the United States Constitution initially guaranteed.

The unending revolts of the newly economically empowered working class in Europe did not fare as well without a non-

---

[1] Article VII of the Constitution of the United States of America.

politicized Church culture that reconciles all societal castes. The revolutionaries of the French Revolution, for example, attempted to rely upon the ideals of Thomas Hobbes and Jean-Jacques Rousseau (1712-1778), as the revolutionaries sought to construct a social contract that reconciles all classes under a centralized State. Instead of holding that Y'haweh endowed individuals with the talents to cultivate and enjoy their natural right to property, the French revolutionaries cultivated a document entitled the Declaration of the Rights of Man and Citizen, which emphasizes that all men are born free and equal; therefore, the revolutionaries sought to preserve freedom and equality by requiring all who enter into political society to accept prohibitions upon the free exercise of their abilities. The revolutionaries deemed unequal material conditions as a threat to the state's socially organized and collective life.

Decidedly, like the Roman jurisprudence that we see in ius gentium, the European socialism is suspicious of any social inequality. The fatal flaw in the social contract is that it is a legal fiction that ignores that fact that people do not come into being to exist under the temporality of a profession, which a contractual arrangement defines. In other words, people do not come into being as wage earning market commodities. Rather, people come into being under kindred groups that naturally entail benefactor-beneficiary relationships that the Holy Marriage fulfills as a consequence of the Testator's relationship with us, the Testator's beneficiaries.

The following is the flaw of the social contracts of a centralized state, which stresses the rights of the individual under contract: the social contract ignores the reality that the commercial economy does not perennially guarantee the equality of scarce goods and services. Capitalists then naturally seek to exploit cheap labor forces for commercial gains. For this cause, individuals become perennially disenfranchised, even being bereft of their natural enfranchisement in kindred groups, which the socialist state undermines in favor of the individual.

The Dominance of Protestant Germanic Kindred Groups

To a significantly greater extent than the socialist regimes of Europe, the Protestant cultures in the United States, Great Britain, and Germany mitigated the ills of capitalism and achieved global wealth unparalleled. In the United States, in particular, the laypeople's civic activist Churches fostered healthy marriages, families, and the sense of civic responsibility from which citizens could glean the best values for a harmonious society. Because of a healthy political culture, the American federal republic could retain peaceful political turnover, peaceful signing of petitions, peaceful taxing of income, and peaceful exercise of free speech. In the American political environment, specialization and the division of labor proliferated, and public education quickly followed. Then a wonderful burst of imagination and invention persisted.

As the Protestant nations cornered markets to increase their wealth, innovation, and power; they spread Western culture around the world. Industrialization started in Protestant Great Britain. Then industrialization flourished in the environs of the free Churches of the United States. As a consequence, the English language is now the international language of commerce.

Championing industrialization, the United States, Great Britain, and Germany developed large scale industries in steel, mining, and oil. Among the industrial nations, huge factories generated a variety of affordable foodstuff, seasoning, tools, and other instruments that surpassed the basic needs of life. Sophisticated corporate forms emerged with life-spans that extended beyond individual sole proprietors. Also, the capitalist corporations created new relationships between men and women, often challenging kindred family roles between providers and beneficiaries. Socially transforming inventions sprung from Protestant countries: for example, the harnessing of electricity, locomotion, automobiles, controlled-powered air-flight, computers, nuclear power, and modern science.

Despite their unparalleled achievements, the Protestant Germanic kindred groups have ironically become a threat to their constitutional freedoms and free market economies because of some Germanic Protestants' inability to appreciate, fully, how the Church has cultivated, unified, and transformed the Germanic tribes' cultural identity. Many Europeans in general have viewed non-European nations as inferior; therefore, instead of liberally cultivating the gospel amongst non-Europeans, Europeans have exploited the non-Europeans for commercial gain. The southern states of the United States have enslaved Africans for vast commercial gain, while European countries have exploited India, Africa, and the Americas for commercial profits.

The ill effect of the "European racial supremacy" attitude is that socialists have made vast inroads into winning public opinion in order to delegitimize Europe's Christian heritage, in general. Tragically, most African Americans fail to celebrate how many Germanic, Anglo-Saxon Americans fought against slavery and championed the civil-rights movements. Secular-socialists have successfully used the horrors of slavery to besmirch the cultural superiority that the Protestant Church has cultivated among the Germanic kindred groups, overall. As the southern States continued to oppress African Americans after the American Civil War, secular socialists transformed the cultural dynamic of the northern States by incorporating socialist leaning, non-Protestant Europeans into the cultural fabric. Thus, in the same way that the 19th Century northern Churches have pioneered the freeing of African slaves in the United States, as well as pioneered urban charities that have become the foundation of contemporary social-service organizations, the northern Churches have pioneered the 20th Century Civil Rights movement, only to inspire decolonization movements around the world, under socialist regimes.

The greatest misfortune for the liberated non-German kindred groups of Africans, Native Americans, Indians, and other groups, is that they have been liberated into a commercial world where they solely maintain wage earning identities under the exploitive vicissitudes of commercial contracts, without their respective ethnicities having the advantage of experiencing the same cultural maturation that the Germanic kindred groups fail to appreciate. In other words, as the freed non-European peoples immediately transition from kindred group status to individual wage earners without their experiencing the high cultural etiquette of Christian Kings, the urbane propriety of Christian aristocracies, and Christian democracy's patriotic fervor of liberty under God; non-Europeans experience a profound psychological impediment: instead of experiencing the upward societal mobility of the Western experience, non-Europeans try to associate their kindred relationships with the kindred experiences of their oppressors who have benefited from the biblical Testaments' maturing of Germanic kindred groups unto the liberty of the Mashiach, whose kindred group is actually Jewish. To be more specific, we note that the Church presently maintains a primarily European identity that fails to liberate billions of non-European populations that are only now transitioning from agricultural economies and the corresponding kindred groups to industrial economies; where liberalism frustrates the emergent world with artificial life-styles choices that only the contractual arrangements of a centralized and impersonal-bureaucratic government allow.

The Anti-*Christ*

In the light of some Europeans' failure to acknowledge the fruit of the gospel, we must conclude the following: whether they are socialists or libertarian capitalists, the secularists deceive themselves into believing that they have been at the heart of social progress. Eventually, the brazen acts of impropriety committed by their financial institutes will so alarm them that they will say, "We have considered all things, but we have not considered the value of our faiths."

Still, never willing to believe in or reconcile themselves with the resurrected purity of Lord Yehoshua, they will create a religion of the state that conceals their selfish aspirations as they only seek economic prosperity for the global classes. In this manner, they will finally discover that prodigious man who is politically sagacious enough to convince all major Western powers to join together under a secular government that he represents, upon seven continents.

We must unquestionably identify this multifaceted government as the New Rome—the bestial last stage of human government, which does not govern its people by an eternal truth but unnaturally governs by the whims of human appetite: an equating of all lifestyles. All the same, our hope remains sound, because we know of our good end. Even though the secularization of the West progressively culminates into the likeness of a global beast, we see evidence of the light of our reconciliation with Y'haweh shining beyond. We see the opportunity to liberate the preaching of the gospel from the perspective of the Jewish kindred group, which Y'haweh himself cultivated amongst the family of nations. Thus, a new common ground between devout Christians and Jews presents itself in the effort to buttress the effects of secularization that snares the weak elements of both Christian and Jewish peoples, whose elect ultimately share a common hope for the return of him who will redeem Yerushalayim. Thereby, a new opportunity presents itself for the Church to assess the order of history with an accountable doctrinal approach that transcends culture to perceive the true benevolence of the Mashiach.

Also, with our orthodox judgment, we have the objective means to demonstrate how Y'haweh expressed the worlds. Likewise, we have the objective means to affirm the free standing of our spirits and souls.

Having confidence in our good end, we must not be astonished to see the final insult by the unredeemed against the mercy seat of Y'haweh, when the secularists' anti-savior tries to suppress Church freedom and the Jewish State, in an attempt to ensure the dominion of his secular state. Initially, he will exploit the vulnerability of the Church by blaming the devout of the Church for the excesses of the wolves of the Church. As well, he will cultivate friendships with those who have become indifferent to the sound liberating doctrines of the Church. Finally, not believing in the free physicality and standing of our personal perspectives, which give us the natural jurisprudence of personal conscience unto Y'haweh, who enables the elect to secure a just society; the anti-savior will seek to control the security and welfare of all conflicting peoples by requiring them to have their personal history embedded on their persons, in order for them to participate in the global economy.

At such a time, the global classes will not accept the truth of Y'haweh, because they will cling to their idols, while they come into direct conflict with the elect of the Church who will continue to proclaim the single truth: the leaders and the privileged will covet their power and social status above sincere empathy and charity. At the same time, the middle and working classes will lusts for the wine of the Whore of Babylon's popular culture above sobriety, sincere brotherly love, and the persistent, selfless, and faithful search for the knowledge of Y'haweh: even as Lord Yehoshua says, "[A]s it was in the days of Noach, so shall it be also in the days of the Son of man. They did eat, they drank, they married wives, they were given in marriage, until the day that Noach entered into the ark, and the flood came, and destroyed them all . . . Even so shall it be in the day when the Son of man is revealed."[1]

Finally, the anti-savior will stand in the Most Holy Place of the Temple that stands upon Mount Tziyon, thinking that he is defying Christian and Jewish extremism. By committing such an outrageous act, he will insult Y'haweh who places his name in the tumultuous land to reflect his glory since he alone brings his Holy Spirit's lasting peace to the land.

To this end, Lord Yehoshua will return and destroy any remnant of the global beast, after he redeems and resurrects his elect Gentiles and after he elects 144,000 virgins of the children of Yisra'el, whom he has empowered to observe his Law and finally receive him. Executing his justice upon the land, while he graciously redeems his chosen with his Holy Spirit, the Lord Yehoshua will destroy Leviathan—the global secular beast—that will arise from the sea of many cultures and peoples:

---

[1] Luke 17:26-30

> In the day that the Lord with his sore and great and strong sword shall visit leviathan the piercing serpent, even leviathan that crooked serpent; he shall lay leviathan that is in the sea.[1]

Essentially, what we must conclude before we look beyond this world and gaze beyond the stars, into the Kingdom of Heaven, is that Lord Yehoshua must destroy all the pride of human ingenuity, which Leviathan represents. For this single purpose, Y'haweh must demonstrate the necessity of his grace to his redeemed by allowing Lord Yehoshua to give those of humanity whom he has not sealed with his Holy Spirit one last chance to choose him over their own aspirations.

And so, for a thousand years, Lord Yehoshua will reign over the fourth interim tabernacle in peace with his elect over the unbelievers, to validate the justice of Y'haweh's Law, which the nations had perennially denied. Following, the Lord will allow Satan to tempt the unbelievers successfully. Then when they foolishly rebel from his interim government by seeking their own satisfaction (and, thereby, bringing strife back into the world), Lord Yehoshua will condemn them, eternally. Correspondingly, he will readily underscore the supreme benefit of Y'haweh's grace, through which the elect receive the Holy Spirit that empowers them to be satisfied with Y'haweh's eternal government.

The Totality of Y'haweh

At long last, we may now conclude our journey, with a description of how the whole body of true worshippers will experience the salvation knowledge of the Lord, after the judgment: they will see their sins passed unto others, and they will rejoice in him who upholds their consciences by being resurrected again to fulfill the pleasure of Y'haweh. Finally, after the judgment, we the elect will possess the salvation knowledge—a common understanding that we can find no lasting fulfillment in any place other than the fulfillment of Y'haweh. And so, watching the golden city perish in our hearts,

---

[1] Isaiah 27:1

we will finally see the true glorious City, New Yerushalayim, descend from beyond the stars, finding her resting place upon the purified mountains of Tziyon.

O rejoice! Eden has returned to us with meaning and purpose: the Holy Couple finding fulfillment in the appreciation of one another, in love.

For sure, only now may we conclude our unfolding of the truth of Y'haweh by describing his and our fulfillment. To accomplish this, we have but to complete our understanding by gazing upon the source of the Holy Spirit's river of truth: even "a river, whereof the streams shall make glad the City of God, the holy place of the tabernacles of the most High."[1]

Poignantly, the river springs forth from the Holy Spirit's tree of life. We see that Y'haweh situated the tree of life at the center of the Holy City, in order for the tree to be nourished by his glory. For this purpose, we must first recognize the fact that we may only approach the source of the river when we no longer need to negotiate the valleys of deprivation, to gain an appreciation for the benevolent hand of the heavenly groom: we approach when Y'haweh no longer has to make low the mountains of our vanities, by his using the revelations of his power and justice. Indeed, we approach the source when we are able to appreciate his humility, meekness, and the abundance of his love that we see in creation's limitations and Lord Yehoshua's simplicity.

Too, we will find the source of the river when we no longer need a law that encourages us to first love Y'haweh and then our neighbor. At such a time, we will no longer need prophets to encourage us to fight the good fight; moreover, at such a time, we will no longer need the prophets to censure us when we forsake the good pleasure of all. As well, when we approach the source of the river, we will not need teachers to give us understanding, because we will all possess a profound sense of fulfillment and beauty, in the Holy Spirit. At such a time, everything in creation will advertise all utility for our minds' inspection. At that moment, we will give all

---

[1] Psalm 46:4

power and glory to Lord Yehoshua the benefactor of all, unto Y'haweh's glory. For sure, we will arrest the source of the river when our faith and hope (which look past our temporal, self-centered lives) find fulfillment in Y'haweh's eternal love, even our finding that Y'haweh has written us into the Book of Lord Yehoshua's eternal life.

Decidedly, at the source of the Holy Spirit's river of truth, our souls spring forth from the loud and cacophonic sarcophagus of this world into a lively place where there is a symphony of Lord Yehoshua's light and understanding: a place that greets our hopeful expectations with such a sense of fulfillment that dramatically surpasses our imaginations. In Lord Yehoshua's Kingdom, we will see the light and glory of Y'haweh that is quintessential beauty and brilliance.

Only now we may note that nothing in creation is like Y'haweh's glory: creation merely reflects the glory of Y'haweh because his truthful form speaks order into the worlds; therefore, if one saw the glory of Y'haweh, he or she would literally see the fabric of creation instantaneously burning away, with all human vanity, because nothing challenges Y'haweh's splendor.

If one could see the glory of Y'haweh, one's soul would then spring forth from his or her frail form. Then Y'haweh would pierce every nerve of the person with his consciousness, integrating the person's dynamic perspective to recreate the person's soul in his presence. One would then feel as though he or she were suspended in a sea of crystal-clear glass, springing forth from a brilliantly white and metaphysically appearing singularity. In the spirit, one would see brilliant white light sparkling out of a central point, enveloping all creation in a sphere. The light rays are crystal like geometrical emanations, interrupting any monotonous patterns with the pure clarity of intelligence, only to titillate one's senses in such a way that one hears the beautiful symphony of life in his or her heart. Indeed, this silent symphony is what inspires the Angels' song.

Furthermore, when one sees the glory of Y'haweh and hears his symphony of life within their souls, one hears the Word of Y'haweh directly communicating purity, intricate design, brilliance, regalia, abundance, beauty, meaning, and of all love—his will to be appreciated for what he truly is: the everlasting love and life that we corporately experience within the peaceable Mashiach, who is the shinning of Y'haweh's glory. And so, when one sees the glory of Y'haweh, all things become crystal clear as the knowledge of Y'haweh's glory arrays itself before the soul. At that moment, one does not ignorantly seek salvation knowledge by pursuing an understanding of the shadowy forms of physical necessity or pleasure; moreover, one's subjective soul does not allow its subjective misconceptions to cloak Y'haweh's eternal glory; because one's soul then beholds the outshining of a perfect relationship, as Y'haweh communicates his love in all things that manifest everyone's physical and spiritual life. In fact, herein is where we find the Holy Marriage of the appreciative and elect souls.

Standing before the glory of Y'haweh, one feels a profound sense of history, as though one were reminiscing over the triumphs and downfalls of his or her life: one feels the relationships that Y'haweh cultivated with the saints throughout time; and so, one feels a sense of the vanquished grief, which the saints endured to gain the higher knowledge's sense of appreciation. At the same time, one feels a profound sense of charity and affability: without, one witness quintessential beauty; because within, one instinctively understands how the light of Y'haweh expressed his order; gained the singular affections of his worshippers; and, finally, satisfied the intimate communion between him and his bride with the abundance of his gentle Holy Spirit.

Thus, the reason why we cannot encompass the glory and beauty of Y'haweh in this world is because, as it happens, nothing can envelope his glory but our eternal state of satisfaction, which Lord Yehoshua secures for us, whom the Holy Spirit grafts into Lord Yehoshua's eternal body. For this cause, in the resurrected body of Lord Yehoshua, we will find that Lord Yehoshua houses the glory of Y'haweh in the Holy City that celebrates his peace. Indeed, the City's cornerstone is Lord Yehoshua, its foundations are the prophets and Apostles, and its building blocks are we who rejoice in the mercy of the Lord.

For this cause, Y'haweh symbolically inscribes our new names in the precious white stones of the City[1]: spiritually, the precious stones are they that Satan could not appreciate when he embodied them as a cherub; as well, the precious stones are they that the high priest of the Levites wore upon his garment, which depicted the Body of the Mashiach. The design of the stones directly complements the crystal like glorious emanations of Y'haweh, which he wonderfully arrays and then instantly terminates in our hearts. So being a part of Lord Yehoshua's faithful body in the Holy City, we will faithfully receive the glory of Y'haweh, which communicates his love and fidelity unto us through the wonders of creation. Thus, the stones—the building blocks of the equitable, cube shaped City—represents the aesthetic beauty of the City that acclaims the triumph of all who abide there, unlike Leviathan's perverse art that covetously celebrates the proud reigns of monarchs; the privileges of aristocrats; the license of democrats; and the greed of capitalists. In contrast, the stones of the City effectively represent an enduring place where inequitable rulers cannot tax or dispossess us of our wealth. To be sure, the stones represent a place where the Lord eternally celebrates and validates our lives. Lastly, the stones mark the place of our enduring habitation: a place that will have stood the fire of Y'haweh's outshining, which will have burned away[2] the vanities of the world to reveal Y'haweh's glory within the hearts of the redeemed. For sure, the stones mark a place where the Lord and our peers accept us with open arms and acknowledge our gifts and talents, which the Lord redeemed to get us there.

Upon the Mount Tziyon, the City sits, "for Y'haweh has chosen Tziyon; he has desired it for his habitation [saying], 'this is my rest forever: here will I dwell; for I have desired it. I will abundantly bless her provision: I will satisfy her poor with bread. I will also clothe her priests with salvation: and her saints shall shout aloud for joy.'"[3]

---

[1] Revelations 2:17
[2] Reference 1 Corinthians Chapter 3
[3] Psalm 132:13-16

For sure, in a chorus with the psalmist, the saints will cry out, "Beautiful for situation, the joy of the whole earth is mount Tziyon . . . the city of the great King"[1]; because from the City runs Y'haweh's glorious river of the Holy Spirit to water the face of the new earth. The greatly desired eternal Sabbath day of Y'haweh's love's fulfillment commences: all the physical and spiritual relationships of Y'haweh's law are in harmony, and we can but then proclaim unto Y'haweh the words of the ensuing song:

> All Thy works with joy surround Thee; earth and Heaven reflect Thy rays, Stars and angels sing around Thee, Center of unbroken praise; Field and forest, vale and mountain, blossoming meadow, flashing sea, Chanting bird and flowing fountain, call us to rejoice in Thee.[2]

It is certain that the true worshipping saints will eternally experience the glory of Y'haweh; however, for now we can only confidently declare to those whose hearts are open and submissive (to the lamb of Y'haweh) that the Choir of Saints have found the wellspring of life and an open door of paradise: momentary weeping at the grave will eternally turn to song.

Let us, therefore, possess this pearl of truth in our hearts. And let us bolster our faith. Let us now confidently seek the purposes of Y'haweh by humbly obeying the Law through Lord Yehoshua, the lamb, who fulfills all things for us. Then when the pains of life pass away and when the temptations of this world no longer endure, we will hear the Good Lord saying, "'Well done my good and faithful servant'; even though the world passes away, my love and charity abides still. 'Come now into the joy of your Lord'[3]: a Holy Marriage that will endure forever."

Amen

---

[1] Psalm 48:2
[2] *Hymn to Joy* by Henry Van Dyke
[3] Matthew 25:21